A GRAMMAR OF EPIGRAPHIC HEBREW

SOCIETY OF BIBLICAL LITERATURE
Resources for Biblical Study

Edited by
Marvin A. Sweeney

Number 23
A GRAMMAR OF
EPIGRAPHIC HEBREW

by
Sandra Landis Gogel

A GRAMMAR OF EPIGRAPHIC HEBREW

by

Sandra Landis Gogel

Society of Biblical Literature
Resources for Biblical Study

Scholars Press
Atlanta, Georgia

A GRAMMAR OF EPIGRAPHIC HEBREW

by

Sandra Landis Gogel

Library of Congress Cataloging-in-Publication Data

Gogel, Sandra Landis, 1952–
A grammar of epigraphic Hebrew.

(Resources for biblical study ; no. 23)
Bibliography: p.
Includes index.
1. Hebrew language—Grammar—1950–
2. Inscriptions, Hebrew—Palestine. I. Title.
II. Title: Epigraphic Hebrew. III. Series.
PJ4564.G69 1989 492.4'5 88-32703
ISBN 1-55540-287-9
ISBN 1-55540-288-7 (pbk.)

Printed in the United States of America
on acid-free paper

ACKNOWLEDGEMENTS

I would like to take this opportunity to thank the many people who have helped me in the preparation of this book. First and foremost, I wish to express my deep appreciation to Professor Dennis Pardee of the University of Chicago who introduced me to Hebrew epigraphy and Northwest Semitic philology. My deepest thanks to him for directing my dissertation, upon which this book is based, with constant aid and encouragement. His comments provided on this manuscript before publication were also extremely helpful.

With fond memories, I would like to thank the late Professor Gosta Ahlström who provided insight and support during the preparation of my dissertation. Special thanks are also due to Professors Carolyn Killean and Norman Golb from the University of Chicago for instilling in me a firm knowledge of Hebrew and furthering my education in Hebrew studies and who also gave me much help during my doctoral studies.

I also wish to acknowledge my friends and colleagues at the Institut d'Études Sémitiques du Collège de France: André Lemaire, Pierre Bordreuil, Bernard Delaveau and Catherine Fauveaud. A note of gratitude is due to Felice Israel who read an early manuscript and offered valuable comments and additions. Any and all remaining errors are my own and not those of my generous readers.

I am grateful to Dennis Ford, Gregory Glover, Steve McKenzie and the staff at Scholars Press for their expert assistance in the publication of this book. Finally, I wish to acknowledge the constant help and support of my husband, Bob, who has been the utmost mentor and friend, as well as technical editor and supervisor of this book during the past years.

To my four children, Sarah, Michael, Rachel and David, my source of inspiration, I say thank you.

I dedicate this book to my mother, Ethel. G. Landis and to the memory of my father, Albert Landis, both of whom offered so much encouragement to me during my studies at the University of Chicago and during the preparation of this book.

Dr. Sandra Landis Gogel

Paris, France
July, 1998

TABLE OF CONTENTS

TABLES

Table **Page**

ABBREVIATIONS

Grammatical Terms

abs	Absolute
Adj	Adjective
Adv	Adverb
AOT	Adverb of Time
AP	Active Participle
ART	Definite Article
Card.	Cardinal Number
Conj	Conjunction
cs	Construct State
DA	Definite Article
D Adj	Demonstrative Adjective
D elem	Divine Element
DN	Deity Name
DO	Direct Object
DOM	Direct Object Marker
DPron	Demonstrative Pronoun
EOLPN	Element of Locative Name
EOPN	Element of Proper Name
f.pl.	Feminine Plural
f.s.	Feminine Singular
Gen	Genitive Clause
Hiph	*Hiphil*

Grammatical Terms
(continued)

I	Infinitive
IML	Internal *mater lectionis*
Imp	Imperfect
Impv.	Imperative
Inf. Abs.	Infinitive Absolute
Inf. Con.	Infinitive Construct
Interr. part.	Interrogative Particle
Juss	Jussive
LPN	Locative Name
m.l.	*matres lectionis*
Mod	Modal
m.pl.	Masculine Plural
m.s.	Masculine Singular
N	Noun
Neg	Negation
Niph	*Niphal*
Nom	Nominal Clause
NR	*nomen rectum*
NRe	*nomen regens*
Num	Numeral
Ordn	Ordinal Number
OS	Object Suffix
Part	Participle
Part of ent	Particle of Entreaty
PartP	Participle Phrase
Perf	Perfect
PN	Proper Name
Pred	Predicate
PredN	Predicate Nominative
Prep	Preposition

Grammatical Terms
(continued)

PrepP	Prepositional Phrase
Pron	Pronoun
PP	Passive Participle
PS	Possessive Suffix
RC	Relative Clause
RPron	Relative Pronoun
RS	Relative Sentence
S.I.	Seal Impression
Sub	Subject
suff pron	Suffixed Pronoun
Temp	Temporal Phrase
V	Verb
VPred	Verbal Predicate
YHWH	Yahweh

Journals and Other Studies Noted in the Footnotes

AASOR	*Annual of the American School of Oriental Research*
AION	*Annali dell'Istituto Orientali di Napoli*
Av NN	Avigad, "New Names on Hebrew Seals," *EI* 12 (1975)
BA	*Biblical Archaeologist*
BAR	*Biblical Archaeology Review*
BASOR	*Bulletin of the American Schools of Oriental Research*
BCat	Bordreuil, *Catalogue des sceaux ouest-sémitiques inscrits*, 1986
BDB	Brown, Driver and Briggs, *Hebrew and English Lexicon of the Old Testament*, 1907
BIES	*Bulletin of the Israel Exploration Society*
BJPES	*Bulletin of the Jewish Palestine Exploration Society*
B/L	Bordreuil/Lemaire
BN	*Biblisch Notizen*
BO	*Bibliotheca Orientalis*
BSOAS	*Bulletin of the School of Oriental and African Studies*
CIS	*Corpus Inscriptionum Semiticarum, Part I: Phoenician Inscriptions*, 1881--
CBQ	*Catholic Biblical Quarterly*
EHO	Cross and Freedman, *Early Hebrew Orthography*, 1952
EI	*Eretz Israel*
Grammar	Blau, *A Grammar of Biblical Hebrew*, 1976
HAR	*Hebrew Annual Review*
HB	Avigad, *Hebrew Bullae from the Time of Jeremiah*, 1986
HHL	Pardee, *Handbook of Ancient Hebrew Letters*, 1982
Hest.	Hestrin
HUCA	*Hebrew Union College Annuals*
IEJ	*Israel Exploration Journal*
IPN	Noth, *Die israelitischen Personennamen im Rahmen der gemeinsemitischen Namengebung*, 1928
JAOS	*Journal of the Americal Oriental Society*
JBL	*Journal of Biblical Literature*

Journals and Other Studies Noted in the Footnotes
(continued)

JNES	*Journal of Near Eastern Studies*
JPOS	*Journal of the Palestine Oriental Society*
JQR	*Jewish Quarterly Review*
JSS	*Journal of Semitic Studies*
KAI	Donner and Röllig, *Kanaanïsche und aramïsche Inschriften*, 1962
MLAHE	Zevit, *Matres Lectionis in Ancient Hebrew Epigraphy*, 1980
NEATC	*Near Eastern Archaeology in the Twentieth Century*
PEQ	*Palestine Exploration Quarterly*
R	Reifenberg
RB	*Revue Biblique*
SANSS	Herr, *The Scripts of Ancient Northwest Semitic Seals*, 1978
Studies	Janssens, *Studies in Hebrew Historical Linguistics Based on Origen's Secunda*, 1982
TA	*Tel Aviv*
TSSI	Gibson, *Textbook of Syrian Semitic Inscriptions, Vol I: Hebrew and Moabite Inscriptions*, 1971
UF	*Ugarit-Forschungen*
VT	*Vetus Testamentum*
VTSup	*Vetus Testamentum*, Supplements
ZAW	*Zeitschrift für die alttestamentliche Wissenschaft*
ZDMG	*Zeitschrift der deutschen morgenländischen Gesellschaft*

Texts and Text Locations

A	Arad
Aj	Ajrud
Gib	Gibeon
HU	Ḥorvat Uza
KBL	Khirbet Beit Lei
KEK	Khirbet el-Kom
KEM	Khirbet el-Meshash
KH	Ketef Hinnom
L	Lachish
MHY	Meṣad Ḥashavyahu
MO	Moussaïeff Ostracon
NY	Naḥal Yishai
papMur	Murabbaʿat Papyrus no. 17
RR	Ramat Rachel
S	Samaria
Sam C 1101	Samaria "Barley Letter"

THE PROVENIENCES OF THE INSCRIPTIONS

Legend

1	Arad
2	Beersheba
3	Beth Shean
4	Beth Shemesh
5	En Gedi
6	Gezer
7	Gibeon
8	Hazor
9	Hebron
10	Ḥorvat Uza
11	Jerusalem
12	Ketef Hinnom
13	Khirbet Beit Lei
14	Khirbet el-Kom
15	Khirbet el-Meshash
16	Kuntillet Ajrud
17	Lachish
18	Megiddo
19	Meṣad Ḥashavyahu
20	Murabbaʿat
21	Naḥal Yishai
22	Ophel
23	Ramat Rachel
24	Samaria
25	Shechem
26	Siloam
27	Silwan
28	Tel Dan
29	Tell Amal
30	Tell Beit Mirsim
31	Tell Ira
32	Tell en-Nasbeh
33	Tell Qasile

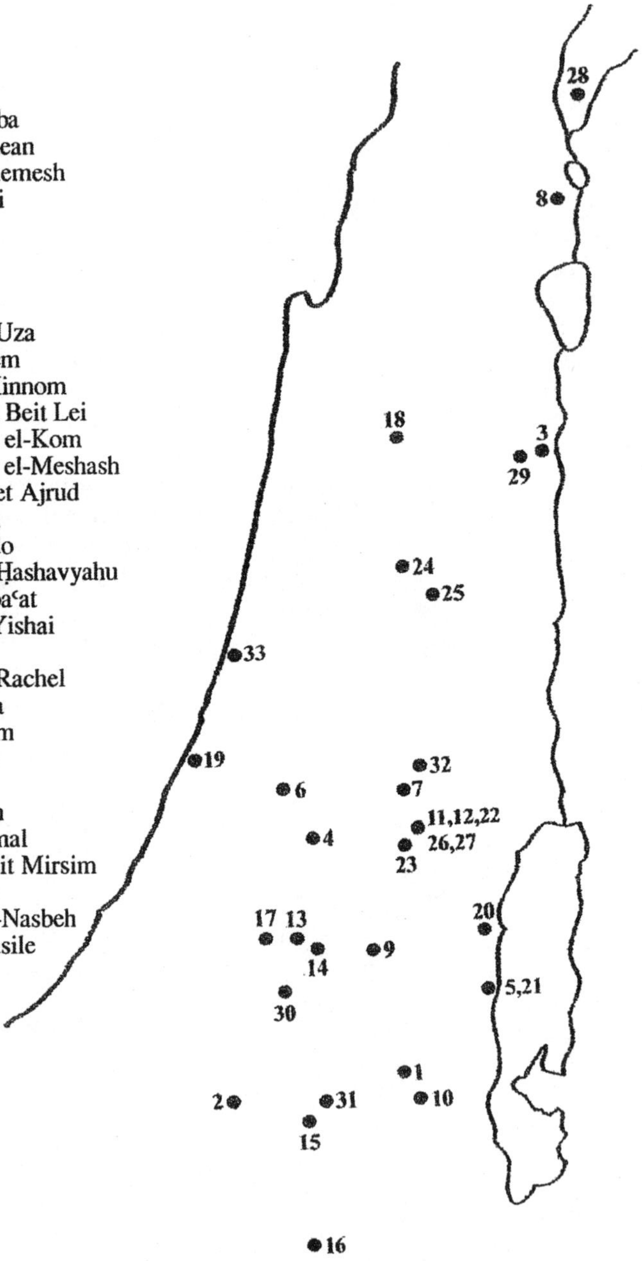

PREFACE

This book provides a grammar of the extra-biblical Hebrew inscriptions of Palestine which have been attributed by various archaeological, historical, and paleographic analyses to the period between the tenth and the sixth century B.C. These pre-Persian inscriptions comprise a corpus of epigraphic Hebrew inscriptions (including ostraca, graffiti, and seals) which previously has never been studied comprehensively. While studies of the better known epigraphic Hebrew inscriptions have been attempted, this book covers the entire corpus. In addition, the seal inscriptions and the personal names have been systematically compared with the longer inscriptions for the first time.

Cross and Freedman's *Early Hebrew Orthography*[1] did examine a portion of the corpus described in this grammar, although their primary focus was the orthography, and not the grammar, of the inscriptions. Cross and Freedman did not analyze all of the inscriptions which were known at that time; since then, many important new inscriptions have been discovered.

One objective of the present work is to test Cross and Freedman's hypotheses in the light of the new material. A careful analysis of all the known epigraphic Hebrew inscriptions, including the seals and other recent discoveries, provides a more comprehensive picture of the evolution of Hebrew orthography.

---

[1]F.M. Cross and D. Freedman, *Early Hebrew Orthography: A Study of the Epigraphic Evidence*, American Oriental Series 36 (New Haven: American Oriental Society, 1952).

André Lemaire's *Inscriptions hébraïques: Les Ostraca* is a very important study of the Hebrew ostraca.[2] This work, however, is devoted primarily to the historical aspects of the Hebrew texts written on the ostraca. Lemaire's insights are used often to support specific points in this book.

A monograph written by Ziony Zevit[3] is the first synthesis of both inscriptions and seals, but solely for the purpose of an orthographic and phonological study of *matres lectionis*. His interpretations provide valuable insights regarding *matres lectionis* as discussed in Chapter 2.

The 1991 publication of the corpus and concordance of "ancient" Hebrew inscriptions by G.I. Davies[4] serves as a useful comparative resource to the material presented in the Appendix of this book.[5]

This study of epigraphic Hebrew grammar is organized as follows. After an introduction which provides the historical context, the major sections include phonology, morphology, syntax, as well as a lexicon. The transliterations and translations of the epigraphic Hebrew inscriptions (texts and seals) are found in the Appendix.[6] The main focus is on morphology which contains an exhaustive treatment of epigraphic Hebrew verbs (e.g., verbal stems, finite forms, simple and derived stems), pronouns, nouns (including numerals), and particles (e.g., adverbs, prepositions, conjunctions, and interjections).

---

[2]A. Lemaire, *Inscriptions hébraïques, tomb I: Les ostraca. Littératures anciennes du Proche-Orient 9* (Paris: Editions du Cerf, 1977).

[3]Z. Zevit, *Matres Lectionis in Ancient Hebrew Epigraphy*, American Schools of Oriental Research Monography Series, no. 2 (Cambridge, Mass.: American Schools of Oriental Research, 1980).

[4]G.I. Davies, *Ancient Hebrew Inscriptions. Corpus and Concordance* (Cambridge: Cambridge University Press, 1991.)

[5]Davies' work does not suggest any fundamental changes in the grammatical analysis that this book provides. The corpus is virtually the same as that of Davies with the following exceptions: he includes a few non-Hebrew inscriptions as well as some post-exilic Hebrew inscriptions.

[6]Unless it is necessary as a syllable divider (e.g., Murabbaʿat), ʾ and ʿ are not indicated in the English transliterations (e.g., Ajrud, Aḥiyahu). Also, the pure English convention of a proper noun or locative is used when one exists. For those names where an English convention does not exist and where confusion is possible, diacritics are used (e.g., Ḥasadyahu, Ḥeleṣyahu, Aḥiyahu).

The present study is a comprehensive analysis of all known epigraphic Hebrew inscriptions including those of the larger collections found at Samaria (102 ostraca), Arad (112 inscriptions), and Lachish (32 texts, excluding inscribed weights and seals).[7] It also includes the seals found at numerous sites throughout Palestine, the over 400 epigraphic Hebrew seal impressions collected (though not studied in depth) by Francesco Vattioni,[8] as well as those which have been discovered and published in more recent years (including the more than 200 Hebrew bullae published by Avigad in 1986).[9]

Other important studies of seals extensively consulted for this grammar include Larry G. Herr's *The Scripts of Ancient Northwest Semitic Seals*,[10] *Inscribed Seals* by Ruth Hestrin and Michal Dayagi-Mendels,[11] as well as publications by Pierre Bordreuil and André Lemaire.[12]

---

[7]Table 1 (pp. 23-25) and the Appendix include only legible inscriptions.

[8]F. Vattioni, "I sigilli ebraici," *Biblica* 50 (1969): 357-88; "I sigilli ebraici II," *Augustinianum* 2 (1971): 447-54; "Sigill ebraici. III." *Annali dell'istituto orientali di Napoli* 28 (1978): 227-54.

[9]N. Avigad, *bwlwt ʿbrywt mymy yrmyhw* [Hebrew Bullae from the Time of Jeremiah] (Jerusalem: *hḥbrh lḥqyrt ʾrṣ-yśrʾl wʿtyqwtyh, 1986); Hebrew Bullae from the Time of Jeremiah. Remnants of a Burnt Archive* (Jerusalem: Israel Exploration Society, 1986).

[10]L. Herr, *The Scripts of Ancient Northwest Semitic Seals*, Harvard Semitic Monographs 18 (Missoula, MT: Scholars Press, 1978). See J. Naveh's review of *The Scripts of Ancient Northwest Semitic Seals*, by L. Herr, in *BASOR* 239 (Summer, 1980): 75-76, with the severe strictures voiced there.

Naveh criticizes the use of Herr's collection of West Semitic seals as a handbook, since it contains printing errors (e.g., *ʿšyhw* instead of *ʾšyhw* in seals 5-7 (Herr, pp. 84-85), omits certain seals (e.g. Vattioni, nos. 55, 189-190, 212), and uses paleographic dating techniques, which, according to Naveh (p. 75) are "overconfident," or "too narrow." Naveh is correct to suggest that Herr's work should be made more exact by a revision; nevertheless, Herr's paleographic dating techniques are equal or superior to those of previous students of the seals, and his work is useful in that it includes most of the seals (he omits relatively few) and is an easy reference tool. Naveh's complaints about Herr's work (e.g., his lack of professional ethics in crediting previous authors or his overlooking of some secondary literature on the seals) do not dismiss or discredit the importance of Herr's work for a study of epigraphic Hebrew seals.

[11]R. Hestrin and M. Dayagi-Mendels, *Inscribed Seals, First Temple Period. Hebrew, Ammonite, Moabite, Phoenician and Aramaic* (Jerusalem: Israel Museum, 1979).

[12]Among these publications are: P. Bordreuil and A. Lemaire, "Trois sceaux nord-ouest sémitiques inédits," *Semitica* 24 (1974): 25-34; "Nouveaux

In addition to the seals, the grammar contains an analysis of various other epigraphic Hebrew inscriptions from Beersheba, Beit Shean, Gezer, Gibeon, Hazor, Ḥorvat Uza, Jerusalem, Ketef Hinnom, Khirbet Beit Lei, Khirbet el-Kom, Khirbet el-Meshash, Kuntillet Ajrud, Meṣad Ḥashavyahu, Murabbaʿat, Nahal Yishai, the Ophel, Ramat Rachel, Samaria, Siloam, Silwan, Tell Amal, Tell Beit Mirsim, Tell Ira and Tell Qasile.

The purpose of this book is to collect and to analyze the Hebrew epigraphic material. Biblical Hebrew provides a useful perspective for analytical purposes and figures prominently in comparisons between epigraphic and biblical Hebrew. Although this grammar does not pretend to be a comparative study between epigraphic and biblical Hebrew, it does provide the basis for future research for such a comparison.

Though not as extensive as some textual corpora from the ancient Near East, the corpus of epigraphic Hebrew inscriptions is large enough to permit a thorough treatment of the language, yet small enough to allow a detailed analysis. This grammar presents epigraphic Hebrew in a clear framework that provides scholars and students with a readily available guide and language tool never before available.

---

sceaux hébreux, araméens et ammonites," *Semitica* 26 (1976): 45-63; "Nouveau groupe de sceaux hébreux, araméens et ammonites," *Semitica* 29 (1979): 71-84; "Nouveaux sceaux hébreux et araméens," *Semitica* 32 (1982): 21-34; P. Bordreuil, *Catalogue des sceaux ouest-sémitiques inscrits de la Bibliothèque Nationale du Musée du Louvre et du Musée biblique de Bible et Terre Sainte (Paris: Bibliothèque Nationale, 1986).*

The following publications appeared after the final manuscript of the present book was completed: R. Deutsch and M. Heltzer, *Forty New Ancient West Semitic Inscriptions* (Tel Aviv: Archaeological Center Publication, 1994), *idem*, *New Epigraphic Evidence from the Biblical Period* (Tel Aviv: Archaeological Center Publication, 1995), and N. Avigad, *Corpus of West Semitic Stamp Seals*, edited by Benjamin Sass (Jerusalem: Hebrew University of Jerusalem, Israel Exploration Society, 1997).

These works are important primarily for the study of epigraphic Hebrew seals and proper names. While they have been reviewed by the present author and are cited in the Bibliography, the Hebrew forms discussed in those works are not specifically treated in this grammar. They will appear in a later edition of this book.

1. INTRODUCTION

1.1 Sources for the Study of Epigraphic Hebrew

Epigraphic Hebrew is the term used here to describe the language of Israel and Judah from the 10th-6th centuries B.C. Except for a few dialectical differences, the texts from the North and the South show similar orthography and morphology. The epigraphic Hebrew texts from the North date primarily from the ninth-eighth centuries, while most of the Southern texts are from the seventh-sixth centuries. There are also more texts from the South than from the North.

Epigraphic Hebrew texts from both Judah and Israel form a cohesive body of material which exhibit certain characteristics setting it apart from other neighboring languages. However, there are definite orthographic and morphological similarities with Phoenician, as well as with Moabite and Aramaic. Biblical Hebrew syntax and morphology remain the closest comparative material to the epigraphic Hebrew inscriptions.

If analyzed critically, the Masoretic text is a reliable source when compared to epigraphic Hebrew because Masoretic Hebrew reflects a later stage of the language represented by epigraphic Hebrew texts. Masoretic Hebrew differs phonologically both from Qumranic and Mishnaic Hebrew (ca. 50 B.C.-200 A.D.); for example, within the former, *ʾaleph, hê, ʿayin* and *ḥet* were preserved, and not weakened, as they were in post-biblical Hebrew.[1]

---

[1] E. Y. Kutscher, *The Language and Linguistic Background of the Isaiah Scroll (IQIsa^{a}),* Hebrew Original, 1969 (Leiden: Brill, 1974), pp. 505-7, 510-11; 1971:cols. 1586, 1595-96. For Mishnaic Hebrew, cf. M. Bar-Asher,

The Masoretic text developed from a Proto-Masoretic text type[2] which was linked with certain of the Qumran texts. These latter texts are representative of the oldest biblical manuscripts, and when compared to the Masoretic text, conform orthographically to it.[3] The Qumran texts under discussion, 4Q Exod, 4Q Sam,[4] and 4Q Jer, date to the period from ca. 250-200 B.C..[5] These texts represent, in several ways, a more archaic prototype of the Hebrew text inherited by the Masoretes which, by the third century B.C., consisted both of the consonantal text and of *m.l.*;[6] vowel markings were added to the text after the sixth century A.D.[7]

Consequently, the Masoretic text is most likely part of a later tradition, the roots of which can be traced to the biblical Qumran texts of the third century B.C., and probably back even further in history to the time period of epigraphic Hebrew. Therefore, if used prudently, the Masoretic biblical texts can be used for comparative

---

qwbs mʾmrym blšwn ḥzl [Anthology of Articles Concerning Rabbinic Hebrew], 1972.

[2]M. H. Goshen-Gottstein, "Hebrew Bible Manuscripts: Their History and Their Place in the *HUBP* Edition," *Biblica* 48 (1967): 245-49; Z. Zevit, "The Linguistic and Contextual Arguments in Favor of a Hebrew 3 m.s. Suffix -Y," *UF* 9 (1977): 327-38; Zevit, *MLAHE*, pp. 8-9.

[3]For the orthographic conformation of Exod[f] and Jer.[a] to the Masoretic text, see D. Freedman, "The Massoretic Text and the Qumran Scrolls: A Study in Orthography," *Textus* 2 (1962): 202, 203, 211.

[4]Both Qumran texts 4QSam[a], cited extensively by P. K. McCarter in *Anchor Bible I Samuel* (Garden City, NY: Doubleday, 1980), and 4QSam[c], published by E. C. Ulrich, "4QSam[c] A Fragmentary Manuscript of 2 Samuel 14-15 from the Scribe of *Serek Hay-yaḥad* (1QS)," *BASOR* 235 (1979): 1-25, are characterized by the use of *matres lectionis*, perhaps even more extensively than in the Masoretic text.

[5] Zevit, *MLAHE*, p. 8; Freedman, "Massoretic Text and Qumran Scrolls: A Study in Orthography," *Textus* 2, pp. 202, 205, 211.

[6]E.g., 4Q Exod[f]: *ʾwtw* (*ʾōtō*); *ʿwlm* (*ʿōlām*); 4Q Jer[a]: *ntwš* (*nātōš*); *ʾzwr* (*ʾēzōr*). See Freedman, "Massoretic Text and Qumran Scrolls," *Textus 2*, pp. 99-100.

[7]The following studies deal with the complexities of the relationship of the Qumran texts and the Masoretic text: M. H. Goshen-Gottstein, *Text and Language in Bible and Qumran* (Jerusalem: Orient Pub. House, 1960); S. Z. Leiman (ed.), *The Canon and Masorah of the Hebrew Bible: An Introductory Reader* (New York: Ktav Pub. House, 1974); S. Talmon and F. M. Cross (eds.), *Qumran and the History of the Biblical Text* (Cambridge: Harvard University Press, 1975).

purposes to conduct a philological and historical examination of the epigraphic Hebrew inscriptions.[8]

1.2 The Inscriptions

The Gezer Calendar, found in 1908, is considered by many scholars (notably Albright, Freedman and Cross) to be the earliest decipherable epigraphic Hebrew inscription.[9] If this interpretation of

---

[8]Zevit, *MLAHE*, p. 10.

[9]Cf. W.F. Albright, "The Gezer Calendar," *BASOR* 92 (1943): 16-26; Freedman, "Massoretic Text and Qumran Scrolls," *Textus* 2, pp. 87-102; F. M. Cross, "Newly Found Inscriptions in Old Canaanite and Early Phoenician Scripts," *BASOR* 238 (1980): 14.

Contrary to the view of Albright, Freedman, and Cross, some scholars contend that the Gezer inscription may not represent the earliest epigraphic Hebrew inscription. G. Garbini has argued for the interpretation of the Gezer ostracon as Phoenician. His position is linguistically plausible. A comparison of the scripts of the Phoenician and epigraphic Hebrew inscriptions with the script of the Gezer inscription suggests a close resemblance between the Gezer and the Phoenician scripts (see n. 11, p. 9).

The Gezer calendar is defective orthographically and it is clear that the philological interpretation of this inscription is not solid enough to permit a definitive conclusion as to whether it represents the earliest inscription in epigraphic Hebrew.

Nevertheless, in this grammar, the Gezer calendar is included in the corpus of epigraphic Hebrew inscriptions for two reasons: 1) it is considered by most scholars to be Hebrew and 2) evidence which indicates that the Gezer inscription is not Hebrew (rather, that it is Phoenician) is not strong enough to refute its identification as the earliest Hebrew inscription. This grammar follows Cross's interpretation as the most likely one to date: his work indicates that a palaeological, archaeological and philological basis exists for the identification of the Gezer inscription as Hebrew.

In addition to the articles by Albright, Freedman, and Cross which have been mentioned earlier in this note, the following articles deal with the Gezer calendar: S. Birnbaum, "The Dates of the Gezer Tablet and of the Samaria Ostraca," *PEQ* 74 (1942): 104-8; L. Finkelstein, "A Talmudic Note on the Word for Cutting Flax in the Gezer Calendar," *BASOR* 94 (1944): 28-29; J.G. Février, "Remarques sur le calendrier de Gézer," *Semitica* 1 (1948): 33-41; A.M. Honeyman, "The Syntax of the Gezer Calendar," *Journal of the Royal Asiatic Society* (1953): 53-58; G. Garbini, "Note sul «calendario» di Gezer," *AION* 6 (1954-56): 123-30; Wolf Wirgin, "The Calendar Tablet from Gezer," *EI* 6 (1960): 9-12; B.D. Rahtjen, "A Note Concerning the Form of the Gezer Tablet," *PEQ* 93 (1961): 70-72; J.B. Segal, " 'YRḤ' in the Gezer 'Calendar'," *JSS* 7

the Gezer ostracon is accepted, it is also the oldest linear text in alphabetic Hebrew, a fact which sets it apart from other texts such as the Izbet Ṣarṭah inscription and other earlier Palestinian inscriptions which, at present, remain unintelligible (except for an abecedary).

The Gezer Calendar represents pure consonantalism, a characteristic inherent in Phoenician and the Proto-Canaanite family,[10] and its script resembles those of the tenth century

---

(1962): 212-21; S. Talmon, "The Gezer Calendar and the Seasonal Cycle of Ancient Canaan," *JAOS* 83 (1963): 177-87; A. Lemaire, "*Zamīr* dans la tablette de Gézer et le Cantique des Cantiques," *VT* 25 (1975): 15-26.

[10]The philological interpretation of the Gezer Calendar is not solid enough to permit a certain conclusion regarding the use of *m.l.* in tenth century Hebrew epigraphy.

The final *waw* at the end of the noun *yrḥw* is attested four times in this inscription. The interpretation of this suffix is varied; the main views are that the *waw* represents a *m.l.* as an archaic nominative dual construct -*ō*, or *aw*, that it is a *m.l.* for an archaic nominative plural construct -*ū*, or the purely consonantal third masculine singular possessive suffix on a dual noun, pronounced -*ēw*.

For the interpretation that the *waw* represents -*ō*, cf. H.L. Ginsberg, "Observations on the Lachish Documents," *Bulletin of the Jewish Palestine Exploration Society* 3 (1935): 49. See W. F. Albright's criticisms in "The Gezer Calendar," *BASOR* 92(1943): 22, and J.C.L. Gibson, *TSSI*, p. 3. The interpretation of Ginsberg that the *waw* of *yrḥw* represents -*ō* must be abandoned, for nowhere in the epigraphic Hebrew corpus does final *waw* represent -*ō*. See sec. 3.2.2.1, p. 159, n. 186 in this grammar for a discussion of *hê* (not *waw*) as the third masculine singular pronominal suffix and *m.l.* for -*ō* in epigraphic Hebrew. For the interpretation that *waw* represents -*aw* in the Gezer inscription, cf. A. Lemaire, "*Zamīr* dans la tablette de Gézer et le Cantique des Cantiques," *VT* 25 (1975), p. 17. For *ū*, cf. G. Garbini, "Note sul «calendrio» di Gezer," *AION* 6 (1954-56), pp. 123-30; Gibson, *TSSI*, p. 3. For the interpretation that *waw* represents -*ēw*, cf. W. F. Albright, "The Gezer Calendar," *BASOR* 92 (1943): 22-24; "The Oracles of Balaam," *JBL* 63(1944): 209-11; Cross and Freedman, *EHO*, p. 57.

For a discussion of -*w* as the third masculine singular pronominal suffix on plural and dual nouns, see sec. 3.2.2.1, pp. 160-61, n. 189 in this grammar. The evidence from epigraphic Hebrew indicates that -*w* is the third masculine singular suffix on plural nouns (e.g., *ʾnšw*, "his people," L 3:18) and prepositions which act as though they are plurals *ʾlw*, "to him," MHY 1:13). The same orthography (-*w*) should probably be considered as the suffix also for dual nouns (e.g., *yrḥw*). Valid arguments exist for the pronunciation of this suffix as -*aw* (uncontracted diphthong) or *ēw* (contracted diphthong); cf. sec. 3.2.2.1, pp. 160-61, n. 189. Since the orthography of *qṣ* (without *yod*) in the Gezer inscription reflects the contraction of the -*ay* diphthong, perhaps the spelling of *yrḥw* (without *yod*) likewise reflects this linguistic feature.

Phoenician inscriptions from Byblos.[11] The spelling of the word *qṣ*, *qēṣ*, "summer-fruit" (and possibly *yrḥw*, *yarḥēw*, "his/its (?) two months") reflects the contraction of the *ay* diphthong,[12] which is either a Phoenician or a North Hebrew (cf. the Samaria ostraca) linguistic feature.

Palaeographically, the Gezer Calendar has been dated to the second half of the tenth century when Gezer was an Israelite city (1Kings 9:16), but epigraphers nevertheless have been unable to determine with certainty whether the script and language of this inscription are Phoenician or Hebrew. Cross[13] points out that the rudimentary features of certain letters (*mem*, *resh*, *ʾaleph*, *waw*, *zayin*, *kaf*) within the inscription suggest a tenth (as opposed to eleventh) century date for the inscription and provide palaeographic evidence for the hypothesis that the Gezer Calendar provides the first glimpse of "the emergent Hebrew script."[14]

The form *pšt*, which Albright took as *pištā* without *m.l.*, represents a further orthographic problem in the Gezer Calendar. Cf. Albright, "Gezer Calendar," *BASOR* 92 (1943), p. 22, and n. 34, following S. Yeivin, *The History of the Jewish Script* I (Jerusalem, 1939), p. 59. Albright's assumption is very doubtful, but if he were correct, this would be an excellent example to prove that *m.l.* were not used in tenth century Hebrew.

[11]It is helpful to look at the actual scripts.

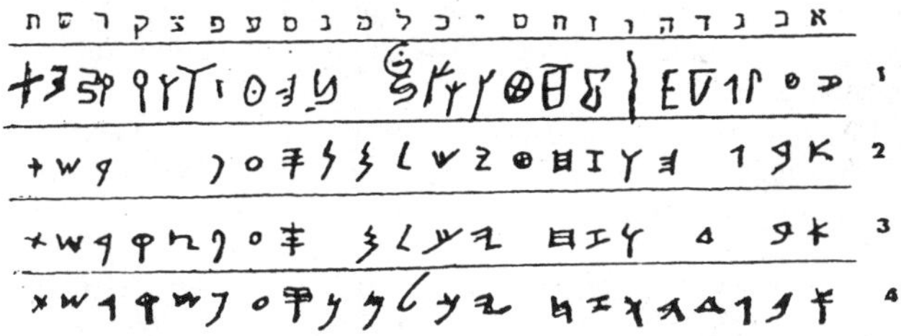

L. 1
L. 2
L. 3
L. 4

Line 1 represents Proto-Canaanite (Old Palestinian) letters from the Izbet Ṣarṭah abecedary (12th c.); line 2 represents the Phoenician alphabet from the Ahiram Sarcophagus (10th c.); line 3 represents the letters from the Gezer Calendar (late 10th c.); and line 4 represents the letters from the Samaria ostraca (8th c.).

[12]Cross and Freedman, *EHO*, pp. 46-47.

[13]Cross, "Inscriptions in Old Canaanite and Early Phoenician," *BASOR* 238 (1980), p. 14, esp. p. 18, n. 16.

[14]According to Cross, "Inscriptions," *BASOR* 238 (1980):14, "I believe that the first rudimentary innovations that will mark the emergent Hebrew Script can be perceived in the Gezer Calendar, but they are faint at

Beyond the recognition of its listing of agricultural activities assigned to the months of the year, the purpose of the Gezer Calendar is disputed.[15] In any event, the tablet appears to be complete and the text has been fitted carefully into the allotted space.

Y. Aharoni has dated five ostraca (Arad 76-79, 98) to the tenth century.[16] These inscriptions, however, are either short (no. 98), or badly preserved on broken sherds (nos. 76-79). On two of these ostraca (nos. 77, 78), only one letter is visible. If the Gezer Calendar is to be regarded as a Hebrew inscription, it is the longest and best-preserved representative of tenth-century Hebrew. However, only when further tenth century inscriptions are discovered will it be easier to establish the early forms of the epigraphic Hebrew language, especially with regard to phonology.

Ninth century epigraphic Hebrew consists of several inscriptions and a few seals. One seal is thought possibly to be a forgery (Herr 161),[17]another perhaps Philistine (Herr 163), [18] while one other seal, containing a final *m.l.*, and therefore important phonologically, was dated by Cross and Freedman[19] to the ninth century because of its archaic *mem*. This seal has been ignored for

---

best...the cluster of Hebrew features here described [in a discussion of Hebrew inscriptions from Gezer, Ajrud and Nimrod in the 10th-9th centuries] represent salient elements in the emergence of a full-blown, independent script tradition in Israelite scribal circles."

[15]From a farming point of view, the actual sequence of farming activities is curiously recorded in that the list of duties begins in the middle of the farming season, during the fruit harvest; nevertheless, it does coincide with the fall-to-fall calendar.

According to Talmon, the Gezer Calendar is best understood as an official document which presents the farming seasons in the lowlands of Palestine in proper chronological sequence. He views the inscription as having been drawn up by the royal administration for tax-collection purposes; cf. "The Gezer Calender and the Seasonal Cycle of Ancient Canaan," *JAOS* 83 (1963): 177-87.

[16]Cf. Y. Aharoni, *ktwbwt ʿrd* [Arad Inscriptions] (Jerusalem: Bialik Institute, 1975), pp. 98, 100, 112, 215-16.

[17]Herr, *SANSS*, p. 148. This seal is from the Moshe Dayan Collection, from an unknown provenience.

[18]Ibid., pp. 149-50. This seal, from an unknown provenience, is from the S. Mossayoff Collection.

[19]Cross and Freedman, *EHO*, pp. 47-48, following W. F. Albright (cf. *EHO*, n. 19).

some reason by later studies.[20] An ostracon from Beth Shean is dated to the ninth/eighth centuries, but it only contains one word (*byt*).[21] The first four inscriptions from Hazor are dated to the mid-ninth century. The forms of the letters are very similar to Phoenician; however, the few letters which may be seen (in inscriptions 1, 2, and 4) are insufficient for lexical analysis. Inscription 3 shows the word *bt*, probably "*bat*-measure," the capacity of the storage jar upon which it had been incised. Several incised sherds from Arad have also been dated to the ninth century (numbers 67-70, 80, 95, 100-103).[22] Of these, number 101 reads *ḥṣy*, where the *yod* is possibly a final *m.l.* for *-ī*.[23] This word has been compared with *ḥṣy* in an inscription from Beersheba, *ḥṣy lmlk*, in giving the translation, "a half-measure."[24] The dating of the inscriptions from Kuntillet Ajrud has also been set at the end of the ninth and first half of the eighth century.[25] These texts will be discussed below.

As new inscriptions come to light, a firmer link between the Gezer Calendar of the tenth century and the more abundant material from the eighth century may be established. With the early eighth century, the study of epigraphic Hebrew inscriptions takes on a wider dimension. The dialectical differences between Israel and Judah can begin to be identified. The main inscriptions from the early/mid eighth century are the Samaria ostraca,[26] the first of which

---

[20]For example, Zevit, *MLAHE*, p. 11, does not include this seal in his corpus.

[21]Zevit, *MLAHE*, p. 11. J. Naveh, "The Scripts in Palestine and Transjordan in the Iron Age," ed., J.A. Sanders, *Near Eastern Archaeology in the Twentieth Century: Essays in Honor of Nelson Glueck* (Garden City, NY: Doubleday, 1970), p. 278, suggests an Aramaic origin for this inscription.

[22]Aharoni, *ktwbwt ʿrd* [Arad Inscriptions], pp. 8, 11, 107, 117-18, 216.

[23]One cannot be absolutely certain that the *-y* is a *mater lectionis*. The third root consonant was historically *yod*. Even if the *-y* is a *m.l.*, it might be explained as historical writing.

[24]Aharoni, *ktwbwt ʿrd*, p. 111.

[25]Z. Meshel, *Kuntillet ʿAjrud: A Religious Centre from the Time of the Judean Monarchy on the Border of Sinai* (Israel Museum Cat. No. 175, 1978), p. 124; also, "Did Yahweh Have a Consort?" *BAR* 5, no. 2 (1979): 34.

[26]The Samaria ostraca consist principally of 63 dockets belonging probably to the reign of Jeroboam II. Another 45 ostraca are deemed illegible by Reisner and 42 by Kaufman, while the present grammar includes 89 legible ostraca. Cf. G.A. Reisner, *Israelite Ostraca from Samaria* (Boston: E.O. Cockayne, 1924) and I.T. Kaufman, "The Samaria Ostraca: A Study in Ancient

were uncovered in 1910 by the Harvard-Samaria team, the two Tell Qasile ostraca, (found on the surface of the site, a bit north of Tel Aviv, in 1948-50), and the Kuntillet Ajrud inscriptions (from a late ninth-early eighth century Judean fortification in northeast Sinai, excavated in 1975-76).

While the Samaria and Qasile inscriptions are written on pottery sherds, the Ajrud finds include inscriptions on plaster walls, on large pithoi and on stone bowls. The inscriptions are votive in nature, and several deity names are mentioned, including Asherah, Baʿal, El, and YHWH. Proper names at Ajrud show the theophoric element *-yw* at the end of the name, although *-yhw* has been said to be the over-riding feature of Judean proper names.[27] Several abecedaries were found at Ajrud showing the *pê* before *ʿayin* order which is also found in the Izbet Ṣarṭah abecedary.[28] The *pê-ʿayin*

Hebrew Palaeography," (Ph.D. dissertation, Harvard University, 1966). The Samaria ostraca were found in the storage rooms of the royal palace and describe shipments of wine and oil brought in by farmers from various places presumably as taxes. This material was the main source for the study of the Hebrew dialect spoken in the Northern Kingdom.

[27]Z. Zevit has written an article which deals with proper names ending with *-yhw*, although in it, he concentrates on the *-yhw* versus *-yh* (rather than with *-yw*) names, the distribution of these suffixes on proper names, and the dating of names bearing these suffixes. Cf. "A Chapter in the History of Israelite Personal Names," *BASOR* 250 (1983): 1-16.

[28]The twelfth century Izbet Ṣarṭah inscription represents the oldest and most complete linear alphabet of twenty-two letters (in line 5).

For G. Garbini's view of Izbet Ṣarṭah, the reader is directed to the following articles: "Sull'alfabetario di ʿIzbet Sartah," *Oriens Antiquus* 17 (1978): 286-95; "Storie e problemi dell'epigrafia Semitica," *Napoli* (1979): 89-92. For additional articles on this inscription, cf. A. Demsky, "A Proto-Canaanite Abecedary Dating from the Period of the Judges and its Implication for the History of the Alphabet," *TA* 4 (1977): 14-27; M. Kochavi, "An Ostracon of the Period of the Judges from ʿIzbet Ṣarṭah," *TA* 4 (1977): 1-13; A. Demsky and M. Kochavi, "An Alphabet from the Days of the Judges," *BAR* 4, no. 3 (1978): 22-25; A. Lemaire, "Abécédaires et exercises d'écolier en épigraphie nord-ouest sémitique," *Journal Asiatique* 266 (1978): 221-35; J. Naveh, "Some Considerations on the Ostracon from ʿIzbet Ṣarṭah," *IEJ* 28 (1978): 31-35; J. Teixidor, "Bulletin d'épigraphie sémitique," *Syria* 56 (1979): 353-405; J. P. Siegel, "The Evolution of Two Hebrew Scripts," *BAR* 5, no. 3 (1979): 28; F. M. Cross, "Newly Found Inscriptions in Old Canaanite and Early Phoenician Scripts," *BASOR* 238 (1980): 8-12; J. Naveh, "The Greek Alphabet: New Evidence," *BA* 43, no. 1 (1980): 25; A. Dotan, "New Light on the ʿIzbet Ṣarṭah Ostracon," *TA* 8, no. 2 (1981): 160-72.

Two important features can be detected in the Izbet Ṣarṭah inscription: its characteristic of a left to right direction for the abecedary text and a reverse scheme is therefore not an error at Ajrud; rather it is part of an earlier alphabetic tradition.

Several more epigraphic Hebrew texts ascribed to the late eighth-early seventh century permit an even more extensive examination. Falling within this time-frame are the inscription from an ivory pomegranate from Jerusalem, as well as the votive tomb inscriptions from Khirbet el-Kom, Nahal Yishai and Silwan.

An ivory pomegranate, bearing an inscription from the First Temple Period, was found in Jerusalem. This object, displayed in the Israel Museum, is thought to come from Solomon's temple and has been dated to the second half of the 8th century B.C.[29]

The Khirbet el-Kom inscriptions come from the village of Khirbet el-Kom, eight and one half miles west of Hebron. The first inscription, incised on stone, bought in Jerusalem in 1967, was traced back to the original site, and was determined to have come from the wall of a tomb chamber (Tomb I). Another inscription, as well as graffiti, also come from the chamber walls of Tomb I, while Tomb II contained one longer text inscribed on a pillar and described as a graffito by the excavator. The remainder of the inscriptions from Khirbet el-Kom come from a decanter, a bowl and a plate.[30]

ḥet-zayin and *pê-ʿayin* order within its alphabet. The former feature is otherwise unattested in epigraphic Hebrew while the latter is attested four times. Both Demsky and Cross suspect a scribal error for the *ḥet-zayin* order in the Izbet Ṣarṭah inscription; cf. "Proto-Canaanite Abecedary," *TA* 4 (1977): 17-18 and "Inscriptions in Early Canaanite and Early Phoenician," *BASOR* 238 (1980): 13.

The *pê-ʿayin* order in the abecedary is well documented in biblical acrostics and appears, as well, in four ninth-eighth century Hebrew abecedaries found by Meshel at Kuntillat Ajrud. The *pê-ʿayin* sequence thus exhibits a long history and illustrates a local scribal tradition which dates back at least to the twelfth century.

For the *pê-ʿayin* order in biblical acrostics, cf. M. Löhr, "Alphabetische und alphabetisierende Lieder im Alten Testament," *ZAW* 25 (1905): 173-98; J. Boehmer, "Ein alphabetisch-akrostichisches Rätsel und ein Versuch es zu lösen," *ZAW* 28 (1908): 53-57; P.A. Munch, "Die alphabetische Akrostichie in der jüdischen Psalmendictung," *ZDMG* 90 (Neue Folge Band 15, 1936): 703-10; N. K. Gottwald, *Studies in the Book of Lamentations* (Chicago: Allenson, 1954), pp. 23-32. For the examples of abecedaries from Kuntillet Ajrud, cf. Meshel, "Consort," *BAR* 5, no. 2 (1979): 31.

[29] A. Lemaire, "Une inscription paléo-hébraïque sur grenade en ivoire," *RB* 88, no. 2 (1981): 236-39.

[30] W. G. Dever, "Iron Age Epigraphic Material from the Area of Khirbet el-Kôm," *HUCA* 40/41 (1970): 139-205.

The inscription from Naḥal Yishai is a Hebrew graffito, written in black ink, which was found in a burial cave near En Gedi in the Judean hills. This graffito was written on a pillar-like stalactite and contained nine lines.[31]

The Silwan Tomb inscriptions, now in the British Museum, were discovered in 1870, but were not deciphered until 1953. These lapidary inscriptions were incised in the rock on both sides of the facade of a small, rock-cut tomb in Silwan Village, east of Jerusalem. The third inscription from Silwan, discovered by A. Reifenberg in 1946, was also inscribed in the rock above the facade of another rock-cut burial chamber.[32]

Besides the tomb inscriptions mentioned above, there are several other epigraphic Hebrew texts ascribed to the late eighth-early seventh centuries. These include the inscriptions from Hazor, Arad, Samaria (C 1101), Beersheba, Siloam, Wadi Murabbaʿat, and the Ophel.

The Hazor texts (numbers 5-8) were discovered in 1956, and consist of proper names preceded by the *lamed* of ownership. All of the inscriptions were incised (except number 6, which was painted) on whole pottery vessels (now broken) to record the owner's name and in some cases, the contents of the vessels.[33]

Twelve ostraca from Arad (numbers 59-66, 87, 92-94) which were unearthed from Stratum 9, date to the late eighth century. The contents of these inscriptions, most of which are very fragmentary, consist of proper names (Arad 59-60, 64), numerals (Arad 60, 65, 87), or the *lamed* of ownership plus proper name (Arad 92-93). Three inscriptions contain instructions either to "send" (Arad 62, 66), or "give" (Arad 60) a commodity. The remaining inscriptions from Stratum 9 are largely illegible (Arad 63, 66, 94).[34]

Also ascribed to the late eighth century are several fragmentary ostraca from the Samaria expedition of 1932. Among

---

[31]P. Bar-Adon, "An Early Hebrew Inscription in a Judean Desert Cave," *IEJ 25* (1975): 226-32.

[32]N. Avigad, "The Epitaph of a Royal Steward from Siloam Village," *IEJ* 3 (1953): 137-52.

[33]Y. Yadin, *The James A. de Rothschild Expedition at Hazor, Hazor II, An Account of the Second Season of Excavations, 1956* (Jerusalem: Magnes Press of the Hebrew University, 1960), pp. 70-75.

[34]Y. Aharoni, *ktwbwt ʿrd* [Arad Inscriptions] (Jerusalem: Bialik Institute, 1975).

these is the incised pottery sherd, broken on the left side, Samaria C 1101. Sometimes called the "Barley Letter," this inscription is written in the cursive script and may have been a memorandum of some sort.[35]

The decipherable inscriptions from Beersheba include three ostraca, three graffiti, and two seals. Ostracon 1, the most important of the ostraca, is a palimpsest of five legible lines which were written in black ink. All of the graffiti were incised on pottery vessels before they were fired.[36]

The Siloam Tunnel inscription, discovered in 1880, was incised on a tunnel wall which connected the Gihon Spring to the Siloam pool at the southeast end of the temple mount area of Jerusalem. Carved in the time of Hezekiah, the inscription commemorated the successful completion of the tunnel.[37]

Murabbaʿat Papyrus no. 17, found in 1952 in a cave about eighteen kilometers south of Qumran, also falls within the late eighth-early seventh centuries.[38] It is the only element of the epigraphic Hebrew corpus to be recorded on papyrus. It is a palimpsest: the later inscription is part of a letter (the earliest one preserved in epigraphic Hebrew), while the underlying text appears to be a list of names, patronymics and a quantity of some commodity allotted to them.[39]

---

[35]W.F. Albright, "Ostracon C 1101 of Samaria," *PEQ* 68 (1936): 211-15. See also A. Lemaire, "L'ostracon C 1101 de Samarie. Nouvel essai." *RB* 79 (1972): 565-70.

[36]Y. Aharoni, *Beer-Sheba I, Excavations at Tel Beer-Sheba, 1969-1971 Seasons* (Tel Aviv: Tel Aviv Institute of Archaeology, 1973), spec. pp. 71-78.

[37]H. Donner and W. Röllig, *KAI*. Band II (Wiesbaden: Otto Harrassowitz, 1962), p. 189. See also G. Levi della Vida, "The Shiloaḥ Inscription Reconsidered," *Beihefte zur Zeitshrift für die alttestamentliche Wissenschaft* 103 (1968): 162-66.

[38]J.T. Milik, in P. Benoit *et al.*, *Discoveries in the Judean Desert II. Les Grottes de Murabbaʿât* (Oxford: Clarendon, 1961). See also F. M. Cross, Jr., "Epigraphic Notes on Hebrew Documents of the Eighth-Sixth Centuries B.C.: II. The Murabbaʿat Papyrus and the Letter found Near Yabneh-Yam," *BASOR* 165 (1962): 34-46.

[39]This text gives some indication of the common use of papyrus in Judah, cf. *Encyclopedia Judaica*, vol. 2 (Jerusalem: Keter, 1972), s.v. "Alphabet, Hebrew," by J. Naveh, p. 682. In addition to this palimpsest papyrus, about twenty clay sealings of papyrus rolls, dating to the sixth century B.C., have been found, mostly at Lachish, cf. Israel Museum. *ktwbwt msprwt*

The Ophel 2 inscription, found in 1978, has likewise been assigned a date in the late eighth century. This inscription, though partially broken on the left, was incised in stone and is thought by the excavator to have been carved in the wall of a public building.[40]

Three additional ostraca from the Ophel were discovered in 1964 and have been dated to the end of the eighth-beginning of the seventh century.[41] The inscriptions mention oil or grain and the quantities of these commodities which were either given or received.

Another incised ostracon from the period under discussion is an inscription on a wine decanter from the Hebron area. The jar was purchased in Jerusalem in 1968.[42] Also ascribed to the late eighth-early seventh century is an incised ostracon from Ramat Rachel[43] containing a proper name with patronym.

The Jerusalem Jar inscription is made up of three lines of formal cursive writing in ink and dates from the late eighth-early seventh centuries. It is on a fragment of the shoulder of a storage jar found at site F in the excavations in the Jewish quarter of Jerusalem in 1971.[44] Also from Jerusalem are two other inscriptions on pithoi,[45] as well as Hebrew seals ascribed to the late eighth-seventh century.[46]

Many other seals have been dated to the late eighth-early seventh centuries, including Herr 2, 3, 10, 13-16, 20, 31-33, 35, 40, 43, 47-50, 52-53, 57-59, 62-63, 65, 69-70, 72-77, 81, 85-86, 88,

---

[Inscriptions Reveal], Catalogue no. 100, ed. Efrat Carmon (Jerusalem: Israel Museum, 1973), p. 36.

40Y. Shiloh, "City of David: Excavation 1978)," *BA* 42 (1979): 170.

41A. Lemaire, "Archaeological Notes. 1: Les ostraca paléo-hébreux des fouilles de l'Ophel," *Levant* 10 (1978): 156-61.

42N. Avigad," Excavations in the Jewish Quarter of the Old City of Jerusalem, 1971 (Third Preliminary Report)," *IEJ* 22 (1972): 193-200.

43Y. Aharoni," Excavations at Ramat Rahel, Seasons 1959 and 1960," *Rome Universita Centro Di Studi Semitici, Serie Archaeologica* 2 (1962): 1-91; "Chronique archéologique: Ramat Rahel," *RB* 70 (1963): 572-74.

44N. Avigad, "Excavations in the Jewish Quarter of the Old City," *IEJ* 22 (1972), pp. 193-200.

45B. Mazar, *The Excavations in the Old City of Jerusalem Near the Temple Mount, Preliminary Report of the Second and Third Seasons 1969-1970* (Jerusalem: Israel Exploration Society, 1971), p. 28.

46N. Avigad, "Excavations in the Jewish Quarter of the Old City, 1970 (Second Preliminary Report)," *IEJ* 20 (1970): 131. Y. Yadin, *Jerusalem Revealed, Archaeology in the Holy City 1968-1974)* (Jerusalem: Israel Exploration Society, 1975), p. 43.

90-91, 101(?)[47], 102-103, 105-106, 114-115, 118 (?), 119, 122-123, 125, 127, 129, 130-131, 133-136, 138, 142-143, 146 (?), 148, 150, 153, 155-156, 157(?), 159-160;[48] Hestrin 40, 46, 55, 57, 60, 79;[49] Bordreuil/Lemaire 26 (1976) seals 1, 5-7, 10-15, 17-19, bulla 21,[50] and many more simply ascribed to the seventh century. Additional seals and bullae which are ascribed an eighth-seventh century date are: the bullae of Baruch and Jerahmeel,[51] *Śar Haᶜir* bullae,[52] Avigad's seals with New Names,[53] Bordreuil / Lemaire seals 2-4, 8-9, 16 and bulla 23, and several of Bordreuil's seals from his *Catalogue*.[54]

The Arad inscriptions, found in 1962, consist of writing in ink on pottery sherds in eighty-eight instances (Arad 1-88). Also part of the Arad cache are sixteen incised sherds (Arad 89-104), and five seals (Arad 105-9). In 1976, excavators found three additional ostraca written in ink (numbers 110-12). The Arad inscriptions date to the end of the eighth century (Arad 41-46, 49-57, 89-91, 109), and primarily to the late seventh-early sixth centuries, with a few assigned to the tenth through mid-eighth centuries. The bulk of inscriptions from Arad date to the late seventh-early sixth centuries, from Strata 6 and 7. The Arad inscriptions are listed in table 1.

---

[47]The use of a question mark (?) indicates an uncertainty of some kind associated with the form or inscription.

[48]Herr, *SANSS*, pp. 83-148.

[49]Hestrin and Dayagi-Mendels, *Inscribed Seals*, pp. 64-103.

[50]P. Bordreuil and A. Lemaire, "Nouveaux sceaux hébreux, araméens et ammonites," *Semitica* 26 (1976): 45-63.

[51]N. Avigad, "Baruch the Scribe and Jerahmeel the King's Son," *IEJ* 28, nos. 1-2 (1978): 52-56, plate 15; also *BA* 42, no. 2 (1979): 114-18.

[52]N. Avigad, "The Governor of the City," *IEJ* 26 (1976): 178-82; *śr-hᶜyr* [The Governor (*Śar Haᶜir*)]," *Qadmoniot* 10, no. 2-3/38-39 (1977): 68-69; "*bwlh šnyyh šl śr-hᶜyr* [On 'A Second Bulla of a *Śar Haᶜir']*," *Qadmoniot* 11, no. 1/41 (1978): 34-35.

[53]N. Avigad, "*šmwt ḥdšym bḥwtmwt ᶜbryym* [New Names on Hebrew Seals]," *EI* 12 (1975): 66-71.

[54]Bordreuil and Lemaire, "Nouveaux sceaux hébreux, araméens, et ammonites," *Semitica* 26 (1976), pp.45-63. P. Bordreuil, *Catalogue des sceaux ouest-sémitiques inscrtis de la Bibliothèque Nationale, du Musée du Louvre et du Musée biblique de Bible et de Terre Sainte* (Paris: Bibliothèque Nationale, 1986), pp. 45-55.

Arad 40 has been dated by Aharoni[55] and Lemaire[56] to the end of the eighth century (ca. 701), although there is a dispute about the date. Pardee, like Holladay, fixes the date to the mid-late seventh century, Holladay on the basis of pottery evidence and Pardee on the basis of orthography and palaeography.[57] Zevit follows the earlier date, and also ascribes Arad 50 to this period.[58] The dispute which arose over the dating of the Arad inscriptions hinges on the date of Stratum 7, and whether tool marks on the casement wall from this level were made by a claw-chisel tool from the sixth century[59] or the seventh century.[60] The determination that the tool in question could well have been used in the earlier century, based on its appearance in Assyrian reliefs from the eighth century studied in the British Museum, created many counter-arguments.[61] The issue regarding the dates of Arad 40, as well as Stratum 7, thus remains unsettled.

Two plaques of sheet-silver, discovered in a repository of a burial cave at Ketef Hinnom, a site located on the western necropolis of the Old City of Jerusalem, bear incised inscriptions dated to the mid-seventh century.[62] The Ketef Hinnom inscriptions are votive in nature and mention YHWH and the priestly benediction.

The fragmentary Ophel 3 inscription, discovered in 1982, appears to contain the beginnings of four lines of Hebrew text. The

---

[55] Y. Aharoni, *ktwbwt ʿrd* [Arad Inscriptions], pp. 8, 72-76.

[56] A. Lemaire, *Inscriptions hébraïques,* p. 171.

[57] D. Pardee, *HHL*, p. 31; J. S. Holladay, "Of Sherds and Strata: Contributions toward an Understanding of the Archaeology of the Divided Monarchy," eds. F. M. Cross, W. E. Lemke, and P. D. Miller: *Magnalia Dei, The Mighty Acts of God. Essays on the Bible and Archaeology in Memory of G. E. Wright* (Garden City, NY: Doubleday, 1976), pp. 275, 281, n. 26.

[58] Zevit, *MLAHE*, pp. 18-19.

[59] The sixth century date is maintained by Y. Yadin, "A Note on the Stratigraphy of Arad," *IEJ* (1965): 180 and C. Nylander, "A Note on the Stonecutting and Masonry of Tel Arad," *IEJ* 17 (1967): 56-59.

[60] E.g., Y. Aharoni " 'The Persian Fortress' at Lachish–An Assyrian Palace?" *BIES* 31 (1967): 89-90.

[61] Zevit, *MLAHE*, p. 18, n. 9.

[62] Cf. G. Barkay, *Ketef Hinnom: A Treasure Facing Jerusalem's Walls* (Jerusalem: The Israel Museum, 1986), pp. 29-36 and "The Priestly Benediction on Silver Plaques from Ketef Hinnom in Jerusalem," *TA* 19(1992): 139-92.

text, which is engraved in limestone and is only partially legible, has been assigned a seventh century date.[63]

The late seventh-early sixth centuries are represented in epigraphy by the bulk of the epigraphic Hebrew inscriptions. The preponderance of material is from Judah. The texts come from Khirbet el-Meshash (late seventh century), Meṣad Ḥashavyahu (late seventh century), the Moussaïeff collection (second half of seventh century), Arad (late seventh-early sixth century), Ḥorvat Uza (late seventh-early sixth century), Ophel (late seventh-early sixth century), Gibeon (late seventh-early sixth century), Lachish (early sixth century), and Khirbet Beit Lei (sixth century). Numerous seals are also assigned to this period.[64]

The Khirbet el-Meshash ostracon was found during the second campaign in room 737 at Khirbet el-Meshash (Tel Masos) in the eastern Negev, fifteen kilometers east of Beersheba, in 1974. It contains five legible lines of text, written in ink, with several proper names followed probably by patronyms (too worn to read).

The ostraca from Meṣad Ḥashavyahu were discovered in 1960 at a site about 1.7 kilometers south of Yavneh Yam (Minet-Rubin). The main inscription was found during the first campaign. It was in six pieces and with it were found two other ostraca written in ink, and an incised sherd. Later the same year, four more ostraca (one which fit the main inscription from the first campaign) and an inscribed weight were discovered. The longest inscription, containing fourteen lines written in ink, has been called the "Reaper's Complaint." Three of the remaining shorter ostraca contain proper names, and two contain references to the shekel. The last merely shows a hieratic numeral.

An ostracon was discovered during the second season of excavations carried out near the fortress gatehouse at the site of Ḥorvat Uza in the eastern Negev.[65] The inscription consists of four lines of text and is a list of names, patronyms and place-names.

---

[63]J. Naveh, "A Fragment of an Ancient Hebrew Inscription from the Ophel," *IEJ* 32 (1982): 195-98.

[64]For example, the corpus of Hebrew bullae published by Avigad date to the time of Jeremiah, cf. Avigad, *Hebrew Bullae from the Time of Jeremiah. Remnants of a Burnt Archive* (Jerusalem: Israel Exploration Society, 1986).

[65]I. Beit-Arieh, "*ʾstrqwn ʾḥqm mḥwrbt ʿwzh* [The Ostracon of Aḥiqam from Ḥorvat ʿUza]," in *Eretz Israel: Archaeological, Historical, Geographical Studies*. Vol. 18, ed. B. Mazar and Y. Yadin (Jerusalem: The Israel Exploration Society, 1985), pp. 94-96.

Two recently published ostraca from the Moussaïeff collection have been identified as epigraphic Hebrew texts dating from the second half of the seventh century. Moussaïeff Ostracon 1 (MO 1) is a receipt for a donation of three silver shekels to the Temple of YHWH while MO 2 is a record of a petition of a widow for some portion of her late husband's property. Both inscriptions are written on pottery and are of unknown provenience.[66]

The Ophel 1 inscription was discovered in 1924 and, although poorly preserved, appears to be a list of proper names, patronyms, and place-names. The text is written in ink on pottery.

Another inscription from the Ophel, no. 675b, was discovered in 1961. The text itself is fragmentary and difficult to read; nine lines of text yield only two certain readings. Based on palaeographic evidence, this inscription has been dated to the early sixth century.[67]

The chronology and interpretation of the stamped Judean jar handles from Gibeon have been disputed, but they were certainly in use during the late seventh and into the early sixth century.[68] Cross extends the date broadly to the sixth century.[69] Fifty-six jar inscriptions were discovered during the 1956-57 excavations at el-Jib, ancient Gibeon, and another five in 1959 (Cross makes the total sixty, rather than sixty-one, as he takes two from the 1959 campaign

---

[66]These ostraca have been included in the corpus of this grammar because they make important contributions to our knowledge of pre-exilic Judean Hebrew. Cf., P. Bordreuil, F. Israel. and D. Pardee, "Deux ostraca paléo-hébreux de la collection Sh. Moussaïeff," *Semitica* 46 (1997): 49-76; H. Shanks, "Three Shekels for the Lord," *BAR* 23 (1997): 28-32; "King's Command and Widow's Plea. Two New Hebrew Ostraca of the Biblical Period," *Near Eastern Archaeology* 61:1 (1998): 2-13; B. Lang, "The Decalogue in the Light of the Newly Published Palaeo-Hebrew Inscription (Hebrew Ostracon Moussaïeff no. 1)," *JSOT* 77 (1998): 21-25. The dating of these ostraca to the second half of the seventh century by Bordreuil, Israel and Pardee is not accepted by all scholars. The authenticity of the ostraca is questioned by Berlejung and Schüle. Cf., A. Berlejung and A. Schüle, "Erwägungen zu den neuen Ostraka aus der Sammlung Moussaïeff," *Zeitschrift für Althebraistik* 11 (1998): 68-73.

[67]A. Lemaire, "Archaeological Notes.1: les ostraca paléo-hébreux des fouilles de l'Ophel," *Levant* 10 (1978): 156-58.

[68]J. B. Pritchard, *Hebrew Inscriptions and Stamps from Gibeon* (Philadelphia: University of Pennsylvania Museum, 1959). For references, see Zevit, *MLAHE*, p. 23, n. 34.

[69]F. M. Cross, "Epigraphic Notes on Hebrew Documents of the Eighth-Sixth Centuries, B.C.: III. The Inscribed Jar Handles from Gibeon," *BASOR* 168 (1962): 23.

to be from one handle). The inscriptions, which identify the owner of the jar and sometimes the place "Gibeon," were incised on handles after firing. Eighty jar handles stamped with the royal "lammelek" seal, as well as seven private seal impressions and an inscribed weight were also found in the Gibeon campaign.

The Lachish ostraca from the early sixth century include the eighteen found in 1935, an additional three from the 1938 season, one from 1966, seven from the 1973-77 campaign, and three from the 1978-83 season. The *terminus ad quem* for Lachish is ca. 588/6, when the site was destroyed by the Babylonians. The bulk of the correspondence was probably written shortly before the Babylonian invasion of 588, perhaps in the summer of 589 B.C.[70] All of the inscriptions are recorded in ink on pottery.

In 1965, an ink inscription on stone was discovered by P. Canfora, containing a proper name and patronym, while Aharoni, in 1966, found several seals, weights, and a rectangular ostracon.[71]

The Canfora inscription, known both as the Lachish XXII and Lachish V ostracon, contains ten lines of writing, in ink, on pottery, with a list of the names of the recipients of a quantity of an unspecified commodity. This find also dates from the Level 2 destruction.

In the campaign carried out at Lachish from 1973-77, David Ussishkin (1978) uncovered many new seals, as well as ostraca (numbers XXIII-XXX), all but two of which are assigned to the early sixth century. In the 1978-83 campaign, inscriptions XXXI and XXXII were discovered and the decanter bearing inscription XXX was restored.[72]

At a site only eight kilometers from Lachish, Khirbet Beit Lei, several graffiti incised on the limestone walls of a burial cave were discovered in 1961. Naveh first suggested a date of ca. 700

---

[70]For a discussion of the dating of the Lachish correspondence and bibliography, see Lemaire, *Inscriptions hébraïques*, p. 143 and Pardee, *HHL*, esp. p. 104. This grammar includes 29 legible ostraca from Lachish in the Appendix.

[71]Y. Aharoni, "Trial Excavation in the 'Solar Shrine' at Lachish, Preliminary Report," *IEJ* 18 (1968): 164-69.

[72]D. Ussishkin, "Excavations at Tel Lachish, 1973-1977, Preliminary Report," *Tel Aviv* 5, no. 1-2 (1978): 81-97, "Excavations at Tel Lachish 1978-1983: Second Preliminary Report," *Tel Aviv* 10, no.2 (1983): 97-175, esp. pp. 157-60. Inscription XXX was published by André Lemaire, "A Note on Inscription XXX from Lachish," *Tel Aviv* 7, nos. 1-2 (1980): 92-94.

for these inscriptions, but in 1968, assigned a sixth century date.[73] Gibson suggests a post-exilic date.[74] The reading of line 2 of Inscription 1 is also debated, being interpreted differently by Cross, Naveh (followed by Zevit), and Lemaire.[75]

Table 1 gives the century of the epigraphic Hebrew inscriptions and the datings (when available) of various scholars. The first column at the left of the table simply refers to the number of legible epigraphic Hebrew inscriptions. The inscriptions are listed chronologically from the earliest (Gezer) to the latest (Khirbet Beit Lei).

Table 1 illustrates that the late eighth-early seventh centuries is the period having the most sites from which epigraphic Hebrew finds come, while the late seventh and early sixth centuries yield the greatest number of actual texts. Any analysis of the Hebrew of the tenth and ninth centuries must await new discoveries since these two centuries lack both variety of sites as well as actual numbers of texts discovered.

---

[73]J. Naveh, "Old Hebrew Inscriptions in a Burial Cave," *IEJ* (1963): 87-88; "A Paleographic Note on the Distribution of the Hebrew Script," *Harvard Theological Revue* 61 (1968): 74, n. 38.

[74]Gibson, *TSSI*, p. 57.

[75]Cross, "The Cave Inscriptions from Khirbet Beit Lei," in *NEATC* (1970), pp. 301-302; Naveh, "Old Hebrew Inscriptions in a Burial Cave," *IEJ* 13 (1963), pp. 68-74; Zevit, *MLAHE* pp. 30-31; A. Lemaire, "Prières en temps de crise: Les inscriptions de Khirbet Beit Lei," *RB* 83 (1976): 558-60.

TABLE 1
DATES OF THE EPIGRAPHIC HEBREW INSCRIPTIONS

No. of inscriptions	Inscription	Century	Datings
1	Gezer	late 10th	Gibson:10th Cross: 925 Albright: 925
2-6	Arad 76-79, 98	late 10th	Aharoni: 920
7-10	Hazor (1-4)	mid 9th	Gibson: 9th Yadin: 9th
11-20	Arad (67-70, 80, 95, 100-103)	9th	Aharoni: 9th
21	Beth Shean	9th/8th	–
22-37	Kuntillet Ajrud	late 9th/ early 8th	Hestrin: 2nd half of 9th/ 1st half of 8th
38-125	Samaria	early 8th	Cross: 778-770
126-27	Qasile	early 8th	–
128	Ivory pomegranate from Jerusalem	late 8th	–
129-34	Khirbet el-Kom	late 8th/ early 7th/ mid 7th	Dever. 8th Cross: 700 Lemaire: 750
135	Nahal Yishai	late 8th/ early 7th	Cross: 700
136-38	Silwan	late 8th/ early 7th	Zevit:last part of 8th Cross:7th
139-42	Hazor (5-8)	late 8th	–
143-55	Arad (59-66, 87, 92-94, 99)	late 8th	

TABLE 1 (continued)

No. of inscriptions	Inscription	Century	Datings
156	Sam C 1101	late 8th	–
157-62	Beersheba	late 8th	–
163	Wadi Murabbaʿat (papMur)	late 8th/ early 7th	Cross:early 7th Gibson: 650
164	Ophel 2	late 8th	Shiloh: late 8th
165-67	Ophel a,b,c	late 8th/ early 7th	–
168-70	Jerusalem Jar	late 8th/ early 7th	–
171	Ramat Rachel	late 8th/ early 7th	–
172-91	Arad (40-46,49-57, 89-91, 107)	late 8th/late 7th	Zevit: 701 Lemaire: 701 Aharoni: 701 Holladay: 600
192-93	Ketef Hinnom	mid 7th-	
194	Ophel 3	7th	Naveh: 7th
195	Khirbet el-Meshash	late 7th/ 2nd half of 7th	–
196-201	MHY	late 7th/2nd half of 7th	Cross: 630 Gibson: 630
202-03	Moussaïeff	2nd half of 7th	Bordreuil, Israel, Pardee: 2nd half of 7th Cross, McCarter: 9th-8th

TABLE 1 (continued)

No. of inscriptions	Inscription	Century	Datings
204-47	Arad[a]	late 7th/ early 6th	Pardee: 630-595
248-50	Ḥorvat Uza	late 7th/ early 6th	–
251	Ophel 1	late 7th	Gibson: late 7th Cross: 7th
252	Ophel no. 675b	early 6th	–
253-312	Gibeon	6th/ early 6th	Albright: 600 Cross: 6th Gibson: 2nd half of 7th Pritchard: 700 Avigad: 700
313-41	Lachish	early 6th	Cross: 589 Albright: 589-588 Gibson: 588-586 Pardee: 589
342-48	Khirbet Beit Lei	6th	Cross: 6th

[a]Stratum VII: 31-37, 47, 86, 97, 105-108; Stratum VI: 1-24, 30, 84, 85, 110-12

New texts and seals continue to be found which increase our knowledge about epigraphic Hebrew. New forms may be added to the framework of this grammar in order to provide the most up-to-date picture of epigraphic Hebrew.

Often, these new discoveries are proper names on seals. It is an incorrect assumption that seals, although much more plentiful than either ostraca or texts on other materials, do little to increase our knowledge about grammar because they only provide new proper names to the epigraphic Hebrew corpus. For example, seals cited by Bordreuil and Lemaire assist the understanding of epigraphic Hebrew phonology and morphology, as in *mrymwt*, in contrast to *mrmwt* (Arad 50), and *qwlyhw*, in contrast to *qlyhw/qlyw* (Herr 133, Sam C 1012).[76]

In addition to discoveries of seals, new ostraca continue to be found which provide valuable insights. For example, an ostracon from the Ophel, dating to ca. 700 B.C., contributes two new words (and one more which was already attested) to the epigraphic Hebrew corpus.[77] Two newly published ostraca from the Moussaïeff collection contribute several new nominal and verbal forms as well as syntactic constructions to the epigraphic Hebrew corpus.[78]

Scholars also continue to study inscriptions which have been found previously and offer new readings and interpretations of certain words or phrases which elucidate key points of epigraphic Hebrew grammar.

For example, Cross's and Miller's reading *ʾlhykh*, "your God," at Khirbet Beit Lei, if correct, proves for the first time the vocalization *-ka* for the second masculine singular pronominal suffix. The long form of the suffix is unprecedented elsewhere in epigraphic Hebrew.[79]

In summary, on-going research and study of epigraphic Hebrew, as well as new discoveries, will provide an increasing level of understanding of the grammar of epigraphic Hebrew.

---

[76] P. Bordreuil and A. Lemaire, "Nouveaux sceaux hébreux et araméens,"*Semitica* 32 (1982): 29-30. P. Bordreuil, *Catalogue des sceaux ouest-sémitiques inscrits*, p. 53.

[77] J. Naveh, "A Fragment of An Ancient Hebrew Inscription from the Ophel," *IEJ* 32 (1982): 195-98. The new words are *mtḥt*, "under, below" and *byrkty*, "in the back of, the recesses of." The form which was previously attested is *hmym*, "the water."

[78] See p. 20, n. 66 in this grammar.

[79] E.g., "your God," is *ʾlhyk* in Lachish 6:12-13. The second masculine singular pronominal suffix is normally written *-k* in epigraphic Hebrew. For the reading *ʾlhykh* at Khirbet Beit Lei, cf. F.M. Cross, "The Cave Inscriptions from Khirbet Beit Lei," in *NEATC* (1970), p. 301 and P.D. Miller, Jr., "Psalms and Inscriptions," *VTSup* 32 (1981): 321.

2. PHONOLOGY

Chapter 2 examines several aspects of phonology. First, the relationship between epigraphic Hebrew and outside sources is reviewed for the purpose of reconstructing a phonology. The second aspect covers the phonetic system detailing the individual sounds and characters of epigraphic Hebrew. The chapter concludes with an in-depth analysis of *matres lectionis*.

2.1 Epigraphic Hebrew and Outside Sources

Epigraphic Hebrew consists of a system of consonants and an occasional use of semi-vowels as *matres lectionis*, but contains no diacritics denoting vowels as does biblical Hebrew. Due to this fact, the determination of a system of phonology for epigraphic Hebrew is complex and far from certain. A reconstruction of the phonetic system is further complicated by the fact that outside source materials are limited. These sources are often far removed chronologically from the period of the corpus, and are viable only when used with discretion in reconstructing the phonetic system in epigraphic Hebrew.

While the pronunciation of epigraphic Hebrew depends upon evidence furnished by loan words and transliterations into foreign alphabets (chiefly Greek and Akkadian), the actual number of borrowings from Hebrew in other languages is limited. Greek sources are rather late for this corpus, because the earliest of these date to the third century B.C. Therefore, any phonological conclusions (especially regarding the status of short vowels in epigraphic Hebrew) based on source material which dates, at best, to three hundred years after the *terminus ante quem* of this corpus, should be viewed as tentative.[1] When these sources show features which are posited to be Proto-Hebrew features, it is difficult to determine whether those features were part of the language at the time of the inscriptions studied here.

Gerard Janssens has made a major contribution in the study of Hebrew historical grammar in his book on Origen's Secunda.[2] The second column of Origen's Hexapla, frequently referred to simply as the Secunda, consists of a Greek translation of the Hebrew text in column one (column one is missing from the few extant fragments of the Hexapla). The pronunciation based on the transliteration of the Hebrew text in Greek letters is important because the material studied by Janssens is considered to pre-date the Babylonian, Tiberian, and Palestinian traditions.

The Secunda is thought by Janssens to have been used by Hellenistic Jews to adapt the text of the Bible for synagogue usage. Although the date of the material is not certain (it is thought to date somewhere between the second century B.C. and the first century A.D.), it is plausible that the Hebrew transliterations derived from the Greek of the Secunda are the oldest known coherent and vocalized Hebrew and probably the first attempt to vocalize the Hebrew consonantal texts. As such, it represents a source for the study of Hebrew vowels which offers an earlier pronunciation of Hebrew than that found in the three traditional systems. It is also more useful than the Septuagint for the study of Hebrew historical

---

[1]On the subject of Hebrew transcription in Greek, and the inability to adduce an accurate phonology based on these transliterations in the comparative source, cf. E. A. Speiser, "The Pronunciation of Hebrew According to the Transliterations in the Hexapla," *JQR* 16 (1925-1926): 361-62.

[2]G. Janssens, *Studies in Hebrew Historical Linguistics Based on Origen's Secunda*, Orientalia Gandensia 9 (Leuven, Belgium: Uitgeverij Peeters, 1982).

linguistics because the Septuagint only occasionally provides separate words in transcription.

The study of the Secunda is important for epigraphic Hebrew because the Hebrew transliterations from the Greek are closer to the time of epigraphic Hebrew than is Masoretic Hebrew. It suggests how epigraphic Hebrew phonological rules may have operated.

A few of Janssens' conclusions for the Hebrew behind the Greek text of the Secunda will illustrate the value of his analyses. For example, Janssens concludes that laryngeals were pronounced at the time of the Secunda.[3] This is contrary to the theory defended by Sperber[4] that the laryngeals had disappeared in Hebrew before the time of Jerome and were reintroduced later, in Masoretic Hebrew, due to Arabic influence.

Regarding spirantization, Janssens concludes that there was no distinction between stops and spirants in the transliterations of the Secunda or the Septuagint,[5] although by the time of Jerome, some letters were spirantized (e.g., *p* was pronounced *f*).[6]

The data from the Secunda suggest that the *shewa* existed in the Hebrew from this period and that there were three types: the *shewa quiescens*, *shewa mobile*, and *shewa medium*. According to Janssens, this is in contrast to Masoretic Hebrew which distinguishes two types, the *shewa quiescens* (to mark the absence of a vowel), and the *shewa mobile* (to mark a reduced vowel).

Janssens also provides various phonological rules which were in use in the Hebrew based on the transliterations of the Secunda and gives a summary of these rules for the pronunciation of the Hebrew. For example, in a closed stressed syllable, Proto-Hebrew *a* is pronounced in the Secunda as *ä*; in an open, unstressed syllable, *a* is reduced to *ə* in pretonic position.[7]

---

[3]Janssens, *Studies*, p. 43.

[4]A. Sperber, "Hebrew based upon Greek and Latin Transliterations," *HUCA* 12/13 (1937-38): 103-274.

[5]Janssens, *Studies*, p. 48.

[6]Ibid., p. 46.

[7]Ibid., pp. 132-33.

Based on Janssens' work, phonological rules for Hebrew from the period ascribed to the Secunda (the second century B.C. to the first century A.D.) can be developed. The vocalization patterns of the Hebrew of the Secunda cannot be adopted as having necessarily been present in epigraphic Hebrew, yet the evidence presented by the Secunda shows features which are posited as Proto-Hebrew features. These features were certainly part of the Hebrew language at a time preceding the period of the Secunda.

James Barr[8] discusses the importance of classical sources for Hebrew grammar and the merits for and against establishing a relationship between the two for the purposes of reconstructing epigraphic Hebrew phonology based on Greek sources. Barr notes that modern scholarship has placed much importance on the Hebrew transcriptions into Greek and Latin characters for which there is ample evidence in classical sources from the third century and after. Scholars have felt that these transcriptions can give the history of Hebrew in pre-Masoretic times. Yet he points out that one cannot be certain that these sources reflect the true state of Hebrew phonology. Barr states[9] that while Jerome approached Hebrew with an analysis biased by the Latin phonemic system, the older transcriptions might represent not an approach to Hebrew biased by Greek phonemics, but an approach to Greek transcription biased by Hebrew (and Aramaic) phonemics.

One cannot be sure either that translators, such as Jerome, were accurate with regard to the way in which they transcribed Hebrew words. These translators were often better versed in their mother tongue than in Hebrew, and, as Barr points out, there is no evidence that Jerome was particularly interested in phonology.[10] Barr suggests that the phonetic analyses and information such as that which Jerome provides is no doubt limited and "rudimentary."[11]

---

8 J. Barr, "St. Jerome and the Sounds of Hebrew," *JSS* 12 (1967): 1-36.

9 Ibid., p. 4.

10 Ibid., p. 35.

11 Ibid., p. 36.

Barr's discussion of Jerome's merits as an analyst suggests that when dealing with outside sources in an attempt to reconstruct the phonology of a limited corpus such as that of epigraphic Hebrew, one must keep in mind that it is valid only to create a broadly based reconstruction. This is because the sources of comparison with epigraphic Hebrew upon which one is relying date from three hundred or more years after the *terminus ante quem* of the epigraphic Hebrew corpus.

Yet the conclusion which can be drawn from the work of both Janssens and Barr is that Greek (and Latin) are useful as sources for the study of Hebrew phonology. Certain Proto-Hebrew features suggested by Greek and Latin transcriptions were certainly part of the Hebrew language at a time preceding the time of these sources.

Neo-Babylonian and Neo-Assyrian, which are close chronologically to the corpus analyzed in this grammar,[12] permit only a limited discussion of phonology in epigraphic Hebrew.[13]

---

[12]Texts from these two periods date, for the most part, between the tenth and the sixth centuries, while the Neo-Babylonian Murašû documents date to the fifth century.

[13]A good secondary source for Akkadian transcriptions of Hebrew proper names is M. Coogan's *West Semitic Personal Names in the Murašû Documents* (Missoula, MT: Scholars Press, 1976). Coogan discusses proper names from the 730 tablets written in Neo-Babylonian found at Nippur, which date to the fifth century. The West Semitic proper names from these tablets, then, are removed by one century from the time span of the epigraphic Hebrew corpus. A monograph dealing with Hebrew proper names found in extra-Biblical sources has been written by M. Heltzer and M. Ohana, but Lipinski has voiced severe strictures with regard to several of their analyses of proper names. Cf. M. Heltzer and M. Ohana, *Massōret ha-šĕmōt ha-ʿibrīyyīm ha-ḥūṣ-miqrāʾyīm mitteqūp̄at Bayt Riʾšōn ʿad hătīmat ha-Talmūd* [Extra-biblical Hebrew names from the Period of the First Temple through the Talmudic Period] (Haifa: Haifa University Press, 1978) = *Studies in the History of the Jewish People and the Land of Israel. Monograph Series*, vol. II.; E. Lipinski, "Etudes d'onomastique ouest-sémitique," *BO* 37, no. 1/2 (1980): 3-4.

In addition to the works by Coogan, Heltzer and Ohana, and Lipinski mentioned in the preceding paragraph, the following articles and books provide a bibliography of secondary sources for the evidence of Akkadian transliterations of West Semitic names. Cf. E.Y. Kutscher, *A History of the Hebrew Language* (Leiden: E.J. Brill; Jerusalem: Magnes Press, 1982), pp. 60-63; A. Malamat, "On the Akkadian Transcription of the Name of King Joash," *BASOR* 204

Although the corpus of Akkadian transliterations of West Semitic proper names is an important independent source for the study of epigraphic Hebrew phonology, few of these transliterations correspond to attested epigraphic Hebrew names.[14] For this reason, the determination of epigraphic Hebrew phonology from a study of Akkadian is uncertain.[15]

With regard to the status of short vowels in epigraphic Hebrew and the determination of when reduction of short vowels in open, unstressed syllables took place, Stephan Kaufman's work on dating the phenomenon in Aramaic is important.[16] Kaufman has dated the beginning of the quantitative reduction of short vowels in open, unstressed syllables to the Achaeminid period (late 6th century) for Aramaic. During the Neo-Babylonian and Imperial Aramaic

---

(1971): 37-39; A.R. Millard, "Assyrian Royal Names in Biblical Hebrew," *JSS* 21 (1976): 1-14, esp. p. 4; R. Zadok, *The Jews in Babylonia during the Chaldean and Achaemenian Periods according to the Babylonian Sources* (Haifa: Haifa University Press, 1979) = *Studies in the History of the Jewish People and the Land of Israel. Monograph Series*, vol. III.; *On West Semites in Babylonia during the Chaldean and Achaemenian Periods. An Onomastic Study* (Jerusalem: H.J. & Z. Wanaarta and Tel Aviv University, 1977).

[14]For example, Akkadian transcriptions for the biblical Hebrew forms *yw*ʾ*š* and *yhw*ʾ*š* discussed by Malamat in "On the Akkadian Transcription of the Name of King Joash," *BASOR* 204 (1971) have limited relevance for epigraphic Hebrew since neither of these two proper names is attested in epigraphic Hebrew. However, the locative name "Samaria" (*samerināya*), from an early eighth century stele which is discussed by Millard in "Assyrian Royal Names in Biblical Hebrew," *JSS* 21 (1976): 4, is relevant because this word is attested in epigraphic Hebrew.

[15]Kutscher attempted to answer phonological questions based on an analysis of the Hebrew name *hwš*ʿ and its transliteration in Assyrian (*Ausi*ʾ). He concluded that due to the limited corpus of Hebrew material in Akkadian transliterations, it was impossible to answer the phonological questions he had posed (cf. Kutscher, *A History of the Hebrew Language*, pp. 62-63).

[16]S. A. Kaufman, *The Akkadian Influences on Aramaic* Assyriological Studies, no. 19 (Chicago and London: The University of Chicago Press, 1974), pp. 146-51; "The History of Aramaic Vowel Reduction," in *Arameans, Aramaic and the Aramaic Literary Tradition*, ed. M. Sokoloff (Ramat-Gan: Bar Ilan University Press, 1983), pp. 47-55; "On Vowel Reduction in Aramaic," *JAOS* 104 (1984): 87-95.

periods, then, reduction of short vowels (in open, unstressed syllables) was a feature of Aramaic. In reaching this conclusion, Kaufman largely drew upon Akkadian transcriptions of Aramaic words. He posited that most Akkadian loanwords in Aramaic should be treated as having the correct reflex of the posited Akkadian form, both with respect to the quantity and quality of the vowel.

The evidence of the Akkadian loanwords points to a date for vowel reduction to the period of Imperial Aramaic. From the beginnings of vowel reduction in the late sixth century, this manner of pronunciation spread throughout all dialects, and there was, during these periods, a gradual reduction from full vowel to zero. Total reduction of *shewa* to zero was completed, according to Kaufman, by the third century A.D.

The corpus of Hebrew words attested by Akkadian transcriptions is not large enough to attempt a similar methodology to prove vowel reduction for epigraphic Hebrew since the evidence is limited to proper names. Any conclusions drawn would be very uncertain since many analogic changes may take place in proper names.

Coogan[17] concluded, on the basis of the evidence of West Semitic names attested in Neo-Babylonian, that there is no systemic evidence in West Semitic names either for vowel reduction or for representation of the West Semitic *shewa.*

Since Aramaic became the *lingua franca* of the Near East, it may have influenced Hebrew with regard to the reduction of short vowels in open, unstressed syllables; that is, vowel reduction may have begun in Hebrew at the same time or soon after it began in Aramaic. The conclusion which may be drawn is that the reduction of short vowels in Northwest Semitic post-dates the *terminus ante quem* of the epigraphic Hebrew corpus.

---

[17]Cf. Coogan, *West Semitic Personal Names in the Murašû Documents*, p. 107.

2.2 The Phonetic System in Epigraphic Hebrew

2.2.1 Introduction

The epigraphic Hebrew alphabet indicates only consonantal phonemes, one phoneme per sign (the exception is the sign ***W***, which probably denotes two phonemes, *š*/*ś*).[18]

The consonants in epigraphic Hebrew are represented by the twenty-two letters of the alphabet, the order of which is known from the Ugaritic and Isbet Ṣarṭah abecedaries, as well as from early biblical alphabetic poems.[19] Part of the order of the alphabet is also indicated by a text from Kuntillet Ajrud, which demonstrates the order *pê-ayin*.

Table 2, on the next page, contains the consonants in epigraphic Hebrew, their names, and transliteration, as well as the accepted correspondence of the consonants to Proto-West Semitic. The script chosen for the column representing epigraphic Hebrew is that of the Siloam inscription, ca. 700. The Siloam script was chosen because it represents the earliest epigraphic Hebrew script which contains the most representatives for the twenty-two letters of the alphabet. It also represents a lapidary script rather than a cursive one, and lacks only the *ṭet* and *samech*.

---

[18]See sec. 2.2.1, pp. 36-39, on the phonemes /š/, /ś/, and /s/.

[19]Cf. A. E. Cowley, *Gesenius' Hebrew Grammar as Edited and Enlarged by the Late E. Kautzsch*, (Oxford: Clarendon Press, 2nd Eng. ed. 1910, 15th impression, 1980), p. 29.

TABLE 2
CONSONANTS IN EPIGRAPHIC HEBREW

Proto-Semitic	Epigraphic Hebrew	Name	Transliteration
ʾ	𐤀	*ʾaleph*	*ʾ*
b	𐤁	*bet*	*b*
g	𐤂	*gimel*	*g*
d	𐤃	*dalet*	*d*
h	𐤄	*hê*	*h*
w	𐤅	*waw*	*w*
ḏ/z	𐤆	*zayin*	*z*
ḫ/ḥ	𐤇	*ḥet*	*ḥ*
ṭ	𐤈	*ṭet*	*ṭ*
y	𐤉	*yod*	*y*
k	𐤊	*kaf*	*k*
l	𐤋	*lamed*	*l*
m	𐤌	*mem*	*m*
n	𐤍	*nun*	*n*
s	𐤎	*samech*	*s*
ǵ/ʿ	𐤏	*ʿayin*	*ʿ*
p	𐤐	*pê*	*p*
ẉ/ḍ/ṣ/	𐤑	*ṣade*	*ṣ*
q	𐤒	*qof*	*q*
r	𐤓	*resh*	*r*
š/ś/ṯ	𐤔	*śin/shin*	*ś/š*
t	𐤕	*taw*	*t*

The scripts from the Hebrew seals and Lachish ostraca, as well as the Moabite, Phoenician and Canaanite scripts, help to determine the form for the letter *ṭet* (a circle containing a symmetrical cross). The letter *samech* may be added to table 2 based on the *samech* in the scripts from Gezer, Samaria, Meṣad Ḥashavyahu, Lachish, and the seals. The *samech* in both Phoenician and Moabite also serves as a model. From these comparisons, a *samech* from Siloam would have consisted of one long vertical stroke with three short parallel strokes crossing it horizontally in its upper half (₮).

In epigraphic Hebrew, many of the Proto-West Semitic phonemes have shifted. Of the supposed twenty-nine Proto-Semitic phonemes, twenty-three continued to exist in Hebrew, since epigraphic Hebrew *z*, *ḥ* *ṣ*, and *š* represent the coalescence of two or three Proto-Semitic phonemes.

The epigraphic Hebrew alphabet, in comparison with other alphabets and phonetic inventories, is itself evidence for the following consonant mergers: the two palatals, *ǵ* and *ḫ* coalesced with the laryngals *ʿ* and *ḥ* respectively (*ǵ* › *ʿ* and *ḫ* › *ḥ*);[20] also, *ḏ* › *z*; *ṯ* › *š*. Another change which took place between Proto-Semitic and epigraphic Hebrew was the coalescence of the two emphatic spirants with the emphatic sibilants, *ḍ* › *ṣ*, *ẓ* › *ṣ*. The absence of miswritings in epigraphic Hebrew and the continuation of a corresponding consonantal inventory in later Hebrew dialects indicate that, with the exception of *š*/*ś*, the signs were not interchanged (as in Old Aramaic, for example).[21]

By analogy to Masoretic Hebrew, one may posit that in epigraphic Hebrew, *ś* and *š* were represented by the same sign. In Masoretic Hebrew, *ś* and *š* are differentiated by means of diacritics, and the double pronunciation there is certain. In epigraphic Hebrew, however, there are no diacritics and the pronunciation of the character denoting *ś* and *š* is not certain.

In most cases, words which are attested in epigraphic Hebrew find their identical match in Masoretic Hebrew where the *ś*/*š* distinction is marked by diacritics. The many similarities between

---

[20] See discussion on *ḥ* and *ʿ*, sec. 2.2.2, pp. 42-44.

[21] Ibid.

epigraphic and biblical Hebrew forms established by orthography, morphology and syntax indicate that biblical Hebrew is a reliable model for the phonetic status of *ś* and *š* in epigraphic Hebrew. The hypothesis which follows this logic is that *s* and *ś* were pronounced distinctly from *š* in epigraphic Hebrew because the Masoretes differentiated *ś* from *š*, and that this distinction was based on a phonetic tradition.

Nevertheless, there is some dispute as to whether *ś* existed in Proto-Semitic, and if it existed, whether it converged with *š*. There is no evidence in epigraphic Hebrew of any confusion between *ś* and *s*, as in Phoenician (*ʿśr* and *ʿsr*, "ten").[22]

---

[22]In Phoenician, Z. Harris (*A Grammar of the Phoenician Language*, p. 22), insists that ***W*** was always pronounced *š*, but he takes too lightly the Phoenician evidence for the word "ten" which is written both with 𐤎 and ***W***. This evidence points to a similarity between the sounds of *samech* and *śin* in Phoenician. Furthermore, this confusion indicates that *śin* was pronounced *s* and that it was historically distinct from *š*.

Harris admits (*A Grammar of the Phoenician Language*, p. 22) that the pronunciation of ***W*** in Phoenician is open to question. He states, however, that "we cannot infer that ***W*** and ***O*** were normally confused in Phoenician...single cases cannot be made the basis of phonetic discussion." He cites Albright ("Notes on Early Hebrew and Aramaic Epigraphy," *JPOS* 6 (1926): 83, n. 16) who suggests the reading *ʾsr* for *ʾśr* is due to Aramaic influence.

The writing *ʿsr* (instead of *ʿśr*), though rare, comes both from Phoenician proper and neo-Punic. While the Phoenician corpus, like that of epigraphic Hebrew, is small, even a few examples of a confusion between two letters can be indicative of an underlying phonetic principle. In this case, the principle is that *ś* and *š* were phonetically distinct in Phoenician.

To date, there are no examples in epigraphic Hebrew which illustrate a confusion in writing *s* and *ś*; however, on the basis of Phoenician and biblical Hebrew, *ś* was phonemically different from both *š* and *s* in epigraphic Hebrew.

Counter-arguments by Diem–that the grapheme *š* became *š* and *ś* under Aramaic influence (which dates this process to the post-exilic period)–may not be accepted. Cf. W. Von Diem, "Das Problem von *ś* im Althebräischen und die Kanaanaische Lautvershiebung," *ZDMG* 124 (1974): 221-52.

Biblical Hebrew itself shows confusion of *ś* and *s* in pre-exilic texts and this points to the fact that *ś* was realized differently from *š* during this period of confusion. Cf. J. Blau, *On Pseudo-Corrections in Some Semitic Languages* (Jerusalem: Israel Academy of Sciences and Humanities, 1970), pp. 23-24, 114-25, 119; "'Weak' Phonetic Change and the Hebrew *Śîn*," *HAR* 1 (1977): 87-88, 100-102; Zevit, *MLAHE*, p. 5.

Without relying upon biblical Hebrew as a model, however, one cannot be sure how the phoneme /*ś*/ was pronounced in the time of epigraphic Hebrew (in biblical Hebrew, it came to be pronounced like a *samech*). Three reasons serve to illustrate the view that /*ś*/ was not simply a bi-form of /*š*/ which developed in Hebrew (and Aramaic). First, /*ś*/ and /*š*/ in Hebrew correspond to two separate consonants in Arabic; second, three different phonemes which exactly parallel those in Hebrew are preserved in South Arabic; and third, /*š*/ and /*ś*/ never interchange (except in foreign loans).

If the people who "spoke" epigraphic Hebrew had all three phonemes, and differentiated *ś* from *š*, they employed one sign for two phonemes using *š* (**W**) polyphonically for both *ś* and *š* instead of adding a new sign to the accepted alphabet. They chose the **W** apparently because the pronunciation of /*ś*/ was close to that of /*š*/.[23]

An examination of the vocalized material from biblical Hebrew shows that some time in the history of *ś*/*š*/*s*/, the pronunciation of /*ś*/ came closer in pronunciation to /*s*/, ultimately merging with it. The *terminus ante quem* for this merger was the period ascribed to the later books of the Bible, as illustrated by several biblical attestations in which *ś* and *s* are occasionally interchanged (e.g., *śkr*, "hire," spelled with *samech* in Ezra 4:5; *skrym*, *sōkĕrîm*, "they hire"). In later Hebrew, most original *ś* roots are spelled with *samech* (e.g., *spq*, *et cetera*).[24]

From Jerome's explanations of the pronunciation and transliteration of the sibilants, it is clear that he pronounced **W** as /*ś*/ in all cases, and was unaware of the differentiation between *shin* and *śin*.[25] Also, due to the nature of the Latin alphabet, the Hebrew

---

[23]It is also possible that **W** was chosen over 𐤎 through the influence of the parent language of Hebrew. While *ś* might have been closer in pronunciation in epigraphic Hebrew to *s*, in the parent language, **W** was used to mark *ś*. Cf. J. Blau, "'Weak' Phonetic Change and the Hebrew *Śîn*," *HAR* 1 (1977): 87, n. 72.

[24]Cf. E.Y. Kutscher, *A History of the Hebrew Language*, pp. 14, 118-19; E. A. Speiser, "The Pronunciation of Hebrew Based Chiefly on the Transliterations in the Hexapla," *JQR* 23 (1932-33): 243, n. 75.

[25]A. Sperber, *A Historical Grammar of Biblical Hebrew* (Leiden: E.J. Brill, 1966), p. 172.

sibilants *samech*, *ṣade*, and *shin* are rendered by only one letter, *s*. The result is that two different words (e.g., *ʾšr* and *ḥṣr*) may be transliterated identically.[26]

In Greek, the same process was at work; one grapheme (σ) was generally (but not exclusively) used to transliterate the Hebrew sibilants *z*, *s*, *ṣ*, *š*/*ś*.[27] It was not easy for the speaker of Greek (or Latin) to find in the alphabet of his own language satisfactory representations for Semitic sibilants. Nevertheless, speakers of Greek such as Origen took it upon themselves to record into Greek script as accurately as possible transliterations based on the Hebrew which they heard. Speiser credits Origen with "orthophonic" tendencies.[28]

The simplest explanation, and the one deemed reasonable by Blau,[29] is that which assumes a separate Proto-Semitic phoneme /*ś*/ for Hebrew *ś* which continued to exist in South Arabic, early Aramaic, Arabic (in a changed form), Geʾez, and epigraphic Hebrew. However, one must acknowledge the discrepancies and difficulties (these are discussed both by Blau[30] and Speiser[31]) associated with tracing the origin of biblical *ś*. It is reasonable to conclude that because Masoretic Hebrew marks a distinction between *ś* and *š*, so did epigraphic Hebrew.

However, one must not lose sight of the fact that the evidence from epigraphic Hebrew does not prove that the three sounds, transliterated by *s*, *ś*, and *š*, were present. The consonantal text of epigraphic Hebrew shows only 𐤎 and ***W***. *S* and *š* are well established in Hebrew from its inception, but *ś* is altogether different.

---

[26] A. Sperber, *A Historical Grammar of Biblical Hebrew* (Leiden: E.J. Brill, 1966), p. 172.

[27] Speiser, "The Pronunciation of Hebrew," *JQR* 23 (1932-33): 250.

[28] Ibid., pp. 363-64. Janssens dates the Secunda to before Origen (*Studies*, pp. 13, 22-23).

[29] Blau, "'Weak' Phonetic Change and the Hebrew *Śîn*," *HAR* 1 (1977): 88.

[30] Ibid., pp. 87-88.

[31] Speiser, "The Pronunciation of Hebrew," *JQR* 23 (1932-33): 241-50.

2.2.2 The Pronunciation of Consonants

Hebrew transliterations into Greek (and Latin) cannot help to determine the exact age of spirantization in epigraphic Hebrew with certainty, but they offer important contributions to the discussion of the phonemes */bgdkpt/*. In biblical Hebrew (and Aramaic), these phonemes may be pronounced either 1) as stops (like English plosives) where they are marked by a *dagesh*, or 2) as fricatives, after a vowel or half-vowel (e.g., */b/~/v/*; *bayit* versus *bĕvayit*. However, epigraphic Hebrew evidence yields no internal proof for the phonemic realization of these consonants.

Although Speiser[32] gives a date of ca. 1000 for the beginning of spirantization, it is possible only to say that the earliest date of this double pronunciation of the *b,g,d,k,p,t* consonants was sometime during the second half of the first millennium B.C..[33]

When one looks to Greek or Latin transcriptions to elucidate this double pronunciation of *b,g,d,k,p,t*, the special conditions of both the transcribed and the transcribing language must be considered to avoid misinterpretation. This was the case for P. Kahle, when he determined that because the Greek and Latin of Origen and Jerome, respectively, deviated in their transcription, the double pronunciation of *b,g,d,k,p,t* was artificial.

On the basis of Greek (and Latin) transcriptions, Kahle[34] showed that, at least in Mishnaic Hebrew, the phonemes under discussion were pronounced solely as fricatives *[v]*, *[f]*, *et cetera*, and that the phonemic distinction of stops/fricatives (e.g., *b*/*v*) was only introduced later by the Masoretes (whom he credits as "language reformers") through Aramaic influence. However, as

---

[32]Cf. Speiser, "Progress in the Study of the Hurrian Language," *BASOR* 74 (1939): 5, n.10.

[33]Kutscher, *A History of the Hebrew Language*, p. 21.

[34]P. E. Kahle, *The Cairo Geniza* (Oxford: Oxford University Press, 1959), p. 179.

Kutscher[35] points out, Kahle did not realize that the Greek sources omit certain phonemic realizations because the Greek language, lacking certain phonemes, also lacks graphemes to denote them.

The Greek alphabet was simply inadequate for transliterating some Hebrew sounds (in this case, fricatives). In addition, most of these transcriptions are limited to proper names (with the exception of Origen's transcription of texts, and words quoted by Jerome) which increases the difficulty of the analysis of phonetic structures.

Barr[36] argues that the distinction between stops and spirants did in fact exist in the time of Jerome and that the distinction between the two pronunciations is allophonic.[37] The evidence from Hebrew transcriptions in Latin has been used to posit that the different pronunciations for stops/spirants did not exist, while, according to Barr,[38] perhaps it did exist, but the Latin transcribers chose to ignore it.

Harris[39] contends that one cannot be sure whether or not spirantization preceded or post-dated the borrowing of the alphabet by the Greeks, because the Greek alphabet could not represent (or accommodate) the spirants.

Uncertain is Speiser's contention that since the stops and the spirants of Hebrew share the same symbols, spirantized *b,g,d,k,p,t* do not go back as far as the invention of the North Semitic alphabet.[40] It cannot yet be proven that if the double pronunciation of the *b,g,d,k,p,t* could be dated to the invention of the alphabet, these phonemes would have been represented by separate signs.

---

[35]Kutscher, *A History of the Hebrew Language*, p. 22 and "Contemporary Studies in North-Western Semitic," *JSS* 10 (1965): 24-36.

[36]Cf. J. Barr, "St Jerome and the Sounds of Hebrew," *JSS* 12 (1967): 9.

[37]Cf. S. Morag, *The Vocalization Systems of Arabic, Hebrew, and Aramaic*, p. 24.

[38]Barr, "St Jerome and the Sounds of Hebrew," *JSS* 12 (1967): 9.

[39]Z. Harris, *Development of the Canaanite Dialects*, American Oriental Series 16 (New Haven: American Oriental Society, 1939), p. 66.

[40]Speiser, "The Pronunciation of Hebrew," *JQR* 16 (1925-1926): 368-70.

In addition to Harris and Speiser, other scholars have expressed varying opinions as to the date of the beginning of the process of spirantization: anywhere from the fifteenth century B.C. to the first century A.D.[41] The transcriptions of the phonemes */bgdkpt/* in Greek (and Latin) do not adequately serve to date this process with certainty due to irregularities and deviations in the transcriptions. Therefore, the lack of sufficient, reliable data pertaining to this phonetic process leaves open the question of the actual beginning of spirantization.

That *ḫ* coalesced to *ḥ* (and *ǵ* › ʿ) in epigraphic Hebrew is also open to debate. The work of J.W. Wevers,[42] based on Old Greek transcriptions of the second century B.C., suggests that *ḥ* and *ḫ* were phonemically distinct and that in epigraphic Hebrew the *ḥet*-sign may have been polyphonous. Zevit[43] concurs and takes the theory one step further by applying the same arguments against coalescence of *ǵ* to ʿ in pre-exilic times. This theory supports that of Lipinski[44] who concludes that the grapheme ʿ was still polyphonous by the Greek/Roman period.

This argument is strengthened by Greek and Latin transcriptions which, except for a few inconsistencies, show χ for *ḫ*, γ for *ǵ*, and zero (Ø) for *ḥ* and ʿ.

---

[41]R. Eisler dates spirantization to the fifteenth century, B.C.; cf. *Die Kenitischen Weihinschriften der Hyksoszeit in den Sinaibergwerken und der Ursprung des Alphabets* (Freiburg: Herdersche Verlagshandlung, 1919), p. 32; new rev. ed., *Die Kenitischen Weihinschriften der Hyksoszeit im Bergbaugebiet der Sinaihalbinsel und einige andere unerkannte Alphabet denkmaler aus der Zeit der XII. bis XVIII. Dynastie* (Hildesheim: Verlag. Dr. H.A. Gerstenberg, 1975).

For additional bibliography for those who date spirantization to later periods, cf. Speiser, "The Pronunciation of Hebrew," *JQR* 16 (1925-1926): 371, and nn. 15, 16.

[42]J.W. Wevers, "*Ḥeth* in Classical Hebrew," in *Essays on the Ancient Semitic World*, eds., J.W. Wevers and D.B. Redford (Canada: University of Toronto, 1970), pp. 110-12.

[43]Zevit, *MLAHE*, p. 5.

[44]E. Lipinski, "Etudes d'onomastique ouest-sémitique," *BO* 37 no. 1/2 (1980): 4.

Harris[45] has explained the non-representation of *ḥ* and ᶜ in the Septuagint merely as illustrations of "the range of actualization" of the phonemes /*ḥ*/ and /ᶜ/. Moscati[46] theorizes that the various transcriptions date from different periods and do not reflect any real phonetic difference. Loewenstamm's[47] research has allowed the most latitude for both counterarguments. He suggests that Greek reflects the coalescence both of *ǵ* to ᶜ and of *ḫ* to *ḥ*, while allowing that the earlier tradition of polyphonous graphemes was still remembered. According to his theory, "every χ/γ in the Septuagint parallels *ḫ*/*ǵ* while those with a vowel sign or zero parallel not only *ḥ*/ᶜ but also *ḫ*/*ǵ* which had disappeared."[48]

Harris[49] argues that phonemes are not remembered once they have become obsolete in a dialect, and that Greek χ and γ cannot be used to prove that *ḫ* and *ǵ* were phonemes in Hebrew, because they occur often in words containing etymological *ḥ* and ᶜ.

As evidence, Harris cites transcriptions of Hebrew words in Egyptian from the tenth century which indicate that *ḫ* › *ḥ*. His first example, *bt ḥ(w)rn*, "Beth Ḥwrn," from the Sheshonq list,[50] with a probable etymological *ḫ* according to Harris, cannot be accepted as definitive proof that *ḫ* › *ḥ* since the word is written *ḥrn* in Ugaritic

---

[45]Harris, *Development of the Canaanite Dialects*, p. 63.

[46]S. Moscati, *An Introduction to the Comparative Grammar of the Semitic Languages* (Weisbaden: Harrassowitz, 1964), p. 40.

[47]J. Blau, "*dkdwq mswwh ḥdš šl hlšwnwt hšmywt* [Review of S. Moscati *et alia*, An Introduction to the Comparative Grammar of the Semitic Languages]" *Lešonenu* 30 (1966): 141, following S.A. Loewenstamm (cf. Blau, "*dkdwq*").

[48]Blau summarizes Loewenstamm's position on *ḥ*/*ḫ* qnd ᶜ/*ǵ* and points out that only the material for *ḥ*/*ḫ* has been examined by the latter and found to be in support of this theory. Cf. Blau, "*dkdwq mswwh ḥdš šl hlšwnwt hšmywt* [Review of S. Moscati *et alia*, An Introduction to the Comparative Grammar of the Semitic Languages]," *Lešonenu* 30 (1966): 141.

[49]Harris, *Canaanite Dialects*, p. 63.

[50]This list comes from the reign of Sheshonq I, biblical Shishak, who attacked Palestinian cities in the tenth century B.C.; cf. W.F. Albright, "Egypt and the Early History of the Negeb," *JPOS* 4 (1924): 145; Harris, *Canaanite Dialects*, p. 63.

(not *ḫrn*). To prove the coalescence of *ǵ* to *ʿ*, Harris cites the transliteration *ša-ʿa-ru*, "gate" (‹ *ṯaǵru*), from the twelfth century inscription of Ramses IX. This example may indicate that the coalescence of *ǵ* to *ʿ* had already taken place by the time of epigraphic Hebrew.

Loewenstamm's and Wever's works leave open the possibility that *ḥ* and *ḫ*, and possibly *ʿ* and *ǵ*, were phonemically distinct in epigraphic Hebrew, and that the graphemes *ḥet* and *ʿayin* accented distinct allophones. The fact that epigraphic Hebrew has only one sign for *ḥet* and one for *ʿayin* (no distinct graphemes for *ḫ* and *ǵ*) proves nothing about the phonemic or phonetic convergence of these sounds in epigraphic Hebrew; rather, it proves only their graphic convergence in the alphabet borrowed by the Hebrews. The inconsistency of the Greek data suggests, however, that the *ʿ*/*ǵ* and *ḥ*/*ḫ* fusions were complete by the time of both biblical and epigraphic Hebrew.

Table 3 relies upon comparative Semitics in assigning the various phonetic categories for the consonants in epigraphic Hebrew. Each group in table 3 categorizes the supposed place of articulation of each consonant:

TABLE 3
PHONETIC CATEGORIES FOR THE CONSONANTS

Category	Consonants
laryngals/glottals	*ʾ*, *h*
pharyngals	*ʿ*, *ḥ*
palatals/velars	*g*, *k*, *q*
dentals	*d*, *ṭ*, *t*
labials	*b*, *p*
sibilants	*z*, *s*, *š*, *ś*, *ṣ*
sonantas	*l*, *m*, *n*, *r*
semi-vowels	*w*, *y*

2.2.3 Changes of Consonants

2.2.3.1 Assimilation

Assimilation occurs when one consonant, generally *nun*, which closes a syllable, assimilates to the following consonant (which begins the next syllable) and forms a strengthened consonant with it. Assimilation is frequent in epigraphic Hebrew in cases where the *nun* assimilates in prepositions, verbs and nouns.

Prepositions (in adverbial phrases)

mšm (= **min šam*), "from there," A 17:4.

mzh (= **min zeh*), "from here," A 13:2; L 3:18.

Verbs

The root for each attested verb is given below in parentheses. Following it are the actual attestation, its meaning in English, and the provenience of the form. The forms are listed alphabetically according to the root.

(*ngd*) *lhg[d]*, "to inform," L 3:1-2

hgd, "it was reported," L 3:13

(*nṭh*) *hṭh*, "he has given his attention to," A 40:4

(*nkh*) *hkw*, "they struck," Siloam 4

(*nṣl*) *ḥṣlyhw*, "YH has delivered," or "deliver, O YH!" Gib S.I̊. 2; L 1:1; Jerusalem Seal 6:2; Hest. 59:1-2, 60:1, *ḥṣlyh̊w*, L Seal 16:2.

(*nqh*) *nqty*, "I am innocent, clean," MHY 1:11
(*ntn*) *ᵓtnnhw*, "I will give it," L 3:12

ttn, "you shall give," A 1:10, 18:6, *[tt]n*, MHY 13:1

ytnw, "they will give," Ajrud 7:2

nttm, "I sent them," A 40:10

(w)ntt, "you are to give (it)," A 2:7-8

Nouns

The root of each noun is given below in parentheses. Following each root is the actual form of the noun attested in epigraphic Hebrew, and the English meaning and one provenience for each form. The reader is directed to the Lexicon for a complete list of restored forms and additional proveniences. Nouns are listed alphabetically according to the root.

(*ḥnṭ*) *ḥṭm*, "wheat," A 3:1.

(*nśᵓ*) *mśᵓ*, "a (mule)-load of," A 3:4
mśᵓt, "signals," L 4:10

(*ᶜnh*) *ᶜt*, "now, even now," L 2:3.

(*šnh*) *št* (‹ **šant*), "year," S 1:1.

As the forms from epigraphic Hebrew illustrate, assimilation of *nun* is well attested. However, there is also evidence for assimilation of *lamed*, as the verb form which follows (from MHY 1:8) attests. It also shows, by its singularity, the infrequency with which this practice is attested in epigraphic Hebrew:

(*lqḥ*) (*w*)*yqḥ* (for **yilqaḥ*), "and he took," MHY 1:8.[51]

2.2.3.2 Commutation

Commutation between consonants may occur when two consonants are homorganic (produced with the same place of articulation). The commutation of *ʾaleph* and *ʿayin*, both gutterals, is demonstrated in epigraphic Hebrew in the forms *rgʾ* (A 31:2, 68:3, *r̊g̊ʾ* S 78:1), and *rğʿ* (S 1:4), "calm," ="(the deity) has calmed", and perhaps also with the palatals *q* and *k* in the proper names *šknyhw* (Av NN 4:1-2) and *šqnyw* (R 9:2 = Herr 111), "YH has dwelled."

2.2.3.3 Syncope

Syncope occurs in the case of the definite article *hê*, e.g., *lmlk* (for *lhmlk*), "to the king," Tell Qasile 1:1; L 5:10.

A largely pre-epigraphic Hebrew phenomenon is one in which *waw* and *yod* elide in Verbs III-weak and the resulting form demonstrates syncope. In epigraphic Hebrew, two forms derived from the roots *ʿny* and *ʿśy*, demonstrate elision of *waw*/*yod* before vocalic afformatives; e.g., *yʿnw*, "they will testify," MHY 1:10, 11; *tʿśw*, "you will do," L 6:9.

The syncope of *waw*/*yod* between short unaccented vowels is a feature also of Verbs III-weak, as attested by epigraphic Hebrew *hyh*, "he was," Siloam 1 and *ʿśh*, "he did," Lachish 4:3.

---

[51]The imperfect of *lqḥ* occurs without *l* in other West Semitic languages, in addition to epigraphic and biblical Hebrew; e.g., Moabite *ʾqḥ* (Mesha 17:20); Phoenician/Punic *yqḥ* (CIS 165:20); Yaudic *yqḥ* and *yqḥw* (Hadad 10, 12); Old Aramaic *yqḥ* (Sefire iB 27) and *tqḥ* (Sefire iii:2); Imperial Aramaic *yqḥwnh* ([with the third feminine singular objective suffix], Cowley 67:18); cf. C. F. Jean and J. Hoftijzer, *Dictionnaire des inscriptions sémitiques de l'ouest* (Leiden: E.J. Brill, 1965), p. 139.

2.2.3.4 Prothetic *ʾaleph*

The prothetic *ʾaleph* is not common in epigraphic Hebrew. When it does occur, it seems to precede a two-consonant cluster. The possible examples are *ʾkzb*, a locative name (from the root *kzb*, "to deceive, lie"), Lachish 8:6 and *ʾkzy[b]*, Lachish 22:10, *ʾpṣḥ*, a proper name meaning "joyous, cheerful," Samaria 31a:2, *ʾ̊p̊ṣ̊ḥ̊*, Samaria 90:2, *ʾprḥ*, a proper name meaning "young bird," Av (*EI* 9) 4:1; Hest. 51:1, and *ʾškr*,[52] Kadesh Barnea, a masculine singular noun, from the root *škr*, meaning "offering, tribute, present." A final restored form *ʾš[ḥr]*, a proper name related to the root *šḥr*, "black, blackness," Samaria 13:3-4, is another form demonstrating the prothetic *ʾaleph.*

The locative and preposition *m‹ʾ›śrʾl*, "from *‹ʾ›śrʾl*," from Samaria 42:1, 48:1, indicates the absence of a prothetic *ʾaleph*, in contrast to the biblical counterpart *ʾśryʾl* (1 Chron. 7:14; Num. 26:31; Josh. 17:2) and *ʾśrʾl* (1 Chron. 4:16). The epigraphic Hebrew form seems to indicate that the *ʾaleph* opening a syllable after a sonant was elided, dropped from the orthography and the preceding vowel was compensatorily lengthened.[53]

2.2.3.5 Diphthongs

Regarding diphthongs, most epigraphic Hebrew evidence indicates that *aw* contracted to *ō* in the North: *ḥrn* (*ḥōrōn* ‹

---

[52]The form occurs in an ostracon from Kadesh Barnea and is parallel to biblical *ʾškr* in Psalm 72:10 and Ezek. 27:15; cf. R. Cohen, "*hḥpyrwt bqdš brnʿ bšnym 1976-1982* [The Excavations at Qadesh Barnea, 1976-1982]," *Qadmoniot* 16, no. 1/16 (1983).

[53]Cf. M. Noth, *IPN*, p. 167; W.F. Albright, "The Site of Tirzah and the Topography of Western Manaasseh," *JPOS* 11 (1931): 249-250; F.M. Cross, "Epigraphic Notes on Hebrew Documents of the Eighth-Sixth Centuries B.C.:I. A New Reading of a Placename in the Samaria Ostraca," *BASOR* 163 (1961): 14; "Epigraphic Notes on Hebrew Documents of the Eighth-Sixth Centuries B.C.:II. The Murabbaʿat Papyrus and the Letter Found near Yabneh-Yam," *BASOR* 165 (1962): 36, n. 10.

*$ḥawrōn$), Qasile 2:1,[54] as did the diphthong *ay*, which contracted to *ē: yn* (**yayn* › *yēn*), often at Samaria. The spelling *byt* at Beth Shean and Qasile 2:1 indicated one of two alternatives. Either the diphthong was uncontracted in these areas, or the *yod* represents a *m.l.* for *ē* in a historical spelling (**bēt*).

2.3 *Matres Lectionis* in Epigraphic Hebrew

The following section of this grammar discusses the positions of various scholars regarding the system of *matres lectionis* in epigraphic Hebrew, presents an evaluation of their ideas, and traces the use of both internal (medial), and external (final) *m.l.* in epigraphic Hebrew from the tenth through the sixth centuries.

The commonly accepted view is that the system of representing vowels by certain consonants (these consonants in this usage are known as *matres lectionis*), in either medial or final position, came

---

[54]See Cross and Freedman, *EHO*, p. 48, who posit *ḥōrōn* ‹ *ḥawrān*. Zevit (*MLAHE*, p. 11 and n. 6) points out that *ā* shifted to *ō* already by the end of the Amarna age. In any event, there is no difference between the derivations of these commentators and all agree that not only is the shift *ā* › *ō* reflected in this form, but also that the diphthong has probably contracted based on the form in Moabite.

The locative is spelled *ḥwrnn* in Moabite (an anomaly in itself since all *aw* diphthongs in the medial positions [as well as many cases of the *-ay* diphthong in medial position] in the Mesa inscription are reduced); cf. Cross and Freedman, *EHO*, p. 43. Etymologically, *ḥrn* may be connected to a root *ḥwr*, "cleft, valley, between hills." As Zevit points out (p. 11, n. 6), *ḥrn* could also represent the deity name, and the Moabite form, with *waw*, could indicate a *m.l.* in the ninth century.

Tell Qasile, on the coast, is geographically a northern site, but there is disagreement among scholars as to whether the pronunciation represented in the sherd is that of this coastal site, or of the biblical site of Beth Horon, presumably in the district of Ephraim, at the border between Israel and Judah. See Zevit, *MLAHE*, p. 12; Gibson, *TSSI*, p. 17; B. Maisler, "Excavations at Tell Qasile," *BJPES* 15:1-2(1949): 8-18; "Two Hebrew Ostraca from Tell Qasile," *JNES* 10(1950): 265-67, esp. 266. Finally, if Gezer/Samaria do not represent Northern Hebrew, Qasile may indicate that diphthongs were retained in the North as well as in the South.

about in Hebrew through the borrowing of an Aramaic orthographic practice in the ninth century. At this time, epigraphic Hebrew developed the pattern of using final *m.l.*, and introduced the practice of incorporating the internal vowel letters somewhat later. This view is that of Cross and Freedman in *Early Hebrew Orthography*, published in 1952. Another tenet of their scheme for *m.l.* in Hebrew orthography supposed that Hebrew orthography was purely consonantal in the tenth century. In Phoenician, Ugaritic, and Proto-Canaanite (Proto-Sinaitic and Old Palestinian), no internal or final *m.l.* were represented in the orthography. The Gezer Calendar was the chief foundation for their arguments regarding Hebrew orthographic practice in the tenth century.

Cross and Freedman hypothesized the appearance of final *m.l.* only in the ninth century when the practice was adopted from the Arameans.[55] Final *m.l.* occurred in Hebrew during this century, as in both Aramaic and Moabite, and increased in usage over time. Internal *m.l.*, which occur for the first time in eighth-seventh century Aramaic texts, occur for the first time in sixth century Hebrew inscriptions, according to Cross and Freedman,[56] and appear sporadically during this century. The only known medial *m.l.* was *yod* representing long *-ī*. With regard to the diphthongs, Cross and Freedman noted that in the North, the contraction of the diphthong had occurred with *ay* › *ê*, as well as *aw* › *ô*, while in the South, the diphthong remained uncontracted with *yod* and *waw* retaining their consonantal character.[57]

Although certain of the patterns outlined by Cross and Freedman remain valid today, their initial timetable for the appearance of *m.l.* had to be dismissed, and it, in fact, needed emendation immediately after the publication of their monograph. This was evident later that year when the monumental Silwan Tomb inscription, dating to the late eighth-early seventh century, was deciphered and it showed an internal *m.l.* in line 2 (*ʾrwr* = **ʾārūr*, "cursed"), with medial *waw* for *-ū*. Only certain of Cross and

[55]Cross and Freedman, *EHO*, p. 57.
[56]Ibid.
[57]Ibid.

Freedman's original tenets regarding epigraphic Hebrew are accepted as completely valid; namely, that final *m.l.* preceded internal *m.l.* and that there was a geographical distinction between the North and South with regard to diphthongs.

The epigraphic Hebrew evidence from the tenth and ninth centuries (however scant it may be) suggests that Hebrew did, in fact, employ final *m.l.* before it included internal *m.l.* The introduction of internal *m.l.*, however, was possibly introduced into Hebrew earlier than Cross and Freedman anticipated (mid ninth-early eighth centuries instead of the late eighth century), but this fact is not proven beyond a doubt.[58] The status of diphthongs, as Cross and Freedman defined them, remains valid today.

Another treatment of *matres lectionis* is that of L.A. Bange,[59] who agrees in principle with the general theory of Cross and Freedman (in recognizing that *m.l.* arose from the historical spelling of the original consonants: *ʾaleph*, *hê*, *yod*, and *waw*).[60] He differs, however, with regard to the time scheme involved with the introduction of vowel letters. While Cross and Freedman hold that final *m.l.* appeared in the ninth century and were introduced earlier than internal *m.l.*, Bange sees *m.l.*, both final and medial, coming into the orthography at the same time, three hundred years later, in the sixth century.[61]

Bange discusses three phases for the origin of vowel letters. Stage I, extending from the origins of consonantal alphabetic script to the tenth century, was a period of full consonantal orthography with *yod* and *waw* only used only as full consonants. Stage II, extending from the end of the tenth to the end of the seventh century, was a period in which there was "semi-consonantal" orthography in such languages as Yaʾudic, Moabite, early Aramaic and epigraphic Hebrew. This period was characterized by the use of *hê*, *waw*, and

---

[58]See discussion on internal *matres lectionis* beginning in sec. 2.3.3, p. 61 of this grammar.

[59]A. Bange, *A Study of the Use of Vowel-Letters in Alphabetic Consonantal Writing* (Munchen: Verlag UNI-druck, 1971).

[60]Ibid., p. 140.

[61]Ibid.

yod as "off-glides" in accented, long, open syllables, and *ʾaleph* as a glottal stop in short, accented open syllables, as well as a diphthongization of vowels corresponding to a shift in the position of the main stress of words in open accented syllables. Stage III in Bange's scheme extended forward from the sixth century, in Aramaic and Hebrew. During this period, *ʾaleph*, *hê*, *waw*, and *yod* were no longer functional as consonants alone, rather historical spelling gave rise to *m.l.*[62] These letters occurred in open, unaccented or closed syllables, where they could not represent "off-glides."[63]

Thus, in differing with the early work of Cross and Freedman, Bange sees the development of vowel-letters not in terms of Cross and Freedman's two stages: 1) characterized by purely consonantal orthography, and 2) characterized by the use of *m.l.*, but rather in terms of three stages. Those three stages are 1) characterized by full consonantal orthography, ca. 1700-1000 B.C., 2) characterized by full and semi-consonantal orthography, ca. 1000-600 B.C., and 3) characterized by the appearance of the first *m.l.*, both internal and external, "due to historical spelling and by analogy with it," ca. 600 B.C., and onwards.[64]

In Zevit's study of the *m.l.*,[65] Bange's theories are examined and labeled as inconsistent in the light of more recent discoveries since the time of the publication of Bange's dissertation (e.g., the Arad letters).[66] The notion of "off-glide," which is a key concept in Bange's explanations of the origin of *m.l.*, is seen as useful in dealing with the orthographic changes between Bange's first and second stage, but not between the second and third stages.[67] The data, which is sparse at best, reveals more inconsistency than consistency in the employment of "off-glides." Zevit concludes that "the notion remains useful in explaining the origin of some final

---

[62]Bange, Vowel Letters, pp. 139-40.

[63]Ibid., p. iii of abstract.

[64]Ibid.

[65]Zevit, *MLAHE*, p. 8, n. 32.

[66]Ibid.

[67]Ibid.

m.l., but not in explaining the development of all *m.l.* in all Northwest Semitic languages."[68]

Zevit[69] also criticizes Bange's rejection[70] of the usefulness of comparative Semitics in dealing with the subject under discussion. Zevit is correct in doing so, as proof for theories such as those which Bange proposes may be determined only through a thorough comparison of sister Semitic languages.

A modified timetable was suggested in 1975 by Cross and Freedman which reflected an updated scheme for the development of *m.l.* in epigraphic Hebrew.[71] Accordingly, final *m.l.* first made their appearance in Hebrew not later than the ninth century, while internal *m.l.* occurred rarely, not later than the second half of the eighth century; by the sixth century, they were still sporadically used.[72]

Zevit re-examined many of the tenets of Cross and Freedman's early work and set up a new scheme regarding *m.l.* in Hebrew.[73] Whereas the two earlier authors saw the system of *m.l.* appearing in Aramaic first in the tenth century and being adopted by the neighboring Hebrews and Moabites later on, Zevit cites both Ugaritic and Phoenician examples of *m.l.*. In the former, he mentions that final *m.l.* represented by the letters *yod*, *hê* and *ʾaleph* sporadically occurred early in Ugaritic.[74] Internal *m.l.* also occurred in Ugaritic, according to Zevit, with *yod* representing *-ī* as a pure *m.l.* (Zevit does, however, see the possibility of taking this letter as

---

[68]Ibid.

[69]Zevit, *MLAHE*, p. 7.

[70]Bange, *Vowel Letters*, p. 2.

[71]F. M. Cross and D. Freedman, *Studies in Ancient Yahwistic Poetry*, a dissertation submitted to John Hopkins University, Baltimore, MD, 1950. Society of Biblical Literature Dissertation Series 21 (Missoula, MT: Scholars Press, 1975), p. 182. Cross's and Freedman's remarks in *Studies* serve to accommodate the new data from epigraphic Hebrew since the time of the publication of their 1950 thesis and to update and add to the principal affirmations presented in *EHO*.

[72]See H. Van Dyke Parunak, "The Orthography of the Arad Ostraca," *BASOR* 230 (1978): 25-31.

[73]Zevit, *MLAHE*.

[74]Ibid., p. 3.

the contracted diphthong -*ē*[75] and *waw* representing a *m.l.* for -*ū* in the Ugaritic word *kwt*. The Ugaritic examples of *m.l.* are not commonplace by any means, but if correctly interpreted, dispel the notion that *m.l.* only occurred in Northwest Semitic orthography after the second millennium.[76]

Phoenician, one of the most conservative of languages, even shows rare instances of the use of *m.l.* after the ninth century (*šmnh*, "eight," 7th c., and a form open to question: *rʾš*, "head," 9th c.).[77]

The lack of *m.l.*, with only rare exceptions, in both Ugaritic and Phoenician, shows that there was no system for representing vowels in the orthography. Aramaic, on the other hand, widely exhibits the use of consonants as *m.l.* and in contrast to more conservative, rigid languages, adopted the principle of polyphony after it borrowed the Phoenician script in the tenth century.

---

[75]Ibid.

[76]See D. Pardee, Review of Zevit's *Matres Lectionis in Ancient Hebrew Epigraphs*, *CBQ* 44 (1982): 503-4. Pardee points out that the concept of *m.l.* in Ugaritic is as yet unsolved [Zevit assumes that it is solved], and that the problem of proving *m.l.* exist in this language hinges on disproving the claims that the forms in question are afformative particles rather than *m.l.* To do this, one would need to refute the theories of K. Aartun, *Die Partikeln des Ugaritischen 2 Teil. Prapositionen, Konjunktionen* (Alter Orient und Altes Testament 21/2, Kevelaer: Butzon & Bercker; Newkirchen-Vluyn: Neukirchener Verlag, 1978)., also, *l. Teil. Adverbien, Verneinungspartikeln, Bekraftigungspartikeln, Hervorhebungspartikeln* (Alter Orient und Altes Testament 21/1, Kevelaer: Butzon & Bercker; Neukirchen-Vluyn: Neukirchener Verlag, 1974).

[77]The form *šmnh* is from a 7th century plaque from Arslan Tash, the script of which is Aramaic. The *m.l.* in this form might well be explained as due to Aramaic influence since Aramaic influenced the palaeography of this inscription; cf. F. M. Cross and R.J. Saley, "Phoenician Inscriptions on a Plaque of the Seventh Century B.C. from Arslan Tash in Upper Syria," *BASOR* 197 (1970): 42, 45.

Zevit (*MLAHE*, p. 4), citing Cross and Freedman (*EHO*, p. 19), considers the *ʾaleph* in *rʾš* from the Kilamuwa inscription (ca. 825 B.C.) as a *m.l.* for *ō*; See H. Donner and W. Röllig, *KAI*, Band I (Wiesbaden: Otto Harrassowitz, 1962), pp. 30-34, text 24:15, 16. However the *ʾaleph* is historical (though it had probably quiesced), and is not a true *m.l.* in the strictest sense of the term.

The epigraphic Hebrew writing system, which also developed after the adoption of a Phoenician-like alphabet, exhibits the same principle of polyphony. This practice is shown by the use of the grapheme *šin* to represent both phonemes *śin* and *šin*. Zevit cites two other possible examples of this practice, the phoneme *ḥet* representing *ḫ* and *ḥ*, and *ʿayin*, *ʿ* and *ǵ* on the basis of Greek and Latin transcriptions.[78]

In dealing with *m.l.* in epigraphic Hebrew, one must be careful to separate out the historical writings from true innovative use of a consonant which is not part of a historical lexeme or morpheme to represent a pure long vowel. A major criticism of Zevit's work is that he does not always separate out forms on this basis, and moreover, appears all too willing to accept the notion of *m.l.* in words in which the status of the consonant as true consonant or *m.l.* is questionable. Zevit's criteria for discerning a consonant from a *m.l.* hinge on two main points: 1) non-etymological/consonantal *ʾaleph*, *hê*, *waw*, and *yod* are considered to be *m.l.* and 2) if graphemes satisfy this first step, "they are considered *m.l.* only when evidence indicates that a sound change occurred and that the grapheme conforms to a historical and not a phonetic spelling."[79]

As Pamela Bruton[80] notes, Zevit's criteria are valid, but he does not apply them strictly enough. He sometimes uses single examples which he claims show undisputed proof of the use of *m.l.*, but which derive no such support from other analogous words, nor can they possibly be explained as evidence of scribal error.[81]

Furthermore, Zevit draws conclusions from too little evidence when he postulates the dates for the contraction of the *aw* diphthong

---

[78]Zevit, *MLAHE*, p. 5, n. 22.

[79]Ibid., p. 8.

[80]P. Bruton, Review of *Matres Lectionis in Ancient Hebrew Epigraphs* by Z. Zevit, in *JNES* 42 (1983): 163-65.

[81]Ibid., p. 163. Bruton cites the example of *šmydʿ* which Zevit accepts unequivocally as a form with internal *m.l.*, but which is not necessarily to be so analyzed (see sec. 2.3.3, p. 63-64, n. 101). Zevit's examples for the contraction of the *aw* diphthong are likewise questionable.

in the North.[82] Although one must be prudent with Zevit's analyses, his work is a useful synthesis of the data [83] pertaining to the use of *m.l.*, especially from the eighth to the sixth centuries, and offers many sensible treatments of specific orthographic/phonological problems.

2.3.1 The Inscriptions and *Matres Lectionis*

Until further texts are discovered which may be dated to the tenth century with certainty, an exact detection of *m.l.* in the early development of epigraphic Hebrew cannot be adequately determined.[84]

Unfortunately, the ninth century epigraphic evidence is almost as scanty as that from the tenth century. Only a few seals have been dated to the ninth century, and those with a good deal of uncertainty. Several fragmentary texts on ostraca (Hazor 1-4 and possibly the Beth Shean Ostracon [ascribed to the ninth-eighth centuries]) show a few letters; the forms of these appear close to Phoenician in style, but little more about them can be said. Five inscribed sherds from Arad have been assigned to the ninth century, one of which, Arad 101, may contain a final *m.l.* for long ī (*ḥṣy*), although *yod* could represent historical writing for it is etymological in nature. The Ajrud inscriptions, which show final and possibly internal *m.l.* as well, belong to the mid-ninth/early eighth century and are discussed below among early eighth century finds.

Herr 161, a possible Hebrew seal, reads *lzryw hrbt*, **lazērīyaw harabbātī*(?), "Belonging to Zeriyaw, the Rabbatite."

---

[82]For a discussion of Zevit's treatment of the diphthong in such epigraphic Hebrew words as *ḥrn*, *ywyšb*, *šmryw* and *ytm*, cf. Bruton, "Review," p. 164.

[83]Zevit's list of examples containing *m.l.* or those which bear on a discussion of the diphthongs is not totally complete. He omits many key forms, including *zh* (MHY 1:9); *ky* and *zdh* (Siloam 1:3); *hbyt* (Silwan 2:1); *yśbʿw* (Ajrud 7:1); *ytnw* (Ajrud 9); *ḥmyʾhl* (Hest. 34:1); *dʾr* (Herr 57); *mykyhw* (Herr 119:2); *yhwd[h]* (Arad 40:13); *wmqyn[h]* (Arad 24:12).

[84]Cf. the discussion of the Gezer Calender in sec. 1.2, pp. 7-9, nn. 9-10, and sec. 3.2.2.1, p. 160, n. 189.

This seal, which could be a forgery, does not have a final *m.l.* represented in the orthography of the gentilic, if the interpretation of the word is correct. Albright, Cross and Freedman give a ninth century date to a seal which they claim shows two definite *waw matres lectionis* for *-ū*.[85] The seal is mentioned in Diringer's *Le iscrizioni antico-ebraiche palestinesi*,[86] *lšm*ʿ*yhw bn zryhw*, "Belonging to Shemayahu, son of Azaryahu." Although the seal had been dated to the eighth-seventh century, Diringer claimed that an earlier date was plausible.[87] If the Shemayahu Seal is correctly dated to the ninth century, it represents the earliest possible example of a *m.l.* in epigraphic Hebrew orthography.

The data from the early-mid eighth century pertaining to the development of *m.l.* in epigraphic Hebrew, as well as other principles of Hebrew orthography, is more abundant. The inscriptions falling within this range come from Samaria, Tell Qasile, Ajrud, and Beth Shean. Also, there are several seals containing *matres lectionis* which may be dated to this period: Herr 30, *lmnḥm ywbnh* (Ramat Rachel); Herr 38, *lbky šlm* (Beth Shemesh); Herr 45, *lḥsd*ʾ *yrmyhw* (Beth Shemesh); Herr 79, *l*ʾ*ryhw* (bought: Jerusalem); Herr 89, *lzkr hwš*ʿ (unknown provenience); Herr 108, *lyrmyhw* (unknown provenience); Herr 121, *lntnyhw bn* ʿ*bdyhw* (es-Soda, near Tartus); and Herr 140, *lš*ʿ*l yš*ʿ*yhw* (unknown provenience; bought: Jerusalem).[88]

When dealing with proper names in epigraphic Hebrew, one is uncertain of the orthographic conventions followed. In the case of determining *m.l.*, a *waw* or *yod* in the form may be historical, rather than a *m.l.* (e.g., proper names with preformative *yw-*, afformative

---

[85]Cross and Freedman, *EHO*, pp. 47-48.

[86]Diringer, *Le iscrizioni antico-ebraiche palestinesi* (Florence, Italy: Felice le Monnier, 1934), pp. 199-200, with earlier bibliography. The seal, from an unknown provenience, was first published by Melchior de Vogúë, *Intailles à légende sémitiques*, (= *Mélanges d'archéologie orientale*), part III (Paris, 1868), pp. 131-40, n. 34. The most recent reference is in Bange, *Study of the Use of Vowel-Letters*, pp. 112-13. Zevit, curiously, does not mention this seal.

[87]Diringer, *Le inscrizioni antico-ebraiche palestinesi,* pp. 199-200.

[88]Herr, *SANSS*, pp. 96, 99-100, 103, 118-19, 121-22, 133-34, 140-41.

-yhw, or elements containing *waw/yod* which derive from Verbs I-weak or Verbs III-weak).

Independent verbs are the best indication of empirical evidence for *m.l.*, however, at least in the eighth century, these forms are scant.

Many of the forms cited in the following section are unequivocal examples of words containing *m.l.*; others are presented only as possible, or in some cases, probable evidence for *m.l.* For instance, all *-yhw* proper names are not certain examples of forms containing *m.l.* (*waw* for *ū*) in the strictest sense, as *-yhw* may have been vocalized *yahwē* (where the *waw* is etymological), rather than *-yahū*. Proper names beginning with *yw-*, the short form of the deity name, may have been pronounced *yô* (with *waw* as *m.l.* for *ō*), or *yaw-* (the *waw* was etymological and not a *m.l.*). Zevit[89] accepts the two affixes, *-yhw* and *yw-* in proper names as definitely containing *m.l.* (at least for *-yhw*), but this assumption is not absolutely certain.

The forms below are offered in two groups—those which are probable or virtually certain to be representative of the *m.l.* in question, followed by those forms which are possible, though by no means certain.

From an analysis of available data, the following conventions operated in epigraphic Hebrew during the first half of the eighth century.

2.3.2 Final *Matres Lectionis*

2.3.2.1 Final *m.l. yod* represented long *-ī*

> *ʾdny*, "my lord" (Ajrud 15:2);[90] *bʿlmʿny*, "the Baʿalmeʿonite" (S 27:3).

---

[89]Zevit, *MLAHE*, pp. 12. He follows other authors in this assumption, especially Cross and Freedman, *EHO*, pp. 48, 51, 53, 54, 57 (for *-yhw*), and Diringer, *Le iscrizioni*, p. 46 (for *yw-*).

[90]This independent noun is certainly "my lord" (biblical *ʾădōnî*), rather than "my lords" (biblical *ʾădōnay*). Although the text of Ajrud 15:2 is broken after this word, the singular suffixes on *brktk*, "I hereby bless you (m.s.)," Ajrud

yḥwʿly (S 55:2).[91]

2.3.2.2 Final *m.l. waw* represented long *-ū*

yśbʿw, "they will be satisfied"[92] (Ajrud 7:1); *ytnw*, "they will give" (Ajrud 7:2).

yhw (or *yhw[h]* ?) (Ajrud 13); *[ʾ]ḥ̊yhw* (Qasile 1:3); *yrmyhw* (Herr 45, 108); *ʾryhw* (Herr 79); *ntnyhw* (Herr 121);*ʿbdyhw* (Herr 121); *yšʿyhw* (Herr 140).[93]

2.3.2.3 Final *m.l. hê* represented long *-ā*

mʾh̊, "one hundred" (Qasile 1:2).[94]
ḋlh (S 38:3); *ʾzh* (S 2:3); *ḣglh* (S 47:1); *nʿh* (S 50:1); *ʿdh* (Ajrud 2); *ʿdnh* (Ajrud 13); *ywʿśh* (Ajrud 14).

15:4, and *yšmrk*, "may he keep you (m.s.)," Ajrud 15:7, point clearly to the fact that it is the singular suffix, rather than the plural one which is attested on the form in question.

[91]Cross and Freedman, *EHO*, p. 49, accept this form as having a final *yod m.l.* (for *-ī*). However, the element *ʿly* probably derives from the final weak root *ʿly*, in which case, the final *yod* would represent the original consonant, rather than a *m.l.*.

[92]The semantics of *yśbʿw* are not certain. The form could represent the third masculine plural *niphal* imperfect from *šbʿ*, "to swear," (="they will swear"), or, more likely, the *qal* (or possibly *piel*) imperfect, "they will satisfy (themselves), be satisfied with," (*brk ymm wyśbʿw*, "blessed be their day and may they be satisfied"). In any case, the final *waw* is a true *m.l.* for long *ū*.

[93]As mentioned in sec. 2.3.1, p. 58, if the *waw* in *-yhw* names is etymological, *yhw* may have been pronounced *yahwē*.

[94]This form is the only independent noun in this group. The forms which follow *mʾh* are proper names and locatives.

During the late seventh-early sixth centuries, epigraphic Hebrew shows several excellent examples of *hê* used as a *m.l.* for *ā* : *ydʿth*, "you knew," L 2:6, 3:8; A 40:9; *[w]ktbth*, "you are to write," A 7:5-6; *šlḥth*, "you have sent," L 5:4, and *ʾlhykh*, "your God," Khirbet Beit Lei 1:1; cf. P. D. Miller, Jr., "Psalms and Inscriptions," *VTSup* 32 (1981): 21.

2.3.2.4 Final *m.l.* *hê* represented long -*ē*

qṣh (S 5:2, *et cetera*).

2.3.2.5 Final *m.l.* *hê* represented long -*ō*

ʾšrth, "his consort" (Ajrud 14).[95]

---

[95]However, one cannot be certain that -*ahu* › *ô*. Zevit (*MLAHE*, p. 17) discusses this form in the Khirbet el-Kom inscription where the same spelling occurs. He follows A. Lemaire, "Les inscriptions de Khirbet el-Qôm et l'Ashérah de YHWH," *RB* 84 (1977): 595-608, in taking the *hê* as the *m.l.* for the third masculine singular pronominal suffix *ō*. He argues that the *hê* is neither consonantal nor a defectively written suffix -*ahu*, because, at least in the Khirbet el-Kom inscription, the final vowel *ū* is represented by *waw* in the proper name *ʾryhw*.

Two problems exist with Zevit's analysis. The first is that *ʾryhw* may, in fact, represent *ʾūr(ī)yahwē* (the *waw* is etymological), and second, the final vowel of *hu* was probably historically short.

D. Pardee in "The Judicial Plea from Mẹad Ḥashavyahu (Yavneh Yam): A New Philological Study," *Maarav* 1/1 (1978): 46, discusses the *hê* suffix, or lack of it, in the Meṣad Ḥashavyahu inscription: *ʾt qṣr*, where the absence of *hê* indicates either 1)scribal error, or 2)that the scribe was not consistent in his use of final *m.l.* If the third masculine singular pronominal suffix was still pronounced -*ahu* in the late seventh century, the first explanation would make more sense; however, if final *hê* was a *m.l.* for *ō*, the situation described in explanation two would be the more likely.

Three additional articles deal with the form *ʾšrh*, especially *lʾšrth*, from Ajrud and Khirbet el-Kom in an effort to elucidate the meaning and significance of this form and to explain the ending -*h*. See Lemaire, "Who or What was Yahweh's Asherah?," *BAR* 10/no. 6 (Nov. Dec., 1984): 42-51, W.G. Dever, "Asherah, Consort of Yahweh? New Evidence from Kuntillet ʿAjrud," *BASOR* 255 (1984): 21-37, and Z. Zevit, "The Khirbet el-Qom Inscription Mentioning a Goddess," *BASOR* 255 (1984): 39-47.

Zevit's analysis of *lʾšrth* at Khirbet el-Kom as "O Asherata" (*BASOR* 255 (1984): 44-45), on the argument that the *hê* stands as a *m.l.* for *ā* as a "double feminization" of the name is out of the question. He uses as proof only three proper names from the Bible (*yoṭbātāh*, Num 33:33; *timnātāh* (Hosh. 19:43) and *ʾeprātāh* (Micah 5:1), and his examples are all locatives. The word *Asherah* in the epigraphic Hebrew texts is not a locative. The remainder of Zevit's evidence (p. 46) is inconclusive as well, and his analysis of the initial

2.3.2.6 Final *m.l.* *ʾaleph* represented long -*ā* [96]

bʿlʾ (S 1:7, *et cetera*); *ʾšʾ* (S 22:2, *et cetera*); *grʾ* (S 30:3); *ḥnʾ* (S30:3); *ʾḥmʾ* (S 32:3, *et cetera*); *ʾlʾ* (S 38:3); *bʿrʾ* (S 45:2, *et cetera*); *ʾḥʾ* (S 51:3); *ʿyrʾ* (Ajrud 1); *ḥsdʾ* (Beth-Shemesh Seal 1).

2.3.3 Internal *Matres Lectionis*

While one must agree with the philologists who describe the evidence for internal *m.l.* in the early-mid eighth century as anomalous, the few forms which can be interpreted as possibly containing an internal *m.l.* are presented below. It must be stressed that epigraphic Hebrew does not provide sufficient evidence to prove beyond a doubt the existence of internal *m.l.* during this period.

---

lamed as a vocative relies on scant evidence, while epigraphic Hebrew evidence supports the view that the preposition *lamed* is never used as a vocative.

In *BASOR* 255 (1984): 21-37, Dever fails to deal with the suffix (*hê*) on the epigraphic Hebrew forms. Instead, he says (p. 30) that he "leave(s) the grammatical problem to specialists," like Zevit, a man whose grammatical solution to the problem is questionable at best.

Evidence from epigraphic Hebrew confirms that *hê* represents the third masculine singular pronominal suffix. The grammatical problem of "how can a proper name take a pronominal suffix?" may be addressed by noting that the deity name can take the definite article: *hʾšrh*. One might then posit that if the deity name can take a definite article, it can take a suffix. It can also be interpreted, as does Lemaire, that *ʾšrth* implies the "personification" of the goddess, and is, grammatically speaking, a noun. This interpretation offers no deterrent to the acceptance of *hê* as the pronominal suffix.

Even with all this in mind, the early eighth century use of the *m.l.* *hê* representing long -*ō* (Ajrud 14), although probable, is not certain.

[96]All of the following forms are proper names. The *ʾaleph* appears to be hypocoristic in these names, as the element preceding it may be analyzed as a substantive. One may determine, therefore, that the hypocoristic ending which is independent of the primary nominal element is vocalic, rather than consonantal.

The following examples could possibly demonstrate the use of internal *waw* representing long ō: *ywyš̊ᶜ* (S 36:3);[97] *ywntn* (S 45:3); *ywbnh* (Herr 30); *hwšᶜ*(Herr 89).[98]

The theophoric element of the first three examples is pronounced either as *yaw-* or *yō-*, and represents the elision of *hê* even at the beginning of names. Scholars, notably A. Cody, have discussed the possibility that, based on Akkadian transcriptions, the diphthong *aw* contracted to ō in initial, unaccented syllables.[99] This

---

[97]The reading of the second element of this proper name is uncertain. The most likely reading is *ywyšᶜ*. G. A. Reisner, *Israelite Ostraca from Samaria* (Boston: E.O. Cockayne, n.d.), p. 21, reads *ywyšb*, Noth, *IPN*, p. 106, n. 1; 189, reads *ywyšr̊*, and I. T. Kaufman, "The Samaria Ostraca: A Study in Ancient Hebrew Palaeography" (Ph.D. dissertation, Harvard University, 1966), p. 143, does not transcribe the final letter. Zevit (*MLAHE*, p. 12) reads *ywyšb*, pronounced **yawyašib*, following P.K. McCarter, "Yaw, Son of Omri: A Philological Note on Israelite Chronology," *BASOR* 216 (1974): 5 or **yōyašib* (See Diringer, *Le Iscrizioni*, p. 46). In any event, it is the first element of this proper name which is important for the present discussion.

[98]The form *hwšᶜ* is derived from a Verbs I-weak root (*wšᶜ*), therefore the *waw* in the form *hwšᶜ* may stand for the original root consonant, and may not be a *m.l.*. It also is possible that by the end of the eighth century B.C., the shift from *aw* › ō in unaccented syllables had taken place in Judah, as was already common practice in Phoenicia, Moab, and Israel. Where this contraction took place, originally consonantal *waws* were retained in the orthography, and were eventually taken as *matres lectionis* for long ō in the medial position.

[99]Cf. A. Cody, "A New Inscription from Tell al-Rimah and King Jehoash of Israel," *CBQ* 32 (1970): 338-39, on the proper name Jehoash (*Ia-ʾa-su*) from the stela of Adad-Nirari III (from Tell Al-Rimah) has observed that the *a* in the first syllable *Ia-* suggests that the pronunciation of the vowel ō (‹ *aw*) in the name *yôʾās* was heard by the Assyrians as / ɔ̄ /. In this case, Cody surmises that *aw* had already shifted to ō in unstressed syllables in the north; also Zevit, *MLAHE*, p. 13, n. 16.

However, A. Malamat, "On the Akkadian Transcription of the Name of King Joash," *BASOR* 204 (1971): 39, offers a different transliteration for the name *Iu-ʾa-su*, based on neo-Assyrian inscriptions. His interpretation of the pronunciation of the first syllable *Iu-*, instead of *Ia-*, discounts the interpretation of Cody. In Malamat's own words, Cody "put the cart before the horse" when he (Cody) suggested the shift from *aw* › ō in ca. 800 B.C., basing this hypothesis on his pronunciation of the name Joash in Hebrew. As Zevit points out, however, Malamat's transcription for the proper name does not discount the hypothesis in favor of the elision of *hê* and the contraction of the *aw* diphthong.

interpretation, however, is not certain. Considering the theophoric element at the end of a word, one posits that *yahu* › *yaw* appears to be the norm, with the diphthong remaining uncontracted.

One sporadic occurrence of the medial *m.l. waw* used to represent the vowel -*ū* is seen possibly in the word *kwr* (S 49:4).[100]

Internal *m.l. yod* may have represented long -*ī* in two examples from the early eighth century: *šmydʿ*(S 36:2, *et cetera*);[101] *ʿyrʾ*

It is clear from Zevit's discussion (*MLAHE*, p. 13, n. 16) of the views of Cody and Malamat, as well as of S. Norin ("*Jô-Namen und Jehô-Namen*," *VT* 29 (1979): 87-97) and P. K. McCarter ("Yaw, Son of Omri: A Philological Note on Israelite Chronology," *BASOR* 216 (1974): 5-7) that he also supports the contention that initial *yw-* represents the elision of *hê* and a contracted diphthong.

Neither reading can be used in favor of an argument for an uncontracted form (*yaw-ʾaš*).

100*(m)kwr*, "(from) Kur," is a locative name of a town. The reading *kwr* (*kour*) is proposed by Kaufman, "Ancient Hebrew Palaeography," p. 138 in place of Reisner's *krr* (cf. Reisner, *Israelite Ostraca from Samaria*, plate XIII and p. 21, and *ksr* (cf. G. A. Reisner, C. S. Fisher and D. G. Lyon, *Harvard Excavations at Samaria*, 2 vols. (Cambridge: Harvard University Press, 1924)).

Lemaire (*Inscriptions hébraïques*, p. 57) identifies *kwr* with "Kur," southwest of Samaria. He relates the form to the root *kwr* (="creuset, fournaise"), parallel to the biblical masculine singular *qūl* base noun *kwr* (*kûr*), "smelting pot, furnace." The Bible mentions the locative name *kwr ʿśn* (*kôr ʿāśān*), 1 Sam. 30:30 (*kwr* as a *qāl* base noun)), although the form *kwr* is taken by Brown, Driver and Briggs as the *ketib* of *bwr ʿśn* (*bôr ʿāśān*), "pit of smoke" (see *BDB*, pp. 92, 468).

By morphology alone, the form *kwr* could also be an infinitive absolute (*kôr*) or the imperative/infinitive construct (*kûr*), either of *kwr* I, "to be or make round," or *kwr* II, "bore, dig, hew." However, these parts of speech are not commonly proven for locatives. The *qūl* base noun discussed above, with the internal *m.l.* (*waw* for long *ū*) appears the most likely solution.

101This form is not certain as proof for this *m.l.* Either the perfect or imperfect of *ydʿ* would have a *yod.* *Šmydʿ*, a clan name, may be vocalized either of two main ways, *šemyadaʿ* (see Lemaire, *Inscriptions hébraïque*, p. 61), or *šemîdaʿ*, following the biblical proper name in Joshua 17:2, 1 Chron. 7:19 and Nu. 26:32 (*šĕmîdāʿ*). See Reisner, "Israelite Ostraca from Samaria," p. 24; Albright, "The Site of Tirzah and the Topography of Western Manasseh," *JPOS* 11 (1931): 251; Cross, "Epigraphic Notes on Hebrew Documents of the Eighth-Sixth Centuries B.C.: I. A New Reading of a Place Name in the Samaria Ostraca," *BASOR* 163 (1961): 13, 14.

(Ajrud 1).[102]

During the late eighth-seventh century, within which much of the extant epigraphic Hebrew inscriptions fall, the same patterns prevail which were discussed as having developed by the mid-eighth century. Material from the late eighth-seventh century shows more widespread use of final *m.l.*, and especially of internal *m.l.* The convention of using *ʾaleph* (and *waw*?)[103] to represent a final vowel appears during this period in the form *lʾ* (*lōʾ* or *lāʾ*), Meṣad Ḥashavyahu 1:12, 14, unless this spelling reflects Aramaic influence.[104]

Zevit (*MLAHE*, pp. 13-14) notes that in Samaria 57, the *yod* was omitted in the form *šmdʿ*, due to scribal error. Following Bange (*Vowel Letters*, p. 116), Zevit points out that this error in Ostracon 57 indicates that the *yod*, present in all other attestations of this name in epigraphic Hebrew, is a *m.l.* for *ī*. Both Zevit and Bange cite other proper names from epigraphic Hebrew which indicate that the *yod* was not commonly written, but they fail to consider closely the fact that the *yod* in *šmydʿ* is not necessarily to be considered a "case ending" on the noun *šem*, "name," as much as it is the first root radical of *ydʿ* "know," the perfect or imperfect of which could demonstrate a consonantal *yod*.

[102]This proper name occurs in the Bible *(ʿîrāʾ)*, 2 Sam. 20:26, 23:26, 38; 1 Chron. 11:28, 40, 27:9. Noth (*IPN*, p. 230) translates "Eselsfullen," "male ass," or "ass foal," and compares the form to the masculine singular biblical noun *ʿyr* (*ʿayir*), "male ass" ("young and vigorous"), and to *ʿyrh (ʿîrōh)*, "his ass" in Gen. 49:11.

[103]The status of the *waw* in *rʿw*, "his fellow," Siloam 1:2, 3, 4, as an example of final *waw* representing *ō*, is open to question. One must exercise caution as the only other forms written like this in epigraphic Hebrew are plurals, *ʾnšw*, "his people," L 3:17-18, or duals, *yrḥw*, "his two months," Gezer 1:1, 2, 6 (this latter form is itself the subject of much debate). Evidence from biblical Hebrew indicates the epigraphic Hebrew form should be considered a III-*hê* noun: *rʿhw* (*rēʿēhû*).

[104]*Lʾ* could have been pronounced *lōʾ* with the *ʾaleph* as a *m.l.* for *ō*, or, if *lʾ* in epigraphic Hebrew reflects Aramaic influence, the writing would reflect the Aramaic pronunciation */lā/*. Charting the writings of the negative particle determines when and where it was first written with *ʾaleph*. In Ugaritic, the spelling is *l*. The negative particle was written without *ʾaleph* in Old Aramaic (ca. 750), as attested by the Sefire inscription. Later Aramaic texts from the 6th-5th century (e.g., the Bauer-Meissner Papyrus, the Elephantine texts) contain the form *lʾ*, pronounced *lāʾ*. See C. H. Gordon, *Ugaritic Textbook* (Roma: Pontificium Institutum Biblicum, 1965), pp. 108, 425; Ludwig Koehler

According to Zevit,[105] another late eighth-seventh century practice which was not attested earlier was the use of *ʾaleph* as an internal *m.l.* for long -*ō*. Three late eighth-seventh century examples of this practice (the first two are mentioned by Zevit) are *zʾt* (Silwan 1:1, 3), *rʾš* (Siloam 6), and *dʾr* (Herr 57).[106] However, all of these are apparently historical writings. They do not qualify, therefore, as *m.l.* in the strictest sense of the term. *Lʾ* remains the only example, then, of a form containing *ʾaleph* as a true *m.l.*, unless the spelling reflects Aramaic influence.

The contraction of the diphthong *aw* › *ō* took place in Israel during the eighth century (e.g., *ḥrn*, Tell Qasile), but it is not clear

---

and Walter Baumgartner, *Lexicon in Veteris Testamenti Libros* (Leiden: E.J. Brill, 1958), p. 466; C. F. Jean and J. Hoftijzer, *Dictionnaire des inscriptions sémitiques de l'ouest*, p. 133.

[105]Zevit, *MLAHE*, p. 18, n. 27; p. 21, n. 47; p. 25.

[106]The spelling of the feminine demonstrative in Phoenician is most frequently *z*, but also *zʾ* and *ʾz*. The Moabite spelling as in Hebrew is *zʾt* (Meša 3). Zevit (*MLAHE*, p. 18 and n. 8) considers the *ʾaleph* as a *m.l.* for *ō* and cites the biblical feminine demonstrative pronoun *zōh* attested in Judges 18:4, 2 Sam. 11:25 and 1 Kings 14:5 in the expression *kzh wkzh (kāzōh wĕkāzeh)*, and independently in 2 Kings 6:19, Ez. 40:45, *et cetera*, as the archaic, original form of *zʾt*.

However, the *ʾaleph* in *zʾt* is apparently historical. J. Blau, in his article "Short Philological Notes on the Inscription of Mešaʿ," *Maarav* 2/2 (Spring, 1980): 143-57, posits the consonantal *ʾaleph* for *zʾt*, based on an original Canaanite *zʾ* (**zaʾa*) and *zʾt* (**zaʾat* › **zāt* › *zōt*). He offers Proto-Semitic *huʾa/hiʾa*, "he/she" as examples containing the *ʾaleph* consonant (*ʾa*).

The *ʾaleph* in *rʾš*, "head," is historical writing. According to Zevit (*MLAHE*, p. 21), who follows Z. Harris in *Development of the Canaanite Dialects*, p. 42, the *aleph* had quiesced by or during the Amarna Age: **raʾš* › **rāš* › *rōš* and represents the medial vowel *ō* in Siloam.

It should be noted that the word *dʾr* mentioned in N. Avigad, "The Priest of Dor," *IEJ* 25 (1975): 101-7, seal 4:2 (=Herr 57) is spelled with *ʾaleph* in Phoenician (in the Eshmunʿazar inscription); see S. Segert, *A Grammar of Phoenician and Punic* (Munchen: Verlag C.H. Beck, 1976), p. 287; Donner and Röllig, *KAI*, p. 23), and apparently with signs that imply an actual *ʾaleph* pronunciation in Akkadian (*duʾru*; see Avigad, "Priest of Dor," *IEJ* 25 (1975): 102, and Donner and Röllig, *KAI*, p. 23 (Akkadian: *Du-ʾ-ri*). Both *dʾr* and *dwr* occur in the Bible.

that this diphthong contracted in Judah by the eighth-seventh centuries.

Zevit cites the forms *tld*, *ytm*, *ym*, and *ql*, written without *waw*, to prove that the contraction of the diphthong had occurred in Judah, but there are cases where the *waw* is written in the forms from this early period, e.g., *hwšʿ* (Driver Seal 1, *et cetera*),[107] *mrmwt* (Arad 50),[108] *bʿwd* (Siloam 1:1, 2),[109] *mwṣʾ* (Siloam 1:5),[110] *hwšʿyhw* (Meṣad Ḥashavyahu 1:7, *et cetera*).[111] Even though Zevit cites the forms containing *waw* as proof to substantiate his claim that the change from *aw* › *ō* had already taken place in Judah in the eighth-seventh centuries, the syllable containing *waw* in these forms may have been pronounced *aw* (in this case, the diphthong would not yet have contracted) just as plausibly as *ō* (in the case that the diphthong would have contracted).

For three of the four epigraphic Hebrew forms without *waw* expressed in the writing (namely, *ytm*, *ym* and *ql*), the absence of the *waw* can be explained in ways other than stating that it proves the contraction of the *aw* diphthong. Zevit cites the form *ytm* from an eighth century seal from Elath as the earliest definitive example for the contraction of the *aw* diphthong in the eighth century in the south, but the authenticity of the seal (i.e., whether it is, in fact, a Hebrew seal) in which this form occurs is disputed.[112] Furthermore, *ytm* cannot be used to prove the contraction of the *aw* diphthong since, on the basis of the biblical Hebrew name *yātōm*, the /*ō*/ is not from /*aw*/. A case has been made by Cross and

---

107 But the root is Verbs I-weak: *wšʿ*, therefore the *waw* may be consonantal.

108 The status of the *waw* in *-mwt* is not certain. See sec. 3.1.4.1, p. 104, n. 72 on the *qal* infinitive absolute . The form could be vocalized **mĕrîmāwet māwet* (*māwet* corresponding to *baʿal* of *mĕrîbaʿal* [see p. 72, n. 129], unless the deity name was only *mōt*).

109 *ʿwd* is a disputed form, but plausibly *ā* ›*ō*, if not, **ʿawd*.

110 But the root is Verbs I-weak: *wṣʾ* (**mawṣaʿ*).

111 See n. 107 above.

112 Herr identifies the seal bearing the name *ytm* as Edomite rather than Hebrew, and dates it to the first half of the 7th century; cf. Herr, *SANSS*, p. 163 (rather than to the 8th century; cf. Zevit, *MLAHE*, p. 14).

Freedman that the forms *ql* and *ym* may relate to biblical Aramaic *qāl* (not *qawl* › *qōl*) and Proto-Hebrew *yām* (not *yawm* ›*yōm*) respectively.[113]

The form which Zevit cites as a fourth example, *tld*, from the Beersheba ostracon,[114] appears to represent the contraction of the *aw* diphthong, but there are some difficulties. The form is probably, but not certainly, a geographic noun, unattested elsewhere in Northwest Semitic outside of biblical Hebrew. In biblical Hebrew, however, the form is spelled with *waw* (Josh 15:30 *ʾltwld* and 1 Chron. 4:29 *twld*). Zevit analyzed the evidence and defined the *waw* in the biblical forms as etymological *waw* functioning as a *m.l.* in a historical spelling.[115] The lack of *waw* in the Beersheba form could indicate that the *waw* has contracted (**tawlád* › *tōlád*).[116]

The problem with Zevit's acceptance of *tld* as proof for the contraction of the *aw* diphthong is that the etymology of this word is uncertain and proper nouns in general are subject to difficulties in analysis. The ostracon itself, from which Aharoni read *tld*, is described by him as a palimpsest and several lines of writing were visible on the inner side (where the word *tld* appears). Since Aharoni was able to discern only two locative designations, one abbreviation, and some hieractic numerical signs, one cannot use a form from this ostracon as proof for such a major linguistic change as the contraction of the *aw* diphthong.

The hypothesis that in epigraphic Hebrew the *aw* diphthong had probably not contracted to *ō* in Judah in the eighth-seventh century is supported by Ammonite evidence. The preservation of the diphthong *aw* in Ammonite is likely expressed in writing by the *waw*. This is in contrast to the diphthong *ay*, which contracted to *ē* and left no residual reminder in the orthography.[117]

---

[113]Cross and Freedman, *EHO*, pp. 50, 53.

[114]Cf. Y. Aharoni, *Beer-Sheba I, Excavations at Tel Beer-Sheba, 1969-1971 Seasons* (Tel Aviv: Tel Aviv University, 1973): 71-73.

[115]Zevit, *MLAHE*, p. 19.

[116]Ibid.

[117]D. Sivan, "On the Grammar and Orthography of the Ammonite Findings," *UF* 14 (1982): 225.

Although it is not certain, internal *waw* may have represented long *ō* by the seventh century. An internal *waw* has been read by Barkay[118] in the restored noun *š[l]wm* which occurs in the mid seventh century inscription from Ketef Hinnom. If further studies of this inscription substantiate this reading, the form *š[l]wm* could then be offered as evidence for the change *ā* › *ō*.

The strongest evidence for the change *ā* › *ō* is *ḥwrṣ*[119] but

---

[118]G. Barkay, *Ketef Hinnom*, pp. 30, 35. It is difficult to accept *š[l]wm* as proof that *waw* represents *ō* until the future publication of the Ketef Hinnom inscription (which Barkay mentions on p. 29) is made available. Barkay himself admits that his present publication does not "offer a full and convincing reading of all parts of the inscription" (p. 29), and indeed, the line drawings are often difficult to interpret along with the corresponding transliteration.

[119]While it is often difficult to interpret forms which function as proper names in a language, the evidence, though limited, indicates that *ḥwrṣ* should be interpreted as a participial form from a strong root. This form illustrates an internal vowel and functions also as an example of the linguistic change *ā* › *ō*.

Two other participial forms in Northwest Semitic epigraphy furnish supporting evidence for these statements: *šwḥr* (on two Ammonite seals dated to the 6th or 7th century) and *ḥwnn* (on an epigraphic Hebrew [or Aramaic] seal). For a discussion and bibliography of all three proper names, cf. G. B. Sarfatti, "Hebrew Inscriptions of the First Temple Period—A Survey and Some Linguistic Comments," *Maarav* 3/1 (1982): 61-62. For additional references for the proper name *šwḥr*, cf. J. Naveh, "*ktwbwt knʿnywt wʿbrywt*" [Canaanite and Hebrew Inscriptions (1960-1964)], *Lešonenu* 30 (1965): 80; N. Avigad, "Ammonite and Moabite Seals," pp. 287 in *Near Eastern Archaeology in the Twentieth Century: Essays in Honor of Nelson Glueck*, ed. by J.A. Sanders (Garden City: N.Y. Doubleday, 1970); P. Bordreuil, "Inscriptions sigillaires ouest-sémitiques I: Epigraphie ammonite," *Syria* 50 (1973): 182; Herr, *SANSS*, p. 64; Zevit, *MLAHE*, p. 25, n. 44; D. Sivan, "On the Grammar and Orthography of the Ammonite Findings," *UF* 14 (1982): 225; K. Jackson, *The Ammonite Language of the Iron Age* (Chico, CA: Scholars Press, 1983). For the proper name *ḥwnn*, cf. C. C. Torrey, "A Few Ancient Seals," *Annual of the American Schools of Oriental Research* 3 (1923): 105; D. Diringer, *Le iscrizioni*, nos. 21, 22; Naveh, "Canaanite and Hebrew Inscriptions," *Lešonenu* 30 (1965): 80; Herr, *SANSS*, p. 187 [Herr considers the seal as a possible forgery]; D. Sivan, "Ammonite Findings," *UF* 14 (1982): 225.

All three forms have been read as participles; cf. Zevit on *ḥwrṣ*, *MLAHE*, p. 27, and *šwḥr*, p. 25 [the reader should check individual references several other forms are offered as possible supporting evidence: *ʿwpy* (Khirbet el-Kom 1:1),[120] *śwkh* (Gibeon Seals, Lachish Seal

---

given above for *šwḥr* and *ḥwnn*]. The *ō* in Northwest Semitic participles derived from an original *a* in Proto-Semitic **qā̆tilu* forms (Bauer and Leander, *Historische Grammatik*, pp. 317-18) and if *ḥwrṣ*, *ḥwnn*, and *šwḥr* are correctly interpreted as participles, then the *waw* is a *m.l.* representing *ō* ‹ *ā*.

The interpretation of the name *šwḥr* is problematic according to Jackson (*Ammonite Language*, p. 90) and the same statement is made by Zevit on *ḥwrṣ* (*MLAHE*, p. 27). The chief difficulty connected with *ḥwnn* is that Herr identifies the seal on which the word is inscribed as a modern forgery (*SANSS*, p. 187). The question of the authenticity of the *ḥwnn* seal and the date of the Ammonite seals led Sarfatti ("Hebrew Inscriptions," *Maarav* 3/1 (Jan., 1982): 63) to doubt these forms as "iron clad" evidence for the use of *waw* as a *m.l.* for *ō*, but he does admit that they "hint in that direction."

[120]The etymology of *ʿwpy* is not certain. The *waw* may be a *m.l.* (either for *ō* or *ū*); see Zevit, *MLAHE*, p. 22.

The epigraphic Hebrew proper name has a parallel form in the Bible,*ʿwpy* (*ʿôpay*), the *ketib* of Jer. 40:8. According to A. Lemaire ("Les inscriptions de Khirbet el-Qôm et L'ashérah de YHWH," *RB* (1977): 596), the *yod* ending is hypocoristic, and the form is related to the middle weak *ʿw/yp*, "to be dark," meaning "ténébreux" ("dark" › "gloomy, swarthy"). This was also the analysis proposed by W. G. Dever, "Iron Age Epigraphic Material from the Area of Khirbet el-Kom," *HUCA* 40/41(1970): 152, n. 15, who also noted that some Greek transcriptions of this proper name indicate the pronunciation *ʿūpay* (*waw* as *m.l.* for *ū*).

Noth's interpretation (*IPN*, p. 230), that *ʿwpy* means "bird," and is related to the middle weak root *ʿwp*, "to fly," and the biblical noun *ʿwp* (*ʿôp*), "fowl(s), bird(s)," seems likely.

15:1-2),[121] and *hkws* (Arad 38:1).[122]

Zevit[123] accepts all of these forms as certain examples for the hypothesis that *waw* functioned as a *m.l.* for *ō* in the seventh century, but none of the forms (except *ḥwrṣ*) can be used as proof positive for the linguistic change *ā* › *ō*.

The late eighth-seventh century epigraphic material shows a much wider use of the medial *waw m.l.* to indicate -*ū* than was apparent in the early eighth century: *ʾrwr* (Silwan 2:2); *ʾwryhw* (A

---

[121]Herr, *SANSS*, p. 89, no. 14, reads *šwk*. The *hê*, however, is fairly clear if one examines the form in Seal 9 (see D. Diringer, "On Ancient Hebrew Inscriptions Discovered at Tell ed-Duweir (Lachish)-I," *PEQ* 73 (April, 1941): 47 and plate IV, fig. 2).

The etymology of this word is not certain. The form is known from the Bible as *śwkh* (*śôkōh*, Jos. 15:35, etc., a locative name, but Diringer ("Ancient Hebrew Inscriptions," *PEQ* 73 (1941): 48) mentions that it also occurs as a proper name in 1 Chron. 4:18. The form is possibly related to such biblical forms as *śwk* (*śôk*), a masculine singular noun, "branch, brushwood," in Judg. 9:49, *śwkh* (*śôkōh*), "his branch," or the feminine singular *śwkh* (*śôkāh*), Judg. 9:48 (*śwkt ʿṣym, śôkat, ʿēṣîm*, "branch of the trees").

As Zevit (*MLAHE*, p. 23) points out, the *waw* of the epigraphic Hebrew form is probably etymological, although he gives this as an example of medial *waw* as *m.l.* for *ō* (p. 25). Cross and Freedman do not posit the existence of the *m.l.* in this form (cf. Cross and Freedman, *EHO*, p. 51, no. 43, **śawkō*).

[122]*Hkws* is a possible additional example of an epigraphic Hebrew form with *m.l.* (for *ō*) not cited by Zevit. Arad 38 is dated to Stratum VII (i.e., to the late seventh century) on the basis of its writing style by Aharoni, *Arad Inscriptions*, p. 69. The *waw* is taken as a *m.l.* for *ō* by reason of comparison with parallel forms in biblical Hebrew. In epigraphic Hebrew, *hkws* is viewed as a proper name consisting of the definite article and masculine singular noun (biblical *kws*, "owl," Lev. 11:17; Deut. 14:16; Ps. 102:7), comparable to another biblical proper name composed of the definite article and masculine singular noun, *hqwṣ*, 1 Chron. 24:10 (see Aharoni, *Arad Inscriptions*, p. 69). It is not certain that the *waw* in *hkws* is a *m.l.* since the root and etymology of the epigraphic Hebrew (*hkws*) and biblical Hebrew (*kws*) forms are unknown.

In the case of *hkws*, the proper name would identify its owner with an animal (this type of proper name is most common in the Bible [see Noth *IPN*, pp. 229-30], and in epigraphic Hebrew), and the bearer of *hqwṣ* would have a plant name (also a fairly common biblical phenomenon; [see Noth, *IPN*, pp. 230-31]).

[123]Zevit, *MLAHE*, pp. 17-25.

31:2); *swsh* (A 32), *yhwd[h]* (A 40:13); *ʾbšwʿ* (Herr 162:1-2); *bwzy* (Herr 12:2).[124]

This period also furnishes more examples of the medial vowel *ī* as represented by *yod*: e.g., *ʾyš* (A 40:7-8), *ʾyšy* (MO 2:3), *ḥmyʿdn* (Avigad New Names 1:1), *ḥmyʾhl* (Hest. 34:1),[125] *zyp* (Beersheba Seal 5:1; Gibeon Seals), *ʾḥyqm* (A31:5),[126] *mykyhw* (Herr

---

[124]Biblical *bûzî*, Ezek. 1:3, a proper name and gentilic. For a more detailed discussion of this form, refer to sec. 3.3.2.1, p. 183, n. 218 on masculine singular gentilics.

[125]*Ḥmyʿdn*, "my husband's father (=DN) is delight," and *ḥmyʾhl*, "my husband's father is (a) shelter," are two proper names (of females, see Hestrin and Dayagi-Mendels, *Inscribed Seals*, pp. 50-51) composed of the elements *ḥmy*, "my father-in-law," and masculine singular nouns *ʿdn*, "delight" (biblical *ʿeden*) or *ʾhl*, "tent, shelter."

The *yod* in the epigraphic Hebrew names is a *m.l.* for *ī*, as in another proper name *ʾbyḥy*, "my father lives," A 39:11, and possibly in *ʾḥyʾm*, "my brother rules, prevails," A 35:3, and *ʾḥyqm*, "my brother rises," A 31:5 (but see next note).

[126]"My brother rises, has arisen." Also, Vattioni 210 (*ʾḥqm*), Avigad (*IEJ* 13) Seal 2:2 (=Herr 129), and biblical *ʾḥyqm* (*ʾăḥîqam*), 2 Kings 22:12, 14, *et cetera*. The *yod* in *ʾḥyqm* in epigraphic Hebrew is probably a *m.l.* for *ī*, unless the word is analyzed as *ʾḥ* + *yqm*, noun plus imperfect.

119:2)[127] *syl*ʾ (Herr 122:1),[128] and *mrymwt* (B/L (32) 1982 Seal 11).[129]

The internal *m.l. ʾaleph* may also have been used to represent *-ā* in the seventh-sixth century as shown in the word *myʾmn* (*miyāmīn*).[130]

---

[127]The seal bearing this name *mykyhw* (biblical *mîkāyāhû*), "who is like YH?" is dated to the last half of the eighth century by Herr (*SANSS*, p. 133). Several analogous biblical names occur (all with the *m.l.* in the first syllable): *mykyhw* (*mîkāyāhû*), 2 Chron. 17:7, etc., *mykyh* (*mîkāyah*), Jer. 26:18 (*ketib*), etc., *mykh* (*mîkah*), Judg. 17:5, etc., *mykʾl* (*mîkāʾēl*), Num. 13:13, etc. The epigraphic Hebrew form (and biblical forms) is analyzed as the interrogative, written *plene*, *my* (*mî*), "who," plus the preposition *k-* ("like"), plus the theophoric element. The name occurs in epigraphic Hebrew without the *m.l.* in *mkyhw*, Jerusalem Jar 1:2; B/L (26) 10:2, and in other hypocoristic names: *mky*, R 9:1 (=Herr 111); A 110:2; *mkl,* L 19:3, and *mkʾ*, Hazor 5, "Who is like (DN)."

[128]The etymology of this proper name is unclear. The *yod* may be a *m.l.* Morphologically, this form corresponds to the biblical *slʾ* (*sillāʾ*), 2 Kings 12:2 (written without *m.l.*), described by Brown, Driver and Briggs (*BDB*, p. 698) as a "word in (unintelligible) designated location." The *Interpreter's Dictionary of the Bible*, vol. 4, ed., G. A. Buttrick (Nashville: Abingdon Press, 1962), p. 352, describes *slʾ* as "possibly a quarter or suburb of Jerusalem; mentioned in connection with the house of Millo."

The root *slʾ*, "weigh," occurs in the Bible only in the *pual* participle *hmšlʾym* (*hamĕšullāʾîm*), "the reckoned ones, the ones weighed, given a value," Lam. 4:2 (also *slʾ* in Sabatian, "consecrate, devote"). Perhaps, *sylʾ* in epigraphic Hebrew means something along the order of "(DN) has valued (me)," where the form relates to the *piel* perfect.

[129]Cf. P. Bordreuil and A. Lemaire, "Nouveaux sceaux hébreux et araméens," *Semitica* 32 (1982): 29-30. The same proper name occurs without *yod* in Arad 50:1 (*mrmwt*).

The etymology of *mrymwt* (B/L (32) 1982) Seal 11), is uncertain, but an extant form supporting the hypothesis that the *yod* is a *m.l.* for *ī*, is *mrybʿl* (1 Chron. 9:40), "Baʿal is my advocate" (cf. *BDB*, p. 937). However, biblical *mrmwt* (*mĕrēmōt*, Neh. 12:3, *et cetera*), is everywhere written without *yod*.

[130]*Myʾmn* appears to be a proper name and is known from two epigraphic Hebrew seals: Hest. Seal 94:1 (see Hestrin and Dayagi-Mendels, *Inscribed Seals*, p. 119), and with an uncertain reading in Lachish V Seal 4:2 (see Y. Aharoni, "Trial Excavation in the 'Solar shrine' at Lachish," *IEJ* 18 (1968): 166). The closest biblical comparison to this name is from Neh. 10:8, *mymn* (*miyāmīn*) and Neh. 12:5, *mymyn* (*miyāmîn*). Other analogous forms come from Nippur (*minyamin*), and Dura-Europos (*mnymn*).

By the first decade of the sixth century, epigraphic Hebrew orthography shows no new innovations except perhaps a wider extension for the use of the internal *yod m.l.* for *-ī: wmqyn[h]* (A 24:12); *hbqydm* (A 24:14-15); *hʿyr* (A 24:17); *lhʿyd* (A 24:18); *ʾyš* (L 3:9-10); *hʿyrh* (L 4:7); *htšʿyt* (L 20:1); and *ʾkzy[b]* (L 22:10 = L V Ost. 1:10). Internal *waw m.l.* for long *ū* is attested in *hsws* (Arad 111:5),[131] *qrbʾwr* (Arad 24:14), and possibly *yhwdh* (KBL 1:2). Clearly, by the sixth century, what were once innovations in epigraphic Hebrew had now become accepted practice and part of an orthographic system.

R. Zadok has confirmed the analysis that the *ʾaleph* functions as a *m.l.* in this form. He connects the form *miyyāmîn* on page 77 of Coogan's *West Semitic Names in the Murašû Documents* (a form which Coogan analyzed as meaning "southerner, lucky") with *myʾmn* on the Hestrin seal, and cites evidence for the *plene* spelling *-ya-* in Aramaic, Old Persian, and Babylonian (cf. Coogan, *West Semitic Personal Names*, pp. 104-5; R. Zadok, "Review of *West Semitic Personal Names in the Murašû Documents* by M. D. Coogan" in *IEJ* 28 (1978): 290-91.

One might cite evidence from epigraphic Hebrew and Phoenician which indicates that the element *ʾmn* (in *myʾmn*) might be construed as a verbal element (*ʾmn*, "support, confirm" in biblical Hebrew). The analogous proper names under discussion are: *ywʾmn*, Avigad Seal 10:1 (epigraphic Hebrew) and *ʾlʾmn*, *ʿbdʾmn* (Phoenician; cf. Benz, *Personal Names in the Phoenician and Punic Inscriptions*, p. 270).

One might argue that *my ʾmn* be analyzed as the interrogative (*my*, "who") plus verbal element (*ʾmn*), "Who supports?" The difficulty with this interpretation is that proper names which have as an element the interrogative word *m(y)*, "who" (Akkadian, *mannu-* or *mi-*), also have the preposition *-k-*, "like," as the second element, followed by a theophoric, not verbal element; e.g., *mykyhw*, *mykʾl* (biblical Hebrew), *m(y)kyhw* (epigraphic Hebrew), *mi-ka-ya-a-ma* (Akkadian); also *man-nu-ki-i-i-la-hi-i* and *man-nu-ki-i-la-hi-Dirgir* (Akkadian), *mngʾnrt* (Ammonite, = *mannu-kī-Inurta*, "Who is like Inurta?" cf. Coogan, *West Semitic Personal Names*, pp. 28-29, 76; N. Avigad, "Seals of Exiles," *IEJ* 15 (1965): 224.

[131]Zevit, *MLAHE*, p. 29, dates this ostracon to the early sixth century following A.F. Rainey, "Three Additional Hebrew Ostraca from Tel Arad," *Tel Aviv* 4 (1977): 97, who associates the inscription with Arad Stratum VI.

2.3.4 Conclusion

Until further texts are discovered, the question of the first introduction of internal *m.l.* into epigraphic Hebrew will remain unanswered. At present, the earliest proven date for the inclusion of internal *m.l.* into epigraphic Hebrew is the late eighth century with such forms as *ʾrwr* (Silwan 2:2), *ḥwrṣ* (Herr 90), and *mykyhw* (Herr 119). Research awaits new material dating to the tenth and ninth centuries in order that a more balanced picture of the use of *m.l.*, internal and external, may be presented. Until then, the corpus of epigraphic Hebrew texts will remain one-sided, with most of the extant material dating from the late eighth through the sixth centuries. Other aspects of epigraphic Hebrew grammar, besides the use of *m.l.*, including specific questions of phonology also await future discoveries for their proper elucidation.

3. MORPHOLOGY

3.1 The Verb

3.1.1 Introduction

The epigraphic Hebrew verbal system is primarily based upon the principle of tri-consonantalism: each verb is composed of three radicals which, taken together, constitute the root.[1]

Added to each root are various affixes which together with prefixes, infixes and suffixes, form patterns. This grammar follows the traditional nomenclature in identifying the common verbal patterns in epigraphic Hebrew by the names commonly ascribed to them by grammarians of biblical Hebrew.

---

[1]The so-called "weak" roots are already in the time of epigraphic Hebrew, severely de- or non-triconsonantalized. For instance, it is difficult to derive some forms of Verbs II-*waw*/*yod* from tri-consonantal patterns, and it is likely that part of this verbal root type may have originated in bi-consonantal roots. See J. Blau, *A Grammar of Biblical Hebrew* (Wiesbaden: Harrassowitz, 1976), p. 61.

3.1.2 Verbal Stems

The verbal stems extant in epigraphic Hebrew are:

qal: The simplest verbal pattern.
niphal: The passive of *qal*.
piel: The intensive/factive of the *qal*.
pual: The passive of *piel*.
hiphil: The causative of the *qal*.
hophal: The passive of *hiphil*.
pilpel: The pattern of reduplication, often not studied as a separate pattern, but as a bi-form of *piel*.[2]

3.1.3 Finite Forms

In epigraphic Hebrew, there are two main finite types, one consisting of the root or a form thereof plus suffixes, which denotes completed, punctual acts; it is called the Perfect in this grammar. The second is called the Imperfect, which is a form of the root plus prefixes and some suffixes; it denotes incompleted, durative acts. The inflection of each verb cited on the following pages is expressed both for the perfect and the imperfect by the three radicals *q.t.l.*, used conventionally by grammarians to denote a tri-literal root. Within this grammar, all paradigms will be given in terms of this root. Where the forms are given for each finite form in the following section, a hyphen indicates that a particular form is as yet unattested. The discovery of additional Hebrew texts will enable future students of epigraphic Hebrew to add to the basic framework presented in this grammar.

[2]While there are many "sub-patterns" in biblical Hebrew, *pilpel* is the only attested sub-pattern in epigraphic Hebrew.

Prefixes and suffixes of perfect and imperfect

The suffixes and prefixes are given in table 4.

TABLE 4
SUFFIXES AND PREFIXES

SINGULAR	**3 masc.**	**3 fem.**	**2 masc.**	**2 fem.**	**1**
Perfect	Ø[a]	*-t*[b]	*-t, -th*[c]	–	*-ty, -t*[d]
Imperfect	*y-*	–	*t-*	–	–
PLURAL	**3 masc.**	**3 fem.**	**2 masc.**	**2 fem.**	**1**
Perfect	*-w*	–	*-tm*	–	–
Imperfect	*y...w*	–	*t...w*	–	*n-*

[a] Ø stands for a verbal form with no suffix.

[b]The *taw* suffix is attested for the third feminine singular perfect from third weak roots only. One would not, on the basis of biblical Hebrew, expect the *-t* on the third feminine singular perfect of non-third weak roots.

[c]There are five certain examples of perfects with suffix *-t* (two others, A 3:5 and A 40:5 are probable) and five with the ending *-th*.

[d]There are six, possibly seven (A 40:5) examples of perfects with suffix *-ty*, and three with the ending *-t*.

Waw-consecutive

The term *waw*-consecutive refers to the special *waw* which occurs before both the perfect and imperfect forms, in situations where one is replaced by the other as a normal feature of Hebrew syntax.[3] In a particular sequence, the *waw*-consecutive perfect verb will correspond to the imperfect in meaning. The opposite is also true: the waw-consecutive plus imperfect verb may, in certain syntactic environments, correspond to the perfect. The term *waw-*

[3]For examples and discussion of the *waw*-consecutive plus perfect/imperfect in epigraphic Hebrew, cf. pp. 87-88, 224, 260-67, 278, 289 in this grammar.

consecutive is not unique to epigraphic Hebrew; indeed, it is derived from biblical Hebrew.

3.1.3.1 Other forms

Imperative and jussive

Besides the indicative verbal forms, epigraphic Hebrew contains modal forms. The Imperative, or command form, corresponds with respect to form and suffixes (on plurals) to the imperfect, but without prefixes.[4] The Jussive resembles the third masculine singular imperfect in form but occasionally is a shorter form, both as an independent verb and as an element in epigraphic Hebrew proper names.[5]

Infinitives and participles

The four finite indicative verbal forms (perfect, *waw*-consecutive imperfect, imperfect, and *waw*-consecutive plus perfect), and the modal forms (imperative and jussive), are joined in epigraphic Hebrew by several non-finite forms, the infinitives and participles, which exhibit a dual verb-noun character.

(1) *Infinitives construct and absolute.* There are two types of infinitives in epigraphic Hebrew: the Construct and the Absolute. The infinitive construct occurs both with the introductory *lamed*, "to" (as in *lqrʾ* "to read," L 3:10), as well as without this prefix (e.g., *qrʾ*, "to read," L 3:9), and exhibits verbal-nominal functions. The infinitive absolute functions primarily as an adverb and is not governed by prepositions (e.g., *[š]lḥ* , with the perfect, "I hereby send," papMur 17a:1; *ntn*, "give!" A 1:2).

(2) *Active and passive participles.* The traditional terms Active Participle and Passive Participle are used in this grammar and correspond in form and function to those of biblical Hebrew (e.g., active participle *ʾwrr*, "a curser," KBL 6:1; passive participle *ʾrwr*, "cursed (be)," Silwan 2:2). Participles are nominal in morphology, but may function syntactically either as a noun (for example, in the construct state), or as a verb (for example, by

---

[4]Cf. pp. 96-102 in this grammar.

[5]Cf. pp. 93-96, esp. nn. 51, 52 (pp. 95-96), p. 141, n. 148 in this grammar.

governing a direct object). Sentences with participles as predicates behave like nominal clauses in their aspectual relationship to a finite verb, in word order (the subject may either precede or follow the participle), and in negation (with the negative marker, e.g., *ʾyn* rather than *lʾ*)[6]

3.1.3.2 Personal pronouns governed by verbs

Personal pronouns governed by verbs may either occur separately from the verb, attached to the particle *ʾt-* or may be attached to the verb as a pronominal suffix. The suffixes are given in table 5.

TABLE 5
PRONOMINAL SUFFIXES ON VERBS

Singular				
1	2 masc.	2 fem.	3 masc.	3 fem.
-n, -ny	*-k*	–	*-h, -w*	–
			-hw	
Plural				
1	2 masc.	2 fem.	3 masc.	3 fem.
-n	–	–	*-m*	–

[6]For examples illustrating each use of the participle mentioned above, refer to the relevant section of this grammar, beginning with the discussion of the participle on p. 106.

3.1.4 Simple Verbal Stems

3.1.4.1 *Qal* (and its relationship to the other verbal stems)

The Perfect

Not all of the possible forms of the perfect paradigm are attested in epigraphic Hebrew. Only one feminine form, the third feminine singular, is attested in epigraphic Hebrew, and this is for Verbs III-weak (*hyt*, Siloam 1:3). The first common plural verb is never attested in epigraphic Hebrew. Two orthographies are attested for the first common singular and second masculine singular perfects–one spelling is *plene* with final *mater lectionis*, and the other without the *m.l.* (e.g., *ktbty*, "I wrote," L 4:3, and *šlḥt*, "I sent," papMur 17a:1). Other forms (excluding the third feminine singular perfect *hyt*, which represents an archaic phonology and orthography for Verbs III-weak)[7] are consistent with biblical Hebrew. The third masculine singular perfect verb occurs both as the first or the second element of epigraphic Hebrew proper names (e.g., *ʾḥz(yhw)*, "(DN) has grasped," AvNN 19:2 and *(yhw)ʾḥz*, Av (*EI* 9) 15:1). It may also constitute a complete proper name, as an independent proper name consisting of that form alone, as in *ʾḥz*, "(DN) has grasped," S 2:5, Ushna Seal 1:2.

(1) *Inflection.* The full inflection of the root *qtl* is given on the next page in table 6 to the extent that the perfect forms are attested in epigraphic Hebrew.

---

[7]Unless it is spelled defectively while pronounced roughly as in biblical Hebrew, i.e., *hāyĕtā*.

TABLE 6
***QAL* PERFECT**

	Singular	Plural
3 m.	*qtl*	*qtlw*
3 f.	**qtlh*[a]	–
2 m.	*qtlt; qtlth*	*qtltm*
2 f.	–	–
1 c.	*qtlty; qtlt*	–

[a]The form **qtlh* for the third feminine singular perfect is hypothetical, even though it is the form expected from biblical Hebrew. There are no attested forms in epigraphic Hebrew other than *hyt*, from Verbs III-*hê*. Since *hyt* lacks a final *m.l. hê*, as is common in biblical Hebrew among third feminine singular perfects from the strong root type, the form *qtl* (rather than *qtlh*) could be posited. However, *hyt*, since it is the sole third feminine singular *qal* perfect attested in epigraphic Hebrew, is not sufficient enough evidence to rule out *qtlh*. In either event, until a specific third feminine singular verb from a strong root is attested in epigraphic Hebrew, both forms remain unproven.

(2) *Forms.* This section describes the extant verbs in the perfect. The inflection of the forms is similar to biblical Hebrew. All lists of forms are complete, unless there is a statement to the contrary.

First common singular. The *yod mater lectionis* for the morpheme *ī* of the first common singular form is more often attested than not.

Table 7, found on the following page, contains the epigraphic Hebrew attestations of perfects ending in the suffixes -*ty*, or -*t*, as well as those perfects attested with object suffixes.

TABLE 7
FIRST COMMON SINGULAR *QAL* PERFECTS

	Form	Meaning	Reference
Suffix *-ty*			
	ktbty	"I wrote"	L: 4:3[a]
	mlkty	"I reigned"	A 88:1
	nqty	"I am innocent"	MHY 1:11
	qrʾty	"I read"	L 3:12
	q[r]ʾty	"I read"	L 12:4[b]
Suffix *-t*			
	klt	"I finished"	MHY 1:8
	šlḥt	"I sent"	papMur 17a:1
	brkt	"I bless"	Ajrud 14:1
Perfects with Object Suffixes			
	brktk	"I bless you"	A 16:2-3
	brkt[k]	"I bless [you]"	A 40:3
	nttm	"I sent, gave them"	A 40:10

[a]*[wktbt]y*, "I (hereby write)," is restored in Arad 40:5.

[b]For the restoration *[ntt]y*, "I gave," A 40:12-13, cf. Pardee, *HHL*, pp. 63, 242.

Second masculine singular. The second masculine singular perfect has one of two possible suffixes: *-t* or *-th*. Attestations in epigraphic Hebrew are contained in table 8 on the following page.

TABLE 8
SECOND MASCULINE SINGULAR PERFECTS

	Form	Meaning	Reference
Suffix *-t*			
	ʾm[rt]	"You ordered"	A 40:5
	(w)hsbt	"You send (them) out"	A 2:5-6
	[whš]bt	"You should return"	MHY 1:14
	(w)lqḥt	"You are to take"	A 3:8, 17:3-4
	(w)ntt	"You are to give"	A 2:7-8
	(wṣrr[t]	"You are to bind"	A 3:5
Suffix *-th*			
	ydʿth	"You knew"	L 2:6, 3:8; A40:9[a]
	(w)ntth	"You are to entrust"	MO 2:4
	ntth	"You have given"	MO 2:7
	[w]ktbth	"You are to write"	A 7:5-6
	šlḥth	"You have sent"	L 5:4[b c]

[a]In two instances, L 2:6, 3:8, this form occurs with the negative particle *lʾ*.

[b]The readings *šlḥth* with final *hê* is disputed, but probable (see discussion below).

[c]The second masculine singular *piel* perfect *dbrth,* "You spoke," MO 2:5 is a further example of the plene writing of the pronominal element in epigraphic Hebrew (see table 20, p. 127, n. a, and following text).

Table 8 illustrates that the second masculine singular perfect with *-t* suffix, while attested with more of a variety of roots, is only slightly more common than those forms with *-th* suffix. In addition, two of the *-t* suffixes are restored.

The discussion which follows concentrates on the problem of the morphology of the second masculine singular perfect. Forms having the suffix *-t* are discussed first, followed by those with the suffix *-th*, and finally, an orthographic discrepancy which occurs in the Bible is discussed.

The question arises why, in epigraphic Hebrew, some verbal forms have the *-th* ending with the *mater lectionis* for long *ā,* while others occur without the *hê*. A.F. Rainey has suggested that the final *hê mater lectionis* in second masculine singular verbs can perhaps be explained by the shift in accent of *waw*-consecutive forms.[8] It has been noted by Paranuk[9] and Zevit[10] that the verbs with the orthography *-t* are all preceded by *waw*-consecutive, which, in biblical Hebrew, shifted the accent from *qatā́lta* to *(we)qataltā́*.

An exception to this, however, is Arad 40:5, *ʾl ʾšr ʾm[rt]*, "...to what you ordered," where *ʾm[rt]* is not preceded by *waw*-consecutive, yet has been restored with the short ending by Aharoni[11] and Pardee.[12] This form would be an exception to the *waw*-consecutive plus accent-shift rule, if the restoration were accepted. Perhaps the form in question is better restored *ʾm[rth]*, a restoration which is possible due to the space after the *mem* which is sufficiently large to accommodate all of these letters.

Two forms which possibly weaken Zevit's and Paranuk's theory are the *waw*-consecutive plus perfect *wntth*, "You are to entrust," MO 2:4 and *[w]ktbth*, "You are to write," A 7:5-6, where a *waw*-consecutive (although restored in A 7:5-6) precedes the verb with *-th* suffix.[13] According to Zevit,[14] some time after the sixth century, the "defective" spelling (*-t*) on verbs tended to prevail over those with *-th*.

The second masculine singular perfect may have a final *hê mater lectionis* representing the final vowel *-ā* in the orthography (see table 8).

In explaining the form *ydʿth* in Lachish 2:6, Cross and Freedman translate "Thou hast [not] known it," where "the suffix

---

[8]A. F. Rainey in *Arad Inscriptions* by Y. Aharoni (Jerusalem: The Israel Exploration Society, 1981), p. 22. Pardee has criticized this view in his review of the Arad Inscriptions, cf. "Review of the *Arad Inscriptions* by Yohanan Aharoni," *JNES* 44/1 (1985): 67-71.

[9]Parunak, "Orthography of the Arad Ostraca," *BASOR* 230 (1978): 26.

[10]Zevit, *MLAHE*, pp. 31, 32.

[11]Aharoni, *Arad Inscriptions*, p. 72.

[12]Pardee, *HHL*, p. 63; "Letters from Tel Arad," *UF* 10 (1978): 323-24.

[13]See Pardee, "Letters from Tel Arad," *UF* 10 (1978): 305 on Arad 7:5-6. The *waw*-consecutive plus perfect syntax posited for A 7:5-6 corresponds to that of RES 1543:3, *wktbt msprm ʾrbʿm wšlš*, "You are to write forty-three letters;" Cf. J. Février, "Le *waw* conversif en punique," *Hommages à André Dupont-Sommer* (Paris: Librairie d'Amérique et d'Orient, 1971), p. 192.

[14]Zevit, *MLAHE*, p. 32.

(*ô*) is retrospective."[15] They do not discuss *ydʿth* in Lachish 3:8 and *š̊l̊ḥ̊t̊h̊* in Lachish 5:4 is restored by them without the *hê*: *[šl]ḥt*, "Thou hast sent."[16] The *plene* orthography *šlḥth* was proposed by Ginsberg and later accepted by Michaud.[17] The Arad examples of the second masculine singular perfect with *hê* ending lend credence to the interpretation which sees the *hê* as a *m.l.* and not as a suffix.

Parunak,[18] however, following Cross and Freedman, reads the *hê* as the third masculine singular pronominal suffix and a *m.l.* for *-ō* , and maintains that all attested second masculine singular perfects in epigraphic Hebrew are regularly apocopated. He further asserts that the context of Arad 7 and 40 and the prior conclusions of Cross and Freedman favor the solution that the *hê* in question is a pronominal suffix.

Aharoni,[19] although he offers no discussion of the subject, treated the *hê* at the end of the forms in question as the second masculine singular perfect suffix *-th* and a *m.l.* for *-ā*, rather than as a pronominal accusative suffix in both Arad inscriptions, and is followed by Pardee[20] and Zevit.[21]

The solution reached by Aharoni, Pardee, and Zevit is more likely than that of Cross, Freedman and Parunak. Paranuk's arguments for the *hê* as pronominal suffix falter in that he accepts Cross and Freedman's theory, and uses as his main argument Arad 7:6, where he translates *ktbth lpnk* as "Write it before you" rather than "Write before you" solely because the former seems to him a "smoother construction." The interpretation of *-h* as a suffix is not especially likely in context, however, for there is no explicit single antecedent for the suffix: *ntn lktym lʿśry b / lḥdš ʿd̊ hššh lḥdš̊ b/ /// [w]ktbth lpnyk*, "Give the Kittim for the (period from) the first (day) of the tenth (month) until the sixth (day) of that month three *bat*-measures (of wine ?). [And] make a record (of it)," Arad 7:2-6.

---

[15]Cross and Freedman, *EHO*, p.53, no. 54.

[16]Ibid., *EHO*, p. 55, no. 81.

[17]H.L. Ginsberg, "Lachish Notes," *BASOR* 71 (1938): 26; Henri Michaud, "Les ostraca de Lakiš, conservés à Londres," *Syria* 34 (1957): 46, 47.

[18]Parunak, "Orthography of the Arad Ostraca," *BASOR* 230 (1978) 28.

[19]Y. Aharoni, *Arad Inscriptions*, pp. 23, 75.

[20]Pardee, "Letters from Tel Arad," *UF* 10 (1978): 305, 323, 325 (on Arad 7:5-6, 40:9); *HHL*, pp. 40, 63.

[21]Zevit, *MLAHE*, p. 19, no. 32; p. 28, no. 74; pp. 31-32.

Paranuk also treats Arad 40:9, a text unfortunately broken right after the form in question, *ydʿth*, in the same way, simply giving his translation as compared to Aharoni's. He does not mention the comparable Lachish verbs or use them as proof for his conclusion, other than accepting Cross and Freedman's theory which was based on the Lachish evidence. Again, there is no explicit single noun before *ydʿth* to serve as an obvious antecedent.

If Paranuk were to have reviewed the Lachish material closely, especially with regard to syntax, he would have found one clear example of the long ending *-th* on the verb *ydʿth* which can only be viewed as the second masculine singular perfect ending, with the *hê* acting as a *m.l.* for long *ā*. This is Lachish 3:8, which Cross and Freedman did not mention in *Early Hebrew Orthography*. The phrase reads *wky ʾmr ʾdny lʾ ydʿth qrʾ spr*, "And (in it) my lord said, 'Don't you know how to read a letter?'"[22] It is not likely that the *hê* ending on *ydʿth*, grammatically, syntactically, or stylistically, would be a pronominal suffix ("You know *it*") in this sentence, as the predicate is directly followed by the infinitive construct and then by the direct object *spr* which is clearly stated.

A similar argument can be given to demonstrate that the *hê* in these verbs is a *m.l.* in other Lachish examples. Following Pardee,[23] the direct object *dbr* is also present in Lachish 2:6, *dbr ʾšr lʾ ydʿth*, "...anything you do not know" (*-h* could be a resumptive suffix but that is far from necessary). Although the text is broken in parts, Lachish 5:4 probably also should be construed as showing the verb with long perfect suffix *-th* followed by a direct object in line 5: *š̊l̊ḥ̊t̊h̊ ʾl ʿbdk ʾ[t] hs[prm]*, "You have sent your servant [the(se) letters]."

The second masculine singular perfect afformative also occurs in two different forms in the consonantal text of the Bible: *-t* and *-th*. In several examples, the *plene* suffix appears in pre-Exilic texts while its counterpart, without *m.l.*, appears in post-Exilic texts: *glyth* (2 Sam. 7:27) and *glyt* (1 Chron. 17:25); *whyth* (2 Sam. 10:11) and *whyyt* (1 Chron. 19:12); *wnplth* (2 Kings 14:10) and

---

[22]Others divide the text in L 3:4-9 differently by taking *wky* (in *kyʾmr*, L 3:8) not as the beginning of a new sentence, rather as a necessary element in the continuation of a long sentence begun in line 4 and linked to *ky* in line 6. Cf. H. Michaud, "Le témoignage des ostraca de Tell Douweir concernant le prophète Jérémie," *Revue des Etudes Sémitiques* (1941): 51.

[23]Pardee, *HHL*, pp. 79-80.

wnplt (2 Chron. 25:19), although the opposite phenomenon is true: *wntt* (1 Kings 8:39) and *wntth* (2 Chron. 6:30).

This variation in biblical Hebrew orthography is explained by Cross and Freedman[24] as reflecting the loss of the final vowel in popular speech (the orthography *-t*), and its retention in the more elegant, older form in the literary language (the orthography *-th*). The Masoretes have recorded and normalized the form *-th* throughout the biblical text with the pointing *tā*. They hold further that this dual tradition manifests itself (in epigraphic Hebrew) by the short form which is predominant in the orthography, and the long form which is standard in the vocalization.[25]

Such a statement regarding epigraphic Hebrew forms cannot be retained for the following reasons: first, the *-t* suffix is not significantly more frequent than the *-th* suffix on second masculine singular perfects. On the basis of this evidence, one may not speak about earlier (older) versus later (newer) forms of the suffix, (i.e., that *-th* preceded *-t*) as both forms occur in the same locale (Judah), during the same time periods (7th-6th century for both suffixes). That one suffix was more common than another in speech or in writing is a topic not substantiated by evidence from epigraphic Hebrew. Moreover, all other things being equal, one would expect *-tā* to be the older form and thus, perhaps, the more plausible form for the seventh-sixth centuries. In any case, if Cross and Freedman's hypothesis is to be applied to epigraphic Hebrew, one would have to posit that the old form *-tā* was still in use alongside the newer form *-t*. It is just as plausible, however, to consider the hypothesis that the variation in orthography is due to the nature of the vowel in question as being only secondarily long.[26]

In so far as the *waw*-consecutive is concerned, the evidence from epigraphic Hebrew suggests that *waw*-consecutive preceded both *-th* and *-t* perfects. The form *wntth*, "You are to entrust," MO 2:4 illustrates the *waw*-consecutive which is visually attested before a *-th* perfect (see table 8).

---

[24]Cross and Freedman, *EHO*, p. 66.

[25]Ibid., *EHO*, p. 67.

[26]Pardee, "Letters from Tel Arad," *UF* 10 (1978): 292-93.

This principle is also operative in biblical Hebrew, as *waw* is attested there several times before third masculine singular perfects ending both with *-th* and *-t*.

Third masculine singular. The third masculine singular perfect form is consistent with biblical Hebrew and is the most common verb form attested in the perfect. It occurs frequently as an independent verbal form. Several examples representing the *qal*, *piel*, and *hiphil* stems are given below. This list in not exhaustive, though it is representative:

> *bqš*, "He tried to obtain," A 40:12; *zkr*, "He has remembered," L 2:4; *(w)ydᶜ*, "He will know," L 4:10; *hyṭb*, "He favored," Ajrud 7:2; *lqḥ*, "He took," MHY 1:9; *ntn*, "He gave," L 4:11; *hyh*, "It, he was," A 111:5; *qrʾ*, "He read," L 6:13; *šlḥ* , "He sent," L 4:2; *mt*, "He died," MO 2:2.

a) *Perfect with object suffixes.* The third masculine singular perfect is attested with object suffixes in the following forms:

> *ktbh*, "He has written it (?)," KEK 3:1; *lqḥh*, "He has taken him," L 4:6; *(w)hbqydm*, "He is to hand them over," A 24:14-15; *(w)ṣwk*, "He orders you," A 3:2-3; *šlḥh*, "He has sent it," L 3:21.

> *hgln(yh)*, "(YH) has carried me away into exile," R 17:2 (Herr 61).[27]

b) *Third masculine singular as proper name or element thereof.* The lists of epigraphic Hebrew names which follow are representative, though not exhaustive for each subsection under discussion. For a complete transliteration and reference of each attested proper name connected with the third masculine singular

[27]This proper name consists of the third masculine singular *hiphil* perfect, plus the first common singular object suffix, followed by the divine element.

perfect, the reader is directed to the Lexicon at the end of this grammar.[28]

In its independent form as a proper name, the third masculine singular perfect is very common:

> ʾḥz, "(DN) has grasped," S 2:5; *brʾ*, "(DN) has created," RR Seal 4:2; *ḥml*, "(DN) has spared," AV NN 15:2.

It also appears as the first element of proper names:[29]

> *ʾḥz(yhw)*, "(YH) has grasped," Av NN 19:2; *ʾmr(yhw)*, "(YH) has said," Beersheba Graffiti 2:2; *brk(yhw)*, "(YH) has blessed," A 22:1; Tel Ira 1:1.

Finally, it appears in epigraphic Hebrew as the second element of a proper name:

> *(yhw)ʾḥz*, Av (*EI* 9) 15:1; *(ʾḥ)ʾmr*, L Seal 11:2; *(ʾl)yšʿ*, S 1:4.

Third feminine singular. The third feminine singular perfect verb is rare in epigraphic Hebrew and is attested by one absolute form of the verb *hyh* in the form *hyt* (**hāyāt* or **hāyĕtā* in Siloam 1:3 which may be the older form of the third feminine singular perfect of Verbs III-weak. The *ketib* in 2 Kings 9:37 is *hyt* (for the regular biblical *hyth* **hāyĕtāh*), while *ʿśt* (instead of *ʿśth* **ʿāśĕtāh*) appears in Leviticus 25:21. Because *hyt* is the only third feminine perfect attested in epigraphic Hebrew, it is not possible to determine whether the phonology of the third feminine

---

[28]In proper names, the theophoric element is expressed in the following manner: if the deity name is not expressed orthographically, (i.e., *ʾḥz*) the abbreviation DN (= deity name) is used (*ʾḥz*, "(DN) has grasped"). If the theophoric element is written as *yhw/yh/yw*, the abbreviation YH (for YHWH) is used. Deity names such as *ʾl*, *mwt*, and *bʿl* are assigned a translation value which more closely fits with the transliteration of the word and the pronunciation of that word as it is known from biblical Hebrew, e.g., *ʾl* = deity El, God; *mwt* = Mot; *bʿl* = Baʿal. A theophoric element not known from biblical Hebrew is expressed simply in terms of the transliteration (e.g., *šʿ*= deity *šʿ* [for a discussion by Avigad and notes by Albright that *šʿ* is in fact an Aramaic deity name, cf. N. Avigad, "Seals and Sealings," *IEJ* 14 (1964): 190-91]).

[29]The full form of the name is given, with the extraneous element in parentheses. This practice is also repeated for proper names, the second element of which is a third masculine singular perfect. The representation of all proper names in this grammar adhere to this practice.

singular perfect would have been *qātělā* or *qātāt (*i.e., $C_1\breve{a}C_2$+ *āt)* (i.e., *hāyětā* vs. *hāyāt*). Orthographically, the first vocalization could be expected to be represented in epigraphic Hebrew by *qtlh*, the form indicated by biblical Hebrew, but it is possible, though unproven, that the *hê* was always lacking, as in the attested Verbs III-weak form.

Second/third masculine plural. The second masculine plural and third masculine plural verb forms in epigraphic Hebrew are consistent with biblical Hebrew orthography. The second masculine plural form ends with *-tm* (*šlḥtm*, "You are to send," A 24:13), and the third masculine plural ending is *-w* (*hkw*, "they struck," Siloam 1:4, *mnw*, "they counted," Ophel b:2, and *šlḥw*, "they sent," A 61:1).

The Imperfect

In all cases where the imperfect is attested in epigraphic Hebrew, the forms correspond to biblical Hebrew. Only one feminine imperfect is attested (A 24:20).

(1) *Inflection.* Table 9 illustrates the inflection of the *qal* imperfect.

TABLE 9
***QAL* IMPERFECT**

	Singular	**Plural**
3 m.	*yqtl*	*yqtlw*
3 f.	*tqtl*	–
2 m.	*tqtl*	*tqtlw*
2 f.	–	–
1 c.	*ʾqtl*	*nqtl*

(2) Forms. This section describes the extant verbs in the imperfect. The inflection of forms is similar to biblical Hebrew. All lists of forms are complete, unless there is a statement to the contrary.

First common singular. Only one verb is attested for the first common singular form, and it is a *pê-nun* verb with object suffix and energic *nun*, *ʾtnnhw*, "I will give it,"[30] L 3:12, with the regular *ʾaleph*-preformative of the first person singular.

Second masculine singular. The second masculine singular imperfect has the preformative *t*- and is attested eight times in several epigraphic Hebrew verb stems: in *qal*, *tktb*, "You will write," L 6:8-9, *tšlh*, "You will send," A 16:10, *tš[l]ḥ* , A 13:1-2, *tšmʿ*, "You will listen," papMur 17a:2 and *ttn*, "You will give," A 1:10, 18:6; in *piel*, *tʾḥr*, "You wait, tarry," A 2:6; and in *niphal*, *tdhm*, "You will be silent," MHY 1:14.

Third feminine singular. The single example of the third feminine singular imperfect occurs in A 24:20, *tbʾ*, "she will come."

Third masculine singular. The third masculine singular imperfect has the expected *y*- preformative and represents two moods–the indicative, as well as the jussive. The third masculine

---

[30]The interpretation of the form follows that of Pardee, *HHL*, p. 86. Lemaire (*Inscriptions hébraïques*, p. 103) suggests that the form may be a *piel* imperfect from the root *tnh*, "to repeat," while Cross derives it from the root *tnn* (comparing the biblical word *ʾetnan* and Ugaritic *ʾitnanu*, "fee") and translates the phrase in L 3:12-13, *ʾtnnhw [ʾ]l mʾwm[h]*, as "I would pay him (no) fee." Cf. F. M. Cross, "A Literate Soldier: Lachish Letter III," in *Biblical and Related Studies Presented to Samuel Iwry*, ed. by Ann Kort and Scott Norschauser (Winona Lake, Ind.: Eisenbrauns, 1985), p. 46.

Both the interpretations of Lemaire and Cross seem less likely than that adopted above since the root *ntn* is commonly attested in epigraphic Hebrew, while verbal forms derived from the roots *tnh* and *tnn* are rare or unattested in the Bible. Further, the meaning of the derived noun *ʾetnan* in biblical Hebrew and *ʾitnanu* in Ugaritic suggests the fee paid to a harlot or a conjugal price. This narrow definition cannot fit the text from Lachish, and one is forced to assign a more general sense to the verb. In any case, whether *ʾtnnhw* derives from the root *ntn*, *tnh*, or *tnn*, the *ʾaleph*-preformative of this word establishes the form of the first common singular imperfect in epigraphic Hebrew.

singular person is the most common form of the imperfect, and occurs not only as the independent verbal form and in one element proper names, but also as the first and second elements of proper names.

The attested independent verbal forms in *qal* are: *ybʾ*, "It will come," L 3:11,[31] *ydʿ*, "He should know," A 40:13, *(w)yqḥ*, "And he took," MHY 1:8, *(w)yhy*, "May he be," Ajrud 15:8, *yʿbr*, "It passes, will pass," A 5:12-13, *ypth*, "He will open," Silwan 2:3,[32] *(w)yqṣr*, "He reaped," MHY 1:4, *yšʾl*, "May (YH) ask," A 18:2-3, Aj 16:1 and *yšlḥ*, "He will send," L 18:1,[33] and *yšmʿ*, "May he hear," MHY 1:1.

In *piel*, the independent verbs are: *yšlm*, "May (YH) restore," A 21:4, *(w)ykl*, "He finished," MHY 1:5, *ydbr*, "He may say," papMur 17a:2, *ybkr*, "May (YH) favor," L 2:5, and *ybrk*, "May he bless," Ajrud 15:6-7.[34]

The form *yšmʿ* occurs in *hiphil*: "May YH cause to hear," Lachish 2:1.[35]

The *niphal* imperfect occurs once: *ylqḥ*, "He, it will be taken," A111:4.

Lamed-hê forms include: *yqrh*, "It will happen," A 24:16, *ymḥh*, "He will efface," NY 1:1,[36] *ymnh*, "He should measure, count out," Sam C 1101:3, and *(w)yhy*, "May he be," Ajrud 15:8. *Yhy*, and *yrʾ*, "May (YH) cause to see," L 6:1, are the only *lamed-hê* jussives attested in epigraphic Hebrew.[37]

The third masculine singular imperfect/jussive forms which occur in epigraphic Hebrew proper names are: *yʾwš*, "YH grants," L 2:1, 6:1,[38] *yʾzn*, "May YH hear," A 59:5 (*yʾz̊n̊*, A 58:4), *yšpṭ*, "May YH judge," A 53:1, *yḥml*, "May YH be compassionate,"

---

[31]Also *[y]b̊[ʾ]*, L 4:9; *wybʾ*, MHY 1:7; and *y‹b›ʾ*, L 5:9.

[32]Also *yp̊[tḥ]*, Silwan 3:2.

[33]Also *y[šlḥ]*, A 5:10-11.

[34]Also *ybr[k]*, KH 1:1-2, 2:5 and *ybr̊kk*, "May he bless you (m.s.)," MO 2:1.

[35]The *hiphil* also occurs in L 3:2, 4:1, 5:1, 8:1, 9:1 and MO 2:1-2. The *niphal* of this root is possible, but uncertain because it is largely restored: *[wyšm]ʿ* "there was heard," Siloam 2.

[36]Also *‹y›mḥh*, KBL 4:2.

[37]*Yhy* and *yrʾ* are the only apparent (proven) jussives in epigraphic Hebrew, i.e., jussive forms visible in the strictly consonantal orthography. The form *yrʾ* is a *hiphil* as is *yrʾk*, L 5:7, the same verb with a pronominal suffix.

[38]Also *y[ʾ]w[š]*, L 3:2.

KEK decanter, and *yš'l*, "May YH ask" (or *hiphil*, "give, grant"), Herr 41:2. The third masculine singular verb occurs (if so, probably in the indicative form) in one possible place-name: *[y]gwr*, "(YH) dwells," A 42:1.

Proper names which have third masculine singular verbs as a first element include: *ygdl(yhw)*, "(YH) is great," Hest. 61:2, *yḥml(yhw)*, "May (YH) be compassionate, spare," Av NN 14:1-2; Herr 149:1-2, *yrḥm('l)*, "May (El) have compassion," Av (1978) Bulla of Jerahmeel 2:1, *y'zn(yhw)*, "May (YH) hear," A 39:9; L 1:3; Av (*EI* 9) 6:1; Tell en Nasbeh 3:1 (*y'z̊n(yhw)*, L 1:2), *yšmʿ('l)*, "May (El) hear," Herr 48:1,[39] *yprʿ(yw)*, "May (YH) let (go) free," R 21:1-4 (Herr 69), and as a second element: *(yhw)yšmʿ*, "May (YH) hear," Naveh 1:1 (Herr 98).

The third masculine singular verb also occurs with suffixes: *yšmrk*, "May he keep you (m.s.)," Ajrud 15:7[40] and *ybr̊kk*, "May he bless you (m.s.)," MO 2:1.

A problem that exists for the proper classification of epigraphic Hebrew verbal forms is that few forms are morphologically distinctive as indicatives or jussives. Only a few third masculine singular verbs can be identified as jussives, on the basis of semantics.

For example, *y'wš* and *[y]gwr* may be vocalized as indicatives or as jussives based on their morphology, as imperfects, **yā'ûš* and **yāgûr*, as jussives, **yā'ôš* or **yāgôr*. In either case, both verbs derive from middle weak roots, *'wš*, "grant, give" and *gwr*, "dwell." As the first form is a proper name, and the latter a proper or place name, semantics are not a criterion for distinguishing the indicative from the jussive. Judging from biblical Hebrew, however, the *m.l.* *-w-* would be more likely to stand for *-ū-* than for *-ō-* in middle weak roots.[41]

The *waw* in *y'wš* was suggested to be consonantal by Cross and Freedman [42] but it is more likely a *mater lectionis* for *ū* or *ō*.[43]

---

[39]Also *yš̊mʿ̊('l)*, Hest. 57:1; *ẙšmʿ('l)*, Hest. 77; *ẙ[šmʿ]'l*, A 57:2.

[40]Also, *w[y]šmrk*, "and (may he) keep you," KH 2:6-7; *[wy]šmrk*, KH 1:2-3.

[41]Examples from two roots in biblical Hebrew suffice to illustrate this point: from *šwb*: *yšwb* (*yašûb*, Hosea 11:5, etc.) and *yšb* (Psalm 146:4, etc.); jussive *yšb* (Judges 7:3, etc.); from *qwm*: indicative *yqwm* (*yāqûm*, Exod. 21:19); jussives *yqm* (Gen. 27:31), *wyqm* (Job 22:28, etc.); cf. *BDB*, pp. 877, 996.

[42]Cross and Freedman, *EHO*, pp. 51-52.

[43]Zevit, *MLAHE*, p. 29.

Pardee[44] suggests by inference that *y'wš* is more likely the indicative (*waw* as *m.l.* for *ū*), while Zevit,[45] following Cross and Freedman, explains *y'wš* as the *qal* jussive, pronounced *ya'ōš*.[46]

These two names are likely hypocoristic.[47] In epigraphic South Arabic, imperfect verbal forms may be written *plene* or defectively.[48] This evidence affects the argument as to mood, since a compound name spelled with *waw* in the verbal element derived from a II-weak root might sway the argument in favor of the indicative rather than jussive. A verbal form containing *waw* in a compound proper name (as in *y'wš'l*), is likely analyzed as the indicative rather than jussive verbal form, as the jussive would not be expected to be written *plene*. This statement is supported by a biblical analogy, an attested proper name *yšbʿm (yāšobʿām* 1 Chron. 11:11, *et cetera)* containing a verbal element from the II-weak root *šwb*. The first element *yšb-*, which is not written *plene*, may likely be explained as a jussive.

The conclusion drawn from the preceding discussion is that there is no firm morphological criterion for distinguishing an indicative from a jussive, outside of drawing inferences from biblical Hebrew, in forms such as *y'wš* and *ygwr*, beyond pointing out that epigraphic Hebrew evidence for the pronunciation of an internal *waw m.l.* in an accented syllable is likely to be *ū*, indicating the indicative (rather than *ō* for the jussive). While few verbal forms are attested which have internal *waw* as *m.l.*, those verbal forms that are attested (e.g., *'rwr*, **'ārûr*, passive participle), as well as forms representing other parts of speech do indicate that the *waw* (as *m.l.*) in an accented syllable likely represents *û*: *qrb'wr* (**(qrb)'ûr*), A 24:14; *hsws* (**hassûs*), A 111:5. The claim that the same *m.l.* in an unaccented syllable more likely represents *ô* is not supported by epigraphic Hebrew evidence. Only *ḥwrṣ* (**ḥôrēṣ*)[49]

---

[44]Pardee, *HHL*, p. 80.

[45]Zevit, *MLAHE*, p. 29.

[46]Zevit incorrectly gives **yā'ūš* as his first vocalization for the form *y'wš* for he goes on to explain the form as a jussive. *Yā'ūš*, however, cannot represent the vocalization of the jussive; rather, the vocalization is that of the indicative.

[47]Cf. Pardee, *HHL*, p. 80.

[48]A.F.L. Beeston, *A Descriptive Grammar of Epigraphic South Arabian* (London: Luzac, 1962), p. 27. See also Zevit, *MLAHE*, p. 29, n. 12.

[49] *'wrr*, **'ōrēr*, "curser," KBL 6 would be a second example to substantiate the statement above were it not for the fact that the form is possibly to be considered an error for *'rwr*, **'ārûr* (cf. Zevit *MLAHE*, p. 30), or *'rr* (cf. A.

may support this claim, but it is in all likelihood an Egyptian name. In any case, a single example cannot alone support the assertion that *waw* always represents *ô* in unaccented syllables in epigraphic Hebrew.

Epigraphic Hebrew evidence seems to indicate that internal *waw* in stressed syllables represented *ū*. On the basis of biblical Hebrew, if the *waw* in such forms as *y'wš* or *ygwr* was to be vocalized *ū*, they should be classified as indicatives rather than as jussives.

Four third masculine singular forms, *y'r*, "May (YH) cause to shine," KH 2:8,[50] *(w)yhy*, "May he be," Ajrud 15:8; *yr'*, "May (YH) cause to see," L 6:1;[51] and *(w)ykl*, "And he finished," MHY 1:5,[52] may be labeled as jussives on the basis of morphology, orthography, and analogy to biblical Hebrew.

Lemaire, "Prières en temps de crise: les inscriptions de Khirbet Beit Lei," *RB* 83 (1976): 562). Cf. p. 68 (n. 119) and p. 109 in this grammar.

[50]Also *[y']r*, KH 1:3-4.

[51]*Y'r*, *yr'* and *yhy* are orthographically and contextually explicit jussives.

One might argue that *y'r* in epigraphic Hebrew represents the *hiphil* indicative (biblical Hebrew *y'yr*, e.g., Job 41:24) written defectively, or the *niphal* imperfect (biblical Hebrew *(w)y'r*, 2 Sam. 2:32), were it not for strong comparative evidence from biblical Hebrew which substantiates the claim that the form represents the *hiphil* jussive. The supporting biblical evidence comes from Numbers 6:25, the passage which contains the priestly blessing. The phrase in which *y'r* occurs in epigraphic Hebrew, *y'r yh[wh] pnyw 'lyk*, exactly parallels the biblical phrase, a phrase in which *y'r* is the *hiphil* jussive.

Yr' occurs in epigraphic Hebrew both as an independent verb (L 6:1) and as a proper name (Avigad 11:1). Morphologically, *yr'* and *yhy* are comparable to, but distinctive from, the *hiphil* and *qal* indicatives, *yr'h* and *yhyh* respectively, known from biblical Hebrew (*yr'h*, Isa. 30:30 and *yhyh*, Gen. 1:29). The biblical jussives from the roots *r'h* and *hyh*, *(w)yr'*, 2 Kings 11:4 and *(w)yhy*, Gen 1:3), exhibit the same orthography as the epigraphic Hebrew forms. Cf. pp. 78, 141, n. 148 in this grammar.

[52]In biblical Hebrew, the *waw*-consecutive and jussive may denote the English "past," so possibly *(w)ykl*, "and he finished" (*ykl*, a *piel* form from the Verbs III-*hê* root *klh*, "finish," as *wayyekal*, Gen 2:2). In light of the problems of interpretation of forms taken to be from the same root (*ykl*) in epigraphic Hebrew (namely *kl* in MHY 1:6 and perhaps *klt* in MHY 1:8), the interpretation of *(w)ykl* is not certain; cf. A. Lemaire, "L'ostracon de Meṣad Ḥashavyahu (Yavneh-Yam) replacé dans son contexte," *Semitica* 21 (1971): 64-68; W.F. Albright, "Palestinian Inscriptions," in *Ancient Near Eastern (Supplementary) Texts (and Pictures)*, ed., J.B. Pritchard (1969), p. 568. The form in question is classified as a jussive mainly for semantic and orthographic reasons. See Pardee, *HHL*, p. 21 on Meṣad Ḥashavyahu 1, lines 5, 6, 8: "No solution yet suggested fits the norms of the seventh century B.C. orthography, and *klh* 'finish'

Indicatives from Verbs III-weak in epigraphic Hebrew end in *hê* (e.g., *yqrh*, "It will happen," A 24:16; *ymḥh*, "He will efface," NY 1:1; *ymnh*, "He will count out, measure," Sam C 1101:3), while two certain jussives from this root type, *yhy* and *yrʾ*, shows a short form without the *hê*. This distribution is the same as in biblical Hebrew, where *qal*, *niphal*, *piel*, and *hiphil lamed-hê* verbs show apocopated jussive forms.[53]

First common plural. The first common plural imperfect has the preformative *nun* and occurs twice in *qal*: *nrʾh*, "We see," L 4:12, and *nʿśh*, "We are to do," L 9:8, and once in *hiphil*: *nšb*, "We will return (word)," A 111:4.

Second and third masculine plurals. The second masculine plural imperfect verb is attested once: *tʿśw*, "You will do," L 6:9, while the third masculine plural imperfect is attested four times in epigraphic Hebrew: in *qal*, *(w)ylkw*, "(The water) flowed," Siloam 1:4, *ytnw*, "They will give," Ajrud 7:2, *yśbʿw*, "They will be satisfied (?)," Ajrud 7:1, and in *piel*, *yʿnw*, "They will testify," MHY 1:10, 11.

The Imperative

Because of the relatively small number of attested epigraphic Hebrew imperatives, the *qal*, as well as the other verbal stems, are discussed together in this section.

(1) *Inflection.* The inflection of the imperative is found in table 10 on the next page.

---

fits best semantically." The form cited is orthographically that of the jussive, *wykl* (*wayyekal*), if from *kly/klh*, and corresponds to biblical Hebrew morphology and orthography.

[53] A.E. Cowley, *Gesenius*, p. 131.

TABLE 10
IMPERATIVE

	Singular	**Plural**
m.	*qtl*	*qtlw*
f.	–	–

(2) *Forms.* Although no feminine imperatives and few second masculine plural forms are attested in epigraphic Hebrew, the masculine singular imperative is frequent.

Imperatives as independent forms. Evidence for imperatives as independent forms with or without an object suffix exists in four verbal stems:

qal: *ʾmr*, "Say!" Ajrud 14:1, 15:2-3; *bʾ*, "Enter!" A 17:1-2; *ḥtm*, "Seal!" A 17:5-6; *ktb*, "Write!" A 1:3-4; *qrʾ*, "Read!" L 6:5; *šlḥ* , "Send!" A 5:2; *spr*, "Calculate!" A 3:6-7; *tn*, "Give!" A 4:3; *q[ḥ]*, "Take!" A 12:1; *qm*, "Arise!" L 13:1. One *qal* imperative occurs with the third masculine object suffix: *šlḥnw*, "Send it!"

niphal: *hšmr*, "Beware!" L 3:21.

piel: *ʾmṣ* , "Strengthen!" A 88:2 and *nqh*, "Absolve!" KBL 2:1 (2x).

hiphil: *hpqḥ* , "Open!" L 3:4, *hwšʿ*, "Save!" KEK 3:3, KBL 3:1, *hšb*, "Return (word)!" L 9:4, and *hqšbw*, a second masculine plural imperative, "Pay attention!" Sam C 1101:2.

Imperatives as proper names or as elements thereof. The imperative was in use as the first element of proper names, but is never found as the second element. The second masculine singular imperatives which occur in proper names are as follows:

ḥkl-, "Wait for!" (*ḥkly[hw]*, "Wait for YH!" L 20:2).

p̊n-, "Turn!" (*p̊n*ʾ*l*, "Turn, O (El)," Beersheba 1:2). The reading of the *pê* in *pnʾl* is uncertain, though possible. If this reading is correct,[54] the form may be analogous to two biblical names containing the plural imperatives: *pnwʾl* (Gen. 32:32, *et cetera*) and *pnwlyh* (1 Chron. 4:4, *et cetera*), "Turn to YH!"[55]

ʾš-, "Give!" (*ʾšnʾ*, "Give, O (DN)!" Ushna Seal 1:1, Hest. 40:1).

šb-, "Return!" (*šbʾl*, *šby*, *šbnʾ*, *šbnyh*, *šbnyw*, *šbnyhw*, "Return, O (DN)!", RR Seal 1:2, *et cetera*).

dml-, "Wait on, be silent to!" (*dmlʾ*, *dmlʾl*, *dmlyhw*, "Be silent to DN!" Gib 21, *et cetera*.[56]

---

[54]Cf. Lemaire, *Inscriptions hébraïques*, p. 272. The original excavator of the Beersheba ostracon, Aharoni, read *mntld*, "from Tolad," an altogether different interpretation of the letters; cf. Aharoni, *Beer-Sheba I, Excavations at Tel Beer-Sheba, 1969-1971 Seasons*, p. 71.

[55]B. Porten, " 'Domlaʾel' and Related Names," *IEJ* 21 (1971): 48.

[56]Suggestions for the meaning of *dml-* related names include "Wait on (God)," (Siegfried Horn, "An Inscribed Seal from Jordan," *BASOR* 189 (1968): 43), and "Be silent before (God)" (B. Porten, " 'Domlaʾel'," *IEJ* 21 (1971): 48). A biblical parallel with the imperative and preposition is Psalm 37:7, *dwm lyhwh*, "Be silent to" (i.e., "Be resigned to") YH."

The "Wait on the Lord" etymology was suggested by J. C. Greenfield commenting on name *dmlʾ*, and is accepted by Pritchard, *Hebrew Inscriptions and Stamps from Gibeon*, p. 11.

Gordon follows the interpretation offered by Virolleaud (who examined a form *da-ma-al-la* in a Seleucid Babylonian text), that the element *dml* connotes a deity; cf. *Ugaritic Textbook*, p. 385. Gordon cites three Ugaritic texts where *dml* occurs (1004:20; 1010:6; 1106:34). In the first and last of these three texts, he suggests that *dml* refers to a deity, while in text 1010:6, *bt dml* may refer not to a temple, but to simply a place.

The interpretation of *dml* as a deity in Ugaritic suggests that epigraphic Hebrew proper names which contain the *dml* element might be interpreted to mean "Dml (is God)," or "O DML!;" e.g., *dmlʾ* (compare epigraphic Hebrew *bʿlʾ*, which possibly means "O Baʿal," S 1:7, etc.); *dml(ʾl)* (compare epigraphic Hebrew *ẙhẘ(ʾl)*, L V 4:1), and *dml(yhw)* (compare *ʾl(yhw)*, Gezer (?) seal 1:1 and *mlkyhw* [if *mlk* is taken as a deity name]). One should keep in mind, however, that human names consisting of two divine elements are extremely rare if they exist at all: "Milku is YHWH," or "Damalla is YHWH" are unexpected.

qwl-/ql-, "Pay homage to," (*qwlyhw*, *qlyhw* and *qlyw*, "Pay homage to DN!", BCat 53, Herr 133:1 and Sam C 1012:2 respectively). This form is not certain to represent the imperative.[57]

hwšʿ-, "Save!" (*hwšʿyhw*, *hwšʿm*, "Save, O DN!", Jerusalem Seal 2:1, *et cetera*).[58]

a) *Imperatives with prepositions in proper names.* Commonly, proper names in epigraphic Hebrew (and elsewhere) consist of up to two elements, a verbal or nominal element plus the theophoric name. However, several of the proper names mentioned above are unusual combinations in that a third element, here a preposition, also occurs within the proper name. The names under discussion contain a masculine singular imperative which is linked with an internal prepositional *lamed*, "for, to" in *ḥkl-*, *dml-*, and perhaps *ql-*. The first of these, *ḥkl-*, is seen as the masculine singular imperative from the *piel* root *ḥkh*, "Wait!" plus the preposition. *Dml-* is the masculine singular imperative from the root *dmm*, "Be silent!" plus the same preposition, and *ql-* is the verbal imperative from the root *qwl*, "Speak all, say › pay homage!" with elision of the *lamed* of the preposition.[59]

b) *Imperatives with the particle of entreaty or energic nun in proper names.* Evidence from epigraphic Hebrew suggests that particles may serve to link together two existing elements of a proper name. The following examples from epigraphic Hebrew illustrate the joining of the imperative with the particle of entreaty

---

[57]See n. 59.

[58]Cf. pp. 143-45.

[59]Porten, " 'Domlaʾel'," *IEJ* 21 (1971): 47, 49, follows Albright's original suggestion to relate *ql* in the name *qlyhw* to Ugaritic (*ql*, "fall" ["fall down to, pay homage to"]) and Akkadian (*qalu*) cognates. Also see Horn, "An Inscribed Seal from Jordan," *BASOR* 189 (1968): 41-43. Bordreuil, citing the Aramaic proper names, *QWYLYH* and *QWL*, prefers to treat the form *qwlyhw* as *QW-L-YHWH*, "Espère en YHWH;" cf. *Catalogue des sceaux ouest-sémitiques inscrits*, p. 53. These names may not necessarily mean "voice of X-deity," i.e., as announcing the birth/fate of the child in question.

(or energic *nun* and *ʾaleph* affix): *ʾš*-, in the proper name *ʾšnʾ*, "Give, O (DN)![60] and *šb*-, in the proper name *šbnʾ*, "Return, O (DN)!".[61] Both of these masculine singular imperatives derive from the middle weak roots, *yʾwš* and *šwb* respectively. The form, sense, and vocalization of the latter two epigraphic Hebrew names as imperatives are well-established by Akkadian and Neo-Babylonian.[62]

The masculine singular imperative. The masculine singular imperative occurs twice as an independent proper name, once in *piel*: *bqš*, "Seek (DN)!" Hest. 83:2, and once in *hiphil*: *hwšʿ*, "Save, (O DN)!" Driver Seal 1. This latter proper name is either to be taken as the imperative (biblical *hwšʿ*) or as derived from the third masculine singular perfect verb (biblical *hwšyʿ*, "He saved"). The name is attested in biblical Hebrew as *hwšʿ* (*hōšēaʿ*), Numbers 13:8, *et cetera*. The nature of the medial *waw* will be considered at the end of the discussion on imperatives.

The masculine plural imperative. The masculine plural imperative occurs in two proper names, *hwdwyhw* (L 3:17) and *yrʾwyhw* (Av NN 5:1).

---

[60]Arguments in favor of the particle of entreaty center upon the orthography of the word itself, *ʾšnʾ*, which ends with *nʾ*. However, the *nun* could be energic and the *ʾaleph* the hypocoristic ending.

ʾšnʾ is a hypocoristicon for a proper name such as *ʾšnyhw*, and consists of the *qal* imperative from the root *ʾwš*, "to give," (attested in Ugaritic) plus the *-nʾ* ending. This was first suggested by W.F. Albright in n. 1, pp. 28-29 of C. Torrey's article "A Hebrew Seal from the Reign of Ahaz," *BASOR* 79 (1940). A lesser possibility exists that *ʾšnʾ* consists of a noun plus a hypocoristic *ʾaleph* suffix, "gift of (God)."

[61]For the semantics of this name, see A. Demski, *Encyclopaedia Biblica*, s.v. Shebnaʾ (Hebrew); Hestrin and Dayagi-Mendels, *Inscribed Seals*, p. 33. For the earliest discussion, cf. Albright in Torrey's "A Hebrew Seal from the Reign of Ahaz," *BASOR* 79 (1940): 28-29, n. 1.

[62]Akkadian *šubna-ilu* (ca. 2000-1600 B.C.) and Neo-Babylonian *šu-bu-nu-ia-a-ma* (5th c.) establish vocalization for *šbnʾ* (*šubnaʾ* and probably *ʾšnʾ* (*ʾušnaʾ*), The vocalization of *šbnʾ* is only approximately fixed by this transliteration, as pointed out by Albright; cf. Albright in Torrey's, "A Hebrew Seal from the Reign of Ahazm," *BASOR* 79 (1940): 28-29, n.1; "The Lachish Letters after Five Years," *BASOR* 82 (1141): 17; Koehler and Baumgartner, *Lexicon in Veteris Testamenti Libros*, p. 942. See also Porten, " 'Domlaʾel'," *IEJ* 21 (1971): 47, following Noth (*IPN*, p. 32), who unquestionably accepts the fact that *šb*- names contain the verbal imperative.

The imperative, *hwdw-*, "Praise, thank (YH)!" (of *hwdwydw*), may be vocalized either as **hawdû-* or **hôdû-* depending on the nature of the medial *waws* (consonantal or *m.l.*). The second *waw* which would represent a final *m.l.* for long *ū* in an independent verbal form is pronounced *-aw* in the biblical name *hwdwyh*, *hôdawyāh*[63] (‹*hawdayū* ?)[64] (Ezra 2:40), and *hwdwyhw*, *hôdawyāhû* (the *qere* of *hdywhw* in 1 Chron. 3:24).[65] The Septuagint has a form *hwdwyhw* that suggests an original *hôdûyāhû* with two internal *matres lectionis*, the first representing the contraction of the dipththong *aw* › *ō* and the second *waw* the *m.l.* for long *ū*.[66]

The imperative, *yrʾw-*, "Fear (YH)!" (*yrʾwyhw*, Av NN 5:1) exhibits the *m.l.* for long *ū*, *yirʾū-*. The analogous biblical name is *yrʾyyh* from Jer. 37:13, 14, but the verbal element of this form has been taken to be from the root *rʾh* and the proper name is ascribed the meaning "May YH see the newborn child and deliver him."[67] Avigad[68] admits the possibility of considering both *yrʾw-* and *hwdw-* as masculine plural imperatives.

The negative of the imperative. The negative of the imperative is:

a) *ʾl* + imperfect: for immediate, specific commands such as:

ʾl tʾḥr, "Don't delay." A 2:6 and *ʾl tšmʿ*, "Don't listen (to)," papMur 17a:2.

---

[63]The biblical form is difficult in terms of analysis as the second masculine plural imperative because of the vocalization of the second *waw*.

[64]See Pardee, *HHL*, p. 86.

[65]*Hwdwyh* occurs at Elephantine; see A. Cowley, *Aramaic Papyri of the Fifth Century B.C.* (Oxford: Clarendon Press, 1923), inscriptions 1:9, 2:2, 3:2, 10:22, 19:10, 20:18, 22:112, 127, 65:18, along with *hwdw* (Cowley 12:4, 22:39, 34:3, 42:6). Also, see P. Grelot, *Documents araméens d'Egypte* (Paris: Les Editions du Cerf, 1972), p. 472, whose vocalization is *hôdawyah* (or *hôdûyah*) for the first name and *hôdaw* for the second.

[66]For the semantics of the name, see Porten, " 'Domlaʾel'," *IEJ* 21 (1971): 47-48; J.J. Stamm, "Ein Problem der altsemitischen Namengebung," *Fourth World Congress of Jewish Studies* (1967): 141-47, esp. p. 142; Noth, *IPN*, p. 32.

[67]N. Avigad, "New Names on Hebrew Seals," *EI* 12 (1975): 67; Noth, *IPN*, p. 198; BDB, p. 909.

[68]Avigad, "New Names on Hebrew Seals," *EI* 12 (1975): 67.

b) *lʾ* + imperfect: for durative, non-specific commands: "You shall, must, not do such-and-such (ever!):

wlʾ yšlḥ, "And you must not send," A 16:10, and possibly, *wlʾ tdhm*, "You must not remain silent," MHY 1:14[69]

Particle of entreaty with the imperative. The particle *nʾ* may follow any imperative form, as possibly in *hpqḥ [nʾ] ʾt ʾzn ʿbdk*, "(Please) open your servant's ear = please explain to your servant," L 3:5, and certainly *qrʾ nʾ*, "(Please) read," L 6:5.

The Infinitive

(1) *Inflection.* The inflection of the infinitives construct and absolute is found in table 11.

TABLE 11
INFINITIVES CONSTRUCT AND ABSOLUTE

Infinitive Construct	Verb Type
qtl	Strong Verb
qtʾ	Verbs III-*ʾaleph*
qtt	Verbs I-*nun, qal*
hqtl	Verbs I-*nun, niphal*
htl	Verbs I-*nun, hiphil*
ql	Hollow Verb
qtt	Verbs III-*hê*

Infinitive Absolute	Verb Type
qtl	Verbs III-*nun*, Verbs III-laryngalis

[69]MHY 1:14 is badly damaged at this point and for this reason, it is difficult to explain precisely the function of this negative and imperative sequence.

(2) *Observations on the infinitive construct and representation by verbal stems.* Infinitive constructs are attested from several root types: Hollow, I-nun, III-*hê*, III-*ʾaleph*, and *qal* roots consisting of three regular consonants or containing a third guttural. There are four stems represented by the forms: *qal*, *piel*, *niphal*, and *hiphil*.

Strong verbs and verbs containing laryngals and pharyngals. The infinitives from this group attested in epigraphic Hebrew are the *qal* forms:

> *lʾmr*, "to say, saying," *lšlḥ* , "to send," and *lšmʿ* , "to hear," the *piel* infinitive *lʿśr*, "to give a tithe," Ophel b:3, as well as the restored *hiphil* infinitive *[whš]qṭ* (biblical *lhšqyṭ*), "to weaken, pacify, allay."

Verbs III-ʾaleph. Verbs III-*ʾaleph* are represented in epigraphic Hebrew by the root *qrʾ*, "to read" in the infinitive form *lqrʾ* at Lachish.

Weak verbs. There are three types of weak verbs:

a) *Verbs I-nun.* Comprising the *prima-nun* category of infinitives attested in epigraphic Hebrew are the *qal* infinitive *lqḥt* (from the root *lqḥ*), "to take ,"[70] L 3:18, the *qal* infinitive *ltt* (from the root *ntn*), "to give," MO 1:2, the *niphal* infinitive *lhn[qb]*, "to be tunneled through," Siloam 1:2,[71] and *hnqbh* (with the possessive suffix), "to being tunneled through," Siloam 1:1 (2x), 1:3-4, and the *hiphil* infinitive *lhg[d]*, (biblical *lhgyd*), "to inform," L 3:1-2.

b) *Hollow verbs (II-waw/yod).* *Lhʿyd*, the *hiphil* infinitive from the root, *ʿwd*, "to warn," A 24:18, exhibits an internal *mater lectionis*, whereas there is no internal vowel marker in the *qal* form *lbʾ*, (biblical *lbwʾ*), "to enter," from L 3:11. *Šwb* is the root of the

---

[70]In biblical Hebrew, the verb *lqḥ* behaves as a Verb I-*nun* in the imperfect and imperative, where the *lamed* assimilates, and for this reason, is included with this verb type in biblical grammars. The same logic is employed in this grammar; see Cowley, *Gesenius*, pp. 174-75.

[71]Biblical *lĕhinnāqēb*, if it were to occur.

restored infinitive *lhš[b]*, "to return," MHY 1:12:13 (biblical *lhšyb*).

c) *Verbs III-hê*. Verbs *III-hê* are represented in the inscriptions by the *qal* infinitive *lʿśt* "to make," A 1:8, L 13:1 (restored in A 5:6), and the *piel* infinitive *lrpt* (biblical *lĕrappōt*, if it were to occur), "to weaken, slacken," L 6:6 from the root *rph*.

Observations on infinitives absolute. The infinitive absolute, which in biblical Hebrew is often written *plene*, is written defectively in all cases in epigraphic Hebrew,[72] thus making the form indistinguishable from the infinitive construct, at least in strong roots.

However, one example of the infinitive absolute, from Verbs I-*nun*, *ntn*, "Give," A 1:2, 2:1, 7:2, 8:1, 11:2 (restored in A 10:2, 14:2) is distinguishable from the infinitive construct for morphological reasons. Thus, *ntn* proves the category of infinitive absolute for epigraphic Hebrew. The infinitive construct from this

---

[72]An exception may be *-mwt* (e.g., *mrmwt*, A 50:1, *mrymwt*, B/L 32 (1982) Seal 11), but the *waw* may be consonantal.

The form *-mwt* may represent the theophoric element, biblical *môt*, or *māwet*, the noun "death." The first interpretation is based on the biblical proper names containing this element (*mrmwt, mĕrēmôt*, Ezra 8:33, 10:36, etc.; *mrmt, mĕrēmōt*, Neh. 12:3). This element also occurs in a feminine Ammonite name *ʿnmwt*; see Herr, *SANSS*, p. 63, no. 13; A. Reifenberg, *Ancient Hebrew Seals* (London: The East and West Library, 1950), p. 43.

That *-mwt* in epigraphic Hebrew represents the theophoric *Mot* is accepted by Aharoni, *Arad Inscriptions*, p. 87, and Lemaire, *Inscriptions hébraïques*, p. 211.

If one accepts the notion that the *waw* in the form *-mwt* in the epigraphic Hebrew names is not consonantal, one may morphologically equate *mwt* to the infinitive construct (biblical *mût*) or absolute (biblical *môt*).

According to the second interpretation of the form *-mwt* mentioned above (i.e., that *-mwt* represents the noun *māwet*), it is possible to interpret the *waw* in *-mwt* as consonantal. As pointed out by Gesenius (Cowley, *Gesenius*, p. 194, n. 1), the view that the *waw* in middle weak verbs like *mwt*, was consonantal is supported by the consonantal treatment of the *waw* in *piel*, as well as in certain middle weak nouns (*mwt*, *māwet*, "death").

The assumption for the element *-mwt* is that the form is *mawt* › *môt* in Ugaritic and Phoenician. For Hebrew the problem is whether *m(w)ṯ* is a native Hebrew deity with the expected Hebrew form of the name *mấwet*, or the Phoenician/Canaanite deity with the Phoenician pronunciation *môt*. The Masoretic vocalizations would indicate the second possibility, but they may be cacophonic or simply deformed.

root is *ltt*, MO 1:2, where the *nun* assimilates,[73] while the infinitive absolute is always characterized by the presence of the *nun* (biblical *ntwn*, *nātôn*, Deut. 15:10, and *ntn*, *nātōn*, Num. 21:2).

To determine the presence of the infinitive absolute, both morphology and syntax must be examined. In epigraphic Hebrew, two verbal forms are most certainly infinitives absolute for syntactic and comparative reasons: *ntn* (Arad 1:2, *et cetera*) and *[š]lḥ* (papMur 17a:1).

That *ntn*, "Give!" in Arad 1:2 is an infinitive absolute[74] on syntactic grounds is supported by biblical Hebrew, where the infinitive absolute can take the place of an imperative, although there, the verbal sequence which commonly follows is a perfect consecutive. In Arad 1:4, the verb completing the *ntn* sequence *(w)ktb*, is probably an imperative.[75] A biblical parallel for this syntax is Nahum 2:2: *nṣwr mṣwrh ṣph drk ḥzq mtnym ʾmṣ kḥ mʾd*, "Guard the ramparts, watch the way, strengthen yourself, make yourself very powerful."[76]

[Š]lḥ , although also written defectively, is probably an infinitive absolute, as it is followed directly by a perfect *šlḥ šlḥt*, a

---

[73]However, the form *ntn* also occurs twice as the strong formation of the infinitive construct as *ntn* (*nĕtōn*, Num. 20:21; *nĕton-*, Gen. 38:9).

[74]The only other possibilities would be the third masculine singular perfect, or first common plural imperfect, neither of which make sense syntactically with the rest of the text. It is also unlikely that *ntn* represents the "strong" imperative. For the view that *ntn* represents the imperative rather than the infinitive, cf. G. Sarfatti, "Hebrew Inscriptions of the First Temple Period– A Survey and Some Linguistic Comments," *Maarav* 3/1 (Jan., 1982): 71.

[75]From context, *wktb* could be either an imperative or a second infinitive absolute (the third masculine singular perfect and infinitive construct are ruled out for contextual or syntactic reasons). Since there is no way to distinguish between these two (imperative or infinitive absolute), it is preferable to analyze *wktb* as *w-* before the imperative on the basis of biblical Hebrew. A biblical parallel for the Arad phrase *wktb šm hym* is Ezek. 24:2, with *ktb* as imperative: *kĕtōb lĕkā ʾet šem hayyôm*, "Write down the date".

[76]Another possible parallel biblical phrase is *habbêṭ yāmîn ūrĕʾēh*, "Look right and see!" This second citation, from Psalm 142:5, more closely parallels the sequence than does the phrase in Nahum since the *waw* is present before the imperative in Psalm 142. This sequence: infinitive absolute plus *w* plus imperative could be accepted were it not for the fact that *hbyṭ* (*habbêṭ*) is possibly to be taken as an imperative (rather than an infinitive absolute); cf. *BDB*, p. 613; Cowley, *Gesenius*, p. 346.

sequence common in biblical Hebrew: e.g., Num. 22:37, *hlʾ šlḥ šlḥty ʾlyk lqrʾ lk*, "Didn't I really send to you to call you?"[77]

The Participle

Epigraphic Hebrew exhibits both the Active and Passive Participle. The greatest number of both occur in *qal.* Other verbal stems are represented as well, and are discussed in sections 3.1.5.2, 3.1.5.3, 3.1.5.4, and 3.1.5.5. of this grammar.[78]

(1) *Inflection*

TABLE 12
ACTIVE PARTICIPLE

	Singular	Plural
m.	*qtl* *qwtl*	*qtlm*
f.	*qtlt*	–

(2) *Forms.* The active participle in epigraphic Hebrew occurs in its absolute form with masculine singular and plural forms, as well as in proper names.

[77]However, see Pardee, *HHL*, p. 122: "Though the verb *šlḥ* is a regular feature of both Hebrew and Aramaic epistolary formulae, this is the only infinitive absolute and perfect formulation in a letter, again indicating that the reading may be incorrect."

Others have read papMur 17a:1 differently; cf. Y. Aharoni, "Three Hebrew Ostraca from Arad," *BASOR* 197 (1970): 30, n. 44; however, the fact that *[š]lḥ šlḥt* as infinite absolute plus perfect is the only such attested formulation in epigraphic Hebrew, in no way diminishes its importance. If the reading is correct, it may be the first known example of this formulation in the relatively small corpus of epigraphic Hebrew material.

[78]Cf. for the *niphal* participle, pp. 125-26, the *piel* participle, pp. 135-36, the *pual* participle, p.137, and the *hiphal* participle, pp. 147-49.

Participle as independent verb. The non-proper name active participles, which all occur in *qal*, include the masculine singular forms:

> *yšb*, "He is staying," A 18:10,[79] *qṣr*, "He is reaping, working at the harvest," MHY 1:3,[80] *qr[ʾ]*, "(The one) calling out," Siloam 2-3,[81] and *šlḥ*, "(He) is sending," L 4:8.[82]

Three masculine active participles occur with the definite article: one in a prose text, *hbʾ*, "(The one) which came," L 3:19, and two substantivized participles *hspr*, "the scribe," Avigad

---

[79]*Yšb* is a problematical word whose meaning and place in the syntax depends at least partially on the sense given to *šlm* in Arad 18:8. The interpretation of Aharoni (*Arad Inscriptions*, pp. 39-40) and Pardee ("Letters from Tel Arad," *UF* 10 (1978): 317-18) that *yšb* is a masculine singular active particle is the most convincing. For a summation of the problems connected with this form; see Pardee, "Letters from Tel Arad," *UF* 10 (1978): 317-18.

[80]The syntax of Meṣad Ḥashavyahu 1:2-4 where this form occurs in the phrase *ʿbdk qṣr hyh ʿbdk bḥṣr ʾsm*, "Your servant is reaping (working at the harvest); your servant was in Hasar-Asam," has been analyzed differently by some authors, who have chosen to see here a *casus pendens* and periphrasis, "as for your servant, your servant was reaping, your servant, in Hasar-Asam."

I.N Vinnikov, "O vnov' otkrytoj nadpisi k jugu ot Jaffy," *Archiv Orientalni* 33 (1965): 546-52; J. Naveh, "*ktwbwt knʿnywt wʿbrywt* (1960-1964)" [Canaanite and Hebrew Inscriptions], *Lešonenu* 30 (1965): 80; Lemaire, "Meṣad Ḥashavyahu," *Semitica* 21 (1971): 61, 63; and Pardee (*HHL*, p. 21) and others, analyze the text as two phrases, each containing one *ʿbdk–ʿbdk qṣr* as a nominal sentence, and *hyh ʿbdk bḥṣr ʾsm*, as a verbal sentence. While *qṣr* could be the third masculine singular perfect, "reaped," the form is best understood syntactically as the masculine singular *qal* active participle, "your servant is reaping."

For the same basic syntax, but with a different view of the function of the active participle, cf. Lemaire, "Meṣad Ḥashavyahu," *Semitica* 21 (1971): 61, 63 (*qṣr*: "reaper"). See Lemaire, *Inscriptions hébraïques*, pp. 259-69.

[81]The main verb in Siloam 1:2 is restored, but whether one reads the *niphal* perfect *[nšm]ʿ*, "and was heard"; Diringer, *Le Iscrizioni*, p. 84; S. Moscati, *L'Epigrafia ebraica antica 1935-1950* (Roma: Pontificio Istituto Biblico, 1951), p. 40; Donner and Röllig, *KAI*, p. 34, no. 189, or *waw*-consecutive and *niphal* imperfect (*[wyšm]ʿ*, "and was heard,"; Gibson, *TSSI*, p. 22), the syntax requires *q[r]ʾ* to be an active participle, "calling."

[82]The use of the negative *ʾyn* instead of *lʾ* before *šlḥ* is proof that *šlḥ* is a *qal* active participle rather than a finite verb form. The reading of *ʾyn[n]y* (Lachish 4:7-8) is accepted by W.F. Albright, "Postscript to Professor May's Article," *BASOR* 97 (1945): 26; F.M. Cross, "Lachish Letter IV," *BASOR* 144 (1956): 24-26; Lemaire, *Inscriptions hébraïques*, p. 112; Pardee, *HHL*, p. 92.

(1978) Baruk Seal 1:3; Herr 110:3 and *hrpʾ*, "the healer," Jerusalem Bulla 4:3.[83]

There is one certain example of the masculine form with a pronominal suffix: *ḥrpk*, with the second masculine singular possessive suffix, "He who insults you, your (m.s.) scorner," KBL 7:1-2.[84]

One certain substantivized masculine singular active participle occurs in the construct state: *khn*, "priest of," Avigad (*IEJ* 25) 4:4,[85] and another possible second example should be mentioned: *qn*, "acquirer, owner of," Jerusalem Jar 1:3.[86]

---

[83]Y. Shiloh, "*Qwṣt bwlwt ʿbrywt mʿyr dwd* [A Group of Hebrew Bullae from the City of David]," in *Eretz Israel: Archaeological, Historical and Geographical Studies*, Vol. 18, ed. B. Mazar and Y. Yadin (Jerusalem: The Israel Exploration Society, 1985), pp. 80, 83; "A Group of Hebrew Bullae from the City of David," *IEJ* 36 (1986): 29, 32.

[84]Before 1978, the form *šmrn*, from Ajrud 14:2, was analyzed solely as the masculine singular active participle plus the first masculine plural possessive suffix, "He who guards us, our guardian," but this interpretation can no longer be accepted with certainty. J.A. Emerton, "New Light on Israelite Religion: The Implications of the Inscriptions from Kuntillet ʿAjrud," *ZAW* 94 (1982): 2-20, following M. Gilula, "*lyhwh šmrn wlʾšrth* [To Yahweh Shomron and his Asherah]," *Shnaton: An Annual for Biblical and Ancient Near Eastern Studies* 3, ed., M. Weinfeld (1978-9): 129-37, interprets *šmrn* as the geographic name, "Samaria;" therefore *yhwh šmrn*, "YHWH of Samaria." This reading of *šmrn* as a locative is certainly possible, based on the parallel inscription *yhwh tmn*, "YHWH of Teman (Yeman)" (see Emerton, "New Light on Israelite Religion," *ZAW* 94 (1982): 3, etc.).

The reading of *šmrn* as "Samaria" instead of "our guardian," is now adopted by Z. Meshel; see M. Weinfeld, "*ywmn prswmym*, Review of Z. Meshel, *kwntylt-ʿgrwd, ʾtr mqwdš mtqwpt hmlwkh bgbwl syny* [Kuntillet ʿAjrud: A Religious Centre from the Time of the Judean Monarchy on the Border of Sinai], in *Shanaton* 4 (1980): 280-84, esp. p. 284.

[85]*Khn* is a lexicalized participle which is more nominalized than other participles (e.g., *hspr*, *hḥṣbm*); the *qal* finite forms of *khn* are rare or unattested in biblical Hebrew.

[86]The reading from the Jerusalem Jar inscription 1:3 is uncertain (see N. Avigad's "Excavations in the Jewish Quarter of the Old City of Jerusalem," *IEJ* 22 (1972): 195-96). Avigad reads *qn ʾrṣ*, "creator of Earth," but the second letter may be a *waw* rather than a *nun*. For the meaning of *qnh* as "acquirer, owner" [as opposed to "creator"], cf. P. Katz, "The Meaning of the Root *QNH*," *Journal of Jewish Studies* no. 3 (1954): 126-31; Ahlström, *Aspects of Syncretism in Israelite Religion, Horae Soederblomianae* V (Lund: C.W.K. Gleerup, 1963) p. 71.

One *plene* form of the masculine singular active participle, ʾ*wrr*, "a curser," KBL 6:1, was originally read by Naveh,[87] but the *waw* was dismissed (as a first attempt at a *resh* by the scribe) by A. Lemaire.[88] Zevit suggests that ʾ*wrr* is perhaps an error for ʾ*rwr*.[89]

One may never be sure of scribal error, but if ʾ*wrr* may, in fact, be assigned as an active participle, then this form serves to prove the long vowel (*m.l.* for *ō*) for the first syllable in the epigraphic Hebrew active participle. Further evidence for the masculine singular participle written *plene* may be provided by the proper name *ḥwrṣ*, "(DN) decides, determines," Herr 90:1, though this name is now identified as Egyptian.[90] It must be noted, however, that all three examples of the active participle of the particular verb ʾ*rr* in biblical Hebrew exhibit defective orthography.[91] This fact proves little, however, for the *qal* participle is very rarely written with *m.l.* in the Bible, no matter from what verb it derives.

Participles as proper names or elements thereof. Both masculine and feminine singular active participles are attested in epigraphic Hebrew proper names.

a) *Masculine singular active participle.* Masculine singular active participles which are epigraphic Hebrew proper names, or elements of proper names: *ḥwrṣ*, "(DN) decides, determines, Herr 90:1,[92] *mkbr-* (*mkbrm*), "one who makes many," Hazor 5,[93] *lḥš*, "whisperer," Av (*EI* 9) 14:1,[94] *mnḥm*, "comforter," A 72:1, *et*

---

[87]Naveh, "Old Hebrew Inscriptions in a Burial Cave," *IEJ* 13 (1963): 81, and fig. 10 (p. 82).

[88]"Prières en temps de crise: Les inscriptions de Khirbet Beit Lei," *RB* 83 (1976): 562.

[89]Zevit, *MLAHE*, p. 30.

[90]Cf. sec 2.3.3, p. 68, n. 119 and sec. 3.1.4.1, pp. 94-95, n. 49 in this grammar.

[91]Zevit, *MLAHE*, p. 30, n. 19.

[92]If Hebrew, this form is empirical evidence for the *qal* active participle in epigraphic Hebrew, but cf. n. 90 above.

[93]Others read *mkbdm*, a *piel* plural participle. cf. sec 3.1.5.5, p. 145, nn. 164-66.

[94]*Lḥṣ* occurs only once in epigraphic Hebrew, on a seal of unknown provenience which Herr labels "undistinguishable" (cf. Herr *SANSS*, p. 185). It is possible that this seal is not Hebrew, but it is nevertheless included in the

cetera,[95] *mnšh*, "May (DN) cause to forget," Avigad (*IEJ* 13) 1:2,*ʿbd-* (*ʿbdyhw*), "servant of," Herr 99:2, *et cetera,*[96] *ʿdd*, "restorer," Hest. 94:2,[97] *(h)šrq*, a proper name with definite article, "the whistler, piper, hisser," Ophel 2.[98]

b) *Feminine singular form of the active participle.* One feminine singular participle is attested in epigraphic Hebrew: *nʾhbt*, "lovely, beloved, delight," Herr 117:1.[99]

Plural Forms of the Participle. Only masculine plural forms of the active participle are attested in the inscriptions or on seals: *yklm*, "we are able," A 40:14,[100] *hqṣrm*, a masculine plural

---

corpus based on the original analysis of the seal made by Avigad; cf. *"qbwṣt ḥwtmwt ʿbryym* [A Group of Hebrew Seals]" *EI* 9 (1969): 7.

[95]Also: *mnḥm* (B/L (26) 6:2; Hest. 34:2); *lmnḥm* (RR Seal 2:1; Jerusalem Seal 4:1; Hest. 78:1; *mnḥm̊* (Ain Shems 5:1); *mnḥ̊m* (Herr 53:1 (Judeideh)); *mn[ḥm]* (Sam. C 1012:5); *lmnḥ[m]* (Hest. 46:1).

[96]Also: *ʿbdyhw* (Herr 121:2, 124:1, 145:1; Hest. 74:1; A 10:4); *ʿbdy[hw]* (A 27:2); *[ʿ]bdẙhw* (MHY 3:7) ; *ʿ̊bd̊[yhw]* (A 49:8; Beersheba Seal 4:1; *ʿbdyw* (S 50:2; Ajrud 13).

ʿbd- is classified as an active participle on the basis of biblical Hebrew proper names which attest to the active participle form of the root *ʿbd* (*ʿōbēd* and *ʿōbēd ʾĕdōm* (cf. *BDB*, p. 714), but a case could be made that the form *ʿbd-* in epigraphic Hebrew is a segolate noun, *ʿbd* (*ʿebed*), also on biblical analogy (proper names *ʿebed, ʿebed melek, ʿăbēd nĕgô, ʿabdāʾ* and *ʿabdĕʾēl*; cf. *BDB,* pp. 714-15.)

[97]The proper name *ʿdd* in epigraphic Hebrew corresponds to the biblical *ʿdd* (*ʿôdēd*), 2 Chron. 15:1 and *ʿdd* (*ʿōdēd*), 2 Chron. 15:8, 28:9, taken to mean "restorer" on the basis of the *Polʿēl* stem, "restore, relieve," (see *BDB*, pp. 728-29), but probably better viewed not as a proper name in the Bible, rather as "seer, prophet," the active participle, on the basis of Aramaic *byd ḥzyn wbyd ʿddn*, "through prophets and soothsayers;" cf. Donner and Röllig, *KAI* (1964), no. 202 A 12. For the interpretation of *ʿôdēd* as "seer, prophet," a non-proper name, cf. B. Kedar-Kopfstein, "Semantic Aspects of the Pattern *Qôṭēl*," *HAR* 1 (1977): 162.

[98]One may not be certain whether the form is *hšrq* or *hśrq*. The latter form seems less likely since *śrq* is not attested in biblical Hebrew except for limited adjectival/nominal forms (cf. *BDB*, p. 977), while the root *šrq* is attested several times as a verbal *qal* perfect and imperfect, and as a feminine noun (cf. *BDB*, p. 1056).

[99]*Nʾhbt* is the feminine singular *niphal* participle (root *ʾhb*). Only the masculine plural participle is attested for this stem in biblical Hebrew (*hanneʾĕhābîm*, "lovely, loveable," 2 Sam. 1:23).

[100]This form is far from certain, however, since no verbal adjective is attested for *ykl* in biblical Hebrew.

active participle with definite article, "those who are harvesting, harvesters," MHY 1:10, *šmrm*, "we are (have been) watching," L 4:11, and *hḥṣbm*, "the stone-cutters," Siloam 1:4, 6.[101]

(3) *Nominalization and the function of active participles.* Most of the epigraphic Hebrew forms cited above permit a word about nominalization of participles. The classification of *qōtēl* forms which was devised and charted by Kedar-Kopfstein[102] is very useful to this discussion. In his article, he analyzed the semantic aspects of the active participle in Hebrew and grouped individual participial forms into specific classes, thereby determining the gradations of nominal and verbal characteristics each form possessed. A synopsis of his main points is useful for an understanding of nominalization in epigraphic Hebrew.

First, on two opposite sides of the pole, the *qōtēl* pattern contains forms which function predominantly as substantives and other forms which function chiefly as predicates. In between these two extremes, fall the *qōtēl* forms in which the nominal and verbal forces interact with each other in varying gradations of intensity. Those participal forms which are more nominal than verbal are put in a class on the nominal pole, the members of which have no radical cognates (these are the most nominal *qôtēl* forms) or signify a profession. *Qōtēl* forms which exhibit "mixed" verbal characteristics may either be 1) connected with a verbal root in a derived stem, or, 2) equated with the participle in the *qal* conjugation. Some of these *qōtēl* forms denote professions or terms of agent, others signify temporary activities. The *qōtēl* forms which function chiefly as verbal forms denoting action are at the other extreme of the chart. In assessing the conclusions drawn from Kedar-Kopfstein's article and analyzing the epigraphic Hebrew evidence in the light of his work, one finds evidence for five classes (instead of nine, which Kedar-Kopfstein determines for biblical Hebrew). These classes are illustrated on the following page in table 13.

---

[101]This form could, however, represent a *qattāl* noun.

[102]Kedar-Kopfstein, "Semantic Aspects of the Pattern *Qôṭēl*," *HAR* 1 (1977): 155-76.

TABLE 13
CLASSES OF USAGE OF THE ACTIVE PARTICIPLE

Nominal					**Verbal**
Class[a]	**b**	**d**	**e**	**g**	**i**
Examples from Epig. Hebrew	*khn* *lḥš* *ʿdd*	*mkbr* *mnšh* *mkbr* *mnḥm*	*ḥṣbm* *spr* *ʿbd* *rpʾ* *šrq*	*qṣr(m)* *ḥrp* *ʾyn šlḥ*	*yšb* *šmrm* *qr[ʾ]*
Formal Features	no radical cognates	connected with verbal roots in derived stems	identical with participle of *qal* conjugation		verb
Signification	profession term of agency			temporary activity	predicate denoting action

[a]The letters corresponding to each separate class are labeled here using the same convention as Kedar-Kopfstein's chart in order to show which classes are represented by the epigraphic Hebrew evidence. Epigraphic Hebrew shows no examples for Kedar-Kopfstein's classes **a** (the extreme side of the nominal pole), **c** (those *qōtēl* nominalized forms derived from nouns), **f** (*qōtēl* forms which denote a permanent feature of the subject in character or behavior), or **h** (*qōtēl* forms which attributively denote action).

The five classes of *qōtēl* forms which are attested in epigraphic Hebrew are:

Class **b**. The epigraphic Hebrew *qōtēl* forms *khn*, *lḥš*, and *ʿdd* belong to this class and signify the holder of an office or profession. *Lḥš* is to be understood as "diviner" (similar to *ḥōzîm* in Isa. 56:10), while *ʿdd* is a *qōtēl* form denoting a similar profession, that of "seer, prophet."[103] Class b active participles are the most nominalized *qōtēl* forms in epigraphic Hebrew since they can be linked to few or no attested verbal forms, either in

[103]Kedar-Kopfstein, "Semantic Aspects of the Pattern *Qôṭēl*," *HAR* 1 (1977): 162.

epigraphic or in biblical Hebrew,[104] and thereby have an uncertain etymology.

Class **d**. The epigraphic Hebrew forms ascribed to class d are supported by roots which appear in the derived stems, but not necessarily in *qal*. The lexemes of this class denote mainly behavioral or personal traits; e.g., *mnšh*, "someone who causes another to forget (misfortune); *mnḥm*, "comforter."

Class **e**. Class e contains *qōtēl* forms which maintain and identify with the *qal* conjugation and specifically function verbally as a *qal* active participle. All of the epigraphic Hebrew examples in this class function as terms for professions; *ḥṣb*, "stone-cutter," *spr*, "scribe," *ʿbd*, "servant" (if it is correctly analyzed as an active participle); *rpʾ*, "healer," [105] *šrq*, "whistler, piper."[106]

Class **g**. *Qal* participles which function substantively to denote temporary activities belong in class g. The *qōtēl* forms *qṣr* and *qṣrm*, attested in epigraphic Hebrew, denote the temporary activities of the agricultural seasons. The form *ḥrp*, "scorner," is assigned to class g by analogy to the *qōtēl* forms discussed by Kedar-Kopfstein which function as terms for wrong-doers,[107] and because "scorning" is a temporary activity. Also included in class g are negative statements, such as *ʾyn* plus *šlḥ* in Lachish 4:7-8, *wʿbdk ʾyn[n]y šlḥ* , "Your servant cannot send."[108]

Class **i**. The *qōtēl* members of class i function as predicates denoting action as in *ʾl msʾt lkš nḥnw šmrm*, "We are watching for the signals of Lachish," L 4:10-11 and *byt yhwh hʾ yšb*, "He is staying in the temple of YHWH," Arad 18:9-10. In Kedar-Kopfstein's own words, "Suffice it to say that the verbal

---

[104]For example, *khn* is more nominalized than either *hspr* or *hḥṣbm*, as the *qal* finite forms of this root are rare or unattested in biblical Hebrew.

[105]As in Gen. 50:2, "healer, physician."

[106]Even if it is incorrect to treat *šrq* as with a *shin* rather than *sin*, *śrq* could also be classified as an active participle, "carder (of flax)." Since, however, no *qal* forms of the root *śrq* are attested in biblical Hebrew, epigraphic Hebrew *śrq* would probably be treated as a member of class b (rather than class e) in Kedar-Kopfstein's chart.

[107]Kedar-Kopfstein, "Semantic Aspects of the Pattern *Qôṭēl*," *HAR* 1 (1977): 169.

[108]Ibid.

potentiality of the *qōtēl* reaches its realization in this class."[109] The active participles which comprise class i are the forms which exhibit the most verbal (in contrast to nominal) characteristics.

(4) *Inflection of the Passive Participle.* The inflection of the passive participle in epigraphic Hebrew follows in table 14.

TABLE 14
PASSIVE PARTICIPLE

	Singular	Plural
m.	*qtl* *qtwl*	–
f.	–	–

(5) *Forms.* Epigraphic Hebrew contains several passive participle forms from the base *qatūl*, and others which, on the basis of analogy with corresponding biblical Hebrew forms, are conjectured to be from the *qattūl* base.[110] All of the forms are masculine singular, and occur as verbal forms, as well as proper names:[111]

---

[109] Kedar-Kopfstein, "Semantic Aspects of the Pattern *Qôṭēl*," *HAR* 1 (1977): 171.

[110] *Qatūl*, the regular base for passives in biblical Hebrew (see H. Bauer and P. Leander, *Historische Grammatik der hebräischen Sprache des Alten Testamentes* (Hildesheim: Georg Olms, 1965), p. 472), is exhibited by epigraphic Hebrew forms *ʾrwr/ʾrr*, *brk*, and *rḥṣ*.

Qattūl is not the regular passive particle base in biblical Hebrew, rather it is an intensified or extended form of the *qal* passive participle (*qatūl*); see Bauer and Leander, *Historische Grammatik*, p. 480. Several epigraphic Hebrew proper names (e.g., *zkr*, *ydʿ*, *nḥm*, and *šlm*) derive from this base, as well as the independent verbal form *ḥnn*.

[111] The passive participle is statistically more common as a proper name than as the independent verb, by a margin of almost two to one (approximately fifty-three proper names to thirty verbal forms).

Independent verbs: *ʾrwr*, "cursed be," Silwan 2:2; *ʾrr*, NY 1:1; KBL 4:1, 6 (?), 7, *ʾr[r]*, KBL 5; *brk*, "blessed be," NY 1:4, 6, 7; Ajrud 4:1, 6:1, 13; Sam. Ost. C 1101:1, 2 (PN ?), *b̊rk*, KEK 3:2; *ḥnn*, "favored," KBL 2:1; *rḥṣ* , "refined, washed," S 16a:3, 16b:3, 17a:3, 18:3, 19:3, 20:3, 21:3, 53:3, 54:2-3, 55:3, 72:2, 82:1-2, *r[ḥ]ṣ* , S 59:1-2, *[rḥṣ]*, S 17b:3.

Proper names: *zkr*, "Remembered (of DN), or "(DN is) remembered," A 67:5; KEM 1:1; Avigad 9:1-2; Herr 89:1, 144:1, *zkr*, S 31a:3, *[z]kr*, A 38:7, 48:3, *bʿl{ʿ}zkr*, S 37:3; *ydʿ*, (DN is) known," L 3:20; *nḥm*, "Comforted (of DN)," A 16:10, 17:1, 8; B/L (26) 15:2; R 18:2 (Herr 126); Gib S.I. 2; L V 2:1; L Seal 12:1 (7x); Av (*EI* 9) 9:1; Jerusalem Seal 6:1; *nḥm* (L Seal 16:1); *nḥ̊m*, Herr 118:1. *[n]ḥm* (?), TBM Sherd 6; *šʾl*, "Desired (of DN)," Av NN 16:2, Avigad 5:1; *šlm*, "One in covenant of peace," A 35:3, 44:1; L 3:20; B/L (26) 10:3, 15:1; R 11:1 (Herr 136); Ain Shems 7:2; L Seal 11:1; Herr 66:1 (Tell el Judeideh); *šlm*, Sam C 1101:1; L Seal 7:1; *šl‹m›* (?), KEK Plate 6; *mšlm*, A 110:1; L Seal 9:1 (7x); Gib S.I. 5; *m̊šlm*, A 39:3; *m[šl]m*, Gib S.I. 6.

Participles as independent forms. The verbal forms include the form *ʾrr*, "cursed (be)," at Nahal Yishai and Khirbet Beit Lei, but more interesting, the same word occurs as *ʾrwr*, at Silwan, i.e., with the internal *waw mater lectionis,* and proving the *qatūl* base for the passive participle in epigraphic Hebrew.

The wish formula which is semantically contrary to *ʾrr*, namely *brk*, "blessed (be)," occurs at Nahal Yishai, Khirbet el-Kom, and three times at Ajrud.

Another passive participle used as an independent verbal form comes from another inscription from Khirbet Beit Lei. It is the masculine singular passive participle and adjective *ḥnn*, "favored."[112] A common passive participle which appears frequently in the inscriptions from Samaria is *rḥṣ*, "washed."[113]

---

[112]*Ḥnn*, an independent passive participle in epigraphic Hebrew, occurs as a proper name in biblical Hebrew (*ḥānûn*), 2 Sam. 10:1, etc., and as an adjective (*ḥannûn*), Exod. 34:6, etc.; see *BDB*, p. 337. The form there, and presumably in epigraphic Hebrew, represents the *qattūl* base (see discussion below). Cf. Bauer and Leander, *Historische Grammatik*, p. 480.

[113]*Rḥṣ* is a masculine singular passive participle from the root *rḥṣ*, "to wash," although the form is unattested in biblical Hebrew. A. Lemaire (*Inscriptions hébraïques*, pp. 31, 46) defined it as such, but with the meaning "raffinée" (= "refined"). D. Diringer, *Le iscrizioni antico-ebraiche palestinesi*, p. 38, translates *rḥṣ* as "(oil of) purification," where *rḥṣ* relates to an attested singular noun in biblical Hebrew *rḥṣy*, "my washing," Ps. 60:1. While this analysis makes sense by the fact that the biblical example occurs in construct state *syr rḥṣy*, "my washing-pot," and all of the epigraphic Hebrew examples of *rḥṣ* occur after the noun *šmn*, "oil," one biblical noun is hardly concrete proof that *rḥṣ* in epigraphic Hebrew is a noun.

As a passive participle, *rḥṣ* would literally mean "washed," but, as pointed out by Lemaire (*Inscriptions hébraïques*, pp. 46-47), the form must explain a quality of "oil" (*rḥṣ* is always attested with *šmn*, "oil," in epigraphic Hebrew). Furthermore, Hebrew epigraphy shows distinct parallelism between the adjective *yšn*, "old," and *rḥṣ* in the Samaria corpus, and because the former describes a quality of "wine," the latter should do the same with regard to "oil." "Washing" oil was a traditional technique practiced in antiquity (see Lemaire, *Inscriptions hébraïques*, p. 47, and R. M. Savignac, "Review of *Le iscrizioni antico-ebraiche palestinesi* by D. Diringer," *RB* 44 (1935): 292, n. 2; Sarfatti has discussed *rḥṣ* as a problematic form; cf. G. B. Sarfatti, "Hebrew Inscriptions of the First Temple Period–A Survey and Some Linguistic Comments," *Maarav* 3/1 (1982): 75).

Lawrence Stager argued convincingly, primarily on archaeological and ethnographic grounds, that *šmn rḥṣ* is "washed oil." The term refers to a technique by which olive oil was extracted or separated, thereby being processed into a quality product. It was not, as Sasson asserted, "refined oil" implying something beyond simply "washed" or "bathed." Cf. L. Stager, "The Finest Olive Oil in Samaria," *JSS* 28 (1983): 241-45. For a discussion of Sasson's views, as well as the citations of the scholars who treat *rḥṣ* as a noun, rather than as a passive participle, Cf. V. Sasson, "Studies in the Lexicon and Linguistic Usage of Early Hebrew Inscriptions", Ph.D. dissertation, New York University, 1979 (Ann Arbor, MI: University Microfilms International, 7925520, 1980), pp. 65-75; "*šmn rḥṣ* in the Samaria Ostraca," *JSS* 26 (1981): 1-5.

E. Lipinski analyzes *rḥṣ* as an active participle meaning "toilet oil, oil for cleansing," on the basis of Akkadian, but Stager, op. cit., p. 241, n. 1 demonstrates that biblical Hebrew forms do not support Lipinski's interpretation; cf. E. Lipinski, Review of *Textbook of Syrian Semitic Inscriptions, I*, by J.C.L. Gibson, in "North-west Semitic Inscriptions," *Orientalia Lovaniensia periodica* 8 (1977): 85-86.

The passive participle as proper name or element thereof. With the exception of the proper name *šʾl*,[114] the remaining forms of this general type attested in epigraphic Hebrew apparently come from the *qattūl* base, and comprise proper names or appear as elements of such.

The reasons for positing the existence of *qattūl* are based primarily on biblical Hebrew where *qattūl* personal names are attested, and there, *qattūl* appears to be an intensified form of *qatūl*, the base of the regular *qal* passive participle. Biblical proper names which correspond to those of epigraphic Hebrew include *ydʿ* (*yaddûaʿ*), *nḥwm* (*naḥ(ḥ)ûm*), and *šlwm* (*šallûm*).[115]

Besides the proper names, epigraphic Hebrew exhibits one independent passive participle, *ḥnn*, "favored," KBL 2:1, which may, also on the basis of biblical Hebrew, be conjectured to represent a *qatūl* base (simple passive participle) or a *qattūl* base (adjectival form). Since none of the attested epigraphic Hebrew proper names is written *plene* (as in the Bible), the interpretation for the proper names from this base can be questioned, as one could analyze the forms (except *mšlm*) instead as perfects.[116]

---

[114]*Šʾl*, meaning "Desired (of DN)," is attested on two of Avigad's seals. The root *šʾl* is attested in biblical Hebrew in *qatūl* proper names (*šʾwl*, 1 Sam. 9:2, etc.). Cf. *BDB*, p. 982; cf. Noth, *IPN*, pp. 136, 216, 257.

[115]Bauer and Leander, *Historische Grammatik*, p. 480.

[116]*Zkr*, *nḥm*, *šlm*, *ydʿ*, and *šʾl* on the basis of biblical Hebrew parallel attested proper names, could represent third masculine singular perfects. *Zkr* as a *qal* perfect could signify "(DN) has remembered" and could represent a hypocoristicon for such attested epigraphic Hebrew/biblical names as *zkryhw* and *zkryh* (2 Kings 15:8, 14:29, etc.), *nḥm*, "(DN) has comforted," as in biblical *nḥm* (*naḥam*), 1 Chron. 4:19, or a hypocoristicon for *nḥmyh[w]* (Neh. 1:1, etc.), *ydʿ*, "(DN) has known (cared about)," as in 1 Chron. 2:28 (*yādāʿ*), *šʾl*, "(DN) has asked (desired)," as in Ezra 10:29 (*šĕʾāl*), and *šlm*, "(DN) has replaced (a dead infant by a new one)," as in Gen. 46:24 (*šillēm*), a *piel* perfect form. In the Bible, all of these proper names have corresponding forms written *plene* in the *qattūl* form. This form of these specific proper names is far more common than the perfect form. Therefore, on the basis of frequency in the Bible, the epigraphic Hebrew *zkr*, *nḥm*, *ydʿ*, *šʾl* and *šlm* probably, though not definitely, represent participles rather than perfects in epigraphic Hebrew.

The proper name *mšlm* (A 110:1, etc.) probably represents the masculine singular *pual* participle, corresponding to biblical *mšlm*, 2 Kings 22:3, etc.. Morphologically, this form is most certainly not a perfect and must be a participle, either *piel* ("DN restores, makes safe," biblical *mĕšallēm*, Deut. 7:10), or *pual*. *Mšlm* is more likely a *pual* participle meaning, "One in covenant of peace," as the form occurs in biblical Hebrew and is attested there more frequently than *mĕšallēm*. It must be admitted, however, that any one example

However, the non-proper name *ḥnn*, mentioned above, is clearly not a perfect, rather it is conjectured to be an adjective: *nqh yhwh ḥnn*, "Absolve (us), O gracious YHWH!" KBL 2:1, where it is an attribute of God, as in the biblical phrase in Exodus 34:6, *yhwh ʾl rḥwm wḥnwn*, "O YHWH, merciful and gracious God."[117]

Zkr, "(X) is remembered (of/by DN)" is a common name in epigraphic Hebrew. It occurs in the absolute form at Arad, Khirbet el Meshash, Samaria and on several seals and is also the second element of a proper name *bʿl{ʿ}zkr* from Samaria.

The proper name *nḥm*, "Comforted," is attested on several seals from such places as Gibeon, Lachish and Jerusalem, as well as on inscriptions from Arad and Tell Beit Mirsim.

The root *šlm* is even more popular than the previous two verbal roots for epigraphic Hebrew proper names. Two proper names, *šlm* and *mšlm*, derive from this root. Both *šlm* and *mšlm* are passive participle forms, the former from the *qal* stem, the latter from the *pual* stem. *Šlm*, "One in covenant of peace,"[118] occurs on several seals, including those found at Tell el Judeideh, Lachish and Ain Shems, and on inscriptions from Arad, Lachish and Samaria. The form *šl*, from a Khirbet el-Kom plate inscription may also stand for *šl‹m›*.[119]

---

in epigraphic Hebrew may be derived from one or another of the bases just discussed.

[117]*Ḥnn* in the Khirbet Beit Lei inscription may be conjectured to be a *qattūl* base form which acts as an adjective and corresponds to biblical *ḥannûn*; see Bauer and Leander, *Historische Grammatik*, p. 480. If *ḥnn* is to be interpreted as an attributive adjective in KBL 2:1, one might expect *hḥnn* (YHWH is definite). The "participle"/adjective *ḥnn* is not definite in KBL 2:1 (as in Exod. 34:6) and there is no intervening *ʾl* as in Exod. 34:6. *Ḥnn* in KBL 2:1 modifies YHWH, a proper noun in a vocative phrase, and, as pointed out by Lemaire, *ḥnn* is used attributively to describe YHWH in Psalms 111:4, 116:5, 145:8, 2 Chron. 30:9, etc., cf. Lemaire, "Prières en temps de crise: Les inscriptions de Khirbet Beit Lei," *RB* 83 (1976): 566.

[118]This meaning is one of several offered by commentators relating the form (as a *qattūl* passive participle) to often attested biblical proper names (2 Kings 15:10, 13, 14, 15, etc.) *šlm* (*šallūm*) and *šlwm* (šallûm). These forms relate to a root *šlm*, "to be in covenant of peace," *BDB*, p. 1023. However, an etymology related to the proper name *šlm* (*šillēm*), "(DN) has replaced (a dead infant by a new one)," Gen. 46:24; Num. 26:49, where *šlm* may be parsed as a third masculine singular *piel* perfect is possible. Cf. A. Lemaire, "Inscription paléo-hébraïque sur une assiette," *Semitica* 27 (1977): 22, for a discussion of *šlm*. For *šillēm*, see Noth, *IPN*, p. 174; Lemaire, *Inscriptions hébraïques*, p. 105.

[119]For *šl* as an abridged form of *šl‹m›*, see Lemaire, "Inscription paléo-hébraïque sur une assiette," *Semitica* 27 (1977): 22.

The proper name *mšlm* representing the only non-*qal* passive participle attested in epigraphic Hebrew, occurs at Arad, Lachish and Gibeon.[120] One less frequently attested proper name which may be derived from the *qattūl* base is *ydʿ*, "(DN) is known," from Lachish 3:20.[121]

3.1.5 Derived Verbal Stems

3.1.5.1 Introduction

In epigraphic Hebrew, as in other Northwest Semitic languages, other forms exist alongside the basic *qal* stem, the "simple" conjugation of the preceding section. The same root which appears in *qal* may also occur in the derived stems with changes occurring in the prefix elements or stem patterns. The six derived verbal stems attested in epigraphic Hebrew, for which we may use the names of traditional Hebrew grammarians, are:

niphal	*hiphil*
piel	*hophal*
pual	*pilpel*

Not all roots known from *qal* occur in all six forms and not all roots occurring in the derived stems appear in *qal* even though they may be attested as nouns or adjectives.

Though to date the evidence for derived verbal stems in epigraphic Hebrew is at best minimal, certain limited observations about the characteristics of each stem are possible. Where the forms are presented in the morphological section for each verbal form, a hyphen indicates that a particular form is as yet unattested. As additional epigraphic Hebrew texts are discovered, new forms may be added to the basic framework presented in this grammar.

---

[120]Noth, *IPN*, p. 174, on *mšlm*, "replaced (= given) (by God in the place of a dead infant);" Grelot, *Documents araméens d'Egypte*, p. 479. The passive participle *mĕšullām*, "one in covenant of peace," is a common biblical proper name; cf. *BDB*, p. 1024.

[121]As a birth name, *ydʿ* may in fact be explained as the third masculine singular *qal* perfect, "(DN) has known (› cared about)"; see Lemaire, *Inscriptions hébraïques*, p. 105. The reason for ascribing this name the *qattūl* base is that the root *ydʿ* is attested in biblical Hebrew in *qattūl* proper names: *ydwʿ*, Neh. 10:22, etc., cf. *BDB*, pp. 396.

3.1.5.2 *Niphal*

The first derived verbal stem, *niphal*, is characterized by the use of the *nun*-prefix on a root. This prefix is only discernible on the participle and perfect since the *nun* assimilates to the first root letter in the imperfect, imperative and infinitive construct (though the imperative and infinitive construct are discernible as being from a derived stem by the prefixed *hê* which occurs on both).

In biblical Hebrew, *niphal* verbs, which may be generally characterized as medio-passive, may be described in more detail as indicating incomplete passiveness (the subject receives the action from an undisclosed agent), reflexivity (where someone does something to himself), reciprocity (plural subjects perform reciprocal acts), or result (the state of the subject which has been produced by the verbal action named by the root is described).

In epigraphic Hebrew, the phrases containing a *niphal* verb may be characterized by each of the categories above. Also, it is important to note that the *niphal* conjugation is represented by almost all of the verbal categories: the perfect (the form attested is the first common singular), the imperfect (the second and third masculine singular), the imperative (the masculine singular form), the active participle (the feminine singular form), and the infinitive construct.

All of the forms except one (*tdhm*) correspond to a *qal* verb in biblical Hebrew, although in others (the roots *nqh* and *nqb*), the *qal* is little known in biblical Hebrew.

The Perfect

(1) *Inflection*. Table 15 gives the inflection of the *niphal* perfect in epigraphic Hebrew.

TABLE 15
***NIPHAL* PERFECT**

	Singular	Plural
3 m.	–	–
3 f.	–	–
2 m.	–	–
2 f.	–	–
1 c.	*nqtlty*	–

(2) *Forms.* This section describes the extant verbs in the *niphal* perfect.

First common singular. Only one form for the perfect *niphal* is attested in epigraphic Hebrew: *nqty*, "I am innocent, clean," MHY 1:11.[122] The form *nqty* shows the regular assimilation of the first root consonant that is expected in the *niphal* perfect (**niqqêtī* ‹ **ninqaytī*), as well as the final *mater lectionis* for long *ī*.

The Imperfect

(1) *Inflection.* Table 16 illustrates the inflection of the *niphal* imperfect.

[122]The form is attested in biblical Hebrew, with both long vowels written *plene*: *nqyty* (*niqqêtî*), Judges 15:3. The root *nqh* appears primarily in the *niphal* and *piel* conjugations in the Bible, with only one infinitive absolute attested in the *qal*.

TABLE 16
***NIPHAL* IMPERFECT**

	Singular	Plural
3 m.	*yqtl*	–
3 f.	–	–
2 m.	*tqtl*	–
2 f.	–	–
1 c.	–	–

(2) *Forms*. This section describes the extant verbs in the *niphal* imperfect.

Third masculine singular. The verb *ylqḥ* occurs in a broken text and, on the basis of the presence of the *l*, has been classified as the *niphal* imperfect, "He, it will be taken," in the phrase *[ ]ylqḥ nšb dbr[ ]*, "...be taken, we will return word...," Arad 111:4[123]

Second masculine singular. The form, *tdhm*, "You must be silent," MHY 1:14, occurs with the negative adverb *lʾ* in an imperative sense.[124]

The Imperative

(1) *Inflection*. Table 17 illustrates the inflection of the *niphal* imperative.

---

[123]In biblical Hebrew, the form would be vocalized *yillāqaḥ*.

[124]The reading *wlʾ tdhm* in MHY 1:14 (the last legible letters on the left side of the ostracon) is uncertain, as is the interpretation of the phrase itself because the continuation of the phrase (in line 15) is missing from the ostracon. Also, the use of *lʾ* rather than *ʾl* in what from the preceding context appears to be a strong point-in-time negative imperative is unusual.

The root *dhm* has no *qal* in the Bible, and occurs only once as the third masculine singular *niphal* perfect in Jer. 14:9, "astounded," but is connected etymologically with the verb *dwm*, "to be silent," as in *ʾîš nidhām*, "silent man."

TABLE 17
***NIPHAL* IMPERATIVE**

	Singular	Plural
m.	*hqtl*	–
f.	–	–

(2) *Forms*. One *niphal* imperative is attested in epigraphic Hebrew.

Second masculine singular. The *niphal* imperative is represented by the independent verb *hšmr*, "Beware!" L 3:21. This form illustrates that in epigraphic Hebrew, the *niphal* imperative is marked by an initial *hê*, and probably has a zero-ending for the masculine singular form.

The Infinitive

(1) *Inflection*. Table 18 illustrates the inflection of the *niphal* infinitive construct.

TABLE 18
***NIPHAL* INFINITIVE CONSTRUCT**

Infinitive Construct	Verb Type
hqtl	Strong Verb
–	Verbs III-ʾ*aleph*
hqtl	Verbs I-*nun*
–	Hollow Verbs
–	Verbs III-*hê*

(2) *Forms*. The extant *niphal* infinitives construct occur with and without prepositions.

Without introductory preposition. With pronominal suffix: *hnqbh*, "it's being tunneled through," Siloam 1:4 (?), 6.

With introductory preposition. *lhn[qb]*, "to be tunneled, cut through," Siloam 1:2.

(3) *Discussion of nqb.* The root *nqb* occurs in the *niphal* conjugation three times in the Siloam inscription, once with the preposition *l-* before the form and twice with a suffix. The root means "to pierce, bore" in the Bible, and occurs in this capacity in the *qal*, but the biblical *niphal* forms have the meaning "prick off, designate."

The first instance of this root in the Siloam inscription is in the first line where it is the first legible word of the inscription: *hnqbh*, "its being tunneled through." The form *hnqbh* has been much disputed, but one viable solution, based on the morphologically identical form *hnqbh* from Siloam 1:3-4, is to analyze the form as the *niphal* infinitive with the third masculine (or feminine ?) singular pronominal suffix. The true status of the form in line 1, however, cannot be fixed with certainty, given the incomplete section of text preceding this word.[125]

---

[125]*Hnqbh* in Siloam 1:1 may be analyzed as either a definite article plus noun, or, as accepted here, the *niphal* infinitive plus suffix ending. This latter view is the opinion also of W.F. Albright, "Review of 'The Babylonian Genesis: the Story of Creation'" by A. Heidel, *Journal of Biblical Literature* 62 (1943): 370, *bĕyôm hinnāqĕbô(h)*, "when the tunnel (probably *néḡeb*) was pierced through," following A. Fischer, "Zur Siloahinschrift," *ZDMG* 56 (1902): 800-809. Also see Cross and Freedman, *EHO*, p. 49 (**hinnaqibô*); Zevit, *MLAHE*, p. 19, who discusses both alternatives: (**hinnaqibō*, a verbal noun) or (**naqūbā*/**naqībā*, "tunnel").

For other alternatives to vocalization and *hnqbh* as a noun, see H. Torczyner, "*ktwbt hšlwḥ, lwḥ gzr wḥrs hʿwpl* [The Siloam Inscription, Gezer Calendar, and Ophel Ostracon]," *Bulletin of the Jewish Palestine Exploration Society* 7 (1939): 1-9; followed by J. A. Soggin, "Un passage difficile dans l'inscription de Siloe," *VT* 8 (1958): 298 and n. 1; I. Livni, "*lktbt hšlḥ* [The Siloam Inscription]," *Bulletin of the Jewish Palestine Exploration Society* 9 (1942): 114 (**hanneqibbah*) using parallels of *šmṭh* (*šĕmiṭṭah*) and *qhlh* (*qĕhillāh*), etc.; Gibson, *TSSI*, p. 23 (**nqabā* or **niqbā* , "act of piercing"); V. Sasson, "The Siloam Tunnel Inscription," *PEQ* 114 (1982): 111-16, esp. pp. 113-14. Sasson (p. 114) argues unconvincingly that *hnqbh* in line 1 of the Siloam Inscription is the definite article and *qiṭlâh* noun (**niqbâh*), basing his assumptions for vocalization on the "*qiṭlâh*" noun *nqrh*, which means "quarried ground." Sasson does, however, correctly analyze the other forms of the root *nqb* which occur in this inscription (*hnqbh*, line 1b and line 3-4) as *niphal* infinitives with the third person singular suffix.

The Participle

(1) *Inflection of the participle.* Table 19 illustrates the inflection of the *niphal* participle.

TABLE 19
***NIPHAL* PARTICIPLE**

	Singular	Plural
m.	–	–
f.	*nqtlt*	–

(2) *Forms.* One *niphal* participle occurs in epigraphic Hebrew.

Feminine singular. The *niphal* participle in epigraphic Hebrew is marked by an initial *nun*, and the feminine singular form ends in *taw*. The participle which occurs in *niphal* is the only feminine participle attested in epigraphic Hebrew: *nʾhbt,* "lovely, beloved," Herr 117:1. To the extent that proper names may be used to reconstruct the morphology of a spoken language, this form illustrates that the *niphal* feminine participle ended in *-t* as in biblical Hebrew (*niqṭélet*). This participle also represents one of the few feminine[126] proper names in epigraphic Hebrew.

Only the masculine plural active participle from this root is attested in the Bible: *nʾhbym* (*neʾĕhābîm*) in 2 Sam. 1:23, and it is

For the older discussion of the form and the various viewpoints regarding it, see Diringer, *Le iscrizioni antico-ebraiche palestinesi,* p. 85, and Moscati, *L'epigrafia ebraica antica*, pp. 40, 41. For the *hê* as *m.l.*, see Zevit, *MLAHE*, p. 19, n. 38.

[126]The term "feminine" is used here to mean both that *nʾhbt* is the name of a woman, *lnʾhbt bt dmlyhw*, "For Neʾehebet daughter of Domlayahu," Herr 117:1-2, and also that it is a name which is feminine in form. For other specifically female names (names of women), some of which are not feminine in form, see Hestrin and Dayagi-Mendels, *Inscribed Seals*, pp. 43-51.

also the only *niphal* verbal form attested in the Bible from this root. The name also occurs at Elephantine: *nʾhbt*, "aimable."[127]

3.1.5.3 *Piel*

Morphologically, *piel* and *qal* are indistinguishable (except for the participle). Verbs taken to be *piel* in epigraphic Hebrew are so analyzed on the basis of biblical Hebrew, where a certain root occurs rarely if at all in *qal*, but frequently in *piel*.[128]

The Perfect

(1) *Inflection.* Table 20 on the next page illustrates the inflection of the *piel* perfect.

[127]Grelot, *Documents araméens d'Egypte*, p. 483. Grelot parses the form as the feminine singular passive participle form of *nʾhbt*. See also Cowley, *Aramaic Papyri of the Fifth Century*, p. 298.

[128]For example, the root *rḥm* is attested as *qal* in biblical Hebrew (Ps. 18:2), "love," but is far more frequent in the *piel* (Ps. 103:13, etc.), "have compassion." For this reason, *rḥm* from the epigraphic Hebrew proper name *yrḥm(ʾl)*, "May (God) have compassion," Av (1978) Bulla of Jerahmeel 2:1, is herein classified as a *piel*.

TABLE 20
***PIEL* PERFECT**

	Singular	Plural
3 m.	*qtl*	–
3 f.	–	–
2 m.	*qtlt; qtlth*[a]	–
2 f.	–	–
1 c.	*qtlt*	–

[a]The second masculine singular *piel* perfect *dbrth,* "You spoke," MO 2:5 is an example of the plene writing of the pronominal element and may be compared to the masculine *qal* singular perfects, *ydʿth, šlḥth* and *ktbth* (see table 8, p. 83 and following discussion).

(2) *Forms*. This section describes the extant verbs in the *piel* perfect.

Third masculine singular.

Independent verbal forms include: *bqš*, "He tried to obtain, sought," A 40:12; *kl*, "He finished," MHY 1:6; *nsh*, "He has tried," L 3:9.

Independent verb plus suffix: *(w)ṣwk*, "He orders you (m.s.)," A 3:2-3.

Element of proper name: *brk(yhw)*, "(YH) blesses," A 22:1, 108:1; Avigad (1978) Baruk Seal 1:1;[129] *šn(yw)*, "(YH) has changed, repeated," R 8:1 (Herr UD 3).

[129]The title of Avigad's seal as "Baruk" may lead one to analyze *brk* in *brk(yhw)* as the *qal* passive participle, rather than a *piel* form. Biblical Hebrew attestations for *brk*-proper names yield the following forms: *bārûk* (*qal* passive

Second masculine singular.

Independent verb forms include: *dbrth,* "You spoke," MO 2:5

Independent verb plus suffix: *ṣwtny*, "You gave me orders," A 18:7-8.

First common singular. Forms include:

Independent verbal form: *brkt*, "I (hereby) bless," Ajrud 14:1; *klt*, "I finished," MHY 1:8.

Independent verb plus suffix: *brktk*, "I (hereby) bless you (m.s.)," A 16:2-3, 40:3.

(3) *Discussion of the piel perfect.* The *piel* perfect in epigraphic Hebrew consists of singular verb forms. The third masculine singular form is most common and is represented by regular roots and third weak roots. There are two third masculine singular forms which are first elements of proper names.

From the point of view of orthography, the form *kl*, MHY 1:6, is problematic in that it lacks the final *hê mater lectionis* common in third weak verbs for the final vowel *ā*. The *piel* verb *nsh* illustrates the final *hê*. *Kl* is problematic in epigraphic Hebrew, both as an infinitive absolute[130] and as a *piel* perfect (where the *hê m.l.* is absent). The hypothesis here (MHY 1:6) is that it is a *piel* perfect from a III-weak root.[131] Analysis of epigraphic Hebrew third weak perfect verbs (not necessarily in *piel*), shows that the evidence for the final *-h* is so overpowering on

---

participle), *bārak(ʾēl)* (*qal* or *piel* [~ *bērak*, Gen. 24:1] perfect), and *yĕberek(yāhû)*, seen as analogous to *yebārek(yāhû)* by Brown, Driver and Briggs (*BDB*, p. 140). The verbal element of this proper name (*ybrkyhw*) is probably to be analyzed as the *piel* imperfect. The attested biblical forms which are orthographically closest to the epigraphic Hebrew name are *brkyh* and *brkyhw* (*berekyāh(û)*); cf. *BDB*, p. 138, which might be explained as apocopated *piel* forms. *BDB* cite *brkyh* and *brkyhw* as short forms for the imperfect *ybrkyhw*, but *brk* (in *brkyhw*) could also correspond to the perfect (~ *bērēk*, Psalm 10:3).

[130] Cf. *Kl* in the Gezer inscription, see sec. 3.1.5.3, pp. 134-35, n. 142.

[131] See Pardee, "Meṣad Ḥashavyahu," *Maarav* 1/1 (1978): 41-42.

independent verbs and as second elements of proper names that *kl* simply has to be looked upon as anomalous.

However, one could cite the proper names *pn* (‹ *pnh*), "(DN) has turned," L Seal 19:1 and *śr* (‹ *śrh*), "(DN) has persisted," Herr 68:1 (Samaria) as further evidence for the omission of *hê* in third masculine singular perfect forms. Further, if *nsh* is not included as a *piel*, another hypothesis would state that *hê* is regularly omitted in third masculine singular *piel* perfects from third-weak roots.

Unfortunately, the evidence from epigraphic Hebrew does not, in and of itself, prove this hypothesis beyond a doubt as the following discussion will show. D. Diringer[132] analyzes *pn* as a hyporisticon analogous to the biblical proper names *pnwʾl* and *pnyʾl*, "Turn, O EL!" and *śr* could likewise be a hypocoristic name related to biblical *śryhw/śryh*, "YH persists, perseveres." However, the reading of *pn* on the Lachish Seal is uncertain, and *śr* could be analyzed as a masculine singular *qall* noun, "chief, governor, ruler, official, prince," as in the epigraphic Hebrew phrase *śr hʿr*, "governor of the city," Avigad (1976) 3:1; Barkay (1977)1:1 (=Avigad 1978),[133] or from *śrr*, "be, act as a prince, rule" (*śryhw*, "YH rules as prince," Avigad (1978) Seal 1:1; Av NN 11:1). Neither *pn* nor *śr* may be used as proof for the omission of *hê* in third masculine singular perfects from Verbs III-weak. *Kl* remains an anomaly within Hebrew epigraphy until fresh evidence becomes available.

Hebrew epigraphy provides evidence that third masculine singular perfects from third weak roots never exhibit a final *hê* when the verb is the first element of proper names. One assumes, on the basis of Masoretic vocalization (e.g., *bnyhw*, *bĕnāyāhû*), that the *yod* in each form is uniquely from the deity name.

In epigraphic Hebrew, however, final *hê* occurs when the third weak verb is the second element of a proper name (e.g., *ywbnh*, "YH has built;" *ʾldlh*, El has adorned," *et cetera*). The one exception to this is Lachish 7:2, *ʾḥʿš*, a name the reading and etymology of which are uncertain, and the root of the final element is more likely derived from Verbs II-weak (rather than from *ʿśh*).

The *hê* suffix of the third masculine singular third-weak perfect is always present in independent proper names with no suffix (e.g.,*ʿdh*, "(DN) has adorned," Ajrud 2), and in all other third

---

[132]Diringer, *Le Iscrizioni Antico-Ebraiche*, p. 51.

[133]Also, *śr ʿr*, "governor of the city," Ajrud 3:1.

masculine singular perfect independent verbal forms (besides *kl*) attested in epigraphic Hebrew (e.g., *hyh*, "It, he was," MHY 1:3, *et cetera*; *hṭh*, "He has applied himself, given his attention to," A 40:4; *ʿśh*, "He has done, did," A 21:3, *et cetera*).

The second masculine singular *piel* perfect is represented by the *plene* form *dbrth,* "You spoke," MO 2:5 and by a form with object suffix, *ṣwtny*, "You gave me orders," A 18:7-8.

The verbs *brkt* and *klt* provide evidence that in *piel* first common singular perfect forms, epigraphic Hebrew shows no orthographic indicator for final long vowels (in contrast to epigraphic Hebrew *qal and niphal* stems). An epigraphic Hebrew example for the first common singular *piel* verb with suffix is *brktk*, "I (hereby) bless you."

The Imperfect

(1) *Inflection.* Table 21 gives the inflection of the *piel* imperfect in epigraphic Hebrew.

TABLE 21
***PIEL* IMPERFECT**

	Singular	**Plural**
3 m.	*yqtl*	–
3 f.	–	–
2 m.	*tqtl*	–
2 f.	–	–
1 c.	–	–

(2) Forms. This section describes the extant verbs in the piel imperfect.

Third masculine singular. Forms include:

Independent verbal form: *ydbr*, "He will say, speak," papMur 17a:2; *ybkr*, "May (DN) treat as a first-born," L 2:5; *ybrk*, "May he bless (you)," Ajrud 15:6-7;[134] ; *yšlm*, "May (DN) restore," A 21:4 *(w)ykl*, "He finished," MHY 1:5.

Element of proper name: *yhl[l(ʾl])*, "May (El) praise," Ajrud 14 (?); *yḥw(ʿly)*, "May (DN) preserve, restore to life," S 55:2, *yḥw(ʿl[y])*, S 60:1; *yrḥm(ʾl)*, "May (El) have compassion," Av (1978) Bulla of Jerahmeel 2:1.[135]

Second masculine singular. Independent verbal form: *tʾḥr*, "You wait, tarry," A 2:6 (with negative adverb).

Only the second and third masculine singular imperfect piel verbs are attested in epigraphic Hebrew. The second masculine singular is represented by one form only: *tʾḥr*. The third masculine singular *piel* imperfect however is frequent among regular and third weak verbs, with one possible geminate root *(hll)* also

---

[134]Also, *ybr[k]*, KH 1:1-2, 2:5 and *ybr̊kk*, "May he bless you (m.s.)," MO 2:1.

[135]The form, *yhl[l(ʾl])*, "may (God) praise," Ajrud 14, is offered as a possible additional example to this category although the form is largely restored and remains open to question.

The root *rḥm*, which is also attested in the *qal* in biblical Hebrew, is far more commonly attested there as a *piel* (in non-proper names). With regard to *rḥm* in Hebrew proper names, the *qal* of this root is attested as an independent proper name by the perfect (*rḥm*, *raḥam*, 1 Chron. 2:44) and passive participle (*rḥwm/rḥm*, *rĕḥûm*, Ezra 2:2, *etc.*), while the *piel* is attested in compound names (personal and geographic) in the imperfect (*yrḥmʾl*, *yeraḥmĕʾēl* and *yrḥmʾly*, *yeraḥmĕʾēlî*, 1 Chron. 2:9, etc. [However, the form *yeraḥm-* is not a regular *piel* form]). *Rḥm* is also attested frequently in the biblical proper name *yrḥm* (*yeroḥām*), in form a *poel.*

Yrḥmʾl (mentioned above as being attested in epigraphic Hebrew) is attested eight times in biblical Hebrew (cf. *BDB*, p. 934). The *rḥm* element of this proper name is a *piel* imperfect, and it is for this reason that *rḥm* is classified as *piel* in epigraphic Hebrew.

attested. Three of the third masculine singular piel verbs are first elements of proper names. One verb has been restored with a possible second masculine singular object suffix.

The form *yḥw-* may be the piel jussive from *ḥw(h)* in which the diphthong is preserved because it is derived from the triphthong *-aww, -aw ‹ -awwiy(u).*[136] The epigraphic Hebrew proper name from which *yḥwʿly,* Samaria 55, 60, "May the Most High restore to life, preserve," is taken[137] may be compared to biblical *yḥwʿly* (2 Chron. 29:4, *ketib*), Egyptian Aramaic *yḥwʿly*[138] Phoenician *yḥwmlk*, and Punic *yḥwʾln.*[139]

The Imperative

(1) *Inflection.* Table 22 gives the inflection of the *piel* imperative.

TABLE 22
***PIEL* IMPERATIVE**

	Singular	Plural
m.	*qtl*	–
f.	–	–

[136]See Cross and Freedman, *EHO*, p. 49. The diphthong *aw* regularly contracts in the North (*aw › ô*), but not in the South.

[137]Based on syntax and semantics, three possibilities exist for the epigraphic Hebrew form *yḥwʿly*: 1) that it represents a locative name parallel to *krm htl*, "the vineyard of the mound," and therefore, *krm yḥwʿly,* "the vineyard of *yḥwʿly*; 2) that it represents a masculine singular gentilic, "the inhabitant of *yḥwʿl*," or 3) that it represents the proper name. This latter interpretation is the most likely, based on the comparative evidence cited above.

[138]Grelot, *Documents araméens d'Egypte*, p. 497.

[139]Benz, *Personal Names in Phoenician and Punic*, p. 27.

(2) *Forms.* This section describes the extant verbs in the *piel* imperative.

Second masculine singular. Forms include:

Independent verbal forms: *ʾmṣ* , "Strengthen!" A 88:2; *nqh*, "Absolve!" KBL 2:1 (2x).

Proper name: *bqš*, "Seek (DN)!" Hest. 83:2.

Element of proper name: *ḥk-*, "Wait (for DN)!" L 20:2.

Piel imperatives are not marked morphologically by prefixes and the masculine singular forms are not marked by suffixes. All *piel* imperatives are so classified on the basis of comparative biblical forms.

The Infinitive

(1) *Inflection.* Table 23 on the next page illustrates the inflection of the *piel* infinitives.

TABLE 23
PIEL INFINITIVES CONSTRUCT AND ABSOLUTE

Infinitive Construct	Verb Type
–	Strong Verb
qtl	Verbs I-Gutteral
–	Verbs III-*ʾaleph*
–	Verbs I-*nun*
–	Hollow Verbs
qtt	Verbs III-*hê*

Infinitive Absolute	Verb Type
ql	Hollow Verb

(2) *Forms*. The extant infinitives construct and absolute in the *piel* are given below.

Infinitive construct. *ʿśr*, "to give a tithe," Ophel b:3;[140] *rpt*, "to weaken," L 6:6.[141]

Infinite absolute. *kl*, "finishing," Gezer 1:5.[142]

---

[140] *Lʿśr* is analyzed as a *piel* infinitive by A. Lemaire, "Archaeological Notes. 1: Les ostraca paléo-hébreux des fouilles de l'Ophel," *Levant* 10 (1978): 159. He cites as supporting biblical evidence the verbal forms from the root *ʿśr* which occur in Gen. 28:22 and Deut. 14:22.

[141] While the root *rph* occurs in the Bible, the infinitive construct is not attested there.

[142] The form *kl* is problematic. Suggestions include taking *kl* from the root *kwl*, as a masculine singular noun *kēl*, or as a *qal* infinitive absolute *kôl*, "measuring." Cf. D. Diringer and S.P. Brock, "Words and Meanings in Early

The Participle[143]

(1) *Inflection.* Table 24 illustrates the inflection of the *piel* participle.

Hebrew Inscriptions," in *Words and Meanings: Essays Presented to David Winton Thomas*, eds., P. R. Ackroyd and B. Lindars (Cambridge: University Press, 1968), p. 42; Gibson, *TSSI*, p. 3; J.B. Segal, " '*Yrḥ*' in the Gezer 'Calendar'," *JSS* 7 (1963): 219; J. G. Février, "Remarques sur le calendrier de Gézer," *Semitica* 1 (1948): 35-36; Donner and Röllig, *KAI*, no. 182.

Others take the form as from the root *klh*, as a *piel* perfect *killâ*, "He finished" or, as accepted here, as the *piel* infinitive absolute *kallē*, "finishing." Cf. J. Naveh, "A Hebrew Letter from the Seventh Century B.C.," *IEJ* 10 (1960): 134; S.S. Yeivin, "The Judicial Petition from Meẕad Ḫashavyahu," *BO* 19 (1962): 5; H.L. Ginsberg, "Review," *BJPES* II (1935): 49; A. Lemaire, "L'ostracon de Meṣad Ḥashavyahu (Yavneh-Yam) replacé dans son contexte," *Semitica* 21 (1971): 65.

Another suggestion, although far less likely, for the etymology of this word was that of G. Garbini, "Sur Note sul 'calendario' di Gezer," *AION*, n.s. Vi (1954-56): 124, who derived *kl* in the Gezer Inscription from *klʾ*, "chiudere, rinserrare," (= "incarcerate, imprison" › "store grain").

For a discussion of the word *kl* and the problems connected with it with special emphasis on the form *kl* at Meṣad Ḥashavyahu, see Pardee, "Meṣad Ḥashavyahu," *Maarav* 1/1 (1978): 41-42.

In a private communication, Pardee has suggested that others of the verbs (besides *wkl*) in the Gezer Calendar may also be infinitives absolute (e.g., *ʾsp* (Gezer 1:1), as in biblical *ʾāsōp*, "gathering," Jer. 8:13, etc.).

The first of these alternatives (*wkl* as a perfect) is doubtful on the basis of the syntax of the Gezer inscription, including parallels set up by the rest of the inscription, and the fact that there are no finite indicative verbal forms in the inscription. With these points in mind, *kl* should be a noun or verbal noun (infinitive absolute), "measuring," or "finishing." Beyond this point, *kl* remains essentially enigmatic.

Commentators have cited the Gezer form in their analysis of *kl* at Meṣad Ḥashavyahu, and referred to the fact that both texts, the harvest plays a key role. Generally, any solution offered regarding *kl* in Meṣad Ḥashavyahu is extended to include the Gezer form also. Lemaire, "L'ostracon de Meṣad Ḥashavyahu," *Semitica* 21 (1971): 64-68, has argued very forcefully that whatever *kl* may be, it is the same in both inscriptions.

Pardee ("Meṣad Ḥashavyahu," *Maarav* 1/1 (1978): 41-42) has offered an acceptable argument that *kl* (from *klh*, "finish") best fits the sense of the Meṣad Ḥashavyahu. After extending the usage of the root *klh* (in both texts associated with the harvest) to Gezer, one discerns that the only form from which this root syntactically fits the text is that of the *piel* infinitive absolute.

[143]Both the active and passive participles in epigraphic Hebrew begin with *mem* and are orthographically indistinguishable. Participial forms in epigraphic Hebrew are classified as active (*piel*) or passive (*pual*) on the basis of biblical Hebrew; cf. sec. 3.1.5.4, p. 137, and n. 145.

TABLE 24
***PIEL* PARTICIPLE**

	Singular	**Plural**
m.	*mqtl*	–
f.	–	–

(2) *Forms*. Two *mem*-preformative proper names represent the *piel* active participle.

Masculine singular. Proper names:

mnḥm, "comforter," A 72:1, *et cetera*, and *mnšh*, "he who causes (someone) to forget," Av (*IEJ* 13) 1:2.[144]

[144]Based on Genesis 41:51, Noth (*IPN*, pp. 64, 211, 222) explained the meaning for the last proper name as "May YH cause (someone) to forget (the death of a former child)." Based on this interpretation, *mnšh* may be given a more substantive meaning: "One who causes to forget (e.g., some misfortune)."

Genesis 41:51 yielded this conclusion: *wyqrʾ ywsp ʾt šm hbkwr mnšh ky nšny ʾlhym ʾlhym ʾt kl ʿmlly wʾt kl byt ʾby*, "And Joseph named his first born Menasseh 'because God made me forget all my troubles and all my father's house.'"

3.1.5.4 *Pual*

The Participle

(1) *Inflection.* Table 25 represents the inflection of the *pual* participle.

TABLE 25
***PUAL* PARTICIPLE**

	Singular	Plural
m.	*mqtl*	–
f.	–	–

(2) *Forms.* One pual participle is attested in epigraphic Hebrew.

Masculine singular. Proper name: *mšlm*, "One in covenant of peace," A 110:1, *et cetera.*[145]

[145]The participle, *mšlm*, "One in a covenant of peace," A 110:1, *et cetera*, is treated as passive on the basis of biblical Hebrew. This form derives from the root *šlm* and is common in the Bible (*mešullām*, Isa. 42:19 [independent verb], and 2 Kings 22:3, 1 Chron. 3:19, Neh. 11:7, etc. [proper name]), and at Elephantine (Cf. Cowley, *Aramaic Papyri of the Fifth Century*, p. 298).

On the basis of the biblical proper name, *mšlm* in epigraphic Hebrew is taken as passive, rather than active, even though the active participle would be orthographically identical in epigraphic Hebrew. See Noth, *IPN*, p. 174 and T. Nöldeke, *Encyclopaedia Britannia*, 1911 ed., s.v., "Semitic Languages," 1 Sp. 3294.

Extra-biblical evidence that the form *mšlm* is passive, rather than active, comes from the Akkadian name *Ištar-mušallimat*, according to Noth (*IPN*, p. 174, no. 1). However, *mušallimat* is an active participle in Akkadian., cf. F. Delitzsch, *Assyrisches Handwörterbuch* (Leipzig: J.C. Hinrichs'sche Buchhandlung, 1896), p. 256; W. Von Soden, *Grundriss der akkadischen Grammatik*, Pontifical Biblical Institute Analecta Orientalia (Rome, 1931-) 33/47, rev. ed., 1969, pp. 13, 110.

3.1.5.5 *Hiphil*

The Perfect

(1) *Inflection.* Table 26 illustrates the inflection of the *hiphil* perfect.

TABLE 26
***HIPHIL* PERFECT**

	Singular	Plural
3 m.	*hqtl* *hqtyl*	*hqtlw*
3 f.	–	–
2 m.	*hqtlt*	–
2 f.	–	–
1 c.	–	–

(2) *Forms.* This section describes the extant verbs in the *hiphil* perfect.

Third masculine singular. Forms include:

Independent verbal forms: *hṭh,* "He has inclined (his heart), applied (himself), given (his attention to)," A 40:4; *hyṭb*, "He favored," Ajrud 11:1; *hšb*, "He has returned," L 5:6.

P. Grelot, following Noth, translates *mšlm* as "replaced" (="given by God in the place of a dead infant"). Cf. *Documents araméens d'Egypte*, p. 479.

Independent verbal form with suffix: *(w)hbqydm*, "He is to hand them over," A 24:14-15.[146]

Element of proper name: *hṣl-*, "delivers," Gib S.I. 2; L 1:1, *et cetera.*

Element of proper name plus pronominal suffix: *hgln-*, "(DN) carried me away into exile," R 17:2 (Herr 61).

Second masculine singular. Independent verbal form:

(w)hsbt, "You should send (them) out," A 2:5-6; *([w)hš]bt)*, "You should return," MHY 1:14.

Third masculine plural. Independent verbal form:

hkw, "They struck," Siloam 1:4.

---

[146]The form *hbqydm* is interesting in that it shows the apparent root *bqd*, a dialectal variant of commonly attested biblical Hebrew *pqd*. This is one of two examples of the *b/p* interchange in epigraphic Hebrew.

The second example of this interchange between *bet* and *pê* comes from the same inscription, Arad 24:18, *bnbškm* (instead of *npškm*).

Hbqydm, which comes from a text characterized by extensive use of *matres lectionis* (Arad 24:14-15), proves that the stem vowel of the third person forms of the *hiphil* perfect was *-ī*.

The Imperfect

(1) *Inflection.* Table 27 illustrates the inflection for the *hiphil* imperfect.

TABLE 27
***HIPHIL* IMPERFECT**

	Singular	**Plural**
3 m.	*yqtl*	–
3 f.	–	–
2 m.	–	–
2 f.		–
1 c.	–	*nqtl*[a]

[a]*nqtl* is the assumed form for a strong verb. Only one first common plural *hiphil* imperfect, from a weak verb, is currently attested: *nšb,* "We will return (word)," A 111:4. Also, the text of A 111:4 is badly broken and cannot provide with certainty the context of the form in question.

(2) *Forms.* The next section describes the extant verbs in the *hiphil* imperfect.

Third masculine singular. Forms include:

Independent verbal forms: *y‹b›ʾ*,[147] "He will bring," L 5:9.

Jussive:[148] *yʾr*, "May (DN) cause to shine," KH 2:8; *[yʾ]r*, KH 1:3-4; *yrʾ*, "May (DN) cause to see," L 6:1; *yšmʿ*, "May (DN) cause to hear," L 2:1, 3:2, 4:1, 5:1, 8:1, 9:1 and MO 2:1.[149]

Independent verbal form with suffix: *(w)yʿlhw*, "He has taken him up," L 4:6-7, *yrʾk*, "May (DN) cause you to see," L 5:7.

Proper name: *yʾzn*, "May (DN) hear," A 59:5, *yʾz̊n̊*, A 58:4, *yrʾ*, "May (DN) cause to see," Avigad 11:1.[150]

Element of proper name: *yʾzn(yhw)*, "May (YH) hear," A 39:9; L 1:3; Av (*EI* 9) 6:1; Tell en Nasbeh 3:1, *yʾz̊n(yhw)*, L 1:2; *yqm(yhw)*, "May (YH) establish," A 39:1, *et cetera*, *(ʾḥ)yqm*, A 31:5; *(ʾl)yqm*, "May (El) establish," RR Seal

---

147The restoration is originally that of Michaud, "Les ostraca de Lakiš conservés à Londres," *Syria* 34 (1957): 48-49. It was rejected by Gibson (*TSSI*, pp. 44-45), but accepted by Lemaire (*Inscriptions hébraïques*, p. 117) and Pardee (*HHL*, pp. 96-97).

148The jussive is given a separate status from that of the imperfect, as *yʾr* and *yrʾ* establish the form of the independent *hiphil* jussive in epigraphic Hebrew. Cf. pp. 78, 93-96, esp. nn. 51, 52 (pp. 95-96) in this grammar.

149 *Yšmʿ* while classified here as a jussive for semantic reasons, is not marked as such by orthography.

150This form may be the *qal* jussive, rather than *hiphil*, "May (DN) see, look upon." Although the form is orthographically identical to the attested independent jussive, the analysis of proper names is not as certain as, for instance, an independent verbal form, especially if a given form may possibly occur in two stems and one can derive a sensible meaning in both.

8:1, *et cetera*;[151] *(ʾl)yʾr*, "May (El) enlighten," A 21:2; *(ʾl)yšb*, "May (El) restore," A 1:1, *et cetera.*[152]

First common plural. Independent verbal form: *nšb*, "We will return (word)," A 111:4.

Since there is no orthographic indicator for an internal long vowel in epigraphic Hebrew *hiphil* imperfects (in contrast to the usual orthography in Masoretic Hebrew), *qal* and *hiphil* imperfects are morphologically indistinguishable. Those forms labeled here as *hiphil* are treated as such on the basis of semantics, rather than orthography. (The vocalic elements of the morphology must, of course, be reconstructed in the absence of *matres lectionis*.)

The Imperative

(1) *Inflection.* Table 28 illustrates the inflection of the *hiphil* imperative.

[151]The forms *kn* from the epigraphic Hebrew proper name *ywkn* (RR Seal 8:2; TBM 1:2; Ain Shems 2:2) and *-qm* from *yhwqm* (Av NN 12:1, 13:1), *ywqm* (Herr 131:2), and *ʾḥqm* (Av (*IEJ* 13) Seal 2:2) may be interpreted as third masculine singular *qal* perfects (*-kān* and *-qām* respectively) analogous to biblical *ʾdnyqm (ʾădōnîqām)*, *ʾḥyqm (ʾăḥîqām)*, *yhwrm* (*yĕhôrām*), *ywrm* (*yorām*) and *yrm* (*yōrām*), or as abbreviations for *hiphil* imperfects, *-kn* (*-kin*) for *-ykn* (*-yākīn*) as in the biblical proper names *ywykyn*, *yhwykyn*, and *yhwykn*, and *-qm* (*-qīm*) for *-yqm* (*-yāqīm*) as in biblical *ywyqym*, *yhwyqym*, and *ywqym*.

[152]Other attestations of *yqm(yhw)* include Herr 105:1-2; B/L (26) 8:2; Gezer (?) Seal 1:2; *yqm(ẙh̊w)*, A 59:2; *yqm̊[yhw̥])*, A 74:3, 80:2., for *(ʾl)yqm*, Hest. 91:1; TBM 1:1; Beth-Shemesh 2:1; *(ʾl)yqm̊ , Av (EI 9)* 7:1., for *(ʾl)yšb*, A 2:1, 3:1, 4:1, 5:1, 6:1, 7:1, 8:1, 11:1, 16:2, 17:2, 18:1-2, 105:1, 106:1; B/L (26) 17:1; *([ʾl])yšb*, A 47:1; *(ʾl)yšb̊*, A 24:2; *(ʾl)yš[b]*, A 64:2; *([ʾl]yš[b]*, A 14:1; *(ʾl)‹ẙ›šb̊*, A 107:1; *(ʾl)yš̊b̊*, A 38:5; *([ʾl)y]šb*, A 10:1, 12:1; *(ʾl)yš[b]*, L 22:8; L V Ost. 1:8.

TABLE 28
***HIPHIL* IMPERATIVE**

	Singular	Plural
m.	*hqtl*[a]	*hqtlw*[b]
f.	–	–

[a]One epigraphic Hebrew form from a strong root, *hpqḥ*, permits us to posit the inflection *hqtl*. Due to the uncertainty of the passage which precedes *hpqḥ* in Lachish 3:4, the form has been the subject of several interpretations. However, syntactically, *hpqḥ* fits in clearly with the text of line 5 as an imperative. See Pardee, *HHL*, p. 85, after R. de Vaux, "Les Ostraca de Lachiš," *RB* 48 (1939):190-91.

[b]The form *hqtlw* is based on a strong verb, *qšb*, attested in Sam. C 1101:2–*hqšbw*, "Pay attention!"

2) *Forms.* This section describes the extant verbs in the *hiphil* imperative.

Masculine singular. Forms include:

Independent verbal form: *hwšʿ*, "Save!" KEK 3:3; KBL 3:1; *hpqḥ*, "Open!" L 3:4;[153] *hšb*, "Return (word)!" L 9:4.

Independent verbal form with pronominal suffix: *hd̊ʿm*, "Inform them!" Sam C 1101:2.[154]

---

[153]The root *pqḥ*, "open (usually the eyes)," but also once "open (the ears)" in Isaiah 42:20, is not attested in *hiphil* in the Bible (rather in *qal* and *niphal*), but the *piel/pael* occurs frequently in Aramaic and post-biblical Hebrew, and Modern Hebrew has the *hiphil* of this root. This distribution points to a fair amount of latitude exhibited by this root in various stems, at least in diachronic terms.

[154]*Dalet* is probably the second letter of this word, following Michaud, *Sur la Pierre et L'Argile* (Neuchatel: Delachaux and Niestle, 1958) and Gibson, *TSSI*, p. 15, since the stroke of the letter in question is not as long as that of the *resh* in lines 1 and 3. The form is read and interpreted differently by E.L. Sukenik, "Inscribed Hebrew and Aramaic Potsherds from Samaria," *PEQ* 65 (1933): 152-54 (*hrʿm*, "the two shepherds"), Albright, "Ostracon C1101 of Samaria," *PEQ* 68 (1936): 211-15 (*hp̊ʿm*, "this time, now"), and A. Lemaire,

Proper name: *hwšᶜ*, "Save (O DN)!" Driver Seal 1; L Seal 8:1; Herr 89:2; Hest. 78:2.

Element of proper name: *hwšᶜ*(yhw), "Save (O YH)!" MHY 1:7; L 3:1; R 3:1 (Herr 87); Hest. 72:1, 73:1-2; *hwšᶜ(*m), "Save (O Paternal Uncle, protector)," Jerusalem Seal 2:1.

Masculine plural. Forms include:

Independent verbal form: *hqšbw*, "Pay attention!" Sam C 1101:2.

Element of proper name: *hwdw(yhw)*, "Praise (YH)!" L 3:17.

Hwšᶜ is either the masculine singular *hiphil* imperative **hawšaᶜ* or **hōšaᶜ* "Save (O DN)!" the third masculine singular perfect, **hawšīaᶜ* or **hōšīaᶜ* "(DN has) saved," or the infinitive absolute **hawšēaᶜ* or **hōšēaᶜ*, "Save (O DN)!"

Hwšᶜ must be analyzed as the imperative when it occurs as an independent verbal form (Khirbet Beit Lei 3:1) and probably also in Khirbet el Kom 3:3, although the syntax and sense of line three is problematic,[155] and most likely also when it is a proper name or element thereof.[156]

A review of the vocalization and sense of *hwšᶜ*- as an element of a proper name in epigraphic Hebrew by various scholars reveals that most take the verbal element as the third

---

"L'ostracon C1101 de Samarie. Nouvel essai," *RB* 79 (1972): 565-70 *(h̊rᶜmh̊,* "fais les paître," p. 569) and in *Inscriptions hébraïques*, p. 246 ("donne-leur de la nourriture").

[155]Lemaire, "Les Inscriptions de Khirbet el-Qôm et L'ashérah de YHWH," *RB* (1977): 599, 602, reads *hwšᶜ* as the third masculine perfect, "he has saved," but W. Dever, "Iron Age Epigraphic Material from the area of Khirbet el-Kom," *HUCA* 40/41 (1969-70): 162, reads perhaps "salvation to him."

[156]In all but two cases (Lachish 3:1 and MHY 1:7) where *hwšᶜ*- occurs in ostraca, the form occurs as an element of a proper name, *hwšᶜyhw* (R 3:1 = Herr 87; Hest. 72:1, 73:1-2), *hwšᶜm* (Jerusalem Seal 2:1), as an independent proper name (L Seal 8:1; Herr 89:2; Hest. 78:2), and with the introductory preposition: *lhwšᶜ* (Driver Seal 1) on seals.

masculine singular perfect.[157] Noth,[158] basing his views on the biblical *hôšaʿăyāh* and *hôšēʿa*, takes both forms as third masculine singular perfects, although he admits the possibility of taking them as imperatives.[159]

Hwšʿ-, when it is an element of a proper name like *hwšʿyhw,* while perhaps a perfect, is more probably an imperative (based on biblical vocalization, i.e., *-a-* stem vowel rather than *-ī).*

Simply on the basis of orthography, *hwšʿ* could represent the perfect (biblical *hôšīʿa*), imperative *(hôšaʿ),* or the infinitive absolute *(hôšēʿa).* The meaning of the proper name has good sense in any of these three verbal categories: "(DN) has saved" (perfect), "Save (O DN)!" (imperative and infinitive absolute). In this instance, the infinitive absolute can be explained as having the sense of (=taking the place of) the imperative, as does the epigraphic Hebrew infinitive absolute *ntn* (often at Arad).

The vocalization ascribed to the proper name *hwšʿ* in the Bible *(hōšēaʿ)* is that of the infinitive absolute,[160] although Noth analyzes the biblical proper name as a perfect or imperative.[161] In support of taking *hwšʿ* in epigraphic Hebrew (and biblical Hebrew) as other than the infinitive absolute is the fact that the infinitive absolute is not a common element of proper names, Either in epigraphic Hebrew or in the Bible, although the same may be said of the imperative in independent names.

There is no orthographic indication of the stem vowel in the epigraphic Hebrew *hiphil* imperatives from strong roots (*hqšbw*, biblical *hqšybw*), while in imperatives derived from some weak verbs (*hwšʿ* and *hwdw-*), the presence of original diphthongs, or,

---

[157]See Pardee, "Meṣad Ḥashavyahu," *Maarav* 1/1 (1978): 47, "Hoshayahu" (biblical *hôšaʿăyā*, also Lemaire, "L'ostracon de Meṣad Ḥashavyahu," *Semitica* 21 (1971): 61; *Inscriptions hébraïques*, pp. 261, 264, "YHWH a procuré le salut" (*Inscriptions* hébraïques, p. 264), and "YHWH a sauvé," "YHWH a libéré" (*Inscriptions hébraïques*, p. 102); Hestrin and Dayagi-Mendels, *Inscribed Seals*, p. 96; Zevit, *MLAHE*, pp. 22, 25; Cross and Freedman, *EHO*, p. 53, and Cross, "Epigraphic Notes on Hebrew Documents of the Eighth-Sixth Centuries B.C. II. The Murabbaʿat Papyrus and the Letter found Near Yabneh-Yam," *BASOR* 165 (1962): 43, n. 32 (*hawšiʿyahu*).

[158]*IPN*, pp. 21, 32, 176.

[159]Ibid., p. 32.

[160]Cf. *BDB*, p. 446 (*hôšēaʿ*, 1 Sam. 25:26, etc.). The proper name *hwšʿ* in epigraphic Hebrew has been vocalized by Hestrin and Dayagi-Mendels (*Inscribed Seals*, p. 102) as *Hosheʿa*, and Zevit (*MLAHE*, p. 17) as *hawšēaʿ* or *hōšēaʿ*. This is the vocalization of the biblical infinitive absolute.

[161]Cf. Noth, *IPN*, pp. 22, 32, 36, 176.

perhaps, the presence of long vowels, is indicated by the consonantal element of the (original) diphthong.[162]

The form of the third masculine plural imperative is distinguished from other forms by the *m.l. waw* (*hqšbw* and *hwdw-*). All epigraphic Hebrew *hiphil* imperatives have the prefix *hê*. The *hiphil* perfect and imperative (the masculine forms, singular and plural) are orthographically indistinguishable. Criteria for establishing a form as one or the other then, rests largely upon semantics and context, or, in the case of proper names, on biblical parallels, rather than on orthography.

The Infinitive

(1) *Inflection.* Table 29 illustrates the inflection for the *hiphil* infinitive construct.

TABLE 29
***HIPHIL* INFINITIVE CONSTRUCT**

Infinitive Construct	Verb Type
hqtl	Strong Verb
–	Verbs III-ʾ*aleph*
htl	Verbs I-*nun*
hql *hqyl*	Hollow Verbs
–	Verbs III-*hê*

The *hê* preceding the first root consonant is the morphological feature of the *hiphil* infinitive in epigraphic Hebrew. The *plene* form *lhʿyd* establishes the form of the *hiphil*

[162]The internal *waw* may represent the contracted diphthong *-ō*. Other epigraphic Hebrew imperatives from weak roots are not marked for long vowels: *hdʿm* (biblical *hwdyʿm, hôdîʿēm*), and *hšb*. In the Bible, this latter verb occurs both with and without the *yod mater lectionis* (*hšyb*, 2 Kings 8:6; *hšb*, Gen. 20:7, etc.).

infinitive construct in epigraphic Hebrew, with *-ī* as the stem vowel.

(2) *Forms.* The infinitives construct extant in epigraphic Hebrew are listed below.

Infinitives construct. Forms with introductory preposition include:

lhg[d], "to inform," L 3:1-2 (Verbs I-*nun*); *lhʿyd*, "to warn," A 24:18 (middle weak root); *lhš[b]*, "to return," MHY 12-13 (middle weak root); *[lhš]qt*, "to weaken, pacify," L 6:6-7 (strong root).[163]

The Participle

(1) *Inflection.* Table 30 illustrates the inflection for the *hiphil* participle.

TABLE 30
***HIPHIL* PARTICIPLE**

	Singular	Plural
m.	*mqtl*	–
f.	–	–

(2) *Forms.* This section describes the extant *hiphil* participles.

Masculine singular. Forms include:

Independent proper name: *mwqr*, "(DN) makes rare, precious," Tel Ira 1:3.

[163] *[Lhš]qt* is restored at the crucial point which prohibits a certain argument in favor of taking the form as specifically a *hiphil* infinitive.

Element of proper name: *mkbr-*, "The one who makes many (is exalted)," Hazor 5.[164]

The *hiphil* participle in epigraphic Hebrew has a prefix *mem*. Orthographically, it is indistinguishable from the *piel* and *pual* participles.

The first element of the epigraphic Hebrew proper name *mkbr(m)*, "the one who makes many is exalted," Hazor 5, is probably a masculine singular *hiphil* participle from the root *kbr*, "be much, many" (in *hiphil*, "to make many, great").[165] The form, *mkbrm*, is composed of two elements: *mkbr* + *rm*.[166]

The loss of one letter (a second *resh*) in these forms may merely represent the regular orthography of long consonants. The

---

[164] A new reading by Naveh has stirred a discussion of this word; cf. J. Naveh, "*lmkbrm ʾw lmkbdm?* ['Belonging to Makbiram' or 'Belonging to the Food-Servers'?]," *EI* 15 (1981): 301-2. Naveh cites the shorter stroke of the fourth letter after the *lamed* as proof that it should be read as *dalet* rather than *resh*, hence *mkbdm*, not *mkbrm*. He interprets the form as a piel plural participle, *mĕkabbĕdim*, "food/drink servers," citing as supporting evidence, the ninth century Aramaic inscriptions *ltb[ḥ]yʾ* and *lšqyʾ*. These latter two forms designate certain categories of officials or personnel whose positions required serving food/drink.

Naveh's arguments for reading the Hebrew form as *mkbdm* are not entirely convincing; he himself calls attention to the fact that *mkbd* does not occur in biblical Hebrew as an adjective with the meaning of "server of food or drink." Further, Naveh's suggestion that ninth century Aramaic evidence supports his reading of *mkbdm* over *mkbrm* is weak. Finally, the absence of a long foot on the letter in question does not necessarily indicate a *dalet* instead of a *resh* in Hebrew epigraphy. As Naveh himself points out (p. 301), the leg of the *dalet* is generally shorter than that of a *resh*; it is not always so.

The word *mkbr̊m* is read in an eighth century Phoenician inscription by B. Delavault and A. Lemaire. They hesitate between the reading *mkbrm* and *mkbdm*; cf. "Les inscriptions phéniciennes de Palestine," *Rivista di Studi Fenici* 7 (1979): 8-9.

[165] *Mkbr* is classified here as a *hiphil* participle, rather than *piel* or *pual* (whose forms also begin with *mem*, and are morphologically indistinguishable from the *hiphil*) on the basis of biblical evidence. The root *kbr* only occurs in *hiphil* in the Bible and then it is attested rarely. The masculine singular active participle occurs once in Job 36:31 with substantive force: *ytn ʾkl lmkbyr*, "he gives food in abundance."

[166] This interpretation was first suggested by Y. Yadin, Hazor II (Jerusalem: Magnes Press, 1960), p. 72. His own first suggestion, however, was to analyze *mkbrm* as *mkb* (as a theophoric appellative) plus *rm* (also as a theophoric element). This latter hypothesis is unlikely as *mkb* occurs nowhere else as a deity name (or as any other word, for that matter).

pronunciation consisted not of two separate sounds, but of one long one (*makbīrrām*). The spelling could therefore contain one sign instead of two identical consonants. The orthographic conclusion which follows, then, is that in epigraphic Hebrew, long consonants are never written twice.

Outside of epigraphic Hebrew, analogous forms exhibiting single writing of double consonants are the biblical *mšlmwt* = *mšlm* + *mwt*[167] and Phoenician *mlkty* = *mlk kty and dʿmlk* = *dʿm mlk.*[168]

One must distinguish between the phenomenon of single writing of geminated consonants in normal prose and in proper names. In the former, the phenomenon is called haplography (as in *ḥyhwh*, L 3:9), where one would expect the two identical consonants to have been written twice. In proper nouns, however, the two elements are permanently joined (having had historically no vowel between the two like consonants), and one would not expect the two consonants to have been written twice (because they were not perceived as two words and were not pronounced twice).

The form of the proper name *mwqr* is a masculine singular active participle from the root *yqr*; in *hiphil*, this root is causative, "to make rare, precious," as in "(DN) makes precious." The *waw* is expected in the *hiphil* participle derived from Verbs I-*yod.*[169]

3.1.5.6 *Hophal*

(1) *Forms*. Only one epigraphic Hebrew form is definitely a *hophal* form. One other form is dubious. The perfect is

---

[167]2 Chron. 28:12 and Neh. 11:3; cf. Yadin, *Hazor*, p. 72, n. 19.

[168]The convention of writing one sign for what has become a long consonant existed in Phoenician; see Z. Harris, *A Grammar of the Phoenician Language* (New Haven: American Oriental Society, 1936), p. 30. *Dʿmlk* is the proper name *dʿmmlk*, "the supporter is King" (see Harris, *A Grammar of the Phoenician Language*, p. 96); also *mlkty* for *mlk kty*, "King of Kitti" (Harris, Ibid., p. 118).

This practice is possibly attested also at Elephantine (see Yadin, *Hazor*, n. 17, and "A Hebrew Seal from Tell Jemmeh," *Eretz Israel* 6 (1960): 54).

[169]The form *mwqr* occurs in a census document found by excavators at Tel Ira, near Beersheba; cf. I. Beit-Arieh, "A First Temple Period Census Document," *PEQ* 115/2 (1983)105-8. There are no known biblical or extra-biblical attestations of this name, except one occurrence of the name engraved on the rim of an eighth century tripod from Nimrod. The closest biblical parallel for a hiphil participial proper name is *mwlyd (môlîd*, 1 Chron. 2:29), also from Verbs I-*yod.*

represented by the word *hgd*, "It has been reported," L 3:13.[170] The form, from the Verbs I-*nun* root *ngd*, is consistent with the biblical verb *huggad* (Josh. 9:24, *et cetera*).

The place name *yhẘd̊h̊*, "Judah," is attested twice in epigraphic Hebrew: *yhẘd̊h̊*, KBL 1:2 [171] and *yhwd[h]*, A 40:13. The *plene* orthography of the Arad form is certain (the internal *waw mater lectionis* for long *ū*). The etymology of the word is uncertain,[172] although *yhwdh* has been taken as the third masculine singular *hophal* imperfect from the root *ydh*, "to thank, praise," meaning "praised, object of praise."[173]

---

[170]The criteria for analysis as a passive comes from biblical Hebrew, where *hophal* is the passive of *hiphil*. *Hgd* morphologically resembles the epigraphic Hebrew *hiphil* perfect (e.g., *hyṭb*), the biblical *hiphil* perfect (*higgîd*, Gen. 3:11, etc.), imperative (*haggēd*, 2 Sam. 18:21, etc.) or infinitive absolute (*haggēd*, Judges 14:12, etc.), or the biblical *hophal* infinitive absolute (huggēd, Jos. 9:24, etc.), or perfect (*huggad*, Jos. 9:24, etc.).

By semantics alone, the meaning of *hgd* in epigraphic Hebrew (Lachish 3:13) is passive: *wlʿbdk hgd lʾmr*, "and to your servant, it was told." Lachish 3 provides no antecedent for *hgd* as an active *hiphil*, rather, the syntax is correct with *hgd* analyzed as a *hophal* (e.g., *wygd lyhwsʿ lʾmr*, "and it was told to Joshua," Jos. 10:17).

In choosing between the perfect and infinitive absolute, the former is more likely if again the reasoning is based upon comparative biblical evidence, where the infinitive absolute *hgd* always precedes the perfect (e.g., *hgd hgd ly, huggēd huggad lî*, "It was told to me," Ruth 2:11, and Jos. 9:24), but the perfect may occur alone (*hgd ly, huggad lî*, Isa. 21:2, and *whgd lk, wĕhuggad lĕkā*, Deut. 17:4).

[171]Naveh, "Old Hebrew Inscriptions in a Burial Cave," *IEJ* 13 (1963): 83 (followed by Gibson, *TSSI*, pp. 57-58 and Zevit, *MLAHE*, p. 30, no. 108), first read *yhd̊*, "Judah." Cross, in a later study, "Khirbet Beit Lei," in *NEATC* (1970), p. 301 and n. 8, noticed the faint *hê*: *yhdh̊*, "Judah," and Lemaire, "Khirbet Beit Lei," *RB* 83 (1976): 558-59 read *yhẘd̊h̊*. This reading is accepted here, although it remains uncertain (cf. Zevit, *MLAHE*, p. 30, n. 20).

[172]L. Koehler and W. Baumgartner, *Lexicon in Testamenti Libros*, p. 367. See W.F. Albright, "A Revision of Early Hebrew Chronology," *JPOS* 1 (1920-1921): 68; J. Lewy, "The Old West Semitic Sun-God Ḥammu," *HUCA* 18 (1944): 479; *BDB*, p. 397.

[173]See G.A. Buttrick, ed., "Name," *Interpreters Dictionary of the Bible*, vol. 3 (Nashville: Abingdon Press, 1962), p. 505, and W. Borée, *Die alten Ortsnamen Palastinas* (Hildesheim: Georg Olms Verlagsbuchhandlung, 1968), p. 101, who analyzes the form as a *hophal* third masculine singular imperfect with locative ending.

3.1.5.7 *Pilpel*

(1) *Forms.* One reduplicated root occurs in epigraphic Hebrew: *klkl-*, "He has sustained, nourished," the first element of the proper name *klklyhw*, Av NN 6:1-2.[174]

3.1.6 Conclusion

Principally, epigraphic Hebrew verbs follow the rules of triliterality, and lend themselves to a comprehensive study of verbal stems (only *hithpael* is as yet unattested) and root type. Finite and other verbal forms are attested for each stem and are proven by the evidence at hand. Even though particular attestations of certain forms (such as the first common plural *qal* perfect) are not as yet a part of the textual evidence, the material which is available to us, proves the existence of the major finite and infinite forms (perfect, imperfect, imperative, *et cetera*).

Within this particular subset, epigraphic Hebrew orthography indicates certain aspects of some specific forms, e.g., the masculine singular *qal* passive participle, as *ʾrwr*, "cursed (be)," the final vowel of the first common singular *qal* perfect, as *ktbty*, "I wrote," the preformative of the masculine singular *piel*

[174]The Bible has the proper name *klkl* (*kalkōl*), 1 Kings 5:11 and 1 Chron. 2:6, and the proper name *klklyh* occurs at Elephantine. Biblical *klkl* (*kalkōl*) is a hypocoristicon for epigraphic Hebrew *klklyhw*, "God has sustained;" see Avigad, "New Names on Hebrew Seals," p. 68. The base of *kalkōl* is *qalqul* or *qalqāl*; see Bauer and Leander, *Historische Grammatik*, p. 482. For the form at Elephantine, cf. Cowley, *Aramaic Papyri of the Fifth Century*, p. 292. Grelot, *Documents araméens d'Egypte*, p. 476, on *klklyh*, discounts Noth's analysis for the derivation of *klkl*, preferring the interpretation also adopted in this grammar (*klkl* from *kwl*, "(DN) has sustained"). Avigad ("New Names on Hebrew Seals," *EI* 12 (1975): 68) claims that the name *klklyh* at Elephantine is problematic–the final *hê* is unclear and there is uncertainty regarding whether it is a proper name.

Noth related the etymology of the biblical proper name to Arabic, and gave the meaning "small, fat," while Albright related it to the Akkadian name of a plant. Cf. Noth, *IPN*, p. 226, no. 794, cites Arabic *kulkulun*, "klein und dick." However, *klkl* is best interpreted as coming from the root *kwl*, "comprehend, contain," as a masculine singular *pilpel* perfect verb meaning "sustain, support, nourish." This interpretation is often reflected in the *pilpel* of this verb in the Bible (Gen. 45:11, etc.), cf. *BDB*, p. 465. Avigad, "New Names on Hebrew Seals," *EI* 12 (1975): 68, cites both Gen. 45:11 and Gen. 50:21 as biblical examples of the *pilpel* verb in question, plus the direct object in a phrase having the sense of "sustaining, supporting and nourishing" someone.

active participle, *mnḥm*, "he who comforts," the assimilation of *n*- in the third masculine singular *niphal* imperfect *ylqh*, "he, it will be taken," and the stem vowel of the third masculine singular hiphil, as in the suffixed form *hbqydm*, "he is to hand them over," to name but a few.

3.2 The Pronoun

3.2.1 The Personal Pronoun

3.2.1.1 The Independent personal pronoun

Three independent subject pronouns are attested in epigraphic Hebrew. Two additional pronouns are partially restored. Table 31 illustrates these pronouns.

TABLE 31
INDEPENDENT PERSONAL PRONOUNS

	Singular	**Plural**
3 m.	*hʾ*	–
3 f.	–	–
2 m.	*ʾ[t]*	–
2 f.	–	–
1 c.	*ʾny*, *ʾnk[y]*	*nḥnw*

(1) *Forms.* Both singular and plural independent personal pronouns are attested in epigraphic Hebrew.

Singular. *ʾny* "I," is attested as one form of the first common singular subject pronoun in epigraphic Hebrew.[175]

ʾny mlkty bk[l...], "I became/have become king in all...," A 88:1.

ʾnky, "I," the second of the biblical forms, was proposed by Pardee[176] (*ʾnk[y]*, L 6:8) for epigraphic Hebrew, but is not proven, due to the broken nature of the text in which this form occurs.

The second masculine singular subject pronoun "you" has been restored in an inscription from Kuntillet Ajrud.[177] The form is not certain, however, as the text is broken after the *ʾaleph*.

hšlm ʾ[t],[178] "Is it well with you?," Ajrud 15:3.

The third masculine singular subject pronoun "he" is attested three times in epigraphic Hebrew, twice as an independent form *hʾ* at Ajrud 13 and Arad 18:10, and once (Arad 40:12) with the coordinating conjunction, *whʾ*.[179]

---

175 *ʾny* occurs also in biblical Hebrew (as well as in Phoenician, Moabite and Akkadian), where *ʾny* is one of two words representing the first common singular subject pronoun.

176Cf. *HHL*, pp. 100, 315, 244.

177Cf. D. A. Chase, "A Note on an Inscription from Kuntillet ʿAjrud," *BASOR* 246 (1982): 63.

178The restoration *ʾ[t]* is that of Chase, "A Note on the Inscription from Kuntillet ʿAjrud," *BASOR* 246 (1982): 65 and n. 15. The form of the pronoun *ʾt*, "you," without *-h mater lectionis* occurs also in biblical Hebrew (e.g., Psalm 6:4, etc.)

179*Hʾ* is also the independent subject pronoun in Phoenician, Moabite and Old Aramaic, cf. Jean and Hoftijzer, *Dictionnaire des inscriptions sémitiques de l'ouest*, p. 61.

The *ʾaleph* of *hʾ* could be historical, a final *m.l.* for *-ū*, or a consonant (**huʾa*). That the *ʾaleph* may have been original and an indication of a consonantal pronunciation is supported by Ethiopic *weʾĕtû*(= *huʾa-tu*) and Assyrian *ya-u-a* (for *yhwʾ*); see Cowley, *Genenius*, p. 107, n. 6a. On the other hand, Ugaritic shows only *w* (*hw*).

Waw is not used to mark the internal vowel *-ū* as it frequently is in biblical Hebrew. Cf. Zevit, *MLAHE*, pp. 28, 31, who admits the uncertainty connected with the *ʾaleph*, and vocalizes *hʾ* as **hūʾ* or **hū*.

brk hʾ lyhw‹h›, “Blessed be he to YHWH,” Ajrud 13.

byt yhwh hʾ yšb, “He is staying in the house of YHWH,” A 18:9-10.

whʾ hmktb bqš [wlʾ ntt]y, “And he tried to obtain the report [but I would not give (it to him)](?),” A 40:12.

Plural. The first common plural *nḥnw*, “we,” occurs once in epigraphic Hebrew, at Lachish:[180]

wydʿ ky ʾl mśʾt lkš nḥnw šmrm, “And he will know that we are watching the Lachish (fire-) signals ,” L 4:10-11.

3.2.2 Pronominal Suffixes

3.2.2.1 The Possessive suffix

The possessive suffix in epigraphic Hebrew occurs on singular and plural nouns and has a genitive relation with these nouns. Table 32 gives the extant suffixes for singular and plural nouns in epigraphic Hebrew.

The *waw* is used, not as a medial *m.l.*(-*ū*, but as a final *m.l.* in this word (Old Aramaic: *hw*, “he”). For a discussion of the etymology of *hwʾ*, see Cowley, *Gesenius*, p. 107. The *ʾaleph* of the biblical form is interpreted by Gesenius as a possible orthographic addition closing the final long vowel.

[180]The regular biblical form is *ʾnḥnw*, but *nḥnw* occurs several times in the Bible (Gen. 42:11, Exod. 16:7-8, Num. 32:32, and Lam. 3:42).

TABLE 32
FORMS OF THE SUFFIXED PERSONAL PRONOUN

		On Sing. Nouns	On Plural Nouns	Meaning
Sing.				
	1c.	*-y*	*-y*	"my"
	2 m.	*-k*	*-yk, -ykh*	"your"
	2 f.	–	–	"your"
	3 m.	*-h, -w, -yw*[a]	*-w, -yw. -yh*[b]	"his"
	3 f.	–	–	"her"
Plur.				
	1c.	–	–	"our"
	2 m.	*-km*	–	"your"
	2 f.	–	–	"your"
	3 m.	*-m*	–	"their"
	3 f.	–	–	"their"

a *ʾḥyw*, "his brother," MO 2:7-8 is understood as the masculine singular noun *ʾḥ* plus the third masculine singular pronominal suffix, as in biblical Hebrew *ʾḥyw*, Gen. 4:2, *et cetera* (note the alternative biblical form as well: *ʾḥyhw*, Jer. 34:9). This interpretation rests on the premise that in epigraphic Hebrew, masculine plural nouns with this suffix are not normally written with *yod* (i.e., *ʾnsw*, "his people", L 3:17-18 [note, however, the possible exception *pnyw*, "his face", KH 2:9]).

bThere is a possible problem associated with the form *-yh* from KEK 3:3 as mentioned on pp. 157-58 in n.182.

(1) *Forms*. This section illustrates the possessive suffixes on attested nouns which are grouped by person, number, and gender.

First common singular suffix. The first common singular suffix occurs on singular and plural nouns, as well as in proper names:

a) *Singular nouns.* *ʾdny*, "my lord," L 2:1; *qṣry*, "my harvest," MHY 1:9; *kṣʾty*, "when I leave (according to my leaving)," A 16:3; *ʾyšy*, "my husband," MO 2:3.

b) *Plural nouns.* *ʾḥy*, "my comrades," MHY 1:10,11.

c) *Proper names.* *ʾby*, "my father," A 39:11; *ʾḥy*, "my brother," A 39:6 (also *ʾḥy-*, A 35:3); *ḥmy*, "my father-in-law," Av NN 1:1, *et cetera*; *ml⟨ʾ⟩ky*, "my messenger," A 97:1 (?); *s[m]ky*, "my support," L Seal 21:1 (?).

Second masculine singular suffix. The second masculine singular suffix occurs on singular and plural/dual nouns:

a) *Singular nouns.* *ʾḥk*, "your brother," A 16:1; *mbytk*, "from your house," A 16:4; *bytk*, "your house," A 16:2, *et cetera*; *bnk*, "your son," A 21:1; *bḥtmk*, "with your seal," A 13:3, 17:6-7; *ḥrpk*, "your scorner," KBL 7:1-2; *ʿbdk*, "your servant," L 2:3-4, *et cetera*; *ʾmtk̊*, "your maidservant," MO 2:2; *ydk*, "your hand," MO 2:3; *šlḥk*, "your sending," L 3:7; *šlmk*, "your welfare," A 18:3.

b) *Plural/dual nouns.* *ʾlhyk*, "your God," L 6:12-13; *ʾlhykh*, "your God," Khirbet Beit Lei 1:1; *ydyk*, "your two hands," L 6:6; *lpnyk*, "before you," A 7:6.

Third masculine singular suffix. The third masculine singular suffix occurs on singular and plural/dual nouns:

a) *Singular nouns.* *ʾm̊th*, "his maidservant," Silwan 2:2; *wlʾšrth*, "and to his Asherah," Ajrud 14:2, 15:6; KEK 3:5; *lbh*, "his heart," A 40:4; *hnqbh*, "it's being tunneled through," Siloam 1, 3-4; *ʿbdh*, "his servant," MHY 1:2, *et cetera*; *rʿw*, "his fellow," Siloam 1:2, 3, 4.[181]

---

[181] The suffix *-w* on a singular noun derived from Verbs III-*yod* is unusual and poses many questions. The biblical noun *rʿ (rēaʿ)*, "friend, companion," is attested one hundred and fifteen times with the third masculine

b) *Plural/dual nouns*. *yrḥw*, "his two months," *wʾnšw*, "and his people," L 3:17-18; *mṣryh*, "from his enemies," KEK 3:3.[182]

---

singular suffix *-hw (ēhû)*, but once with *-w (ô)* in Jeremiah 6:21. Since the origins of this noun are found in the root *rʿh*, the suffix expected on all singular nouns forms is the former *(-hw)*; see J. Barth, *Die Pronominalbildung in den semitischen Sprachen* (Hildesheim: Georg Olms, 1967; reproduced from the first ed., Leipzig, 1913), p. 49, par. 19b and Blau, *A Grammar of Biblical Hebrew*, p. 25, par. 7.2.1.5.2.

Cross and Freedman (*EHO*, p. 50 and n. 28) vocalize the epigraphic Hebrew *rʿw* as *reʿew* ‹ *rēʿēhū*, based on syncope of the *hê*. Zevit (*MLAHE*, p. 20, n. 17) asserts that Cross and Freedman should consider the *-w* of *rʿw* as a *m.l.* for *ô*; see Zevit, op. cit.

Both Cross and Freedman, in later studies, modify their analyses of the suffix on the noun in question, the former positing the shift from *-uhu › -ū › -ō*, the latter positing the development *uh › aw › ō* (but, as pointed out by Zevit [*MLAHE*, p. 20, n. 17], there is "no phonetic explanation for the development *uh › aw › ō* which he [Freedman] posits."); see Cross, "The Cave Inscriptions from Khirbet Beit Lei," in *NEATC*, 1970, p. 305, n. 3, and Freedman, "The Massoretic Text and the Qumran Scrolls: A Study in Orthography," *Textus 2* (1962): 93.

Although the final step in both analyses is possibly correct (that *-w* in the third masculine singular pronominal suffix represents a *m.l. ō*), the development to that point remains questionable; see Zevit, *MLAHE*, p. 20, n. 17.

Zevit (op. cit., pp. 19-20) posits a possible, though unproven solution for the suffix in question on *rʿw* when he relates this noun to the singular biblical nouns *ʿēṣ*, *ʿēd*, *lēah*, and *dēaʿ* which commonly used the *-w* suffix. In this instance, the epigraphic Hebrew form *rʿw* would be best viewed as a new singular (absolute *rēaʿ*), based on the plural *rēʿīm*, but as a back-formation of such, and which was no longer considered specifically linked to Nouns III-*yod*.

For further discussion of the form *rʿw* in epigraphic Hebrew, see D. Pardee, "Review of *Matres Lectionis* in *Ancient Hebrew Epigraphs* by Z. Zevit," *CBQ* 44 (1982): 503-4. Pardee remains unconvinced that *-w* in epigraphic Hebrew functioned as a *m.l.* for the third masculine singular suffix on singular nouns. He correctly points out that this uncertainty will remain (re: *rʿw*) until a completely clear form occurs which demonstrates this specific suffix. The preponderance of Biblical evidence for the etymology of *rʿ*, "friend," from a III–*yod* root and a comparison with plural forms (*ʾnšw* = "his men") favor Pardee's position.

[182]*[ʿṣmtw]*, "his bones," Silwan 2:2 is a restored plural noun with pronominal suffix.

The form and analysis of *mṣryh* is that of Lemaire, "Khirbet el-Qôm," *RB* 84 (1977): 599, 601. As Lemaire himself points out, line 3 of this inscription poses serious problems of reading and interpretation.

Lemaire's reading involves major syntactic difficulties. According to him, the line reads *wmṣryh. lʾšrth. hwšʿ lh*, "et ‹par son ashérah;› de ses ennemis {par son ashérah}, il l'a sauvé (ou sauve-le)." Lemaire's strongest argument is his emphasis upon biblical parallels such as Psalm 34:7, *ūmikkol ṣārōtāyw hōšīʿō*, and Psalm 44:8, *kī hōšaʿtānū miṣṣārēynū* placement in the

Second masculine plural suffix. The second masculine plural suffix occurs on singular nouns:

Singular noun. bnkm, "your son," A 40:1; *nbškm*, "your lives," A 24:18.

Third masculine plural suffix. The third masculine plural suffix is possibly attested in epigraphic Hebrew on a singular noun.

Singular noun. ymm, "their day," Ajrud 4:1.[183]

The first common singular possessive suffix is attested in epigraphic Hebrew as *-y* on singular and plural nouns. The possessive suffix is present on the infinitive construct in the form *kṣʾty*, "when I leave" (specifically, "when (it is) my leaving"), A 16:3. The first common singular possessive suffix is not attested on feminine nouns.

The second masculine singular possessive suffix is likewise attested on masculine and feminine nouns and corresponds with the biblical form *-k* on singular nouns (*ʿbdk,* "your servant;" *ʾmtk̊*, "your maidservant;" MO 2:2; *ydk,* "your hand;" MO 2:3) and *-yk* on plural/dual nouns (*ʾlhyk*, "your God;" *ydyk*, "your two hands;" *lpnyk*, "before you"). One epigraphic Hebrew form, *ʾlhykh*, KBL 1:1, illustrates the long form of the second masculine singular suffix.[184]

---

epigraphic Hebrew phrase of *lʾšrth* between the suffixed noun and verb is difficult to explain contextually. Lemaire compares the suffixed noun *mṣryh* to the biblical *mṣryw*, "his enemies," as in Deut, 33:7 etc., but the regular third masculine singular suffix on plural nouns in epigraphic Hebrew is *-w* (biblical *-yw*). If, however, Lemaire's reading is correct, *ṣryh* reveals an uncontracted diphthong on a plural noun before a third masculine singular pronominal suffix, otherwise not attested in epigraphic (Judean) Hebrew.

The Khirbet el-Kom inscriptions are dated to the 8th-7th century B.C., leaving open the possibility that the spelling of *-yh* in *mṣryh* represents archaic writing (for -yhw). Biblical Hebrew attests to a third masculine singular suffix (*-yhw, -êhû*) on plural nouns in Habbakuk 3:10 (*ydyhw*, "its [m.s.] hands") and Job 24:23 (*ʿynyhw*, "his eyes"); cf. Cowley, *Gesenius*, p. 258.

[183]The interpretation of *ymm* is open to question. The final *mem* could represent the suffix under discussion, although it perhaps represents the ending of a plural noun "days," or an adverbial ending. See also p. 161 in this grammar.

[184]The reading of *ʾlhykh* instead of *ʾlhy kl*, "God of all (the earth)," is that of F.M. Cross, "The Cave Inscriptions from Khirbet Beit Lei," in *NEATC*

The third masculine singular possessive suffix is attested in epigraphic Hebrew on singular nouns most commonly as *-h* (*lbh*, "his heart"), although the suffix occurs as *-w* on one noun (*rʿw*, "his fellow").[185]

The suffix *-h* is also attested on an infinitive construct *hnqbh*, "its being tunneled through."[186]

On plural nouns, the third masculine singular suffix in epigraphic Hebrew is attested both as *-w*[187] as in *wʾnšw*, "and his people," Lachish 3:18, and as *-yw*, as in *pnyw*, "his face," KH 2:9; *-yw* is the standard orthography in biblical Hebrew (e.g.,*ʾnšyw*).[188]

(1970), p. 301, and P.D. Miller, "Psalms and Inscriptions," *VTSup* 32 (1981): 321.

[185]See pp. 156-57, n. 181 in this grammar. Zevit (*MLAHE*, p. 21, no. 53) posits a second epigraphic Hebrew singular noun with the *-w* pronominal suffix: *qṣrw*, "his harvest," Meṣad Ḥashavyahu 1:6, and challenges other interpretations, notably that of Pardee, "The Judicial Plea from Meṣad Ḥashavyahu (Yavneh Yam)," *Maarav* 1/1 (1978): 45-46, who takes the *w*, not as a pronominal suffix on *qṣr*, but rather as a conjunction before the verbal form which follows it. Pardee's syntactic arguments seem the most convincing and the lack of frequent evidence for the third masculine singular pronominal suffix (*-w*) in epigraphic Hebrew dispel Zevit's interpretation of *qṣrw* in Meṣad Ḥashavyahu 1:6.

[186]In contrast to epigraphic Hebrew, the most frequent orthography of the third masculine singular suffix in biblical Hebrew is not *h, but -w* (for *-ô*), with *waw m.l.* for long *ō*, while the feminine suffix in biblical Hebrew is *-h (-āh).*

The *hê* suffix on singular nouns in epigraphic Hebrew may indicate the use of *hê* as a *m.l.* for *ō* in pre-biblical times, *ahu › aw › ô*. On the other hand, the absence of the *waw* as *m.l.* for *ō* in pre-Qumranic texts might lead one to vocalize a *hê* suffix possibly as containing consonantal *hê*. One possible and one tentative epigraphic Hebrew form do little to dismiss this notion; the suffixed noun *rʿw* in the Siloam inscription possibly contains the *waw m.l.* for *ō*, and *qṣrw (qaṣīrō)*, "his harvest," in Meṣad Ḥashavyahu 1:6 is a less likely example. By Qumranic times, historical *-ahu* in final position had become *ō (ahu › aw › ô)*, and *waw* had all but replaced *hê* as the *m.l.* for *ō* in the third masculine singular suffix.

In epigraphic Hebrew times, however, the suffix *-w* was the norm only on plural nouns (and possibly singular nouns from III-weak roots). The statement by Cross ("Cave Inscriptions from Khirbet Beit Lei," in *NEATC*, 1970, p. 301) that "*Waw* does not become a vowel letter for *ō* before the fourth century in Hebrew" cannot yet be verified for lack of data. All that may be stated with certainty is that *-h* is the common third masculine singular pronominal suffix on singular nouns before the texts from Qumran.

[187]Biblical *-a(y)w.*

[188]On the basis of the Masoretic vocalization without *yod,* as well as the then attested Judean form written without *yod*, *ʾnšw*, "his men," Lachish

The orthography *-w* is also attested on the dual noun *yrḥw*, "his two months" and is restored on the feminine plural noun *[ʿṣmtw]*, "his bones."[189]

3:18, the third masculine singular pronominal suffix on a masculine plural noun has been reconstructed on lines similar to the Masoretic form. Cf. Cross and Freedman, *Early Hebrew Orthography*, p. 54 and Andersen and Forbes, *Spelling in the Hebrew Bible*; Dahood Memorial Lecture, *BibOr 41* (1986).

The form with *yod* included in the orthography, *pnyw*, "his face," KH 2:9, is evidence for:

1) a very archaic historical spelling in which the *yod* is not assumed to be pronounced.

2) a seventh century Judean Hebrew pronunciation that included consonantal *yod*; cf. Barkay, "The Priestly Benediction on Silver Plaques from Ketef Hinnom in Jerusalem," *TA* 19 (1992) :165)

3) a seventh century Judean pronunciation including a vowel for which *yod* was the correct *mater lectionis* (Cross and Freedman [*EHO*, pp. 54-55] assumed that it was the correct northern Hebrew form) or

4) a very early instance of secondary graphic insertion of *yod* according to the theory of Andersen and Forbes (cf. *Spelling in the Hebrew Bible*, p. 62); also Pardee, "Review of *Spelling in the Hebrew Bible: Dahood Memorial Lecture* by Francis I. Andersen and A. Dean Forbes," *CBQ* 50 (1988): 276-80.

Mention must also be made not only of nouns (e.g., *ʾnšw*), but also prepositions that show forms like plurals (e.g., *ʾlw*, "to him," MHY 1:13 [biblical *ʾlyw*]).

189Cross ("The Cave Inscriptions from Khirbet Beit Lei," in *NEATC*, 1970, p. 304, n. 3) states with confidence that the *waw* of *yrḥw* stands for *-êw (yarḥêw)*, "the articular suffix added to a plural or dual noun." The pattern *ayhū › êhū › êw* for the pronominal suffix pertains to Israelite for certain, but also may pertain to Judahite for plural and dual nouns, according to Cross and Freedman (*EHO*, p. 54). The two do admit the possibility of an *-aw*, rather than *-êw* pronunciation for the form at Lachish (*EHO*, pp. 54-55).

Zevit (*MLAHE*, pp. 29-30, nn. 13-15) suggests the development *ayhū › ayū › ayō › āw* for the ending of *ʾnšw*, mostly on the basis of biblical Hebrew where the *-ay* diphthong in unstressed syllables essentially remains uncontracted.

Zevit's second suggestion for *ʾnšw*, that the waw is rather the third masculine singular pronominal suffix on a singular collective noun (*ʾanōšō)* based on the biblical parallel in Isaiah 24:6, is not likely. The absolute plural noun *ʾnšm*, "men" occurs (A 24:19) while the collective *ʾnš* does not. In fact, the collective "men" is *ʾyš* in epigraphic Hebrew; cf. Arad 40:8; Pardee, *HHL*, p. 64.

The form *ʾnšw* may be vocalized **ʾanašêw* or **ʾanašaw*. In Northern Hebrew, the suffix would likely have been pronounced *-êw* (as in Gezer *yrḥw*, "his two months;" **yarḥêw*, but in Judean Hebrew, the suffix may have been pronounced **-aw*, since the diphthong of the plural construct was preserved in the South (**-ayhū › *-aw*) .

The plural possessive suffixes occur only on singular nouns. Before a new interpretation of the word *šmrn* by Gilula and Emerton, the *-n* of this form was posited as the first common plural possessive suffix.[190]

The second masculine plural possessive suffix is attested in epigraphic Hebrew as *-km* (e.g., *bnkm,* "your son").

Although not as decisive as evidence, one epigraphic Hebrew form, *ymm*, "their day," may illustrate that the third masculine plural possessive suffix on singular nouns is *-m* (as also in biblical Hebrew). While this is the opinion of Meshel,[191] the form *ymm* is ambiguous, for in the text of Ajrud 4 (*brk ymm wyśbᶜw*), the final *mem* may conceivably represent the masculine plural ending (*ymm*, "days"), or an adverbial ending, as in biblical Hebrew *ywmm* (*yô mā m*), "in the day time, by day," or "continually" (but usually in conjunction with *lylh*, e.g., *ywmm wlylh*, Exod. 13:21). The meaning of Ajrud 4 is consistent with the rendering of *-m* in *ymm* as adverbial, "(May he) be blessed continually and be satisfied."[192]

In the view of Cross and Freedman (*EHO*, pp. 54-55), the plural form **-êw* would have extended to the Southern dialect as implied by the writing *-yw* in the Masoretic text. The yod here would be a *mater lectionis* representing *ê* and would not be explained as an example of historical spelling *per se*.

In other words, the *"ketib"* of the Masoretic text would represent Israelite pronunciation (*-*ê*), while the Masoretic pointing would suggest Judean pronunciation **-aw*. The orthography implies a reading **-ê,* while the vocalization is *-āw*. According to this theory, the Masoretic vocalization would derive from the Judean pronunciation, while the orthography would represent North Israelite reading. Cross and Freedmann suppose a general extension of the *-*ê* form in the orthography, and a similar, subsequent levelling through of the *-*āw* form in the vocalization.

Regarding the problem presented by the form *pnyw* (KH 2:9), see the preceding note.

[190]*Šmrn* had been treated as a participle plus the possessive suffix meaning "our guardian" (biblical *šmrnw*). However, a new analysis of this word is now accepted by most commentators; cf. pp. 108, n. 84.

[191]Cf. Meshel, "Kuntillet ᶜAjrud" (Israel Museum Cat. 175), 1978, n.p.; "Did Yahweh Have a Consort," BAR 5, no. 2 (1979): 30.

[192]This interpretation, however, requires a different separation of words in the text. The letters after the final *waw* in *wyśbᶜw* are missing, but it is possible that the *waw* began the following word (*wyśbᶜ w*..., hence, "May he be satisfied, and...," in lieu of the plural *wyśbᶜw* [since *brk* is in the singular]). The discounter to this reading is, however, that there are markers in Ajrud 4 which separate the words, and no marker appears between the *ᶜayin* and *waw* of *wyśbᶜw*.

Two other Ajrud texts (Ajrud 5 and 6) show a word divider between the two *mems* in similar votive passages, *brk.bˁl.bym.ml [ ]* and *šm.ˀl.bym.ml[ ]*, indicating that the second mem is not a possessive suffix; rather, it belongs to the following word.

3.2.2.2 The Object suffix

In epigraphic Hebrew, as in biblical Hebrew, a pronominal direct object may be suffixed directly to a verb rather than to the object marker *ˀt*:[193]

> *qrˀty ˀth*, "I read it," L 3:12, but *lqḥh*, "He took him," L 4:6.

> *ṣrr[t] ˀtm*, "Bind them!" A 3:5-6, but *nttm*, "I gave (= sent) them," A 40:10.

Four object suffixes are attested in epigraphic Hebrew. These are the first common singular, second and third masculine singular, and third masculine plural forms.

---

[193]The relative frequency of verbs with the direct object marker *ˀt* and verb plus the object suffix is more than two to one in favor of the latter in epigraphic Hebrew. There are seven attestations of the verb plus unattached object marker:

wṣrr[t] ˀtm	"Bind them"	A 3:5-6
wtn ˀ[tm]	"Give [them]"	A 12:2
ḥtm ˀth	"Seal it"	A 17:6
wšlḥtm ˀtm	"Send them"	A 24:13
qrˀty ˀth	"I read it"	L 3:12
q[r]ˀty [ˀ]th	"I read it"	L 12:4
brkt ˀtkm	"I bless you"	Ajrud 14:1

Note the use of the same verb, one with unattached, the other with attached object markers, in the following attested pairs in epigraphic Hebrew, usually showing a difference which explains the usage of one form or the other:

wtn ˀ[tm], "Give [them]," and *ˀtnnhw*, "I will give it."

wšlḥtm ˀtm, "Send them," and *šlḥh*, "He sent it," (and *šlḥnw*, "Send it").

brkt ˀtkm, "I bless you," and *brktk*, "I bless you."

Table 33 illustrates the object suffixes which occur on verbs in epigraphic Hebrew:

TABLE 33
OBJECT SUFFIXES ON VERBS

	Perfect	Imperfects	Imperative	Meaning
Sing.				
1c.	*-ny, -n*	–	–	"me"
2 m.	*-k*	*-k*	–	"you"
2 f.	–	–	–	"you"
3 m.	*-h*	*-hw*	*-(n)w*	"him"
3 f.	–	–	–	"her"
Plur.				
1c.	–	–	–	"us"
2 m.	–	–	–	"you"
2 f.	–	–	–	"you"
3 m.	*-m*	–	*-m*	"them"
3 f.	–	–	–	"them"

(1) *Forms.* This section describes the object suffixes on perfects, imperfects, and imperatives.

First common singular suffix. These suffixes include:

a) *On perfects. ṣwtny,* "You gave me orders," A 18:7-8.

b) *On proper names. hgln-*, "(DN) carried me away into exile," R 17:2 (Herr 61).

Second masculine singular suffix. These suffixes include:

a) *On perfects. brktk,* "I bless you," Ajrud 15:4; A 16:2-3, 21:2, 40:3; *wṣwk,* "And (he) orders you," A 3:2-3

b) *On imperfects/jussives. yrʾk,* "May (YH) cause you to see," L 5:7; *wyšmrk,* "And may he keep you," Ajrud 15:7;[194] *ybr̊kk,* "May (YH) bless you," MO 2:1.

Third masculine singular suffix. These suffixes include:

a) *On perfects. ktbh,* "He has written it (?)," KEK 3:1; *lqḥh,* "He has taken him," L 4:6; *šlḥh,* "He has sent it," L 3:21.

b) On the energetic form of the imperfect. *ʾtnnhw,* "I will give it," L 3:12.

c) *On imperatives. wšlḥnw,* "And send it!" A 4:2.

Third masculine plural suffix. These suffixes include:

a) *On perfects. nttm,* "I sent them," A 40:10; *whbqydm,* "And he is to hand them over," A 24:14-15.

b) *On imperatives. hdʿm,* "Inform them!" Sam. C 1101:2.

3.2.3 Demonstratives

(1) *Forms.* The following section describes the various usages of the demonstrative.

---

[194] Also *w[y]šmrk,* KH 2:6-7 and *[wy]šmrk,* KH 1:2-3.

TABLE 34
DEMONSTRATIVES

	Singular		Plural	
masc.	*zh*	"this"	–	"these"
fem.	*z't*	"this"	–	"these"
masc.	–	"that"	–	"those"
fem.	–	"that"	–	"those"

Both *zh* and *zʾt* occur as demonstrative pronouns, while the masculine singular form functions also as a demonstrative adjective.

Demonstrative adjective. The demonstrative adjective in epigraphic Hebrew has a usage parallel to that of the adjective: The attributive demonstrative adjectives follow the noun which they modify and agree with it in number, gender, and definiteness. Only the masculine singular demonstrative adjective is attested in epigraphic Hebrew as an attributive:

h̊ḥdr hzh, "this (burial)-chamber," KEK 1:3.

hʿt hzh, "this season," L 6:2.[195]

[hš]m̊n hzh, "this oil," A 13:2.

Demonstrative pronoun. In epigraphic Hebrew, *zh* and *zʾt* may also have the status of a pronoun. Both the masculine singular and feminine singular demonstrative pronouns are attested:

---

195 *ʿt* is principally a feminine noun in biblical Hebrew (e.g., *bʿt hhyʾ*, Jos. 5:2, etc.) and is seldom masculine, and then mostly in late texts (e.g., *lʿtym mzmnym*, "for appointed times," Ezra 10:14; *bʿtym hhm,* "and in those times," 2 Chron. 15:5; Dan. 11:14).

wzh hyh dbr hnqbh, "And this was the way in which it was tunneled out," Siloam 1:1.

zʾt̊ [qbrt šbn]ẙhw, "This is the [tomb of Sheban]yahu," Silwan 2:1.

[wz]ʾt h[r]ʿh ʾš[r] ʾd[m], "And this is the evil wh[ich] the Edom[ites have done]," A 40:14-15.

ʾrwr hʾdm ʾ̊šr ypt̊ḥ̊ ʾt̊ z̊ʾ̊t "Cursed be the man who opens this (tomb)," Silwan 2:2-3.

In Siloam 1, Silwan 2, and possibly Arad 40, the demonstrative pronoun acts as the subject of the sentence in apposition to a substantive. In Siloam 1:1, *zh* agrees with *dbr* in the syntactic unit: demonstrative pronoun + pronoun + perfect predicate + predicate noun in construct state.

Silwan 2:1 is largely restored in this section of the inscription, although it is likely that the feminine singular demonstrative pronoun *zʾt* is followed by the feminine singular noun *qbrt* in construct state based on the parallel inscription from Silwan 3: *qb̊r̊t...ʾšr yp̊[tḥ]*, "...the tomb of...who o[pens]"

Arad 40:14-15 is also restored in the section of the text under examination. One interpretation is that the feminine demonstrative pronoun should be restored *[wz]ʾt hrʿh* "and this is the evil..." to agree with the feminine noun *rʿh*, but it has also been suggested[196] that *ʾt hrʿh ʾšr*, composed of the direct object marker plus definite article and noun, followed by the relative pronoun, is satisfactory and even has a parallel in biblical Hebrew (1 Kings 11:25).[197]

The demonstrative pronoun also occurs in epigraphic Hebrew as the direct object in Silwan 2:2-3. *Zʾt* in this phrase is the direct object of the verb *ypth̩*, "will open," and its antecedent in the phrase is *qbrh*, "tomb, burial-chamber," restored in line 1.

---

[196]P.E. Dion (collaborator), in *Handbook of Ancient Hebrew Letters* by D. Pardee (Chico, CA: Scholars Press, 1982), p. 65.

[197]*Wʾt hrʿh ʾšr hdd (wĕʾet hārāʿāh ʾăšer hădād)*, "and the evil which Hadad...," 1 Kings 11:25 (*ketib*); however, the suggested emendation of the phrase (*qere*) is *wzʾt hrʿh ʾšr ʿśh hdd (wezōʾt hārāʿāh ʾăšer ʿāśāh hădād)*, "and this is the evil which Hadad did;" see R. Kittel, *Biblia Hebraica* (Stuttgart: Wurttembergische Bibelanstalt, 1937), p. 529.

The demonstrative *zh*, "this," functions as a quasi-adverb in Meṣad Ḥashavyahu: *zh ymm*, "at this time...," MHY 1:9. In this expression, *zh* modifies a time-term and *zh ymm* may be an adverbial phrase "at this time, now," analogous to biblical Hebrew's *zeh yāmîm rabbîm* in Josh. 22:3.[198]

The Demonstrative plus preposition

The demonstratives may combine with prepositions (in epigraphic Hebrew *k-* and *m-*) to form an adverbial phrase.

The demonstrative pronoun occurs with the preposition *k-*, "like, as," in Lachish 5 and 6:

> *my ʿbdk klb [ky] š̊l̊ḥ̊t̊h̊ ʾl ʿbdk ʾ[t] hs̊[prm] kz̊ʾ[t]*, "Who is your servant but a dog that you have sent your servant these letters? [= have sent your servant's letter in this fashion ?]" L 5:3-4.
>
> *[lm]h̊ tʿśw kzʾt*, "Why are you acting thus?" L 6:9-10.

Kzʾt has the special adverbial meaning, "thus" (as has been discussed) in Lachish 6 and "the like of this" = "things such as these," in Lachish 5 after the verb *šlḥ*. A similar biblical phrase to Lachish 5 is Judges 13:23–*wkʿt lʾ hšmyʿnw kzʾt*, "...nor should he have told us such things as these (= told it to us after this fashion)."

The demonstrative and *m-*, "from," denote another adverbial phrase in epigraphic Hebrew:

> *wʾ[t] hwdwyhw bn ʾḥyhw wʾnšw šlḥ lqḥt mzh,* "And he has sent (messengers) to take Hawdawyahu, the son of Ahiyahu and his men from here," L 3:16-18.

---

[198] *Zh*, in the expression *zh ymm*, is certainly an example of a demonstrative which functions as a quasi-adverb, since it does not agree in number with the noun (*ymm*) that it "modifies." For *zh ymm* and the function of *zh* as a quasi-adverb, cf. F. A. Pennacchietti, "Sono già due anni che nel paese cʾè la carestia" (Gen. XLV, 6): I sintagmi temporali ebraici introdotti dal pronome ze e la lora traduzioni in siriaco, arabo ed etiopico," *Vicino Orient* 3 (1980): 225-42. See also Cowley, *Gesenius*, pp. 442-43 (136d), where *zh* (in analogous biblical phrases) is designated as a demonstrative pronoun functioning as an enclitic of time.

Mzh occurs in the locative sense "from here," in Lachish 3 and occurs often with this sense in biblical Hebrew as well (Gen. 37:17, 42:15, 50:25, *et cetera*).

3.2.4 The Relative Pronoun

The relative pronoun in epigraphic Hebrew is *ʾšr*. This particle of relation brings the clause introduced by it into relation with an antecedent phrase or clause.

3.2.4.1 The Relative pronoun as substantive

The following examples from epigraphic Hebrew illustrate that the relative clause may be substantivized (be used without an antecedent *per se*). In fact, *ʾšr* includes its own pronominal antecedent, whether in the nominative or oblique cases as in Numbers 22:6–*wʾšr tʾr ywʾr*, "He whom you curse, is cursed."

In the first three examples below, *ʾšr* has the meaning "(he) who," and functions as the subject of the sentence:

> *ʾrr ʾšr ymḥh̊*, "Cursed be he who effaces," NY 1:1.
>
> *ʾrr ‹ʾ›šr ‹y›mḥh*, "Cursed be he who effaces," KBL 4:2.
>
> *ʾ̊šr yp̊[tḥ]*, "he who o[pens]," Silwan 3:2.

(1) *Kl ʾšr*. The next set of phrases also contain the relative pronoun which includes its pronominal antecedent, but the referent is inanimate and *ʾšr* is preceded by *kl*, "all." The epigraphic Hebrew phrases function in a similar manner to the biblical phrases in Genesis 1:31, *wyrʾ ʾlhym ʾt kl ʾšr ʿśh,* "and God saw everything that he made," and Isaiah 63:7, *kʿl kl ʾšr gmlnw yhwh*, "according to all that which YHWH has bestowed on us."

The three examples below contain the phrase *kl ʾšr*, "all that which, whatever":

> *kkl ʾšr šlḥ ʾdny kn ʿśh ʿbdk*, "Your servant has done all that which my lord send (word to do)," L 4:2.
>
> *ktbty ʿl hdlt kkl ʾšr šlḥ̊ [ʾdny ʾ]ly*, "I have written down all that which my lord has sent to me," L 4:4.

wk̊l ʾš[r], "whatever," A 21:7.

(2) *ʾl ʾšr*. Arad 40 illustrates the relative pronoun governed by the preposition *ʾl* with the meaning "to what, that which:"

> *wʿt ḥṭh̊ [ʿ]bdk [l]bh ʾl ʾšr ʾm[rt]*, "And now your [ser]vant has applied himself to what (all that which) you ord[ered]," A 40:4-5.

(3) Unmarked adverbials. The relative in Lachish 9 occurs without an accompanying preposition (probably *ʿl*, "about," is latent in the construction):

> *hšb̊ [l]ʿbdk dbr byd̊ šlm̊yhw ʾšr nʿśh mḥr*, "Return word [to] your servant through the intermediary of Shelemyahu (about) what we are to do tomorrow," L 9:4-9.

This example suggests that the morphological/syntactic inclusion of a preposition governing the relative is not a fixed grammatical rule for epigraphic Hebrew.

3.2.4.2 The Relative with antecedents

In epigraphic Hebrew, the relative *ʾšr* may represent the simple subject of the sentence or the direct object of a verb. In this case, the relative clauses have antecedents, i.e., they serve as attributes and have an adjectival function. This type of relative phrase is also common in biblical Hebrew: *mkl mlʾktw ʾšr ʿśh*, "from all the work which he had done," Genesis 2:2 and *ʾšr btwk hgn*, "(The tree) which is in the middle of the garden," Genesis 3:2. The following examples from epigraphic Hebrew contain relatives with antecedents:

> *hpqḥ [nʾ] ʾt ʿyn̊ ʿbdk lspr ʾšr šlḥ ʾd[ny] lʿbdk ʾmš*, "Please explain to your servant (the meaning of) the letter which my lord sent to your servant yesterday," L 3:4-5.

> *kl sp̊r ʾšr ybʾ ʾly ʾm qrʾty ʾth*, "Any letter which might come to me, I can read it," L 3:11-12.

wyd' ky 'l mś't lkš nḥnw šmrm kkl h'tt 'šr ntn 'dny, "He will know that we are watching for the signals of Lachish according to all the signals (code) which my lord gave (us)," L 4:10-11.

yšlḥ ['lb[dk h]spr 'šr šlḥ 'dny [l]'zr[y]hw, "Your servant will send the letter which my lord sent to Azaryahu," L 18:1.

m'wd hqmḥ [hr]'[šn ']šr[ ], "From the first (batch of) meal, which...," A 5:3-4.

[wz]'t hr'h 'š[r] 'd[m 'śth], "[And th]is is the evil whi[ch] the Edo[mites have done]," A 40:15.

'rwr h'dm 'šr ypth 't z't, "Cursed be the man who opens this (tomb)," Silwan 2:2-3.

In the preceding phrase, the antecedent (the definite noun, *h'dm*, "the man, the one") is stated, which sets this relative phrase slightly apart from its parallels at Naḥal Yishai and Khirbet Beit Lei.

Four epigraphic Hebrew phrases contain the relative pronoun *'šr* and its antecedent *dbr*:[199]

'l tšm' lk[l] dbr 'šr ydbr 'lyk, "Don't listen to w[hat X] will say to you," papMur 17a:2.

ybkr yhwh 't '[dn]y dbr 'šr l' yd'th, "May YH favor my lord with knowledge of anything you do not already know," L 2:5-6.

hšb [l]'bdk dbr byd šlmyhw 'šr n'sh mḥr, "Return word to your servant through the intermediary of Shelemyahu (about) what we are to do tomorrow," L 9:4-9.

wldbr 'šr ṣwtny šlm, "With regard to the matter about which you gave me orders; everything is fine," A 18:6-8.

---

[199]In the papMur example, *ydbr* has a specific antecedent (*kl dbr*), while in Lachish 2:5-6, *dbr* is clearly the direct object of *yd'th*. *Dbr* in Lachish 9:5-6 is the traditional "accusative of respect."

This last example, from Arad 18, is interesting in that the formula of lines 6-8, *dbr* + *ʾšr* + ṣwh occurs often in the Bible (Exod. 16:32, 35:4; Lev. 17:2; Josh. 8:35) with regard to orders to be immediately given out or as a reminder of those previously given out.

(1) *ʾšr and the prepositional phrase.* The title: *ʾšr ʿl hbyt.* The following examples showing the antecedent type of *ʾšr* phrase are those containing the relative marking a following prepositional phrase as an attribute. The title *ʾšr ʿl hbyt* signifies "royal steward," literally, "the one over the house:"[200]

lgdlyhw [ʾ]šr ʿl hbyt, "Belonging to Gedalyahu, royal steward," L Seal 6:2.

zʾt̊ [qbrt šbn]ẙhw ʾšr̊ ʿl hbyt, "This is [the tomb of Sheban]yahu, royal steward," Silwan 2:1.

[l]ydw ʾšr [ʿ]l hbyt, "Belonging to Yiddo, royal steward," Avigad Hecht Seal 1:1-2

lʾdnyhw ʾšr ʿl hbyt, "Belonging to Adoniyahu, royal steward," Avigad HB 1,2

lntn ʾšr [ʿ]l ‹h›byt, "Belonging to Natan, royal steward," Avigad HB 3

---

[200]Cf. T.N.D. Mettinger, *Solomonic State Officials: A Study of the Civil Government Officials of the Israelite Monarchy* (Lund: CWK Gleerups Fölag, 1971). Mettinger explains the phrase *ʾšr ʿl hbyt* as signifying one who is "house-minister" (pp. 70-79) and whose function it is to be both a "major-domo," as well as the administrator of the royal estate. Cf. p. 213, n. 275 in this grammar.

Scott Layton, in an article on the subject of *ʾšr ʿl hbyt,* explains the title as that of a royal official of the government whose duties included overseeing the king's palace. He posits that over time, the position grew to such importance as to have become one designation of the highest senior officials in the state. Cf. Scott C. Layton, "The Steward in Ancient Israel: A Study of Hebrew (*ʾĂŠER) ʿAL-HABBAYIT* in its Near Eastern Setting," *JBL* 109/4 (1990): 633-49.

(2) *ʾšr and the possessive.* Epigraphic Hebrew parallels biblical Hebrew in that the relative pronoun may govern the preposition of ownership, *ʾšr l-*, "which belongs to:"

ʾšr lb̊n̊ [ ], "which belongs to Ben[ ]," A 8:9.

Arad 17:2, Sam. Ost. 1936, and Arad A 29:7 also contain the relative pronoun, but the texts containing it are badly broken and do not permit further discussion.

3.2.5 Interrogatives

3.2.5.1 Interrogative pronouns

The extant interrogative pronouns in epigraphic Hebrew are *my*, "who," and *lmh*, "why".

my

The interrogative pronoun *my*, "who," is attested in the inscriptions three times as an independent form, and once in a proper name. This form occurs in identical phrases in Lachish 2, 5, and 6: *my ʿbdk klb...*, "Who is your servant (but) a dog..."

More common than the independent form of this pronoun is its use as the first element of several epigraphic Hebrew proper names. In Herr 119:2, the orthography shows the internal *m.l.*, an unusual feature of proper names in general: *mykyhw*, "Who is like YH?" Four additional proper names which contain the morphological component *my* (although without *plene* orthography), are abbreviated forms of the same name *(mykyhw)*. All are composed of the interrogative pronoun *m(y)*, "who," the preposition *k-*, "like," plus either the theophoric ending (e.g., *mk(yhw)*, B/L (26) 10:2), or a hypocoristic ending (e.g., *m̊k̊l̊* , L 19:3; *mky*, Herr 111; A 110:2; *mkʾ*, Av (*IEJ* 25) 4:2).

lmh

Lmh, "why," a form which is largely restored, is attested once in epigraphic Hebrew at Lachish: *[lm]h̊ tʿśw kzʾt*, "Why are you doing thus?" L 6:9-10.

3.2.6 Indefinite Pronoun

One indefinite pronoun, *m'wm̊[h]*, "anything," is partially restored in Lachish 3:12-13–*[ʾḥ]r ʾtnnhw [ʾ]l mʾwm̊h*, "I can recount all the de[tails] (contained in it)." A similar phrase *(ʾl mʾwmh)* is not found in the Bible and the etymology of *mʾwmh* is disputed.[201] The original meaning of *mʾwmh* may have been "point" › "something."[202] The general sense of the expression at Lachish is fairly clear from the context of the phrase: *mʾwmh*, "to the most minute detail, down to the smallest point."[203]

3.2.7 The Definite Article

The definite article is discussed with the pronouns because it developed from a deictic element, and its demonstrative force is still preserved in cases like *hym*, "today," Arad 24:19.[204]

The definite article in epigraphic Hebrew, *h-*, "the," is written together with a following substantive or attributive. The use of the definite article *h-* shows that it was widely known throughout epigraphic Hebrew, is quite regular, and is a basic feature of the language agreement between nouns and the adjectives or demonstratives modifying them.

The definite article *h-* occurs in proper names: *hgbh*, "the locust;" *hkws*, "the owl," and in locatives: *hmṣh*, "the drainage area (?);" *htl*, "the mound." In these epigraphic Hebrew proper and locative names containing the definite article, the definite article is part of the name and not attached to it secondarily.

In the example *hʿyrh*, "to the city," from Lachish 4:7, the definite article is attached to a noun to which the locative suffix is

---

201 In the Bible, *mʾwmh* usually occurs in negative phrases and is not attested in prepositional phrases (see *BDB*, pp. 548-49). Suggestions for the etymology of *mʾwmh* include taking the form as an old accusative form from *mʾwm*, in the sense of "speck, particle" (Cowley, *Gesenius*, p. 250).

202 Lemaire, *Inscriptions hébraïques*, p. 103.

203 Ibid. Lemaire is followed by Pardee, *HHL*, p. 84, "I can repeat it [down] to the smallest det[ail]."

204 The pronominal element from which the article developed is thought to have been either *han-*, see Blau, *A Grammar of Biblical Hebrew*, p. 43, or *hal-*, cf. Cowley, *Gesenius*, pp. 111-12.

also attached. The word takes on an adverbial meaning, and the *h-* does not signify "the," but "to, in the direction of."[205]

In construct state chains, *hê* as the definite article precedes final nouns only, whatever the number of nouns in the chain. The *hê* does not occur before final proper names.

Some epigraphic Hebrew texts show the absence of the definite article in noun phrases where it is syntactically expected.

While the definite article is lacking in Ajrud 3:1–*lśr ʿr*, "belonging to the governor of the city," two seal inscriptions bearing the same phrase show the definite article: *śr hʿr*, "the governor of the city," Barkay (1977) 1:1 and Avigad (1978) 3:1.[206]

The definite article is noticeably absent in several texts from Samaria. The common means of stating the date in the Samaria Ostraca was the formula *bšt* + *h-* + ordinal number. When the number is not written out, but is instead written in hieratic numerals, the definite article is used before the number even though it is expressed by a symbol: *h(ḥmš ʿśrh)*, in Samaria 24,

---

[205]*Hʿyrh* is biblical as well (1 Kings 14:12, etc.). The article occurs on a similar biblical form, *hbyth*, "homeward," Gen. 19:10, but is not necessarily required (*byth*, Psalm 68:7). Epigraphic Hebrew shows the latter form only, *byth*, "to the house of," A 17:2, which could not, of course, take the definite article because it is in the construct state.

[206]Two additional texts, from Lachish 13:3 and Arad 40:10-11, although broken or unclear, may likewise indicate the lack of a required definite article.

Lachish 13:3–*ʾt ʾšpt (ʾrbʿ)*, "quivers, 4," is curious in that there appears to be the definite direct object marker, yet no article before the noun. Since the text is broken before these words, it is difficult to comment further. Usually when a quantity of some substance is being discussed, there is also a recipient of that quantity mentioned and no definite article. It is possible that the phrase was something like "Give them the quivers, 4." In this case, the definite article is required. It is also possible that the word *ʾt* in this text is simply the preposition "with" in a phrase like "Give them the bow with quivers, 4. See Lemaire, *Inscriptions hébraïques,* pp. 130-31.

It is also possible according to Pardee (*HHL*, p. 109) that Lemaire's reading of the four strokes after *ʾšpt* as a numerical designation is incorrect, and that the phrase should be read *ʾt ʾšpt* X, "the quiver(s) of X," with the feminine noun *ʾšpt* in construct state after the direct object marker. In this case, we would not expect the definite article before the noun, as *ʾšpt* would then be the *nomen regens*, before which the definite article may not occur.

In Arad 40:10-11, *[bṭrm y]rd ym*, "before evening," one would expect the definite article before *ym* (functioning a *nomen rectum*), as the sender of the letter in this text specifically states that he sent the letter back before evening of a definite day. See Lemaire, *Inscriptions hébraïques*, p. 208; Pardee, *HHL*, p. 65; "Letters from Tel Arad," p. 325.

31a, 34, 43, 44, and 45. However, it is even more common before hieratic numerals to omit the definite article completely: *bšt (ḥmš ʿśrh)*, "In (the fifteenth) year," Samaria 22, *et cetera*, and *bšt (šlš ʿśrh)*, "In (the thirteenth ?) year," Samaria 63:1. This pattern seems to be an orthographic phenomenon; i.e., when the number was written with a symbol, it was not required that the definite article be written.

In the previous examples, the absence of the definite article in epigraphic Hebrew is notable. There is one text, Arad 2:1-3, where the definite article is present (in line 3), but it is not clear why it is so:

> *ntn lktym b(tm šnym) yyn lʾrbʿt hymm*, "Give the Kittim two *bat*-measures of wine for the four days."[207]

3.2.8 Conclusion

Epigraphic Hebrew texts yield the following types of pronouns: the independent personal pronoun, the demonstrative pronoun, the relative pronoun, the interrogative pronoun, and the indefinite pronoun. Pronominal suffixes in epigraphic Hebrew consist of the possessive suffixes (on nouns) and object suffixes (on verbs). A close examination of the corpus of pronouns and pronominal suffixes in epigraphic Hebrew illustrates that very few forms of the pronoun are presently attested in the language. For instance, only three non-restored forms of a probable total of at least ten[208] independent pronouns have been attested with certainty.

With regard to pronominal suffixes, the actual number of attested suffix forms is limited, and while possessive suffixes outnumber object suffixes, future discoveries of both suffix types

---

[207]The reason for the definite article is unknown, however, one speculation is that the Kittim were receiving supplies for a specific four-day trip. See Pardee, *HHL*, p. 33; "Letters from Tel Arad," pp. 297-98; Lemaire, *Inscriptions hébraïques*, p. 161.

[208]The number ten is based on biblical Hebrew, where there are ten principal independent personal pronouns. The term "principal" refers to the most commonly attested independent personal pronouns: *ʾny, ʾth, ʾt, hwʾ, hyʾ, ʾnḥnw, ʾtm, ʾtn, hm, hn,* rather than to the secondary, less commonly attested forms *ʾnky, ʾtnh, nḥnw, ʾnw, hmh and hnh.* Cf. Lambdin, *Introduction to Biblical Hebrew* (New York: Charles Scribner's Sons, 1971), p. 82. In epigraphic Hebrew, only *ʾny, hʾ* and *nḥnw* are attested as unrestored independent pronouns.

are needed in order to complete the lists of forms in tables 32 and 33.

Especially important for increasing our understanding of pronouns within epigraphic Hebrew grammar will be the addition of feminine suffixes of both possessive and object types, since, to date, no attestations of feminine singular or plural pronominal suffixes exist for epigraphic Hebrew.

By contrast to those forms of the pronoun mentioned already, the definite article, which developed from a pronominal element, is widely attested in epigraphic Hebrew.

3.3 The Noun

3.3.1 Nominal Patterns

3.3.1.1 Introduction

Attested nouns in epigraphic Hebrew provide evidence for vowel patterns (due to the presence of *m.l.*), as well as several affix patterns. With regard to vowel patterns, empirical evidence exists in epigraphic Hebrew for the *qīl, qūl, qatūl* nominal patterns, and nouns with *-ī* and *-īt* suffixes. Reduplicated, and quadraconsonantal nouns, as well as *ʾaleph*, *mem*, and *taw* preformative nouns are all patterns attested in epigraphic Hebrew.

In this section, the transliteration of each noun is given first in each class, followed by the biblical vocalization (if the relevant form is attested), as a reference point, and then the proto-vocalization. The list of forms for each class represents all nouns extant in epigraphic Hebrew for that particular nominal pattern.

The class assigned to the epigraphic Hebrew form is the same class to which its biblical counterpart has been assigned by biblical grammarians. The historical derivations below provide the history of the biblical form, and the epigraphic Hebrew form is demonstrated to be the same for the several patterns mentioned above (i.e., *qīl, qūl, et cetera*). The nominal patterns discussed below derive from traditional grammars, with special emphasis upon Bauer and Leander's *Historische Grammatik der hebräischen Sprache*, and Klaus Beyer's *Althebräische Grammatik.*[209]

3.3.1.2 Nouns with two radicals and a long vowel

qīl (Masoretic: *qīl*). *ʾyš* and *ʾš* *ʾīš* < *ʾīš*, "man;" *ʿyr* and *ʿr* *ʿīr* < *ʿīr*, "city."

Both *ʾyš* and *ʿyr* with *yod m.l.* are empirical epigraphic Hebrew evidence for the *qīl* nominal pattern.

---

[209]Bauer and Leander, *Historische Grammatik*, pp. 445-506; Beyer, *Althbräische Grammatik* (Gottingen: Vandenhoeck & Ruprecht, 1969), pp. 42-53.

qūl (Masoretic: *qūl*). *sws sūs* ‹ *sūs*, "horse;" *ʾwr* and *ʾr ūr*‹ *ʾūr*, "flame, light;" *ṣr ṣūr* ‹ *ṣūr*, "cliff, rock;" *kwr kūr*‹*kūr*, "smelting pot, furnace."

qūlat: swsh sūsâ ‹ *sūsat*, "mare."

Sws, ʾwr, kwr, and *swsh* with *waw m.l.* for *ū* stand as empirical evidence for the *qūl* nominal pattern in epigraphic Hebrew.

3.3.1.3 Nouns with three radicals and second vowel long

qatūl (Masoretic: *qatūl*). *ʾrwr ʾārūr* ‹ *ʾarūr*, "cursed;" *brk bārūk* ‹ *barūk*, "blessed;" *ʿbr ʿābūr* ‹ *ʿabūr*, "yield, produce;" *rḥṣ rāḥūṣ* ‹ *raḥūṣ*, "washed."

ʾrwr with *waw m.l.* stands as empirical epigraphic Hebrew evidence for the *qatūl* pattern.

3.3.1.4 Reduplicated nouns

qalqal (qalqall)

glgl gilgal ‹ *galgal,* "wheel."[210]

qataltāl

šḥrḥr šeḥarḥōr ‹ *šaḥarḥār*, "dark one."

3.3.1.5 Quadraconsonantal roots

Four consonants with two syllables

ʿkbr ʿakbōr, "mouse;" *prʿš parʿōš*, "flea;" *śmʾl śĕmōʾl* ‹ *śimʾāl*, "left."[211]

---

[210]But Noth, *IPN*, p. 23, compares *glgl* with Arabic *gulgulun* to mean "small bell".

[211]One may presume a proto-form *śamʾal* (Arabic *śáḿʾal*) for epigraphic Hebrew *śmʾl*; however, the biblical pronunciation *śĕmōʾl* is traced to the proto-form *śimʾāl* (cf. Blau, *A Grammar of Biblical Hebrew*, p. 23).

Four consonants with three syllables

smdr sĕmāder, "blossom of grape."

3.3.1.6 Nouns with prefixes

Prefix *ʾaleph*

ʾprḥ ʾeprōaḥ, "young bird;" *ʾkzb/ʾkzy[b]*, "Akzib;" *ʾpṣḥ*, "joyous, cheerful;" *ʾš[ḥr]*, "black;" *ʾškr*, "offering." The *ʾaleph* in these forms is likely prothetic.[212]

Prefix *mem*

maqtal, miqtal (Masoretic: *maqtāl, miqtāl*). *mktb miktāb* < *miktab*, "letter;" *mlʾk malʾāk* < *malʾak*, "messenger;" *mpqd mipqād* < *mipqad*, "roll call, muster;" *mšmr mišmār* < *mišmar*, "guard;" *mtn mattān* < mattan, "gift;" *mśʾ maśśāʾ* < *maśśaʾ*, "load;" *mṣʾ mōṣāʾ*< *mawṣaʾ*, "source;" *mnḥ mānōaḥ* < *manuaḥ*, "rest;" *mqnh miqneh* < *miqnay*, "creature;" *mʿśh*

---

[212]In epigraphic Hebrew, the prothetic *ʾaleph* occurs before an initial two-consonant cluster; cf. sec. 2.2.3.4, p. 48. The prothetic *ʾaleph* was not common in epigraphic Hebrew.

The analysis of the derivation of one of the examples given above, *ʾprḥ*, indicates that the *ʾaleph* in the form is likely to be prothetic. This word occurs in the Bible (*ʾeprōaḥ*) as an attested masculine singular noun, "young one, young bird," but also attested are the proper name *prwḥ* (*pārûaḥ*, 1 Kings 4:17) and the feminine plural active participle *prḥwt* (*pōrĕḥôt*, "flying things, birds"), implying a masculine singular *prḥ* (*porēaḥ*), "flying thing" (the root of these forms being attested *prḥ*, "to fly"). From the forms cited above, one may speculate that the *ʾaleph* of the epigraphic Hebrew *ʾprḥ*, perhaps pronounced **ʾeprūaḥ* or **ʾeprōaḥ*, (as well as the identical biblical noun, for that matter), is probably prothetic.

For another interpretation of the meaning of *prwḥ* (and implications for the meaning of *ʾprḥ*), see Noth, *IPN*, p. 229, who takes the biblical proper name *pārûaḥ* as "happy, cheerful," analogous to Arabic *farūḥ*. However, the noun *ʾprḥ*, "young bird," attested three times in the Bible is, by all indications, certainly the exact orthographic match of the epigraphic Hebrew form, a proper name carrying with it an identification with an animal (see N. Avigad, "*qbwṣt ḥwtmwt ʿbryym* [A Group of Hebrew Seals]," *EI* 9 (1969), p. 3. This identification of proper names with animals is common in epigraphic Hebrew, as well as other Northwest Semitic languages (for biblical Hebrew, see Noth, *IPN*, pp. 229-330).

maʿaśeh ‹ *maʿśʹay*, "deed; *mḥsh maḥseh* ‹ *maḥsay*, "refuge."[213]

maqtalat: *mlʾkh mĕlāʾkâ* ‹ *malʾākâ*,[214] "work."

maqtallat: *mʿdnh maʿădannâ* ‹ *maʿdannat*, "delight."

maqtil (Masoretic: *maqtēl*). *mʿśr maʿăśēr* ‹ *maʿśir*, "tithe;" *mgn magēn* ‹ *maginn*,[215] "shield."

Prefix *taw*

taqtūl (Masoretic: *taqtūl*). *tnḥm tanḥūm*, "consolation."

taqtilat. *tsbt* ‹ *tasibbat* (in construct state in L 4:9), "tour, rounds of."

3.3.1.7 Nouns with suffixes

Suffix *-ī* (originally *-iy(y)*)

Gentilics. *yhdy yĕhūdī*, "Judean;" *kty kittī*, "the Kitti;" *qsry qērōsī*, "the Qerosite;" (see sec. 3.3.2 for further examples).

Ordinals. *rbʿy rĕbīʿī*, "fourth;" *ʾśry ʾaśīrī* "tenth."

Suffix *-īt* (Masoretic *-yt, -īt*)

Feminine Singular Ordinals. *šlšt šĕlīsīt*, "third;" *rbʿt rĕbīʿīt*, "fourth;" *tšʿyt* and *tšʿt tĕšīʿīt*, "ninth;" *ʿśrt ʿaśīrīt* "tenth."

Tšʿyt in Lachish 20:1 stands as empirical evidence for nouns with the suffix *-īt* in epigraphic Hebrew. The *yod* is an internal *m.l.* for *-ī*.

---

[213] See Bauer and Leander, *Historische Grammatik*, p. 491, for a discussion of preformatives from Verbs III-weak.

[214] Ibid., pp. 218, 490.

[215] Ibid., p. 492.

3.3.2 Gentilics

Substantives in epigraphic Hebrew have a *yod* afformative which converts a noun into an adjective. Its primary distribution is on ordinal numbers and on gentilic substantives. The attested epigraphic Hebrew forms of the suffix are: masculine singular, *-y (-î)*, feminine singular, *-t* and *-yt* (*-ît* ‹-*iyt*) and masculine plural, *-ym* (*-iyyîm* or *îm*).

The forms of the gentilic in epigraphic Hebrew provide evidence for a "close" morphological relationship with biblical Hebrew, since the gentilic forms of the latter are morphologically identical to those of epigraphic Hebrew.

Ordinals in epigraphic Hebrew, specifically those for "tenth" and "fourth," exhibit both masculine singular, as well as feminine singular forms:

> *ʿśry*, A 7:3, 7-8, and *ʿśrt*, S 1:1, 2:1-2, 3:1, 13:1, 16a:1, 16b:1, 17d:1, 18:1, 19:1, 21:1, 51:1, 52:1, 54:1, 55:1, 72:1, 17b:1 (restored), "tenth," and *rbʿy*, Ophel 2:3, *rbʿt*, L 29:1, "fourth."

Two additional feminine ordinals are represented by *tšʿyt,* L 20:1, and *tšʿt,* "ninth," [216] and *šlšt,* " third, " A 20:1.

[216] *Tšʿt is* attested more often: *tšʿt*, S 6:1, 9:1, 10:1, 12:1; *t̊šʿt*, S 8:1; *tšʿ̊t*, S 4:1; *t[š̊ʿt]*, S 5:1; *tš̊[ʿt]*, S 100:1; *tš[ʿt]*, S 14:1.

The inflection for the gentilic in epigraphic Hebrew is illustrated in table 35.

TABLE 35
INFLECTION OF THE GENTILIC

	Singular	**Plural**
masc.	*-y*	*-ym*
fem.	*-t, -yt*[a]	–

[a]The affix *-t* is much more common in epigraphic Hebrew than the affix *-yt*; cf. the numerous attestations of *ʿśrt, tšʿt et cetera* versus the singular example of *-yt* in *tšʿyt* (L 20:1).

Epigraphic Hebrew exhibits several gentilics which refer to patronyms or tribal names and which include mostly masculine singular forms, with the exception of one masculine plural form. All of the singular gentilics end in *yod* (a final *m.l.* for *-î [‹-iy(y)]*) except the form *hrbt*. Two masculine singular gentilics presumably stem from feminine singular nouns: *bʿlt*, "Baʿalat," and *rbt*, "Rabbat." Of the two masculine plural gentilics, *ktym*, "Kittim," provides evidence for the affix of the masculine plural gentilic, *-ym* (*ktym*, "Kittim"), a form which is consistent with biblical Hebrew.[217]

---

[217]A second epigraphic Hebrew masculine plural gentilic represents defective writing: *ʾdmm*, "Edomites," biblical *ʾdmym*. This problematic form is from a text of broken context: Arad 3:12. The suggestion that the form should be read "Edomites" is originally that of Aharoni, *Arad Inscriptions*, pp. 18, 19, but, as pointed out by Pardee, "Letters from Tel Arad," *UF* 10 (1978): 302, *ʾdmm* could stand for the plural of *ʾdm*, "man" (as in Phoenician), a plural of *ʾdm*, "red," or the like. In 1978, Pardee ("Letters from Tel Arad," op. cit., p. 302) judged the reading "Edomites" as probable, on the basis of the mention of Edom in Arad 24 and 40, but in his *Handbook of Ancient Hebrew Letters* (c. 1982, p. 35), he discounted this earlier reading. On the basis of the plene spelling for *ktym*, "Kittim," (Arad 1, 2, 4, 5, 7, 8, 10, 11, 14), never *ktm*, the word for Edomites, should be written *ʾdmym* in epigraphic Hebrew.

3.3.2.1 Masculine singular gentilics

bwzy, "The Buzite," Herr 120:2,[218] bᶜlmᶜny, "The Baᶜalmeᶜonite," Samaria 27:3,[219] *hbᶜlty*, "The Baᶜalatite," Arad 60:1-2,[220] *hyhd[y]*, "The Judean," Samaria 51:3,[221]

---

[218]Cf. C. C. Torrey, "A Few Ancient Seals," *AASOR* 3 (1923): 105; Herr, *SANSS*, p. 133. The location of a place named Buz is uncertain, although Noth determined that it was probably an Aramaean territory or tribe. Cf. Noth, *IPN*, no. 249, p. 232, and n. 4: "der Buzit...zu dem aramäischen Lande Bazu." According to *The Interpreter's Dictionary of the Bible*, vol. 1 (Nashville: Abingdon Press, 1962), p. 477, Buz was an Arabian tribe or territory of uncertain location.

The proper name *bwzy* is known from Ezek. 1:3 and *bwz* from Gen. 22:21 (Nahor's genealogy) and 1 Chron. 5:14. *Bwz* also occurs as a masculine singular noun "contempt" in the Bible and *bwzy* as a gentilic adjective occurs in Job 32:2, 6. The tribal name Buz is mentioned in Jeremiah 25:23 (= Arab place) along with Dedan and Tema; cf. *BDB*, p. 100.

[219]*Bᶜlmᶜwn* occurs in Num. 32:38, 1 Chron. 5:8, and Ezek. 25:9 as the locative place name; cf. *BDB*, p. 128; also *byt bᶜl mᶜwn*, Jos. 13:17. Another locative place name which is analogous is the biblical *mᶜwn*, while *mᶜwnym* is possibly a related gentilic (Judg. 10:12). The locative is *mᶜwn* (*māᶜôn*), as in Jos. 15:15, etc., and the gentilic *mᶜwn* (*māᶜôn, ketib*), although the writer possibly intended the latter as *mᶜwnym (mĕᶜûnîm)*; cf. *BDB*, pp. 587, 733.

[220]The form is problematic and read differently by Aharoni (*Arad Inscriptions*, p. 90) who reads *kkl...hnṭlty*, "As all...four (?)...I weighed (carried a load, loaded)," with *nṭlty* corresponding to the biblical usage of *nṭl* (e.g., Isa. 40:15, *yṭwl, yiṭṭôl* (*ketib*)); cf. Koehler-Baumgartner, *Lexicon in Veteris Testamenti Libros*, p. 612. Lemaire (*Inscriptions hébraïques*, pp. 216, 217) presumably reads the letters in question as *hbᶜlty* (he transcribes as *Habaᶜalty*), but he offers no explanation of this form. One assumes from his treatment of the letters before this word (*kprh*), that Lemaire interprets the form in question as a gentilic ("Kephirah [a proper name], the Baᶜalatite").

Based on the attested biblical locative *bᶜlt (baᶜălāt), hbᶜlty* may be a masculine singular gentilic with a definite article, "the one from Baᶜalat," or "the Baᶜalatite." The epigraphic Hebrew form possesses the definite article and is reflected in the Bible in the locative place name *bᶜlt*, a city of Dan, in Josh. 19:44, 1 Kings 9:18, and 2 Chron. 8:6. Also, *bᶜlh*, another locative name appears in Josh. 15:9, 10, 11, 24, and 1 Chron. 13:6. The form *bᶜlty* could derive from the feminine noun *bᶜlh* ("mistress") and be viewed as a gentilic adjective referring to one from the place *bᶜlt* or *bᶜlh*.

[221]This form consists of the definite article and gentilic adjective. The text of Sam. 51:2 is broken after the *dalet* of *yhd[y]*. Because the gentilic ending is restored, this form is not certain to represent the plene form. I. T. Kaufman, "The Samaria Ostraca: A Study in Ancient Hebrew Palaeography," 1966, p. 144, reads *hyhw*, but G. A. Reisner, "Israelite Ostraca From Samaria," 1924, p. 21, reads *dalet* instead of *waw* (after the *hê*) and restores the *yod (yhd[y]*, "Judean." Lemaire, *Inscriptions hébraïques*, p. 36, reads "Hayehud(y)." As Lemaire (p.

lkšy, "Belonging to Kushi, the Kushite," Herr 109:1,[222] *hrbt*, "The Rabbatite," Dayan 3:1-2 (Herr 161),[223] *hkty*,

---

52) points out, Yadin ("Aha of Yahud," *Bulletin of the Israel Exploration Society* 16 (1951): 61-63) is not correct to relate the form under discussion to a village "Yehud," located nine kilometers from Samaria, rather, the term refers to the people who originally came from a certain region.

[222]Analogous forms occurs in Phoenician, Aramaic, and in biblical Hebrew as *kwšy* (Jer. 36:14; Zeph. 1:1) and *kwš* (Ps. 7:1). See Noth, *IPN*, p. 232, no. 803; Grelot, *Documents araméeens d'Egypte*, p. 477, states that Phoenician *kšy* (*kûšî*) is either a Hebrew or Aramaic name which may be analyzed as a gentilic form of *kûš*, and means "the Kushite." Benz, *Personal Names in the Phoenician and Punic Inscriptions*, p. 335, also cites Egyptian *kš*, "Nubian."

Besides the proper names *kšy* and *kwš*, the gentilic adjective (*kwšy*) is attested often in the Bible *(kûšî)*, Jer. 13:23 and thirteen more times. The feminine singular and masculine plural forms are attested, though less often (see *BDB*, p. 469).

[223]*Hrbt* consists of the definite article and gentilic adjective (written defectively). The seal from which this word comes is dated to the ninth century B.C. Herr, *SANNS*, pp. 148-49, lists this seal, from the Dayan Collection, as a possible forgery. For the original publication of this seal, see Y. Aharoni, "Three Hebrew Seals," *Tel Aviv* 1 (1974): 157-58. This author does not question the authenticity of the seal, which he dates to the tenth or early ninth century.

The first interpretation for the epigraphic Hebrew form is that *hrbt* may refer to the locative place name *rbh* which occurs in the Bible. Attestation of the locative *rbh* (*rabbāh*), identified with modern Amman, is not uncommon in the Bible. Cf. *BDB*, p. 913; 2 Sam. 11:1, 1 Chron. 20:1 (2x); Amos 1:14; Jer. 49:3; Ezek. 25:5; Jos. 13:25; in a compound locative phrase, *rbt bny ʿmwn* (*rabbat bĕnê ʿammôn*), 2 Sam. 12:26, 27; 17:27; Deut. 3:1; Jer. 49:2; Ezek. 21:25; with locative afformative, *rbth* (*rabbatah*), 2 Sam. 12:29. Another locative *hrbh* (*harabbah*), Jos. 15:60, refers to a city in Judah, the site of which is uncertain. A third locative, *hrbyt* (*hārabbît*), Jos. 19:20 is thought to refer to modern Raba, a city not far from Nablus; cf, *BDB*, p. 914. Aharoni ("Three Hebrew Seals," *Tel Aviv* 1 (1974): 158) vocalizes the epigraphic Hebrew form as a gentilic *hārabbātī*, "the Rabbatite," and, since the seal on which it appears is supposedly from Judah, he identifies the city associated with the gentilic as that mentioned in Joshua 15:60 (Khirbet Hamida, in the Kiriat-Yearim district). According to him, this locality is attested as *r-b-t* in Egyptian topographic lists, and as Rubute in the el-Amarna correspondence. Cf. Y. Aharoni, "Rubute and Ginti-kirmil," *VT* 19 (1969): 137-45.

A second interpretation for *hrbt* in epigraphic Hebrew is that it relates to a form known from Phoenician, *rbt* (*rabbat*), "lady, goddess. Cf. Harris (*A Grammar of the Phoenician Language*, p. 146) and S. Segert (*A Grammar of Phoenician and Punic*, p. 302). This form is also the second element in the Phoenician proper name *ʿbdrbt*. Cf. Harris, *A Grammar of the Phoenician Language*, p. 130 (from *CIS*, Part I, 2262); Benz, *Personal Names in Phoenician and Punic*, p. 408. *Rbt* is a feminine singular noun, "lady, goddess," commonly attested in Phoenician (cf. Harris, *A Grammar of the Phoenician Language*, p.

The Kitti," Arad 17:9,[224] *nby*, "The Nobite (?)," Avigad

146), and occurs with the definite article in the phrase *hrbt bʿlt nbl* (CIS 1.2). To posit the analogy of the form *hrbt* on the epigraphic Hebrew seal with Phoenician *hrbt*, "the lady" is to infer that *zryhw* (the proper name on Seal 161) was the name of a female.

Although most of the attested names of females have endings other than -*yhw* or -*yw* (cf. Herr, *SANSS*, p. 148, who reads *zryw*), one other epigraphic Hebrew proper name ending with -*yhw* (*ʿmdyhw*) is that of a female, cf. Hestrin and Dayagi-Mendels, *Inscribed Seals*, pp. 45-51.

Harris (*A Grammar of the Phoenician Language*, p. 146) cites the locative *rbt* (in Phoenicia ?), but the form is reconstructed and has not actually been found in Phoenician inscriptions.

With the Hebrew and Phoenician evidence in mind, one may be inclined to agree with Aharoni that *hrbt* in the Dayan Seal is related to a locative *rbh* (from the Bible), derived from the root *rbb*, "to be great, populous" (cf. *BDB*, p. 913), and is analogous to a biblical feminine noun (not attested) or adjective, vocalized along the lines of the biblical forms as *hārabbātī*, "the Rabbatite" (base *qallat*). However, if the antiquity and genuineness of the seal is upheld, one also should accept as plausible the similarities with the Phoenician word for "lady," as well as the possibility that *zryhw* is the name of a female. The solution, then, of taking *lzryhw hrbt* as meaning "belonging to *Zeriyaw*, the Lady," seems to be just as likely as following the interpretation of Aharoni. In either case, the seal exhibits many strange forms of letters which do not fit in clearly with what is known of the early Hebrew script; cf. Herr, *SANSS*, pp. 148-49.

[224]The form consists of the definite article and gentilic adjective. In biblical Hebrew, only the plural form of this word is attested. Cf. *BDB*, p. 508.

NN 20:2,[225] *(wl)qrsy*, "(And to) the Qerosite," Arad 18:5.[226]

---

[225]Avigad, "New Names on Hebrew Seals," *EI* (1975): p. 71; Hestrin and Dayagi-Mendels, *Inscribed Seals*, p. 109. Avigad relates *nby* to the locative place name *nb*, "Nob;" however, the etymology of this word is uncertain. According to Avigad ("New Names on Hebrew Seals"), *nby* is a name of a south-Arabic origin, analogous to biblical *nbywt* (Gen. 25:13, etc.) and related to the locative *nōb* (Isa. 10:32); see *BDB*, p. 611. *Nb*, "Nob" corresponds to *nby*, "Nobite" (a correspondence between a locative and gentilic), just as *kwš (kûš*, Isa. 11:1, etc.) relates to *kšy* (*kûšî* Jer. 13:23, etc.); see *BDB*, pp. 468-69, 526.

The form *nby* also appears in a seal impression (no. 6, line 3) from a clay bulla found in the excavations of Lachish V. In this grammar, this impression is referred to as Lachish V 6:3 to indicate that the find comes from the publication of Aharoni on Lachish V and refers to line 3 of find no. 6. Aharoni mistakenly states that the combination *nby* does not fit any known personal name and he therefore restores an *ʾaleph* to the form (*nby[ʾ]*, "prophet"); cf. Y. Aharoni, *Investigations at Lachish, the Sanctuary and the Residency* (Lachish V) (Tel Aviv: Gateway Publishers, Inc., 1975), pp. 21, 22.

[226]The form consists of the conjunction, preposition, and gentilic noun and is related to the biblical names *qrs* (*qēros*), Ezra 2:44 and *qyrs* (*qêros*), Neh. 7:47. Cf. *BDB*, p. 902. For the reading as a gentilic, see Aharoni, *Arad Inscriptions*, p. 38; Lemaire, *Inscriptions hébraïques*, p. 180. *Qrsy* denotes one of the biblical *nĕtînîm*; see Aharoni, *Arad Inscriptions*, p. 38; B.A. Levine, "The *Netînîm*," *JBL* 82 (1963): 207-12; "Notes on a Hebrew Ostracon from Arad," *IEJ* 19 (1969): 50, 51.

3.3.2.2 Masculine Plural Gentilics

> *ktym*, "Kittim," (the plural of *kty*), A 1:2, 2:1-2, 4:1, 7:2, 14:2, *ktym̊*, A 11:2, *k̊t̊[y]m̊*, A 8:1-2, *[k]t[ym]*, A 5:6-7, *[kt]ym*, A 10:2.[227]

The consistent writing with *yod* in these forms (unless *ʾdmm* is a counter example), [228] may indicate that the gentilic plural ending had not yet monophthongized in epigraphic Hebrew (*-iyyīm* › *-îm*).[229]

3.3.3 The Inflection of the Noun

3.3.3.1 Gender

Epigraphic Hebrew nouns are either masculine or feminine. The masculine noun occurs, for the most part,[230] without an

---

[227]The form *ktym* is well known from the Bible (*ktym/ktyym*, *BDB*, p. 508) and the Dead Sea Scrolls. According to Aharoni (*Arad Inscriptions*, pp. 12-13), the term refers to Greek or Cypriotic mercenaries. This view is followed by most others (cf. Lemaire, *Inscriptions hébraïques*, p. 156; Gibson, *TSSI*, pp. 50, 52; Pardee, *HHL*, p. 31, etc.).

[228]*ʾdmm*, Arad 3:12. The form occurs with coordinating conjunction *w-* and may mean "Edomites." The uncertainty is based on the fragmentary condition of lines 11 and 12 in Arad 3. Also, the absence of the *yod* (biblical *ʾdmym*; cf. epigraphic Hebrew *ktym*) indicates that we should perhaps look for another interpretation for *ʾdmm*, as the ending for the plural gentilic, as evidenced by *ktym*, is *-ym*. Cf. sec. 3.3.2, esp. p. 182, n. 217.

[229]See Pardee, "Letters From Tel Arad," *UF* 10 (1978): 293. In the Bible, both *ktyym* and *ktym* are attested. That the *yod* is consonantal is likewise the opinion of D. Freedman, "The Orthography of the Arad Ostraca," *IEJ* 19 (1969): 52, who reads *lakkittiyyim*, as in Isa. 23:12, Jer. 2:10 and Ezek. 27:6. The *yod* of *ktym* is identified as the gentilic and the vocalization of Freedman is followed by Parunak, "The Orthography of the Arad Ostraca," *BASOR* 230 (1978): 25, 27.

[230]Note the masculine singular noun *qrʾh*, "partridge" with a *-h* ending. It is proven masculine by its occurrence in a patronymic sequence *ḥ[z]qyhw bn qrʾh*, "*Ḥizqiyahu*, son of *Qoreh*," Ophel 1:1. That *qrʾh* should be the name of the father, see Hestrin and Dayagi-Mendels, *Inscribed Seals*, p. 9. The form corresponds to the masculine singular biblical noun (and proper name) *qrʾ (qōrēʾ)*, 1 Chron. 26:1, (and *qwrʾ*, 1 Chron. 9:19, 2 Chron. 31:4). The afformative *-h* in the epigraphic Hebrew noun is a *m.l.* for -ē. See Donner and Röllig, *KAI*, p. 188, no. 190; Gibson, TSSI, p. 26; Lemaire, *Inscriptions hébraïques*, p. 240.

ending (e.g., *sws*, "horse," A 111:5), while feminine singular nouns most commonly end with *-h* (e.g., *nḥlh,* "inheritance," MO 2:4-5; *-swsh*, "mare," A 32:1), derived from -at.[231]

This morphology is consistent with biblical Hebrew. The old *-at* ending is regularly retained in epigraphic Hebrew in the construct state (e.g., *mʾh*, "one hundred," Qasile 1:2, absolute; *m[ʾ]t*, "one hundred of," Siloam 1:5-6, construct). The old feminine ending *-t*, on the other hand, is, as in biblical Hebrew, retained in certain environments in both the absolute and construct states: e.g., *bt*, "daughter of," Avigad (1978) Lyre 1:2; Avigad NN 1:2; TBM (sherd) 2 (?); Naveh 1:2 (Herr 98); Herr 117:1-2, 143:2; Hest. 34:2; *št*, "year"[232](in *bšt htšʿt*, "in the ninth year," S 9:1), although this ending is not exclusive to feminine absolutes (i.e., *ʿt*, "time," a masculine singular in *hʿt hzh*, "this season.[233]

Other epigraphic Hebrew nouns are feminine in gender because the meaning of the word naturally denotes a feminine being: *ʾšt*, "wife of," *ʾmth,* "his maidservant," *bt*, "daughter of."

Some epigraphic Hebrew zero-ending nouns are feminine in gender for no obvious reason; e.g., *ʿr/ʿyr*, "city," *ʾrṣ*, "earth" take feminine modifiers in biblical Hebrew,[234] but no empirical evidence exists in epigraphic Hebrew to prove this gender.

In biblical Hebrew, parts of the body that come in pairs are generally feminine.[235] One could hypothesize that in epigraphic Hebrew, the morphology of the pair *yd* (singular), "hand," and *ydt* (plural), "hands, monuments" proves the feminine gender for parts

---

[231]Cf. Cowley, *Gesenius*, p. 222.

[232]The feminine singular noun *št* (**šat*) deserves special mention. The form is dialectical, occurring only in northern texts. In the northern form, attested at Samaria, the *nun* has assimilated: **šat ‹ šant*. The regular biblical form is *šānāh ‹ šanat*; this form is not, however, attested in epigraphic Hebrew, either in the North or South.

[233]The masculine demonstrative adjective proves that the noun *ʿt* is masculine in epigraphic Hebrew. This is in contrast to the biblical word *ʿt* which is more frequently feminine and occurs rarely, in mostly late texts (i.e., Ezra 10:14, *lʿtym mzmnym, lĕʿittîm mĕzumānîm*; see *BDB*, p. 773. It is probable that *zh* is not to be pronounced *zo (feminine) as the form of epigraphic Hebrew feminine demonstrative is everywhere *zʾt (zʾōt).* It is to be noted though that zʾt in Silwan 2:1, 3 is the demonstrative of a restored feminine noun *qbrh*, "tomb," and in Arad 40:14-15, the feminine noun *rʿh* "evil" is evident but the word *[z]ʾt* is restored.

[234]See Lambdin, *Introduction to Biblical Hebrew*, p. 3; Blau, *A Grammar of Biblical Hebrew*, p. 65.

[235]See Cowley, *Gesenius,* p. 392, n. n.

of the body that come in pairs. The necessary evidence would rest on *ydt*, a plural analogous orthographically to biblical *ydt*, *yādōt* (Gen. 47:24, *et cetera*) and semantically to *yd* in 2 Sam. 18:18.[236] Technically, however, the *-t* ending on *ydt* proves nothing of the sort, and could, in fact, resemble other biblical masculine plural nouns such as *ʾbwt (ʿābôt)*, "fathers," Exod. 12:3, *et cetera*, and *nhrwt* (*nĕhārôt*), "rivers," Isa. 19:6, *et cetera*.

Epigraphic Hebrew epigraphy exhibits the morphology of the masculine and feminine gentilics. The afformatives *-y* (for masculine) and *-t*/*-yt* (for feminine) convert a substantive into an adjective, including names of people or countries and numerals to form patronymics or tribal names, and figure also in ordinal numbers.

The suffix *-y* appears on masculine gentilic nouns (e.g., *bʿlmʿny*, "The Baʿalmeʿonite," S 27:3; bʿlty, "The Baʿalatite," A 60:1-2), while the feminine afformative is *-t* (*ʿśry*, "tenth," (masculine); *ʿśrt*, "tenth," (feminine))[237] or *-yt* (tšʿyt, "ninth")[238].

---

[236]The letters *ẙd̊t̊* are visible in Ophel 1:3; see Milik, "Notes d'épigraphie et de topographie palestiniennes," RB 6 (1959): plate 13, and his comments to this effect on pp. 550-51. Milik is followed by Lemaire, *Inscriptions hébraïques*, pp. 239-41: *ydt*, "steles," but not by others; cf. Gibson, *TSSI*, p. 25, who, along with others, reads *yh̊ẘ[špṭ]*.

The epigraphic Hebrew feminine plural ending is *-t* ; (see sec. 3.3.3.2, pp. 190-92); hence, *ydt* may possibly be a feminine plural, and *yd* a feminine singular. Other epigraphic Hebrew nouns that are parts of the body which come in pairs may be feminine (e.g., *zrʿ*, "arm," *ʿyn*, "eye"), but this assumption is again based on comparative biblical evidence where these words generally function as feminines (see Cowley, *Gesenius*, p. 392, n. n). Note, however, that both *zrʿ*, "arm," and *ʿyn* "eye" also occur as masculines in the Bible (*zrʿ*, Isa. 17:5, etc., *ʿyn*, Zech. 3:9, *etc*.).

[237]Also, *rbʿy* (Ophel 2:3) and *rbʿt* (Lachish 29:l), "fourth." The gentilic nouns which denote patronyms or tribal names in epigraphic Hebrew indisputably show the *yod m.l.* (*ī*) on masculine singular forms, but no feminine counterpart is attested. However, gentilics which function as ordinal numbers exhibit both masculine and feminine forms (e.g., "tenth" and "fourth" above).

[238]The form *tšʿyt* shows internal evidence for the *-ît* ending in feminine ordinals, and thus it follows also, in feminine singular gentilics. In summary, epigraphic Hebrew exhibits a group of nouns known as gentilics, which end in *-y (-ī)* for the masculines, and *-(y)t* (*-īt*) for the feminines. For a more detailed discussion of gentilics in epigraphic Hebrew (including also the masculine plural form), see sec. 3.3.2 above, beginning on p. 181.

3.3.3.2 Number

Three categories of number exist in epigraphic Hebrew: singular, plural, and dual. The singular has a zero-ending for the masculine and *-h* or *-t* ending for the feminine.[239] Like the feminine singular, the plural and dual in epigraphic Hebrew exhibit special endings.

The epigraphic Hebrew masculine plural ending is *-m* (biblical *-(y)m*, *-īm*). The following pairs of epigraphic Hebrew forms illustrate the singular versus plural opposition: *khn*, "priest," Avigad (*IEJ* 25) 4:4 and *khnm*, "priests," Lemaire "grenade" inscription (*RB* 88); *spr*, "letter," L 3:9, *et cetera*, and *hsprm*, "the letters," L 5:6-7; *qṣr*, "harvestor, the one harvesting," MHY 1:3 and *hqṣrm*, "the harvestors," MHY 1:10; *ym*, "day," L 5:9, *et cetera*, and *ymm*, "days," MHY 1:9, *et cetera*; *bn*, "son," L 1:1, *et cetera*, and *bnm*, "sons," MO 2:3; *hkty*, "the Kitti," A 17:9 and *ktym*, "Kittim," A 10:5; *ṭb*, "good," L 1:2, *et cetera*, and *ṭbm*, "good," L 6:6.

The feminine plural afformative in epigraphic Hebrew is probably *-t*,[240] as is indicated by the epigraphic Hebrew form *ʾmt*, "cubits," Siloam 1:2. Most feminine plurals in biblical Hebrew are marked by *-(ô)t* and the feminine plural morpheme in epigraphic Hebrew may be assumed to have been the same. In biblical Hebrew, there are feminine plurals not marked by *-ôt* (e.g., *nāšîm*, "women," *ʿārîm*, "cities") and there are *-ôt* endings which

---

[239]See sec. 3.3.3.1, pp. 187-89.

[240]A final epigraphic Hebrew form considered an adjective displays the ending *-wt*, which possibly exhibits internal evidence for the feminine plural ending *-ōt*. The word in question occurs once as a proper name, *yrymwt*; see P. Bordreuil and A. Lemaire, "Nouveaux sceaux hébreux, araméens et ammonites," *Semitica* 26 (1976): 46.

Lemaire considers the name a noun signifying "le corpulent," following Noth (*IPN*, p. 226) who take *yrymwt* in the Bible as an adjective from a *qatīl* base meaning "fat, stout." He, however, notes that the *-wt* ending is hypocoristic and under no circumstances should be regarded as a plural.

It is also reasonable to note the element *-mwt*, possibly signifying the deity *mōt* (?), in *yrymwt*, just as in another epigraphic Hebrew proper name *mrmwt*. This is the suggestion of L. Koehler and W. Baumgartner, *Lexicon in Veteris Testamenti Libros*, p. 405, who identifies the proper name as elements *yry* (= *yrw*) and *mwt*, and compares it to the analogous biblical forms *yrwʾl* (*yĕrûʾēl*) and *yryʾl* (*yĕrîʾēl*). Another analogous biblical name not mentioned by Koehler and Baumgartner is *yryhw* (*yĕriyyāhû*). Of course if *yrymwt* contains the theophoric element, the form does in no way prove the feminine plural ending for epigraphic Hebrew.

do not mark feminine gender (e.g., *ʾābôt*, "fathers," *nĕhārôt*, "rivers").

In order to prove conclusively the morphology of the feminine plural in epigraphic Hebrew, forms must be identified that are indicated to be feminine plurals by markers other than the *-t* afformative, such as modifiers (e.g., known feminine plural adjectives, verbs, or the plural demonstrative). However, only one epigraphic Hebrew form *(ʾmt)* occurs with such a modifier (the cardinal number *šlš*).

Of four nouns which may be regarded as feminine plurals on the basis of biblical Hebrew, only one may be labeled a feminine plural in epigraphic Hebrew with certainty. These nouns are *mśʾt*, "signals," L 4:10, *ʾšpt*, "quivers," L 13:3, *ʾtt*, "signs, indications," L 4:11, and *ʾmt*, "cubits," Siloam 1:2.

Morphologically, *mśʾt*, in the phrase *ʾl mśʾt lkš nḥnw šmrm*, on the analogy of biblical Hebrew *mśʾt* (Gen. 43:34) could be a feminine plural, "We are watching for the signals of Lachish;" however, the same could be said for the feminine singular construct (biblical *mśʾt*, as in Judges 20:38: *mśʾt* hʿšn, "uprising of smoke, smoke signal[s]), "signal of Lachish."[241]

ʾšpt, "quivers," may be a feminine plural noun (the biblical singular counterpart is *ʾšph [ʾašpāh])*, especially if the strokes after this word in Lachish 13:3 are numerical[242] However, another plausible interpretation of Lachish 13:3 takes *ʾšpt* as the feminine singular construct.[243]

The form *ʾtt* seems likely to be a plural. This conclusion is based on the parallelism of L 4:10, *mśʾt lkš*, "Lachish (fire)-signals," and the writing with two taws, which is analogous to biblical *ʾwtwt (ʾôtôt)*, "signs." However, the biblical *ʾwt (ʾôt)* is

---

[241]There is also a problem of semantics in comparing the epigraphic Hebrew form as a plural to the biblical word. From the context of Lachish 4, it is the meaning of the biblical singular construct ("signals"), rather than that of the plural ("portions, burdens"), which better fits the meaning of *mśʾt* in epigraphic Hebrew.

For *mśʾt*, see G. Dossin, "Signaux lumineux au pays de Mari," *Revue d'assyriologie et d'archéologie orientale* 35 (1938): 174-186.

[242]For this interpretation, see Lemaire, *Inscriptions hébraïques*, pp. 130-31.

[243]For the alternative *ʾt ʾšpt X*, "the quiver of X," cf. Pardee, *HHL*, p. 109. Cf. also p. 174, n. 206, in this grammar.

attested both as a masculine and feminine noun.[244] This fact clouds the certainty of assigning the feminine gender to the epigraphic Hebrew form, since the latter form is not modified in such a way as to indicate the gender of this noun.

The final noun in the discussion of feminine plurals in epigraphic Hebrew is *ʾmt*, a form which can be shown to be a feminine plural on the basis of other epigraphic Hebrew forms, including a modifier. In the same inscription in which *ʾmt* occurs (Siloam), *ʾmh*, the feminine singular form occurs twice (lines 5 and 6), and also *šlš*, the cardinal number which modifies feminine nouns, occurs before *ʾmt* ("three cubits"). *ʾmt*, then, stands as empirical evidence for the feminine plural in epigraphic Hebrew, a form which ends in *taw*.

There is no empirical evidence that nouns of feminine gender may have *-m* endings. It is, however, likely that nouns such as *ḥṭm*, "wheat," and *śʿrm*, "barley," which are feminine plurals in the Bible, would have also been of feminine gender in epigraphic Hebrew.

Besides singular and plural, the dual, a third number in epigraphic Hebrew, is used to denote objects which occur in pairs. The epigraphic Hebrew dual ending is *-ym*. This fact is proven by the epigraphic Hebrew forms: *mʾh*, "one hundred," absolute, *m[ʾ]t*, "one hundred of," construct, and the dual, *mʾtym*, "two hundred," as well as by the singular *yd*, "hand," and dual *ydyk*, "your (m.s.) hands (strength, power)."

The dual ending is appended to a ground form, and in epigraphic Hebrew, one form, *mʾtym* illustrates the feminine singular stem and dual ending. In the feminine, the old *-at* ending is retained before the dual afformative, just as in biblical Hebrew (e.g., *sph*, "lip," *śĕpātaym*, "two lips").

The *yod* in both duals in epigraphic Hebrew can either indicate that the diphthong *-ay* did not reduce (and the vocalization for the dual ending is therefore **-aym*[245]/ or *-ayim*), or that the unaccented diphthong *ay* reduced to *ê*.

The use of the dual is restricted to substantives which come in pairs (especially dual body parts; e.g., *ydyk*, "your (m.s.) two

---

[244] *BDB*, p. 16. Even the plural is attested as a masculine: *lšny hʾtwt hʾlh* (*lišnêy hāʾōtôt hāʾēleh*), "these two signs," Ex. 4:9. However, the feminine plural also exists: *hʾtwt hgdlwt hʾlh* (*hāʾōtôt hagĕdōlôt hāʾēleh*), "these great signs," Josh. 24:17.

[245] See Cross and Freedman, *EHO*, pp. 54, 56.

hands"), and some numerals (*mʾtym*, "two hundred;" *šnym*, "two"), and geographic names (e.g., *mṣrym*, "Egypt").

The epigraphic Hebrew orthography of the dual noun in construct state is *ydy*, "the hands of, power of, strength of," L 6:7.[246]

3.3.3.3 Construct State

In epigraphic Hebrew, a noun may be proclitic and form a "stress unit" with a following noun, the two nouns called technically the *nomen regens* and *nomen rectum*, respectively.[247]

The latter form remains unchanged in its form, while the noun before it undergoes a morphological change.[248] The *nomen regens* is dependent upon the *nomen rectum* and is said to be in the construct state, while the *nomen rectum* is said to be in the absolute state.[249]

Epigraphic Hebrew masculine singular nouns in construct state show no consonantal modification (e.g., *bgd ʾbdk*, "your servant's garment;" *nbl yn yšn*, "a jar of old wine;" *dbr hmlk*, "the king's order").[250]

---

[246]For the pronunciation of *ydy* as *yaday*, cf. Cross and Freedman, *EHO*, p. 56; Gibson, *TSSI*, p. 46. This vocalization assumes that 1) /a/ in propretonic open syllables has not reduced, and 2) unaccented *-ay* has not gone to *ê*. Zevit, on the other hand, would probably vocalize *yĕdê*, just as he vocalizes other construct plurals and duals (see *MLAHE*, p. 30, n. 104 and p. 27, n. 72) as though the *-ay* diphthong has contracted by the sixth century in the South.

[247]See Blau, *A Grammar of Biblical Hebrew*, p. 66 and Cowley, *Gesenius*, p. 247.

[248]For example, note the construct phrase *m[ʾ]t ʾmh* in the phrase *wm[ʾ]t ʾmh hyh gbh hṣr*, "The rock was one hundred cubits high," from Siloam 1:5-6. In this example, the *-h* of the *nomen regens* (*mʾh*) shows the retention of the older form with *-t* before the *nomen rectum*, while the *-h* of the latter form remains unchanged.

[249]Cowley, *Gesenius*, p. 247.

[250]In biblical Hebrew, the masculine singular noun (also feminine singular nouns which have no consonantal ending, such as *ʿyn*, "eye of" and *ʿyn*, "spring of" [see below]) is differentiated in the absolute and construct states only by vowel pattern. Vowel patterns are not observable in epigraphic Hebrew. Yet, the statement that epigraphic Hebrew singular nouns in construct state show no consonantal modification is accepted as true, at least *prima facie*, based on comparative biblical evidence.

Epigraphic Hebrew examples of masculine singular nouns in construct state are: *bn*, "the son of," Hazor 6:2, etc. (see Lexicon for numerous other

The masculine singular noun (and all nouns for that matter) as *nomen regens* may be introduced by a preposition or conjunction, but never by the definite article, which may only appear before a definite *nomen rectum*.[251] Examples in epigraphic Hebrew which illustrate this fact with regard to the preposition include *bʾrh*, "in the way of," Ajrud 7:1, *lbn*, "for the son of," A 10:4, *lgdr*, "belonging to the enclosure of," Gib 51, *bḥm*, "in the heat of," MHY 1:10, *bṭb*, "in the good(ness) of," L 5:8, *mynn*, "from the wine of," A 1:9, *bym*, "on the day of," Ajrud 5:1, 6:1, *mytr*, "from the surplus of," A 5:13-14, *bk[l]*, "in all of," A 88:1, *bnbl*, "in a jar of," S 53:2, 72:2, *mʿwd*, "from what is left of," A 5:3, *bʿmq*, "in the valley of," Ophel 2, 3, *bśd‹h›* (?), "in the field of," Ophel 1, *lśr*, "belonging to the commander of," Ajrud 3:1.

The fact that the definite article occurs before the *nomen rectum* in the construct state is illustrated by the following phrases: *šm hym*, "the date" (literally, "the name of the day)," A 1:4, *śr*

references), *gbh*, "the height of," Siloam 1:6, *gdr*, "walled plot of," Gib. 1, 7, 8, 10, 14-16, 19, 25, 31, 32, 34, 36, 51, 54, 55, 59, 61; (*gdr*), Gib. 3; (*gd[r]*), Gib. 9, 18; (*[gd]r*), Gib. 2; (*[gd]r*), Gib 17; (*g[dr]*), Gib 60; (*‹g›dr*), Gib. 11, *zhb*, "gold of," Tell Qasile 2:1; *zrʿ* "grain, seed of (?)," L 5:10; *kl*, "all of," KBL 1:1; MHY 1:10; (*bk[l]*), "in all of," A 88:1; *ksp*, "the money of," A 16:8; *krm*, "the vineyard of," S 20:1; 53:2; 54:1-2; 58:2; 60:1; 61:1; 72:1; (*kr[m]*), S 73:2; *lb*, "the heart of," L 3:6; *mlk*, "the king of," A 88:3; (*mlk*), A 40:13, *mśʾ*, "a mule load of," A 3:4; *nʿr*, "steward of," Avigad Naar Seal 1:1, 2:2; TBM 1:1; (*[nʿ]r*), Ain Shems 2:2; (*[nʿ]r*), RR 8:2; *[sp]r*, "the letter of," L 6:3-4; (*[s]pr*), 16:4; *ʿbd*, "servant of," L 3:19; Megiddo Seal 1:2; Ushna Seal 1:1-2; Hest. (1974) Hebron 1:3; Tell en Nasbeh 3:2; Herr 4:2-3; *ʿwd*, "yet, still, anymore of," A 2:7, (*mʿwd*), A 1:5, 5:3; *ʿṣd*, "cutting, hoeing of," Gezer 1:3; *ql*, "the voice of," Siloam 1:2; *qṣr*, "the harvest of," Gezer 1:4; *rʾš*, "head of," Siloam 1:6; *śr*, "the commander, captain, governor of," A 26:2; L 3:14; Av (1978) 3:1; (*śr*), Barkay (1977) 1:1 (=Avigad 1978); Ajrud 3:1; *šm*, "the name of," A 1:4; Ajrud 5:1; *byt*, "the house of," A 18:9; L 20:1 (?); L 4:5; Tell Qasile 2:1; L 22:10; L V Ost. 1:10; *(byt)*, Beersheba 1:3; *yn/yyn*, "wine of," (*yn*, S 53:1, 54:1, 62:1, 72:1, 73:2; (*[y]n*) S 20:1-2; *yyn*, Avigad Wine Decanter 1 (?); *ʿyn*, "the eye of," L 3:5. A final example, *[ʿ]yn*, "the spring of," is uncertain as an example of construct state because Arad 71 is badly broken. Although Aharoni reads as though a proper name, *ʾdn gdy[hw]*, (*Arad Inscriptions*, p. 96), the visible letters could possibly be read *[ʿ]yn gdy*, "Ain Gedi."

[251]This rule is true for all nouns in epigraphic Hebrew; e.g., *lʾrbʿt hymm*, "for (the) four days," A 2:2-3; *bktp hṣ[r]* on the side of the rock," Silwan 1:1; *btsbt hbqr*, "during the morning rounds," L 4:9; *byd hkty*, "into the hand of (to) the Kitti," A 17:9.

hṣbʾ "the commander of the army," L 3:14, *ʿbd hmlk*, "the king's servant," L 3:19.

The masculine singular noun occurs in the construct state as the first element of a locative place name, e.g., *byt*, "the house of," A 18:9; Lemaire's ivory "grenade"[252] (*byt yhwh*), L 4:5 *(byt hrpd)*, Tel Qasile 2:1 *(byt ḥrn)*, L 22:10 (= L V Ost. 1:10) (*byt ʾkzy[b])*, *krm*, "the vineyard of," S 20:1, 53:2, 54:1-2, 58:2, 61:1, 72:1 *(krm htl)*, S 55:1-2, 60:1 *(krm yḥwʿly)*, 73:2 *(kr[m])*, *ḥṣr*, "the village of," MHY 1:3-4 *(ḥṣr ʾsm)*, A 32:1 *([ḥṣr] swsh)*.

The construct state for masculine singular nouns also appears in proper names, as the first element, e.g., *ʾš-*, "gift of," L 22:6; L V Ost. 1:6; A 17:3, 35:2, 51:1, 105:2, 106:2, 107:2; B/L (26) 12:1-2; *ʾ̊š̊* -, "Jerusalem Jar 3:1, *[ʾ]š-*, A 40:11 (likewise the proper name *ʾšʾ*), *gr-*, "sojourner, newcomer, guest (?) of," Av (*EI* 9) 8:2; R 5:1 (?) (=Herr 83), *zr-*, "circlet of (?), crown of," Dayan 3:1-2, *ḥl-*, "strength/fortress, rampart of," Ajrud 8, *mʿś-*, "work of," Av (*EI* 9) 7:2, Hest 77:1, Herr 149:2, Seal of Maʿaseyahu 1:1, *mqn-*, "creature of," Herr 116:1, A 60:4, 72:1, *mtn-*, "gift of," L 1:5, B/L (26) 9:2, 11:2, Jerusalem Seal 1:1, *m̊tn-*, Tell en Nasbeh 2:2,ʿbd-, "servant of" (likewise the proper names *ʿbd* and *ʿbʾ-*), A 10:4, Herr 99:2, 121:2, *et cetera* (see Lexicon for complete list of references), *ʿgl-*, "calf of," S 41:1, *šlm-*, "thanksgiving offering of," A 108:3, R 3:2 (= Herr 87), Tel Ira 1:4.

Feminine singular nouns having the *m.l. -h* in the absolute, have *-t* in the construct: *mʾh*, "one hundred," Tel Qasile 1:2, *m[ʾ]t,* "one hundred of," Siloam 1:5-6, *ʾšt*, "wife of," R 7:1-2 (Herr 36), *qbrt*, "the tomb of," Silwan 3:1,[253] *šmʿt,* "tidings of," L 3:3, 4:2, *šm̊ʿt*, L 2:2, *[šm]ʿt*, L 8:1-2, *š[mʿt]*, L 9:2, *[šmʿt]*, L 5:2, and *tsbt*, "tour, rounds of," L 4:9.

Feminine singular nouns ending in *taw* and those without a feminine marker show no (consonantal) modification in the construct, e.g., *bt*, "daughter," Avigad (1978) Lyre 1:2 (*lmʿdnh bt hmlk*, "for Maʿadanah, daughter of the king"), Avigad NN 1:2; TBM (sherd) 2 (?), Naveh 1:2, Herr 117:1-2, 143:2, Hest. 34:2, *yd*, "hand of," A 24:15 (*whbqydm ʿl yd ʾlyšʿ*, "He is to hand them over to [into the hand of] Elisha"), *byd*, A 17:9, *byd̊*, L 9:6-7,

---

[252]A. Lemaire, "Une inscription paléo-hébraïque sur grenade en ivoire," *RB* 88, no. 2 (1981): 236-39.

[253]If the restoration is correct, *[qbrt]*, Silwan 2:1, would be an addition to this group.

[by]d, A 24:13-14, *ʿyn*, "the eye of," L 3:5 (*ʿyn ʿbdk*, "your servant's eye").

As the first element of a locative place name, epigraphic Hebrew has *bʾr-*, "well of," A 3:3-4 *(bʾr šbʿ)*, S 1:2 (*bʾrym*, "west well," or possibly the dual, "two wells") and *gt-*, "wine press of," S 14:1-2 *(gt prʾn)*.

One epigraphic Hebrew proper name contains a possible feminine singular construct form: *dlt-*, "door of (= womb of)," Av NN 8:1 *(dltyhw)*, however the form in question could be a perfect from *dlh*, "pull, draw, lift up."[254]

---

[254]For the epigraphic Hebrew proper name *dltyhw*, see Avigad, "New Names on Hebrew Seals," *EI* 12 (1975): 68. *Dltyhw* may, in fact, be analogous to the biblical proper name *dlyhw* and verb *dlytny*, "You have lifted me up," (Psalm 30:2).

The difficulty with this analysis is the absence of empirical biblical data for the second masculine singular perfect in proper names; the only form directed to the masculine singular subject is *ʾlyʾth*, "you (m.s.) are my God," 1 Chron. 25:4. Coogan, *West Semitic Personal Names in the Murašû Documents*, pp. 19-20, 71, cites a name from this same root (*dlh*) which uses the second masculine singular *qal* perfect plus the first person singular suffix: *dalātānī*.

A second, though less plausible possibility is to relate *dlt-* to the feminine singular noun *dālît*, "branch, bough (of YH)," as in *dlytyw/dlywtyw* (Ezek. 19:11, Jer. 11:16, etc.).

Another possibility for *dltyhw* is to trace its etymology to the feminine singular noun *dlt*, "door." This noun is attested in Proverbs 8:34, *ʾšry ʾdm šmʿ ly lšqd ʿl dltty ywm ywm lšmr mzwzt ptḥy*, "Happy is the man who listens to me, watching daily at my doors, guarding my gates," in a phrase (*lšqd ʿl dltty*) which functions metaphorically to signify man's faith and wisdom in God.

Avigad, "New Names on Hebrew Seals," *EI* 12 (1975), suggests that the parallelism between *dlt* and *ptḥ* in Proverbs 8:34 may establish a connection between the attested biblical proper name *ptḥyh* (1 Chr. 24:16, etc.), and *dltyhw*.

The former name may refer to "opening the womb" (i.e., a birth name, "May (DN) open (your maid-servant's womb)," or "(O DN), open my womb!"). Perhaps, then, *dlt* also refers to the womb. In fact, this assumption finds a parallel in the Bible. In Job 3:10, *dlt* refers to the aperture of the womb, *dlt btny*, and this analogy is certainly important for establishing *dltyhw* as a birth name, meaning "(Open) the womb (of your maid-servant), O DN!" or the like.

The biblical example from Job 3:10 provides evidence for taking *dlt* (in *dltyhw*) as though it is a verbal noun of some kind. However, this hypothesis can be accepted if one argues that *ptḥ* in proper names is not just a verbal noun ("opening [of the womb] is YHWH"), rather, that it is a more concrete notion like *delet*.

The meaning of the absolute noun *dlt*, which is attested in epigraphic Hebrew (Lachish 4:3), has also been the subject of debate with the most current sense given being that of a column of writing in a papyrus scroll (cf. *dlt* in Jer. 36:23); cf. Pardee, *HHL*, p. 92, for a summation and partial bibliography. Victor Sasson has concluded that *dlt* at Lachish referred to a writing tablet made out of

Epigraphic Hebrew masculine plural nouns in construct state end with *yod* as in biblical Hebrew, e.g., *bny*, "the sons of," A 16:5, 49:1, 2, 4, 16, L 16:4 (?), *dbry*, "the words of," L 6:5, *hrẙ* "the mountains of," KBL 1:1-2, *spry*, "the letters of," L 6:4. The same is true of epigraphic Hebrew duals: *ydy*, "the hands (power, strength) of," L 6-7. Neither masculine plural nor dual nouns in construct state are attested in a proper or locative name in epigraphic Hebrew.

Only one restored feminine plural noun appears in the construct state. It is the noun coupled with a conjunction, *ẘʿ̊ṣm[t]*, "and the bones of," Silwan 2:2. There is not sufficient room in Silwan 2:2 to reconstruct *-wt*. This is consistent with the fact that epigraphic Hebrew evidence points only to the *-t* afformative for the feminine plural.

3.3.4 Numerals

3.3.4.1 Cardinal numbers

Tables 36 and 37 illustrate the extant cardinal numbers in epigraphic Hebrew. Table 36 gives the numerals attested below one hundred, while table 37, lists those attested numerals which are equal to or greater than one hundred.

---

leather. He discounts all earlier interpretations for *dlt* (including that which argues for *dlt* as a column of writing in a scroll); cf. "Studies in the Lexicon and Linguistic Usage of Early Hebrew Inscriptions," pp. 76-88.

TABLE 36
NUMBERS FROM 1-100

With fem. nouns	With masc. nouns	No.
–	*šnym*	2
šlš	–	3
–	*(h)ššh*	6
šbʿ	–	7
ʿśr	–	10
–	*šl̊šh ʿś̊r*	13
–	*š̊m̊nh̊ ʿśr*	18

TABLE 37
NUMBERS FROM 100-1000

Form	No.
*mʾh̊ (m[ʾ]*t, construct)	100
mʾtym̊	200
ʾlp, ʾl̊[p	1000

The cardinal numbers are rarely written out in epigraphic Hebrew and are usually expressed in the form of hieratic numerals. However, the cardinal numbers which do in fact occur as written forms illustrate certain morphological features.

Cardinal numbers under ten are variable according to gender agreement. This statement is based more on biblical Hebrew, where the evidence is abundant, but is probably also true in epigraphic Hebrew. The evidence from three epigraphic Hebrew texts, Siloam 1:2 and Arad 7 and 8, which contain the cardinal numbers "three", "six", "thirteen", and "eighteen" illustrates the following points. If the noun is feminine (Siloam 1:2), the numeral has a zero-ending (*šlš ʾmt*, "three cubits"). If the noun to which the numeral refers is masculine, as in *ym*, "day" (which is implied though not expressed in written form in Arad 7 and 8) the cardinal number ends in *hê*; e.g., *(h)ššh*, "the sixth (day)," *(h)šl̊šh ʿś̊r*, "the thirteenth (day)," *(h)šm̊nh̊ ʿśr*, "the eighteenth (day)". These last three forms are in the absolute state, as is shown by the use of the definite article and by the *-h* ending.

The numerals of one hundred and above are invariable for gender agreement. This fact is proven by Siloam 1:5: *bmʾtym̊ ẘʿlp ʾmh wm[ʾ]t ʾmh*, "twelve hundred cubits...one hundred cubits," where *ʾlp* (presumably a masculine noun as in biblical Hebrew), and *m[ʾ]t* (a feminine noun in construct state; *mʾh*, "one hundred," *mʾt*, " one hundred of ") both modify the feminine singular noun *ʾmh*, "cubit."

The data on numerals below one hundred is as follows. The number "two," *šnym*, occurs once, at Arad 7:7, in a temporal phrase. The noun to which the cardinal refers (*ym*, "day") is not expressed by the text. The form *šnym* is a dual and agrees with the gender of its noun; in this case, it modifies a masculine noun (unstated *ym*).

The number "three" is attested once as *šlš* in Siloam 1:2 where it modifies a feminine plural noun: *wbʿwd šlš ʾmt lhn[qb]*, "And while there were yet three cubits (of rock) to be tunneled through."

The two forms, *šbʿ and ʿśr*, from the stone plaque fragment discovered in the Ophel[255] may be separate cardinal numbers, "seven" and "ten" respectively, but because the inscription is broken on both sides of the tablet, other possibilities exist for the interpretation of these words. Another possibility is to restore line 2 as: *šbʿ ʿśr[h]*, the cardinal number "seventeen," which precedes

[255] Y. Shiloh, "City of David: Excavation 1978," *BA* 42 (1979): 170.

feminine nouns[256] or as the excavator points out,[257] as two masculine singular segolate nouns: *śbʿ (śōbaʿ)*, "abundance," and *ʿšr (ʿōšer)*, "riches." However, the ordinal *rbʿy*, "fourth," in line 3, may be an indication of the numerical nature of the text.

The cardinals "thirteen" and "eighteen" are the only numerals from eleven to nineteen which are attested in epigraphic Hebrew. Both numbers are from temporal expressions (Arad 8:2-3 and 3-4) and modify the unstated masculine singular noun *ym*, "day." The forms of the cardinals themselves are masculine, as numbers from eleven to nineteen, like those under ten, are variable according to gender agreement. The two numerals illustrate that numerals above ten and below twenty consist of two units, the first unit being a number from one to nine, and the second unit being the number "ten" (*ʿśr* is the masculine word for "ten").

The cardinal number "one hundred" occurs twice in epigraphic Hebrew; once with the masculine singular noun *šmn*, "oil," where it occurs after the noun, and is to be taken with another numeral, *ʾlp*, "one thousand;" *lmlk ʾl̊[p] šmn wmʾh̊*, "for the King: one thousand one hundred (units of) oil," Tell Qasile 1:1-2. The form of the numbered item in this phrase is as normally in the Bible after "one thousand" and "one hundred," that is, with the noun in the singular,[258] although according to regular biblical word-order, the noun should come after the second number or be repeated there.

The cardinal number "one hundred" occurs in construct state in Siloam 1:5, where it precedes the feminine singular noun *ʾmh*, "cubit;" *wm[ʾ]t ʾmh hyh gbh hṣr ʿl rʾš hḥṣb[m]*, "(At this point), the rock was one hundred cubits high over the head(s) of the hewers." Again, the noun is in the singular and follows the cardinal number. This is a common pattern in biblical Hebrew, although it is by no means the only pattern.[259]

The dual form of *mʾh, mʾtym*, "two hundred," occurs once in epigraphic Hebrew and is paired with *ʾlp*, "one thousand," just as *mʾh*, "one hundred," was in Tell Qasile: *wylkw hmym mn hmwṣʾ ʾl hbrkh bmʾtym̊ ẘʾlp ʾmh*, "And the water flowed from the spring to the pool a distance of twelve hundred cubits," Siloam

---

[256]As in Gen. 37:2–*šbʿ ʿśrh šnh*, "seventeen years;" cf. Blau, *A Grammar of Biblical Hebrew*, p. 99.

[257]Shiloh, "City of David," *BA* 42 (1979): 170.

[258]Cowley, *Gesenius*, p. 433.

[259]Ibid., pp.433-34.

1:4-5. *M'tym*, "two hundred," the smaller number, occurs before *'lp*, "one thousand," in this inscription, while in biblical Hebrew, the larger number usually comes first: *'lp (w)m'tym*, "twelve hundred."[260] *M'tym* exhibits the same form as in biblical Hebrew *(m'tym, mā(')tayim)*.

3.3.4.2 Ordinal numbers

Ordinal numerals from three through ten are formed from corresponding cardinals by adding the afformatives *-y* to the masculine and *-t* (or *-yt*) to the feminine. Based on the evidence from biblical Hebrew and the fact that the ordinal form varies from the expected cardinal form in epigraphic Hebrew, it can be assumed that there was also an internal vowel variation between the cardinal and ordinal forms. The ordinal "first" consists of a different word derived from the same root as biblical Hebrew *rō(')š*, "head, beginning" with a *-n* affix. Table 38 illustrates the ordinals attested in epigraphic Hebrew.

TABLE 38
ORDINAL NUMBERS

Masculine	Feminine	Meaning
r'šn	–	"first"
–	*šlšt*	"third"
rbʿy	*rbʿt*	"fourth"
–	*tšʿt, tšʿyt*	"ninth"
ʿśry	*ʿśrt*	"tenth"

The ordinal number "first" is attested in the masculine form *r'šn*, from Arad 1:6–*mhqmḥ hr'šn*, "of the first meal."

Rbʿy, "fourth," occurs in a broken context in Ophel 2:3, [ ]*rbʿy w*[ ], "...fourth and...," while its feminine counterpart *rbʿt* is

[260]Cowley, *Gesenius*, p. 434, n.i.

attested in Lachish 29:1, *brbᶜt*, "in the fourth [year]." The masculine ordinal ends in -y, while the feminine ends in *-t*, or *-yt* (*tšᶜyt*, "ninth").

The ordinal "tenth" also occurs in both the masculine and the feminine forms. The feminine ordinal *ᶜśrt* is much more common than the masculine form *ᶜśry*[261] in epigraphic Hebrew.

The form *tšᶜyt*, "ninth," from Lachish 20:1, is the only example of an ordinal exhibiting internal *yod* in the suffix (*m.l.* for long -ī); e.g., biblical *tĕšîᶜît*. This form is most important for it establishes the quality and quantity of the second vowel of the ordinal in epigraphic Hebrew.[262]

3.3.5 Adjectives

The attributive adjective in epigraphic Hebrew follows the noun that it modifies and agrees with it in number, gender and definiteness (e.g., *hqmḥ hrʾšn*, "the first meal," A 1:6).

The masculine singular adjective has a zero-ending (e.g., *yn yšn*, "old wine," S 5:3, *et cetera*), and the masculine plural adjectival affix is *-m* (e.g., *dbry h[śrm] lʾ ṭbm*, "The [officials'] statements are not good," L 6:6 and *[m]ᶜnym tḥtnm*, "[from] Lower Anim," A 25:2).

If the substantive is immediately connected with the *nomen rectum* and stands in construct state, the adjective follows the latter, as in the previous example and in Lachish 3:7–*lb ᶜbdk dwh*, "the heart of your servant is sick" (› "your servant has been sick at heart"). In both instances, the adjective functions predicatively and is not marked for definiteness.

A detailed listing of adjectives attested in epigraphic Hebrew is included in the Lexicon at the following entries: *ʾbr-*, *ʾmṣ*, *ʾpṣh*, *ʾš[ḥr]*, *bwzy*, *bᶜlmᶜny*, *bᶜlty*, *dwh*, *zkʾ*, *ḥy*, *ḥnn*, *ṭbm*, *ṭb-*, *ybš*, *yhd[y]*, *yšn*, *kšy*, *-ᶜz*, *ᶜlynm*, *ᶜšn*, *ṣdq*, *qdš*, *rʾšn*, *rb-*, *rbt*, *šḥrḥr*, *tḥtnm*.

---

261 *Hᶜśrt*, "the tenth (year)," S 1:1, 2:1-2, 3:1, 13:1, 16a:1, 16b:1, 17a:1, 18:1, 19:1, 21:1, 51:1, 53:1, 54:1, 55:1, 72:1; (*[hᶜ]śrt*), S 17b:1; (*h̊ᶜ[śrt]*), S 20:1; *ᶜśr̥y*, (+ *b-*), "(in the) tenth (month)," A 7:7-8; *ᶜśr̊y* (+ *l-*), "(of the) tenth (month)," A 7:3.

262 *Tšᶜt* (without *plene* spelling) occurs more often than *tšᶜyt*: *htšᶜt*, "the ninth," S 6:1, 9:1, 10:1, 12:1; (*ht̊šᶜt*), S 4:1; (*[h]tšᶜt*, S 8:1; (*htš̊[ᶜt]*), S 100:1; (*h̊tš[ᶜt]*), S 14:1; (*ht[šᶜt]*), S 5:1.

3.3.6 Conclusion

The previous section on substantives begins with a discussion of noun types in epigraphic Hebrew. The main nominal patterns which are proven by *matres lectionis* in epigraphic Hebrew, and which are discussed in more detail above, are the *qīl*, qūl, and *qatūl* patterns, as well as nouns with the suffixes *-ī* and *-īt*. Other nominal patterns for which the evidence is explicit are *ʾaleph*, *mem*, and *taw*-preformatives, reduplicated forms, and quadriconsonantals. The masculine gentilics, both singular and plural, as well as the feminine singular gentilic are proven by *matres lectionis*, as is the *-y* ending of ordinal numerals.

The preceding section on substantives also assembles the empirical evidence for numerous grammatical features of epigraphic Hebrew regarding the inflection of the noun (gender, number and construct state), gentilics, numerals (cardinals and ordinals), and adjectives.

3.4 The Particle

The particles in epigraphic Hebrew consist of adverbs, prepositions, conjunctions and interjections. These parts of speech express the relationship between words, one to another, and may serve to connect sentences. In most instances, particles are derived from original nominal, pronominal, and verbal forms.[263]

3.4.1 Adverbs

3.4.1.1 Introduction

In epigraphic Hebrew, forms which are used as adverbs fall into two principle groups, short independent forms and those independent forms which are more complex, consisting of a combination of two different parts of speech. Often these "complex" adverbs consist of a preposition plus a noun or another adverb, e.g., *kymm*, "according to the days" › "a few days ago (?)," *bṭb*, "in good(ness)" › "pleasantly, well."

Specific epigraphic Hebrew forms cited in this section are classified as adverbs on internal grounds. Also, most of the epigraphic Hebrew forms find a counterpart in biblical Hebrew.

Although all epigraphic Hebrew adverbs are independent forms, many of which are combinations of other parts of speech, the short forms, including temporal and locative adverbs, as well as the negatives *ʾl, ʾyn* and *lʾ*, comprise an important group and are more frequent in the language than "complex" adverbs.

Some short independent adverbs were originally substantives; e.g., *hym*, "the day" › "today," *mḥr*, "tomorrow," while other adverbial forms consist of a noun plus locative suffix, *hʿyrh*, "to the city."

While the etymology of most adverbs is clear, a few others, labeled by Gesenius as "primitive",[264] are of uncertain origin: e.g., *lʾ*, "not," *šm*, "there," *ʾl*, "don't."

The several types of adverbs attested in epigraphic Hebrew are grouped below according to their respective category.

---

[263]Cowley, *Gesenius*, pp. 103, 293.

[264]Ibid., p. 294.

3.4.1.2 Prepositions as preformatives

kym (preposition plus a noun used as an adverbial accusative in the unit *ʿt kym*), "this day; about this time, now," L 2:3 (2x); L 4:1, and restored in L 5:2-3, 3; L 8:2.

kymm (preposition plus noun), "according to the days (= a few days ago," MHY 1:5, 7.

mʾz (preposition plus adverb), "since, from the time of," L 3:7; *[m]ʾz*, L 6:13.

mzh (preposition plus adverb), "from here," L 3:18; A 13:2.

mšm (preposition plus adverb), "from there," A 17:4.

bʿwd (preposition plus adverb), "while yet," Siloam 1:1, 2.

bṭb (preposition plus noun), "in good › pleasantly, well," L 5:8.

3.4.1.3 Substantives as "adverbial accusatives"

mʾd, "very (much)," A 111:3.

hym, "the day › today," A 24:19; L 5:9; L 4:8 (restored).

ymm, "(A few) days (ago)," MHY 1:9.

mḥr, "tomorrow," A 2:6; L 9:8-9.

ʿwd, "yet, still," A 2:7,*ʿẘd̊*, A 21:8.

mhrh, "quickly," A 12:3; 17:5.

3.4.1.4 Pronouns used in an adverbial sense

zh in *mzh*, "from here," L 3:18; A 13:2.

3.4.1.5 Interjections/presentatives

hnh (demonstrative particle), "surely, lo, indeed," A 24:18; L 6:5.[265]

3.4.1.6 Negatives

ʾl, "don't," A 2:6; papMur 17a:2.

lʾ, "not," MHY 1:12; L 2:6, 3:8, 4:12, 6:6, *l[ʾ]*, L 6:14, *[lʾ]*, A 40:8, *wlʾ*, MHY 1:14; A 16:10; *[wlʾ]*, A 40:12.

ʾyn, "(there) is not," L 4:5, *ʾyn̊*, Silwan 2:1.

The latter negative adverb *(ʾyn)* takes pronominal suffixes: *ʾy[nn]y*, "I am not," L 4:7-8, *[ʾy]nnw*, "We are not," A 40:13-14.

3.4.1.7 Adverbs with inflectional suffix *hê*

Some adverbs are formed by the addition of the inflectional suffix *hê* (in most cases attached to a noun) which determines the form as a locative:

byth, "to the house of," A 17:2.

mṣrymh, "to Egypt," L 3:16.

hʿyrh, "to the city," L 4:7.

šmh, "(to) there," A 24:20; L 4:8, 8:7.

3.4.1.8 Short adverbs

Short adverbial forms are: *kn*, "so, thus," L 4:3, and the interrogative *hê* in the forms *hʾl* (the interrogative particle plus negative adverb), "Will (you) not?, won't you?," L 6:8, *hʾl* (interrogative particle plus preposition), "Is it true that (someone will send something) to (someone)?," L 5:9, and *hšlm*

[265]For a discussion of *hn*, cf. p. 230, n. 302.

(interrogative particle plus substantive), "Is it well (with you)?," Ajrud 15:3.[266]

3.4.1.9 Miscellaneous adverbs

ʾmn, "it is so,[267] truly, verily," MHY 1:11.

gm, "moreover, truly, yea," L 3:10.

3.4.1.10 Locative adverbs

[p]ḥ, "here," Silwan 2:1.

šm, "there," L 4:5 (also *šmh*, A 24:20; L 4:8; 8:7, and *mšm*, A 17:4).

3.4.1.11 Temporal adverbs

[ʾḥ]r, "afterwards," L 3:12 (probably substantive in origin).[268]

ʾmš, "yesterday," L 3:6.

ʿt,[269] "now, even now," L 2:3 (2x); 4:1, *[ʿt]*, L 5:2, 3; 8:2, *wʿt*, A 1:1-2, 2:1, 3:1, 5:1-2, 7:1-2, 8:1, 10:1, 11:2, 16:3, 18:3, 21:3, 40:4; L 4:2; papMur 17a:2, *[w]ʿt*, A 17:1, *w[ʿt]*, A 6:1; L 3:4, 9:3, *[wʿt]*, A 14:1; L 5:6, 6:8.

---

[266]Cowley, *Gesenius*, p. 296. Gesenius views the interrogative particle as possibly a short form of *hl* (*hal*).

[267]Pardee, *HHL*, p. 22.

[268]*BDB*, p. 29.

[269]Gesenius (Cowley, *Gesenius*, pp. 251, 561) analyzes the biblical counterpart of the epigraphic Hebrew *ʿt*, which is *ʿth*, as having the *hê* adverbial ending, used temporally (rather than a determination of a locative). The form minus *hê* occurs rarely in the Bible (the *ketib* in Ezek. 23:43 and Ps. 74:6), and everywhere in epigraphic Hebrew, indicating that the inflectional suffix *hê* is reserved in epigraphic Hebrew as the locative determinator. On the pronunciation and analysis of *ʿt*, see Pardee, "Letters From Tel Arad," *UF* 10 (1978): 292-93.

3.4.2 Prepositions

3.4.2.1 Introduction

In epigraphic Hebrew, forms which are used as prepositions fall into two principle groups: those represented by independent forms, and those which consist of a single prefixed consonant.

Epigraphic Hebrew "complex" prepositions developed from a substantive attached to a preposition: e.g., *lpny*, "in the face of," › "before," *mʿwd*, "from what is left," *byd*, "into the hand of" › "through, by the intermediary of."

Prepositional phrases (which have an adverbial function) develop when a substantive is combined with a preposition: e.g., *bʿwd*, "in the duration of " › "during, while, yet," *lnṣḥ*, "to perpetuity, everlastingness" › "(for)ever," *kym*, "this day, about this time" ›"now."

3.4.2.2 Independent prepositions

The following prepositions occur as independent forms in epigraphic Hebrew:

ʾl

The preposition *ʾl* occurs twenty-four times (plus three restored forms) in epigraphic Hebrew. It occurs at Siloam three times with the meaning "toward, in the direction of:"

> *ʾš ʾl rʿw*, "Each man toward his fellow worker," Siloam 1:2.
>
> *[wyšm]ʿ ql ʾš q[r]ʾ ʾl rʿw*, "The voice of a man could be heard calling toward (to) his fellow worker," Siloam 1:2-3.
>
> *wylkw hmym mn hmwṣʾ ʾl hbrkh*, "The water flowed from the spring to the pool," Siloam 1:4-5.

Yadin has commented extensively on the preposition *ʾl* in the Lachish letters in an attempt to disprove the theories of Rainey and Aharoni as to the function of *l-* in the Samaria ostraca. *ʾl*, not *l-*, Yadin concludes, introduced the addressee in Hebrew epigraphy.[270]

In Lachish 4:10-11, *ʾl* is coupled with the verb *šmr*, "watch" and means "for," or, as proposed by Yadin, "over:" *ky ʾl mśʾt lkš nḥnw šmrm*, "We are looking at (Yadin: "tending") the signals of Lachish."[271] The preposition also appears with the verb *šlḥ*, "send something to someone," at Lachish. The phrase here means "send (a letter) to (your servant)," and the same verb and preposition are seen in Lachish 3:20, 21; 5:4. Two more verbs are linked with the preposition *ʾl*: *šwb*, "return something to someone" is attested in the Lachish 5:6-7 phrase *hšb ʿbdk hsprm ʾl ʾdny*, "Your servant (hereby) returns the letters to my lord," and the verb *ktb*, "write to someone," appears in Arad 40:5-6–*[wktbt]y ʾl ʾdny*, "I (hereby) write to my lord."

Another usage of the preposition *ʾl* occurs in Arad 40:5–*wʿt hṭh̊ [ʿ]bdk [l]bh ʾl ʾšr ʾm[rt]*, "And now, your servant has applied himself to what you ordered." In this phrase, the preposition is linked with the relative pronoun *ʾšr* and means "to what, to that which."

The preposition *ʾl* occurs once in epigraphic Hebrew in the interrogative *ʾl*, "Is it true that (someone will do something) to (someone)," in Lachish 5:9-10–*hʾl ʿbdk y‹b›ʾ ṭbyhw zrʿ lmlk̊*, "Will Tobyahu be sending royal grain to your servant?"

---

[270]Y. Yadin, "Recipients or Owners: A Note on the Samaria Ostraca*," *IEJ* 9 (1959): 186; "A Further Note on the Samaria Ostraca," *IEJ* 12 (1962): 64; "A Further Note on the *Lamed* in the Samaria Ostraca," *IEJ* 18 (1968): 50.

[271]Cf. Y. Yadin, "The Lachish Letters–Originals or Copies and Drafts?," in *Recent Archaeology in the Land of Israel*, eds., H. Shanks (English ed.) and B. Mazar (Hebrew ed.) (Washington, D.C.: Biblical Archaeology Society, 1984 [Eng. edition], Jerusalem: Israel Exploration Society, 1981 [Heb. edition]), pp. 179-86. Evidence from biblical Hebrew supports Yadin's hypothesis that *šmr ʾl* means "watch over" in Lachish 4. *Šmr* plus *ʾl* is not found with the sense "watch for" in the Bible, but *šmr* takes the preposition *ʾl* to signify "watch over" in 1 Sam. 26:15 and 2 Sam. 11:16.

ʾt

The epigraphic Hebrew preposition *ʾt*, "with," occurs once in Arad 24:19-20–*hʾnšm ʾt ʾlyšʿ*, "The men (must be) with Elisha."[272]

ʿm

A second preposition meaning "with" occurs twice in epigraphic Hebrew, in Arad 3:4–*ʿm mśʾ ṣmd ḥmrm*, "with a pair of pack donkeys," and Ajrud 15:8–*wyhy ʿm ʾd[n]y*, "May he be with my lord."

lpny

This form occurs in Meṣad Ḥashavyahu 1:5-6–*wykl wʾsm kymm lpny šbt*, "Your servant reaped, finished, and stored (the grain) a few days ago, before Shabbat" (or "before stopping"). *Lpny* is, in all likelihood, a preposition, in the sense of a "complex" preposition, composed of the preposition *l-*, "to," and the noun *pny* (‹ *pānīm*, "face").[273]

---

[272]Pardee discusses Arad 24:19-20, and interprets the meaning of *ʾt* as "with," rather than "to;" cf. Review of *Arad Inscriptions* by Y. Aharoni in *JNES* 44/1 (1985): 70.

[273]See Pardee, "The Preposition in Ugaritic," *UF* 8 (1976): 306, 308-9, commenting on the "complex preposition" *lpn* in Ugaritic; Blau, *A Grammar of Biblical Hebrew*, p. 81.

lqrt

The preposition *lqrt*, which occurs in Siloam 1:4, is a third weak infinitive construct form used as a preposition, meaning "toward." The absence of *ʾaleph* is in contrast to biblical Hebrew *(lqrʾt)*.[274]

mʾt

Mʾt, from Lachish 3:20, is a form composed of the preposition *mn*, "from," prefixed to the preposition *ʾt*, "with" giving *mʾt* the sense "from." The form is common in biblical Hebrew and presupposes the transferral of a concrete object from

---

[274]E.Y. Kutscher, "Inscriptions of the First Temple Period," *Sepher Yerushalayim*, ed., M. Avi-Yonah (Jerusalem: Bialik Institute, 1956), p. 169 identifies *qrh* as the root of *lqrt* and states that biblical *lqrʾt* represents a blend of roots *qrh* and *qrʾ*.

Biblical *lqrʾt* is analyzed as an infinitive construct from the root *qrʾ*, "encounter, befall" by Brown, Driver and Briggs, *BDB*, p. 896, who also connect to it *lqrt* from Siloam 1:4, meaning "to meet, opposite" › preposition, "toward, against." W. F. Albright ("A Reexamination of the Lachish Letters," *BASOR* 73 (1939): 21, n. 35) identifies *lqrt* in Siloam as the phonetic spelling for the more original form which preserves the older spelling *lqrʾt*, found in the Bible.

As Gesenius points out for biblical Hebrew (Cowley, *Gesenius*, pp. 69-70), there may be rejection of a weak consonant (in this case, *ʾaleph*) in the middle of a word when *šewa* precedes that consonant, e.g., *mwm* for *mʾwm*, but this *ʾaleph* is retained in biblical *lqrʾt.* He further points out that while the root of *lqrʾt* is *qrʾ*, the *qal* infinitive construct is analogous to Verbs III-weak.

K. Beyer (*Althebräische Grammatik*, p. 68) vocalizes *lqrt* in Siloam as *laqrot* as though the root is III-weak (*qry/qrh*), and is followed by Gibson (*TSSI*, p. 23), who takes the form as from *qry* (**qrot*), rather than from *qrʾ*.

On the subject of quiescent *ʾaleph*, other forms can be noted: epigraphic Hebrew *kṣʾty*, "when I left," A 16:3, and biblical *yṣty*, "I came out," Job 1:21. In the former, the *ʾaleph* is retained, indicating perhaps that if the root of *lqrt* were *qrʾ*, the *ʾaleph* would have been written, while in the second, syncope has taken place. This practice of syncope with *ʾaleph* is not uncommon, however, in biblical Hebrew (cf. Cowley, *Gesenius*, p. 80, for multiple examples for Verbs III-*ʾaleph*).

From the conclusions of the authors cited above, it can hypothesized that the derivation of the epigraphic Hebrew form *lqrt* is either from *qrʾ*, but the quiescent *ʾaleph* is not written (as *mwm/mʾwm*) as it is in the particular form *lqrʾt* in the Bible, or that the epigraphic Hebrew form is derived from *qry/qrh* and is a regular infinitive construct of this root type.

From epigraphic and biblical Hebrew examples, there is no semantic reason to derive *lqr(ʾ)t* from *qrʾ*, "to call." Kutscher's argument is the more logical one; the root of *lqrt* is *qrh*.

one person to another, just as this phrase exhibits: *wspr ṭbyhw ʿbd hmlk hbʾ ʾl šlm bn ydʿ mʾt hnbʾ*, "In regard to the letter of Tobyahu, servant of the king, which was sent to Shallum, son of Yaddua, from the prophet," Lachish 3:19-20.

mn

The preposition "from" in epigraphic Hebrew is attested three times by its independent form *mn*, and only in the previously mentioned compound *ʾt* with assimilation of the *nun*. *Mn* occurs before nouns in Siloam 1:5–*hmym mn hmwṣʾ*, "the water from the spring," and at Arad 3:2–*tn mn hyyn*, "Give from the wine." In this last example, *mn* means "some of" and is used partitively with the verb *ntn*, "Give some of the wine." At Arad, *mn* is attested with respect to calendar time intervals: *mn hšl̊šh ʿś̊r lḥdš ʿd h̊š̊m̊nh̊ ʿśr lḥdš*, "(for the period) from the thirteenth of the month until the eighteenth of the month," Arad 8:2.

All of the epigraphic Hebrew examples which contain *mn* indicate that the rule for retention of the *-n* in biblical Hebrew (before the definite article) apparently operated in epigraphic Hebrew.

ʿd

The preposition *ʿd* occurs three times with the meaning "until." It is part of a time interval phrase in Arad 7:3-4–*lʿśry b(ʾḥd̊) lḥdš ʿd̊ hššh lḥdš*, "(from) the first (day) of the tenth (month) until the sixth (day) of the month," and Arad 8:2-4–*mn hšl̊šh ʿś̊r lḥdš ʿd h̊š̊m̊nh̊ ʿśr lḥdš*, "from the thirteenth of the month until the eighteenth of the month." Although Lachish 18:1 is part of a broken text, the existing phrase indicates that *ʿd* is probably used here also in its standard temporal usage (*ʿd hʿrb*, "until evening," L 18:1).

ʿl

The preposition *ʿl* occurs in several different contexts. First is the phrase where *ʿl* is part of a royal title, *ʾšr ʿl hbyt*, "He who is over the house, overseer, royal steward," at Silwan 2:1 and Lachish

Seal 6:2. The title refers to a royal official, possibly to the chamberlain of the royal palace.[275]

ʿl means "over, above," and expresses the idea of being suspended over something without however being in contact with it in the phrase *ʿl rʾš hḥṣb[m]*, "over the head(s) of the stone cutters" (Siloam 1:6), while at Lachish 4:3, *ʿl hdlt*, "on the 'panel,'" the use of the preposition seems to denote proximity (English: "by" or "on"). *ʿl* is to be interpreted "over against" and occurs between two nouns in a phrase describing figurative action in Siloam 1:4, *grzn ʿl grzn*, "pick over against pick." With the sense "concerning, about" the phrases include: *ʿl dbr byt hrpd*, "about the matter of Beth-Harapid," Lachish 4:5, and *[ʿ]l mʾwm̊[h]*, "on anything (at all)" › "down to the smallest detail," Lachish 3:13.

Two phrases from Arad which contain the preposition *ʿl* require additional discussion. In the first phrase, *ʿl* precedes a geographic name, while in the second phrase *ʿl* is part of a verb plus preposition idiom: *ʿl bʾršbʿ* in the phrase *wṣwk ḥnnyhw ʿl bʾršbʿ ʿm mśʾ ṣmd ḥmrm*, "Hananyahu (hereby) orders you to Beersheba with a pair of pack donkeys," Arad 3:3-5,[276] and *ʿl yd*

[275]According to Albright, the person designated as *ʾšr ʿl hbyt* was an official who was in charge of the royal property, or a palace chamberlain. Cf. W.F. Albright, "The Seal of Eliakim and the Latest Preëxilic History of Judah, With Some Observations on Ezekiel," *JBL* 51 (1932): 84. The same phrase is attested in biblical Hebrew, "Governor of the Palace," Isaiah 22:15; cf. *BDB*, p. 755; see also T. N. D. Mettinger, *Solomonic State Officials*, Scott Layton, "The Steward in Ancient Israel" (see p. 171, n. 200 of this grammar) and N. Avigad, "New Light on the Naʿar Seals," in *Magnalia Dei: The Mighty Acts of God, Essays on the Bible and Archaeology in Memory of G. Ernest Wright*, eds., F. M. Cross, W.E. Lemke, and P.D. Miller (New York: Doubleday, 1976), p. 298, for a discussion of the royal titles found on seals (e.g., *ʿbd hmlk, bn hmlk, nʿr PN* and *X ʾšr ʿl hbyt*).

[276]*ʿl*, in Arad 3:3-4, has been interpreted variously by others; Aharoni (*Arad Inscriptions*, p. 18)) first interprets *ʿl bʾršbʿ* as "about (the subject of) Beersheba," although he goes on in his discussion to identify the *ṣwh* + *ʿl* idiom as "order a person (to a place, for a task);" cf. Aharoni, *Arad Inscriptions*, p. 18, n. 2.

Another less likely interpretation for the meaning of *ʿl* in Arad 3:3-4 is offered by Lemaire (*Inscriptions hébraïques*, p. 164). He reads *ʿl* as an apocopated imperative from a root III-weak, "Go up to Beersheba!"

ʿl, in the phrase *ṣwk X ʿl bʾršbʿ*, functions to denote direction (therefore parallel in usage to *ʾl*, "to"). The form precedes a geographic name and is part of a verb/preposition idiom. The expression *ṣwh* + *ʿl* is not attested in the Bible, except possibly in Ezra 8:17 (*qere*) with the sense "command (to go)

ʾlyšʿ, "Entrust upon/to the hand of, into the care of, over to, Elisha," in the phrase *whbqydm ʿl yd ʾlyšʿ bn yrmyhw brmt ngb*, "He is to hand them over to Elisha, son of Yirmeyahu at Ramat-Negeb," Arad 24:14-16.

The first example of *ʿl* occurs where analogy would lead us to expect the preposition *ʾl*, "to Beersheba," although biblical Hebrew also shows several instances where *ʿl* is used instead of *ʾl* (e.g., 1 Sam. 1:10; 1 Kings 20:43–*wylk ʿl bytw*, "and he went to, in the direction of his house"). Both *ʾl yd* and *ʿl yd* are attested in biblical Hebrew in the sense "to put someone into the charge or custody of someone else" in the phrase *ʿl yd* from Arad 24:15. The biblical phrase *tnh ʾtw ʿl ydy*, "Entrust him to me," literally, "Put him upon my hand," from Genesis 42:37, is a parallel phrase to that of the epigraphic Hebrew.

bʿd and *ʿmd*

The prepositions bʿd and *ʿmd* occur as first elements of epigraphic Hebrew proper names.

bʿd-, "on behalf of," is part of a proper name on Herr's seal 40:2–*bʿdʾl*, "on behalf of El" from Beth Shemesh.

ʿmd-, "with me," from the proper name *ʿmdyhw*, of unknown provenience (Herr 143), may be the preposition *ʿmd-*, based on the analogous biblical proper name *ʿmnwʾl*, "God is with us." [277] The Bible shows no attestations of proper names from the preposition *ʿm* itself. Noth[278] vocalizes the epigraphic Hebrew seal name as *ʿimmādīyāhû*, "YH is with me."

Another possibility for *ʿmdyhw* is that of taking the form *ʿmd* as from the root *ʿmd*, "stand," either as a perfect, "(DN) stands, endures, is steadfast," or as a participle, "He who stands before" › "attends, serves" › "servant (of DN)." In epigraphic Hebrew (and the Bible), either of these solutions is plausible since proper names

---

to," but this meaning is the most likely interpretation for the reading of Arad 3:3-4. Cf. Pardee, "Letters from Tel Arad," *UF* 10 (1978): 300.

[277] *ʿimmānûʾēl*, "God is with us," Isaiah 7:14. Such a proper name would symbolize God's presence to deliver his people and a declaration of trust and confidence. *ʿmnyh* also occurs at Elephantine (Cowley 22:105); see Cowley, *Aramaic Papyri of the Fifth Century*, p. 304).

[278] Noth, *IPN*, p. 33, also p. 160., cf. Diringer, *Le iscrizioni antico-ebraiche palestinesi*, p. 218 (no. 61).

made up of verbal/nominal elements are more common than those with a prepositional component.[279]

3.4.2.3 Prefixed prepositions

Of the prepositions mentioned above as independent forms, *mn*, "from," frequently occurs in an abbreviated form, *m-*, with the *nun* assimilated to the following consonant:

m-

> *m*ʾ*[šm]*, "from guilt," *m̊bytk*, "from your house," *mgb[*ʿ*]*, "from Geba," *ẘm̊[śm]*ʾ̊*l*, "and (from ›) on the left," *mymn*, "(from ›) on the right."

Three additional prepositions which consist of a single prefixed consonant are among the most frequent prepositions attested in epigraphic Hebrew:

b-

> *b*ʾ̊*rḥ*, "in the way of," *bḥṣr-*, "in Hasar-," *bḥtmk*, "with your seal," *bym*, "on the day (of)," *bšt*, "in the year," *bm*ʾ*tym̊*, "for two hundred," *brmt ngb*, "at Ramat-Negeb."

---

[279]Possible semantic parallels for *ʿmdyhw* "YH stands, endures, is steadfast," are *yhwqm*, "YH arises, has arisen," AvNN 12:1; 13:1; *ʾḥqm*, "(my brother) arises, has arisen," Av (*IEJ* 13) seal 2:2; *yhwkl*, "YH prevails, is able," A 21:1; Herr 63:2; L V 1:1; *knyhw*, "YH endures," A 49:4, L 3:15 (restored); *g̊b[ryhw]*, "(YH) prevails, is strong," A 60:5-6. For *ʿmd* in the sense of "endure" (Ex. 18:23; Ezek. 22:14), "be steadfast" (Deut. 25:8; Ruth 2:7), "persist" (Eccles. 8:3).

In epigraphic Hebrew, proper names commonly consist of a perfect plus the theophoric element; e.g., *ntnyhw*, "YH has given," *ʾmryhw*, "YH has said, commanded, promised," *zkryw*, "YH has remembered," *ʿzryhw*, "YH has helped," *šmʿyhw*, "YH has heard."

ʿmdyhw could also mean "he who stands (before) God," › "servant of God" (*ʿmd* as participle) on the analogy of the proper name *ʿbdyhw*, A 10:4, etc., and the Bible *ʿōbadyāhû*, 1 Kings 18:3, etc., "servant of YH" , as well as the biblical use of *ʿbd*, "attend upon, be(come) servant of," (esp. of God), 1 Kings 17:1, 18:15, etc. (*BDB*, p. 764).

l-

lʾdny, "to my lord," *lʾprḥ*, "belonging to Ephroah," *lbyt*, "for the house of," *lḥdš*, "of the month," *lmlk*, "of the king," *lšlmk*, "about your welfare," *dmlyhw*, "Be silent before YH, be resigned to YH, Wait on YH," *dmlʾl*, "Be silent before El," *dmlʾ*, "Wait on (DN)," *lyhwh*," to YH," *lʾnyhw*, "by *(lamed auctoris)* Oniyahu."

k-

[kym], "at (about) this time, now," *kkl*, "according to everything," *kymm*, "according to the days, a few days ago (?)," *kṣʾty*, "when I left," *mykyhẘ*, "Who is like YH?"

By the fact that the particles above have been reduced to a single radical, they have lost the character of an independent word and may not stand alone. When *b-*, *l-*, or *k-* precede a definite noun, the *hê* (definite article) is always elided.

3.4.2.4 Prepositions with pronominal suffixes

Introduction

Prepositions may, as do nouns, take pronominal suffixes.[280] This rule is true for both epigraphic and biblical Hebrew.

The prepositions *ʾl*, "to," *ʾt*, "with," *ʿm*, "with," *lpny*, "before," *b-*, "in," and *l-*, "to, for," are attested with suffixes in epigraphic Hebrew. The first common singular suffix is *-y*,[281] the second masculine singular suffix is *-k*,[282] the third masculine singular suffix is *-h* (on prepositions that take suffixes as though

280See Cowley, *Gesenius*, p. 300.

281*ʾly*, "to me," A 8:8; L 3:11; (*[ʾ]ly*), L 4:4; *ʾty*, "with me," MHY 1:10; *ʿmy*, "with me," MO 2:4; *ly*, "for me," MHY 1:10, 11; L 3:10.

282*ʾlyk*, "to you," papMur 17a:2; *[ʾl]yk*, KH 2:10; *lpnyk*, "before you," A 7:6; *ʾtk*, "with you (?)," A 16:7 (the broken context of A 16 makes it impossible to tell whether this form is the preposition, or the second masculine singular suffixed form of the definite direct object marker); *mʾtk*, "from (that which) is yours (= with you)," A 5:2, 6:2, 40:8; *(mʾt[k])*, A 9:2; *lk*, "to you," A 5:11; papMur 17a:1.

singular nouns),[283] and *-w* (on prepositions that take suffixes as though plural nouns),[284] the second masculine plural suffix is *-km*,[285] and the third masculine plural suffix is *-hm*.[286] No feminine singular or plural, nor the first common plural prepositional suffixes are attested in epigraphic Hebrew. The prepositional suffixes in epigraphic Hebrew are illustrated on the next page in table 39.

As Blau points out for biblical Hebrew, prepositional suffixes "take forms as if attached to singular noun forms,"[287] and in some instances, they also take forms as if attached to plural nouns. In the case of epigraphic Hebrew, the independent prepositions *ʾt*, "with," and *ʿm*, "with," and the uni-radical prepositions *b-* and *l-* behave as singular nouns, while the prepositions *ʾl*, "to," and *lpny*, "before," behave as plural nouns. These latter two prepositions, when taking pronominal suffixes, deviate slightly in form from those of the type characterized by *ʾt*, *ʿm*, *b-*, and *l-* (e.g., *ʾlyk* and *lpnyk*, with yod preceding the pronominal suffix). The reason for this difference in preposition types is explained that historically, the ground forms of *ʾl* and *lpny* derive from roots III-weak.[288]

(1) *Forms*. The six attested prepositions with pronominal suffixes which occur in epigraphic Hebrew are shown in table 40 on pages 218-19.

---

[283]*lh*, "him," KEK 3:3; Aj 16:1; *ʾ[t]h*, "with him," Silwan 2:2.

[284]*ʾlw*, "to him," MHY 1:13.

[285]*ʾtkm*, "with you," A 24:17; *bkm*, "you," A 24:19.

[286]*lhm*, "for, to them," A 1:8, 2:8, 4:3; (*[l]hm*), A 40:8-9; *ʾl[yhm]*, "to them," L 6:9.

[287]Blau, *A Grammar of Biblical Hebrew*, p. 78.

[288]Cowley, *Gesenius*, p. 304.

TABLE 39
PREPOSITIONAL SUFFIXES

Person/Gender/Number	Suffix
1 c.s.	*-y*
2 m.s.	*-k*
2 f.s.	–
3 m.s.	*-h, -w*
3 f.s.	–
1 c.pl.	–
2 m.pl.	*-km*
2 f.pl.	–
3 m.pl.	*-hm*
3 f.pl.	–

TABLE 40
PREPOSITIONS WITH PRONOMINAL SUFFIXES

	ʾ*t* "with"	**ʿ*m* "with"**	***l*- "to, for"**	***b*- "in"**
1 c.s.	ʾ*ty* (MHY)	ʿ*my* (MO)	*ly* (MHY)	–
2.m.s.	ʾ*tk* (Arad)		*lk* (Arad, KH, papMur)	–
2 f.s.	–		–	–
3.m.s.	ʾ*[t]h* (Silwan)		*lh* (KEK, Aj)	–
3.f.s.	–		–	–
1.c.pl	–		–	–
2.m.pl.	ʾ*tkm* (Arad)		–	*bkm* (Arad)
2.f.pl.	–		–	–
3.m.pl.	–		*lhm* (Arad)	–
3.f.pl.	–		–	–

TABLE 40
PREPOSITIONS WITH PRONOMINAL SUFFIXES
(continued)

	ʾ*l* **"to"**	***lpny*** **"before"**
1 c.s.	ʾ*ly* (Arad, Lachish)	–
2 m.s.	ʾ*lyk* (papMur, KH)	*lpnyk* (Arad)
2 f.s.	–	–
3 m.s.	ʾ*lw* (MHY)	–
3 f.s.	–	–
1 c.pl.	–	–
2 m.pl.	–	–
2 f.pl.	–	–
3 m.pl.	ʾ*l[yhm]* (Lachish)	–
3 f.pl.	–	–

The forms of most of the prepositions are as we would expect from biblical Hebrew (*ʾlw* [biblical *ʾlyw*], "to him").[289] A *yod* appears in the second masculine singular form at Murabbaʿat, Ketef Hinnom, and at Arad, although it is absent at Meṣad Ḥashavyahu in the third masculine singular form.

---

[289] *ʾlk* (biblical *ʾlyk*), "to you (m.s.)," and *ʾl[yhm]*, "to them," are deleted from the main text because they are questionable forms. *ʾlk* merits additional comment because of the difficulty in determining the context of Arad 3:8-9 and *ʾl[yhm]* is largely restored.

For *ʾlk*, cf. Aharoni, *Arad Inscriptions*, pp. 18-19. It is not the reading of *ʾlk* that is in dispute, it is the context of the phrase in lines 8 and 9. In fact, the context is too broken to be sure of the meaning of *ʾlk*. Aharoni reads a possible *mem* after the *kaf* (*ʾlkm*, "to you (m.pl.) (?)"), but the rest of the reverse side of ostracon 3 is too effaced for reading.

Zevit (*MLAHE*, pp. 27-28) uses *ʾlk* as indirect proof for the contraction of the *ay* diphthong in unaccented syllables (as the form is not written *ʾlyk*), but this example remains too uncertain to posit such a theory. E.g., Lemaire, *Inscriptions hébraïques*, pp. 163, 165, and Pardee, *HHL*, pp. 34-35 do not attempt an explanation of this word. The latter does mention *ʾlk* in the discussion of *ʾl[yhm]*, Lachish 7:9, as a form in a line of text too badly effaced to establish a certain context of this word (*HHL*, p. 102).

The fact that both *ʾlyk*, papMur 17a:2 [Zevit does not include the Murabbʿat Papyrus in his corpus, and hence does not mention this form] and *lpnyk*, Arad 7:6, are attested in epigraphic Hebrew (both written with *yod*), weakens Zevit's theory. Zevit's contention that the form *lpnyk* represents the contraction of the *-ay* diphthong and that the *yod* is a *m.l.* for *ē* is by no means certain; cf. Parunak, "The Orthography of the Arad Ostraca," *BASOR* 230 (1978): 25 (**lapanayk*).

The reading of *ʾlk*, if it is to be accepted as the suffixed preposition in Arad 3, and *ʾlyk*, in papMur 17a:2, would be analogous to the biblical forms with and without *yod* (e.g., *ʾlkm*/ *ʾlykm*; *ʾlhm*/ *ʾlyhm*; *ʾlhn*/ *ʾlyhn*).

The third masculine plural form of the preposition *ʾl* has been restored as *ʾl[yhm]* based on space considerations in this particular Lachish inscription. Pardee, "The Judicial Plea from Meṣad Ḥashavyahu," *Maarav* 1/1 (1978): 44-45, in assessing the final *yod* of *lpny* (MHY 1:5), comments that the *yod* which is attested in medial position in such forms as *pnyk* and *ʾlhyk*, "your God," may represent the uncontracted diphthong *-ay* in masculine plural suffixal forms.

In *HHL*, p. 102, Pardee asserts that the suffixed preposition *ʾlyk*, "to you," along with the previously mentioned forms containing internal *yod*, lead us to expect the spelling *ʾlyhm* for the third masculine plural suffixed preposition. His restoration, *ʾl[yhm]*, p. 100, more closely follows that of Cross and Freedman, *EHO*, p. 56, in contrast to the reading *ʾlh[m]* suggested by De Vaux, "Les ostraca de Lachiš," *RB* 48 (1939): 197 and W. F. Albright, "The Lachish Letters after Five Years," *BASOR* 82 (1941): 22.

The third masculine singular form *lh,* "to him"[290] points out one further difference between epigraphic and biblical Hebrew

---

[290] The suffixed preposition in epigraphic Hebrew for "to him" is *lh*, not *lw*. On the reading *lw* at Khirbet Beit Lei, see Cross and Freedman, *EHO*, 46; Cross, "The Cave Inscriptions from Khirbet Beit Lei," in *NEATC*, 1970, p. 301. In the latter article, Cross convincingly dispelled Naveh's original reading of *lw* in the Khirbet Beit Lei inscription A (west wall), line 2: *hry yhd lw*, "the mountains of Judah belong to him" (cf. Naveh, "Old Hebrew Inscriptions in a Burial Cave," *IEJ* 13 (1963): 84), to *ʾrṣh ʿry yhdh wgʾlty yršlm*, "I will accept the cities of Judah, and will redeem Jerusalem." Lemaire, "Prières en temps de crises: Les Inscriptions de Khirbet Beit Lei," *RB* 83 (1976): 558-59, likewise did not read *lw* in line two: *hry yhwdh lʾlhy yršlm*, "the mountains of Judah belong to the God of Jerusalem."

Zevit (*MLAHE*, pp. 30-31) prefers the original reading of Naveh, but his arguments for doing so, are pointless. This is in view of the writing *lh* for "to him," at Khirbet el-Kom (Zevit himself acknowledges the reading of the preposition as *lh* at Khirbet el-Kom in his 1984 article [see discussion which follows], and the preponderance of *hê* (not *waw*) as the third masculine singular pronominal suffix in epigraphic Hebrew, both on prepositions and nouns.

Hebrew epigraphy provides strong evidence that *waw* is the third masculine singular suffix on plural nouns (e.g., *ʾnšw*, "his people," L 3:18 [also *-yw* as in *pnyw*, "his face," KH 2:9]) and prepositions which act as though they are plurals (*ʾlw*, "to him," MHY 1:13). The historical development of this suffix is thought to be **-ayhu › -āhu › -āu › -āw;* see Sarfatti, "Hebrew Inscriptions of the First Temple Period," p. 65.

The chief evidence for the third masculine singular pronominal suffix *hê* on a preposition is *lh*, KEK 3:3 and Aj 16:1 (the *hê* presumably occurs also on Silwan 2:2, but the word *ʾ[t]h*, "with him," is restored). Zevit does not acknowledge this form at Khirbet el-Kom in his 1980 monograph (*MLAHE*, pp. 17-18), presumably because the context of the particular section of this inscription (line 3) is disputed (however, he does read *hwšʿ*, the word preceding *lh*, cf. below). In a more recent article, Zevit does, in fact, read *lh* after *hwšʿ* in line 3, "Save him;" cf. "The Khirbet el-Qôm Inscription Mentioning a Goddess," *BASOR* 255 (1984): 45-46. W. G. Dever, "Iron Age Epigraphic Material from the Area of Khirbet el-Kom," *HUCA* 40/41 (1970): 159-62, reads the appropriate section of text as *wmʾrr yd lʾšr thhwš ʿlh*, "And cursed be the hand of whoever (defaces it)!," where *lh* is read with the preceding *ʿayin*, *ʿlh*, "upon it." Dever (p. 162) points out that this reading is highly objectionable and he offers the reading *hwšʿ lw*, "salvation to him," as another possibility. Lemaire, "Les Inscriptions de Khirbet el-Qôm," *RB* 84 (1977): 599, 602, correctly reads *hwšʿ lh*, "il l'a sauvé" or "sauve-le" ("He has saved him" or "Save him!"), although specific textual difficulties in line 3 remain (especially with respect to how the form *lʾšrth* fits in with the rest of the line).

For *lh* in Aj 16:1, *wntn lh yhw‹h› klbbh*, "And let YHW‹H› give to him as he wishes (=according to his heart)," cf. Moshe Weinfeld, "*ywmn prswmym. nwspwt lktwbwt ʿgrwd* [Further Remarks on the Ajrud Inscriptions)," *Shnaton* 5-6 (1982): 237; "Kuntillet ʿAjrud Inscriptions and Their Significance," "Studi Epigrafici e Linguisici 1 (1984): 125-26; Judith M.

(*lw*, "to him"). The *hê* in epigraphic Hebrew may represent a final *m.l.* for long *ō*,[291] for according to Cross, *waw* did not replace *hê* as a vowel letter for *ō* before the fourth century in Hebrew.[292] Evidence from the epigraphic Hebrew corpus proves that *waw* did not replace *hê* as the third masculine singular suffix by the end of the sixth century. One will note that the prepositional form is similar to the nominal form and that the hypothesis that *-h* = *-ô* is no more plausible here than there.

One of the suffixed prepositions, *mʾtk*, "from (that which) is yours, with you (m.s.)," from four Arad inscriptions, is a compound form.

3.4.3 Conjunctions

3.4.3.1 Introduction

Conjunctions in epigraphic Hebrew connect words, phrases and clauses, express their relations one to another, and may be co-ordinating or subordinating. The most common co-ordinate conjunction in epigraphic Hebrew is *waw*, while subordinate conjunctions in epigraphic Hebrew are *ky*, *ʾm*, *btrm*, *ʾšr*, and *pn*.

Hadley, "Some Drawings and Inscriptions on Two Pithoi from Kuntillet ʿAjrud," *VT* 37 (1987): 187.

Hwšʿ, which is also accepted as the reading in Khirbet el-Kom by Zevit (*MLAHE*, p. 18) is attested in epigraphic Hebrew as the imperative in another votive text, KBL 3:1–*hwšʿ [y]hwh*, "Save (us), YH!," but there, minus the preposition.

In the Bible, the *hiphil* forms of *yšʿ* frequently occur with the preposition *l-* (e.g., Deut. 22:27; Judg. 10:14; 2 Sam. 10:11, etc.), and the imperative coupled with this preposition is attested in Josh. 10:6–*whwšyʿh lnw*, "Save us!"

[291] A second interpretation for the vocalization of the suffix *hê* is that offered by Pardee (see "The Judicial Plea from Meṣad Ḥashavyahu," *Maarav* 1/1 (1978): 40), that is, that the absence of *waw* as a *m.l.* for *-ō* in epigraphic Hebrew could be evidence that the pronunciation of the third masculine singular pronominal suffix was *-ahu* (i.e., that the shift *ahu* › *au*/*aw* › *ô* had not yet occurred). This cannot be proven on the basis of Hebrew epigraphy, of course; only the opposite could be proven, that is, an indubitable writing *-w* would prove that the phonetic shift had taken place.

[292] Cf. Cross, "Cave Inscriptions from Khirbet Beit Lei," in *NEATC*, 1970, p. 301, and n. 3. As originally stated by Cross and Freedman (*EHO*, p. 46), "...final *ō* is always represented by *hê* and never by *waw* in pre-exilic Hebrew inscriptions."

The classification of conjunctions according to their origins is as follows: conjunctions which were originally substantives, or composed of a substantive and a preposition: *bṭrm*; "before;" [293] prepositions which, by addition of *ʾšr* or *ky*, become themselves a compound conjunction: *kʾšr*, "when," *ky ʾm*, "only, for (except);" and certain conjunctions, the origins of which are, in most cases, doubtful: *w*-, "and," and *ʾm*, "if."

3.4.3.2 The Coordinating conjunction *w*-, "and"

By far, the most common conjunction in epigraphic Hebrew is *w*- which is attached to a following word, and means "and." The coordinating conjunction *w*- connects two or more words or clauses.

3.4.3.3 *Waw*-conjunctive and consecutive

Waw-conjunctive and *waw*-consecutive are attested in epigraphic Hebrew with the perfect, imperfect (or jussive) and/or imperative (*waw*-conjunctive only).[294]

3.4.3.4 Subordinate conjunctions

ʾm

The conjunction *ʾm*, "if," occurs in seven phrases in epigraphic Hebrew, and the conjunction *ky ʾm* occurs twice in Lachish 4:9 and Silwan 2:2 (restored).

ʾm is the marker of the protasis of a conditional sentence in epigraphic Hebrew, as in Arad 2:7-8: *ʾm ʿwd ḥmṣ wntt lhm*, "If there is any vinegar left, give (it) to them." An example of a negative protasis: *wʾm lʾ lśr lhš[b ʾt bgd] ʿ̊b̊[dk wtt]n ʾlw rḥ[mm]*, "If the official does (= you do) not consider it an obligation to return [your servant's garment, then hav]e pity upon him," MHY 1:12-14. If the text is properly restored, this is a conditional "If...then" sentence: "And if not *(ʾm lʾ)*, (then) it is (still) incumbent upon you to..."[295]

---

[293]*Bṭrm*, originally, "in the not yet" › "earlier" ›"before."

[294]Cf. pp. 77-78, 87, 260-67, 278, 289 in this grammar.

[295]In the Bible *ʾm* (or *ʾm lʾ*) does not occur in conditional phrases, where the infinitive is in the protasis, and the closest semantic parallel to the Meṣad Ḥashavyahu phrase is Micah 3:1–*hlwʾ lkm ldʿt ʾt hmšpt*, "Is it not

ʾm also marks the conditional in oath formulae, where the apodosis is omitted and *ʾm* functions thereafter as an emphatic negative. In Lachish 3:9-10, *ʾm* occurs after the oath formula and introduces an emphatic negative: *ḥyhwh ʾm nsh ʾyš lqrʾ ly spr*, "As ‹Y›HWH lives, no one has ever tried to read a letter to me." This passage illustrates the function of *ʾm* in the context of oath, as the marker of a negative oath (originally, of course, a conditional clause). In the same inscription (line 11), *ʾm* occurs before a perfect and marks a subordinate clause: *kl spr ʾšr ybʾ ʾly ʾm qrʾty ʾth*, "Any letter which might come to me, when I read it..."

The attestations of *ky ʾm* are found as separate particles in Lachish 4:7-10–*wʿbdk ʾy[nn]y šlḥ šmh ʾt hʿd [hym] ky ʾm btsbt hbqr [y]b[ʾ] wydʿ*, "Your servant cannot send the witness there (today); for if he comes (around) during the morning rounds, he will know..."; and as a compound conjunction in Silwan 2:1-2–*ʾyn [p]h ksp wzhb [ky] ʾm [ʿṣmtw] wʿṣm[t] ʾmth ʾ[t]h,* "There is no silver or gold here, only his bones and his servant-wife's

---

incumbent upon you to know justice?" and 2 Chron. 25:9–*yš lyhwh ltt lk hrbh mzh*, "It is incumbent upon YHWH (in YHWH's power) to give you much more than that." In the Bible, *ʾm* (or *ʾm lʾ*) may be followed by the imperfect or its equivalent in the apodosis, to represent a condition which is regarded as possible or capable of fulfilment in the future (cf. Cowley, *Gesenius*, pp. 493-95). The restoration of the imperfect *ttn* (Pardee, *HHL*, p. 35) or jussive *ytn* (Cross, "Epigraphic Notes on Hebrew Documents of the Eighth-Sixth Centuries B.C.: II. The Murabbaʿat Papyrus and the Letter found Near Yahneh-Yam," *BASOR* 165 (1962): 44) in the apodosis of line 13 coincides with the acceptable verb type expected from biblical Hebrew.

It must be noted, however, that several sections of MHY 1:12-14 are largely restored and that *ʾm lʾ* has been interpreted otherwise than as the conjunction and negative particle by several commentators (cf. Pardee, "The Judicial Plea from "Meṣad Ḥashavyahu," *Maarav* 1/1 (1978): 52-53 for a review of and bibliography for the various interpretations of *ʾm lʾ*). Pardee, following especially Cross (crediting Albright, in "Epigraphic Notes on Hebrew Documents of the Eighth-Sixth Centuries B.C.: II. The Murabbaʿat Papyrus and the Letter found Near Yabneh-Yam," *BASOR* 165 (1962): 45, n. 50) and Lemaire ("L'ostracon de Meṣad Ḥashavyahu," pp. 74-75), argues that *ʾm lʾ* should be regarded as two words, *ʾm lʾ*, rather than a one-word verbal form. Pardee argues against the interpretation of Sasson that *wʾmlʾ* represents the conjunction *w* plus the first common singular *niphal* imperfect of the verb *mlʾ*, "to fill, be full," meaning "to be vindicated" in Meṣad Ḥashavyahu 1:12; Cf. V. Sasson, "An Unrecognized Juridical Term in the Yabneh-Yam Lawsuit and in an Unnoticed Biblical Parallel," *BASOR* 232 (1978): 57-63; D. Pardee, "A Brief Note on Meṣad Ḥashavyahu Ostracon, 1. 12: *wʾmlʾ*, " *BASOR* 239 (1980): 47-48.

bones with him." In Lachish 4:9, *ky ʾm* consists of explanatory *ky* plus *ʾm* marking the protasis of a conditional sentence, while at Silwan 2:2, *ky ʾm* marks an exceptive (limitative) clause, after a negative.

ʾm occurs four times at Arad; however, in three instances, the texts are broken and do not permit an analysis of the context of *ʾm*. In Arad 16:8, the text is broken on both sides of the word *wʾm*. In Arad 21:8, the text is also broken before *wʾm*, but it does occur before *ʿwd*, and thus may be translated "and if yet" although the context is unknown. Arad 28 is also a broken text and ʾm is the only word in line 6. Therefore, it is difficult to be definitive about this phrase.

bṭrm

Bṭrm occurs twice at Arad. The form consists of a preposition and an adverb of time. The phrase in Arad 5:10-13 is *y[šlḥ] lk ʾt hmʿ[śr] b(tm šlšh) bṭrm yʿbr h̊ḥdš*, "He will send you the tit[he ?], three *bat*-measures, before the month passes." The conjunction occurs before the imperfect *yʿbr* in a temporal clause containing the definite noun *hḥdš*, and refers to the future.

kʾšr

Kʾšr, "when," is attested twice at Meṣad Ḥashavyahu: *kʾšr kl [ʿ]bdk ʾt qṣr wʾsm kymm wybʾ hwšʿyhw bn šby wyqḥ ʾt bgd ʿbdk*, "When your [se]rvant had finished his reaping and had stored it a few days ago, Hoshayahu ben Shobay came and took your servant's garment," MHY 1:6-8, and *kʾsr klt ʾt qṣry zh ymm lqḥ ʾt bgd ʿbdk*, "When I had finished my reaping, at that time, a few days ago, he took your servant's garment," MHY 1:8-9. There is no exact parallel from biblical Hebrew for *kʾšr* beginning a temporal clause without the accompanying tense/aspect indicators *wyhy* or *whyh* (cf. biblical Hebrew *wăyĕhî kaʾăšer...way-*).

ky

The conjunction *ky* occurs twelve times in epigraphic Hebrew and twice in the expression *ky ʾm*. In epigraphic Hebrew, *ky* is a subordinating conjunction used to introduce syndetic subordinate clauses.

(1) *ky* and complementary clauses. The following phrases illustrate the function of *ky* as the marker of a complementary

clause (containing the perfect) which is dependent upon an interrogative clause (*my ʿbdk...*, "Who is your servant..."):[296]

> *my ʿbdk klb ky zkr ʾdny ʾt [ʿ]bdh*, "Who is your servant (but) a dog that you have sent to your servant these letters?" Lachish 2:3-4,

> *my ʿbdk klb [ky] šl̊ḥ̊t̊h̊ ʾl ʿbdk ʾ[t] hs̊[prm] k̊z̊ʾ[t]*, "Who is your servant (but) a dog that you have sent to your servant these letters?" Lachish 5:3-6,

> *my ʿbdk klb ky šlḥ ʾdny ʾ[t sp]r hmlk [wʾt] spry hśr[m]*, "Who is your servant (but) a dog that my lord should have sent (him) the king's letter and those of the officials?" Lachish 6:2-4.[297]

Two additional phrases where *ky*, meaning "that," introduces complementary clauses, are Lachish 4:9-11–*ky ʾm tsbt hbqr [y]b̊ʿ[ ] wydʿ ky ʾl mśʾt lkš nḥnw šmrm*, "For if he comes (around) during the morning rounds, he will know that we are watching for the signals of Lachish," and Arad 40:13-14–*ydʿ mlk̊ yhwd[h ky ʾy]nnw yklm lšlḥ ʾt h[ ]*, "The king of Judah should know [that] we [are un]able to send the [ ]."

Lachish 2 associates *ky* with the verb *zkr*, "remember," as in the biblical phrase of Psalm 78:35, while the other two texts, Lachish 5 and 6, deal with a second active verb, *šlḥ*, "send." In Genesis 22:12 and 24:14, *ky* introduces clauses depending on the verb *ydʿ*, "know," as above in Lachish 4:9-11 and in Arad 40. The

---

[296]The function of *ky* to mark complementary clauses is analogous to such biblical phrases (although there the verb after *ky* is the imperfect) as Exod. 3:11–*my ʾnky ky ʾlk ʾl prʿh*, "Who am I, that I should go to Pharaoh?"

[297]Lachish 2, 5, and 6 contain the phrase reminiscent of the El Amarna Texts, though the intent of the words is different. In the Hebrew phrases, the implication is: "Who is your servant (but) a dog, that you should condescend to look so favorably upon him?" A similar phrase occurs in El Amarna, no. 320, lines 20-25, where Widia, the prince of Ashkelon, writes: "Who is the dog that does not listen to the words of the king, his lord, the son of the Sun-god?" The implication in the Hebrew texts is a bit different for in Lachish 2, 5, and 6, the intent of the words is a humble thanks, i.e., "Thank you my lord, for condescending to think of me in this way," while the El Amarna phrase implies, "Anyone who is foolish enough not to mind your words, my lord, is surely nothing but a dog."

perfect occurs in Genesis 22:12–*wyʾmr ʾl tšlḥ ydk ʾl hnʿr wʾl tʿś lw mʾwmh ky ʿth ydʿty ky yrʾ ʾlhym ʾth wlʾ ḥśkt ʾt bnk ʾt yḥydk mmny*, "And He said, 'Don't lay your hand upon the boy, nor hurt him in any way, for now I know that you fear God in that you've not withheld your only son from me,'" while the imperfect appears in Genesis 24:14–*wbh ʾdʿ ky ʿśyt ḥsd ʿm ʾdny*, "In this way, I will know that you have dealt kindly with my lord." The imperfect of ydʿ occurs in Arad 40:13–*ydʿ*...[*ky*], "He should, will know," while Lachish 4:10 illustrates the *waw*-consecutive and perfect: *wydʿ ky*, "and he will know that..."[298]

(2) *ky* and oaths. In epigraphic Hebrew the conjunction *ky* is also used as a presentative to introduce a positive oath. In this usage, *ky* functions differently from *ʾm* which also occurs in a *ḥy yhwh* phrase (written *ḥyhwh* in Lachish 3:9). In the context of oath formulae, *ky* marks a positive main clause, while *ʾm* introduces a negative main clause.[299]

> *ḥy yhwh ʾlhyk k[y m]ʾz qrʾ ʿbdk ʾt̊ hspr[m] l[ʾ] h[y]h̊ ʾb[dk]*, "As YHWH your God lives, surely ever since your servant read the letters, he has been able to think of) nothing (else)," Lachish 6:12-15.

Lachish 12:3-4, which is fragmentary, has been restored as:

> *[ḥ]y yhwh [k]y [ ]ʾy[ ]q[r]ʾty [ʾ]th*, "[A]s YHWH lives, [indeed (ever since)] I [re]ad[i]t"

(3) *ky* and explanatory clauses. The conjunction *ky* introduces explanatory clauses in epigraphic Hebrew:

> *ky lb ʿbd̊[k] d̊ẘh mʾz šlḥk ʾl ʿbdk*, "For (because) your servant has been sick at heart ever since you sent (it) to your servant," Lachish 3:6-8.

---

[298]For *ydʿ* as perfect, see p. 263, n. 23.

[299]On the function of *ʾm* and *ky* in oath formulae, see Cowley, *Gesenius*, pp. 471-72; Pardee, *HHL*, p. 102. In epigraphic Hebrew, the use of *ky* in the context of oath formula is more frequent than the use of *ʾm* (or *ʾm lʾ*) in this context. In the Bible, however, the use of *ky* in a sentence expressing an oath is rare and this function is expressed more commonly by *ʾm* or *ʾm lʾ*, cf. *Gesenius*, p. 471.

wydʿ ky ʾl mśʾt lkš nḥnw šmrm kkl hʾtt ʾšr ntn ʾdny ky lʾ nrʾh ʾt ʿzqh, "He will know that we are watching the Lachish (fire)-signals according to the code which my lord gave us, for (because) we cannot see Azeqah," Lachish 4:10-13.

In both passages above, a causal situation is implied. In Lachish 3:6-7, *ky* introduces a phrase describing the state of being sick at heart which was caused by reading the contents of a letter which the author received. In Lachish 4:10-12, there appears to be a good reason or cause for watching the signals from Lachish–the fact that Azeqah is no longer visible and the enemy may be fast approaching.

(4) *ky* used to introduce a fronted subordinate clause. Two examples from Lachish illustrate the function of *ky* to introduce fronted subordinate clauses:

wky ʾmr ʾdny lʾ ydʿth qrʾ spr ḥyhwh ʾm nsh ʾyš lqrʾ ly spr lnṣḥ, "And regarding the fact that (as for what) my lord said, 'You do not know how to read a letter,' as ‹Y›HWH lives, no one has ever tried to read a letter to me!," Lachish 3:8-10.

wky šlḥ ʾdny ʿl dbr byt hrpd, "In regard to what my lord has written about the matter of Beth-Harapid," Lachish 4:4-5.

Pardee [300] has drawn parallels from Ugaritic for the syntax of *ky* functioning as a subordinating conjunction "regarding, in regard to, since."

---

[300] Pardee, "A New Ugaritic Letter," *BO* 34 (1977): 8, n. 43, with reference to W.L. Moran, "Early Canaanite *yaqtulu*," *Orientalia* n.s. 29 (1960): 17, n. 1.

pn

The conjunction *pn*, "lest, that not," introduces negative final clauses, functions as a marker of a clause expressing a fear or precaution, and is followed by the imperfect. This conjunction occurs twice in epigraphic Hebrew:

> *whbqydm ʿl yd ʾlyšʿ bn yrmyhw brmt ngb pn yqrh ʾt hʿyr dbr*, "He is to hand them over to Elisha, son of Yirmeyahu, at Ramat-Negeb, lest something happen to the city," Arad 24:14-17.

> *hʾnšm ʾt ʾlyšʿ pn tbʾ ʾdm šmh*, "The men (must be) with Elisha lest the Edomites go there," Arad 24:19-20.

In both examples, this conjunction directly precedes the imperfect in a context of incompleted action. Phrases of similar pattern are the most common in biblical Hebrew, although there the range of *pn*-phrases is more varied, including examples of this conjunction before the perfect where the result feared is conceived as having possibly already taken place (i.e., 2 Sam. 20:6), as well as sentences of dissuasive force which begin with *pn*.[301]

3.4.4 Interjections

The interjections in epigraphic Hebrew are:

> *hnh*, "surely, lo, indeed," A 24:18, L 6:5,[302] *nʾ*, the particle of entreaty, L 6:5, *[nʾ]*, L 3:5; MHY 1:12, and *yh*, "O," KBL 2:1.

Hnh is deitic ("behold") at A 24:18 and L 6:5.

---

[301] Cowley, *Gesenius*, pp. 318, 482.

[302] *Hn*, attested twice in epigraphic Hebrew (Arad 21:3; 40:9), is possibly to be considered as an interjection. However, this analysis is uncertain; the form in Arad 40:9 is uncertain because of the broken context of the end of line 9. *Hn* may be a marker of the protasis of a conditional sentence. It is likewise uncertain in A 21:3 whether *hn* is conditional (" if ") or deictic.

*N*ʾ is used to emphasize a warning or entreaty and directly follows the expression to which it belongs (e.g., *my ʿbdk klb ky šlḥ ʾdny ʾ[t sp]r hmlk [wʾ]t spry hśr[m lʾm]r qrʾ nʾ*, "Who is your servant (but) a dog that my lord should have sent (him) th[e] king's [lett]er and [those] of the official[s askin]g (me) to read (them)?," L 6:2-5. Epigraphic Hebrew illustrates that *nʾ* follows the imperative (as is especially common in biblical Hebrew),[303] as in Lachish 6:5 (also possibly in Lachish 3:5, and Meṣad Ḥashavyahu 1:12 [both restored]).

Yh is a vocative particle of entreaty, which directly follows the imperative and precedes the deity name:

nqh yh yhwh, "Absolve O YHWH!," KBL 2:1.[304]

[303]Cowley, *Gesenius* p. 308, n.1.

[304]*Yh* is to be taken to represent an interjection rather than as an apocopated form of the divine element YHWH, on the basis of comparative Semitic sources, especially Ugaritic and Aramaic.

This particle is known from Ugaritic (*y = yâ;* cf. Gordon, *Ugaritic Texts*, p. 109, 407) and Aramaic (*yh*) (also Arabic and late Hebrew). *Yh* occurs in Ahiqar 127, 129 as an exclamation *yh bry*, "O my son," (see Jean-Hoftijzer, *Dictionnaire des inscriptions sémitiques de l'ouest*, p. 105), and is probably dialectic (Ugaritic *ya ʾili-mi*, O El!").

Cross treats *yh* as the particle of entreaty in Khirbet Beit Lei (cf. "The Cave Inscriptions from Khirbet Beit Lei," in *NEATC*, 1970, pp. 302, 306, n. 17), in contrast to the interpretation by Naveh ("Old Hebrew Inscriptions in a Burial Cave," *IEJ* 13 (1963): 87) and Gibson (*TSSI*, p. 58), that *yh* is an apocopated form for the theophoric element (*yah*). Lemaire, in 1976, following Naveh ("Old Hebrew Inscriptions in a Burial Cave," *IEJ* 13 (1963): 86), translates *nqh yh yhwh* as though *yh* is a form of the divine name, "Absolve YH-YHWH!" (see "Prières en temps de crise: Les inscriptions de Khirbet Beit Lei," *RB* 83 (1976): 560). He later explains *yh yhwh* as a "double théonyme, forme courte suivie de *la forme longue" (p. 566).

According to Cross (op. cit., p. 306, n. 17), in classical Hebrew, *yh* may be "hidden behind" a late, short form of the divine name, *yah*, e.g., in such a context as Psalm 130:3. The expression *yh yhwh* is attested in Isaiah 12:2; 26:4, and *yh ʾlhym* occurs in Psalm 68:19.

Given the evidence from comparative sources, e.g., Ugaritic, Aramaic, biblical Hebrew (e.g., Ps. 68:19), Cross's analysis of *yh* as a particle of entreaty is more likely than the analyses of Naveh, Gibson, and Lemaire.

3.4.5 Conclusion

In epigraphic Hebrew, particles are well represented both as independent forms and as proclitics. The evidence from epigraphic Hebrew illustrates that adverbs, prepositions, conjunctions and interjections are generally simple forms, usually composed of one element (e.g., *ʾl*, *ʿl*). Certain more "complex" particles consist of two distinct units (e.g., *lpny)*.

Certain prepositions and adverbs may take suffixes, thereby expressing both number and gender (e.g., prepositions: *lk*, "to you (m.s.)," *lhm*, "to them (m.pl.);" adverbs: forms of the negative *ʾyn*; e.g., *ʾy[nn]y*, "I am not," *[ʾy]nnw*, "we are not"), while only independent non-suffixed forms are attested as conjunctions and interjections in epigraphic Hebrew.

Sentences in epigraphic Hebrew illustrate that particles express interrelationships between words, may connect phrases, and supply secondary information to the phrase.

4. SYNTAX

4.1 Introduction

This chapter deals with the construction of sentences and the function[1] of words, phrases and sentences in epigraphic Hebrew. The limitations placed on the analysis of epigraphic Hebrew syntax are severe, namely: the short time span for the inscriptions (most texts date to between the mid-ninth and early sixth centuries), the lack of royal monumental inscriptions (as were common in Mesopotamia and Egypt), the scarcity of narrative prose, the large proportion of name lists/seals, the absence of poetry, the brevity of individual texts, and the fragmentary state of preservation of many texts.

The main sources for the study of epigraphic Hebrew syntax are the Lachish, Arad, Samaria, and dedicatory inscriptions, while the Siloam inscription and the Meṣad Ḥashavyahu ostracon are also very important to support particular points of epigraphic Hebrew grammar.

First, morphosyntax will be discussed, and emphasis will be placed upon rules of agreement, rules for verbal sequence, *et cetera*,

---

[1]W. Richter, *Grundlagen einer althebräischen Grammatik. B. Die Beschreibungsebenen. II. Die Wortfügung (Morphosyntax)* (EOS Verlag: St. Ottilien, 1979) (hereafter cited as Richter, *Grundlagen B.II.*); III. Der Satz(Satztheorie) (St. Ottilien: EOS Verlag, 1980).

according to the grammatical outline presented in Richter's *Grundlagen einer althebräischen Grammatik.*[1] The second part of the chapter includes a study of the nominal sentence and phrase in epigraphic Hebrew with special emphasis on the Samaria ostraca. Following this section is a discussion of the narrative and word order in verbal sentences in epigraphic Hebrew. The fourth section includes various sentence/phrase types which are attested for epigraphic Hebrew.

4.2 Morphosyntax

This section deals with morphosyntax, or the syntax of short phrases, in epigraphic Hebrew, closely following the format and terminology used in Richter's[2] work on morphosyntax. His systematic presentation, which is based upon modern linguistics, provides an excellent model for a syntax of epigraphic Hebrew.

In the first part of Richter's work, the morphosyntactic relationships between two words are treated. In this section, Richter considered thirteen types of relationships for biblical Hebrew:

1.	definition	8.	prepositional
2.	apposition	9.	interrogative
3.	construct	10.	modal
4.	attribution	11.	conjunctival
5.	annexation	12.	verbal
6.	adverbial	13.	verbal noun
7.	numeral		

The second part of Richter's work studies the various compounds ("complex" constructions) from biblical Hebrew resulting from combinations of the relationships (1-13) listed above (e.g., construct chains).

Due to the limited size of the epigraphic Hebrew corpus and the fact that the evidence of certain constructions in epigraphic Hebrew is limited, it is appropriate to combine under a single

---

[2]Richter, *Grundlagen B.II.*

heading all epigraphic Hebrew examples for both simple and "complex" constructions representing each of the thirteen categories listed above. Therefore, the reader will note, for instance, that under "apposition," both simple, as well as complex, appositional constructions are analysed.

For each of the syntactic constructions discussed, a formula is provided (expressed by abbreviations) which illustrates each type of relationship. Examples from epigraphic Hebrew are used to illustrate each syntactic formula. Rules governing the various constructions are also given.

By analyzing the formulae which Richter cites for biblical Hebrew in terms of epigraphic Hebrew syntax, it is clear that there is much overlap between the two. Morphosyntactic evidence from epigraphic Hebrew corresponds to many of the syntactic formulae cited by Richter for biblical Hebrew; however, the relative paucity of epigraphic Hebrew material limits the number of examples from epigraphic Hebrew to illustrate all of Richter's formulae. There is, however, morphosyntactic evidence for eleven of Richter's thirteen "Verbindungen."[3]

4.2.1 Definition

The syntactic formula for definition in epigraphic Hebrew follows:

Art + ‹N, Adj, Part, DPron, Num›

In epigraphic Hebrew, as in biblical Hebrew, definition is often marked by *hê,* the definite article, which is attached to both singular and plural, masculine and feminine substantives, locative substantives, gentilics, adjectives, participles, demonstrative pronouns and ordinal numerals.[4]

---

[3]Annexation and adverbial constructions (Richter's numbers 5 and 6 in the list given on the previous page) are presently not attested in epigraphic Hebrew.

[4]For specific examples for epigraphic Hebrew, the reader is directed to sec. 3.2.7, beginning on p. 173 and to the Lexicon in this grammar.

The rules governing determination in epigraphic Hebrew are:

4.2.1.1 The definite article most often grammatically determines a construct phrase (it precedes the nomen rectum), e.g., *ʿbd hmlk*, "servant of the king," L 3:19.[5] It was not required in numeric phrases where the number is expressed by a symbol (e.g., *bšt* , "in (the fifteenth) year," Samaria 22:1).

4.2.1.2 In prepositional phrases, the definite article functions to specify a time interval; e.g., *ʿd hššh lhḏš̊*, "until the sixth (day) of the month," A 7:4-5.

4.2.1.3 In definite phrases, the marker of determination follows *ʾt* and precedes the object of an active verb; e.g., *wʿbdk ʾy[nn]y šlḥ šmh ʾt̊ hʿ[d]*, "Your servant is [not] able to send the wit[ness] there," L 4:7-8.

4.2.1.4 An adjectival attributive which modifies a definite substantive is itself marked for definiteness (e.g., *hʿt hzh*, "this season," L 6:2). The attribute immediately follows the noun which it modifies, agreeing with it in number, gender, and definiteness; e.g., *hqmḥ hrʾšn*, "the first meal," A 1:5-6.

4.2.1.5 Nouns with attached pronominal suffixes are determinate. The definite article never marks these phrases as the noun is already made definite by the pronominal suffix; e.g., *bnkm gmr[yhw] wnḥmyhw*, "your sons Gemar[yahu] and Neḥemyahu," A 40:1-2.[6]

4.2.1.6 Proper nouns are definite by signification and no definite article precedes these nouns. In proper names like *hkws*, "the owl,"

---

[5]In one construct phrase, from Ajrud 3:1, *lśr ʿr*, "belonging to the governor of the city," the *nomen rectum* is unmarked for definiteness.

[6]There are no examples in epigraphic Hebrew of "noun + pronoun" modified by a definite object (e.g. *bnk hṭwb* "your good son") to prove this statement. Biblical Hebrew syntax serves as the analogous source that the rule as stated operated in epigraphic Hebrew.

A 38:1, the definite article is part of the name and not attached secondarily to the form.

4.2.2 Apposition

In epigraphic Hebrew, as in biblical Hebrew, appositional phrases consist of two nouns with no conjunctival connector. The nouns (or noun equivalents) refer to the same person or thing and typically stand adjacent to each other. There are ten syntactic formulae which illustrate the rules for apposition in epigraphic Hebrew.

4.2.2.1 ‹PN› + ‹N/abs/›+ (PS)

A proper name precedes an absolute substantive with an attached pronominal suffix, as in L 6:12, *yhwh ʾlhyk*, "YHWH, your God."

4.2.2.2 (prep) + ‹PN› + ‹N/abs/› + ‹PN/cs› + (DA) + ‹N/abs/›

The possessive suffix need not be present (as in formula 4.2.2.1 above), and instead, the marker of definition is a definite article. The absolute noun may be separated from the proper name by an intervening phrase (in this case, *bn mnḥ*) as in Herr Seal 110, *lmʾš bn mnḥ hspr*, "belonging to MʾŠ son of Manoaḥ, the scribe." This phrase actually contains two appositional phrases, *bn mnḥ* and *hspr*, both describing *mnḥ*.

4.2.2.3 (prep) + ‹PN›+ ‹N/NRe/› + (NR)

The type of appositional phrase illustrated by formula 4.2.2.3 is very common in epigraphic Hebrew, not only in seals, but also in the texts from Arad and Lachish (e.g., L 1:1-5; A 22:1, 2, 4; A 24:2, 3). The preposition at the beginning of this type of appositional phrase is not mandatory.

The rule for apposition which is illustrated by this syntax is: a proper name precedes a substantive bound to a following proper noun (personal or geographic name) in a construct relationship. In other words, the appositional noun is also a *nomen regens*. Two examples serve to illustrate:

> *lṣdq bn mkʾ*, "belonging to Ṣadoq, son of Mika," Avigad (*IEJ* 25) 4:1-2

> *[lz]kryw khn dʾr*, "[belonging to Ze]karyaw, priest of Dor," Avigad (*IEJ* 25) 4:3-4

4.2.2.4 ‹N/abs/› + (PS) + PN

An absolute substantive with an attached pronominal suffix precedes a proper name, as in A 21:2, *bnk yhwkl*, "your son Yehukal," A 40:1-2; *bnkm gmr[yhw] wnḥmyhw*, "your sons Gemar[yahu] and Neḥemyahu," and L 3:1, *ʿbdk hwšʿyhw*, "your servant Hawshayahu."

A variation of the syntactic formula above sees a preposition governing the appositional phrase, as in A 18:1-2, *ʾl ʾdny ʾlyšb*, "to my lord Elyashib," and L 2:1 *et cetera*, *ʾl ʾdny yʾwš*, "to my lord Yaush."

4.2.2.5 ‹N/abs/›+ (PS) + (DA) + ‹N/abs›

An absolute substantive with an attached pronominal suffix precedes a second absolute substantive marked for definiteness, as in *ʾdny hśr*, "my lord, the official," MHY 1:1.

4.2.2.6 ‹N/abs/› + (PS) + (Neg) + ‹Pron› + (PS)

An absolute substantive plus a pronominal suffix precedes the particle (of non-existence) plus pronoun. In the example which follows, *ʾynny* consists of the particle (of non-existence) plus a pronoun and an attached suffix: *wʿbdk ʾy[nn]y*,[7] "your servant is [not] able," L 4:7-8.

[7] Note the shift in person from *-k* (on *ʿbdk*, "your servant") to *-(n)y* (on *ʾy[nn]y*, "I am not").

4.2.2.7 ‹N/NRe/› + (NR) + PN

A substantive functioning as a *nomen regens* precedes a proper name (the *nomen rectum* intercedes between the two), as in *śr hṣbʾ knyh̊ẘ*, "the commander of the army, Konyahu," L 3:14-15.

4.2.2.8 (N/NRe/) + ‹N/NR/›+ VP + (DA) +‹N/abs/ʿ› + (Prep)

An appositional relationship exists between an absolute substantive marked for definiteness (*hqṣrm*, see example below) and the *nomen rectum* of a construct phrase. A verbal phrase intervenes between the two, in the example from *Meṣad Ḥashavyahu* 1:10:

> *wkl ʾḥy yʿnw ly hqṣrm ʾty*, "All my companions will testify for me, all who were reaping with me"

In this example, *hqṣrm*, "the reapers," serves as an attributive noun referring to *ʾḥy*, "my brothers." MHY 1:10 illustrates that an attributive noun and its head do not necessarily stand adjacent to one another (here, a verbal phrase intervenes).

4.2.2.9 (prep) + ‹N/abs/› + RS

An absolute substantive in a prepositional phrase precedes a relative clause, marked by *ʾšr*, as in *wldbr ʾšr ṣwtny*, "regarding the matter about which you gave me orders," A 18:6-8, and *lspr ʾšr šlḥ ʾd[ny] lʿbdk ʾmš*, "the letter which [my lo]rd sent to your servant yesterday," L 3:5-6.

4.2.2.10 (DA) + ‹N/abs/› + Num Sign + ‹abbreviated N/NR/›

An absolute noun preceded by the definite article precedes a numerical sign and abbreviated form of the *nomen rectum*, as in *wšlḥ̊ty ʾt h[k]s̊p (šmnt) š(qlm)*, "I will send the [mo]ney, eight shekels," A 16:4-5.

4.2.2.11 "Complex" Compound Apposition-Construct Constructions

A "complex" compound construction contains at least one construct and appositional phrase. The examples given above for formulae 4.2.2.3, 4.2.2.7, and 4.2.2.8 are compound constructions also, but they contain only one construct and one appositional phrase, for a total of only two component parts.

Lachish 3:19-20 serves to illustrate a "complex" compound noun clause containing several appositional and construct phrases:

> *wspr ṭbyhw ʿbd hmlk hbʾ ʾl šlm bn ydʿ mʾt hnbʾ*, "In regard to the letter of Tobyahu, servant of the king, which was sent to Shallum, son of Yada, from the prophet"

The two appositional phrases, *ṭbyhw ʿbd hmlk* and *šlm bn ydʿ*, illustrate the basic syntactic arrangement of formula 4.2.2.3 above:

‹PN› + ‹N/NRe/› + (NR)

4.2.3 Construct State

In epigraphic Hebrew, a proclitic noun forms a "stress unit" with a following noun. The result is the juxtaposition of two nouns functioning to mark a modifying relationship. In construct constructions in epigraphic Hebrew, as in biblical Hebrew, a substantive constitutes the first element of the unit, while a second substantive or proper name constitutes the second element. The second substantive (*nomen rectum*) indicates that the phrase is definite (if it is marked by the definite article, a pronominal suffix, or is a PN), or indefinite (if it is not marked for definiteness). Specifically, the determination of the construct is a function of the *nomen rectum*. A definite *nomen regens* is never marked for definiteness since this is a function of the *nomen rectum*.

These remarks are schematized in the following syntactic formula:

$$\langle N/cs/\rangle \; + \begin{cases} \langle N/abs/\rangle \\ (DA) \; + \; \langle N/abs/\rangle \; + \; (PS) \\ PN \end{cases}$$

The two nouns in a construct phrase function to mark an indefinite phrase if one substantive immediately precedes the second without a marker for determination, as in *nbl yn (yšn)*, "a jar of (old) wine," S 5:3; *šmʿt šlm*, "tidings of peace," L 2:3; *ʿṣd pšt*, "cutting of flax," Gezer 3.

The two nouns in a construct phrase function to mark a definite phrase if one substantive immediately precedes a second and the second substantive is marked, either by the definite article, or an attached possessive suffix, as in *bgd ʿbdk*, "your servant's garment," MHY 1:8; *dbr hmlk*, "the king's order," A 24:17; *wʿṣm[t] ʾmth*, "his servant-wife's bon[es]," Silwan 2:2. In this kind of phrase, the construct governing the definite *nomen rectum* is grammatically determinate. The phrase *(l)śr ʿr*, "(belonging to) the governor of the city," Ajrud 3, seems to furnish an exception to this rule.[8]

A substantive and proper noun combined in a construct phrase function to mark a phrase if the substantive immediately precedes the proper noun. No definite article or pronominal suffix mark these construct phrases since the proper name is already definite by signification;[9] e.g., *yd hkty*, "the hand of (= to) the Kitti," A 17:9; *bny gʾlyhw*, "the sons of Geʾalyahu," A 16:5; *mlk mṣrym;* "the king of Egypt," A 88:3.

The function of some construct phrases is to denote certain locatives in epigraphic Hebrew; as in *byt ḥrn*, "Beth-ḤRN," Tell Qasile 2:1; *byt ʾkzy[b]*, "Beth-Akzi[b]," L 22:10; *byt yhwh*, "House

---

[8]Sarfatti discusses this indeterminate construct phrase in detail, concluding that analogous phrases occur in the *qere* and *ketib* of biblical Hebrew and in Mishnaic Hebrew, and are to be understood as demonstrating colloquial style. Cf. G. Sarfatti, "Hebrew Inscriptions of the First Temple Period," *Maarav* 3/1 (1982): 71-73.

[9]Cf. Blau, *A Grammar of Biblical Hebrew*, p. 93.

of YHWH," L 4:5; *krm yḥwʿly*, "The vineyard of Yeḥawʿeli," S 73:2.

An analysis of adjectival attributes of substantives in construct phrases reveals that attributes which modify the *nomen rectum* conform to the regular rules of agreement between noun and adjective; that is, that the attribute immediately follows the noun which it modifies and agrees with it in number, gender, and definiteness, as in *mʿwd hqmḥ hrʾšn*, "from the rest of the first meal," A 1:5-6; *nbl šmn rḥṣ*, "a jar of refined oil," S 55:2-3.

There is one phrase in epigraphic Hebrew which attests to the adjectival attribute of the *nomen regens*: *spr ṭbyhw ʿbd hmlk hbʾ ʾl šlm bn ydʿ*, "The letter of Tobyahu...which was sent to Shallum," L 3:19-20. In this phrase, a definite active participle (*hbʾ*), functioning as an adjectival attribute (verbal adjective), modifies the *nomen regens* (*spr*) of the first construct phrase (*spr ṭbyhw*). The adjectival attribute of a *nomen regens* may not interfere between the two substantives (the *nomen regens* which it modifies and the *nomen rectum*) and when there is an intervening appositional phrase (in this case, the appositional phrase *ʿbd hmlk* functions also as a construct phrase), the attribute must immediately follow the intervening phrase.

4.2.3.1 Combination Phrases: Construct State

Triple construct chains are attested in epigraphic Hebrew where two *nomina recta* are governed by one construct. The construct chain in epigraphic Hebrew is not extended to more than three nouns. The syntactic formula which corresponds to the evidence from epigraphic Hebrew follows.

$$\langle N/cs/\rangle \;+\; \langle N/cs/\rangle \left\{\begin{matrix} PN \\ \langle N/abs/\rangle \end{matrix}\right.$$

A substantive functioning as the *nomen regens* precedes a second substantive, a form which is followed by the third element in the chain, a personal name, as in *ʿbd̊ byt̊ ʾmṣ̊*, "a servant of the house of Amoṣ," Beersheba 1:2-3, or another substantive, as in *mśʾ*

ṣmd ḥmrm, "a load of (= what can be borne by) a pair of pack donkeys," Arad 3:4-5. The third element in both phrases functions as the *nomen rectum* which determines the whole phrase. No definite article is needed in the phrase from Beersheba since the proper name is definite by signification. No definite article appears in the phrase from Arad because the phrase is indefinite.

In biblical Hebrew, it is uncommon for two *nomina regentia* to precede one *nomen rectum*,[10] and consequently, certain circumlocutions are used (such as the use of the preposition *l*-) to avoid cumbersome syntax. The examples of triple construct chains in epigraphic Hebrew indicate that having two substantives functioning as constructs is the norm. In *ʿbd byt ʾmṣ,* the element *byt* is, in relation to *ʿbd*, a *nomen rectum*, but it is also the noun governing *ʾmṣ* . The element *ṣmd* in *mśʾ ṣmd ḥmrm*, is likewise both governed by *mśʾ* and the form which governs *ḥmrm.*

If two *nomina recta* are governed by one construct, the head noun may be repeated, as in *bnk yhwkl šlḥ lšlm gdlyhw [bn] ʾlyʾr wlšlm bytk*, "Your son Yehukal sends greetings (to) Gedalyahu, [son of] Elyaʾir and to your household," A 21:1-2 (the two *nomina recta* are *gdlyhw* and *bytk*, the *nomen regens* is *(l)šlm*). This rule applies also to biblical Hebrew, e.g., Gen. 37:14, *ʾt šlwm ʾḥyk wʾt šlwm hṣʾn*, "the welfare of your brothers and your flock."

The syntax of this phrase may be formulated as:

(NR1) (NR2)

‹N/cs/› + PN + *w* + ‹N/cs/› + ‹N/abs/›

Substantives which denote quantity may function as *nomina regentia* in epigraphic Hebrew (the same is true for biblical Hebrew[11]), as in *wmlʾ hḥmr yyn*, "A full *homer* measure of wine," Arad 2:4-5. Epigraphic Hebrew *kl* functions in the same capacity

---

[10] Blau, *A Grammar of Biblical Hebrew*, p. 97.
[11] Ibid., pp. 97-98.

where it either precedes a determinate plural noun and means "all," e.g., *kl ʾḥy*, "all my companions," MHY 1:10; or precedes a singular indeterminate noun and means "any, every," *kl sp̊r*, "any letter, document," Lachish 3:11.

4.2.3.2 Construct-Apposition Constructions

Evidence from epigraphic Hebrew indicates that appositional and construct phrases occur together in a compound noun clause. The examples which follow illustrate compound constructions containing construct and appositional relationships among nouns. The first one, listed below, is from Arad 17:2-3.

byth ʾlyšb bn ʾšyhw

C1 A C2

"To the house of Elyashib, son of Eshyahu," A 17:2-3

The two construct phrases, labeled C1 and C2 above, may be diagrammed as follows:

‹N/cs/› + PN[12]

The substantives *byth* and *bn* are both *nomina regentia*, while the proper nouns function as *nomina recta*.

The phrase marked "A" above is the appositional phrase. The *nomen rectum* (*ʾlyšb*) of the first construct phrase is the head noun of the appositional phrase *ʾlyšb bn*, while *bn* is *nomen regens* of the second construct phrase.

---

[12]This formula was cited above in sec. 4.2.3, p. 241 at the beginning of the discussion of construct state phrases.

Several construct and appositional phrases occur in Lachish 3:19-20.[13] The construct and appositional phrases are labeled (A for "apposition;" C for "construct") and numbered.

spr ṭbyhw ʿbd hmlk hbʾ ʾl šlm bn ydʿ mʾt hnbʾ

C1 A1 C2 PartP A2 C3

"The letter of Tobyahu, servant of the king, which was sent to Shallum, son of Yada, from the prophet."

The syntactic scheme for the three construct phrases can be illustrated by two formulae:

1) ‹N/cs/› +	PN	
spr	*ṭbyhw*	Construct phrase 1
bn	*ydʿ*	Construct phrase 3

2) ‹N/cs/›+ (DA) +	‹N/abs/ ›	
ʿbd	*hmlk*	Construct phrase 2

ʿbd (in *ʿbd hmlk*) and *bn* (in *bn ydʿ*) have two functions. They are both *nomina regentia* and an appositional noun (the head of *ʿbd* in the first appositional phrase is *ṭbyhw* and the head of *bn* in the second appositional phrase is *šlm*).

---

13 See sec. 4.2.2.11 under "Apposition," p. 240.

4.2.4 Attribution

Attributives (adjectives, participles, and numerals [ordinals]) in epigraphic Hebrew follow a substantive and agree with it in number, gender and definiteness.

The demonstrative adjective may function attributively in epigraphic Hebrew and have a usage parallel to that of an adjective; in this function, it also follows the noun that it modifies and agrees with it in number, gender, and definiteness.

In phrases containing construct state constructions where an attributive modifies a *nomen regens*, the attributive may not intervene between the two. Instead, it follows immediately after the *nomen rectum*, unless there is an intervening construct phrase (as in Lachish 3:19-20) functioning as an appositive (to the *nomen rectum* of the first construct phrase). In this case, the attribute follows immediately thereafter (see formula 4.2.4.1).

The syntactic formulae which illustrate the epigraphic Hebrew evidence for attribution are given below and on the following page.

4.2.4.1

$$\left.\begin{matrix}(\mathrm{DA}) + \langle \mathrm{N\,/\,abs/} \rangle \\ \mathrm{PN}\end{matrix}\right\} + (\mathrm{DA}) + \langle \mathrm{Adj, Num(Ord), Part} \rangle$$

The evidence from epigraphic Hebrew which follows the syntax of this formula shows that an attribute, namely an adjective, participle, or ordinal number, immediately follows the noun that it modifies (if that noun is not a *nomen regens*), and agrees with it in number, gender, and definiteness.

Examples:

šmn rḥṣ , "refined oil," Samaria 16a:3
yn yšn, "old wine," Samaria 5:3
hqmḥ hrʾšn, "the first meal," A 1:5-6
ʾryhw̥ hʿšr, "Uriyahu, the notable (rich)," KEK 3:1
[m]ʿnym tḥtnm, "[from] lower Anim," A 25:2

4.2.4.2 DA + N + DA + DAdj

The evidence from epigraphic Hebrew indicates that the demonstrative adjective modifies a preceding substantive and agrees with it in number, gender and definiteness, e.g.,

> *h̊ḥdr hzh*, "this (burial-)chamber," KEK 1:3
> *hʿt hẓh*, this season," L 6:2
> *[hš]m̊n hzh*, "this [oi]l," A 13:2

4.2.4.3

$$\langle N / NRe / \rangle + \left\{\begin{matrix} PN \\ N / NR / \end{matrix}\right\} + \left\{\begin{matrix} \text{cs phrase} \\ VP \end{matrix}\right\} + DA + \langle Part \rangle + PrepP$$

> *spr ṭbyhw ʿbd hmlk hbʾ ʾl šlm bn ydʿ*, "The letter of Tobyahu, servant of the king, which was sent to Shallum, son of Yada," L 3:19-20

> *wkl ʾḥy yʿnw ly hqṣrm ʾty*, "All my companions will testify for me, all who were reaping with me," MHY 1:10

As mentioned above, a participle in a noun phrase functioning as an attributive follows the noun which it modifies and adheres to the rules of agreement. The phrase in Lachish 3:19-20 illustrates that if there is an appositional phrase (*ʿbd hmlk*) which modifies a preceding *nomen rectum* (*ṭbyhw*), the appositional phrase intervenes between the phrase containing the *nomen regens* (*spr ṭbyhw*) and its attributive (*hbʾ*). The latter follows immediately after the intervening phrase. In the case of Lachish 3:19-20, *hbʾ* functions not only as an attributive but also to govern a following prepositional phrase.

Hqṣrm, "the reapers," in Meṣad Ḥashavyahu 1:10, serves as an attributive noun referring to *ʾḥy*, "my brothers." The phrase illustrates that a verbal phrase may intervene between an attributive noun and its head. In the case of Meṣad Ḥashavyahu 1:10, an appositional relationship exists between *hqṣrm* and the *nomen rectum* (*ʾḥy*) of a preceding construct phrase. *Hqṣrm* functions not only as an attributive and a noun in apposition, but also, it governs a following prepositional phrase.

4.2.5 Numerals

Since the evidence for numerals and related substantives in epigraphic Hebrew is more limited than in biblical Hebrew, the syntactic formulae for the numerals which are posited below are based primarily upon analogy to biblical Hebrew. The available evidence for numerals from epigraphic Hebrew indicates that many of the same rules of number agreement and word order of numerals to substantives apply both to epigraphic and to biblical Hebrew.

The syntactic rules which relate to the relationship between numerals and substantives follow:

4.2.5.1 The numerals which are attested for epigraphic Hebrew (which are the numerals between two and eighteen and between one hundred and one thousand) indicate that cardinal numbers under ten precede the noun that they modify and are variable according to gender agreement. Numerals under ten also take the object numbered in the plural, as in biblical Hebrew, although in biblical Hebrew, there are exceptions to this rule (e.g., Exod. 16:22, *et cetera*).[14]

The syntactic formula which illustrates this rule is as follows:

‹Num 3-10› + ‹N {/pl abs/}›

as *šlš ʾmt*, "three cubits," Siloam 1:2. Although there is no way of knowing whether *šlš* is absolute or construct in this case, the example proves the word order: numeral plus substantive, and the number (plural) and status (absolute) of the substantive.

---

[14] Cowley, *Gesenius*, pp. 433-34.

4.2.5.2 The order of numeral to substantive is not known for numerals from eleven to nineteen, as the examples from epigraphic Hebrew for numerals within this range function as concrete substantives and the noun numbered is elided in the construction (see examples which follow from Arad 8).

The forms, marked for gender agreement to a latent substantive and preceded by the definite article, function as substantives in the absolute state. The syntactic formula which corresponds to the evidence from epigraphic Hebrew for numerals from eleven to nineteen is as follows:

(DA) + ‹Num/abs/›

The rule relating to the order of words which constitute the numerals from eleven to nineteen is that the first unit consists of a numeral from one to nine in the feminine absolute (agreeing with a latent masculine noun), followed immediately by the numeral ten:

‹Num 3-9 /abs f/› + ‹Num 10›

as in *(h)šl̊šh ʿś̊r*, "thirteen," A 8:2-3 and *(h)š̊m̊nh̊ ʿśr*, "eighteen," A 8:3-4.

4.2.5.3 The numerals from one hundred and upwards take the object numbered in the singular. This rule applies generally to biblical Hebrew, although there, *mʾh*, *mʾtym*, and *ʾlp* may occur with a plural substantive (e.g., *mʾh ʿmwt*, "one hundred cubits", Ezek. 40:27).[15] The related syntactic formulae for epigraphic Hebrew numerals above one hundred are schematized as follows:

---

[15] Cowley, *Gesenius*, p. 435.

4.2.5.3.1 ‹Num 100...›+ ‹N /sing abs/› as in Siloam 1:5-6, *bmʾtym̊ ẘʿlp ʾmh wm[ʾ]t ʾmh*, "twelve hundred cubits...one hundred cubits," where the numeral precedes a singular noun in the absolute state.

4.2.5.3.2 ‹Num 100...› + ‹N /sing abs/› + ‹Num 100› as in Tell Qasile 1:1-3, *ʾl̊[p] šmn wmʾh̊* , "one thousand (units of) oil and (another) one hundred (units of) oil," where the second numeral (*mʾh*), preceded by the conjunction *w*-, follows the noun numbered. According to biblical Hebrew word-order, if the conjunction *w*- were not present, the noun should come after the second number or be repeated there. The conjunction (*w*- in *wmʾh̊)* indicates that the noun (*šmn*) is not repeated. The evidence from Tell Qasile illustrates that the noun numbered precedes the second numeral (if that numeral is preceded by the conjunction *w*-), and is not repeated after it.

4.2.5.4 When numerals precede the substantive, they occur either in the construct state (as the *nomen regens*) or in the absolute. A numeral in the absolute state may follow the noun numbered and function as an apposition, as in Tell Qasile 1:1-2:

> *ʾl̊[p] šmn wmʾh̊* , "one thousand [units of] oil and [another] one hundred [units of] oil"

The formula for numerals as *nomen regens* relates to the number "one hundred", as shown in the following example from Siloam 1:5-6. This is the only certain evidence for a cardinal number functioning in the construct state:

‹Num 100 /cs/› + ‹N /sing abs/›

> *wm[ʾ]t ʾmh hyh gbh hṣr*, "the rock was one hundred cubits high"

4.2.5.5 Often in epigraphic Hebrew, the substantive is latent in the numerical construction, and the numeral functions as a substantive representing a concrete expression from which one element has been elided. The numerals which function in this capacity are in the absolute state, are preceded by the definite article, and end in *-h*.

The evidence from epigraphic Hebrew suggests the formula which follows:

(DA) + ‹Num /abs/›

as in: *(h)ššh*, "the sixth (day)," A 7:4; *(h)šl̊šh̊ ʿš̊r*, "the thirteenth (day)," A 8:2-3; *(h)š̊mnh̊ ʿśr*, "the eighteenth (day)," A 8:3-4.

All of the numerals which attest to this formula end in -h because the noun which is latent in the construction is presumably *ym*, "day," a masculine noun (numerals agreeing in gender with masculine nouns terminate in *hê*).[16]

The rule proposed for numerals below twenty in epigraphic Hebrew is that such numerals, when preceded by the definite article, function in the absolute state, without a numbered noun. The numeral itself functions as the substantive of a concrete expression (from which the principle modified noun has elided).

These numerals illustrate the cardinal form of the number, e.g., *hššh* (if the latent noun is indeed "day"), rather than the ordinal form (biblical *hššy*), which has this quasi-pronominal function.

---

[16]The examples cited above illustrate the rule that in numbering the days of the month in epigraphic Hebrew, the cardinals are used instead of the ordinals. This practice (as well as the omission of the word for "day") is frequent (but not mandatory) in biblical Hebrew, as e.g., *bʾḥd lḥdš*, "the first of the month," Gen. 8:5; *bʾrbʿh lḥdš*, "the fourth of the month," Zech. 7:1. Cowley, *Gesenius*, p. 433. For additional biblical forms, see Cowley, *Gesenius*, pp. 435-36. Two biblical parallels include 2 Kings 18:10–*šnt šš*, "the sixth year," and 1 Kings 15:25–*bšnt štym*, "in the second year." A third biblical parallel, this time for the *b...b* sequence in Arad 7:7–*bšnym lḥdš bʿśry*, "on the second day of the tenth month," is Hag. 1:15–*bĕyôm ʿeśrîm wĕʿarbāʿâ laḥōdeš baššiššî*, "on the twenty-fourth of the sixth month."

4.2.5.6 The ordinal numerals in epigraphic Hebrew function as attributives. They follow the noun which they modify and agree with it in number, gender, and definiteness. The formula for ordinals and related substantives in epigraphic Hebrew is the same as in biblical Hebrew:

$$(\text{DA}) + \langle \text{N}\begin{Bmatrix}/\text{sing}\\ /\text{pl}\end{Bmatrix}\text{abs}/\rangle + (\text{DA}) + \langle \text{NumOrd} / \text{abs}/\rangle$$

as in *mhqmḥ hrʾšn*, "of the first meal," A 1:5-6 and *b̊št htšʿt*, "in the ninth year," S 6:1.

4.2.5.7 When the noun numbered is expressed in written form (only at Samaria), the ordinal occurs with the definite article and follows the noun. However, the noun numbered need not be expressed (e.g., L 20:1, 29:1; A 20:1).

The Samaria Ostraca exhibit the most frequent use of the feminine ordinal in conjunction with the feminine singular noun *št*, "year." Less common is the temporal phrase with the preposition *b-*, "in," and an unstated noun presumed also to be the word for "year."

Other than *rʾšn*, "first," the ordinals in epigraphic Hebrew (masculine and feminine) illustrate the function of ordinals in numbering months and years. This is in contrast to the use ordinals to number days (of the month). In biblical Hebrew, months are also always numbered by ordinals, as are years.

4.2.6 Prepositional Constructions

In epigraphic Hebrew, prepositions precede either substantives/proper name/pronouns or pronominal suffixes.

4.2.6.1 Prep + N/PN/Pron

Examples which illustrate this syntax are:

hʾnšm ʾt ʾlyšʿ, "the men (must be) with Elisha," A 24:19-20

ʾl ʾšr ʾm[rt], "to what you ord[ered]," A 40:5

4.2.6.2 Prep + PS

as in *hqṣrm ʾty*, "all who were reaping with me," MHY 1:10.

4.2.6.3 When the preposition precedes a noun, a definite article, attached to the substantive may intervene, or the substantive may itself take a pronominal suffix. The syntactic expression of this point follows:

Prep + (DA) + N (+ PS)

Epigraphic Hebrew phrases illustrate this formula; e.g., *mn hmwṣʾ ʾl hbrkh*, "from the spring to the pool," Siloam 1:5; *ʾl ʾdny*, "to my lord," L 5:7 (these examples correspond to the formula: Prep DA + N); *ʾš ʾl rʿw*, "each man toward his fellow worker," Siloam 1:2,3 (this example constitutes the syntax: Prep + N +PS).

4.2.6.4 When uni-consonantal prepositions (*b*-, *l*-, or *k*-) precede a definite noun, the definite article elides:

Prep + DA + N -> Prep + N

as in *lmlk*, "of the king (=royal)," L 5:10.

4.2.6.5 Prepositions which are uni-consonantal are attached to a following noun (e.g., *bšt*, "in the year," Samaria 1:1, *et cetera*) or suffix (*ly*, "to me," MHY 1:10), but never stand as an independent word, while prepositions composed of two or more consonants always stand independently.

4.2.6.6 Prepositions precede an infinitive, as in e.g., *kṣʾty*, "when I leave," A 16:3; *lqrʾ*, "to read," L 3:10. The syntactic formula for the evidence above is:

Prep + Inf.

4.2.6.7 The interrogative particle (*h*-) may precede and govern a preposition, e.g., *hʾl*, "is it true that (someone will do something) to (someone)," L 5:9.

4.2.6.8 Prepositions which combine with adverbs in compound forms may function conjunctivally; e.g., *mʾz*, "since, from the time of," L 3:7 (prep + adverb = form functions as conjunction). Prepositions which combine with nouns in "complex" forms function either as prepositions (e.g., *lpny*, "in the face of," [prep + noun])[17] or as adverbs (e.g., *kym*, in the unit *ʿt kym*, "at this very time, this day, now," L 2:3, *et cetera*, where *kym* conforms to the syntax: Prep + Noun).[18]

4.2.7 Interrogative Constructions

The interrogative pronouns *my* and *[lm]h̊* introduce interrogative clauses and always come first in the construction. *My* marks a rhetorical question, while *lmh* requests a reason.

> *my ʿbdk klb ky*, "Who is your servant (but a) dog that..." L 2:3-4, *et cetera*

[17]See sec. 3.4.2, pp. 208-10 in this grammar.
[18]See sec. 3.4.1, pp. 204-5 in this grammar.

[lm]h̊ tʿśw kzʾt, "[Wh]y are you doing this?" L 6:9-10

Any sentence can be transformed into a question by prefixing *h-* to the first word. The interrogative particle (*h-*) is attached to a following preposition or adverb. If the person to whom the question is addressed is mentioned, this person's name or appositional noun directly precedes the form containing the interrogative particle (see Lachish 6 below). The particle *h-* marks a direct simple question when the inquirer is uncertain of the expected response.

hʾl ʿbdk y‹b›ʾ ṭbyhw zrʿ lmlk, "Will Tobyahu be b‹ring›ing royal grain to your servant?" L 5:9-10

ʾdny hlʾ tktb ʾl[yhm], "My lord, won't you write to [them]?" L 6:8-9

4.2.8 Modal Constructions

4.2.8.1 Affirmation

In epigraphic Hebrew, indicative imperfects, jussives, passive participles and imperatives function to mark affirmative volitive modal constructions, and, with the exception of the syntax with an imperfect, constitute the first unit of such constructions. The syntactic formula which follows is that of the most commonly attested modal construction in epigraphic Hebrew. According to this formula, the modal form may precede a noun (e.g., *yšmʿ ʾdny*, "May my lord hear," MHY 1:1-2), proper name/deity name (e.g., *yrʾ yhwh*, "May YHWH cause to see," L 6:1), or pronoun (e.g., *brk hʾ*, "May he be blessed," Ajrud 13:1).

Mod + N/PN/Pron

Mod = indicative imperfect, jussive, passive participle, imperative

Indicative/Jussive[19]

The indicative imperfect, jussive, and perfect function to express optative clauses. The modal form precedes a noun or proper (deity) name and governs a direct object; the object clause begins with the marker of the accusative *ʾt*, as in Lachish 6:1-2, *yrʾ yhwh ʾt ʾdny*, "May YHWH cause my lord to see," illustrating the syntactic formula:

Mod + DN + (DOM) + N (+ PS)

or, the object governed by the modal form can be expressed by an object suffix, as in Lachish 5:7-8, *yrʾk yhwh,* " May YHWH allow you to see (witness)," illustrating the syntax:

Mod (+ Obj. Suff.) + DN

The word order for modal phrases which have no direct object is that the imperfect follows the substantive (in the case of Arad 18, a deity name). In Arad 18, a prepositional phrase follows the modal form: *yhwh yšʾl lšlmk*, "May YHWH concern himself with your well-being," A 18:2-3.

The syntax for non-direct object modal phrases is:

DN + Mod + Prep + N (+ PS)

In modal constructions, multiple modal forms are ordered consecutively with no intervening independent words and are linked by conjunctive *waw*. Object suffixes attached to the modal forms function to express the objects governed by the verb.

---

[19]The jussive is formally identical with the indicative imperfect, except in the case of *yrʾ* and *yhy*, which, as jussives, are distinguishable from the indicative imperfect (*yrʾh* and *yhyh* would be expected), on the basis of biblical Hebrew rules for the formation of jussives and imperfects from Verbs III-weak. The term "imperfect" is used below to refer to forms which do not show an overtly marked difference between the indicative imperfect and the jussive.

The syntactic formula for this "complex" modal construction follows:

Mod (+ OS) + Conj. + Mod (+ OS) + Conj + Mod + PrepP

as in *ybrk wyšmrk wyhy ʿm ʾd[n]y*, "May he bless (you) and keep you, and may he be with my lo[rd]," Ajrud 15:6-9.

Passive Participles

The passive particle expresses mode when followed by a pronoun (independent subject pronoun or relative pronoun) or noun.

Examples for the syntactic formula: PP + Pron/N illustrating the passive participle as modal form are, for the second element as pronoun, e.g., *brk hʾ lyhw‹h›*, "Blessed be he to YHW‹H›," Ajrud 13, a phrase in which the modal form governs a prepositional phrase, and *ʾrr ‹ʾ›šr ‹y›mḥh̊*, "Cursed be ‹he› who will ‹ef›face (this tomb)," KBL 4, *et cetera*. In the last phrase, the modal form precedes a relative pronoun which govern the imperfect; for the second element as noun plus relative pronoun, *ʾrwr hʾdm̊ ʾš̊r yp̊tḥ*, "Cursed be the man who will open," Silwan 2:2-3 (the syntax is: PP + DA + Relative Pron. + Imperfect).

4.2.8.2 Imperative

The imperative occurs in independent volitive clauses which express a command. It is sometimes accompanied by a vocative. The imperative is always the first unit in the modal construction and precedes a deity name, suffixed preposition (functioning as a direct object; [see KEK 3 below]), particle of entreaty, or vocative particle.

The syntactic formula for the imperative as modal is:

Mod + PN =(DN)/ Prep/ *nʾ*/ vocative particle

Examples from epigraphic Hebrew which illustrate this syntax are:

n̊q̊h̊ yhẘh̊, “Absolve (us), YHWH!” KBL 2:1
nqh yh yhwh, “Absolve (us), O YHWH!” KBL 2:1
h̊wšʿ lh, “Save him!” KEK 3:3
qrʾ nʾ, “Read (them)!” L 6:5

4.2.8.3 Wish

The particle *nʾ* functions to determine a model phrase after the imperative:

Imperative + *nʾ*

as in *qrʾ nʾ*, “Read (them)!” L 6:5.

4.2.8.4 Negation

In epigraphic Hebrew, *ʾl*, *lʾ*, and *ʾyn* function as markers of negation. The main distinction with regard to *ʾyn* and *lʾ* is that the former negates nominal clauses, while the latter negates verbal and adjectival clauses. Negative volitive clauses are always expressed by *ʾl* plus imperfect.

The syntactic formulae which illustrate the markers for negation in epigraphic Hebrew are:

a) *ʾl* + Volitive (prefixed form with *taw*)

b) *lʾ* + Perf/Impf/ Infinitive/ Adj

c) *ʾyn* + N

ʾyn + PS + Participle

N + *ʾyn* + PS + Participle

ʾl functions to negate the volitive (*ʾl* + imperfect/jussive = negative imperative) and expresses a prohibition or negative wish; e.g., *ʾl tʾḥr*, "Don't delay!" A 2:6; *ʾl tšmʿ*, "Don't listen," papMur 17a:2.

Lʾ is the negativizer of 1) a nominal prepositional sentence (e.g., *lʾ lśr lhš[b]*, "The official does not consider it an obligation [to return (the garment)]," MHY 1:12-13), 2) indicative verbal sentences (with perfect verbs, e.g., *lʾ ydʿth*, "You do not know," L 3:8, and imperfects, e.g., *lʾ nrʾh*, "We cannot see," L 4:12), 3) adjectives (e.g., *lʾ ṭbm*, "not good," L 6:6).

ʾyn functions to negativize nominal sentences; e.g., *ʾyn̊ [p]h̊ ksp wz̊h̊b*, "there is neither silver nor gold [he]re," Silwan 2:1; *ʾyn šm ʾdm*, "there is no one there," L 4:5-6.

If *ʾyn* follows a definite subject, a resumptive pronominal suffix is attached to it, e.g., *wʿbdk ʾy[nn]y šlḥ* , "Your servant is [not] able to send," L 4:7-8. *ʾyn* may also bear a pronominal suffix which functions as subject of the nominal sentence, e.g., *[ʾy]nnw yklm lšlḥ* , "We [are un]able to send," A 40:13-14. The negative marker *ʾyn* when it takes a pronominal suffix functions to negate participial phrases, e.g., L 4:7-8 and A 40:13-14 above.

ʾl and *lʾ* as modes of negation directly precede the word that they are modifying. In noun phrases marked by *ʾyn*, an adverb (a short word functioning as an enclitic) may intervene between the marker of negation and its noun (e.g., *ʾyn šm ʾdm*, L 4:5-6).

Two conjunctions, *ʾm* and *pn*, function as markers of negation in epigraphic Hebrew.[20] *ʾm* functions as a marker of a negative oath. The particle is attested with the perfect; e.g., *ḥyhwh ʾm nsh ʾyš lqrʾ ly spr*, "As ‹Y›HWH lives, no one has ever tried to read a letter to me," L 3:9-10.

Pn, "lest, that not," introduces a negative final clause, and is immediately followed by the imperfect in a context of incompleted action; e.g., *pn yqrh*, "lest (anything) happen," A 24:16; *pn tbʾ*, "lest (they) come," A 24:20.

---

[20]For a further discussion of *ʾm* and *pn*, and their functions in epigraphic Hebrew, see pp. 223-26, 230 in this grammar.

4.2.8.5 Prolongation

ʿwd functions in epigraphic Hebrew as the marker of prolongation and directly precedes nouns. It may function as the *nomen regens* of construct constructions[21] or as an adverb.

The syntactic construction containing the prolongation marker which is specified by the evidence from Hebrew is :

Conj. *waw* + Conj/prep + prolongation marker + (DA) + N

Epigraphic Hebrew *ʿwd* may function as an abstract equivalent of *šĕʾār*, "remainder,"[22] in construct state, governed both by prepositions and conjunctions:

> *wmʿwd hqmḥ hrʾšn*, "from the remainder of the first meal," A 1:5-6

or, as in Arad 2:7, *ʿwd* may function as an adverb:

> *wʾm ʿwd ḥmṣ*, "If (there is) yet vinegar" › "if there is any vinegar left," A 2:7

4.2.9 Conjunctival Constructions

The widespread use of the coordinating conjunction *waw* in lieu of specifically subordinating conjunctions to connect phrases, clauses, and sentences is a feature of epigraphic Hebrew syntax. Sentences connected by *waw* in epigraphic Hebrew have different functions depending on the word order within a sentence or by the type of verbal form which follows the conjunction.

---

[21]The reader is directed to sec. 4.2.3 beginning on p. 240 (esp. p. 242) for a more detailed discussion of this sentence type.

[22]For *ʿwd* as a noun, cf. G.B. Sarfatti, "Hebrew Inscriptions of the First Temple Period," *Maarav* 3/1 (1982): 74.

Waw connects two principle kinds of sentences in epigraphic Hebrew: conjunctive (a second sentence is consequent to the first), in which *waw* precedes a verbal clause, and disjunctive (a second sentence is not consequent to the first), in which *waw* precedes a non-verbal clause.

Waw precedes a second verbal form (the imperfect, perfect, jussive or imperative) in narrative or volative sequences. A clause introduced by *waw* is thus preceded either by verbal clauses containing a perfect, imperfect, or imperative, or by non-verbal clauses. The formulae for conjunctive clauses in epigraphic Hebrew are given below:

Narrative sequences

1. perfect + *waw* + imperfect

2. imperfect + *waw* + perfect (uncertain)

3. infinitive + *waw* + perfect

Volitive sequences

1. imperative/inf.abs + *waw* + imperative

2. imperative/inf. abs + *waw* + perfect

3. impf + *waw* + impf + *waw* + juss

4. *waw* + perf + *waw* + imperative + *waw* + perf

Volitive Plus *Waw*-conjunctive Perfect Sequence

1. imperative + *waw* + perf + *waw* + impf.

4.2.9.1 Narrative Sequences with *Waw*

Waw functions to join verbs in narrative sequences. Such sequences may continue through several sentences. Each sentence subsequent to the first, and part of the main narrative, begins with the prefixed *waw* and the imperfect or perfect.

1. perfect + *waw* + imperfect

Waw-consecutive marks the sequence Perfect + Imperfect. This narrative sequence functions to mark completed actions. The subject need not be the same in each clause.

Examples:

hkw...wylkw hmym, "They struck...and the water flowed," Siloam 1:4-5

lqḥh šmʿyhw wyʿlhw hʿyrh, "Shemayahu has seized him and brought him up to the city," L 4:6-7

hyh ʿbdk bḥṣr ʾsm wyqṣr ʿbdk wykl, "Your servant was in Ḥaṣar-Asam. Your servant reaped, finished..." MHY 1:3-5

kl...wybʾ hwšʿyhw...wyqḥ , "(Your servant) finished... and along came Hawshayahu...and took," MHY 1:6-8

2. imperfect + *waw* + perfect

In biblical Hebrew, *waw*-consecutive precedes the perfect in narrative sequences beginning with an imperfect. This sequence, imperfect plus perfect, functions to mark incompleted action. In epigraphic Hebrew, however, the evidence for this sequence depends upon Lachish 4, line 10, in which the reading of the first verb is uncertain. The second verb, *(w)yd*ʿ, is likewise ambiguous.[23]

*[y]b̊[ʾ]...wyd*ʿ, "(If) he [co]me[s]...he will know," L 4:9-10

Therefore, the syntax herein described cannot be accepted as evident beyond doubt for epigraphic Hebrew until more certain examples of the "imperfect plus *waw* plus perfect" syntax become available from future epigraphic finds.

3. <u>infinitive + *waw* + perfect</u>

The sequence "infinitive plus *waw* plus perfect" is a variation of the syntax expressed in sequence number 2 above. *Waw*-consecutive precedes the perfect in narrative sequences beginning with an infinitive and marks the future. Formula 3 and the discussion about it are based on the reading of Arad 16:3-4. There is no reason internal to the document in question why the clause in Arad 16 should not be treated as demonstrating the syntax *waw*-consecutive plus perfect.

kṣʾty m̊bytk wšlḥ̊ty, "When I leave your house, I will send," A 16:3-4

---

[23] *Yd*ʿ could represent the perfect (*yādaʿ*) or imperfect (*yēdaʿ*). The reading of *yd*ʿ as a perfect hinges on the restoration of line nine of Lachish 4. The reading *[y]b̊[ʾ]* in this line, and *wyd*ʿ as the *waw*-consecutive and perfect (see Pardee, *HHL*, p. 93) is accepted in this grammar in contrast to Albright and Cross's rendering of the verb as jussive, "and let/may (my lord) know." See W. F. Albright, in *Ancient Near Eastern (Supplementary) Texts (and Pictures)*, ed., J. B. Pritchard (1969), p. 322, no. 279 and F. M. Cross, "Lachish Letter IV," *BASOR* 144 (1956): 25.

H. Torczyner, *Lachish I, The Lachish Letters* (London: Oxford University Press, 1938), p. 200 also read *wyd*ʿ in line 10 as the perfect plus *waw*-consecutive: *wĕyādaʿ*, "then he would know."

4.2.9.2 Volitive Sequences

1A. imperative + *waw* + imperative

Evidence from epigraphic Hebrew indicates that in order to give consecutive commands, each imperative is listed consecutively and each command after the initial one is preceded by conjunctive *waw*.

q[ḥ]...wtn..., "Ta[ke]...and give...," A 12:1-2

1B. infinitive absolute + *waw* + imperative

The infinitive absolute functions as an imperative in volitive sequences in epigraphic Hebrew. The *waw* precedes an imperative or perfect (see examples on the following page under 2B) and follows the infinitive absolute in this sequence. The function of sequence 1B, as in the sequence 1A (imperative plus *waw* plus imperative), is to express consecutive commands.

ntn...wktb..., "Give...and write[24]...," A 1:2-4

---

[24]*Ktb* is not certainly an imperative. The supporting evidence for the sequence "infinitive absolute + *waw* + imperative" rests on the interpretation of this form as an imperative, as *ntn* is attested only before perfect sequences in other Arad texts. Note, however, that the verbal element following the *ntn* phrase is missing in several of the Arad letters due to broken context (e.g., A 11:2).

Ktb in Arad 1:4, is interpreted as the imperative, "Write!," by Aharoni (*Arad Inscriptions*, p. 12), Lemaire (*Inscriptions hébraïques*, p. 155), Gibson (*TSSI*, p. 52), and Pardee (*HHL*, p. 30). The Bible supports this interpretation; the infinitive absolute is followed by imperatives (but without the conjunction) in Nahum 2:2, *nṣwr* (inf.abs.)...*ṣph* (impv.)...*ḥzq* (impv.)..*ʾmṣ* (impv.), "Guard...watch...strengthen...fortify!"

2A. imperative + *waw* + perfect

To express explicit consecution, *waw* plus a perfect follows an initial imperative.

bʾ...wlqḥt, "Go...and take," A 17:1-4

2B. infinitive absolute + *waw* + perfect (+ *waw* + perfect)

A second volitive sequence containing *waw* plus perfect to express consecution is the sequence with initial infinitive absolute (functioning as an imperative) preceding *waw* plus the perfect.

ntn...[w]ktbth, "Give...[and] (then) write (make a record [of it])," A 7:2-6

ntn...whsbt...wntt, "Give...and(then) send...and (then) give," A2:1-8[25]

A volitive sequence in the Moussaïeff Ostracon provides an example of the syntax of the *waw*-consecutive + perfect plus *waw*-consecutive + perfect.

whyh ydk ʿmy wntth byd ʾmtk ʾt hnḥlh, "(I request politely that the following) happen: let your hand be with me and entrust to your maidservant the inheritance," MO 2:3-5

Literally, the *waw*-consecutive formulation *whyh...wntth* in MO 2:3-5 means "and it will be (=let it be)...and (then) give (=entrust)."

---

[25] Arad 24:13-15 furnishes two additional examples of *waw*-consecutive perfects:...*wšlḥtm...whbqydm*, "...and send them...he is to hand them over..." Since parts of the text preceding lines 13-15 are not preserved, the initial verbal form in the sequence is uncertain (although it is likely that it was either an imperative or infinite absolute).

3. imperfect + *waw* + imperfect + *waw* + jussive

Waw functions to connect indicatives/jussives in volitive sequences which express consecution. The *waw* precedes all verbs after the initial one.

ybrk wyšmrk wyhy ʿm ʾd[n]y, "May he bless (you) and keep you, and may he be with my lo[rd]," Ajrud 15:6-9

4. *waw* + perfect + *waw* + imperative + *waw* + perfect

Waw precedes all volitive verbal forms, even the initial one, in sequences containing perfects and imperatives functioning to mark explicit consecution.

wṣrr[t]...wspr...wlqḥt, "Bind...calculate...and take," A 3:5-8

4.2.9.3 The Volitive Plus *Waw*-Conjunctive Perfect Sequence

Attention may be called to the syntax of Arad 3:2-5. In this phrase, *wṣwk* appears to represent the *waw*-conjunctive plus perfect ("X [hereby] orders you"), preceded and followed by volitive forms:

1. imperative + *waw*-conjunctive + perfect + *waw* + perfect

tn...wṣwk...wṣrrt, "Give...and (Hananyahu) (hereby) orders you....and (you are to) bind,"A 3:2-5

Wṣrrt is a *waw*-consecutive second masculine singular perfect in an imperative sequence (*tn* is the imperative).[26] The form *wṣwk* consists of a simple *waw* plus perfect which functions as an

[26]Cf. no. 4 above.

epistolary perfect.[27] As pointed out by Pardee,[28] the volitive semantic context of *ṣwh* permits the following *waw*-consecutive perfect to function as a volitive form.

While two forms from epigraphic Hebrew are possible additional evidence for the sequence: *waw*-conjunctive plus perfect, *wʾsm* in Meṣad Ḥashavyahu 1:5, 6-7, and *wšlḥty* in Arad 16:4,[29] *ʾsm* more likely represents the infinitive absolute, rather than the perfect or imperfect,[30] and *šlḥty* probably demonstrates the syntax *waw*-consecutive plus perfect ("I will send"), rather than *waw*-conjunctive plus perfect syntax ("I sent").[31]

---

[27]Pardee, "Letters from Tel Arad," *UF* 10 (1978): 300; *HHL*, p. 35; "The 'Epistolary Perfect' in Hebrew Letters," *BN* 22 (1983): 34-40. Cf. D. Pardee and R. M. Whiting, "Aspects of Epistolary Verbal Usage in Ugaritic and Akkadian," *BSOAS* 50 (1987): 1-31.

[28]"Letters from Tel Arad," *UF* 10 (1978): 300.

[29]Cf. Pardee, *HHL*, p. 48. Pardee has since revised this analysis and now considers *wšlḥty* as representing *waw*-consecutive plus perfect syntax.

[30]The syntax of the phrase (especially MHY 1:6-7) in which *ʾsm* occurs is subject to debate. Therefore, it is not certain beyond a doubt whether *ʾsm* represents a perfect, infinite absolute or imperfect.

For *ʾsm* as a perfect; cf. L. Delekat, "Ein Bittschriftentwurf eines Sabbatschanders (*KAI* 200)," *Biblica* 51 (1970): 462; Lemaire, "L'ostracon de Meṣad Ḥashavyahu (Yavneh-Yam)," *Semitica* 21 (1971): 68 and Pardee, "The Judicial Plea from Meṣad Ḥashavyahu (Yavneh Yam)," *Maarav* 1/1 (1978): 42.

The form is best argued as an infinite absolute by Cross, "Epigraphic Notes on Hebrew Documents of the Eighth-Sixth Centuries B.C.: II. The Murabbaʿat Papyrus and the Letter Found Near Yabneh Yam," *BASOR* 165 (1962): 44, n. 43; "The Ammonite Oppression of the Tribes of Gad and Reuben: Missing Verses from 1 Samuel II Found in 4Q Samuel[a]," History, Historiography and Interpretaion. Studies in Biblical and Cuneiform Literatures (Jerusalem: Magnes, 1983), pp. 150-151.

For *ʾsm* as the first common singular imperfect with elision of one *ʾaleph*, see Joseph Naveh, "A Hebrew Letter from the Seventh Century, B.C., *IEJ* 10 (1960): 133. Naveh's reading of *ʾsm*; is very unlikely because this interpretation requires a shift from third to first person, in a conjunctive sequence.

The syntactic environment which makes *wʾsm* a plausible *waw*-consecutive involves perceiving the action described by *wʾsm* in Meṣad Ḥashavyahu not as consecutive, rather as coordinate to the principal action (which itself expressed by a *waw*-consecutive form).

[31]See p. 263.

Waw and the Disjunctive Sentence

The sequence *waw* + non-verbal phrase is a common feature of epigraphic Hebrew. In this case, the sentences introduced by *waw* are narratively disjunctive. The main categories for disjunctive sentences introduced by *waw* that a modern analysis may isolate in epigraphic Hebrew are contrastive, initial, and parenthetical.

Waw precedes non-verbal phrases in a volitive conjunctive sequence where the noun phrase precedes the imperative. The syntax is disjunctive, with object/verb word-order. The function of the *waw* is to differentiate between commodities. *Waw* introduces a disjunctive sentence describing what is to be done to a mentioned commodity which is a separate action from that which is prescribed to a previously mentioned commodity. A volitive phrase intervenes between the phrases mentioning the contrasting commodities.

Examples:

wyyn b ⊢/ *tn lhm*, "Give them one *bat*-measure of wine," A 4:3

wšmn ḥ[tm], "S[eal] (a jar of) oil," A 7:8-9

wmʿwd hqmḥ hrʾšn trkb / *qmḥ*, "From the remainder of the first meal, have one *homer*-measure of meal loaded," A 1:5-7

The disjunctive function of *waw* to express initial events or signal a beginning occurs when it precedes the adverb of time or temporal phrases, e.g., *wʿt*, "and now," A 1:1-2, *et cetera*; *wbym hnqbh*, "now, on the day that the tunneling was completed," Siloam 1:3-4.

Waw functions to introduce parenthetical disjunctive clauses which intervene within the narrative to supply supplementary relevant information to the narrative; e.g.,

wbʿwd šlš ʾmt lhn[qb], "and while there were yet three cubits (of rock) to be tun[neled through]," Siloam 1:2

4.2.10 Verbal Constructions

This section refers to the simple verbal phrase which illustrates the finite verb plus infinitive construction. Referring to Richter's formulae, cited for *Verb-Verbindungen*,[32] we find that only his sequence number one (that is, "infinitive absolute plus perfect/imperfect/participle") is partially relevant for the evidence from epigraphic Hebrew.

The evidence from epigraphic Hebrew for the finite verb plus infinitive construction is discussed below:

4.2.10.1 Infinitive absolute + perfect

The infinitive absolute is followed immediately by a finite verb form of the same stem to emphasize or more accurately define the idea expressed by the main verb.

> *[š]lḥ šlḥ̊t̊ ʾt šlm bytk*, "I (hereby) [s]end heartfelt greetings to your household," papMur 17a:1

4.2.10.2 Perfect + infinite construct

A finite verb is followed (usually, but not always immediately) by the infinitive construct to express purpose, goal or result. Examples from epigraphic Hebrew which illustrate this use of the perfect and infinitive construct sequence are listed on the following page.

---

[32]Richter concentrates his discussion on verbal constructions wherein the first verbal element is a modal form; cf. *Grundlagen B.II.*, p. 44. Part of his first sequence, namely, "infinitive absolute + perf" applies to the evidence from epigraphic Hebrew.

ʿbdk hwšʿyhw šlḥ lh̊g[d], "Your servant Hawshayahu (hereby) sends (a letter) to info[rm]," L 3:1-2

lʾ ydʿth qrʾ, "You don't know how to read," L 3:8-9

ḥyhwh ʾm nsh ʾyš lqrʾ ly spr , "As ‹Y›HWH lives, no one has ever tried to read a letter to me," L 3:9-10

4.2.11 Verbal Nouns

The verbal nouns are the infinitives construct and absolute and the participles. Verbal nouns express manner of action in their patterns and have both verbal and nominal functions.

4.2.11.1 Infinitives Construct

The infinitive construct has both nominal and verbal functions. In the latter role, the infinitive construct may take subjects, objects, and verbal adjuncts.

In epigraphic Hebrew, infinitives construct may be introduced by prepositions, most often *l-*, but also *k-*.

The infinitive construct (either preceded by a preposition or standing alone) may govern a noun as a direct object. Further, the infinitival phrase itself serves as an object phrase of a preceding verb or verbal phrase.

Examples:

ḥyhwh ʾm nsh ʾyš lqrʾ ly spr, "As ‹Y›HWH lives, no one has ever tried to read a letter to me," L 3:9-10

lʾ ydʿth qrʾ spr, "You don't know how to read a letter," L 3:8-9

When pronouns serve as subjects of an infinitive construct, they are attached to it as a pronominal suffix:

m'z šlḥk 'l ʿbdk, "Since you sent (=your sending) (the letter) to your servant," L 3:7-8

The infinitive, preceded by the preposition *k*-, in a phrase preceding *waw*-consecutive and the perfect, illustrates a usage well attested in biblical Hebrew. With *k*-, the infinitive functions as a temporal adverbial clause, e.g., *wʿt kṣ'ty m̊bytk wšlḥ̊ty 't h[k]s̊p*, "and now, when I leave your house, I will send the [mo]ney," Arad 16:3-5.

The infinitive construct may function as a substantive in a clause. In the following example, the infinitive serves as the *nomen rectum*, governed by the noun *ym*, within a prepositional phrase denoting temporality: *wbym hnqbh*, "on the day of its tunneling (= the day the tunnel was completed)," Siloam 1:3-4, or as the *nomen rectum* of the phrase governed by a preceding verb, e.g., *wzh hyh dbr hnqbh*, "This was the way of its tunneling (= the way in which it was tunneled out)," Siloam 1:1.

4.2.11.2 Infinitives Absolute

The infinitive absolute functions either as an adverb in epigraphic Hebrew or as a substitute for a finite form.

To emphasize a verbal idea, the infinitive absolute precedes a finite verb, e.g., *[š]lḥ šl̊ḥ̊t 't šlm bytk*, "I hereby [s]end heartfelt greetings to your household," papMur 17a:1.

The infinitive absolute functions as an imperative frequently in the Arad letters. It is used in place of a finite verb and is not dependent on any other verb in the clause; e.g., *wʿt ntn lktym yyn*, "Now, give the Kittim wine," A 1:1-3, *et cetera*.

In biblical Hebrew, the infinitive absolute may function as a substitute for a finite form describing action on par with the main verb. The one possible form in epigraphic Hebrew is not unanimously so analyzed.[33]

---

[33]The form under discussion is *'sm* from the Meṣad Ḥashavyahu ostracon. See p. 267, n. 30 in this grammar.

4.2.11.3 Participles

Participles are verbal adjectives which function as substantives or as verbal forms, or a combination of both.[34] Participles indicate voice, person, number, and gender.

The participle may be used attributively:

wspr ṭbyhw...hbʾ ʾl šlm...," The letter of Tobyahu which came (=was sent) to Shallum," L 3:19-20

wkl ʾḥy yʿnw ly hqṣrm ʾty, "All my companions will testify for me, all who were reaping with me," MHY 1:10

and/or predicatively,

ʿbdk qṣr, "Your servant is working at the harvest,"[35] MHY 1:2-3

hʾ yšb, "He is staying," A 18:10

ʾl mśʾt lkš nḥnw šmrm, "We are watching the Lachish (fire) signals," L 4:10-11

The participle as an attribute or predicate usually indicates a continuing action contemporaneous with a principal frame of action. Participles govern direct objects expressed by a suffixed pronoun, e.g., *ʾrr ḥrpk*, "Cursed be he who insults you (='your scorner')," KBL 7:1-2.

Sentences with participles functioning predicatively identify with nominal clauses in specifying temporality, in word order, and in negation. Regarding temporality, the epigraphic Hebrew participle as verb often expresses on-going action, as in Lachish

---

[34] See the discussion of participles in the morphological chapter of this grammar, pp. 106-19.

[35] For a discussion of this form and the syntax of MHY 1:3, cf. sec. 3.1.4.1, p. 107, n. 80 of this grammar.

4:10-11, *ʾl mśʾt lkš nḥnw šmrm*. With respect to word order, the subject (as either pronoun or noun) in epigraphic Hebrew always precedes the participle (*byt yhwh hʾ yšb*, "He is staying in the temple of YHWH," Arad 18:9-10; *ʿbdk qṣr*, "Your servant is working at the harvest," Meṣad Ḥashavyahu 1:2-3.

Participles as predicates behave like nouns with respect to negation since the negative particle *ʾyn* is used rather than *lʾ*, e.g., *wʿbdk ʾy[nn]y šlḥ*, "Your servant is [not] able to send," Lachish 4:7-8.

Active participles may be used as subjects (*hkw hḥṣbm*, "the hewers struck," Siloam 1:4), and in construct phrases (as *nomina regens*; *ʿl rʾš hḥṣb[m]*, "over the head(s) of the hewer[s]," Siloam 1:6).

4.3 Nominal Sentences and Noun Lists

Francis Andersen,[36] in his survey of biblical nominal clauses, formulated rules for describing the varieties of verbless clauses which are possible in Hebrew and gave a full repertoire of clause types with examples and references.[37] His study provides a useful tool for the study of nominal sentences and noun lists in epigraphic Hebrew.

The nominal sentence is attested frequently in the epigraphic Hebrew inscriptions, particularly in the Samaria ostraca. Nominal sentences characterize the philologically difficult Gezer ostracon and incomplete nominal sentences and various lists consisting of noun phrases occur also on the numerous seals, and ostraca/graffiti. These latter inscriptions often list the names of people and the various commodities or amounts calculated and allotted to them. Nominal sentences and lists of nouns occur also in the inscriptions from

---

[36]F. I. Andersen, *The Hebrew Verbless Clause in the Pentateuch. Journal of Biblical Literature Monograph Series XIV* (Nashville: Abingdon Press, 1970).

[37]Andersen isolated three main types of verbless clauses which he classified by discourse function: the declarative (the most common pattern of nominal clause in the Bible), precative, and interrogative nominal clauses.

Beersheba, Tell Qasile, Hazor, Silwan, Lachish, Arad, Khirbet el-Kom, and Ajrud.

The Samaria ostraca are a fixed body of epigraphic Hebrew material, the syntax of which is stereotyped. The following syntactic arrangement is attested most often in these inscriptions:

Temp + Gen + Nom

The temporal clause serves as the introduction to the inscription, e.g., *bšt htšʿt*, "in the ninth year," Samaria 9:1. Following it is usually a locative prepositional phrase (with *m*-, "from") functioning as an indicator of the origin of the commodity being received, e.g., *mʾzh*, "from Azah," Samaria 2:3. It is then followed by a genitive clause consisting of a preposition governing a proper name (*lʾdnʿm*, "belonging to Adoniam," Samaria 10:2-3), and the inscription often ends with a nominal phrase illustrating *status constructus*, e.g., *nbl yn yšn*, "a jar of old wine," Samaria 12:3-4, naming the specified commodity.

Occasionally, the order of the genitive and nominal elements is reversed; e.g., Samaria 19:2-4– *nbl šmn rḥṣ lʾd̊nʿm*, "a jar of refined oil belonging to Adoniam," or the genitive and locative phrase may be in reverse order (e.g., *lgmr mnʿh*, "belonging to Gomer, from Neʿah," Samaria 50:1).

The *lamed* phrase in the Samaria ostraca can be understood as one which functions as a genitive, "(belonging) to, for," in a phrase indicating the recipient (rather than donor) of a set commodity.[38] However, in epigraphic Hebrew (as in biblical

---

[38]Much has been written about the function of the "*lamed*" in the Samaria ostracon. Cf. Yadin, "Recipients or Owners: A Note on the Samaria Ostraca," *IEJ* 9 (1959): 184-87; Rainey, "Administration in Ugarit and the Samaria Ostraca," *IEJ* 12 (1962): 62-63; Yadin, "A Further Note on the Samaria Ostraca," *IEJ* 12 (1962): 64-65; Aharoni, "The Samaria Ostraca–An Additional Note," *IEJ* 12 (1962): 67-69; Rainey, "The Samaria Ostraca in the Light of Fresh Evidence," *PEQ* 99 (1967): 32-41; Yadin, "A Further Note on the *Lamed* in the Samaria Ostraca," *IEJ* 18 (1968): 50-51; Rainey, "Semantic Parallels to the Samaria Ostraca," *PEQ* 102 (1970): 45-51; F. M. Cross, "Ammonite Ostraca from Heshbon. Heshbon Ostraca IV-VIII," *Andrews University Seminary Studies* 13 (1975): 1-20; W.H. Shea, "The Date and Significance of the Samaria

Hebrew), there exists a wide range of meaning for the preposition *l*- which governs a proper name.

The Samaria ostraca are but one body of textual evidence which illustrates the use of the nominal clause with prepositional phrases functioning as adverbial predicates. The epigraphic Hebrew inscriptions are replete with evidence for this construction, at Arad (e.g., Arad 22)[39] and Lachish (e.g., Lachish 22: 6-7, *lʾš[yhw] (ḥmr) lʿs̊yhw bn [ ]ʾ[ ] (sʾh)*, "Belonging to Esh[yahu], a *homer*; "belonging to Asayahu, son of..., a *seah* (?)", as well as in the short inscriptions:

lpqḥ smdr, "Belonging to Peqaḥ, *SMDR*-wine," Hazor 7:1

lmlk ʾl̊[p] šmn wmʾh̊ ḥ̊yhw," For (belonging to) the King: one thou[sand] one hundred (units of) oil. Ḥiyahu," Tell Qasile 1:1-2

z̊hb ʾpr lbyt ḥrn š(qlm šlšm), "Gold of Ophir for Beth-ḤRN, thirty shekels," Tell Qasile 2:1-2

The principal formulae for the syntax of the nominal sentence in epigraphic Hebrew and examples from the texts which illustrate them are given on the following page.

Ostraca," *IEJ* 27 (1977): 16-27; Rainey, "The *Sitz im Leben* of the Samaria Ostraca," *TA* (1979): 91-94; G. B. Sarfatti, "Hebrew Inscriptions of the First Temple Period," *Maarav* 3/1 (1982): 75-76.

[39]At Arad, the preposition is latent in the construction, as the syntax for the phrases functioning as indicators of receipts of goods are commonly nominal phrases (person's name) plus numerical sign (e.g., A 31). These phrases are simply elliptical ones functioning as a statement of commodity received by a person. The only evidence at Arad for the genitive construction where the prepositional phrase is attested by *l*- and the commodity is also listed, is Arad 22, but the amounts and type of goods received (three and four *homer* measures (?) in lines 3 and 4) are difficult to interpret.

4.3.1 Formulae for Word-order in Nominal Sentences

4.3.1.1 Sub + Pred (+ Adv/PrepP)

This construction illustrates the normal order for the elements within the nominal sentence in epigraphic Hebrew.[40] The examples from epigraphic Hebrew which provide the evidence for this syntax come from Lachish and Silwan.

> *whnh dbry h[śrm] lʾ ṭbm*, "Well, the [officials'] statements are not good," L 6:5-6

> *zʾt [qbrt šbn]yhw*, "This is the [tomb of Sheban]yahu," Silwan 2:1

4.3.1.2 Pred + Sub

Evidence from epigraphic Hebrew suggests that nominal sentences of the type illustrated by formula 4.3.1.2 are not as common in epigraphic Hebrew as those having the subject/predicate order.

Nominal sentences of this particular type indicate that a personal pronoun may function as the subject, and that the predicate precedes it for emphasis in a question, as in Ajrud 15:3–*hšlm ʾ[t]*, "Is it well with y[ou]?," and always with the interrogative pronoun, e.g., *my ʿbdk klb*, "Who is your servant (but) a dog," Lachish 2:3.

---

[40]The order "subject/predicate" is also the common syntactic arrangement for biblical Hebrew nominal sentences; R.J. Williams, *Hebrew Syntax: An Outline* (Toronto and Buffalo: University of Toronto Press, 1967), p. 98. Biblical Hebrew syntax follows that of epigraphic Hebrew very closely, although biblical Hebrew provides numerous additional examples which verify each pattern. The evidence from epigraphic Hebrew, however, provides evidence for the main syntactic formulae which are discussed by biblical Hebrew grammarians. The commonly attested word order sequences in biblical Hebrew (e.g., subject/predicate order for nominal sentences) are also widely attested sequences (relatively speaking) in epigraphic Hebrew.

4.3.1.3 PrepP + Sub

The syntactic sequence illustrated by formula 4.3.1.3 is the common order for the nominal phrase at Samaria, and elsewhere in epigraphic Hebrew (Khirbet el-Kom, Tell Qasile). The nominal sentence under discussion contains the prepositional phrase and subject in the following order:

The prepositional phrase, which functions as the predicate of the sentence, precedes the subject:

> *lʾwpy bn ntnyhw h̊ḥdr hzh*, "Belonging to Ophay, son of Netanyahu (is) this (burial-)chamber," KEK 1:1-3

> *lmlk ʾl̊[p] šmn wmʾh̊*, "For (belonging to) the King: one thou[sand] one hundred (units of) oil," Tell Qasile 1:1-3

4.3.1.4 PrepP + NPred

Formula 4.3.1.4 illustrates the nominal sentence with an initial prepositional phrase and nominal predicate for which Arad 18:6-8 is an example.

> *wldbr ʾšr ṣwtny šlm*, "Regarding the matter about which you gave me orders: everything is fine," A 18:6-8

The sentence from Arad 18 above begins with a hanging prepositional phrase and *šlm* functions as the nominal predicate.[41]

4.4 Verbal Sentences and Phrases

In the following section, verbal sentences and the formulae which illustrate their syntax are discussed. The examples which substantiate the various syntactic issues raised or formulae

---

[41]Cf. Pardee, "Letters from Tel Arad," *UF* 10 (1978): 317.

diagrammed come from a wide range of texts from the epigraphic Hebrew corpus. In addition to the important examples from Arad and Lachish, the inscriptions from Siloam, Murabbaʿat, Khirbet el-Kom and Meṣad Ḥashavyahu figure prominently.

In the second part of the section on verbal sentences and phrases, the definite direct object marker *ʾt* and its function in epigraphic Hebrew will be discussed.

4.4.1 Word Order in Verbal Sentences

The varied formulae which express word order in narrative verbal sentences are given below:

4.4.1.1 V Pred + Sub + (DO)

Formula 4.4.1.1 expresses the usual syntactic arrangement of the epigraphic Hebrew verbal sentence.

In epigraphic Hebrew, the verbal predicate precedes the noun serving as the subject and functions as 1) the *qal/piel* jussive or imperfect, 2) the *qal* perfect (when the verb is not an action verb) or 3) the *hiphil* perfect. This word order is maintained in sentences with a *waw*-consecutive plus perfect/imperfect sequence. The following examples which illustrate formula 4.4.1.1 come from Lachish, Ketef Ḥinnom, Beersheba, Arad, Murabbaʿat, Meṣad Ḥashavyahu, and Siloam:

> *yšmʿ yhwh ʾt ʾdny šm̊ʿt šlm*, "May YHWH give you good news," L 2:1-3 (and the same or similar phrases in L 3:2-3, L 4:1-2, L 5:1-2, L 6:1-2, L 8:1-2, L 9:1-2)

> *hšb ʿbdk hsprm*, "Your servant (now) returns the letters," L 5:6-7

> *yr̊ʾ̊k̊ yhwh hq̊ṣr̊*, "May YHWH allow my lord to witness the harvest," L 5:7-8

yšlḥ [ʿ]b[dk h]spr, “[Your se]rv[ant] will send [the] letter,” L 18:1

yʾr yh[wh] pnyw, “May YH[WH] make his face shine,” KH 2:8-9

wṣwk ḥnnyhw ʿl bʾršbʿ, “Hananyahu (hereby) orders you to Beersheba,” A 3:2-4

yšlm yhwh lʾdn̊[y], “May YHWH reward [my] lord,” A 21:4

ḥṭh̊ [ʿ]bdk [l]bh ʾl ʾšr ʾm[rt], “Your [ser]vant has applied himself to what you ord[ered],” A 40:4-5

ydʿ mlk̊ yhwd[h ky], “The king of Juda[h] should know [that],” A 40:13

ʾ̊m̊r̊[ ]yhw lk, “[X]-yahu (hereby) says to you,” papMur 17a:1

yšmʿ ʾdny hśr ʾt dbr ʿbdh, “May the official, my lord, hear the plea of his servant,” MHY 1:1-2

hyh ʿbdk bḥṣr ʾsm, “Your servant was in Ḥaṣar-Asam,” MHY 1:3-4

wyqṣr ʿbdk wykl wʾsm, “Your servant reaped, finished and stored (the grain),” MHY 1:4-5

hkw hḥṣbm, “The hewers struck,” Siloam 1:4

wylkw hmym, “And the water flowed,” Siloam 1:4-5

4.4.1.2 VPred + Subj + DO + (adverbial accusative)

Formula 4.4.1.2 expresses a variation to the predicate/subject formula for which Lachish 6 is an example: *yrʾ yhwh ʾt ʾdny ʾt hʿt hzh šlm*, "May YHWH make this time a good one for you," L 6:1-2. *ʾt ʾdny* and *ʾt hʿt hzh* function as "double accusatives" of the *hiphil yrʾ*, while *šlm* is an adverbial accusative.[42]

In conjunctival *ky* and *ʾšr* phrases, the order is either "predicate (perfect) plus subject" (e.g., *wky ʾmr ʾdny*, "As for what my lord said," L 3:8), or "predicate plus subject plus direct object" as in *ky zkr ʾdny ʾt [ʿ]bdh*, "that my lord should remember his servant," L 2:4; the same is true after *kkl ʾsr* (e.g., *kkl ʾšr šlḥ ʾdny kn ʿśh ʿbdk*, "Your servant has done everything my lord has sent (word to do)," L 4:2-3, and *kʾšr*, in *kʾsr kl [ʿ]bdk ʾt qṣr*, "When your [se]rvant had finished his reaping," MHY 1:6.

4.4.1.3 Sub + VPred

The examples from epigraphic Hebrew which illustrate the syntactic formula 4.4.1.3 come from Lachish and Arad:

> *ʿbdk hwšʿyhw šlḥ lh̊g[d] lʾ[d]ny y[ʾ]w[š]*, "Your servant Hawshayahu (hereby) [re]po[rts] to my [lor]d Y[a]u[sh]," L 3:1-2

> *ʾḥk ḥnnyhw šlḥ lšlm ʾlyšb*, "Your brother Hananyahu (hereby) sends greetings to (you) Elyashib," A 16:1-2

> *bnk yhwkl šlh lšlm gdlyhw*, "Your son Yehukal sends greetings to Gedalyahu," A 21:1

> *bnkm gmr[yhw] wnḥmyhw šlḥ[w lšlm] mlkyhw*, "Your son Gemar[yahu] and Neḥemyahu (hereby) sen[d greetings to (you)] Malkiyahu," A 40:1-3

---

[42]Cf. Pardee (*HHL*, p. 100) describes *šlm* as an "abstract predicate." The form may also be described as an "adverbial accusative."

yhwh yšʾl lšlmk, "May YHWH concern himself with your well-being," A 18:2-3

4.4.1.4 DO + VPred (+Sub)

This syntactic arrangement is frequent in the epigraphic Hebrew inscriptions. The examples for this sequence come from Lachish and Arad:

hwdwyhw bn ʾḥyhw wʾnšw šlḥ lqḥt mzh, "He has sent (messengers) to take Hawdawyahu, son of Ahiyahu and his men from here," L 3:17-18

wspr ṭbyhw...šlḥh[43] *ʿb⟨d⟩k ʾl ʾdny*, "Your ser⟨vant⟩ has sent the letter of Tobyahu to my lord," L 3:19-21

wsmkyhw lqḥh[44] *šmʿyhw*, "Shemayahu has taken Semakyahu," L4:6

wyyn b / tn lhm, "Give them one *bat*-measure of wine," A 4:2-3

4.4.1.5 Sub + DO + VPred

Formula 4.4.1.5 is attested once, in Arad 40:12.

whʾ hmktb bqš, "He tried to obtain the report," A 40:12, illustrates this unique syntax where the direct object *hmktb* is embedded in the subject/predicate sequence.

---

[43]Note the resumptive pronoun (*h*), "(As for) the letter of Tobyahu, your servant has sent (=forwarded) it."

[44]*Lqḥh* (like *šlḥh* in Lachish 3:21) has a resumptive pronoun (*h*), "As for Semakyahu, Shemayahu has seized him."

4.4.1.6 PrepP + VPred (+ Sub)

Formula 4.4.1.6 illustrates the verbal sentence with the inclusion of a prepositional phrase, in the sequence "prepositional phrase plus verbal predicate (plus subject).

The examples for this sequence come from Siloam and Arad:

wbym hnqbh hkw hḥṣbm, "Now, on the day that the tunneling (was completed), the hewers struck," Siloam 1:3-4

wmʿwd hqmḥ hrʾšn trkb (ḥmr /) qmḥ lʿśt lhm lḥm, "From the remainder of the first meal, have one homer-measure of meal loaded to make bread for them," A 1:5-9

myyn hʾgnt ttn, "Give (them) some of the wine from the *ʾgnt* bowls (craters)," A 1:9-10[45]

4.4.1.7 Unmarked Adverbial + Sub + Pred

While the order "prepositional phrase plus predicate (plus subject)" is the common sequence for epigraphic Hebrew, the syntax "unmarked adverbial plus subject plus predicate" is attested once in Arad 18:9-10, *byt yhwh hʾ yšb*, "He is staying in the temple of YHWH." In this sentence, the first phrase (*byt yhwh*) is the unmarked adverbial (the preposition before *byt* is latent), and the participle acts as the predicate of the phrase.

4.4.2 The Definite Direct Object Marker *ʾt*

Pronouns as objects of a verb are attached as suffixed forms on the object marker. These forms are illustrated on the next page in table 41.

A definite noun or proper name which may be the object of an action verb is preceded by *ʾt*, the object marker. *ʾt* is repeated before the two objects of a causative verb, e.g., *yrʾ yhwh ʾt ʾdny ʾt*

[45]In this phrase, *myyn* is a partitive prepositional phrase functioning as the direct object.

hˁt hzh šlm, "May YHWH cause my lord to see this season in peace," Lachish 6:1-2.

The suffixed forms of the direct object marker are morphologically identical to the suffixed forms of the preposition *ˀt*, "with," e.g., *ˀtkm*, "with you (m.pl.)," A 24:17 and *ˀtkm*, "you (m.pl.)," Ajrud 14:1.

TABLE 41
FORMS OF THE DEFINITE DIRECT OBJECT MARKER

	Singular	**Plural**
1 c.	–	–
2 m.	*ˀtk* "you" A 16:7[a]	*ˀtkm* "you" Aj 14:1
2 f.	–	–
3 m.	*ˀth* "it" A 17:6; L 3:12	*ˀtm* "them" A 3:6; A 24:13
3 f.	–	–

[a]This form is not certain to be a suffixed form of the direct object marker. The broken context of Arad 16:17 enables us to interpret this form either as "you (m.s.)," or as *ˀtk*, "with you" (the suffixed form of the preposition *ˀt*, "with"). These two forms are likely to be identically written in epigraphic Hebrew, as this is the case in biblical Hebrew.

In epigraphic Hebrew, *ˀt* may precede the object of an active verb (when the object follows the verb). The verb precedes the definite direct object marker, and the definite article *h-*, which is attached to the object, immediately follows *ˀt*: *wšlḥ̊ty ˀt h[k]s̊p*, "I will send the [mo]ney," Arad 16:4-5; *y[šlḥ] lk ˀt hmˁ[śr]*, "He will [send] you the tit[he]," Arad 5:10-12; *wˁbdk ˀy[nn]y šlḥ šmh ˀ̊t hˁ[d]*, "Your servant is [not] able to send the wit[ness] there,"

Lachish 4:7-8; *[m]ʾz qrʾ ʿbdk ʾt̊ hspr[m]*, "[Si]nce your servant read the letter[s]," Lachish 6:13-14.

The definite direct object marker *ʾt* may be omitted when the object precedes the verb, as illustrated by Arad 40:12, *whʾ hmktb bqš*, "He tried to obtain the report."

4.5 Special Kinds of Sentences

Special kinds of sentences (clauses and phrases) are discussed in this section. The examples which illustrate the sentences discussed are drawn from the corpus of epigraphic Hebrew inscriptions at large. In order, the following structures will be discussed: complex sentences, conditional sentences, desiderative sentences, circumstantial clauses, restrictive clauses, existential sentences and elliptical phrases.

4.5.1 Complex Sentences

The complex sentence consists of one sentence preceded by a noun phrase referred to by a pronoun in that sentence. The complex sentence construction in epigraphic Hebrew begins with a noun phrase (the subject), which precedes an independent verb/noun sentence in which there is reference to the principal subject by means of a pronoun. The following example from epigraphic Hebrew illustrates the subordinate complex sentence.

> *kl sp̊r ʾšr ybʾ ʾly ʾm qrʾty ʾth [ʾḥ]r ʾtnnhw [ʾ]l mʾwm̊[h]*, "Any letter that might come to me–I can read and recount every det[ail] (contained in it)," L 3:11-13

Two further examples from epigraphic Hebrew serve to illustrate *casus pendens*:

> *wspr ṭbyhw ʿbd hmlk hbʾ ʾl šlm bn ydʿ mʾt hnbʾ lʾmr hšmr šlḥh ʿ̊b‹d›k ʾl ʾdny*, "With regard to the letter of Tobyahu, servant of the King, which was sent to Shallum,

son of Yada, from the prophet and which begins 'Beware,' your ser‹vant› has sent (=forwarded) it to my lord," L 3:19-21

wsmkyhw lqḥh šmʿyhw wyʿlhw hʿyrh, "As for Semakyahu, Shemayahu has seized him and taken him up to the city," L 4:6-7

4.5.2 Conditional Sentences

Conditional sentences are a special form of complex sentence. In sentences where there is a marker for the conditional in the form of a specific particle, that particle is *ʾm*, "if." *ʾm*, which marks the protasis of the sentence, introduces and marks either a nominal clause as in the following example from Arad:

wʾm ʿwd ḥmṣ wntt lhm, "If there is any vinegar left, give (it) to them," A 2:7-8

or a verbal clause, as in Lachish 3:

wgm kl spr ʾšr ybʾ ʾly ʾm qrʾty ʾth [ʾḥ]r ʾtnnhw [ʾ]l mʾwm[h], "Moreover, any letter which might come to me, I can read and recount every det[ail] (contained in it)," L 3:10-13

In L 3:11,the protasis is situated between an introductory object clause and the apodosis.

The syntax of Lachish 4:8-10 has been debated,[46] but the solution which fits best, both semantically and grammatically (if the reading be granted), is that of Pardee.[47] The conditional clause begins in line 9 and is marked by *ʾm* (governed by the causal conjunction *ky*):

---

[46]For a summary of the discussions which centered on L 4:8-10, cf. Pardee, *HHL*, p. 93.

[47]Ibid.

> *ky ʾm btsbt hbqr [y]b̊[ʾ] wydʿ ky ʾl mśʾt lkš nḥnw šmrm*, "For if he [co]me[s around] during the morning tour, he will know that we are watching the Lachish (fire-) signals," L 4:9-11

In conditional sentences containing the oath formula, the apodosis is omitted and *ʾm* comes to serve as an emphatic negative:

> *ḥyhwh ʾm nsh ʾyš lqrʾ ly spr lnṣḥ*, "As ‹Y›HWH lives, no one has ever tried to read a letter to me," L 3:9-10

A negative conditional sentence is marked by *ʾm lʾ* in Meṣad Ḥashavyahu 1:12:

> *wʾm lʾ̊ lśr lhš[b ʾt bgd] ʿ̊b̊[dk] [wtt]n ʾlw rḥm[m whš]b̊t ʾt [bgd ʿ]bdk*, "If the official does not consider it an obligation to retur[n your] servant's [garment, then hav]e pi[ty] upon him [and ret]urn your [se]rvant's [garment]," MHY 1:12-14

Several fragmentary sentences in epigraphic Hebrew in which *ʾm* is attested may indicate conditional sentences (e.g., A 16:8; A 21:8), but the broken text does not permit a conclusive analysis.

ʾm is definitely the main marker of conditional sentences in epigraphic Hebrew, but *hn* may be posited as a second particle marking the conditional if Arad 21:3 is considered as part of a conditional sentence: *wʿt hn ʿśh ʾdny*, "And now, if my lord has done...". The fragmentary condition of Arad 21, from the end of line 3 to the conclusion of the inscription, however, does not provide clear enough evidence to determine whether *hn* marks a conditional or a deictic sentence.

In biblical Hebrew, there are examples of both unmarked and marked conditional sentences.[48] In epigraphic Hebrew, however, conditional sentences are marked by *ʾm* (and *hn* ?). This discrepancy

---

[48]Cf. Cowley, *Gesenius*, pp. 493-95 for a sampling of the biblical examples.

between epigraphic and biblical Hebrew is likely attributable to differences in genre. Unmarked conditionals are perhaps more "literary" than would be expected in the prose letters, *et cetera*, of epigraphic Hebrew.

4.5.3 Desiderative Sentences

Desiderative (optative) sentences are attested frequently in epigraphic Hebrew. Optative sentences may be expressed by the jussive, the passive participle, and the imperative (with and without the particle of entreaty, *nʾ*). The examples from epigraphic Hebrew which illustrate each type of optative sentence are examined below.

4.5.3.1 Optative Sentences Expressed by the Precative Mood (Jussive)

The most common way of expressing the optative sentence in epigraphic Hebrew is by the precative. The examples which illustrate this point come from Lachish, Ajrud, Ketef Hinnom, the second Moussaïeff Ostracon,[49] Arad, and Meṣad Ḥashavyahu:

> *yr̊ʾ̊k̊ yhwh hq̊ṣr̊ b̊ṭ̊b̊ hym*, "May YHWH allow you to witness a good harvest today," L 5:7-9

> *yrʾ yhwh ʾt ʾdny ʾt hʿt hzh šlm*, "May YHWH cause my lord to see this season in peace (= may he make this time a good one for you)," L 6:1-2

> *ybrk wyšmrk wyhy ʿm ʾd[n]y*, "May he bless (you) and keep you, and may he be with my lo[rd]," Ajrud 15:6-9

---

[49]This ostracon provides an entirely new formula: *brk* + *b šlm* to bless someone (so that he be) in (a state of) well-being, which is not attested either in the Bible or in the inscriptions. Mention is made, however, of a close parallel in Ugaritic (*yšlm l šlm*) in P. Bordreuil, F. Israel and D. Pardee, "King's Command and Widow's Plea. Two New Hebrew Ostraca of the Biblical Period," *Near Eastern Archaeology* 61:1 (1998): 12, n.2.

ybr[k] yhwh [wy]šmrk [yʾ]r yhwh [p]n[yw], "May YHWH bles[s (you) and k]eep you. [May] YHWH [shi]ne [his f]ace (upon you)," KH 1:14-18

ybr[k] yhwh w[y]šmrk yʾr yh[wh] pnyw [ʾl]yk w[yś]m lk š[l]wm, "May YHWH bles[s (you)] and keep you. May YH[WH] shine his face [upon] you and [gi]ve you pe[ac]e," KH 2:5-12

ybr̊kk yhwh bšl̊m, "May YHWH bless you in peace," MO 2:1

yhwh yšʾl lšlmk, "May YHWH concern himself with your well-being," A 18:2-3

yšmʿ ʾdny hśr ʾt dbr ʿbdh, "May the official, my lord, hear the plea of his servant," MHY 1:1-2 (the same syntax occurs also in frequently at Lachish, e.g., L 2, *et cetera*)

4.5.3.2 Optative Sentences Expressed by the Passive Participle

brk hʾ lyhw‹h›, "May he be blessed to YHW‹H›," or "Blessed be he to YHW‹H›," Ajrud 13:1, *et cetera*

ʾrr ‹ʾ›šr ‹y›mḥh̊, "May ‹he› who will ‹ef›face (this tomb) be cursed," or "Cursed be ‹he› who will ‹ef›face (this tomb)," KBL 4:1-2, *et cetera*

4.5.3.3 Optative Sentences Expressed by the Imperative

Desiderative imperative sentences contain the second masculine singular form of the verb. The fourth example below (L 6:2-5) is the only example which also contains *nʾ*, the particle of entreaty, as the marker of the desiderative sentence.

n̊q̊h̊ yhẘh̊ ḥnn nqh yh yhwh, "Absolve (us), merciful YHWH, Absolve (us), O YHWH!," KBL 2:1

h̊wšʿ [y]hwh, "Save (us), YHWH!," KBL 3:1

h̊wšʿ lh, "Save him," KEK 3:3

my ʿbdk klb ky šlḥ ʾdny ʾ[t sp]r hmlk [wʾt] spry hśr[m lʾm]r qrʾ nʾ, "Who is your servant (but) a dog that my lord should have sent (him) th[e] king's [lett]er [and tho]se of the official[s] [tellin]g (me) to please read (them)?'," L 6:2-5

4.5.4 Circumstantial Clauses

In epigraphic Hebrew, circumstantial clauses do not begin with the introductory marker *wyhy* or *whyh* as in biblical Hebrew, but have the prepositional/adverbial phrase in first position.

In biblical Hebrew, temporal circumstantial clauses include the aspect indicator in the sequence *wyhy* + *kʾsr* + *wy-*, while no such aspect indicator (*wyhy* or *whyh*) occurs as an introductory word before temporal circumstantial clauses in epigraphic Hebrew. The only instance of *wyhy* in epigraphic Hebrew is from Ajrud 15:8, where the form is the jussive *wyhy*, in the optative phrase *ybrk wyšmrk wyhy ʿm ʾd[n]y*, "May he bless (you) and keep you, and may he be with my lo[rd]," Ajrud 15:6-9.

Meṣad Ḥashavyahu 1:6-9 and the first Moussaïeff Ostracon furnish the syntax for circumstantial clauses in epigraphic Hebrew. Three syntactic constructions exist for the elements in these clauses, all of which indicate past action (see examples which follow).

The placement of *kʾšr* in the Moussaïeff Ostracon at the very beginning of the text is otherwise unknown in extra-biblical texts. *Kʾšr* appears within the body of the text in Meṣad Ḥashavyahu 1:6-8.

4.5.4.1 *kʾšr* + Perfect + *Waw*-Consecutive Imperfect

kʾšr kl [ʿ]bdk ʾt qṣr wʾsm kymm wybʾ hwšʿyhw bn šby wyqḥ ʾt bgd ʿbdk, "When your [se]rvant had finished his reaping and had stored it a few days ago, Hawshayahu ben Shabay came and took your servant's garment," MHY 1:6-8

4.5.4.2 *kʾšr* + Perfect + Perfect

> *kʾšr klt ʾt qṣry zh ymm lqḥ ʾt bgd ʿbdk*, "When I had finished my reaping, at that time, a few days ago, he took your servant's garment," MHY 1:8-9

4.5.4.3 *kʾšr* + Perfect + Infinitive

> *kʾšr ṣwk ʾšyhw hmlk ltt byd [z]kryhw,* "According as Ashyahu the King commanded you to give to [Ze]karyahu," MO 1:1-3

4.5.5 Restrictive Clauses

The restrictive clause is expressed by means of *ky ʾm*, after a negative:

> *ʾyn̊ [p]h̊ ksp wz̊h̊b [ky] ʾm̊ [ʿṣmtw] ẘʿ̊sm[t] ʾm̊th ʾ̊[t]h*, "There is neither silver nor gold [he]re, [on]ly [his bones] and his servant-wife's bon[es] w[ith] him," Silwan 2:1-2

4.5.6 Existential Sentences

The marker for existence, *yš*, known from biblical Hebrew, is presently unattested in epigraphic Hebrew, while *ʾyn*, the negative substantive which is the marker of non-existence, is attested. *ʾyn* occurs in the *status constructus* as the *nomen regens* and acts as a verbal predicate.

ʾyn, in construct state, precedes the substantive, the non-existence of which it predicates, and functions as the negative of the entire noun-clause. The original character of *ʾyn* as a bound form is not readily apparent in epigraphic Hebrew, as in both phrases where it occurs, it is separated from its noun by the insertion of short words acting as enclitics (*[p]h* and *šm*, two adverbs). The examples under discussion are from Silwan and Lachish:

ʾyn̊ [p]h̊ ksp wz̊h̊b, "There is neither silver nor gold here," Silwan 2:1

ʾyn šm ʾdm, "There is no one there," L 4:5-6

4.5.7 Elliptical Phrases

Aposiopesis is a characteristic of the oath formula, in that the apodosis of the conditional phrase is omitted, e.g., *ḥyhwh ʾm nsh ʾyš lqrʾ ly spr lnṣḥ*, "As ‹Y›HWH lives, no one has ever tried to read a letter to me," L 3:9-10

Ellipsis occurs after numerals when certain expressions are omitted (e.g., *ym*, "day," *ḥdš*, "month," *šnh* (?) or *št*, "year"):

lʿśr̊y b / lḥdš ʿd̊ hššh lḥdš̊, "for the (period from) the first (day) of the tenth (month) until the sixth (day) of that month," A7:3-5

bšlšt, "in the third (year)," A 20:1; *btšʿyt*, "in the ninth (year)," L 20:1; *brbʿt*, "in the fourth (year)," L 29:1

Ellipsis possibly characterizes Arad 40:8-9, *wʾyš̊ [lʾ ntn l]hm*, "[He has not given th]em any men," where the antecedent for *lhm* is nowhere mentioned in the text and is possibly latent in the construction.[50]

---

[50] For a discussion of the difficulties connected with the phrase, cf. Pardee, *HHL*, p.64. The reason why ellipsis is not certain to characterize the phrase of Arad 40:89 is because this phrase quite possibly poses a textual, rather than grammatical problem.

4.6 Conclusion

The syntax of epigraphic Hebrew sentences and selected phrases discussed in this chapter is, in most cases, strikingly similar to those of the Bible and despite the limited corpus, epigraphic Hebrew provides evidence for a varied repertoire of sentence/phrase types commonly studied only with reference to biblical Hebrew. The documents in prose indicate that epigraphic Hebrew narrative syntax, which is attested from at least the seventh century B.C., has important parallels with biblical narrative prose.

Further elucidation of epigraphic Hebrew syntax must await future epigraphic discoveries. Examples of extra-biblical poetry would be especially welcome. Not only will such additions increase the size of the corpus for each syntactic structure discussed in the chapter, but they also will provide material for new or different syntactic categories, sentence/phrase types, word order, formulae, *et cetera*. As more material is discovered, our assessment of all facets of epigraphic Hebrew syntax will become more precise.

5. LEXICON

The basic orientation of the lexicon is according to root, rather than form. The attested roots of epigraphic Hebrew are listed in the following pages in alphabetical order. All forms from a given root are listed in one place (e.g., *mnḥm* at *nḥm*), and a cross-reference is also provided at the alphabetically expected slot for forms which do not begin with the root letter (e.g., an entry for *mnḥm* includes an indication of the root entry).

For each entry in the lexicon, the following information is supplied:

1. The root of each verb or the absolute form of the noun, adverb, adjective, *et cetera*,
2. Transcription of the word reflecting the orthography in epigraphic Hebrew,
3. Part of speech and description of the word,
4. Translation,
5. Provenience of the word.

Distinguishable roots of the various words in epigraphic Hebrew are written in capital letters, while particles or words without clearly defined roots appear in lowercase letters. Each root is clearly visible at the left margin of the lexicon, while the additional information cited is divided by commas and semi-colons, with semi-colons to separate the individual citations. Entry forms which appear in proper names are separated from those which appear independently.

Attested forms have been organized under specific headings on the basis of grammar, rather than spelling. For example, under the listing for *ʿbd*, nouns are grouped together first, and are followed by the attested proper names, or in the case of *ntn*, the order is as follows: perfect, imperfect, imperative, infinitive, proper names. In all cases, the proper names appear last. Numerous proper names under one root entry are arranged alphabetically.

Within each sub-group (e.g., perfects), the attested forms are also organized grammatically, according to the traditional order in Hebrew grammars.

The provenience of a certain word includes the inscription or seal from which it comes, followed by the number of the inscription or seal, a colon, and the line of the text in which the word appears.

The conventions for expressing the theophoric element in proper names operated in the preceding chapters of this grammar.

All clear words, as well as incomplete or restored forms for each word, are given under each entry. If the word occurs in a completely perfect state (i.e., no restorations or damaged letters), this form is listed first. All attestations for a given form are supplied, as well as a complete selection of occurrences.

The conventions below are employed to facilitate the reading of the vocabulary:

1. < >	Material added
2. { }	Material to be removed
3. ( )	Addition in English translation
4. [ ]	Restored lacunae
5. x̊	Letter not clear, barely visible

The reader is directed to the list of abbreviations given in the front of this book to facilitate the reading of the Lexicon.

ʾB

ʾbbʿl PN; “Baal is my father;” S 2:4
ʾbgd PN; “my father is fortune;” L 24:1; Seal of Avigad 1:1
ʾbgyl PN; “my father is rejoicing, joy;” Avigad Hecht Seal 8:1
ʾby PN; “my father;” papMur 17b:2; Gezer 1:8 *(ʾby[ ])*
ʾbyhw PN; “YH is my father;” A 27:6; *[ʾ]byhw*, Avigad *HB*
ʾbyw PN; “YH is my father;” S 52:2; Herr 72; BCat 40
ʾbyḥy PN; “my father lives;” A 39:11
ʾbmʿṣ PN; “my father is wrath;” Jerusalem Seal 3:1-2
ʾbʿzr LPN; “my father is help;” S 13:1-2; S 28:1
ʾbšwʿ PN; “my father is salvation;” Herr 162:1-2
ʾbšʿl PN; “my father is a fox;” BCat 44
yhwʾb PN; “YH is (my) father;” A 39:10; A 49:9; *ẙh̊wʾb*, A 59:1; *yhwʾb̊*, Jerusalem Bulla 10:2

ʾBR

ʾbryhw PN; “YH is strong;” Av NN 7:1

ʾbšwʿ See *ʾB*

ʾGN

hʾgnt DA N m.pl.; “the craters;” A 1:10

ʾDM

ʾdm̊ m.s. N; “man, anyone;” L 4:5-6
hʾdm̊ DA N; “the man;” Silwan 2:2
[ʾ]dm PN N; “man;” A 39:1

ʾdm

ʾdm LPN ; “(the) Edom(ites);” A 21:5; A 24:20; *ʾd[m]*, A 40:9-10
ʾdmm m. pl. gentilic adj; “Edomites (?);” A 3:12

ʾDN

ʾdny m.s.N, 1st c.s. PS; “my lord;” L 2:1, 2, 4; L 3:3, 6, 8, 21; L 4:2, 4-5, 12; 5:7; L 6:1, 2, 3, 8; L 8:1, 7; L 12:1, 6; L 17:2; L 18:1, 2; A 21:3; A 26:2, 4; MHY 1; Aj 15:2; MO 2:2; *ʾdnẙ*, A 40:6; NY 1:7; *[ʾd]ny*, L 3:2; L 5:1; *[ʾ]dny*, L 17:3; *[ʾd]n̊ẙ*, L 9:1-2; *[ʾdn]y*, L 4:1; *ʾ[dn]y*, L 2:5-6; *ʾd[n]y*, Aj 15:8-9; *ʾdn[y]*, A 40:10; *ʾdn̊[y]*, A 21:4

ʾDN (continued)

	ʾdnyhw	PN; "YH is (my) lord;" Avigad *HB* 1 + 2, 11, 165;*ʾdny[hw]*, Avigad *HB* 125
	ʾdnyw	PN; "YH is (my) lord;" S 42:3
	[ʾ]dnyḥy	PN; m.s. N, 1st c.s PS + Adj; "my lord lives;" Avigad *HB* 113.
	ʾdnʿm	PN; S 9:2; *ʾdnʿm*, S 10:2-3; S 19:4; *[ʾd]n̊ʿm*, S 11:2; *[ʾdn]ʿm*, S 8:2
ʾdtʾ		
	ʾdtʾ	Fem. PN; f.s. N; "lady;" Ugar./Phoen. name (?); R 7:1 (Herr 36)
ʾhʾb		
	ʾh̊ʾb̊	PN; *hê* written for *ḥet* (?); "father (God) is my tent (=shelter̊)(?);" Hest., p. 113; *ʾhʾb*, R 12:2 (Herr 47)
ʾHB		
	nʾhbt	Fem. PN; f. *Niph* AP; "lovely, beloved, delight;" Herr 117:1
ʾHL		
	ʾwhl	PN; "(DN is my) shelter;" Jerusalem Bulla 29:2
	ḥmyʾhl	PN; *hmy-* + m.s. N; "tent, shelter;" Hest. 34:1
ʾWH		
	hʾtt	DA f.pl. N; "the indications, signs, code;" L 4:11
ʾWM		
	ʾḥyʾm	PN; "my brother has ruled;" A 35:3
	ʾḥʾmh	PN; "my brother has prevailed, ruled;" B/L (26) 8:1
ʾWR		
	yʾr	3rd m.s. *Hiph* Juss V; "may (DN) cause to shine;" KH 2:8; *[yʾ]r*, KH 1:16-17
	ʾlyʾr	PN; "May El cause to shine;" A 21:2
	ʾwryhw	PN IML; "YH is my light;" A 31:2; *ʾẘr̊yhw*, Ophel 1:8
	ʾryhw	PN; KEK 3:1, 2; A 26:1; En Gedi 1:1; Hest. 79:1; Hest. 80:1; Herr 79:1-2; S 50:2; *ʾ̊ryhw*, Herr 48:2; *ʾr̊[yhw]*, A 36:2

ʾWR (continued)		
	ʾry[w]	PN; Sam C 1012:4
	ywʾr	PN; "YH is (my) light, flame;" Av (*EI* 9) 13:1
	qrbʾwr	PN; A 24:14
	qrbʾr	PN; Avigad *HB* 156
ʾWŠ	*ʾšʾ*	PN N CS; "gift (of DN);" S 22:2; S 23:2; S 26:1; S 27:1; S 28:1-2; S 29:1; S 37:3; B/L (24) 2:1; *[ʾ]š̊ʾ*, S 39:3; *ʾš[ʾ]*, S 24:1; *[ʾ]š[ʾ]*, S 102:1
	ʾšnʾ	PN impv V; part. of entreaty; " give, O (DN)!;" Ushna Seal 1:1; Hest. 40:1; *[ʾ]šnʾ*, Avigad Hecht Seal 2:1
	ʾšyhw	PN; "gift of YH;" A 51:1; A 105:2; A 106:2; MO 1:1-2; B/L (26) 12:1-2; Avigad *HB* 33, 110; *ʾšyh̊‹w›*, A 107:2; *ʾšyh[w]*, Avigad *HB* 105; *ʾšy[hw]*, A 35:2; *ʾš[yhw]*, L 22:6; L V Ost. 1:6; *ʾ̊š̊[yhw]*, Jerusalem Jar 3:1; *[ʾ]š[y]h̊w*, A 40:11; *[ʾšyhw]*, A 40:7
	ʾ[šyw]	PN; "Gift of YH;" (or *ʾ[byw]* (?); Aj 14
	yʾš	PN; 3rd imp V; "(DN) grants;" Avigad *HB* 30, 66, 67
	yʾwš	L 2:1; L 6:1; *y[ʾ]w[š]*, L 3:2
	mʾš	PN N (?); "gift (of DN);" Herr 110:1; See Bordreuil, *Syria* 52 (1975); B/L (29) 6:2
ʾz		
	ʾz	Adv; "then"; only in prepositional phrase *mʾz*, "since, from the time of;" L 3:7; L 6:13
ʾzh		
	ʾzh	Prep LPN; "from *ʾzh*;" S 2:3; S 17a:1-2; *ʾz[h]*, S 17b:1
zn		
	-zn	See *ʾZN*
ʾZN		
	ʾzn	N CS; "the ear of," L 3:5
	[ʾ]zn̊[y]	PN N PS (?); "my hearing, ear;" L 20:2
	yʾzn	PN; imp V; *Hiph*; "hears;" A 59:5; Avigad *HB* 152; *yʾz̊n̊*, A 58:4(?)
	yʾzny[h]	PN; "may YH hear;" Jerusalem Bulla 5:2
	yʾznyhw	PN; "may YH hear;" A 39:9; L 1:3; Tell en Nasbeh 3:1; *yʾz̊nyhw*, L 1:2; *yʾzny[w]*, Jerusalem Bulla 48:1; *yʾznyh[w]*, Av (*EI* 9) 6:1
	ywzn	PN; "YH has heard;" B/L (26) 13:1

ʾḤ

ʾḥk	N; 2nd m.s. PS; "your (m.s.) brother;" A 16:1
ʾḥyw	N 3rd m.s. PS; "his brother;" MO 2:7-8
ʾḥy	N; m.pl. PS; "my comrades, brothers;" MHY 1:10, 11
ʾḥʾ	PN N; "brother;" A 49:16; S 51:3; KEM 1:4; Jerusalem Bulla 34:2; *ʾḥ̊ʾ*, A 74:2; Herr 66:2 (Tell el Judeideh); *[ʾ]ḥ̊ʾ*, A 67:4
ʾḥʾb	PN; "(my) brother is 'Divine' father;" L Seal 4:2; Avigad *HB* 16, 17, 18, 19, 60
ʾḥʾmh	PN; "(my) brother rules (?);" B/L (26) 8:1; Avigad *HB* 151
ʾḥʾmr	PN; "(my) brother says, promises, commands;" L Seal 11:2
ʾḥ̊y	PN N PS; "my brother;" A 39:6
ʾḥyʾm̊	PN; "my brother has ruled, prevailed;" A 35:3
ʾḥyhw	PN; "YH is (my) brother;" Ophel 1:2; RR 1; Av (*EI* 9) 11:1; L 3:1; Avigad *HB* 166; Avigad *HB* 13
ʾḥyw	PN; "YH is (my) brother;" Av NN 16:1
ʾḥymh̊	PN; Jerusalem Bulla 45:1
ʾḥyqm	PN; "my brother has arisen;" A 31:5; Avigad Hecht Seal 6:1
ʾḥmʾ	PN; "(my) brother is k(ing);" S 32:3; S 37:2; S 38:2; S 39:2
ʾḥmlk	PN, "(my) brother is king;" A 72:2; S 23:2; S 27:2; S 28:2; S 29:1; S 48:2; Av NN 1:2; Beth Shemesh 4:2; L Seal 3:2; L Seal 9:2 (7x); Hest. 73:2; Avigad *HB* 129; B/L (29) 3:2; *ʾḥ̊mlk*, S 22:2-3; *ʾ̊ḥml̊[k]*, S 24:1; *[ʾ]ḥ̊ml̊[k]*, S 25:2; *‹ʾ›ḥmlk* Herr 146:1
ʾḥqm	PN; "(my) brother has arisen;" Avigad *HB* 14-16; HU 1; *ʾḥq̊m*, Avigad (*IEJ* 13) Seal 2:2; *ʾḥqm̊*, B/L (29) 5:1
ʾḥʾš	PN; "(my) brother has aided, saved;" L Seal 7:2 *[yh]wʾḥ* PN; "YH is my brother;" Avigad *HB* 71-73

ʾḤZ

ʾḥz	PN; perf V; "(DN) has grasped;" S 2:5; Ushna Seal 1:2; Sam C 1220
ʾḥzy	PN; perf V; "(DN) has grasped;" S 25:3
ʾḥzyhw	PN; "YH has grasped;" Av NN 19:2; *ʾ̊ḥzyh̊[w]*, Tell Nasbeh 2:1
yhwʾḥz	PN; "YH has grasped;" Av (*EI* 9) 15:1

ʾḥy

ʾḥy	See *ʾḤ*

ʾḥyʾm

ʾḥyʾm See *ʾḤ*

ʾḥyhw

ʾḥyhw See *ʾḤ*

ʾḥyw

ʾḥyw See *ʾḤ*

ʾḥyqm

ʾḥyqm See *ʾḤ*

ʾḥmʾ

ʾḥmʾ See *ʾḤ*

ʾḥmlk

ʾḥmlk See *ʾḤ*

ʾḥqm

ʾḥqm See *ʾḤ*

ʾḤR

tʾḥr 2nd m.s. imp V; Piel; "you (m.s.) wait, tarry;" A 2:6

[ʾḥ]r Prep; "afterwards;" L 3:12

ʾYN

ʾyn N; particle of negation; "(there) is not;" L 4:5; *ʾyn̊* , Silwan 2:1

ʾy[nn]y 1st c.s. suf. neg. adv; "I am not;" L 4:7-8

[ʾy]nnw 1st c.pl. suf. neg. adv; "we are not;" A 40:13-14

ʾyʿdh

ʾyʿdh PN; "my fat(her) has adorned, decked himself" (*ʾ‹b›yʿdh*) or possibly "where has (He) adorned?" (*ʾy*, **ay(ya)*; interrogative adv as in Phoenician and other NW Semitic names)

ʾYŠ

ʾyš	m.s. N IML; "no one;" L 3:9-10
ʾyš̊y	m.s. N IML, 1st c.s. PS; "my husband;" MO 2:3
hʾyš	DA N IML; "the man;" A 40:7
ʾyš̊	N; "man (collective (?);" A 40:8
ʾš	N; "one, each (man);" Siloam 1:2; Siloam 1:4; (+m-), "(from) a man;" Aj 16:1

ʾkzb

ʾkzb	LPN; L 8:6
ʾkzy[b]	IML; L 22:10 (= L V Ost. 1:10)

$ʾl_1$

ʾl	Neg. adv; "not;" A 2:6; papMur 17a:2

$ʾl_2$

ʾl	Prep; "toward;" Siloam 1:2, 3; "for, over;" L 4:10; "to;" Siloam 1:5; L 2:1; L 3:7, 20, 21; L 5:4, 7; L 6:1; A 1:1; A 2:1; A 3:1; A 4:1; A 5:1; A 6:1, 2; A 7:1; A 11:1; A 17:1; A 18:1; A 40:5, 6, L 5:9; *ʾ̊l̊*, A 24:1; *[ʾ]l*, L 3:13; *[ʾ]l̊*, A 8:1; *[ʾl]*, A 10:1
ʾly	1st c.s. suff. prep; "to me;" A 8:8; L 3:11; *[ʾ]ly*; L 4:4
ʾlyk	2nd m.s. suff. prep; "to you (m.s.);" A 3:9; *[ʾl]yk*, "upon you;" KH 2:10
ʾlk	2nd m.s. suff. prep (?); "to you (m.s.) (?) ;" A 3:9
ʾlw	3rd m.s. suff. prep; "to him," MHY 1:13
ʾl[yhm]	3rd m.pl. suff. prep; "to them;" L 6:9

ʾl

ʾl	See *ʾLH*

ʾlʾ

ʾlʾ	See *ʾLH*

ʾlbʾ

ʾlbʾ	See *ʾLH*

ʾldgn

ʾldgn	See *ʾLH*

ʾldlh

ʾldlh	See *ʾLH*

ʾLH

ʾlhykh	m.pl. N; 2nd m.s. PS ; "your God;" KBL 1:1
ʾlhyk	N; 2nd m.s. PS; "your (m.s.) God;" L 6:12-13
ʾlh̊y	m.pl. N CS; "the God of;" KBL 1:2
ʾl	PN m.s. N; "God;" KEK bowl 5; Aj 5:1; Aj 7:1; Aj 8:1,3
ʾlʾ	PN N; "O God;" S 38:3
ʾlbʾ	PN; "Ba(al) is (my) God;" S 1:6
ʾldg[n]	PN; "God of grain;" Dayan 2:1-2 (forgery (?))
ʾldlh	PN; "God draws out, lifts;" Herr 74:1
ʾlzkr	PN; "God has remembered," B/L (29) 7:2
ʾlḥnn	PN; God is gracious;" Avigad Hecht Seal 8:2
ʾlyʾr	PN; "God enlightens;" A 21:2; B/L (29) 4:1; B/L (32) 1:1
ʾlyhw	PN; "YH is my God;" Gezer Seal 1:1 (Seal of Elijah); Avigad *HB* 27, 85; B/L (29) 3:1; B/L (32) 4:2
ʾlysmk	PN; "God supports;" Avigad *HB* 39
ʾlyʿz	PN; "God is strong;" Avigad *HB* 28, 71
ʾlyṣr	PN; "God forms, fashions (= creates);" Herr 75:1 (Samaria region (?))
ʾlyqm	PN; "God sets up;" RR Seal 8:1; Hest. 91:1; TBM Seal 1:1; Beth-Shemesh 2:1; *ʾlyqm̊* , Av (*EI* 9) 7:1; Jerusalem Bulla 29:1
ʾlyrb	PN; God contends;" L 32
ʾlyrm	PN; "God is exalted;" Avigad *HB* 29
ʾlyšb	PN; "God restores;" A 1:1, A 2:1, A 3:1, A 4:1, A 5:1 A 6:1, A 7:1, A 8:1, A 11:1, A 16:2, A 17:2, A 18:1-2, A 105:1; A 106:1; B/L (26) 17:1; *ʾlyšb̊* , A 24:2; *ʾlyš̊b̊* , A 38:5; *[ʾly]šb*, A 10:1; A 12:1; *[ʾl]yš̊[b]*, A 14:1; *[ʾl]yšb*, A 47:1; *ʾlẙš̊[b]*, A 64:2; *ʾlyš[b]*, L 22:8; L V Ost. 1:8; *ʾl‹y›šb* A 107:1
ʾlyšʿ	PN; "God is salvation;" S 1:4; A 24:15, 19-20; *ʾlyš[ʿ]*, S 1:7; *[ʾly]šʿ*, S 41:1
ʾlm[lk]	N; "my God is king;" (could be *ʾlm[tn]*); Hazor 6:2
ʾlmtn	LPN; S 28:3
ʾlntn	PN; "God has given;" Gib S.I. 5; L 3:15; Hest. 80:2; Jerusalem Bulla 20:1; *ʾl[ntn]*, Gib S.I. 6; *ʾl̊n̊t̊n̊*, L 11:3; *ʾl[nt]n*, Avigad *HB* 30; *ʾln̊t̊[n]*, A 110:1
ʾlsmk	PN; "God supports;" Avigad *HB* 40; Lemaire Seal 3:2
ʾl̊ʾ̊d̊h	PN; "God has adorned;" papMur 17b:3
ʾlʿz	PN; "God is strong;" Avigad *HB* 17 + 18, 72-73, 90
ʾlʿš	PN; "God aids, saves;" Av NN 17:2
[ʾ]lṣd[q]	PN; "God is righteous;" Avigad *HB* 84
ʾl̊ṣ̊r̊	PN; "God is (my) rock;" Beersheba 2:1

ʾLH (continued)

ʾlrm — PN; "(my) God is exalted;" Herr 153:1

ʾlšmʿ — PN; "(my) God has heard;" RR Seal 3:2; Hest. 72:2; Herr 148:1; Herr 152:1; Avigad *HB* 4, 66; B/L (32) 12:1; Jerusalem Bullae 7:1; 10:1; 35:2; Lemaire Seal 6:1; *ʾlšmʿ̊* , Av (*EI* 9) 9:2; *ʾlšm̊[ʿ]*, Avigad *HB* 158; *[ʾl]šmʿ* , Avigad *HB* 159; *ʾ[l]š̊[mʿ]*, Avigad *HB* 160

bʿdʾl — See *bʿd*

dmlʾl — See *DMM*

ṭbʾl — See *ṬWB*

yhwʾl — PN; "YH is God;" L V 4:1

ywʾl — PN; (DN) is God;" Avigad Hecht Seal 10:1

yrḥmʾl — See *RMḤ*

yšmʿʾl — See *ŠMʿ*

šbʾl — See *ŠWB*

ʾlzkr

ʾlzkr — See *ʾLH*

ʾlḥnn

ʾlḥnn — See *ʾLH*

ʾlyʾr

ʾlyʾr — See *ʾLH*

ʾlyhw

ʾlyhw — See *ʾLH*

ʾlysmk

ʾlysmk — See *ʾLH*

ʾlʿdh

ʾl̊ʿ̊d̊h — See *ʾLH*

ʾlyʿz

ʾlyʿz — See *ʾLH*

ʾlyṣr

ʾlyṣr — See *ʾLH*

ʾlyqm

	ʾlyqm	See *ʾLH*

ʾlyrb

	ʾlyrb	See *ʾLH*

ʾlyrm

	ʾlyrm	See *ʾLH*

ʾlyšb

	ʾlyšb	See *ʾLH*

ʾlyšʿ

	ʾlyšʿ	See *ʾLH*

ʾlmlk

	ʾlmlk	See *ʾLH*

ʾlmtn

	ʾlmtn	See *ʾLH*

ʾlntn

	ʾlntn	See *ʾLH*

ʾlsmk

	ʾlsmk	See *ʾLH*

ʾlʿdh

	ʾl̊ʿ̊d̊h	See *ʾLH*

ʾlʿz

	ʾlʿz	See *ʾLH*

ʾlʿš

	ʾlʿš	See *ʾLH*

ʾlṣdq

	ʾlṣdq	See *ʾLH*

ʾLP

	ẘʾlp	Conj m.s. N; “and one thousand;” Siloam 1:5
	ʾl̊[p]	N; “one thousand;” Tell Qasile 1:1

ʾlṣr

ʾl̊ṣ̊r̊	See *ʾLH*

ʾlrm

ʾlrm	See *ʾLH*

ʾlšmʿ

ʾlšmʿ	See *ʾLH*

ʾm

ʾm	Conj; "if;" L 3:9, 11; L 4:9; MHY 1:12; A 2:7; A 16:8; 21:8; *ʾm̊*, A 28:6; Silwan 2:2

ʾMH

ʾmtk	f.s. N 2nd m.s. PS; "your maidservant;" MO 2:4; *ʾmtk̊*, MO 2:2; *ʾm̊th* f.s. N 3rd m.s. PS; "his maidservant;" Silwan 2:2

ʾMM

ʾmh	f.s. N; "cubit(s);" Siloam 1:5, 6
ʾmt	f.pl. N; "cubits," Siloam 1:2

ʾMN

ʾmn	Adv; "verily, truly;" MHY 1:11
yẘʾmn	PN; "YH confirms, supports, nourishes;" Avigad 10:1

ʾMṢ

ʾmṣ	m.s. Piel impv V; "strengthen!;" A 88:2
ʾmṣ̊	PN Adj; "(DN) is strong;" Beersheba 1:3; Tell Dan 1

ʾMR

ʾmr	3rd m.s. perf V; "he said, (thus) says X;" Aj 14:1; L 3:8; papMur 17a:1; *[ʾ]m̊r̊*, Aj 15:1(above line 1)
ʾm[rt]	2nd m.s. perf V; "you (m.s.) ordered;" A 40:5
ʾmr	2nd m.s. Impv; "say!," Aj 14:1; Aj 15:2-3
ʾmr	I (*lʾmr*); "to say, saying;" L 3:14; L 3:20-21; [*ʾmr*], (*l[ʾmr]*); L 6:9; *[ʾm]r*, (*[lʾm]r*); L 6:4-5
ʾ̊m̊r	PN perf V; "(DN) has said;" S 29:3
ʾmryhw	PN;"YH said;" Gib 14-17; Avigad 13 (= Kiryat Yearim 3:2); Avigad *HB* 31; *ʾmr[y]hw*, Gib 61; *[ʾ]mryhw*, Gib 18; *ʾ̊m̊r̊yhw*, Beersheba Graffiti 2:2

ʾMR (continued)

	ʾmryw	PN; "YH said, promised;" Aj 15:1
	ʾḥʾmr	See *ʾḤ*
ʾmš		
	ʾmš	Adv; "yesterday;" L 3:6
ʾny		
	ʾny	1st c.s. subject pronoun; "I;" A 88:1
ʾnky		
	ʾnk[y]	1st c.s. subject pronoun; "I;" L 6:8
ʾnyhw		
	ʾnyhw	PN; "YH is (my) strength, vigor, force;" KEK 3:4
ʾNŠ$_1$		
	ʾnšw	m.pl. N PS; "his people;" L 3:17-18
	hʾnšm	DN N; "the men;" A 24:19; *hʾ[nšm]*, L 6:7
ʾNŠ$_2$		
	ʾšt	f.s. N CS; "wife of;" R 7:1-2 (Herr 36)
ʾNT		
	ʾ[t]	2nd m.s. subject pronoun; "you," Ajrud 15:3
ʾSM		
	wʾsm	Conj inf. Abs. (or perf); "and he stored (the grain);" MHY 1:5, 6-7
	ḥṣr ʾsm	LPN; *ḥṣr* + m.s. N; "granary, storehouse;" MHY 1:4
ʾSP		
	ʾsp	m.s. N; "(olive) harvest;" Gezer 1:1
	ʾsp	PN; perf V; "he gathers, brings together;" Herr 156:1 (Megiddo)
	ʾspẙ	PN; B/L (32) 14:2
ʾply		
	ʾply	PN; perf V (?); "(DN) judges (?);" Av (*EI* 9) 10:1
ʾpṣḥ		
	ʾpṣḥ	PN Adj; "joyous, cheerful;" S 31a:2; *ʾ̊p̊ṣ̊ḥ̊*, S 90:2

ʾpr

ʾpr LPN; Tell Qasile 2:1

ʾprḥ

ʾprḥ PN; m.s. N; "young bird;" Av (*EI* 9) 4:1; Hest. 51:1; Avigad *HB* 19, 21, 23; Jerusalem Bullae 9:1; 17:2; *[ʾ]prḥ* , Avigad *HB* 20, *[ʾ]p̊rḥ̊* , Avigad HB 22

ʾṢL

ʾṣlyhw PN; "YH is noble;" B/L (32) 9:1

ʾrʾ

ʾrʾ See *ʾRH*

ʾrbʿ

ʾrbʿt See *RBʿ*

ʾRH

ʾrʾ PN; m.s. N; "lion (of DN);" Av NN 5:2

ʾryhw

ʾryhw See *ʾWR*

ʾryw

ʾryw See *ʾWR*

ʾRṢ

ʾrṣ f.s. N; "land (?);" Jerusalem Jar 1

hʾrṣ DA f.s. N; "the earth;" KBL 1:1

ʾRR

ʾẘrr m.s. AP IML; "a curser;" KBL 6

ʾrwr m.s. PP IMP; "cursed be;" Silwan 2:2

ʾrr m.s. PP; NY 1:1; KBL 4:1; KBL 7; *ʾr[r]*, KBL 5

ʾŚR

‹ʾ›śr̊ʾl LPN; "(God) is happiness;" S 42:1; *‹ʾ›śr[ʾl]*, S 48:1

ʾšʾ

ʾšʾ See *ʾWŠ*

ʾšt
ʾšt See *ʾNŠ₂*

ʾšḥr
ʾš̊ḥr̊ See *ŠḤR*

ʾšyhw
ʾšyhw See *ʾWŠ*

ʾškr
ʾškr See *ŠKR*

ʾŠM
ʾ[šm] m.s. N (could be f.s. *ʾšmh*); "guilt, any wrongdoing, infraction;" MHY 1:11-12

ʾšnʾ
ʾšnʾ See *ʾWŠ*

ʾŠP (?)
ʾšpt f.pl. N; "quivers;" L 13:3

ʾŠR
ʾšr Relative pron; "which;" A 5:10; A 8:9; A 71:2; L 3:5, 11; L 4:2, 4,11; L 18:1; Aj 16:1; Sam Ost. Exped. 1936; papMur 17a:2; A 18:7 ("concerning which"); MO 2:5; MO 2:6-7; L 2:6; A 29:7, A 40:5 ("that which"); L 9:7-8 ("as to what"); NY 1:1 and Silwan 2:2 ("(he) who"); MHY 1:6, 8 (+ *k-* = "when"); "who (is);" Avigad *HB* 1-3 (*ʿl hbẙt)*; Avigad Hecht Seal 1:1 *([ʿ]l hbyt)*; *ʾšr̊*, Silwan 2:1 (*ʾšr̊ ʾl hbyt)*; *ʾ̊šr*, Silwan 3:2; *[ʾ]šr*, L Seal 6:2 (*[ʾ]šr ʿl hbyt̊*) "which;" A 5:4; *ʾš[r]*, A 21:7; A 40:15; *‹ʾ›šr*, "(he) who;" KBL 4:2; *[ʾšr]*, "that (which);" A 40:6
[ʾš]rḥy PN; "He who (God) lives;" Avigad *HB* 34, 126
[ʾ]šryḥt PN; "He who (God) cuts (off his enemies);" Avigad *HB* 127

ʾšrḥy
ʾšrḥy See *ʾŠR*

ʾšryḥt
ʾšryḥt See *ʾŠR*

ʾšrt

ʾšrt PN (?) f.pl. N; "Divine Goddess; sacred poles;" Aj 7:2

ʾšrth PN f.s. N PS; "his *ʾsrh*, consort (?);" KEK 3:3; Aj 10:1; Aj 14:2; Aj 15:6; *ʾ̊šrt̊h̊*, KEK 3:5

ʾt_1

ʾt Definite DOM; MHY 1:2, 6, 8, 9 (2x), A 5:11; A 16:4, 6, 8, 10; A 24:16; A 40:14; L 2:2, 4, 5; L 3:5; L 4:8, 12; L 6:1-2, 2; L 8:1; L 9:1; L 13:3; papMur 17a:1; MO 2:2; MO 2:4; MO 2:6; *ʾt*, DOM or Prep (?); A 111:3, 9; *ʾt̊*, Silwan 2:3; MHY 1:14; L 6:14; *ʾ[t]*, L 3:16; L 5:5; L 6:3; *[ʾt]*, MHY 1:12,13; A 13:2; A 40:6; L 3:3; L 4:1; L 5:1; L 6:4; Siloam 1:1

ʾtk 2nd m.s. suff DOM; "you (m.s.);" A 16:7; could be suff Prep

ʾth 3rd m.s. suff DOM; "it (m.s.);" A 17:6; L 3:12; *[ʾ]th* L 12:4

ʾtkm 2nd m.pl. suff DOM; "you (m.pl);" Aj 14:1

ʾtm 3rd m.pl. suff DOM; "them;" A 3:6; A 24:13; *ʾ[tm]*, A 12:2

ʾt_2

ʾt Prep; "with" A 24:19; L 3:20 (+ *m-* =from)

ʾty 1st c.s. suff Prep; "with me;" MHY 1:10

ʾtk 2nd m.s. suff Prep (?); "with you (m.s.);" A 16:7; could be suff DOM̊(?); A 5:2; A 6:2; A 40:8 (+ *m-* = "from [that which] is yours [with you]"); *ʾt[k]*, A 9:2 (+*m-*)

ʾ̊[t]h 3rd m.s. suff Prep; "with him;" Silwan 2:2

ʾtkm 3rd m.pl. suff Prep; "with you (m.pl.); A 24:17

ʾt

ʾ[t] See *ʾNT*

ʾtt

hʾtt See *ʾWH*

b		
	b	Prep; "in, at;" A 5:12; A 7:3, 6, 9; A 13:3; A 17:6, 8, 9; A 20:1; A 24:16, 18; A 32:1; A 88:1; A 111:2; L 4:9; L 5:8; L 9:6; L 20:1; L 29:1; MHY 1:3, 10; S 1:1 S 2:1; S 3:1; S 5:1; S 7:1; S 9:1; S 10:1; S 12:1; S 13:1; S 14:1; S 16b:1 S 17a:a; S 18:1; S 19:1; S 20:1 S 21:1; S 22:1; S 23:1; S̊24:1; S 27:1; S 28:1; S 29:1; S 30:1; S 31a:1; S 31b:1; S 32:1; S 35:1; S 37:1; S 38:1; S 39:1; S 43:1; S 45:1; S 46:1; S 48:1; S 49:1; S 50:1; S 51:1; S 52:1; S 53:1, 2; S 54:1; S 55:1; S 56:1; S 58:1; S 59:2; S 61:2; S 63:1; S 72:1, 2; S 73:1; S 80:1; S 100:1; Aj 5:1; Aj6:1; Aj7:1; Ophel 1:1, 2, 3; Ophel 2:2 (?); Siloam 1:1, 2, 3 (2x), 5; Silwan 1:1; MO 1:2; MO 2:1; MO 2:4; MO 2:7; *b̊*, S 6:1; S 16a:1; *[b]*, A 16:5; A 24:13; A 40:10, 11; S 4:1; S 8:1; S 17b:1; S 26:1; S 33:1; S 34:1; S 36:1; S 42; S 44:1; S 47:1; S 73:2
	bkm	2nd m.pl. suff Prep; "you (m.pl.);" A 24:19
BʾR		
	bʾrym	LPN N (?); "west well;" S 1:2
	bʾršbʿ	LPN; "well of seven;" A 3:3-4
BGD		
	bgd	m.s. N CS; "the garment of;" MHY 1:8, 9; *[bgd]*, MHY 1:13, 14
	bgdy	N PS; "my garment;" MHY 1:12
	bgy	PN; NY 1:6
bdyw		
	b̊dyw	PN; "in the hand of YH," or "through the intermediary of YH;" S 58:1
BWʾ		
	ybʾ	3rd m.s. imp V; "(it) will come;" L 3:11; *[y]b̊[ʾ]*, "he will come, he comes;" L 4:9
	(w)ybʾ	Conj; 3rd m.s. imp V; "and he came along;" MHY 1:7
	y‹b›ʾ	3rd m.s. *Hiph* imp V; "he will bring;" L 5:9
	tbʾ	3rd f.s. imp V; "she (the Edomites) will come, go;" A 24:20

BWʾ (continued)

	bʾ	m.s. Impv V; “go to!;” A 17:1-2
	hbʾ	DA m.s. AP; “(the one) which came;” L 3:19
	bʾ	I (+ *l*-); “(to) enter;” L 3:15
bwzy		
	bwzy	PN; gent. Adj; IML; “the Buzite;” Herr 120:2
BṬḤ		
	mbṭḥyhw	PN; “YH is my confidence;” L 1:4
BYT		
	byt	m.s. N CS; “the house of;” A 18:9 (*byt yhwh*); MO 1:4 *(byt yhwh)*; *byt̊*, Beersheba 1:3; *byt*, N CS (?); L 20:1; *byt̊[t]*, *(lbẙ[t yhw]h)*, Jerusalem pomegranate inscription (= Lemaire “grenade” inscription; “Une inscription paléo-hébraïque sur grenade en ivoire,” *RB* 88, no. 2 (1981:236-39).
	byt	EOLPN N CS; L 4:5 (*byt hrpd*); Tell Qasile 2:1 (*byt ḥrn*); MO 1:4; *(byt yhwh)*; *hbyt* Silwan 2:1; Avigad *HB* 1-2 *(ʾšr ʿl hbyt)*; Avigad Hecht Seal 1:2 (*ʾšr [ʿ]l hbyt); hbyt̊*, L Seal 6:2 (*ʾšr ʿl hbyt̊*)
	byt	N; “(the) house;” Avigad *HB* 3 *(ʾšr [ʿ]l byt)*
	[byty]	N PS; “my house;” A 40:11
	bytk	N 2nd m.s. PS; “your (m.s.) house; household;” A 16:2; A 21:2; papMur 17a:1; A 16: 4 (+ *m̊*- =“from your (m.s.) house”)
	byth	N CS Locative; “to the house of;” A 17:2
bky		
	bky	PN N; “camel (?);” Beth-Shemesh 7:1
BKR		
	ybkr	3rd m.s. imp V; Piel; “may (DN) favor;” L 2:5
blgy		
	blgy	PN m.s. N; “(DN is my) brightness;” Herr 80:1; Jerusalem Bulla 1:1; Jerusalem Bulla 20:2

BN

bn N CS; "son of;" Hazor 6:2; L 1:1, 2, 3, 4, 5; L 3:15, 17, 20; L 22:7; A 8:9; A 10:4; A 17:3; A 22:4; A 23:9; A 24:14, 15; A 27:2, 6; A 31:2, 3, 4, 5; A 35:2, 3; A 36:2; A 38:3, 5; A 39:1, 2, 3, 4, 5, 6, 9, 10; A 49:3; A 51:2; A 55:1; A 56:1; A 58:3; A 59:1, 2, 4, 5; A 71:4; A 79:1; A 105:2; A 106:2; A108:2, 3; A 109:2; MHY 1:7; MHY 2:1; KEK 1:1; HU 1, 2, 3, 4; Ophel 1:1; Ophel 1:2; Ophel 1:3; Aj 12:1; Aj 13; Avigad (*IEJ* 13) 1:2; Avigad (*IEJ* 25) 4:2; Avigad (*IEJ* 4) 6:1-2; Avigad (BIES 18) 8:1-2; Avigad (1964) Seal 2:1-2; Avigad (1978) Baruk Seal 1:2; Avigad (1978) Bulla of Jerahmeel 2:2; Av NN 2:2; Av NN 3:2; Av NN 8:2; Av NN 16:2; Av NN 20:2; Jerusalem Seal 5:1-2; Hest. (1974) Hebron 1:2; B/L (26) 4:1-2; 5:2; 6:2; 7:2; 8:2; 10:3; 11:1; 14:1-2; 15:1-2; 17:2; B/L (29) 1:2; 2:2; 4:1-2; 7:2; B/L (32) 3:2; 9:2; 10:1; L V 1:2; 2:1-2; 6:2; 7:2; L V Ost. 1:7; R 3:2 (Herr 87); R 5:2 (Herr 83); R 18:2 (Herr 126); R 20:1-2 (Herr 95); L Seal 2:2; Av (*EI* 9) 1:2; 5:2; 7:2; 10:1; Herr 39:2; 70:1-2; 90:2; 93:2; 99:1-2; 100:1-2; 110:2; 118:1-2; 120:2; 121:1-2; 122:1-2; 131:2; 135:1; 145:2; 148:1-2; 151:2; 152:1-2; Hest. 55:2; 56:2; 57:1-2; 65:1-2; 78:2; 82:1-2; Avigad *HB* 6, 17-21, 28, 30-31, 33, 39-40, 42, 45, 49-55, 57, 59, 63-64, 66, 68 (2x), 69-70, 75, 77, 83, 86, 90, 92-93, 95, 99, 101, 103, 113-115, 117, 119-121, 123-124, 128, 131-132, 136, 138, 143, 148-149, 151-153, 158-159, 164, 169, 176, 180, 184; Avigad Hecht Seals 4:2; 5:1; 10:1-2: 11:2; BCat 45, 50, 52-53, 55, 59; Jerusalem Bullae 1:1-2; 4:2; 5:2; 7:1-2; 8:2; 10:2; 12:2; 13:2; 17:2; 19:2; 20:2; 27:1-2; 28:2; 29:2; 31:1-2; 33:2; 34:1-2; 35:1-2; 50:2; 51:1; *bn̊*, A 35:4; B/L (26) 20:2; L V 6:3; Av (*EI* 9) 15:2; *b̊n*, L Seal 19:1; Herr 94:2; Herr 119:2; Avigad *HB* 134; *b̊n̊*, A 20:2; A 23:7; A 38:4; A 39:7; A 58:2; A 59:3; KEK 2:1; Avigad *HB* 137, 156; *[b]n*, Av (*EI* 9) 6:2; Herr 116:2; Avigad *HB* 7, 25, 43, 67, 73, 79, 80, 108, 133; Jerusalem Bullae 2:2; 23:2; 48:2; *b[n]*, A 22:1, 2; A 23:4, 5; A 27:4; KEM 1:2, 3, 4; B/L (26) 13: 1-2; Av (*EI* 9) 4:1; Hest. 51:1; Avigad *HB* 14, 26, 27, 32, 58, 84, 112, 116, 118, 122, 161, 166, 174; *[bn]*, L 20:2; A 21:1; Avigad *HB* 22-23, 38, 44, 60, 68, 88, 102, 111, 113, 139, 160; *‹b›n*, A 38:2; A 107:2; *b‹n›*, Hest. 94:2

BN (continued)

bn PN N CS; "son (of DN);" Herr 81:1

bnk N 2nd m.s. PS; "your (m.s.) son;" A 21:1

bnkm N 2nd m.pl. PS; "your (m.pl.) son;" A 40:1

bnm m.pl. N; "sons;" MO 2:3

bny m.pl. N CS; "sons of;" A 16:5; A 49:1, 2, 4, 16; L 16:4 (?)

bt f.s. N CS; "daughter of;" Avigad (1978) Lyre 1:2; Avigad NN 1:2; Avigad Hecht Seal 8:1-2; TBM (sherd) 2 (?); Naveh 1:2 (Herr 98); Herr 117:1-2; Herr 143:2; Hest. 34:2

BNH

bnyhw PN; "YH has built;" Avigad *HB* 35; Jerusalem Bulla 31:1; *b̊nyhw*, Avigad Naar Seal 2:1-2; *bn̊yhw*, B/L (26) 3:3; Dayan 1:1; *b̊n̊ẙhw* (?), A 39:9; *bn[yhw]* (?), A 74:4; *b̊nyhẘ*, Hest. 82:1

yhbn̊h PN; "YH has built;" Beth-Shemesh 5:2; *[yhw]bnh*, L 27:1; *[y]hẘbnh*, L 28:1; *ywbnh*, Jerusalem Seal 4:2; RR Seal 2:1

mbn PN N; "creature of (DN);" Shechem Seal level 6

bnyhw

bnyhw See *BN*

b‘d

b‘d’l PN; "on behalf of God;" Herr 40:2

b‘dyhw PN; "on behalf of YH;" Avigad *HB* 36-37

B‘L

b‘l PN m.s. N D elem; "lord;" Aj 8:2; S 12:2

b‘l’ PN m.s. N D elem; "lord;" S 1:7; S 3:3; S 27:3; S 28:3; S 31a:3

b‘lḥnn PN; Ba‘al is gracious;" BCat 50

b‘ l{‘}zkr PN; scribal error; " Ba‘al is to be remembered;" S 37:3

b‘lm‘ny Gentilic Adj; "the Ba‘alme‘onite;" S 27:3

hb‘̊lty DA Gentilic Adj; "The Ba‘alatite;" A 60:1-2

b‘r’ PN; " Ba‘(al) is ex(alted);" ; S 47:1; *b‘̊r̊’*, S 45:2; *b̊[‘r’] (?), S 43:2; b[‘r]’̊* (?), S 46:2-3

’bb‘l PN; S 2:4; see also *’B*

mrb‘l PN; S 2:7; see also *MRR*

‘ṣb‘l PN; MHY 6:1; see also *‘WṢ*

bʿrʾ		
	bʿrʾ	See *BʿL*
bṣy		
	bṣẙ	PN; “in the sha(dow of God);” abbreviation for *bṣlʾl* (?); R 5:2 (Her̊r83)
bṣl		
	bṣl	PN Prep N; “In the shadow (of DN);” A 49:1
BṢQ		
	bṣq	m.s. N; “dough;” A 3:6
bṣr		
	bṣr	PN m.s. N; “fortress, strength;” related to biblical *mbṣr* (?); Av NN 9:2
BQR		
	hbqr	DA m.s. N; “the morning;” L 4:9
BQŠ	*bqš*	3rd m.s. Perf V; “he tried to obtain;” A 40:12
	bqš	PN; Impv V; “Seek (DN)!;” Hest. 83:2
BRʾ		
	brʾ	PN Perf V; “(DN) has created;” RR Seal 4:2
BRK		
	brkt	1st c.s. Perf V; “I (hereby) bless;” Aj 14:1
	brktk	1st c.s. Perf V; PS; “I (hereby) bless you (m.s.);” A 16:2-3; A 21:2; Aj 15:4; *brkt[k]*, A 40:3
	ybrk	3rd m.s. Imp/Juss V; “may he bless (you);” Aj 15:6-7; *ybr[k]*, KH 1:14-15; KH 2:5; L 31:2 (PN ?), *ybr̊kk* “may he bless you (m.s.);” MO 2:1
	brk	m.s. PP; “blessed be;” NY 1:4, 6, 7; Aj 7:1; Aj 8:2; Aj 13; Sam. Ost. C 1101:1, 2 (PN (?)); Sam C 1220; *b̊rk*, KEK 3:2
	brkyhw	PN; “YH blesses;” A 108:1; Avigad (Baruk Seal) 1978 1:1; Tel Ira (*PEQ* 83 (1983)) 1:1; Avigad *HB* 38; Jerusalem Bulla 33:1; *b̊r̊k̊yhw*, A 22:1
	brkh	f.s. N (?); “blessing (?);” A 28:7; *[br]kh*, A 28:1
	hbrkh	DA f.s. N; “the pool;” Siloam 1:5

bt

bt — See *BN*

BTT

bt — m.s. N; "*bat*-measure;" Hazor 3:1; TBM sherd 2

GʾL

gʾlyhw — PN; "YH redeems;" A 16:5; A 39:5; Herr 39:1 (Bet Zur); Avigad *HB* 6

GBH_1

gbh — m.s. N CS; "the height of;" Siloam 1:6

GBH_2

hgbh — PN DA f.s. N; "the locust;" Avigad (1966) 1:2

GBḤ

gbḥ — PN Adj; "bald-headed one," Tel Ira (*PEQ* 83 (1983)) 1:2

GBʿ

gbʿ — LPN m.s. N; "hill;" S 8:1-2

gbʿn — LPN; m.s. N; "hill;" Gib 1, 8, 9, 10, 14, 18, 19, 21, 23, 26, 27, 28, 31, 32, 36, 51, 61; *gbʿ̊n*, Gib 60; *g̊bʿn*, Gib 11; *[g]bʿn*, Gib 25, 29, 30, 34, 54, 55; *[gb]ʿn*, Gib 7, 15; *[gb]ʿ̊n*, Gib 16; *gb[ʿn]*, Gib 56; *[gbʿ]n*, Gib 59

GBR

g̊b[ryhw] — PN; "(YH has pre)vailed, (been st)rong;" A 60:5-6

GDD

gd̊ʾ̊ — PN N; "GD;" A 72:3

gdy — PN; Avigad *HB* 25

gdyhw — PN; "GD is YH (=God);" B/L (29) 1:1; Avigad *HB* 24, 26, 169; Jerusalem Bulla 13:1; *gdẙ[hw]* (?), A 71:3; *[g]dyhw*, Avigad *HB* 23; *[g]dyh[w]*; Avigad *HB* 26

gdyw — PN; "GD is YH (=God);" S 2:2; 4:2; 6:2-3; 16a:2; 16b:2; 17a:2; 18:2; 30:2; 33:2; *[gd]ẙẘ*, S 5:2; *gdẙ[w]*, S 7:2; *[gdy]ẘ*, S 17b:2; *[g]d̊yw*, S 34:2; *gd[yw]*, S 35:2; *gdy[w]*, S 42:3

ʾbgd — PN; "GD (is my father)" Seal of Abigad 1:1; see also *ʾB*

GDH (?)

-gdy EOLPN *[ʿ]yn gdy*; m.s. N; "young goat, kid;" A 71:3

gdyhw

gdyhw See *GDD*

gdyw

gdyw See *GDD*

GDL

g̊dl PN; Perf V; Piel; "(DN) makes great;" or Qal, "YH is great;" Av (*EI* 9) 6:2

gdlyhw PN; "YH is great;" A 21:1; Herr 152:2; L Seal 6:1; Av (*EI* 9) 5:1; Avigad *HB* 5; *gdlẙhw*, Avigad (1964) Seal 2:2; *gd[ly]h̊w*, Avigad *HB* 41

gdl̊yh̊ PN; "YH is great;" A 110:2

ygdlyhw N; "YH is great;" Hest. 61:2

m[gd]lyh[w] PN; "Tower of YH"; Gib 58

GDR

gdr m.s. N CS; "walled plot if, enclosure of;" Gib 1, 7, 8, 10, 14, 15, 16, 19, 25, 31, 32, 34, 36, 51, 54, 55, 59, 61; *g̊dr*, Gib 3; *gd[r]*, Gib 9, 18; *[gd]r*, Gib 2; *[gd]r̊* , Gib 17; *g[dr]*, Gib 60; *‹g›dr*, Gib 11

GWR

[y]gwr LPN 3rd m.s. Imp V; "may (DN) dwell;" A 42:1; *yg̊r*, L 31:5

grʾ PN N; "sojourner, newcomer › guest (of DN);" S 30:3; *g̊r̊ʾ*, A 20:2; *[g]rʾ*, S 36:3; TBM sherd 5

gry PN N; "sojourner, newcomer, guest (of DN);" Dayan 1:2; *grẙ* (?), A 64:1

gryhw PN; "sojourner, newcomer, guest (of DN);" Av (*EI* 9) 8:2; R 5:1 (Herr 83)

GḤM

gḥm PN m.s. N (?); "flame (?);" A 31:6

GLH

hglnyh PN; "YH has exiled me;" R 17:2 (Herr 61)

GLL

glgl PN m.s. N; "small bell;" A 49:3

gm

wgm Conj Adv; "and truly, yea;" L 3:10

GML

gmlyhw PN; "YH is my reward, recompense;" R 20:2 (Herr 95); Avigad Hecht Seal 5:2

GMR

gmr PN m.s. N (?); "(DN) has finished;" S 50:1
gmryh PN; "YH has accomplished;" Jerusalem Bulla 19:1
gmryhw PN; "YH has accomplished;" A 31:8; A 38:3; L 1:1; Jerusalem Bulla 2:1; *g̊mryhw*, A 35:4; *gmr[yhw]*, A 40:1

GNN

mgn PN N; "(DN is my) shield;" Gib S.I. 8; L Seal 10:2 (7x)

GʿL

gʿly PN; Avigad *HB* 39-40

grʾ

grʾ See *GWR*

GRZ

grzn m.s. N; "pick;" Siloam 1:4 (2x)
hgrzn DA m.s. N; "the pick;" Siloam 1:2

gry

gry See *GWR*

gryhw

gryhw See *GWR*

GŠM

g̊šmy PN; Lemaire Seal 4:2

gt

gt pr'n	LPN; "wine press/farm of wild asses;" S 14:1-2
gt prḥ	LPN; "wine press/farm of flowers;" Ophel c:6

d'r

d'r	See *DWR*

DBR

dbr	N; "the matter;" A 18:6-7; *dbr*, "a word;" L 9:5- 6; A 111:4; *[d]br*, L 16:10; *dbr*, "anything, a thing, something;" A 24:17; *dbr*, papMur 17a:2; *dbr*, N (?) (or Piel Impv V (?)); "knowledge, something;" or "tell !;" L 2:6
dbr	N CS; "the matter of;" A 24:17; L 4:5; "the way of;" Siloam 1:1; "the complaint, case, plea of;" MHY 1:2; MHY 1:14
dbry	m.pl. N CS; "the words of;" L 6:5
dbrth	2nd m.s. Perf V; "you spoke; MO 2:5
ydbr	3rd m.s. Impf V; "he may, will say, speak; papMur 17a:2

DGN

'ldg[n]	PN; *'l-* + N D elem (?); "grain, Dagan;" Dayan 2:1-2 (forgery (?))

ddyhw

ddyhw	See *DWD*

DHM

tdhm	2nd m.s. *Niph* Imp V; "you will be silent;" MHY 1:14

DWD

ddyhw	PN; "YH is (my) uncle;" Av NN 2:2

DWH

dwh	Adj; "sick;" L 3:7

DWR

d'r	LPN N; "dwelling-place, habitation, abode;" Avigad (*IEJ* 25) 4:4

DYN

ydnyhw	PN; "YH judges;" A 27:4; Avigad Hecht Seal 11:1

DLH

hdlt DA N; "the door (?), column of writing on a papyrus roll;" L 4:3

dlh PN Perf; "(DN) has drawn up;" Av (*EI* 9) 3:1; *d̊lh*, S 38:3; *d̊lh̊* (?), B/L (26) 22:1

dlyh[w] PN; "[YH] has drawn up;" Avigad Seal 5:1; *dlyh[w]*, Jerusalem Bulla 1:2; *dl[yhw]*, L V Ost. 1:4; L 22:4

dlẙẘ PN; "YW has drawn up;" Hazor 8

ydlyh̊ẘ PN; "may YH draw (me up);" Av (*EI* 9) 2:2

dltyhw PN; "womb of YH;" Av NN 8:1

ʾldlh PN; Herr 74:1; see also *ʾLH*

dmlʾ

dmlʾ See *DMM*

dmlʾl

dmlʾ See *DMM*

dmlyhw

dmlyhw See *DMM*

DMM

dmlʾ PN m.s. Impv V; Prep; "wait on (DN), be resigned to (DN), be silent before (DN)!;" Gib 21; Av NN 18:1; Sam C 1307; *d̊mlʾ*, Gib 26; *dml̊ʾ̊*, Gib 27; *[dm]lʾ*, Gib 28; *dml[ʾ]*, Gib 29

dmlʾl PN; "be silent before God, wait on God, be resigned to God!;" Herr 133:2

dmlyhw PN; "be silent before YH, wait on YH, be resigned to YH!;" Herr 117:2; Herr 151:1; Avigad *HB* 42-43, 170; Jerusalem Bulla 36:2;*[d]mlyhw*, Avigad *HB* 44; *d[mlyhw]*, Avigad *HB* 45; *dmly[hw]*, *dmlẙ[hw]*, Jerusalem Bulla 50:2; Avigad *HB* 46; BCat 59

DRŠ

	dršyhw	PN; "YH seeks;" A 109:1-2; Av NN 15:1-2

h (interr. part.)

	h-	*hʾl*; Interr. part. and Prep; "is it true that (someone will do something) to (someone)?;" L 5:9; *hlʾ*; Interr. part. and neg. part.; "will (you) not?;" L 6:8; *hšlm*; Interr. part. and N; "is it well (with you) (?)" Aj 15:4

hwʾ

	hʾ	3rd m.s. subject pron; "he;" Aj 13; A 18:10; A 40:12

hgbh

	hgbh	See *GBH*

hglnyh

	hglnyh	See *GLH*

HWD

	hwdyh	PN; "YH is (my) splendor, majesty;" Herr 122:2
	hwdyhw	PN; "YH is (my) splendor, majesty;" B/L (26) 1b:1; 9:1

hwdwyhw

	hwdwyhw	See *YDH*

hwšʿ

	hwšʿ	See *YŠʿ*

hwšʿyhw

	hwšʿyhw	See *YŠʿ*

hwšʿm

	hwšʿm	See *YŠʿ*

HYH

	hyh	3rd m.s. perf V; "(it, he) was;" A 111:5; MHY 1:3; Siloam 1:1, 6; *h[y]h̊* , "(there) has been;" L 6:14; *hyh* (+ *w-*) "may (your hand) be (with me), and it will be;" MO 2:3
	hyt	3rd f.s. perf V; "it was;" Siloam 1:3
	yhy	3rd m.s. Juss; "and may he be;" Aj 15:8

hkws

hkws See *KWS*

HLK

wylkw 3rd m.pl. Imp V; "and (the water) went, flowed;" Siloam 1:4

HLL

yhl[ʾl] PN; "he will prai(se God);" Aj 14

hmṣh

hmṣh See *MṢH*

hn

hn See *hnh*

hnh

hnh demons. part.; "look now, lo, indeed;" A 24:18; L 6:5; *hnh̊*, Ophel 675b:2; *hn*; deitic (as *hnh*) or conditional part. (="if"), A 21:3; A 40:9

HRR

hrm m.pl. N; "mountains;" Aj 8:1
hrẙ m.pl. N CS; "the mountains of;" KBL 1:1-2

hṣlyhw

hṣlyhw See *NṢL*

hšʿyhw

hšʿyhw See *YŠʿ*

hšrq

hšrq See *ŠRQ*

htl

htl See *TLL*

w

w	*w*	Conj; "and;" A 1:1, 3, 5; A 2:1, 3, 4, 5, 7 (2x); A 3:1, 2, 5, 6, 7, 8, 12; A 4:2 (2x); A 5:1, 13; A 6:1; A 7:1, 8; A 8:1, 8; A 10:1, 3; A 11:2, 4 (?); A 12:1, 2, 5, 6; A 13:4 (2x); A 16:2, 3, 4, 6, 7 (?), 8, 10; A 17:3, 4, 5; A 18:3, 5, 6; A 21:2, 3, 7, 8; A 24:8 (?), 9 (?), 12, 13, 14, 17; A 26:3; A 29:7; A 33:2, 4, 7; A 40:1, 4, 8, 9, 11, 12; A 111:2, 3, 6 (?), 7; L 3:4 (2x), 8, 10, 13, 16, 17, 19; L 4:2, 4, 6 (2x), 7, 10; L 5:2; L 6:5, 10; L 9:2; L 13:2; L 16:10; MHY 1:4, 5 (2x), 6, 7, 8, 10, 12, 14; papMur 17a:2; Aj 7:1; Aj 8:1 (2x); Aj 10:1; Aj 14:1 (2x); Aj 15:6, 7, 8; Aj 16:1; Ophel 2:1; KEK 3:3; Siloam 1:1, 2, 3, 4, 5; Siloam 2:1; Tell el Qasile 1:2; Gezer 1:5; *ẘ*, Siloam 1:3; Silwan 2:2; *[w]*, A 7:5, 9; A 8:5; A 13:3; A 14:1, 3; A 17:1; A 40: 5, 7, 12, 14; L 5:6; L 6:4, 6, 8 (?); L 9:3; MHY 1:13, 14; Siloam 1:2; MO 2:1; MO 2:3; MO 2:4; MO 2:1; MO 2:6

z' t

	z' t	See *zh*

zdh

	zdh	See ZND

zh

	zh	Conj demonst. pron; "this;" Siloam 1:1; *zh*, m.s. demonst. adv; "this;" MHY 1:9 (*zh ymm*, "at this time"); *zh*, Adv in loc. sense with *m[n]*-: (*mzh*), "from here;" A 13:2; L 3:18
	hzh	demonst. Adj (DA demonst. pron); "this;" KEK 1:3; A 13:2; L 6:2
	z'̊t	f.s. demonst. pron; "this;" Silwan 2:1; L 6:10 (+ *k*-: "thus, like this"); *z'̊t*, Silwan 2:3; *[z]'t*, A 40:14-15; *z'[t]*, L 5:5-6 (+ *k̊* -: "like this")

ZHB

	z̊hb	m.s. N CS; "gold of;" Tell Qasile 2:1
	z̊h̊b	N; "gold;" Silwan 2:1

ZWR (?)

	zryw	PN; "crown of YH;" Dayan 3:1-2

ZKK (?)

*zk*ʾ — PN Adj; (DN) is pure, righteous;" Beth-Shemesh 10a:2; 10b: 2

ZKR

zkr — 3rd m.s. Perf V; "has remembered;" L 2:4

zkr — PN PP; (DN) is remembered" or "remembered one (of DN);" A 67:5; KEM 1:1; HU 2; Avigad 9:1-2; Av NN 6:2; Herr 89:1; Herr 144:1; Avigad *HB* 50; Jerusalem Bullae 4:2; 28:2; *zk̊r*, S 31a:3; *[z]kr*, A 38:7; A 48:3; Avigad *HB* 51

[z]kryhw — PN; "YH remembered;" MO 1:3

zkryw — PN; "YH remembered;" Av (*BIEJ* 18) 8:2; *[z]kryw*, Av (*IEJ* 25) 4:3

ZMR$_1$

zmr — N; "vine-pruning;" Gezer 1:6

ZMR$_2$

zmr — PN Perf V (cf. Phoenician *zmr*; Ugar. *ḏmr*); "(DN) has been strong, courageous, has helped, protected;" S 12:3

zmryhw — PN; "YH has been strong, courageous, has helped, protected;" Herr 107:2 (Egypt)

ZND (?)

zdh — N; "a fissure;" Siloam 1:3

zp

z̊p̊ — LPN; A 17:5

zyp — LPN IML; Beersheba seal 5:1

ZQN

zqn — PN N; "bearded one (?);" Av NN 19:1

zr

zr — See *ZWR*

ZRḤ

zrḥ — Inf. con. (+ *b*-); "(when DN) rises, shines forth;" Aj 8:1

zr̊ḥ — PN; Perf V; "(DN) rises, shines forth;" Avigad *HB* 62

yhwzrḥ — PN; "YH rises, shines forth;" Avigad *HB* 118; *yhwzr̊ḥ*, Hest. (1974) Hebron 1:1-2

zryw

zryw See *ZWR*

ZRʿ$_1$

zrʿ N CS (?); "grain, seed;" L 5:10
z̊rʿ N; "early sowing;" Gezer 1:1-2

ZRʿ$_2$

zrʿ N; "arm, (shoulder, strength)," A 88:2

ḥʾh

ḥʾh PN; Herr 40:1

ḤBʾ

ḥbʾ PN, "(DN) hides › protects (the newborn);" Avigad *HB* 52

ḤGB

ḥgb PN N; "locust;" L 1:3; Avigad *HB* 53-54

ḤGG

ḥgy PN N (?); Adj (?); "born on a feast day" (see Coogan, p. 73), "feast (of DN), festal;" Avigad Naar Seal 2:2; Jerusalem Seal 2:2; Jerusalem Seal 5:1; Herr 41:1 (Ophel); Herr 70:1; Avigad *HB* 55

ḤGL

ḥ̊glh LPN f.s. N; "partridge;" S 47:1; *ḥgl̊[h]*, S 45:1; *ḥ̊g̊l̊[h]*, S 66:1

ḤDR

ḥd[r] m.s. N; "room, chamber (burial chamber);" Silwan 1:1
hḥdr DA N; "the room, chamber (burial chamber);" KEK 1:3

ḤDŠ

ḥdš m.s. N; "(the) month;" A 7:3-4, 5; A 7:7; A 8:3; A8:4; A 17:8; A 32
hḥdš DA N; "the month;" A 5:13

ḥwyhw

ḥwyhw See *ḤWH*

ḤWH

ḥwyhw PN; “YH lives;” B/L (26) 7:2

ḤWL

ḥyl N; “army;” A 24:4
ḥylʾ PN N; (DN) is my strength;” Av NN 3:2; 4:2
ḥlyw PN; “fortress (of YH);” Aj 9
yhwḥyl PN; “YH is (my) strength;” RR Seal 7:1
ẙh̊ẘḥl PN; “YH is (my) fortress;” RR Seal 6:1

ḥwrṣ

ḥwrṣ See *ḤRṢ*

ḤWŠ

ḥ̊šy PN N PS (?); “my enjoyments, delights (?);” A 57:2; Jerusalem Bulla 8:2

ḤZH

yḥzyhw PN; “YH sees, may YH look (with favor); “Avigad Wine Decanter 1; *yḥzy[hw],* A 6:3

ḤZQ

ḥzq PN; “(DN) is strong;” B/L (32) 13:1
ḥzq̊ẙh̊ẘ PN; “YH is my strength;” Hest. (1974) Hebron 1:3-4; *ḥ̊[z]qyhw,* Ophel 1:1; *ḥz̊q̊ [yhw],* TBM sherd 4

ḥṭm

ḥṭm See *ḤNṬ*

ḥṭš

ḥṭš PN; Avigad *HB* 56

ḤYH

ḥy Adj; “as (YH) lives; “ L 6:12 (*ḥy yhwh*); L 12:3 (*[ḥ]y yhwh*); L 3:9 (*ḥyhwh*); A 21:5 (*ḥyh̊[wh]*)
ḥym PN N; “(DN) is life, sustenance;” Herr 159:1
ḥwyhw PN; “YH lives;” B/L (26) 7:2
yḥwʿly PN; “God preserves, lets live, may the Most High restore to life; S 55:2; *yḥwʿl[y]* S 60:1
ʾbyḥy PN; A 39:11
[ʾ]dnyḥy PN; Avigad *HB* 113
ʾšrḥy PN; Avigad *HB* 126; *[ʾš]rḥy,* Avigad *HB* 34
yhwḥy PN; “YH lives;” L V 1:2

ḥ̊yhw

	ḥ̊yhw	PN; ‹ʾ›*ḥ̊yhw* (?) Tell Qasile 1:3

ḥyl

	ḥyl	See *ḤWL*

ḥylʾ

	ḥylʾ	See *ḤWL*

ḥym

	ḥym	See *ḤYH*

ḤKH

	ḥkl	PN; "wait for (DN); B/L (32) 3:2
	ḥkl y[hw]	PN; "wait for YH;" L 20:2

ḤLD

	ḥ̊ldẙ	PN N; "mole, weasel;" A 27:5; A 39:10

ḥlyw

	ḥlyw	See *ḤWL*

ḤLṢ

	ḥlṣ	PN N; "vigor;" S 22:4; S 23:3; S 31a:2; 32:2; S 35:2; Avigad *HB* 60, *ḥlṣ̊*, Avigad *HB* 142; *ḥ̊[lṣ]*, S 49:2; *ḥl̊ṣ*, S 30:2; *[ḥ]l̊ṣ̊*, S 33:2
	ḥlṣyhw	PN; "YH is vigor, strength;" or from Phoen. verb "deliver" (?); R 19:2 (Herr 112); Avigad *HB* 47, *ḥ̊lṣyhw*, Avigad *HB* 157; Lemaire Seal 6:2;*[ḥl]ṣyh[w]*, Avigad *HB* 79

ḤLQ

	ḥlq	LPN N; "portion, possession (of DN), or "(DN is my) portion;" S 22:1; S 23:1; S 27:1; *[ḥ]lq*, S 24:1; *[ḥ l]q*, S 26:1
	ḥlq	PN N; "portion, possession (of DN), or "(DN) is my portion;" Av NN 8:2; Avigad *HB* 57, 149
	ḥlqʾ	PN N; "(DN is my) portion," Lemaire Seal 5:2

ḤLQ (continued)

ḥlqyhw PN; “portion of YH,” or “YH is my portion;” B/L (26) 21:2; Herr 128:2; Hest. 57:2; Av NN 2:1; L Seal 2:1; Hest. 56:1; Avigad *HB* 58-59, 107, 142; Jerusalem Bulla 27:2; *ḥlq̊[y]hw*, Hest. (1974) Hebron 1:2-3; *ḥlqyh[w]*, Hest. 55:1

ḥm

ḥm See *ḤMM*

ḤMD

ḥmdʾ PN N; “desire, choice (of DN);” A 55:1

ḤMH

ḥmyʾhl PN Fem; “my husband's father (=DN) is a shelter;” Hest. 34:1

ḥmyʿdn PN Fem; “my husband's father (=DN) is delight;” Av NN 1:1

ḥmyʾhl

ḥmyʾhl See *ḤMH*

ḥmyʿdn

ḥmyʿdn See *ḤMH*

ḤML

ḥml PN Perf V; “(DN) spares;” Av NN 15:2; Avigad *HB* 83

yḥml PN Imp V; “may (DN) spare;” KEK decanter 4

yḥmlyhw PN; “may YH spare, be compassionate;” Av NN 14:1-2; Herr 149:1-2

ḤMM

ḥm N CS (+ *b*-); “(in) the heat of;” MHY 1:10

ḥmn

ḥmn PN; Herr 43; *ḥ̊mn̊*, Herr 118:2

ḤMṢ

ḥmṣ N; “vinegar;” A 2:7

ḤMR$_1$

hḥmr DA N CS; “the *homer*-measure;” A 2:5

ḤMR$_2$

ḥmrm m.pl. N; “mules, he-asses;” A 3:5

ḥnʾ

ḥnʾ See *ḤNN*

ḥnh

ḥnh See *HNN*

ḤNṬ

ḥṭm N; “wheat;” A 31:1; A 33:1, 2, 3; *[ḥ]ṭ̊m*, A 33:6; *[ḥ]ṭ̊m̊*, A 33:8; *ḥṭ̊[m]*, Beersheba 3:1; *ḥ(ṭm)*, *ḥet* as an abbreviation for “wheat;” A 49:15, 16; *ḥ̊ṭ̊m̊*, A 33:4; *ḥ̊[ṭ]m*, A 33:7

hḥṭm DA N; “the wheat;” MO 2:6; “the (amount of) wheat;” A 3:7

ḥnyhw

ḥnyhw See *ḤNN*

ḤNN

ḥnn m.s. Adj; PP; “merciful;” KBL 2:1

ḥnʾ PN Perf V; “(DN) has favored;” S 30:3

ḥnh PN fem.; Perf V; “(DN) favors;” *PEQ* (1976) (Near Lachish) Seal 1

ḥnyhw PN; “YH has been favorable;” B/L (26) 1a:2

ḥnn PN Perf V; “(DN) has been gracious;” Av (*EI* 9) 2:1; Avigad *HB* 64; *[ḥ]nn*, Avigad *HB* 63; *ḥn[n]* (?), A 38:2

ḥ̊nmlk̊ PN, “The King has been favorable;” Jerusalem Bulla 3:1

ḥnny PN; Avigad *HB* 150

ḥnnyh PN; “YH has been gracious;” Jerusalem Bulla 45:2

ḥnnyhw PN; “YH has been gracious;” Gib 22, 32, 33, 35, 38; 39; 40; 41; 50; 52; A 3:3; A 16:1; KEM 1:3; Hest. 59:2; Hest. 79:2; Herr 93:1; Herr 94:1; Av (1964) Seal 2; Avigad *HB* 61; BCat 53; *ḥ̊nnyhw*, Gib 42; *ḥn̊nyhw*, Herr 44:1 (Beth-Shemesh) *ḥnnyh̊ẘ*, Avigad *HB* 62; *ḥn̊n̊ẙhw*, A 36:4; *ḥnnẙh̊ẘ*, Avigad *HB* 100; *ḥnnyh[w]*, Jerusalem Bulla 34:1; *ḥnny[hw]*, Gib 43; *ḥnn[yhw]*, Gib 51; *[ḥ]nnyhw*, Gib 47; *ḥn[n]yhw*, Gib 57; *[ḥn]nyhw*, Gib 37

ḤNN (continued)

ʾlḥnn See *ʾLH*

bʿlḥnn See *BʿL*

yḥ̊ny PN Imp V; “(DN) favors, has favored;” L Seal 19:2

ḤSD

ḥsdyhw PN; “YH is kind;” RR 2; Herr 153:2

ḤSH

mḥsyhw PN; “(YH) is (my) refuge;” Avigad *HB* 85; *mḥsy[hw]*, Avigad *HB* 80; *m̊ḥsy[hw]*, Jerusalem Bulla 14; *mḥs[yhw]*, A 23:6; *mḥ[sy]hw*, Avigad *HB* 86

mḥ[syw] PN; “[YH] is (my) refuge;” Sam C 1012:1

ḤSR

ḥsr Adj; “lacking, needy (=partly full); A 98:1

ḤṢB

hḥṣbm DA AP; “the hewers;” Siloam 1:4; *hḥṣb[m]*, Siloam 1:6; *[hḥṣbm]*, Siloam 1:1

ḤṢH

ḥṣy N; “half-(measure);” A 101

ḥṣy PN Perf V; “(DN) has apportioned, distributed;” R 20:1 (Herr̊95)

yḥṣ PN; juss. V; “may (DN) apportion, divide;” Herr 104:1

ḤṢR$_1$

ḥṣr ʾsm LPN; N CS; “in *ḥṣr ʾsm*; village of granaries;” MHY 1:3-4

[ḥṣr] LPN (*[ḥṣr] swsh*); N CS; “village of mare(s);” A 32:1

ḤṢR$_2$

ḥṣrt LPN; f.pl. N; “enclosures, courts;” S 18:1; S 23:3; S 25:3-4; *ḥṣrt̊*, S 22:4; *[ḥ]ṣrt*, S 15:1; *[ḥ]ṣ̊rt̊*, S 24:2; *ḥ[ṣrt]*, S 26:2

ḤRN

byt ḥrn LPN; *byt* + DN; Tell Qasile 2:1

ḤRP		
	ḥrpk	m.s. AP; 2nd m.s. PS; "he who insults you, your scorner;" KBL 7:1-2
ḤRṢ		
	ḥwrṣ	PN AP IML; "(DN) decides, determines;" Herr 90:1
ḤŠB		
	ḥšbyhw	PN; "YH has reckoned;" MHY 2:1
ḥšy		
	ḥšy	See *ḤWŠ*
ḤTM		
	ḥtmk	N; 2nd m.s. PS; "your (m.s.) seal;" A 13:3; A 17:6-7
	ḥtm	Impv V; "affix, seal!;" A 4:2; A 17:5-6; *ḥ[tm]*, A 7:8-9; *[ḥ]tm*, A 10:4; *[ḥtm]*, A 13:3
ḥts		
	ḥts	PN; Av (*IEJ* 4) 6:2
ṬWB		
	ṭb	N Abs.; "good, well-being;" L 4:2; L 8:2; *ṭ̊b̊*, L 5:2; *[ṭb]*, "good (news);" L 9:2
	ṭ̊b̊	N CS; "the good(ness) of;" L 5:8 (+ *ḇ*-)
	ṭb	Adj.; "good;" Kadesh Barnea (*Qad.* 16 (61), 1983, p. 12)
	ṭbm	m.pl. Adj; "good;" L 6:6
	ṭbʾl	PN; "God is good;" B/L (26) 18:1-2
	ṭbyhw	PN; "YH is good;" L 3:19; Avigad *HB* 14; *ṭbẙh̊ẘ*, L 5:10; *ṭby[hw]*, Avigad *HB* 65
	ṭbšlm	PN; "ŠLM is good;" L 1:2; En Gedi 3:1; *ṭ[bšlm]* L 7:5-6; [*ṭbšlm]*, Jerusalem Bulla 4:1; *ṭ̊bšlm̊*, Jerusalem Bulla 28:1
ṬRM		
	bṭrm	Prep AOT; "before;" A 5:12; *[bṭrm]*, A 40:10
yʾš		
	yʾš	See *ʾWŠ*
yʾwš		
	yʾwš	See *ʾWŠ*

y'zn

y'zn See *'ZN*

y'znyhw

y'znyhw See *'ZN*

YBB

š'ybb PN (Aramaic Name); "*Š'* (DN) is triumphant, exults;" Av (1964) Seal 1

YBŠ

ẙb̊š PN Adj; "he is withered;" L 19:5

ygdlyhw

ygdlyhw See *GDL*

ygwr

ygwr See *GWR*

YD

yd N CS; " hand of;" Prep N (*byd*); "through the intermediary of (DN), in the hand of (DN);" *yd,* MO 1:2 (+ *b-*); *yd̊* , L 9:6-7 (+ *b-*); *[y]d,* A 16:5-6; A 24:13-14 (+ [*b*-]); EOPN *b̊dyw,* S 58:1

ẙd̊t̊ pl. N; "monuments, stelae;" Ophel 1:2, 3

ydk N 2nd m.s. PS; "your hand;" MO 2:3

ydy Fem. dual N CS; "the hands of, the power of, the strength of;" L 6:7

ydyk Fem. dual N; 2nd m.s. PS; "your (m.s.) hands (=strength, power);" L 6:6

YDH

yhẘd̊h̊ LPN *hophal* Imp V; IML; "(DN) is praised;" KBL 1:2; *yhwd[h],* A 40:13

hwdwyhw PN; "praise YH!, thank YH!;" L 3:17; Avigad *HB* 55:2

YDW

ydw PN; B/L (32) 9:2; Avigad Hecht Seal 1:1

ydlyhw

ydlyhw See *DLH*

ydnyhw

ydnyhw See *DYN*

YDʿ

wydʿ Conj 3rd m.s. Perf V; "and he will know;" L 4:10

ydʿth 2nd m.s. Perf V; "you knew, know;" L 3:8 (with neg.); L 2:6 (with neg); A 40:9

ydʿ 3rd m.s. Imp V; "(he) should know;" A 40:13; L 6:7 (can also be Perf V)

hd̊ʿm m.s. *Hiph* Impv; 3rd m.pl. PS; "inform them!;" Sam C 1101:2

ydʿ PN PP; "he is known;" L 3:20

ydʿyhw PN; "YH knows;" A 31:7; A 39:4; Herr 109:2; Avigad *HB* 68-69; Jerusalem Bulla 12:1; *yd̊ʿyhw*, A 39:5

ydʿyw PN; "YH knows;" S 1:8; S 42:2; *ẙd̊ʿẙw*, S 48:1

šmydʿ LPN, (+ *m-* = "from"); "The Name knows;" S 3:2; S 30:1; S 31a:1; S 37:1; S 38:1-2; S 39:1; S 40:1; S 63:2; S 90:1; *šmyd[ʿ]*, S 36:1; *š[mydʿ]*, S 35:1; *[š]my[dʿ]*, S 34:1; *šmy[dʿ]*, S 33:1-2; *š‹m›ydʿ*, S 32:1; *[šmyd]ʿ*, S 49:1-2; *š̊[mydʿ]*, S 29:1

šmyd[ʿ] LPN; S 62:1; *šm‹y›dʿ*, S 57:2

ydt

ydt See *YD*

yh

yh Part. of entreaty; "O!;" KBL 2:1

yhbnh

yhbnh See *BNH*

YHD

hyhd[y] DA gent. Adj; "the Judean;" S 51:3

yhwʾ

yhwʾ PN; Avigad *HB* 70

yhwʾb

yhwʾb See *ʾB*

yhwʾḥ

[yh]wʾḥ See *ʾḤ*

yhwʾḥz

yhwʾḥz See *ʾḤZ*

yhwʾl

yhwʾl See *ʾLH*

yhwbnh

yhwbnh See *BNH*

yhwdh

yhwdh See *YDH*

YHWH

yhwh PN D elem.; Aj 10:1; Aj 7:2; Aj 14:2; Aj 15:4-5; KEK 3:2; A 16:3; KBL 2:1; L 2:2, 5; L 5:7-8; L 6:1, 12; L 9:1; L 12:3; KH 1:15-17; KH 2:6; MO 1:4; MO 2:1; *yhẘh̊*, KBL 2:1; *ẙhẘh̊*, KBL 1:1; *[y]hwh*, KBL 3:1; *yhw[h]*, L 3:3; L 4:1; *yh[wh]*, KH 2:8-9; *[yhw]h̊*, L 8:1; Jerusalem pomegranate inscription (= Lemaire "grenade" inscription *RB* 88, no. 2 (1981):236-39); *‹y›hwh*, L 3:9; *‹y›h̊[wh]*, A 21:5; *[yhwh]*, L 5:1; *yhw‹h›*, Aj 13:1; Aj 16:1; *[yhw]h̊*, A 21:2-3

yhwzrḥ

yhwzrḥ See *ZRḤ*

yhwḥy

yhwḥy See *HYḤ*

yhwḥyl

yhwḥyl See *ḤWL*

yhwḥl

yhwḥl See *ḤWL*

yhwyšmʿ
yhwyšmʿ See *ŠMʿ*

yhwkl
yhwkl See *YKL*

yhwmlk
yhwmlk See *MLK*

yhwndb
yhwndb See *NDB*

yhwʿz
yhwʿz See *ʿZZ*

yhwʿzr
yhwʿzr See *ʿZR*

yhwqm
yhwqm See *QWM*

yhwrm
yhwrm See *RWM*

yhwšʿ
yhwšʿ See *YŠʿ*

yhllʾl
yhllʾl See *HLL*

ywʾl
ywʾl See *ʾLH*

ywʾmn
ywʾmn See *ʾMN*

ywʾr
ywʾr See *ʾWR*

ywbnh

ywbnh See *BNH*

ywzn

ywzn See *ʾZN*

ywyšʿ

ywyšʿ See *YŠʿ*

ywkn

ywkn See *KWN*

ywntn

ywntn See *NTN*

ywstr

ywstr See *STR*

ywʿzr

ywʿzr See *ʿZR*

ywʿlyhw

ywʿlyhw See *YʿL*

ywʿśh

ywʿśh See *ʿŚH*

ywqm

ywqm See *QWM*

yḥwʿly

yḥwʿly See *ḤYH*

yḥzyhw

yḥzyhw See *ḤZH*

yḥml

yḥml See *ḤML*

yḥmlyhw

yḥmlyhw See *ḤML*

yḥny

yḥny See *ḤNN*

yḥṣ

lyḥṣ See *ḤṢH*

YṬB

hyṭb 3rd m.s. *Hiph* Perf V; "he favored;" Aj 7:2

YYN

yyn N; "wine;" A 1:3; A 2:2, 5; A 4:3; A 8:5; A 10:2; A 11:3

yyn N (CS); "wine (of);" Avigad Wine Decanter 1; L 25:1; A 1:9 (+ *m*- = "from the wine of"); *[yy]n*, L 9:3-4

hyyn DA N; "the wine;" A 3:2

yn N; "wine;" S 5:3; S 6:3; S 10:3; S 11:1; S 12:3; S 13:3; S 14:3; S 101: 3; *y[n]*, S 9:3; S 15:2; S 89:1; *[yn]*, S 1:2 ; S 3:2; S 7:2; S 8:3

yn N CS; "wine of;" S 53:1, S 54:1; S 62:1; S 72:1; S 73:2; *[yn]*, S 20:1

hyn DA N; "the wine;" S 44:3; *hẙn*, S 26:2

YKL

yklm m.pl. AP; "we are able;" A 40:14

yhwkl PN; "YH is able, prevails;" A 21:1; Herr 63:2 (Tell es Safi); L V 1:1; Avigad Hecht Seal 10:2

YLD

mldh LPN (+ *m*-) "(from) Moladah"; HU 2

YM

ym m.s. N; "day;" A 40:11; *ym*, (+ *k*-: "this day, at [about] this time, now);" L 2:3 (2x); L 4:1; *[ym]*, L 5:2-3, 3; L 8:2

ym N CS (+ *b*-: "on the day of);" Siloam 1:3; Aj 8:2,3

hym DA N; "today, now;" A 24:19; *hym*, "the day;" L 5:9; A 1:4; *[hym]*, "today;" L 4:8

ymm N PS; "their day;" Aj 7:1

YM (continued)

	ymm	m. pl. N; "(a few) days (ago);" MHY 1:9; *ymm*, N (+ *k*-: "according to the days [= a few days ago]);" MHY 1:5, 7
	hymm	DA N; "the days;" A 2:3
YMN		
	ymn	N (+ *m*-: "on the right"); Siloam 1:3
	myʾmn	PN; Prep + N; *ʾaleph* as IML; "the right" › southerner, lucky" (see Coogan, p. 77), V 4:2; Hest. 94:1; *[m]yʾmn*, Avigad *HB* 87-88
yn		
	yn	See *YYN*
ynm		
	ynm	PN; A 19:1
YSP		
	ysp	PN; "(DN) adds, increases;" Avigad *HB* 131
YʿL		
	ywʿlyh̊ẘ	PN; "May YH avail, aide;" Lemaire Seal 1:1
yʿś		
	yʿś	See *ʿŚH*
YPH		
	ypẙh̊ẘ	PN; "beauty (is DN);" L Seal 20:2
yprʿyw		
	yprʿyw	See *PRʿ*
YṢʾ		
	ṣʾty	Inf. Con. PS (+ *k*-: *kṣʾty*); "(when) I leave;" A 16:3
	hmwṣʾ	DA N; "the source; spring;" Siloam 1:5
yṣt		
	yṣt	LPN (+ *m*-: "from *yṣt*"); S 9:1-2; S 10:1-2; S 19:2; S 47:2; *ẙṣ[t]*, S 45:3; *ẙṣ̊[t]*, S 67:1; *[y]ṣ̊t̊*, S 80:1

yqmyhw

	yqmyhw	See *QWM*

YQR

	mwqr	PN *Hiph* P; "(DN) makes rare, precious," Tel Ira (*PEQ* 83 (1983)) 1:3

yrʾ

	yrʾ	See *RʾH*

YRʾ

	yrʾwyhw	PN Impv V; "Fear YH!;" Av NN 5:1

yrbʿm

	yrbʿm	See *RBB*

YRD

	yrd	3rd m.s. Perf V; "went down, has come down;" L 3:14
	[y]rd	3rd m.s. Imp V (?); "goes down, will descend;" A 40:10-11

YRḤ

	yrḥ	N (3rd m.s. PS); "(his) month;" Gezer 1:3, 1:4; 1:5; 1:7
	yrḥw	masc. dual N PS; "his two months;" Gezer 1:1 (2x); 1:2; 1:6

yrḥmʾl

	yrḥmʾl	See *RḤM*

yrymwt

	yrymwt	PN Adj; "corpulent, stout, fat;" B/L (26) 3:2

YRK

	yrkty	N CS; (+ *b*-: "in the back of"); Ophel 3:3 (*IEJ* 32 (1982))

yrm

	yrm	See *RMH*

yrmyhw

	yrmyhw	See *RMH*

yršlm

yršlm LPN; “Jerusalem;” KBL 1:2

yšʾl

yšʾl See *ŠʾL*

YŠB

yšb m.s. AP; “he is staying;” A 18:10

yšb PN Imp V (?); Perf V (?); juss. V (?); “may YH dwell, abide, endure;” or “may he cause to dwell (hiph. juss.);” Herr 145:2

yšb LPN; *Hiph* juss. (?); (+ *m*-: “from *yšb*”); “may cause to dwell;” S 48:3

yšmʿʾl

yšmʿʾl See *ŠMʿ*

YŠN

yšn Adj; “old (wine);” S 1:3; S 5:3; S 6:4; S 9:3; S 10:4; S 12:4; S 13:3; S 14:3; S 101:1; *[y]š*n, S 3:2-3; S 7:3; *[yš]n*, S 8:3; *[yšn]*, S 15:2

YŠʿ

h̊wšʿ *Hiph* Impv V; “save!;” KEK 3:3; KBL 3:1

hwšʿ PN inf. Abs. or Impv V; “save (O DN)!;” papMur 17b:1;L Seal 8:1; Herr 89:2; Hest. 78:2; Driver Seal 1; *hwš[ʿ]*, Avigad *HB* 46; *hw[šʿ]*, Avigad *HB* 45

hwšʿyhw PN; “Save O YH!;” or “YH delivered, saved;” MHY 1:7; L 3:1; R 3:1 (Herr 87); Hest. 72:1; Hest. 73:1-2; Avigad *HB* 48, 143-148, 161; *hwšʿyhw*, Avigad *HB* 28; *hw[š]ʿyhw*, Avigad *HB* 41; *hwšʿyh[w]*, Avigad *HB* 43; *[h]wšʿyhw*, Avigad *HB* 44; *hwš{ʿyhw]*, Avigad *HB* 46

hwšʿm PN; “Save, O paternal uncle, protector (=DN);” Jerusalem Seal 2:1

hšʿyhw PN; “Save O YH!;” or “YH delivered, saved;” HU 3

yšʿʾ PN N; “(DN is my) salvation;” Hest. 74:2

yšʿyhw PN; “YH saves;” Herr 140:2; Hest. 60:2; Av (*IEJ* 13) 3:1-2 (Kiryat Yearim); Avigad *HB* 83, 91; Avigad Hecht Seal 3:1; *[y]šʿyhw*, Avigad *HB* 84; *yšʿy[hw]*, Avigad *HB* 91; *yšʿyh[w]*, Seal of Maʿaseyahu 1:2; *yšʿẙhw*, Jerusalem Jar 2:1

*YŠ*ᶜ (continued)

	*yhwš*ᶜ	PN; "YH is salvation;" Herr 100:1; Avigad *HB* 20-21
	*ywyš*ᶜ	PN; "YH has saved;" S 36:3; Sam C 1265
yšpṭ		
	yšpṭ	See *ŠPṬ*
YTM		
	ytm	PN; B/L (29) 7:1
YTR		
	ytr	N CS (+ *m*-); "(and from) the surplus of;" A 5:13-14
k		
	k	Prep; "like, as;" A 16:3; L 2:3 (2x); L 4:1, 2, 3, 11; L 6:10; MHY 1:5, 7; MHY 1:6, 8 (+ -*ʾšr* = "when"); MO 1:1 (+ -*ʾšr* = "as, according as"); *k̊*, L 8:2; *[k]*, L 5:3 (2x), 5
KBR		
	mkbrm	PN; "the one who makes many (=DN) is exalted;" Hazor 5
KHN		
	khn	N AP CS; "priest of;" Avigad (*IEJ* 25) 4:4
	khnm	N; "priests;" Jerusalem pomegranate inscription (=Lemaire "grenade" inscription; *RB* 88), no. 2 (1981):236-39)
KWL		
	klkl	PN; "(DN) sustains, supports, nourishes;" Avigad Hecht Seals 9:1
	klklyhw	PN; "YH sustains, supports, nourishes;" Av NN 6:1-2
KWN		
	knyh̊ẘ	PN; "may (DN) be enduring;" L 3:15; A 49:4
	ywkn	PN; "YH establishes;" RR Seal 8:2; TBM 1:2; Beth-Shemesh 2:2
	yknyhw	PN; "YH establishes;" B/L (32) 3:1
kws		
	hkws	PN DA N IML; "the owl;" A 38:1

KWR

	kẘr	LPN N (?) IML (+ *m̊*- : "from kwr"); "smelting-pot, furnace;" S 49:4

KḤL

	kḥl	LPN (?); N (?); "dark-colored;" Avigad Wine Decanter 1

KY

	ky	Conj; "for;" Siloam 1:3, L 4:12; ky, "though, for;" L 3:6; ky, "and as for what;" L 3:8; *ky*, "with respect to what, and seeing that, since;" L 4:4; ky, "that;" L 2:4; L 4:10; L 6:3; *[ky]*, A 40:13; L 5:4; Silwan 2:2 (*ky ʾm*); ky, "only, for (except);" *ky ʾm*; L 4:9; *k[y]*, "indeed, truly;" L 6:13; *[k]y*, L 12:3

kl

	kl	See *KLL*

KLB

	klb	N; "a dog;" L 2;4; L 5:4; L 6:3; L 12:1
	klb	PN N; "dog;" A 58:2

KLH

	klt	1st c.s. Perf V; "I finished;" MHY 1:8
	kl	3rd m.s. Perf V; "he finished;" MHY 1:6
	ykl	Piel Imp V (+ *w*-); "(and) he finished;" MHY 1:5
	kl	Piel Inf. Abs. (+ *w*-); "(and) finishing (the harvest);" Gezer 1:5

klklyhw

	klklyhw	See *KWL*

KLL

	kl	N (*kl ʾšr*); "everything, whatever;" A 21:7; Aj 16:1 (+ *k*-: "according to everything"); L 4:2, 3; *[kl]*, "all;" A 40:6
	kl	N CS; "all of;" MHY 1:10; "any," L 3:11; (+ *k*-: "according to all of"), L 4:11; *kl̊*, KBL 1:1; *k̊[l]* (+ *b*-: "in all of, over all"); A 88:1; *k[l]*, "any," papMur 17a:2

kn

kn Adv; "so, thus;" L 4:3

knyhw

knyhw See *KWN*

ksʾ

ksʾ PN N; "throne of (DN)," or "(DN is my) throne;" Beth-Shemesh 10a:1; Beth-Shemesh 10b:1

KSL

kslʾ̊ PN; N (?); "confidence (in DN);" Avigad *HB* 132

KSP

ksp N; "silver;" MHY 6:2; Silwan 2:1; MO 1:3; *k̊s̊p*, A 29:6
ksp N CS; "the money of;" A 16:8
h[k]s̊p DA N; "the money;" A 16:5

kpr

k̊p̊r̊h PN N; "young lion;" A 60:1

KRM

krm N CS; "the vineyard of;" S 55:1-2; S 60:1
krm EOLPN N CS; S 20:2; S 53:2; S 54:1-2; S 58:2; S 61:1; S 72:1; *kr[m]*, S 73:2
krmy PN N PS (?); "(DN is) my vineyard;" or "vineyard (of DN);" Avigad *HB* 68; *krm̊y*, L Seal 20:1
krm htl LPN; "vineyard of the mound;" S 53:2; S 54:1-2; S 58:2; S 61:1; S 72:1-2; *krm ht̊[l]*, S 20:2

krmy

krmy See *KRM*

kršn

kršn PN; papMur 17b:3

kšy

kšy PN gent. Adj; "the Kushite;" Herr 109:1

KTB

	hmktb	DA N; "the report;" A 40:12
	[hmktbm]	DA N; "the reports (?);" A 40:9
	ktbty	1st c.s. Perf V; "I have written;" L 4:3; *[ktbt]y* (?), 1st Perf V; "I (hereby) write;" A 40:5
	ktbth	2nd m.s. Perf V; "and you (m.s.) are to write;" A 7:5-6
	ktbh	3rd m.s. Perf V; 3rd m.s. PS; "(he) has written it (?);" KEK 3:1
	t̊ktb	2nd m.s. Imp V; "you (m.s.) will write;" L 6:8-9
	ktb	m.s. Impv V; "write down!;" A 1:3-4

kty

	hkty	DA Gent. N; "the Kitti;" A 17:9
	ktym	m.pl. Gent. N; "Kittim;" A 1:2; A 2:1-2; A 4:1; A 7:2; A 10:5; A 14: 2; *[k]t[ym]*, A 5:6-7; *k̊t̊[y]m̊*, A 8:1-2; *[kt]ym*, A 10:2; *ktẙ[m]*, A 11:2

KTP

	kt̊p	N CS (+ *b*-); "(in) the side, slope of (=shoulder);" Silwan 1:1

l

	l	Prep; "to, belonging to, for, by (KEK 3:4);" A 1:2, 8; A 2:1, 2; A 4:1; A 5:6; A 7:2, 3 (2x), 5, 6, 7; A 8:1, 3, 4, 9; A 10:4; A 11:2; A 16:1, 2, 3, 5; A 17:5, 8; A 18:3, 4, 5, 6; A 21:1, 2, 4; A 22:1, 2, 4, 6; A 24:3 (?), 18; A 32:1; A 40:10, 14; A 60:5; A 89:1; A 91:1; A 92:1; A 93:1; A 95:1; A 105:1; A 106:1; A 107:1; A 108:1; A 109:1; A 111:7; L 3:1, 5, 6, 10 (2x), 13, 14, 15, 20; L 5:10; L 6:6, 9, 10, 15; L 13:1; L 22:k, 2, 3, 4, 5, 6, 7, 8, 9, 10; MHY 1:5, 12 (2x); MHY 2:1; papMur 17a:2; S 1:1; S 2:2; S 3:3; S 4:2; S 5:2; S 6:2; S 7:1; S 9:2; S 10:1; S 12:2; S 13:2, 3; S 14:2; S 16a:2; S 16b:2; S 17a:2; S 18:2; S 19:3; S 21:1; S 22:1; S 23:2; S 24:1; S 26:1; S 27:1; S 28:1; S 30:2; S 31a:2; S 31b:2; S 32:2; S 35:2; S 37:2; S 38:2; S 45:2; S 46:2; S 47:1; S 49:2; S 50:1, 2; S 56:2; S 58:1; S 102:1; Sam 689; Sam C 1142; Sam C 1265; Sam C 1307; Aj 3:1; Aj 4:1; Aj 5:1; Aj 6:1; Aj 8:3; Aj 10:1 (2x); Aj 13:1 (2x); Aj 14:1 (4 x); Aj 15:2, 4, 6; KBL 1:2; KEK 1:1; KEK 2:1; KEK 3:2, 3, 4, 5; KEK 4:1; KEK 6:1; Siloam 1:2, 4; Tell el Qasile 1:1; Tell el Qasile 2:1; Jerusalem Jar 2:1; Jerusalem Jar 3:1; Jerusalem pomegranate inscription

l (continued)

l (=Lemaire "grenade" inscription; *RB* 88), no. 2 (1981): 236-39) Beersheba Graffiti 2:1; 3:1; 4:1; 5:1; Avigad Wine Decanter 1:1; Gib 51 (2x); Gib S.I. 2, 3, 5, 6, 8; Hazor 5, Hazor 7, Hazor 8; MO 1:4; MO 2:5-6; MO 2:7; Aroer Seal 1; Avigad *IEJ* 4 (1954) Seal 5:1, 6:1; Avigad *BIES* 18 (1954) Seal 8:1; 11:1; Avigad *IEJ* 13 (1963) Seal 1:2; Avigad *IEJ* 14 (1964) Seal 1:1; 2:1; Avigad *IEJ* 16 (1966) Seal 1:1; Avigad *IEJ* 18 (1968) Seal 1:1; Avigad *Qadmoniot* 2 (1969) Stone Weight 1; Avigad *IEJ* 25 (1975) Seal 4:1; Avigad *EI* 14 (1978) Seal 1:1; Avigad *IEJ* 28 (1978) Seal 1:1, 2:1 (*Baruk the Scribe and Jerahmeel the King's Son*); Avigad *IEJ* 28 (1978) Lyre Seal 1:1; Avigad (*EI* 9) Seal 1:1, 2:1, 3:1, 4:1, 5:1, 6:1, 7:1, 8:1; 9:1; 10:1; 12:1; 13:1; 14:1; 15:1; Avigad (*EI* 12) New Names Seals 1:1; 2:1; 3:1; 4:1; 6:1; 7:1; 8:1; 9:1; 10:1 11:1; 14:1 15:1; 16:1; 17:1; 18:1; 19:1; 20:1; Avigad Naar Seal 2:1; Beth-Shemesh Seals 1:1; 2:1; 4:1; 5:1; 6:1; 7:1; 8:1; 9:1; 10a:1; 10b:1; Torrey *BASOR* 79 (1940) Ushna Seal 1:1; B/L (24) 2:1; B/L (26) 1a:1; 1b:1; 2:1; 3:2; 4:1; 5:1; 6:1; 7:1; 8:1; 9:1; 10:2; 11:1; 12:1; 13:1; 14:1; 15:1; 16:1; 17:1; 18:1; 19:2; 21:1; B/L (29) 1:1; 2:1; 3:1; 4:1; 6:1; 7:1; 8;1; B/L (32) 1:1; 2:1; 3:1; 4:1; 5:1: 6:1; 7:1; 8:1; 9:1; 11:1; 12:1; 13:1; 14:1; 15:1;Tel Dan Seal 1; Dayan Seals 2:1; 3:1; Driver (*PEQ* 1955) Seal 1; Ein Gedi Seal 1:1; 2:1; Herr Seals 4:1; 39:1; 40:1; 41:1; 43:1; 44:1; 60:1; 62:1; 63:1; 64:1-2; 68:1; 70:1; 74:1; 75:1; 79:1; 80:1; 81:1; 89:1; 90:1; 93:1; 94:1; 99:1; 100:1; 104:1; 105:1; 107:1; 109:1; 110:1; 116:1; 117:1; 118:1; 119:1; 120:1; 121:1; 122:1; 124:1; 131:1; 133:1; 137:1; 140:1; 141:1; 143:1; 144:1; 145:1; 146:1; 148:1; 149:1; 151:1; 152:1; 153:1; 156:1; 159:1; Hest. 34:1; 40:1; 46:1; 51:1; 55:1; 56:1; 57:1; 59:1; 60:1; 61:2; 65:1; 72:1; 73:1; 74:1; 77:1; 78:1; 79:1; 80:1; 82:1; 91:1; 94:1; 96:1; Jerusalem Citadel Seal 1:1; 3:1; 4:1; 5:1; Lachish Seals (Driver) 2:1; 4:1; 5:1; 6:1; 7:1; 10:1; 11:1; 12:1; 13:1; 14:1; 15:1; 16:1; 21:1; Lachish V Seals 1:1; 2:1; 4:1; 6:1; 7:1; Megiddo Seal 1:1; Naveh (*Qadmoniot* 1 (1968-69)), *IEJ* 15 (1965) Seal 1:1; Ramat Rahel Seals 1:1; 2:1; 8:1; 9:1; Ramat Rahel Royal Seals (15 seals); Reifenberg Seals 1:1; 2:1; 3:1; 4:1; 5:1; 6:1; 7:1; 8:1; 11:1; 12:1; 17:1; 18:1; 19:1; 20:1; 21:1; Seal of Elijah 1:1; Bartlett *PEQ* 108 (1976) Seal 1; Stieglitz *IEJ*

l (continued)

l 23 (1973) Seal of Maʿaseyahu 1:1; Hestrin and Dayagi *IEJ* 24 (1974), Servant of King Hezekiah Seal 1:1; Shechem Seal 1; Tel Amal Jar Inscription 1; TBM 1:1, 3, 4; Royal Seals (4 seals); Tell en-Nasbeh 1:1; 3:1; Ophel 675b:3; Avigad *HB* 1-7, 11-15, 17-26, 28-30, 32-33, 36-61, 63-73, 75-107, 109-153, 155-168, 174, 184, 189-90, 196; Avigad Hecht Seals 3:1; 4:1; 5:1; 6:1; 7:1; 8:1; 9:1; 10:1; 11:1; 12:1; HU 1; BCat 40, 44-45, 50, 52, 53, 55; Lemaire Seals 1:1; 2:1; 5:1; 6:1; Jerusalem Bullae 1:1; 2:1; 3:1; 5:1; 7:1; 8:1; 9:1; 10:1; 12:1; 13:1; 14:1; 17:1; 19:1; 23:1; 27:1; 28:1; 29:1; 31:1; 32:1; 33:1; 34:1; 35:1; 36:1; 39:1; 45:1; 48:1; 50:1; l̊, A 21:2; S 42:2; S 48:1; B/L (26) 122:1; Herr 66:1; 135:1; Lachish Seals (Driver) 19:1; Lachish V Shekel Weight 1:1; BCat 59; Lemaire Seal 4:1; *[l]*, A 5:6; A 10:2; A 12:3; A 14:2; A 40:2, 3; L 3:2; L 6:4, 6; L 9:5; L 18:2; L 27; L 28; S 8:2; S 11:2; S 17b:2; S 28:1; S 29:1; S 33:2; S 34:2; S 39:2; Hazor 6:1; Lachish V Seals 3:1; 5:1; 9:1; Jerusalem Bullae 4:1; 20:1; 51:1; Avigad *HB* 27, 31, 34, 38; Avigad Hecht Seals 1:1; 2:1; BCat 57; *[l]*, Prep + *-[m]h̊* = Inter. Pron; "why?;" L 6:9; *l*, Prep (+ *pny* = "before"); MHY 1:5; A 7:6 (+ *pnyk* = "before you [m.s.]")

ly 1st c.s. suf. prep.; "for me;" MHY 1:10, 1:11; L 3:10

lk 2nd m.s. suf. prep.; "to you (m.s.);" A 5:11; papMur 17a:1

lh 3rd m.s. suf. prep.; "him;" KEK 3:3; Aj 16:1

lhm 3rd m.pl. suf. prep.; "for them;" A 1:8; *lhm*, "to them;" A 2:8; A 4:3; *[l]hm* (?) A 40:8-9

lʾ

lʾ Neg. Adv; "not;" MHY 1:12; MHY 1:14; A 16:10; L 2:6; L 3:8; L 4:12; L 6:6; L 6:8; MO 2:3; (Inter. particle and Neg. Adv: *hlʾ*, "will (you) not ?, won't you ?"); *l[ʾ]*, L 6:14; *[lʾ]*, A 40:8, 12

LʾK

mlʾkh N; "work;" L 13:1

mlʾk̊ẙ PN N PS (?); "(DN) is my messenger," or "messenger (of DN);" A 97:1

LBB

lb N CS; "heart of;" L 3:6
lbbh N 3rd m.s. P.S. (+ *k*-: "according to"); "according to his heart;" Aj 16:1
[l]bh N 3rd m.s. PS; "his heart;" A 40:4

LWN

ln 3rd m.s. Perf V; "(he) is staying;" A 40:11

LḤM$_1$

mlḥ[mh] N; "war;" Aj 8:2-3

LḤM$_2$

lḥm N; "(loaves of) bread;" L 9:3; A 1:8-9; A 2:4; A 5:6; *lḥ[m]*, A 6:4
hlḥm DA N; "the bread;" A 3:7-8; A 12:6

LḤŠ

lḥš PN AP; "whisperer;" Av (*EI* 9) 14:1 (=Herr UD #2)

lkš

lkš LPN; "Lachish;" L 4:10

lmh

[lm]h̊ See *l*

LQḤ

lqḥt 2nd m.s. Perf V; "you (m.s.) are to take;" A 3:8; A 17:3-4
lqḥ 3rd m.s. Perf V; "he took;" MHY 1:9
lqḥh 3rd Perf V PS; "he has taken him;" L 4:6
yqḥ m.s. Imp V; "he took;" MHY 1:8
ylqḥ m.s. *Niph* Imp V; "he, it will be taken;"
q[ḥ] m.s. Impv V; "take!;" A 12:1
lqḥt I "(to) take;" L 3:18

LQŠ

lqš N; "late sowing;" Gezer 1:2

mʾb

mʾb LPN; "Moab;" L 8:3-4

Mʾ D

mʾd N; "very much;" A 111:3

Mʾ H

mʾh̊ N; "one hundred;" Tell el Qasile 1:2
m[ʾ]t N CS; "and one hundred (of);" Siloam 1:5-6
mʾtym̊ N; Card. (+ *b*-); "(for) two hundred;" Siloam 1:5

mʾwmh

mʾwm̊[h] Indef. Pron; "anything;" L 3:13

mʾs

mʾs PN; (possible reading *mʾp̊s̊); L Seal 2:2*

mʾš

mʾš See *ʾWŠ*

mʾt

mʾt See *ʾ*t_2

mʾtym

mʾtym̊ See *Mʾ H*

mbn

mbn See *BNH*

mbṭḥyhw

mbṭḥyhw See *BṬḤ*

mgdlyhw

m[gd]lyh[w] See *GDL*

mgn

mgn See *GNN*

MHR

mhrh N as Adv; "quickly;" A 12:3; A 17:5

mwṣʾ

hmwṣʾ See *YṢʾ*

mwqr

	mwqr	See *YQR*

MWT

	mt	3rd m.s. Perf V; "he died;" MO 2:2
	mrmwt	See *MRR*
	mrymwt	See *MRR*

MZH (?)

	mz	N (?); CS (?); "extract, essence of (?); L 30:1

MḤH

	ymḥh̊	3rd m.s. Imp V; "he will efface;" NY 1:1; *‹y›mḥh̊,* KBL 4:2

MḤR

	mḥr	N as Adv; "tomorrow;" A 2:6; L 9:8-9

mḥsyhw

	mḥ̊s̊yhw	See *ḤSH*

mḥsyw

	mḥsyw	See *ḤSH*

MY

	mym	N; "water;" A 111:8
	hmym	DA N; "the water;" Siloam 1:5; Ophel 3:2 *(IEJ* 32*)*

my

	my	Inter. Pron; "who ?;" L 2:3; L 5:3; L 6:2
	mykh	PN; Inter. Pron + Prep; "who is like (DN) ?;" Avigad *HB* 27
	mykyhẘ	PN IML; "who is like YH ?;" Herr 119:2
	mkʾ	PN inter. Pron and Prep; "who is like (DN)?;" Av (*IEJ* 25) 4:2
	mky	PN inter. Pron and Prep; "who is like (DN)?;" R 9:1 (Herr 111); A 110:2; HU 4
	mkyhw	PN; "who is like YH ?;" L 11:4; Jerusalem Jar 1:2; B/L (26) 10:2; Avigad *HB* 90, 92, 96-97; Jerusalem Bulla 32:2; *mkyh[w]*, Avigad HB 91; *mky[[hw]*, Avigad *HB* 94-95; Jerusalem Bulla 8:1; B/L (32) 6:1
	m̊k̊l̊	PN fem.; inter. Pron and Prep; "who is like (DN)?;" L 19:3

my᾽mn

my᾽mn See *YMN*

mykh

mykh See *my*

mykyhw

mykyhw See *my*

mym

mym See *MY*

myrb

myr[b] PN; Avigad *HB* 89

mk᾽

mk᾽ See *my*

mkbrm

mkbrm See *KBR*

mky

mky See *my*

mkyhw

mkyhw See *my*

mkl

mkl See *my*

MKR

mkr PN; "(DN) delivers;" B/L (32) 6:1

mktb

hmktb See *KTB*

mktbm

hmktbm See *KTB*

MLʾ		
	mlʾ	N CS; "and fullness of;" A 2:4-5
mlʾkh		
	mlʾkh	See *LʾK*
mlʾky		
	mlʾk̊ẙ	See *LʾK*
mldh		
	mldh	See *YLD*
MLK		
	mlk	N; "king;" A 24:3; Tell Qasile 1:1; L 5:10
	mlk	N CS; "the king of;" A 88:3; *mlk̊*, A 40:13; *m̊lk*, L 6:10-11
	hmlk	DA N; "the king;" L 3:19; L 6:4; A 24:17; MO 1:2; Avigad (*IEJ* 13) 1:3; Avigad (1978) Bulla of Jerahmeel 2:2; L V 5:2; B/L (29) 1:3; Herr 148: 2 *(bn hmlk)*; Herr 39:2 (Bet Zur) *(bn̊ hmlk)*; Av (*EI* 9) 15:2; Avigad *HB* 6 *(bn hmlk)*; Avigad *HB* 7 *([b]n hmlk)*; Avigad HB 5; Tell en Nasbeh 3:2 *(ʿbd hmlk)*; Avigad (1978) Lyre 1:2; Avigad *HB* 4 *(ʿbd hmlk)*; *h[ml]k*, Aj 14
	mlky	PN; "(DN is) my King;" Jerusalem Bulla 33:1
	mlkyhw	PN; "YH is my king;" A 24:14; A 39:2; A 40:3; Avigad Naar Seal 1:1; Av NN 3:1; R 19:1 (Herr 112); Avigad *HB* 98-99, 120; B/L (29) 2:1; *mlk[yhw]*, Beersheba graffito 3; Avigad *HB* 175; *ml[k]y[hw]*, Avigad *HB* 174; B/L (32) 5:1; B/L (32) 8:1
	ʾḥmlk	PN; "*MLK* is my brother;" See ʾ*Ḥ*
	ḥ̊nmlk̊	See *ḤNN*
	yhwmlk	PN; "YH is king;" Herr 116:2
	mqnmlk	PN; "Creature of *MLK*," Avigad *HB* 109
mlkyhw		
	mlkyhw	See *MLK*
mlkrm		
	mlkrm	See *MLK*

mn

mn Prep; “from;” Siloam 1:5; A 3:2; A 8:2; *m̊n̊*, A 26:2

m A 1:5, 9; A 5:2, 3, 13; A 6:2; A 9:2; A 16:4; A 17:4; A 24:12 (2x); A 25:3, 4; A 40:8; L 3:7, 18, 20; MHY 1:11; S 1:2; S 2:3; S 3:2; S 4:1; S 5:2; S 8:1; S 9:1; S 10:1; S 12:2; S 13:1, 4; S 14:1; S 16a:1; S 16b:1; S 17a:1; S 17b:1; S 18:1; S 19:2; S 21:2; S 22:1, 4; S 23:1, 3; S 25:3; S 26:2; S 27:1; S 28:1; S 29:1, 3; S 30:1; S 31a:1; S 32:1; S 33:1; S 35:1; S 37:1; S 38:1; S 39:1; S 42:1; S 44:1; S 45:1, 3; S 47:2; S 48:1, 3; S 50:1; S 63:2; Siloam 1:3; *m̊*, S 6:2; S 24:2; S 34:1; S 49:4; S 52:1; S 56:1; S 64:1; S 67:1; S 90:1; Siloam 1:3; *[m]*, A 25:2; A 40:9; L 6:13; S 7:1; S 24:1; S 26:1; S 31b:1; S 36:1; S 40:1; S 47:1; S 49:1

MNH

mnw 3rd m.pl. Perf V; “they counted;” Ophel b:2

ymnh 3rd m.s. Imp V; “he should measure, count out;” Sam C 1101:3

mnḥ

mnḥ See *NWḤ*

mnḥm

mnḥm See *NḤM*

mnr

mnr PN; B/L (32) 15:1

mnš

mnš PN; Avigad *HB* 103

mnšh

mnšh See *NŠH*

mnt

m̊n̊t PN (?); S 33:3

mspr

mspr See *SPR*

mʿdnh

	mʿdnh	See *ʿDN*

mʿn

	mʿ n	LPN (+ *m-*); "(from) *mʾn* (Biblical Maon);" A 25:4

mʿśy

	mʿśy	See *ʿŚH*

mʿśyh

	mʿ̊yh	See *ʾŚH*

mʿśyhw

	mʿśyhw	See *ʿŚH*

mʿśr

	hmʿ[śr]	See *ʿŚR*

MṢH

	mṣh	LPN N (?); Gib S.I. 1
	hmṣh	LPN DA; "the drainage area (?);" Avigad Wine Decanter 2:1

MṢR

	mṣr	PN; "Egyptian;" Avigad *HB* 108
	mṣ̊rym̊	LPN f. dual N; "Egypt;" A 88:3
	mṣrymh	LPN Loc. f. dual N; "toward Egypt;" L 3:16

mqdh

	mqdh	LPN (+ *m-*) "(from) Maqqedah;" HU 4

mqnyhw

	mqnyhw	See *QNH*

mqnmlk

	mqnmlk	See *QNH*

mrbʿl

	mrbʿl	See *MRR*

mrmwt

	mrmwt	See *MRR*

mrymwt

mrymwt See *MRR*

MRR

mrbʿl PN; "Baʿal has blessed," or "Baʿal is (my) master, lord;" S 2:7

mrmwt PN; "Mot has blessed," or "Mot is (my) master, lord;" A 50:1

mrymwt PN; B/L (32) 11:1

mśʾ

mśʾ See *NŚʾ*

mśʾt

mśʾt See *NŚʾ*

MŠH

ʾmš See *ʾmš*

mšlm

mšlm See *ŠLM*

mšmr

mšmr See *ŠMR*

mšʿn

mšʿn See *ŠʿN*

mtn

mtn See *NTN*

mtnyhw

mtnyhw See *NTN*

nʾ

nʾ Part of ent; "please;" L 6:5; *[nʾ]*; MHY 1:12; L 3:5

nʾhbt

nʾhbt See *ʾHB*

NBʾ

hnbʾ DA N; "the prophet;" L 3:20; L 16

nby

nby PN; gent.; "(biblical) Nobite;" Av NN 20:2; L V 6:3

NBL

nbl N CS; "a jar, pitcher of;" S 1:2; S 3:2; S 4:2; S 5:3; S 6:3; S 8:2; S 10:3; S 12:3; S 13:2; S 14:3; S 16a:2; S 16b:2; S 17a:2; S 17b:2; S 18:2; S 19:2; S 21:2; S 54:2; S 55:2; S 59:1; (+ *b*-: "in a jar of") S 53:2; S 72:2; *n̊b̊l*, S 89:1; *nb̊l*, Ophel 675b:7; *[n]bl*, S 9:3; S 15:2; *[n]bl̊* , S 11:1; *n̊b̊[l]*, Ophel 675b:9; *[nbl]*, S 7:2; S 20:2; S 73:2

nbš

nbškm See *NPŠ*

ngb

ngb LPN (?) PN (?) N; "Negeb, south;" Gib S.I. 3; Beth-Shemesh 9:2

ngby PN; "southerner;" Avigad *HB* 120

rmt ngb LPN; "south;" A 24:16; rmt *ng̊[b]*, A 24:13

NGD

h̊g[d] I *(lh̊g[d]); Hiph;* "To info[rm];" L 3:1-2

hgd 3rd m.s. *Hophal* Perf V; "it has been reported, was reported;" L 3:13

NDB

n̊d̊byh PN; "YH has been generous, noble;" L V Shekel Weight 1:1-2

n̊dbẙhw PN; "YH has been generous, noble;" A 39:3

yhwndb PN; "YH has been generous, noble;" Av NN 13:2

NWḤ

mnḥ *PN N;* "rest, repose;" Herr 110:2; See Bordreuil, *Syria* 52 (1975), "that which is offered."

nwy

nwy *PN; HU 3*

NWP

[mnpm]	3rd m. pl. *Hiph;* ["wielding"]; Siloam 1:1
š̊ʿnp	PN (Aramaic Name); "*Š̊ʿ* is exalted;" Av NN 20:1

NWR

nrʾ	PN N; "(DN is my) light;" Gib 22, 24, 32, 37, 38, 45, 48, 50, 57; RR Seal 1:1; *nr̊ʾ*, Gib 39; *n[rʾ]*, Gib 40, 42; *[n]rʾ*, Gib 46, 49; *‹n›rʾ*, Gib 47; *n̊r̊ʾ*, En Gedi 2:1
nryhw	PN; "YH is my light;" A 31:4; L 1:5; Av (1978) Seal 1:2; Av (1978) Baruk Seal 1:2; Herr 15:2; B/L (26) 2:2; B/L (32) 2:1; Hest. 65:2; Beersheba graffito 2:1; Avigad *HB* 9, 15, 50, 125-28; Jerusalem Bulla 36:1; *nrẙhw*, Herr 44:2; *[n]ryhw*, L 26:1; *n̊ryhẘ* L V 3:1; *n̊r̊ẙhw*, Avigad HB 122; *n̊r̊yhẘ*, Lemaire Seal 4:1; *nry[hw]*, Avigad *HB* 7

NḤL

hnḥlh	DA f.s. N; "the property, inheritance;" MO 2:4-5

NḤM

nḥm	PN PP; "comforted;" R 18:2 (Herr 126); A 16:10; A 17:1, 8; B/L (26) 15:2; Gib S.I. 2; L V 2:1; L Seal 12:1 (7x); Av (*EI* 9) 9:1; Jerusalem Seal 6:1; Avigad HB 77, 153, 176, 202; Jerusalem Bulla 51:1; *n̊ḥ̊m̊*, Herr 118:1; *n̊ḥm*, L Seal 16:1; *[n]ḥm*, TBM sherd 6; *n[ḥ]m*, Avigad *HB* 121
nḥmyhw	PN; "YH comforts;" A 31:3; A 40:1-2; Herr 119:1; *nḥmẙhẘ*, A 59:3; *[n]ḥmyhẘ*, A 11:5; *nḥmẙh̊[w]*, A 36:2; *nḥmy[hw]*, Avigad *HB* 61
mnḥm	PN AP; "(DN) is a consoler (by giving a child)" (See Coogan, p. 78), "comforter;" A 72:1; Hest. 34:2; B/L (26)6:2; RR Seal; Jerusalem Seal 4:1; Hest. 78:1; Avigad *HB* 101, 103-104, 152; Avigad Hecht Seal 9:2; Beth-Shemesh 5:1; *mn[ḥm]*, Sam C 1012:5; Avigad *HB* 102; *mnḥ̊m*, Herr 53:1; *mnḥ̊m̊*, Avigad HB 100; *mnḥ̊[m]*, Hest. 46:1; *m[n]ḥm*, HU 1
tnḥm	PN N; "consolation;" A 39:4; Gib S.I. 3, 8; L Seal 10:1 (7x); Beth-Shemesh 9:1-2; *tnḥ̊[m]*, Avigad *HB* 168

nḥnw

nḥnw	1st c.pl. subject pronoun; "we;" L 4:10-11

NṬH

hṭh̊ 3rd m.s. *Hiph* Perf V; "(he) has applied himself, given his attention to;" A 40:4

NKH

hkw 3rd m.pl. *Hiph* Perf V; "they struck;" Siloam 1:4

nmṭr

n̊m̊ṭ̊r PN; papMur 17b:1

nmš

nmš PN N; "little mammal, ichneumon;" S 56:2; Tel Amal; Avigad *HB* 122

nmšr

nmšr PN; Avigad *HB* 123-24

NSH

nsh 3rd m.s. *Piel* Perf V; "has tried;" L 3:9

nʿh

nʿh LPN N *(+ m-);* "(from*)* *nʿh;"* S 50:1; *n̊ʿh̊,* S 64:1*;* *n̊ʿh,* S 52:1

nʿmh

nʿmh LPN; MO 2:7

NʿR

nʿr N; "steward, attendant, squire;" A 15:4; A 110:1, 2

nʿr N CS; "steward of;" Avigad Naar Seal 1:1; TBM 1:1; Avigad Naar Seal 2:2; *[n]ʿr,* Beth-Shemesh 2:2; *[nʿ]r,* RR *8:2*

NPŠ

nbškm N PS *(+ b-);* "(for) your (m.pl.) lives;" A 24:18

NṢḤ

nṣḥ N *(+ l-);* "ever;" L 3:10

NṢL

hṣlyhw PN; “YH has delivered,” or “save, O YH!;” Gib S.I. 2; L 1:1; Jerusalem Seal 6:2; Hest. 59:1-2; Hest. 60:1; Avigad *HB* 49, 128*;*

hṣ̊lyh̊ẘ L Seal 16:2; *hṣl[yhw],* Avigad *HB* 168*; [hṣ]lyhw,* Avigad *HB* 197

NQB

hnqbh *Niph* I*;* PS; “it's being tunneled through;” Siloam 1:1 (2x); Siloam 1:3-4

hn[qb] *Niph* I *(lhn[qb]);* “(to) be tunneled, cut through;” Siloam 1:2

NQH

nqty 1st c.s. *Niph* Perf V; “I am innocent, clean;” MHY 1:11

nqh m.s. *Piel* Impv V; “absolve!;” KBL 2:1; *n̊q̊h̊,* KBL 2:1

nrʾ

nrʾ See *NWR*

nryhw

nryhw See *NWR*

NŚʾ

mśʾ N CS; “a (mule-)load of;” A 3:4

mśʾt N; “(fire-)signals;” L 4:10

NŠH

mnšh PN AP; “may (DN) cause to forget;” Av (*IEJ* 13) 1:2; B/L (32) 5:1

NTN

[ntt]y 1st c.s. Perf V*; “I would give (?);”* A 40:12-13

nttm 1st c.s. Perf V; PS; “I sent them (m.pl.);” A 40:10

wntt Conj 2nd m.s. Perf V; “and you give (it);” A 2:7-8

wntth Conj 2nd m.s. Perf V; “may you entrust, give;” MO 2:4; *ntth,* “you have given (it);” MO 2:7

ntn 3rd m.s. Perf V; “he gave, has given;” L 4:11; A 17:8; A 28:2 (or Inf. Abs.); *[ntn],* A 40:8

ʾtnnhw 1st c.s. Imp V; energic nun; 3rd m.s. PS; “I will give it;” L 3:12

NTN (continued)

ttn — 2nd m.s. Imp V; formal Impv V; "you shall give;" A 1:10; A 18:6; *[wtt]n,* Conj 2nd m.s. Imp V; "you shall give;" MHY 1:13

ẙtnw — 3rd m.pl. Imp V; "they will give;" Aj 7:2

tn — m.s. Impv V; "give!;" A 3:2; A 4:1, 3; A 18:4; A 60:4; A 71:1; L 9:3; wtn, Conj m.s. Impv V; "and give!;" A 12:2, 5

ltt — I; "to give, contribute;" MO 1:2

ntn — Inf. Abs.; "give!;" A 1:2; A 2:1; A 7:2; A 8:1; A 11:2; *[ntn],* A 10:2; A 14:2

ntn — PN; "(DN) has given;" Avigad HB 3, 129-130; B/L (29) 6:1; B/L (32) 4:1

ntnyhw — PN; "YH has given;" A 56:1-2; KEK 1:2; KEK 2:1; Avigad Hecht Seal 11:2; Herr 120:1; Herr 121: 1; *n̊t̊n̊ẙ[hw],* A 23:9

ywntn — PN; "YH has given;" S 45:3

ʾlntn — PN; "God has given;" See *ʾLH*

mtn — PN N; "gift (of DN)," or "(DN is giver of) gift(s);" B/L (26) 16:1; B/L (29), 2:2; B/L (32) 2:1; Avigad *HB* 52, 74, 113, 115-118, 134; Avigad Hecht Seal 6:2; *m̊tn*, Avigad *HB* 114

mtnyh — PN; "gift of YH;" BCat 57

mtnyhw — PN; "gift of YH," or "YH (is giver of) gift(s);" Jerusalem Seal 1:1; Avigad *HB* 21, 119; *m̊tnyh̊w*, L 1:5; B/L (26) 9:2; B/L (26) 11:2; *mtnyh[w],* Tell en Nasbeh 2:2

sʾl

sʾl — PN; Avigad *HB* 131

SBB

tsbt — N CS *(+ b -);* "(in) the course of;" L 4:9

hsbt — 2nd m.s. *Hiph* Perf V; "make the rounds, send (them) out;" A 2:5-6

SWS

hsws — DA N IML; "the horse;" A 111:5

-swsh — EOLPN *[ḥṣr] swsh*; N IML; "mare;" A 32:1

sylʾ

sylʾ — PN N IML; "weight, payment (?);" Herr 122:1; Jerusalem Bulla 35:1

sl̉

    sl̉   PN; Avigad *HB* 132

smdr

    smdr   N; "blossom of grape;" Hazor 7:1

SMK

    smk   PN Perf V; "(DN) supports, protects, sustains;" Beth-Shemesh 8:2; L Seal 3:1; Av (*EI* 9) 5:2; Herr 80:2; Hest. 83:1; *[s]mk̊*, B/L (29) 8:1; *s[mk]*, Avigad HB 136

    s[m]ky   PN N (?); Perf V (?); "(DN) is my support;" L Seal 21:1

    smkyh   PN; "YH has sustained;" Jerusalem Bulla 7:2; smkyh̊ ; Lemaire Seal 2:1

    smkyhw PN; "YH has sustained;" L 4:6; L 22:5; Avigad *HB* 119; *smkyhw*, L 11:5; *smkyh̊w*, Av (*EI* 9) 4:2; *smk[yh]w*, Hest. 96:2;   *smk[yhw]*, L V Ost. 1:5; *smk[yhw]*, L 13:2; *[s]mky[hw]*, Avigad *HB 93*

    smk[yw] PN; "YH supports;" Sam C 1012:3

    ʾlsmk   PN; "God supports;" See ʾLH

SʿD

    s̊ʿdyh   PN; "YH supports;" Lemaire Seal 3:1

    sʿdyhw   PN; "YH supports;" B/L 32 (1982) Seal 8:1; *sʿd[yhw]*, Avigad *HB* 133

SʿR

    sʿryhw   PN; "YH rages;" A 31:4; (could be *sʿdyhw*)

SPR

    spr   N; "a letter;" L 3:9, 10; *sp̊r,* L 3:11; *sp̊r̊,* L 7:3,5; *[s]pr,* L 12:2

    spr   N CS; "the letter of;" L 3:19; *[sp]r,* L 6:3-4; L 16:4; *spr,* N (+ *l-*); "(to the) letter;" L 3:5

    [h]spr   DA N; "the letter;" L 18:1

    hspr   DA N AP; "the scribe;" Herr 110:3; Avigad (1978) Baruk Seal 1:3

    spr   LPN N (+ *m-*); "(from) *spr*;" S 16a:1-2; S 16:1-2; S 29:3

    spry   N CS; "the letters of;" L 6:4

    hsprm   DA N; "the letters;" L 5:6-7; *hs̊[prm]*, L 5:5; *hspr[m]*, L 6:14

    spr̥   Impv V; "and calculate the amount of;" A 3:6-7

    msp̊r̊   PN; Avigad *HB* 106

STR

ywstr	PN; "YH protects, hides;" BCat 55

ʿBD

ʿbd	N; "servant;" A 24:6
ʿbd	N CS; "servant of;" L 3:19; Megiddo Seal 1:2; Ushna Seal 1:1-2; Hest. (1974) Hebron 1:3; Tell en Nasbeh 3:2; Herr 4:2-3; BCat 40; Avigad *HB* 5 *(ʿbd hmlk)*; *[ʿ]bd*, Avigad *HB* 4 *([ʿ]bd hmlk)*
ʿbdk	N 2nd m.s. PS; "your (m.s.) servant;" L 2:3-4; L 3:1, 5, 7-8; L 3:13; L 4:3, 7; L 5:3, 4-5, 6, 9; L 6:3, 13-14; L 9:5; L 12:7; MHY 1:2, 3, 4, 8, 9; *ʿbd̊ [k]*, L 3:7; L 17:1; *ʿbd[k]*, L 12:4; *[ʿ]b[dk]*, L 18:1; *[ʿ]bdk*, A 40:4; MHY 1:6, 14; *ʿb‹d›k*, L 3:21; *ʿb̊[dk]*, MHY 1:13; *ʿ[b]dk*, N PS; "your servant;" L 3:6; *ʿ̊[bdk]*, L 6:15
ʿbdh	N 3rd m.s. PS; "His servant;" MHY 1:2; *ʿ[ʿ]bdh*, L 2:5
hʿbdh	DA N; "the work;" A 5:14
ʿb̊d̊	PN N CS; "servant of (DN);" A 72:5
ʿbdʾ	PN; "servant of (DN);" Avigad *HB* 65; S 57:1
ʿbdy	PN N; "servant of (DN);" Avigad 10:2; L Seal 12:2 (7x); L Seal 13:1-2
ʿ̊b̊d̊yh	PN; "servant of YH;" Beersheba Seal 4:1
ʿbdyhw	PN; "servant of YH;" A 10:4; Herr 99:2; Herr 121:2 (es-Soda); Herr 124:1; Herr 145:1; Hest. 74:1; Avigad *HB* 134; *ʿbdy[hw]*, A 27:2; *ʿb̊d̊[yhw]* (?), A 49:8; *[ʿ]bdẙhw*, MHY 3:7
ʿbdyw	PN; "servant of YH;" S 50:2; Aj 13

ʿbdh

hʿbdh	See *ʿBD*

ʿBR

ʿbr	N; "yield, produce;" A 31:10
hʿbr	DA N; "the yield, produce;" A 111:6
yʿbr	3rd m.s. Imp V; "it passes, will pass;" A 5:12-13

ʿGL

ʿglẙẘ	PN; "calf of YH;" S 41:1

ʿd

hʿ[d]	See *ʿWD*

ʿd		
	ʿd	Prep; "until;" L 18:1; A 8:3; *ʿd̊*, A 7:4
ʿDD		
	ʿdd	See *ʿWD*
ʿDH		
	ʿdh	PN Perf V; "(DN) has adorned;" Aj 2
	ʿdyhw	PN; "YH has adorned;" A 58:1; Hest. 56:2; B/L (26) 14:1; Beth-Shemesh 4:1
ʿDN		
	ʿdnh	PN N; "delight;" Aj 13
	mʿdnh	PN fem; N; "delight;" Av (1978) Lyre 1:1
ʿWD		
	hʿ[d]	DA N; "the witness;" L 4:8
	ʿwd	N CS; "yet, still, anymore;" A 2:7; *ʿẘd̊*, "yet, (there) remains;" A 21:8
	ʿwd	*Adv (+ b-);* "while, yet;" Siloam 1:1, 2
	ʿwd	N CS (+ *m-*); "(from) what is left of;" A 1:5; A 5:3
	hʿyd	*Hiph* I *(lhʾyd) ;* IML; "(to) warn;" A 24:18
	ʿdd	PN AP; "restorer, (DN) restores;" Hest. 94:2
ʿWP		
	ʿpy	PN; Avigad *HB* 88
	ʿwpy	PN N (?); IML; KEK 1:1; *ʿwp̊ẙ*, KEK 2:1
ʿWṢ		
	ʿ̊ṣ̊bʿl	PN; "counsel, O Baʾal!;" MHY 6:1; reading uncertain; cf. Lemaire (1977), pp. 268-69
ʿWŠ	*ʿ̊ḥ̊ʿ̊š*	PN; "my brother (See *ʾḤ*) has aided, saved;" L Seal 7:2
	ʾlʿš	PN; "God has aided, saved;" Av NN 17:2
ʿZZ		
	ʿzʾ	PN N; "(DN) is (my) strength;" S 1:5; Hest. 91:2; Av (*IEJ* 4) 6:1; BCat 50; *ʿ̊z̊ʾ̊* (?), A 72:4
	ʿzyhw	PN; "YH is (my) strength;" Hest. 65:1; *ʿzẙhw*, A 20:2; *ʿzyh[w]*, Avigad *HB* 177
	ʿzyw	PN; "YH is (my) strength;" Herr 4:3; BCat 40
	ʿz[yhw]	PN; "(DN) is (my) strength;" TBM sherd 3

ʿZZ (continued)

yhwʿz PN; "YH is mighty;" A 31:3; Avigad *HB* 74; *yhwʿz̊*, R 12:1 (Herr 47: Safi); *[yh]ẘʿ̊z̊*, A 49:7

ʿzqh

ʿzqh LPN; "Azeqah;" L 4:12-13

ʿZR

ʿzr PN N; "(DN is my) help;" Aj 12:1; A 22:2; A 23:8; B/L (26) 12:2; Beth-Shemesh 3:2; Herr 144:2; A 51:2; A 58:3; KEM 1:2; B/L (26) 11:1; Av NN 17:1; Avigad HB 57, 135; Avigad Hecht Seals 7:1; 12:1; Jerusalem Bulla 13:2; Sam C 1142; *ʿz[r]*, L 19:1

ʿzryh PN; "YH helps;" R 18:1 (Herr 126)

ʾbʿzr PN; "my father is help;" S 13:1-2; S 28:1

ʿzryhw PN; "YH helps;" Gib 1, 2; Jerusalem Seal 1:2; En Gedi 1:2; L Seal 1:1-2; Herr 93:2; Herr 128:1; B/L (26) 4:1; Avigad *HB* 63, 137; Jerusalem Bulla 27:1; Lemaire Seal 5:1; *ʿ[zryhw]*, Gib 3; *[ʿ]zryh̊[w]*, Gib 4; Gib S.I. 4; *[ʿ]zryhw*, Gib 5; A 16:6; Herr 65:2 (Tell el-Judeideh); *ʿzr[yhw]*, Gib 6; *ʿz[ryhw]*, Gib 7; *[ʾ]zr[y]hẘ*, L 18:2

ʿzryw PN; "YH helps;" Av (1966) 1:1-2

ʿzrqm PN; "(my) help has arisen;" Avigad *HB* 138-39; Jerusalem Bulla 32:1

ʾbʿzr PN; "my father is help;" S 13:1-2; S 28:1

yhwʿzr PN; "YH is my help;" Herr 99:1; Hest. 61:1

ywʿzr PN; " YH is my help;" papMur 17b:4

ʿḥʿš

ʿḥʿš See *ʾḤ; ʿWŠ*

ʿYN

[ʾ]yn̊ gdy LPN; "spring of young goat(s);" A 71:3

ʿYR$_1$

hʿyr DA N; "the city;" A 24:16-17

hʿyrh DA Loc. N; "to the city;" L 4:7

ʿr N; "city;" (*lśr ʿr*); Aj 3:1; Aj 4:1; Aj 5:1; Aj 6:1

hʿr DA N; "the city;" (*śr hʿr*); Avigad (1976) 3:1; *h̊ʿr*, (*śr h̊ʿr*); Barkay (1977) 1:1 (=Avigad 1978)

ʿYR$_2$

ʿyrʾ PN N; “male ass;” Aj 1

ʿkbr

ʿkbr PN N; “mouse;” Av (*IEJ* 13) 2:1; Herr 94:2; *ʿkb[r]*, Avigad *HB* 140

ʿl

ʿl Prep; “over;” Silwan 2:1; Avigad *HB* 1-2 (*ʾšr ʿl hbyt*); Siloam 1:6; L Seal 6:2; *[ʿ]l*, Avigad Hecht Seal 1:2; (*ʾšr [ʿl]);* Avigad *HB* 3 (*ʾšr [ʿl] byt*); *ʿl*, “on (the door);” L 4:3; *ʿl*, “against;” Siloam 1:4; ʿl, “concerning, about;” L 4:5; *ʿl*, “to;” A 24:15;

ʿLH

yʿlhw 3rd m.s. *Hiph* Imp V; “he has taken him up;” L 4:6-7

ʿlynm m.pl. Adj (+ *m-*); “(from) Upper (LPN);” A 25:3

ʿlyhw PN; “YH goes up, ascends;” Avigad *HB* 35, 141-42

ʿm

ʿm Prep; “with;” Aj 15:8; A 3:4

ʿmy 1st c.s. suf. prep; “with me;” MO 2:4

ʿmdyhw Prep; fem. PN; “YH is with me;” HU 2; Herr 143:1; *ʿmdyh[w]*, Avigad *HB* 93

ʿML

ʿml̊ [yhw] PN; “(DN) toils;” Avigad Hecht Seals 3:2; 4:2; Avigad *HB* 195

ʿMM

ʿm m.s. N (+ *l-*); “(to the) people, nation;” Ophel 675b:3

ʾdnʿm PN; S 9:2; S 10:2-3; S 19:4; *[ʾd]n̊ʿm*, S 11:2; *[ʾdn]ʿm*, S 8:2

ʿMS

ʿms PN; “(DN) has carried (= protected) (in his arms);” Lemaire Seal 2:2

ʿmsyhw PN; MO 2:5-6

ʿMQ

ʿm̊q N CS (+ *b-*); “(in) the valley of;” Ophel 1:2, 3

ᶜnmś

    ᶜnmś   PN Egyptian; S 24:2

ᶜNH₁

    yᶜnw   3rd m.pl Imp V; "they will testify;" MHY 1:10, 11

ᶜNH₂

    hᶜt   DA N; "the season, time;" L 6:2
    ᶜt   AOT; "now, even now;" L 2:3 (2x); L 4:1, 2; A 1:1-2; A 2:1; A 3:1; A 5:1-2; A 7:1-2; A 8:1; A 10:1; A 11:2; A 16:3; A 17:1; A 18:3; A 21:3; A 40:4; papMur 17a:2; MO 2:1; *[ᶜt]*, A 6:1; A 14:1; L 3:4; L 5:2, 3, 6; L 6:8; L 8:2; L 9:3

ᶜnym

    ᶜ̊nym   LPN; A 25:2

ᶜNN

    ᶜnnyhẘ   PN; "YH appears, has presented himself (?);" L V 2:2

ᶜpy

    ᶜpy   See *ᶜWP*

ᶜṣbᶜl

    ᶜṣbᶜl   See *ᶜWṢ*

ᶜṢD

    ᶜṣd   N CS; "cutting of; hoeing;" Gezer 1:3

ᶜṢM

    ᶜ̊ṣm[t]   N CS; "the bones of;" Silwan 2:2
    [ᶜṣmtw]   N PS; "his bones;" Silwan 2:2

ᶜr

    ᶜr   See *ᶜYR*

ᶜRB

    hᶜrb   DA N; "the evening;" L 18:1

ʿrd

ʿrd	LPN N; "Arad; wild ass;" A 99:1 (3x); 3 (written *drʿ*), 4; A 24:12 (+ *m-* = "from Arad"); *ʿ̊rd*, A 48:1; *ʿr[d]*, A 99:2 (written *[d]rʿ*); *ʿ[rd]*, A 99:1

ʿŚH

ʿśh	3rd m.s. Perf V; "has done, did;" A 21:3; L 4:3
[ʿśth]	3rd f.s. Perf V; "she/it has done;" A 40:15
nʿśh	1st c.pl. Imp V; "we shall do, we are to do;" L 9:8
tʿśw	2nd m.pl. Imp V; "you (m.pl.) do, will do;" L 6:9
ʿśt	I (*lʿśt*); "to make;" A 1:8; L 13:1; [*ʿśt*] ([*lʿśt*]) A 5:6
yʿś	PN m.s. Imp V; Jussive V; "may (DN) make, do;" S 48:3
mʿśy	PN N; "work (of DN);" A 22:4
mʿśyh	PN; "deed of YH, work of YH;" Hest. 77:1; *mʿśyh̊*, Av (*EI* 9) 7:2
mʿśyhw	PN; "word, deed of YH;" Herr 149:2; Seal of Maʿaseyahu 1:1; Jerusalem Bulla 48:2: *[mʿ]śyhw*, Avigad *HB* 87; *mʿśʿy[hw]*, Avigad *HB* 105 (2x), 107
ʿśy	PN Perf V; "(DN) has made, done;" Av (*EI* 9) 8:1
ywʿśh	PN; "YH has done;" Avigad 9:1; Aj 14:1
ʿśyhw	PN; "YH has done, made;" L Seal 5:2; Herr 100:2; L 22:7; L V Ost. 1:7; B/L (26) 7:1; Avigad *HB* 32, 34
ʿśyw	PN; "YH has done, made;" Herr 131:1

ʿŚR

ʿśr	*Piel* I *(lʿśr)*; "(to) give a tenth, tithe;" Ophel b:3
ʿśr	Card; "ten (?);" Ophel 2:2 (could be N "riches" (?))
hšl̊šh ʿ̊śr	Card (with DA) "the thirteenth (day);" A 8:3
hšm̊nh̊ ʿśr	Card (with DA); "the eighteenth (day);" A 8:4
ʿśry	m.s. Ordn (+ *b-*); "(in the) tenth (month);" A 7:7-8; *ʿśr̊y*, m.s. Ordn (+ *l-*); "(of the) tenth (month);" A 7:3
hʿśrt	DA f.s. Ordn; "the tenth (year);" S 1:1; S 2:1-2; S 3:1; S 13:1; 16a:1; S 16b:1; S 17:1; S 18:1; S 19:1; S 21:1; S 51:1; S 53:1; S 54:1; S 55:1; S 72:1; *[hʿ]śrt*, S 17b:1; *hʿ̊[śrt]*, S 20:1; *[hʿśrt]*, S 73:1
hmʿ[śr]	DA N; "the tithe (?);" A 5:11-12

ʿŠN

ʿšn	m.s. Adj (?); N (?); "smoking vintage, fermented, red;" L 25:1

ʿŠR

h̊ʿšr DA N; "the rich one, notable;" KEK 3:1

ʿšrt LPN (+ *m-*); "(from) *ʾsrt*;" S 42:4

ʿt

ʿt See *ʿNH*$_2$

pgy

pgy PN; Avigad *HB* 104

PGŠ

pgš 3rd m.s. Perf V (?); "he met;" A 37:2

PDH

pdy PN Perf V; "(DN) has ransomed;" B/L (26) 18:2; *[pd]y* (?), A 55:2; B/L (29) 8:1

pdyhw PN; "YH has ransomed;" A 49:15; B/L (26) 5:2; Av (*EI* 9) 1:1; Avigad *HB* 67, 99, 130, 137, 178; *p̊d̊yhw*, Avigad *HB* 12; B/L (32) 1:2; B/L (32) 7:2

ph

[p]h̊ Loc. Adv; "here;" Silwan 2:1

phʾ

phʾ PN; S 689

PLṬ

plṭh PN; "(DN) has delivered him (?);" BCat 52

plṭyhw PN; "YH has delivered;" B/L (26) 21:1; Avigad *HB* 86, 94, 114, 135, 143-49; Jerusalem Bulla 23:2; *plḥyh̊ẘ*, B/L (29) 5:2; *[p]lṭyhw*, Avigad *HB* 115; *plṭyh[w]*, Avigad *HB* 116; *[p]lṭy[hw]*, Avigad *HB* 116.

pn

pn Conj; "lest;" A 24:16, 20

pn

pn See *PNH*

pnʾl

p̊n̊ʾl See *PNH*

PNH

pnyw	m. N + 3rd m.s. PS; "his face;" KH 2:9
pny	Prep (+ *l*-); "before;" MHY 1:5
pnyk	Prep PS (+ *l*-); "before you (m.s.);" A 7:6
pn	PN; Perf V (?); Impv V (?); (DN) has turned," or "turn, (O DN)!;" S Seal 19:1
p̊n̊ʾl	PN; "turn, O God!;" Beersheba 1:2

PSḤ

psḥ	PN N; "lame one;" Av (*EI* 9) 1:2

ppy

ppy	PN Egyptian; A 72:2

PQD

hbqydm	*Hiph* Perf V PS; p/b interchange; "he is to hand them over;" A 24:14-15
mpqd	N; "roll call, muster;" Tel Ira (*PEQ* 83 (1983)) 1:1

PQḤ

hpqḥ	m.s. *Hiph* Impv V (?); "open!;" L 3:4
pqḥ	PN N; "opening;" L 19:2; Herr 56:1 (Nablus); Hazor 7

pqll

pqll	PN; Herr 90:2

PRʾ

prʾn	EOLPN (*gt prʾn*); "wild asses;" S 14:1-2

PRḤ

p̊r̊ḥ̊	EOLPN (*g̊t̊ p̊r̊ḥ̊*); "flower(s);" Ophel c:6

PRʿ

yprʿyw	PN; "may YH let free;" R 21:1-4 (Herr 69)

prʿš

prʿš	PN N; "flea;" L V 3:2

prpr

prpr	PN; Avigad *HB* 138

pšḥr

pšḥr PN Egyptian; “the son of Horus;” A 54:1; R 7:2 (Herr 36); Avigad *HB* 151-52; *[pš]ḥr*, Avigad *HB* 183

PŠT

pšt N; “flax;” Gezer 1:3

PTḤ

ypt̊ḥ̊ 3rd m.s. Imp V; “will open;” Silwan 2:3; *yp̊[tḥ]*, Silwan 3:2

ptḥ PN; “(DN) opens;” Avigad *HB* 153

ṢBʾ

hṣbʾ DA N; “the army;” L 3:14

ṢBH

ṣby PN N m.s., “gazelle;” papMur 17b:2

ṣby

ṣby See *ṢBH*

ṣbly

ṣbly PN; Hest. 82:2

ṢBR

ṣbr V; “accumulate;” Ophel 2:1

ṢDQ

ṣdq PN; Adj; “just, righteous;” Beth-Shemesh 8:1; A 93:1; Av (*IEJ* 25) 4:1

[ṣd]qyhẘ PN; “YH is righteousness;” Ophel 1:4; *ṣ̊[d]qẙ[hw]*, L 11:6

ṣdqʾ PN; “(DN) is righteous;” Avigad *HB* 139

ṢWH

ṣwtny 2nd m.s. Perf V; 1st c.s. PS; “you gave me orders;” A 18:7-8

ṣwk 3rd m.s.Perf V; 2nd m.s. PS; “he orders you;” A 3:2-3, MO 1:1

ṢWR

ṣr — N (+ *b*-); "(in the) rock, cliff;" Siloam 1:3
hṣr — DA N; "the rock;" Siloam 1:6; *hṣ[r]*, Silwan 1:1
ʾlṣr — PN; "God is (my) rock;" Beersheba 2:1

ṢYD

ṣyd — PN N; "hunter, fisher;" A 52:1

ṢMD

ṣmd — N CS; "couple, pair of;" A 3:4-5

ṢMḤ

ṣmḥ — PN N; "sprout, growth;" A 49:11

ṢMQ

ṣmqm — m.pl. N; "raisons;" L 30:1

ṢPN

ṣpn — PN Perf V; "(DN) has hidden, treasured up;" L Seal 1:1; 8:2; Hest. 90:1; Jerusalem Seal 3:1; B/L (26) 2:1; Jerusalem, Bulla 39:1; *ṣpn*, Beth-Shemesh 3:1
ṣpnyh — PN; "YH has hidden, treasured up;" BCat 57
ṣpnyhw — PN; "YH has hidden, treasured up;" L V 6:2; 7:2; Herr 135:2; Avigad *HB* 53, 155; *ṣpny[hw]*, Avigad *HB* 54; *ṣpny[hw]*, L Seal 22:2; *ṣpnyhw*, L Seal 21:2; *ṣp[n]yhw*, Ophel 1:3; *ṣpn[yhw]*, Avigad *HB* 154; *ṣpn[yhw]* (?), A 59:5

ṣr

ṣr — See *ṢWR*

ṢRR$_1$

ṣrr[t] — 2nd m.s. Perf V; "you are to bind;" A 3:5

ṢRR$_2$

ṣryh — N; 3rd m.s. PS (?) (+ *m*-); "(from) his enemies;" KEK 3:3

QBR

qbrt — N CS; "the tomb of;" Silwan 3:1; *[qbrt]*, Silwan 2:1

qdbš

q[d]bš — PN Egyptian; "Bes has created;" S 1:5

QDŠ

qdš N; “holy (vessel);” A 104:1; Beersheba Graffito l; Hazor bowl stratum Va

qdš N CS; “holy (vessel) of,” Jerusalem pomegranate inscription (=Lemaire “grenade” inscription; RB 88, no. 2 (1981):236-39); *q‹d›š*, A 102, 103.

QWL

ql N CS; “the voice of;” Siloam 1:2

qwlyhw PN; “pay homage to YH!;” BCat 53

qlyhw PN; “pay homage to YH!;” Herr 133:1

qlyẘ PN; “pay homage of YH!;” Sam C 1012:2

QWM

qm m.s. Impv V; “arise!;” L 13:1

ʾḥyqm PN; “my brother has arisen;” A 31:5

ʾḥqm PN; “(my) brother has arisen;” Av (*IEJ* 13) Seal 2:2

ʾlyqm PN; “God sets up, establishes;” Hest. 91:1; RR Seal 8:1; TBM 1:1; Beth-Shemesh 2:1; *ʾlyqm̊*, Av (*EI* 9) 7:1; Jerusalem Bulla 29:1

yhwqm PN; “YH rises, gets up,” or “YH has arisen;” Av NN 12:1; 13:1; Avigad *HB* 12; *yhwq[m]*, Avigad *HB* 171

ywqm̊ PN; “YH rises; gets up,” or “YH has arisen;” Herr l31:2

yqmyhw PN; “YH establishes;” Gezer (?) Seal 1:2; A 39:1; B/L (26) 8:2; Herr 105:1-2; Avigad *HB* 11, 75, 77; *yqmẙh̊w*, A 59:2; *yqmyh[w]*, Avigad HB 172; *yqm[yhw]*, A 74:3; S 80:2

ʿzrqm PN; Avigad *HB* 138, 139; Jerusalem Bulla 32:1

qws

q̊ws EOPN -*q̊ws*, A 26:3

qwsʾ

qwsʾ PN; D elem; Aroer 1 (Edomite Seal according to Herr)

qwsʿnl

[qw]sʿnl PN; A 12:3

qynh

qynh LPN IMP (+ *m*-); “(from) *qynh*;” A 24:12

QYṢ

qṣ N; "summer fruit;" Gezer 1:7

ql

ql See *QWL*

QMḤ

qmḥ N; "meal, flour;" A 1:7; A 12:2; *qm[ḥ],* A 5:5-6; *qm‹ḥ›,* A 8:2; A 112:1,2

hqmḥ DA N; "the meal;" A 1:5; A 5:3

QNH

qn m.s. AP CS (?); "the acquirer, owner of;" Jerusalem Jar 1:3

mqnyhw PN; "creature of YH;" Herr 116:1; Avigad *HB* 154; *mq̊nyhw,* A 60:4; *m̊qnyhw,* A 72:1

qny PN; "YH acquires, owns;" Lemaire jar inscription (*Maarav* 2 (1980):161)

qnyw PN; "YH acquires, owns;" Herr 60:1 (Jerusalem)

qṣ

qṣd See *QYṢ*

QṢH

qṣh LPN (+ *m*-); "(from) *qṣh*;" S 5:2; S 6:2; q[ṣh], S 4:1-2; *[qṣ]h,* S 7:1-2

QSR

qṣr N; "(the) harvest;" Gezer 1:5; MHY 1:6

qṣr N CS; "the harvest of;" Gezer 1:4

qṣry N 1st c.s PS; "my harvest (my quota of grain);" MHY 1:9

hq̊ṣr̊ DA N; "the harvest;" L 5:8; *[hqṣr],* MHY 1:11

qṣr m.s. AP; "(he) is reaping, reaper;" MHY 1:3

hqṣrm DA m.pl. AP; "the harvesters; those who are the harvesters;" MHY 1:10

yqṣr m.s. Imp V; "he reaped;" MHY 1:4

QRʾ

qrʾty	1st c.s Perf V; "I read;" L 3:12; *q[r]ʾty*, L 12:4
qrʾ	3rd m.s. Perf V; "he read;" L 6:13
qrʾ	m.s. Impv V; "read!;" L 6:5
qrʾ	I (*lqrʾ*); "(to) read;" L 3:10; *qrʾ*, Inf. Con.; "to read;" L 3:9
q[r]ʾ	m.s. AP; "(the one) calling out;" Siloam 1:2-3

qrʾh

qrʾh	PN N; "partridge;" Ophel 1:1

QRB

qrbʾwr	PN IML; "*Qrb* is light;" A 24:14
qrbʾ	PN; Avigad *HB* 156

QRH

yqrh	3rd m.s. Imp V; "(it) happens, will happen, befall;" A 24:16
qrt	Inf. Con. as Prep (*lqrt*); "toward;" Siloam 1:4

QRḤ

qrḥ	PN N; "bald one;" A 49:2

QRS

qrsy	gent. N (+ *l*-); "(to) the Qerosite;" A 18:5

QRṢ

qrṣ	PN N; "mosquito;" Ophel 1:3

QŠB

hqšbw	3rd m.pl. *Hiph* Impv V; "pay attention!;" Sam C 1101:2

RʾH

nrʾh	1st c.pl. Imp V; "we see, will see;" L 4:12
yrʾ	3rd m.s. *Hiph* Juss V; "may (DN) cause to see;" L 6:1
yrʾk	3rd m.s. *Hiph* Juss V; 2nd m.s. PS; "may (DN) cause you to see, witness;" L 5:7
yrʾ	PN Juss V; "may (DN) see, look upon;" Avigad 11:1
rʾyhw	PN; "YH sees," Avigad *HB* 157

Rʾš

- *rʾš* — N CS; "the head of;" Siloam 1:6
- *hrʾšn* — DA Adj; "the first (batch of);" A 1:6; *[hr]ʾ[šn]*, A 5:4

RBB

- *hrbt* — DA gent. Adj (?); "the Rabbatite;" Dayan 3:1-2
- *rbyhw* — PN; "YH is great;" R 17:1 (Herr 61)
- *yrbʿm* — PN; "may the paternal uncle (=DN) increase, be many;" Megiddo Seal 1:2; *yrbʿ[m]*, Hazor 6:1

RBʿ

- *ʾrbʿt* — m.s. Card CS (+ *l*-); "(for the) four (of);" A 2:2-3
- *rbʿy* — m.s. Ordn; "fourth;" Ophel 2:3
- *rbʿt* — f.s. Ordn (+ *b*-); "(in the) fourth (year);" L 29:1

rbt

- *hrbt* — See *RBB*

RGʾ

- *rgʾ* — PN Perf V; "(DN) has calmed (?);" A 31:2; A 68:3; *rgʾ* (?), S 78:1

RGʿ

- *rgʿ* — PN Perf V; "(DN) has calmed;" S 1:4

RWM

- *rmt ng[b]* — LPN; "height of the south;" A 24:13
- *rmt ngb* — LPN (+ *b*-); "(at) *rmt ngb*;" A 24:16
- *yhwrm* — PN; "YH is exalted;" L V 9:1

RḤM

- *rḥ[mm]* — N; "mercy;" MHY 1:13-14
- *yrḥmʾl* — PN; "may DN have compassion;" Avigad (Bulla of Jerahmeel) (1978) 2:1 (= Avigad *HB* 8)

RḤṢ

- *rḥṣ* — m.s. PP; "washed;" S 16a:3; S 16b:3; S 17a:3; S 18:3; S 19:3; S 20:3; S 21:3; S 53:3; S 54:2-3; S 55:3; S 72:2; S 82:1-2; *r[ḥ]ṣ*, S 59:1-2; *[rḥṣ]*, S 17b:3; S 73:3

RKB

- *trkb* — 2nd m.s. *Hiph* Imp V; "you will load, you are to load;" A 1:6-7

RMH

yrm PN; Juss (?); N (?); Herr 107:1 (Egypt (?))

yrmyhw PN; "YH loosens (the womb);" A 24:15-16; B/L (26) 6:1; B/L (29) 4:2; L V 6:1; L V 7:1; Av (*EI* 9) 12:1; *yrm̊ẙh̊ẘ*, L 1:4; *yrm̊yhẘ*, Beth-Shemesh 1:2; *yrm̊[yhw]*, Avigad *HB* 78

ʾlyrm PN; see *ʾLH*

rmʿ (?)

rmʿ PN; Herr 62:1 (Ashkelon)

rmt

rmt See *RWM*

rntn

rntn LPN (+ *m-*), "(from) *rntn;*"; HU 3

RʿH

rʿw N 3rd m.s. PS; "his fellow;" Siloam 1:2, 3, 4

Rʿʿ

hrʿh DA N; "the evil (thing);" A 40:15

RPʾ

hrpʾ DA AP; "the healer;" Jerusalem Bulla 4:3 (Shiloh *IEJ* 36, (1986)

rpʾ PN Perf V; "(DN) has healed;" S 24:2; B/L (26) 19:2; Herr 63:1 (Tell es-Safi); *r̊pʾ*, B/L (26) 20:2

rpʾyhw PN; "YH heals;" Avigad *HB* 111; *rpʾ[yhw]*, Avigad *HB* 121

RPD

byt hrpd LPN; *byt* + DA N (?); "the protection (?);" L 4:5

RPH

rpt Piel I (*lrpt*); "(to) weaken, slacken;" L 6:6

RṢH

[r]ṣh 3rd m.s. Perf V; "wanted, agreed;" A 40:6-7

ŚBʿ

yśbʿw	m.pl. Imp V; "they will be satisfied" (or possibly from *šbʿ*, "they will swear"), Aj 7:1

ŚDH

śdh	m.s. N; "field;" Ophel 675b:6; *[ś]d̊h*; Ophel 675 b:1
śdh	N CS "the field of;" MO 2:6; *śd‹h›* (+ *b*-); "(in the) field of;" Ophel 1:1

ŚWK

śwk	PN N LPN (?); "branch, brushwood;" L Seal 15:1-2 (*hê* is restored by Driver: *śwk[h]*)

ŚWM

w[yś]m	Conj; 3rd m.s. Juss V; "and [may he giv]e, [pu]t;" KH 2:10-11

ŚMʾL

[śm]ʾ̊l̊	N (+ *m*-); "(on the) left;" Siloam 1:3

ŚʿR

śʿrm	N; "barley;" Sam. C 1101:3; Gezer 1:4

ŚRH

śr	PN; Perf V (?); N (?); "(DN) has persisted, persevered," or "(DN) is chief;" Herr 68:1 (Samaria); Avigad *HB* 37, 167
śryhw	PN; "YH has persisted," or "YH is chief;" Avigad (1978) Seal 1:1; Av NN 11:1; Avigad *HB* 37, 167
śrmlk	PN; "(my) king persists," or "(my) king is chief;" Av NN 10:2; B/L (32) 12:1

śryhw

śryhw	See *ŚRH*

śrmlk

śrmlk	See *ŚRH*

ŚRR

śr N (+ *l*-); "(to the) official, commander, governor;" MHY 1:12

śr N CS; "the official, commander, governor of;" A 26:2; L 3:14; Av (1978) 3:1; *śr*, Barkay (1977) 1:1 (=Avigad 1978); *śr*, N CS (+ *l*-); "(to the) official, commander, governor of;" Aj 3:1, Aj 4:1, Aj 5:1 Aj 6:1

hśr DA N; "the official, commander;" MHY 1:1; *hś̊r̊*, MO 2:2

hśr[m] DA N; "the officials;" L 6:4; *h[śrm]*, L 6:5

*Š*ʾ*L*

*yš*ʾ*l* 3rd m.s. Imp V; "may (DN) ask;" A 18:2-3; Aj 16:1

*yš*ʾ*l* PN; m.s. Imp V; "may (DN) ask;" Hiph: "give, grant;" Herr 41:2 (Ophel)

*š*ʾ*l* PN PP; "asked for of (DN), dedicated to (DN);" Av NN 16:2; Avigad 5:1

*š*ʾ*lh* PN N; "request, asked for of (DN); "Avigad *HB* 155; Jerusalem Bulla 51:2

*šb*ʾ*l*

*šb*ʾ*l* See *ŠWB*

šby

šby See *ŠWB*

*šbn*ʾ

*šbn*ʾ See *ŠWB*

šbnyh

šbnyh See *ŠWB*

šbnyw

šbnyw See *ŠWB*

šbnyhw

šbnyhw See *ŠWB*

*ŠB*ʿ$_1$

*šb*ʿ Card; "seven;" Ophel 2:2 (could be N "abundance")

ŠBʿ$_2$

šbʿ PN N; "(DN) swears, promises by oath;" S 2:6; Av NN 14:1; *šbʿ* , A 38:4; *[š]bʿ* , Avigad *HB* 202

ŠBR

šbrm m.pl. N; "grain;" Ophel a:2

ŠBT

šbt Inf. Con.; "stopping, quitting time;" MHY 1:5-6 (or possibly N, "Shabbat")

ŠDŠ

hššh DA N; Card; "the sixth (day);" A 7:4

ŠWB

[whš]b̊t Conj 2nd m.s. *Hiph* Perf V; "and you should return;" MHY 1:14

hšb̊ m.s. *Hiph* Perf V; "he has returned;" L 5:6

nšb 1st c.pl. *Hiph* Imp V; "we will return (word);" A 111:4

hšb̊ m.s. *Hiph* Impv V; "return (word)!;" L 9:4; *[hšb]*, "return!;" MHY 1:12

hš[b] *Hiph* I (*lhš[b]*); "(to) return;" MHY 1:12-13

šby PN; "return, (O DN)!;" MHY 1:7:8

šbʾl PN; "return, O God!;" Gib 21

šbnʾ PN Impv V; part. of ent.; "return, (O DN)!;" Avigad (*BIES* 18) 7:1; L Seal 4:1; L Seal 14:1-2; L Seal 15:2-3; RR Seal 1:2; RR Seal 9:1-2; Tell en-Nasbeh 1:1 (3x)

šbnẙh̊ PN; "return, O YH!;" L Seal 17:2; 18:1

šbnyw PN; "return, O YH!;" Herr 4:1, 2

šbnyhw PN; "return, O YH!;" A 60:3; Jerusalem Seal 5:2; Herr 143:2; Av NN 9:1; L V 5:1; Avigad *HB* 49, 96-97, 124; BCat 45; *šb̊nyhw*, Herr 65:1 (Tell el Judeideh); *šbnyh̊w*, Herr 64:1-2 (Gezer); *šbny[hw]*, Avigad *HB* 167; *šb[nyhw]*, A 27:4; *[šbn]yhw*, Silwan 2:1

šwššrʾṣr

šwššrʾṣr PN; "Shamash, protect the king;" Neo-Babylonian name; Naveh 1:2 (Herr 98)

ŠḤR$_1$

šḥrt	N;"black(ness);" L 30:1
šḥrḥr	PN Adj; "dark-one;" Herr 135:1; *šḥrḥ‹r›*, Herr 124:2
ʾšḥr	PN; m.s. Adj (?); "black, blackness;" Avigad *HB* 32; *ʾš[ḥr]*, S 13:3-4

ŠḤR$_2$

šḥr	PN Perf V; "(DN) looks diligently for;" RR Seal 6:2; 9:2; L Seal 14:2; Tell en-Nasbeh 1:2 (3x); Avigad *HB* 22, 24-26, 112; *[š]ḥr*, Avigad *HB* 113; *šḥ[r]*, RR Seal 7:2; Avigad *HB* 95; *[šḥ]r*, Avigad *HB* 23

ŠKM

mškm	Prep LPN N; "from Shechem, shoulder;" S 44:1

ŠKN

šknyhw	PN; "YH dwells, abides;" Av NN 4:1-2

ŠKR

ʾškr	N; "present," Kadesh Barnea; *Qad.* 16 (61), 1983, p. 12

ŠLḤ

šlḥty	1st c.s. Perf V; "I have sent;" ; A 24:18; *šlḥty*, (+ *w*-), "I will send;" A 16:4
šlḥt	"I (hereby) send;" papMur 17a:1
šlḥth	2nd m.s. Perf V; "you (m.s.) have sent;" L 5:4; *šlḥ[th]*, L 4:4
šlḥ	3rd m.s. Perf V; "he (hereby) sends;" A 16:1, 9 (?); A 21:1; A 62:1; *šlḥ*, "he sent, has sent;" (implies "has written"); L 4:2; L 6:3; L 18:2; *šlḥ*, "he dispatched, sent;" L 3:1, 6, 18
šlḥtm	2nd m.pl. Perf V; "you (m.pl.) are to send;" A 24:13
šlḥw	3rd m.pl. Perf V; "they sent;" A 61:1; *šlḥ[w]*, "(they) hereby sent;" A 40:2
tšlḥ	2nd m.s. Imp V; "you (m.s.) shall send;" A 16:10; *tš[lḥ]*, A 13:1-2
yšlḥ	3rd m.s. Imp V; "he will send;" L 18:1; *y[šlḥ]* , A 5:10-11
šlḥ	m.s. Impv V; "send!;" A 5:2; A 6:2; A 13:4; A 14:3; A 17:4-5; L 16:9; *[š]lḥ*, L 16:3
šlḥnw	m.s. Impv V; 3rd m.s. PS; "send it!;" A 4:2; *[šlḥnw]*, A 7:9
[š]lḥ	Inf. Abs.; with Perf V; papMur 17a:1

ŠLḤ (continued)

šlḥk — Inf. Con.; 2nd m.s. PS; "your (m.s.) sending, you sent;" L 3:7

šlḥ — I (*lšlḥ*); "(to) send;" A 40:1

š̊lḥ — m.s. AP; "(he) is sending;" L 4:8

ŠLM

šlm — N; "(in) peace;" L 6:2, 10; L 18:1; *šlm*, "peace, well-being;" L 2:2-3; L 3:3; *šlm̊*, L 9:2; *š̊lm (+ b-)* MO 2:1; *[šl]m̊*, L 5:2; *šlm*, "greeting(s);" (*šlm bytk*); papMur 17a:1; *šlm*, "everything is fine;" A 18:8

š[l]wm — N IML; "Peace, well-being;" KH 2:11-12

hšlm — Interr. + N, "Is it well (with you) (?);" Ajrud 15:3

šlm — N CS (+ *l*-); "(to) greet, ask about the welfare of;" A 16:1-2, 2; A 21:1, 2; *[šlm]*, A 40:2

šlmk — N; 2nd m.s. PS (+ *l*-); "(about) your welfare;" A 18:3

yšlm — 3rd m.s. Imp V; Piel; "may (YH) restore;" A 21:4

šlm — PN PP; "one is covenant of peace," or, as Piel Perf V, "(DN) has replaced (a dead infant by a new one);" A 35:3; A 44:1; L 3:2; Beth-Shemesh 7:2; B/L (26) 10:3; B/L (26) 15:1; R 11:1 (Herr 136); L Seal 11:1; Herr 66:1 (Tell el Judeideh); Avigad *HB* 108, 158-59, 161, 196; *šlm̊*, Sam C 1101:1; L Seal 7:1; *š̊l̊m*, B/L (32) 10:1; *šl[m]*, Avigad *HB* 160

šl — PN (=*šl‹m›* (?)); KEK plate

šlmyhw — PN; "thank-offering of YH," or "YH has recompensed, restored;" Tel Ira (*PEQ* 83 (1983)) 1:4; Av NN 10:1-2; A 108:3; R 3:2 (Herr 87); *š̊l̊m̊yhw*, L 9:7

mšlm — PN PP; "one in covenant of peace;" A 110:1; L Seal 9:1 (7x); Gib S.I. 6; Avigad *HB* 75, 92, 110; Jerusalem Bulla 12:2; *mšlm̊*, B/L (32) 14:1; *mš̊lm*, A 39:3; *m̊š̊l̊m̊*, Avigad *HB* 111; *m[šl]m*, Gib S.I. 6

ŠLŠ

šlš — Card; "three;" Siloam 1:2

hšlʿšh ʿś̊r — DA Card; "the thirteenth (day of the month);" A 8:2-3

šlšt — Ordn (+ *b*-); "(in the) third (year); A 20:1

ŠM

šm	N CS; "the name of;" A 1:4; Aj 8:3
šm	PN N; "(divine) name;" Av (*EI* 9) 11:2
šmyd[ʿ]	LPN; "the Name knows;" S 62:1; *šm‹y›dʿ*, S 57:2; *šmydʿ*, LPN (+ *m-*); "(from) *šmydʿ* ("The Name knows")"; S 3:2; S b31a:1; S 37:1; S 38:1-2; S 39:1; S 90:1; *šmyd̊ʿ*, S 30:1; S 63:2; *š̊mydʿ*, S 40:1; *šmyd[ʿ]*, S 36:1; *š[mydʿ]*, S 35:1; *[š]m̊ẙ[dʿ]*, S 34:1; *šmy[dʿ]*, S 33:1-2; *š‹m›ydʿ*, S 32:1; *[šmyd]ʿ*, S 49:1-2; *š̊[mydʿ]*, S 29:1
šmyh	PN; "the (divine) name is YH;" A 110:1

šm

šm	Adv; "there;" L 4:5; *š̊m̊*, Adv (+ *m-*); "(from) there;" A 17:4
šmh	Loc. Adv; "there;" A 24:20; L 4:8; L 8:7

šmydʿ

šmydʿ	See *ŠM, YDʿ*

šmyhw

šmyhw	See *ŠM*

ŠMN

šmn	N; "oil;" Tell Qasile 1:2; A 4:1-2; A 7:8; A 10:3; A 12:1; A 14:3; A 17:4, 8-9; S 16a:3; S 16b:3; S 17a:2-3; S 17b:2; S 18:2; S 19:3; S 21:2-3; S 53:2; S 54:2; S 55:3; S 59:1; S 72:2; S 73:3; S 82:1; *[š]mn*, S 20:2-3
hšmn	DA N; "the oil;" A 6:5; *[hš]mn*, A 13:2
šmnm	m.pl. N; "oil;" Ophel a:1; Ophel c:1; *šmn̊m* , Ophel c:3; *šmnm̊*, Ophel c:4; *šm̊n̊m̊*, Ophel c:2

ŠMNH

hš̊m̊nh̊ ʿśr	DA Card; "the eighteenth (day of the month); A 8:3-4

ŠMʿ

šmʿt	N CS; "tidings of;" L 3:3; L 4:2; *šm̊ʿt*, L 2:2; *[šm]ʿt*, L 8:1-2; *š[mʿt]*, L 9:2; *[šmʿt]*, L 5:2
tšmʿ	2nd m.s. Imp V (with neg. *ʾl*); "you will listen to, don't listen to;" papMur 17a:2
yšmʿ	3rd m.s. Imp/Juss V; "may (he) hear;" MHY 1:1

ŠMʿ (continued)

yšmʿ 3rd m.s. *Hiph* Imp/Juss V; "may (DN) cause to hear;" L 2:1; L 3:2; L 4:1; L 5:1; L 8:1; L 9:1; MO 2:1-2

[yšm]ʿ̊ (?) 3rd *Niph* Imp V (?); "there was heard;" Siloam 1:2

š̊mʿ I (*lšʿmʿ*); "(to) hear;" A 111:7

šmʿ PN Perf V; "(DN) has heard;" Av (*EI* 9) 10:2; Hest. 55:2; Avigad 8:1; Stone 1; Megiddo Seal 1:1; Herr 137:1; Avigad *HB* 48; BCat 55

ʿlšmʿ PN; "God hears, has heard;" RR Seal 3:2; Herr 148:1; Herr 152:1; Hest. 72:2; Jerusalem Bulla 7:1, 10:1, 35:2; Lemaire Seal 6:1. *ʿlšm̊ʿ*, Av (*EI* 9) 9:2

yhwyšmʿ fem.PN; "YH will hear, may YH hear;" Naveh 1:1 (Herr 98)

yšmʿʾl PN; "may God hear;" Avigad *HB* 79, 89, 101, 164, 173; BCat 52; Jerusalem Bulla 3:2; Lemaire Seal 1:2; *yšmʿʾl̊*; Herr 48:1 (Ophel); *ẙšmʿʾl*, Hest. 77:2; *yšm[ʿʾl]* Avigad *HB* 80, 81, 82; *y[šmʿ]ʾl* (?), A 57:2; *yš̊mʿ̊ʿl*, Hest. 57:1; *yšmʿ̊ʾ[l]*, Avigad *HB* 78; *yš[mʿʾl]*, Avigad *HB* 102

šmʿyhw PN; "YH hears;" ; A 39:2, 7-8; L 4:6; papMur 17b:4; Avigad *HB* 29, 33, 64, 162-63 Jerusalem Bullae 5:1; 23:1 ; *šm̊ʿyhw*, A 27:2; *šmʿyhẘ*, A 31:5; *šmʿyh[w]*, Avigad *HB* 179; *[š]mʿyhw*, Avigad *HB* 38; *šmʿy[hw]*, Jerusalem Bulla 14:1; *šmʿ[yhw]*, L 19:4

šmʿ yw PN; "YH hears;" Aj 12:1

ŠMR

yšmrk Imp V; 2nd m.s. PS; "may he keep you;" Aj 15:7; *[y]šmrk (+ w-)*, "and [may he] keep you," KH 2:6-7; (+ [*w*]-), "[and may he] keep you, " KH 1:15-16

hšmr m.s. *Niph* Impv V; "beware!;" L 3:21

šmrm m.pl. AP; "we (are) have been watching;" L 4:11

mšmr m.s. N (+ *b*-); "(on/in the) guard;" A 111:2

šmrn LPN; "Samaria;" Aj 14:2 (could be AP and 1st c.pl PS: "our guardian")

šmryhw PN; "YH kept, preserved;" B/L (26) 4:2; B/L (26) 5:1; A 18:4

šmryw PN; "YH kept, preserved;" S 1:1-2; S 13:2; S 14:2; S 21:1-2; Herr 67:1 (Samaria)

ŠMŠ

h̊šm̊š̊ DA N; "the sun;" MHY 1:11

ŠNH$_1$

št Prep N (+ *b*-); "(in the) year;" S 1:1; S 2:1; S 3:1; S 4:1; S 5:1; S 6:1; S 7:1; S 9:1; S 10:1; S 12:1; S 13:1; S 14:1; S 16a:1; S 16b:1; S 17a:1; S 18:1; S 19:1; S 20:1; S 21:1; S 22:1; S 23:1; S 24:1; S 27:1; S 28:1; S 29:1; S 30:1; S 31a:1; S 32:1; S 35:1; S 37:1; S 38:1; S 39:1; S 43:1; S 45:1; S 46:1; S 48:1; S 50:1; S 51:1; S 53:1; S 54:1; S 55:1; S 56:1; S 58:1; S 59:2; S 61:2; S 63:1; S 72:1; S 73:1; S 100:1; *št̊*, S 31b:1; *š[t]*, S 49:1; *š̊t*, S 42:1; *[š]t*, S 34:1; *[št]*, S 8:1; S 17b:1; S 33:1; S 36:1; S 44:1; S 47:1

ŠNH$_2$

šnym Card (+ *b*-); "(on the) second (day);" A 7:7

šn̥y̥ẇ PN (forgery (?)); "YH has changed, repeated;" R 8:1 (Herr UD 3)

šʿybb

šʿybb See *YBB*

šʿl

šʿl PN N; "fox;" A 38:2; A 49:14; Avigad Wine Decanter 2; B/L (26) 17:2; Herr 140:1; Avigad *HB* 69, 79, 123, 164; *š[ʿ]l*, Avigad *HB* 174

ʾbšʿl See *ʾB*

ŠʿN

mšʿn PN N; "(DN is my) support;" Avigad *HB* 112

šʿnp

šʿnp See *NWP*

ŠʿR

šʿryhw PN; "YH has opened;" B/L (26) 1b:2

ŠPH (?)

ʾšpt See *ʾSP*

ŠPN

špn PN; Jerusalem Bulla 2:2

ŠPṬ

yšpṭ PN 3rd m.s. Imp/Juss V; "may (DN) judge;" A 53:1

špṭ PN Perf V; "(DN) has judged;" Avigad Naar Seal 1:2; Herr 141:1; *šp̊ṭ* , Avigad *HB* 166

špṭyhw PN; "YH has judged;" B/L (26) 14:2; L Seal 5:1; Hest. 96:1; Avigad *HB* 56; Jerusalem Bullae 39:1; 50:1; *šp̊ṭyhw*, B/L (32) 10:1; *špṭ̊y[hw]*, Avigad *HB* 165; *špṭ[yhw]*, Avigad *HB* 180; *[šp]ṭyhw*, Avigad *HB* 180

šptn

šptn LPN (+ *m*-); "(from) *šptn*;" S 12:2

ŠQṬ

[hš]qṭ *Hiph* I (*[lhš]qṭ*); "(to) weaken, pacify, allay;" L 6:6-7

ŠQL

šq[l] N; "shekel;" MHY 5:1

š[qlm] N Abbrev.; "s(hekels);" Tell Qasile 2:2; A 16:5; A 65:1, 2; A 81:1; MHY 4:1; MHY 6:2; MO 1:5

ŠQN (?)

šqnyh PN; R 9:2 (Herr 111); (could be *qof* written for *kaf*: *šknyh*, "YH lives, abides")

ŠRQ

hšrq PN DA AP; "the whistler, piper, hisser;" Ophel 1:2 (or *hśrq*, "the comber, carder [of flax]")

š̊r̊q̊m AP; "whistlers;" Ophel 1:1; (or *śrqm*, "carders [of flax])"

šš

hššh See *ŠDŠ*

št

št See $ŠNH_1$

ŠTL

štl PN Perf V; "(DN) has planted, transplanted;" RR Seal 5:1

twl

twl LPN (+ *m*-); "(from) *twl*;" S 13:4; S 21:2

TḤT

tḥt	Prep (+ *m*-); "under, below," Ophel 3:1 (*IEJ* 32 (1982))
tḥtnm	m.pl. Adj; "lower;" A 25:2

TLL

htl	EOLPN DA N; "the mound;" S 53:2; S 54:2; S 58:2; S 61:1; S 72:2; S 99:1; *ht̊[l]*, S 20:2; *[htl]*, S 73:2
ht[l]	DA N(+ *m*-); "(from) the mound;" S 56:1

tmn

tmn	LPN; "Teman," Aj 15:5
htm̊n	DA LPN; "the (one from) Teman;" Aj 10:1

tnḥm

tnḥm	See *NḤM*

tsbt

tsbt	See *SBB*

tršš

tršš	LPN; "Tarshish," MO 1:3-4

TŠʿ

tšʿyt	f.s. Ordn (+ *b*-); IML; "(in the) ninth (year);" L 20:1
htšʿt	DA Ordn; "the ninth;" S 6:1; S 9:1; S 10:1; S 12:1; *htš̊[ʿt]*, S 100:1; *h̊tš[ʿt]*, S 14:1; *[h]t̊šʿt*, S 8:1; *htšʿt̊*, S 4:1; *ht[šʿt]*, S 5:1

6. APPENDIX

TEXTS AND SEALS

The Appendix furnishes the transliterations and English translations of the corpus of epigraphic Hebrew inscriptions (including ostraca, graffiti, and seals).[1] The first part of the Appendix is devoted to all non-seals (referred to as "Texts") which are listed in alphabetical order by site[2] beginning with the Arad inscriptions and ending with the Tell Qasile ostraca.

The seals are treated separately in the second part of the Appendix. For reasons of convenience, each group of seals is named either according to the site (if that is relevant) or according to the scholar who has gathered a disparate collection (for example, Avigad, Herr, Reifenberg, *et cetera*).

---

[1]When the traces of a word or letter are too effaced, no English translation is provided.

[2]One exception to this rule is the heading "Avigad" for two wine decanter inscriptions (see 6.1.2 on pp. 402-3) which Avigad described only in general terms as having come from the Hebron area; cf. N. Avigad, "Two Hebrew Inscriptions on Wine-Jars," *IEJ* 22 (1972): 1.

6.1 Texts

6.1.1 ARAD

Arad 1

1	*ʾl . ʾlyšb . w*	1	To Elyashib. And
2	*ʿt . ntn . lktym*	2	now, give the Kittim
3	*yyn . b/ /// w*	3	three *bat*-measures of wine and
4	*ktb . šm . hym .*	4	write down the date.
5	*wmʿwd . hqmḥ*	5	From the remainder of the
6	*hrʾšn . t*	6	first meal,
7	*rkb . / . qmḥ*	7	have one *homer*-measure of meal loaded
8	*lʿśt . lhm . l*	8	to make bread for
9	*ḥm . myyn .*	9	them. It is the wine from
10	*hʾgnt . ttn*	10	the *ʾgnt* bowls (=craters) that you are to give (to them).

Arad 2

1	*ʾl .ʾlyšb . wʿt . ntn l*	1	To Elyashib. And now, give
2	*ktym . b/ // yyn . l*	2	the Kittim two *bat*-measures of wine for
3	*ʾrbʿt hymm w*	3	the four days,
4	ш *lḥm w*	4	Three hundred loaves of bread, and
5	*mlʾ . hḥmr . yyn wh*	5	a full *homer*-measure of wine. Send
6	*sbt mḥr . ʾl tʾḥr .*	6	(them) out tomorrow – don't delay.
7	*wʾm . ʿwd . ḥmṣ . wnt*	7	If there is any vinegar left, give
8	*t lhm*	8	(it) to them (also).

Arad 3

1	*ʾl .ʾlysb . wʿt .*	1	To Elyashib. And now,
2	*tn . mn . hyyn . /// b/ . w*	2	give three *bat*-measures of wine (to bearer).
3	*ṣwk . ḥnnyhw . ʿl b*	3	Hananyahu (hereby) orders you to
4	*ʾršbʿ ʿm . mśʾ ṣ*	4	Beersheba with a pair of pack
5	*md . ḥmrm . wṣrr[t]*	5	donkeys. You are to bind
6	*ʾtm . bṣq . w*	6	them (with a load of) dough and
7	*spr . hḥṭm whl*	7	calculate the (amount of) wheat and the (number of loaves of)
8	*ḥm wlqḥt*	8	bread. (Next) you are the take
Reverse			
9	*[]ʾlk[ ]*	9	to you
10	*ry [ ]*	10	

Arad 3 (continued)

11	*l[ ]///*	11	
12	*wʾdmm . h[ ]*	12	and Edomites
13	*[ ]*	13	
14	*[ ]m[ ]*	14	

Arad 4

1	*ʾl ʾlyšb tn lktym š*	1	To Elyashib. Give the Kittim
2	*mn / ḥtm wšlḥnw w*	2	one (x-measure of) oil. Seal (the jar) and send it. And
3	*yyn b / tn lhm*	3	give them one *bat*-measure of wine.

Arad 5

1	*ʾl ʾlyšb . wʿ*	1	To Elyashib. And
2	*t . šlḥ. mʾtk*	2	now, send some of the meal which
3	*mʿwd hqmḥ.*	3	you have left from
4	*[hr]ʾ[šn ʾ]šr*	4	the [fi]r[st] (batch of) meal, [wh]ich
5	*[ ]qm*	5	[of] mea[l]
6	*[ḥ lʿśt] lḥm l*	6	[to make] bread for
7	*[k]t[ym]ʾt*	7	the [Ki]tt[im].
8	*[ ]h*	8	
9	*[ ]b̊ [ ] hwk [ ]*	9	
10	*[ ]ʾšr . y*	10	He will
11	*[šlḥ] lk ʾt hmʿ*	11	[send] you the tit[he],
12	*[śr] b / /// bṭrm . y*	12	three *bat*-measures, before
13	*ʿbr h̊ḥdš . wm*	13	the month passes. And from the
14	*ytr [ ]hʿbdh*	14	surplus of the work
15	*[ ]ḥ[ ]m[ ]*	15	

Arad 6

1	*ʾl ʾlyšb . w[ʿt]*	1	To Elyashib. And [now,]
2	*šlḥ mʾtk ʾl*	2	send from your supplies to
3	*yḥzy[hw]*	3	Yahzeya[hu]
4	*lḥ[m] [ ]* 	4	three [hundred] (?) loaves of bre[ad]
5	*[ ] hšmn[ ]*	5	the oil
6	*bšl̊[ ]*	6	
7	*[ ]*	7	
8	*[ ]m[ ]*	8	
9	*[ ]*	9	

Arad 7

1	*ʾl ʾlyšb . wʿ*	1	To Elyashib. And now,
2	*t . ntn . lktym .*	2	give the Kittim
3	*lʿśr̊y b/ lḥd*	3	for the (period from) the first (day) of the tenth (month)
4	*š . ʿd̊ hššh*	4	until the sixth (day)
5	*lḥdš̊ b/ /// [w]*	5	of that month three *bat*-measures (of wine (?)). [And]
6	*ktbth lpnyk . b*	6	make a record (of it) on the
7	*šnym lḥdš . bʿś*	7	second (day) of the tenth month.
8	*ry[ ]wšmn ḥ*	8	(Also,) s[eal] (a jar of) oil
9	*[tm wšlḥnw]*	9	[and send it]

Arad 8

1	*[ʾ]l ʾlyšb . wʿt . ntn l*	1	[T]o Elyashib. And now, give
2	*k̊t̊[y]m̊ ⊢/q̊m‹ḥ› . mn . hš*	2	the Kittim one *ḥomer*-measure (?) of meal (for the period) from the
3	*l̊šh ʿś̊r lḥdš .ʿd h̊*	3	thirteenth of the month until the
4	*š̊mnh̊ .ʿśr lḥdš*	4	eighteenth of the month
5	*[w]yyn b̊ / ///*	5	[and] three *bat*-measures of wine
6	*[ ] š*	6	
7	*[ ]ntb[ ]*	7	
8	*[ ]ʾly . w[ ]*	8	to me
9	*[ ]ʾšr lbn[ ]*	9	which belongs to Ben
10	traces only	10	

Arad 9

1	*[ ]b̊ [ ]*	1	
2	*[ ]mʾt[k]*	2	from you[r supplies]
3	*[ ]b / /// b[ ]*	3	three *bat*-measures

Arad 10

1	*[ʾl ʾly]šb . wʿt .*	1	[To Elya]shib. And now,
2	*[ntn lkt]ym . yyn b/ ////*	2	[give the Kitt]im four *bat*-measures of wine
3	*[ ]mʾ[ ]b̊tym . wšmn /*	3	one (*bat*-measure (?)) of oil.
4	*[ḥ]t̊m . lbn ʿbdyhw š̊ [ ]*	4	[Se]al (?) (it) for Ben-Obadyahu
5	*[ ]ktym[ ]*	5	Kittim

Arad 11

1	*ʾl .ʾlyšb*	1	To Elyashib.
2	*wʿt ntn lktẙ[m]*	2	And now, give the Kitti[m]
3	*[ ]b/ // yyn*	3	two *bat*-measures of wine
4	*[ ]w*	4	
5	*m [n]ḥmyḥẘ*	5	[Ne]ḥemyahu

Arad 12

1	*[ʾl ʾly]šb . q[ḥ] šmn / w*	1	[To Elya]shib. Ta[ke] one unit-measure of oil
2	*[ ]// qmḥ wtn .ʾ[tm]*	2	two (unit-measures of) meal and give th[em]
3	*[lqw]sʿnl mhrh . ṣ[ ]*	3	[to Qaw]sanal quickly
4	*[ ]ʾ̊lb[ ]ṣy[ ]*	4	
5	*s[ ]š[ ]wtn[ʾ]*	5	and give
6	*t hlḥm . wb[]ʾyl[ ]*	6	the bread

Arad 13

1	*[ ] . tš*	1	se[nd]
2	*[lḥ ʾt hš]mn hzh*	2	this [oi]l
3	*[wḥtm] . bḥtmk*	3	[and affix] your seal (to it)
4	*[ ]wšlḥ w[ ]*	4	send, and
5	*[y]hw . t[ ]*	5	[-ya]hu

Arad 14

1	*[ʾl ʾl]yš̊[b wʿt]*	1	[To El]yash[ib. And now,]
2	*[ntn l]ktym [ ]*	2	[give the] Kittim
3	*[w]šlḥ / šmn*	3	[and] send one unit-measure of oil.

Arad 15

1	*[ ]ʾ̊ḥ[ ]*	1	
2	*[ ]šb[ ]*	2	
3	*[ ]ʿdy[ ]*	3	
4	*[ ] . nʿr*	4	steward
5	*[ ]hlwʾḥ[ ]*	5	

Arad 16

1 *ʾḥk . ḥnnyhw . šlḥ lšl*	1	Your brother Hananyahu (hereby) sends greetings
2 *m .ʾlyšb . wlšlm bytk br*	2	to (you) Elyashib and to your household. I bless
3 *ktk lyhwh . wʿt kṣʾty*	3	you to YHWH . And now, when I leave
4 *m̊bytk wšlḥ̊ty ʾt*	4	your house, I will send
5 *h[k]s̊p* ıı *š lbny gʾlyhw . [b]*	5	the [mo]ney, eight shekels, to the sons of Geʾalyahu [by
6 *y[d ʿ]zryhw wʾt[ ]*	6	the] interm[ediary of A]zaryahu, and the
7 *[ ]ʾtk whš̊[ ]*	7	with you
8 *ʾt ksp[ ] wʾm[ ]*	8	money and if
9 *[ ]ṣbk [ ] šlḥ[ ]*	9	send
10 *ʾt nḥm wlʾ t̊šlḥ[ ]*	10	Naḥum, and you must not send
11 traces only	11	
12 traces only	12	

Arad 17

1 *ʾl . nḥm . [w]ʿt b*	1	To Naḥum. [And] now, go
2 *ʾ byth .ʾlyšb .*	2	to the house of Elyashib
3 *bn ʾšyhw . wlqḥ*	3	son of Eshyahu and take
4 *t . mš̊m̊ . / šmn . w*	4	one unit-measure of oil from there and
5 *šlḥ. lz̊p̊ mhrh . w*	5	send (it) to Ziph right away.
6 *ḥtm .ʾth bḥ*	6	Affix your seal
7 *tmk*	7	to it.
Reverse		
8 *b* Ƶ //// *lḥdš ntn nḥm š*	8	On the twenty-fourth of the month, Naḥum gave
9 *mn byd hkty .* /	9	oil to the Kitti (for delivery)--one (unit-measure).

Arad 18

1 *ʾl ʾdny .ʾly*	1	To my lord Elyashib.
2 *šb . yhwh yš*	2	May YHWH concern
3 *ʾl lšlmk . wʿt*	3	himself with your well-being. And now,
4 *tn . lšmryhw*	4	give Shemaryahu
5 ↰ *. wlqrsy*	5	one *letek*-measure, and to the Qerosite

Arad 18 (continued)

6	*ttn .* ⊢ *wld*	6	give one *homer*-measure. Regarding
7	*br .ʾšr . ṣ*	7	the matter about which you
8	*wtny . šlm .*	8	gave me orders: everything is fine:
9	*byt . yhwh .*	9	he is staying in
Reverse			
10	*hʾ . yšb*	10	the house (temple) of YHWH.

Arad 19

1	*ynm*	1	Yanum

Arad 20

1	*bšlšt*	1	In the third (year)
2	*g̊r̊ʾ b̊n̊ ʿzẙhw* (or *ẙr̊ḥ. ṣḥ*)	2	Gera, son of Uzziyahu (or: "in the month of *ṣaḥ*")

Arad 21

1 *bnk . yhwkl . šlḥ. lšlm . gdlyhw [bn]*
2 *ʾlyʾr . wlšlm . bytk . brktk l̊[yhw]*
3 *h̊ . wʿt . hn .ʿśh .ʾdny . [ ]*
4 *[ ]yšlm . yhwh . lʾdn̊[y]*
5 *[ ]ʾdm [ ] ḥyh̊ [wh]*
6 *[ ] h [ ]ʿt[ ]*
7 *[ ]ẘkl ʾš[r]*
8 *[ ]wʾm .ʿẘd [ ]*
9 *[ ]ʾš[ ]*
10 *[ ]lḥ[ ]*

1 Your son Yehukal sends greetings to Gedalyahu, [son of]
2 Elyaʾir and to your household. I (hereby) bless you to [YHW]H.
3 And now, if my lord has done
4 May YHWH reward [my] lord
5 Edom as Yah[weh] lives
6
7 whateve[r]
8 and if yet
9
10

Arad 22

1	*lb̊r̊k̊yhw b[n]*	1	For Berekyahu, so[n of]
2	*lʿzr b[n]*	2	For Ezer, s[on of]
3	*[ ]* ⟻////	3	Four *homer*-measures (?)
4	*lmʿśy bn* [ ] ///	4	For Maʿasay, son of [ ] 3
5		5	
6	*lyh[w]*	6	For YH[W]

Arad 23

1	traces only	1	
2	traces only	2	
3	traces only	3	
4	*b[n]*	4	so[n of]
5	*b[n]*	5	so[n of]
6	*mḥ̊s̊[yhw]*	6	Maḥse[yahu]
7	*b̊n̊*[ ]	7	son of
8	*ʿzr*[ ]	8	Ezer
9	*bn*[ ]	9	son of

Arad 24

1 *ʾ̊l̊ [ ]*
2 *ʾlyšb̊ [ ]*
3 *ls[ ]mlk[ ]bm[ ]*
4 *[ ] ḥyl [ ]*
5 *[ ] ks [ ]*
6 *[ ]ʿbd [ ]*
7 *[ ] ṭ [ ]r[ ]*
8 *[ ] wʿ [ ] d [ ]*
9 *[ ]wk[ ]*
10 traces only
11 traces only

Reverse

12 *mʿrd* ר̊ *wmqyn̊[h]*
13 *h . wšlḥtm .ʾtm . rmt ng̊[b by]*
14 *d . mlkyhw bn qrbʾwr . whb*
15 *qydm .ʿl . yd ʾlyšʿ bn yrmy .*
16 *hw . brmt ngb . pn . yqrh . ʾt h*
17 *ʿyr . dbr . wdbr hmlk ʾtkm*
18 *bnbškm . hnh šlḥty lhʿyd*
19 *bkm . hym . hʾnšm .ʾt .ʾlyš*
20 *ʿ . pn . tbʾ .ʾdm . šmh*

Arad 24 (continued)

1 To
2 Elyashib
3 king
4 army
5
6 servant
7
8
9
10
11
12 from Arad fifty (or five) and from Qina[h]
13 and send them to Ramat-Nege[b unde]r
14 Malkiyahu, son of Qerabur. He is to hand
15 them over to Elisha, son of Yirmeyahu
16 at Ramat-Negeb lest (anything) happen to the
17 city . This is an order from the king–a life and
18 death matter for you . Indeed, I have sent (this message) to
19 you today: The men (must be) with Elisha
20 lest (the) Edom(ites) come there.

Arad 25

1	*[ ]* Ч| ·	1	[ ] ten *ḥq3t* of barley
2	*[m]ʿ̊nym . tḥtnm .* Ч *////.*	2	[From] lower Anim, thirty *ḥq3t* of barley
3	*mʿlynm* ε.	3	From upper (Anim), sixty *ḥq3t* of barley
4	*mmʿn* Լ.	4	From Maon, ten *ḥq3t* (of barley)

Arad 26

1	*[ ]ʾryhw [ ]*	1	Uriyahu
2	*[ ]m̊n̊ ʾdny . śr[ ]*	2	from my lord the commander of
3	*[ ]q̊ws wyh[ ]*	3	-qaws and
4	*[ ]ʾdny[ ]*	4	my lord
5	traces only	5	
6	traces only	6	

Arad 27

1	*[ ]yhw*	1	yahu
2	*ʿbdy[hw] bn šmʿ̊yhw*	2	Obadyahu, son of Shemayahu

Arad 27 (continued)

3	[ ]l[ ]	3	
4	*ydnyhw b[n] šb[nyhw]*	4	Yedanyahu, so[n of] Sheba[nyahu]
5	*ḥldy[ ] rʾ*	5	Ḥelday
6	[ ]bn ʾbyhẘ	6	son of Abiyahu
7	[y]hw	7	[ya]hu

Arad 28

1	[br]kh . z[ ]	1	blessing
2	[ ]ntn . bt [ ]	2	gave
3	[ ]tnḥs . ʾḥ[ ]	3	
4	[ ]dn[ ]h[ ]	4	
5	[ ]t[ ]	5	
6	[ ]ʾm̊ [ ]	6	if
7	[ ]brkh . wt̊[ ]	7	blessing and

Arad 29

1	traces only	1	
2	traces only	2	
3	ʿk[ ]lm[ ]s[ ]	3	
4	ʾtb[ ]	4	
5	[ ]l[̊]n̊[ ]b	5	
6	⊢ k̊sp lm[ ]	6	ten (pieces of) silver
7	wʾšr bkb[ ]	7	and that which

Arad 31

1	ḥṭm .	1	Wheat
2	ʾwryhw bn rgʾ / ⊄⅃	2	Uriyahu, son of Ragga, five *seah*-measures, (equals one *letek*)
3	nḥmyhw bn yhwʿz ⊐	3	Neḥemyahu, son of Yehoaz, eight
4	nryhw bn sʿryhw ⌐	4	Neriyahu, son of Seʿaryahu, one *letek*-measure
5	ʾḥyqm bn šmʿyhẘ	5	Aḥiqam, son of Shemayahu, seven
6	gḥm ⌐ ⅄	6	Gaḥam, one *letek*-measure
7	ydʿyhw ⌐	7	Yedayahu, one *letek*-measure
8	gmryhw ⌐	8	Gemaryahu, one *letek*-measure
9	[y]hw ⅃	9	[ya]hu, six (?)
10	/ε .ε ⅃Β ʿbr	10	forty-six (?) *ephot*: total produce

Arad 32

1 *b /// ⅂ lḥdš [ḥṣr] swsh . k[   ]*

1 On the fourth (day) of the month, [Ḥaṣar]-Susah

Arad 33

1	*ḥṭm*	1	wheat *seah*
2	*wḥṭm*	2	fifty-three and wheat
3	*ḥṭm* . *b*	3	wheat *letek*
4	*wḥṭm*	4	and wheat
5	*[ ]*	5	
6	*[ḥ]ṭm* .	6	[wh]eat *seah*
7	*wḥ[ṭ]m*	7	and wh[ea]t
8	*[ḥ]ṭm*	8	[wh]eat

Arad 35

1	*[ ]ʾb*	1	
2	*[ ]bn .ʾšy[hw]*	2	son of Eshya[hu)
3	*šlm bn ʾḥyʾm*	3	Shallum, son of Aḥiam
4	*gmryhw bn [ ]*	4	Gemaryahu, son of

Arad 36

1	traces only	1	
2	*ʾr[yhw] bn nḥmyh[w]*	2	Uri[yahu,] son of Neḥemyah[u]
3	traces only	3	
4	*ḥnnyhw*	4	Ḥananyahu
5	traces only	5	
6	*[ ]* .	6	one (?)
7	*[ ]*	7	five

Arad 37

1	traces only	1	
2	*pgš*	2	he met (?)
3	*[ ]y[ ]*	3	

Arad 38

1	*hkws*	1	Hakkos
2	*šʿl ‹b›n ḥn[n]*	2	Shuʿal, ‹so›n of Ḥana[n]
3	*gmryhw bn[ ]*	3	Gemaryahu, son of
4	*šbʿ bn [ ] /*	4	Sheba, son of one (?)
5	*[ ] bn ʾlyšb* /	5	son of Elyashib, one
6	*ḥnn* //	6	Ḥanan, two
7	*[z]kr* /	7	[Za]kkur, one

Arad 39

1	*[ʾ]dm bn yqmyhw*	1	[A]dam, son of Yeqamyahu
2	*šmʿyhw bn mlkyhw*	2	Shemayahu, son of Malkiyahu
3	*mšlm bn n̊dbẙhw*	3	Meshullam, son of Nedabyahu
4	*tnḥm bn ydʿyhw*	4	Tanḥum, son of Yedayahu
5	*gʾlyhw bn ydʿyh̊w*	5	Geʾalyahu, son of Yedayahu
6	*[ ]yhw bn ʾḥ̊y*	6	son of Aḥi
7	*[ ]yhw b̊n̊ š*	7	son of
8	*mʿyhw*	8	Shemayahu
Reverse			
9	*yʾznyhw bn b̊n̊ẙhw*	9	Yaʾazanyahu, son of Benayahu
10	*yhwʾb bn ḥldẙ*	10	Yehoab, son of Ḥelday
11	*ʾbyḥy*	11	Abiḥay

Arad 40

1 *bnkm . gmr[yhw] wnḥ*
2 *myhw . šlḥ[w lšlm]*
3 *mlkyhw brkt[k lyhw]h*
4 *wʿt . ḥt̊h [ʿ]bdk [l]bh*
5 *ʾl . ʾšr ʾm[rt wktbt]y*
6 *ʾl ʾdnẙ [ʾt kl ʾšr r]*
7 *ṣh . hʾẙš [wʾšyhw b]*
8 *ʾ . mʾtk . wʾyš [lʾ ntn l]*
9 *hm . whn . ydʿth [hmktbm m]*
10 *ʾdm . nttm lʾdn[y bṭrm y]*
11 *rd ym . w[ʾ]š[y]hw . ln [bbyty]*
12 *whʾ . hmktb . bqš [wlʾ ntt]*
13 *y . ydʿ . mlk̊ . yhwd[h ky ʾy]*
14 *nnw . yklm . lšlh .ʾt h[wz]*
15 *ʾt hrʿh .ʾš[r] ʾd[m ʿśth]*

1 Your son Gemar[yahu] and Ne*ḥ*em-
2 yahu (hereby) sen[d greetings to (you)]
3 Malkiyahu. I bless [you to YHW]H.
4 And now, your [ser]vant has applied himself
5 to what you ord[ered]. I (hereby) [write]
6 to my lord [everything that the man]
7 [wa]nted. [Eshyahu has co]me
8 from you but [he has not given]
9 [th]em any men. Surely you know [the reports from]
10 Edom. I sent them to [my] lord [before]
11 [ev]ening. Eshyahu is staying [in my house.]

Arad 40 (continued)

12 He tried to obtain the report [but I would not give (it to him).]
13 The king of Juda[h] should know [that] we [are
14 un]able to send the [ ]. [This]
15 is the evil whi[ch] (the) Edo[m(ites) have done.]

Arad 41

1 *[yh]w* . ᒪ	1 [yah]u, a *seah*-measure
2 *[ ]ʾl . [ ]*	2
3 *[ ]yh[w]*	3 yah[u]
4 *[ ]yhw[ ]*	4 yahu
5 *[ ]q[ ]*	5
6 *[ ]*	6
7 *[y]hw* . ᒪ	7 [ya]hu, a *seah*-measure

Arad 42

1 *[y]gwr* ⌐	1 [Ya]gur, a *letek*-measure
2 ⌐	2 a *letek*-measure

Arad 44

1 *šlm*	1 Shallum
2 *bk*	2

Arad 47

1 *[ʾl]yšb* ///	1 Elyashib, three
2 *[ ]n*	2

Arad 48

1 *ʿ̊rd*	1 Arad
2 *r* . I7 s	2 six
3 *[z]kr* ///	3 [Za]kkur three

Arad 49

base	
1 *bny . bṣl* ///	1 The sons of Baṣal, three
2 *bny . qrḥ* //	2 The sons of Qoraḥ, two
3 *bn . glgl* /	3 The son of Gilgal, one
4 *bny . knyh̊ẘ*	4 The sons of Konyahu
side a	side a
5 /	5 one
6 /	6 one

Arad 49 (continued)

7 *[yh]wʿz* /	7 [Yeho]az, one
side b	side b
8 *ʿbd[yhw]*	8 Obad[yahu]
9 *yhwʾb*	9 Yehoab
side c	side c
10 *[ ]yhw* /	10 yahu, one
side d	side d
11 *[b]n . ṣmḥ* /	11 [s]on of Ṣemaḥ, one
12 *[ ]dʾl[ ]*	12
13 *[ ]ʾ* //	13 two
14 *šʿl* /	14 Shuʿal, one
15 *pdyhw . ḥ(ṭm)* / ∩	15 Pedayahu, eleven measures of) w(heat)
16 *bny .ʾḥʾ . ḥ(ṭm)* ///	16 The sons of Aha, three (measures of) w(heat)

Arad 50

1 *mrmwt*	1 Meremot

Arad 51

1 *ʾšyhw*	1 Eshyahu,
2 *bn ʿzr*	2 son of Ezer

Arad 52

1 *ṣyd*	1 Ṣayyad

Arad 53

1 *yšpṭ .*	1 Yishpot

Arad 54

1 *pšḥr*	1 Pasḥur

Arad 55

1 *bn ḥmdʾ*	1 the son of Ḥemda
2 *[pd]y*	2 [Pad]i

Arad 56

1 *bn nt*	1 The son of
2 *nyhw*	2 Netanyahu

Arad 57

1	*[ ]ʾl*	1	
2	*ḥšy*	2	Ḥushay

Arad 58

1	*ʿdyhw*	1	Adayahu
2	*klb bn[ ]*	2	Kaleb, son of
3	*ʿzr bn[ ]*	3	Ezer, son of
4	*yʾḥṣ[ ]*	4	Yaʾaḥaṣ

Arad 59

1	*yhwʾb bn y[ ]*	1	Yehoab, son of
2	*yqmyhʿw bn [ ]my [ ]*	2	Yeqamyahu, son of
3	*nḥmyhw bn [ ]*	3	Neḥemyahu, son of
4	*ʿmšlm bn [ ]*	4	Ammishalem, son of
5	*yʾzn bn ṣpn[yhw]*	5	Yaʾazan, son of Ṣepan[yahu]

Arad 60

1	*kprh hbʿ*	1	Kepirah the Baʿalatite
2	*lty ///*	2	twenty-seven (?)
3	*šbnyhw /*	3	Shebanyahu, one
4	*mqnyhw . tn*	4	Miqneyahu, give
5	*lgb*	5	to Geba[ryahu]
Reverse			
6	*[ryhw] /*	6	six

Arad 61

1	*šlhw .ʿ[ ]*	1	they sent
2	*[ ]n b //*	2	two
3	*[ ]r*	3	
Reverse			
4	*[ ]w*	4	
5	*[ ]*	5	
6	*[ ]h[ ]*	6	

Arad 62

1	*šlḥ.*	1	he sent
2	*[ ]ḥ. //*	2	two

Arad 64

1	*gry*	1	Geri
2	*ʾlyš[b]*	2	Elyashib

Arad 65

1	*š(klm)*	1	she(kels)
2	*š(klm)* ר	2	she(kels), five

Arad 67

1	*[ ] /*	1	one
2	*[ ]r̊ /*	2	one
3	*[ ]ẙhw //*	3	yahu, two
4	*[ʾ]ḥ̊ʾ //*	4	[A]ḥa, two
5	*zkr /*	5	Zakkur, one

Arad 68

1	*[ ] .*	1	
2	*[ ]ḥl .*	2	
3	*rgʾ*	3	Ragga
Reverse			
4	*w*	4	
5	*ʾš*	5	

Arad 69

1	*[ ]yhw*	1	yahu
2	*[ ]yhw*	2	yahu
3	*[ ]ʿ̊yhw*	3	yahu
4	*[ ]h̊wʾ*	4	
5	*[ ]l*	5	
6	*[ ]ʾln*	6	
7	*[ ]ʾ*	7	

Arad 71

1	*[ ]r . tn .*	1	give
2	*[ ]t̊ .ʾšr l̊[ ]*	2	which
3	*[ʿ]ẙn . gdy*	3	[A]yn Gedi
Reverse			
4	*[ ]ʾ . bn*	4	son of
5	*[ ]p*	5	

Arad 72

1	*m̊qnyhw / mnḥm /*	1	Miqneyahu, one; Menahem, one
2	*ppy /ʾḥmlk /*	2	Pepi, one; Ahimelek, one
3	*g̊d̊ʾ / [ ] ///*	3	Gadda one, three
4	*ʿ̊z̊ʾ̊ ///*	4	Uzza, three
5	*ʿb̊d̊ //*	5	Ebed, two

Arad 74

1	*[ ]*	1	
2	*ʾḥ̊ʾ*	2	Aḥa
3	*yqm̊[yhw]*	3	Yeqam[yahu]
4	*bn̊*	4	Ben

Arad 79

1	*[ ]ʾḥ bn*	1	-aḥ, son of

Arad 80

1	*[ ]ʾ̊b .*	1	-ab
2	*yqm̊[yhw]*	2	Yeqam[yahu]

Arad 81

1	*///š̊*	1	three sh(ekels)
2	*/*	2	one (?)

Arad 83

1		1	
2		2	seven (?)
3		3	*letek*-measure

Arad 87

1	 / /////////	1	fifteen (?)

Arad 88

1	*ʾny . mlky . bk̊[l]*	1	I became King in al[l]
2	*ʾmṣ zrʿ . ẘ [ ]*	2	Strengthen (your) arm and
3	*mlk . mṣr̊ym̊. l̊[ ]*	3	the king of Egypt

Arad 89

1	*lyw[ ]*	1	Belonging to Yaw

Arad 92

1	*lḥnn[ ]*	1	Belonging to Ḥanan

Arad 93

1	*lṣdq*	1	Belonging to Ṣadok

Arad 97

1	*mlʾ̊kẙ*	1	Malaki

Arad 98

1	*ḥsr*	1	(only) partly full (=lacking, needy)

Arad 99

1	*ʿrd ʿrd ʿ[rd] ʿrd*	1	Arad Arad Arad Arad
2	*[d]rʿ*	2	Arad
3	*drʿ*	3	Arad
4	*ʿrd*	4	Arad

Arad 101

1	*ḥṣy*	1	half(-measure)

Arad 104

1	*qdš*	1	holy (thing)

Arad 110

1	*šmyh mšlm . nʿr ʾln̊t̊[n]*	1	Shemiyah Meshullam, steward of Elnata[n]
2	*mky . nʿr . gdlẙh̊ q[ ]*	2	Maki, steward of Gedalyah

Arad 111

1	*d̊ʿ[ ]ʾ̊n̊[ ]*	1	
2	*rt wbmšmr[ ]*	2	and in/on (the) guard
3	*rʾ . mʾd wʾt[ ]*	3	very much. And
4	*ylqḥ nšb dbr[ ]*	4	be taken; we will return word
5	*hyh . hsws[ ]*	5	The horse was
6	*r . hʿbr ẘ[ ]*	6	
7	*wlš̊mʿ. [ ]*	7	and to hear
8	*mym . [ ]*	8	water
9	*ʾt[ ]*	9	the/with

Arad 112

1	*qm‹ḥ›* ε 2	1	Meal sixty-seven
2	*q̊m‹ḥ›* ε.	2	Meal sixty + *ḥqʒt*-measures

6.1.2 AVIGAD

Wine Decanter Inscription 1; Avigad, *IEJ* 22 (1972)

1	*lyḥzyhw yyn kḥl* E	1	Belonging to Yaḥzeyahu dark-colored (?) wine E

Wine Decanter Inscription 2; Avigad, *IEJ* 22 (1972)

1	*hmṣh šʿl*	1	Hammoṣah Shuʿal

6.1.3 BEERSHEBA

Beersheba 1

1	7Λ	1	fifteen
2	*p̊n̊ʾl . ʿbd̊*	2	Penuel, the servant of
3	*byt̊ . ʾmṣ̊*	3	the house of Amoṣ

Beersheba 2

1	*ʾl̊ṣ̊r̊*	1	Eliṣur

Beersheba 3

1	*ḥṭ̊‹m›*	1	whea‹t›

Beersheba 1 Graffiti

1	*qdš*	1	holy (thing)[2140]

Beersheba 2 Graffiti

1	*lnryhw*	1	Belonging to Neriyahu
2	*lʾm̊r̊ẙhw*	2	Belonging to Amaryahu

Beersheba 3 Graffiti

1	*l̊mlk[yhw]*	1	Belonging to Malkiyahu

6.1.4 BETH SHEAN

Beth Shean

1	*byt (?)[ ]*	1	house/temple (of)

6.1.5 GEZER

Gezer 1

1	*yrḥw ʾsp . yrḥw z̊*	1	His two months are harvest. His two months are early
2	*rʿ . yrḥw lqš*	2	sowing. His two months are late sowing.
3	*yrḥ ʿṣd pšt*	3	His month is cutting flax.
4	*yrḥ qṣr śʿrm*	4	His month is harvesting barley.
5	*yrḥ qṣr wkl*	5	His month is harvesting and finishing (the harvest).
6	*yrḥw zmr*	6	His two months are vine-pruning.
7	*yrḥ qṣ*	7	His month is summer-fruit.
8	*ʾby [ ]*	8	Abi

6.1.6 GIBEON

Gibeon 1

1	*gbʿn . gdr . ʿzryhw*	1	Gibon, walled plot of Azaryahu

Gibeon 2

1	*[gd]r . ʿzryhw*	1	[Walled pl]ot of Azaryahu

Gibeon 3

1	*[ ] gdr . ʿ[zryhw]*	1	walled plot of A[zaryahu]

Gibeon 4

1	*[ʿ]zryh[w]*	1	[A]zaryah[u]

Gibeon 5

1	*[ʿ]zryhw*	1	[A]zaryahu

Gibeon 6

1	*[ ]ʿzr[yhw]*	1	Azar[yahu]

Gibeon 7

1	*[gb]ʿn . gdr . ʿz[ryhw]*	1	[Gib]eon, walled plot of Aza[ryahu]

Gibeon 8

1	*gbʿn . gdr . [ ]*	1	Gibeon, walled plot of [ ]

Gibeon 9

1	*gbʿn . gd[r]*	1	Gibeon, walled pl[ot]

Gibeon 10

1	*gbʿn . gdr*	1	Gibeon, walled plot

Gibeon 11

1	*gbʿn ‹g›dr [ ]*	1	Gibeon, ‹walled› plot of [ ]

Gibeon 14

1	*gbʿn gdr ʾmryhw*	1	Gibeon, walled plot of Amaryahu

Gibeon 15

1	*[gb]ʿn . gdr ʾmryhw*	1	[Gib]eon, walled plot of Amaryahu

Gibeon 16

1	*[gb]ʿn . gdr . ʾmryhw*	1	[Gib]eon, walled plot of Amaryahu

Gibeon 17

1	*[gd]r . ʾmryhw*	1	[walled pl]ot of Amaryahu

Gibeon 18

1	*gbʿn . gd[r ʾ]mryhw*	1	Gibeon, walled [plot of A]maryahu

Gibeon 19

1	*gbʿn gdr [ ]*	1	Gibeon, walled plot of [ ]

Gibeon 21

1	*gbʿn . dmlʾ . šbʾl*	1	Gibeon Domla Shubaʾel

Gibeon 22

1	*ḥnnyhw . nrʾ .*	1	Ḥananyahu Nera

Gibeon 23

1	*gbʿn*	1	Gibeon

Gibeon 24

1	*[ ]yhw . nrʾ .*	1	yahu Nera

Gibeon 25

1	*[g]bʿn . gdr . [ ]*	1	[Gi]beon walled plot of

Gibeon 26

1	*dmlʾ gbʿn*	1	Domla Gibeon

Gibeon 27

1	*gbʿn . dmlʾ*	1	Gibeon Domla

Gibeon 28

1	*[dm]lʾ gbʿn*	1	[Dom]la Gibeon

Gibeon 29

1	*[g]bʿn dml[ʾ]*	1	[Gi]beon Doml[a]

Gibeon 30

1	*[g]bʿn*	1	[Gi]beon

Gibeon 31

1	*gbʿn . gdr*	1	Gibeon walled plot

Gibeon 32

1	*gbʿn . gdr ḥnnyhw nrʾ*	1	Gibeon walled plot of Ḥananyahu Nera

Gibeon 33

1	*ḥnnyhw .*	1	Ḥananyahu

Gibeon 34

1	*[g]bʿn gdr*	1	[Gi]beon walled plot

Gibeon 35

1	*ḥnnyhw*	1	Ḥananyahu

Gibeon 36

1	*gbʿn . gdr .*	1	Gibeon walled plot

Gibeon 37

1	*[ḥn]nyhw nrʾ*	1	[Ḥana]nyahu Nera

Gibeon 38

1	*ḥnnyhw nrʾ*	1	Ḥananyahu Nera

Gibeon 39

1	*ḥnnyhw nrʾ*	1	Ḥananyahu Nera

Gibeon 40

1	*ḥnnyhw n[rʾ]*	1	Ḥananyahu Ne[ra]

Gibeon 41

1	*ḥnnyhw*	1	Ḥananyahu

Gibeon 42

1	*ḥ̊nnyhw n[rʾ]*	1	Ḥananyahu Ne[ra]

Gibeon 43

1	*ḥ̊nny[hw]*	1	Ḥananya[hu]

Gibeon 44

1	*ḥnnyh[w]*	1	Ḥananyah[u]

Gibeon 45

1	*nrʾ*	1	Nera

Gibeon 46

1	*[n]rʾ*	1	[Ne]ra

Gibeon 47

1	*[ḥ]nnyhw ‹nr›ʾ*	1	[Ḥa]nanyahu ‹Ne›ra

Gibeon 48

1	*nrʾ*	1	Nera

Gibeon 49

1	*[n]rʾ*	1	[Ne]ra

Gibeon 50

1	*ḥnnyhw nrʾ*	1	Ḥananyahu Nera

Gibeon 51

1	*gbʿn lgdr lḥnn[yhw]*	1	Gibeon belonging to the walled plot, (that is) belonging to Ḥanan[yahu]

Gibeon 52

1	*ḥnnyhw .*	1	Ḥananyahu

Gibeon 54

1	*[g]bʿn gdr*	1	[Gi]beon walled plot

Gibeon 55

1	*[g]bʿn gdr*	1	[Gi]beon walled plot

Gibeon 56

1	*gb[ʿn]*	1	Gib[eon]

Gibeon 57

1	*ḥn[n]yhw . nrʾ*	1	Ḥana[n]yahu Nera

Gibeon 58

1	*m[gd]lyh[w]*	1	Mi[gda]lyah[u]

Gibeon 59

1	*[gbʿ]n . gdr*	1	[Gibeo]n walled plot

Gibeon 60

1	*gbʿn . g[dr]*	1	Gibeon wal[led plot]

Gibeon 61

1	*gbʿn gdr ʾmr[y]*	1	Gibeon walled plot of Amar[ya]hu
2	*hw*	2	

Gibeon 62

1	*[yh]w nrʾ*	1	Nera

6.1.7 HAZOR

Hazor 3

1	*bt z.g/h*	1	*bat*(-measure) (?)

Hazor 5

1	*lmkbrm*	1	Belonging to Makbiram

Hazor 6

1	*[l]ẙrbʿ̊[m]*	1	[Belonging to] Yerobo[am],
2	*bn ʾlm[lk]*	2	the son of Elime[lek]

Hazor 7

1	*lpqḥ. smdr .*	1	Belonging to Peqaḥ, SMDR-wine

Hazor 8

1	*ldlyw*	1	Belonging to Delayaw

6.1.8 ḤORVAT UZA

Ḥorvat Uza 1

1 *[š]lm . lʾḥqm . bn m[n]ḥm*
2 *ʿmdyhw . bn . zkr . mmldh*
3 *hwšʿyhw . bn . nwy . mrntn*
4 *mky . bn . hṣlyhw . mmqdh*

1 [Greet]ings to Ahiqam, son of Me[na]ḥem
2 Amadyahu, son of Zakkur, from Moladah
3 Hoshayahu, son of Nawy, from RNTN
4 Maky, son of Hiṣṣilyahu, from Maqqedah

Ḥorvat Uza 2

1	*ʾlyšb bn ʾprḥ*	1	Elyashib son of Ephroaḥ

Ḥorvat Uza 3

1	*[ ] bn ḥgb [ ] yhwmlk*	1	[ ] son of Ḥagab [ ] Yehomelek

6.1.9 JERUSALEM

Jerusalem Jar Inscription 1

1		1	
2	*mkyhw*	2	Mikayahu
3	*qn ʾrṣ*	3	creator of (?) the earth

Jerusalem Jar 2

1	*lyšʿyhw*	1	Belonging to Yeshayahu

Jerusalem Jar 3

1	*lʾš[yhw]*	1	Belonging to Esh[yahu]

Jerusalem Pomegranite Inscription

1 *lbẙ[t yhw]h̊ qdš khnm*

1 Belonging to the Tem[ple of YHW]H, holy (vessel) of the priests

6.1.10 KETEF HINNOM

Ketef Hinnom 1

1	*[ ] // yh̊w [ ]*	1	
2	*[ ]*	2	
3	*[ ]*	3	
4	*[ʾ]hb hb̊r[yt]*	4	
5	*[wh]ḥ̊sd l̊ʾ̊h[by]*	5	He who loves the cove[nant]
6	*[w]b̊šm̊ry[ ]*	6	[and the] mercy
7	*[ ]]b̊k̊[ ]*	7	
8	*( ]h̊hʿ̊l mš[kb]*	8	
9	*[ ]bh[ ]h mkl*	9	from all
10	*[ ]wmhrʿ [ ]*	10	and from the evil
11	*k̊ybwg̊l*	11	
12	*hky yhwh[ ]*	12	YHWH
13	*[ ]šyn̊m̊w[ ]*	13	
14	*k̊wr ybr*	14	May
15	*[k] yhwh [w]*	15	YHWH bles[s (you) and]
16	*[y]šmrk [y]*	16	[k]eep you. [May]
17	*[ʾ]r yhwh*	17	YHWH [shi]ne
18	*[p]n[yw]*	18	[his f]ace (upon you)

Ketef Hinnom 2

1	traces only	1	
2	traces only	2	
3	traces only	3	
4	traces only	4	
5	*ybr[k]*	5	May
6	*yhwh w*	6	YHWH bles[s (you)] and
7	*[y]šmrk*	7	keep you.
8	*yʾr yh*	8	May YH[WH] shine
9	*[wh] pnyw*	9	his face
10	*[ʾl]yk w[y]*	10	[upon] you and
11	*[ś]m lk š*	11	[gi]ve you
12	*[l]wm*	12	pe[ac]e.

6.1.11 KHIRBET BEIT LEI

K. b. Lei 1

1 *ẙhẘh̊ ʾlhy kl̊ hʾrṣ h*
2 *rẙ yhẘd̊h̊ l̊ʾlhy yršlm*

K. b. Lei 1

1 YHWH, the God of all the earth
2 The mountains of Judah belong to the God of Jerusalem.

or Miller:

1 *[ʾn(k)y] yhwhʾlhykh .ʾrṣh*
2 *ʿr̊y yhd̊h̊ ẘg̊l̊ty yršlm*

1 [I am] YHWH, your God. I will accept
2 the cities of Judah. I will redeem Jerusalem.

K. b. Lei 2

1 *n̊q̊h̊ yhẘh̊ ḥnn . nqh yh yhwh*

1 Absolve (us) merciful YHWH, Absolve (us) O YHWH !

K. b. Lei 3

1	*h̊wšʿ [y]hwh*	1	Save (us), YHWH !

K. b. Lei 4

1	*ʾrr*	1	Cursed be
2	*‹ʾ›šr ‹y›mḥ̊h*	2	‹he› who will ‹ef›face (this tomb)

K. b. Lei 5

1	*ʾr[r]*	1	Cursed be

K. b. Lei 6

1	*ʾrr*	1	Cursed be

or possibly:

1	*ʾwrr*	1	One who curses

K . b . Lei 7

1	ʾrr ḥ	1	Cursed be he
2	rpk	2	who insults you

6.1.12 KHIRBET EL-KOM

K . el-Kom 1

1	lʿwpy . bn	1	Belonging to Ophay, son of
2	ntnyhw	2	Netanyahu
3	h̊ḥdr . hzh	3	(is) this (burial-) chamber.

K . el-Kom 2

1	lʿwp̊ẙ . bʿn̊ . ntnyhw	1	Belonging to Opay, son of Netanyahu

K . el-Kom 3

1 ʾryhw . h̊ʿšr . ktbh
2 b̊rk .ʾryhw . lyhwh .
3 wmṣryh . lʾšrth . hwš ʿ lh
4 lʾnyhw
5   wlʾšrt̊h̊

1 (On behalf of) Uriyahu, the notable, (has) he written it.
2 Blessed be Uriyahu to YHWH ‹and to his Asherah›.
3 Save him from his enemies.
4 (Written) by Oniyahu, (executor)
5 and by his Asherah.

K . el-Kom 4 (decanter)

1	lyḥml	1	Belonging to Yaḥmol

K . el-Kom 5 (bowl)

1	ʾl	1	El

K . el-Kom 6 (plate)

1	lšl	1	Belonging to šl‹m› (?)

6.1.13 KHIRBET EL-MESHASH

K. el-Meshash

1	*zkr*	1	Zakkur
2	*ʿzr b[n]*	2	Ezer, so[n of]
3	*ḥnnyhw b[n]*	3	Ḥananyahu, so[n of
4	*ʾḥʾ b[n]*	4	Aḥa, so[n of]

6.1.14 KUNTILLET AJRUD

K. Ajrud 1

1	*ʿyrʾ*	1	Ira

K. Ajrud 2

1	*ʿdh*	1	Adah

K. Ajrud 3

1	*lśr ʿr*	1	Belonging to the governor of the city

K. Ajrud 4

1	*lśr ʿr*	1	Belonging to the governor of the city

K. Ajrud 5

1	*lśr ʿr*	1	Belonging to the governor of the city

K. Ajrud 6

1	*lśr ʿr*	1	Belonging to the governor of the city

K. Ajrud 7

1 *brk . ymm . wyśbʿw.*
2 *hyṭb . yhwh [ ] ytnw . l[ ]ʾšrt [ ]*

1 Blessed be their day and they will be satisfied
2 YHWH favored [ ] they will give [ ] Asherot [ ]

K. Ajrud 8

1 *wbzrḥ [ ] ʾl [ ] wymsn hrm[ ]*
2 *brk bʿl bym mlḥ[mh]*
3 *lšm ʾl bym mlḥ[mh]*

1 When God shines forth (=appears)
the mountains
2 Blessed be Baal on the day of w[ar]
3 For the name of God on day of w[ar]

K. Ajrud 9

1	*ḥlyw*	1	Ḥelyaw

K. Ajrud 10

1	*lyhwh . htm̊n . wlʾšrth*	1	To Yahweh of Teman and to his Ashera

K. Ajrud 11 (2x)

1	*ṭyklmnspʾṣqršt*	1	Abecedary

K. Ajrud 12

1	*šmʿyw bn ʿzr*	1	Shemayaw, son of Ezer

K. Ajrud 13

1 *lʿbdyw bn̊ ʿdnh brk hʾ lyhw‹h›*

1 Belonging to Obadyaw, son of Adnah. Blessed be he to YHW‹H›.

K. Ajrud 14

1 *ʾmr . [ ]ʾmr . lyhl[lʾl] . wlywʿśh . w[ ] . brkt .ʾtkm . lyhwh . šmrn . wlʾšrth .*

1 Thus says [X], "Say to Yehal[lelʾel] and to Yawasah, [ ] 'I (hereby) bless you by YHWH, of Samaria, and by his Asherah.'"

K. Ajrud 15

	[ʾ]m̊r̊		(Thus) [sa]ys
1	*ʾmryw ʾ*	1	Amaryahu,
2	*mr l .ʾdny*	2	"Say to my lord
3	*hšlm .ʾ[t]*	3	'Is it well with y[ou]?
4	*brktk . ly*	4	I (hereby) bless you by
5	*hwh tmn*	5	YHWH of Teman
6	*wlʾšrth . yb*	6	and by his Asherah. May he

K . Ajrud 15 (continued)

7 *rk . wyšmrk*	7 bless (you) and keep you,
8 *wyhy ʿm .ʾd[n]*	8 and may he be with
9 *y[ ]k*	9 my lo[rd]"

K . Ajrud 16

1 *kl ʾšr yšʾl mʾš ḥnn[ ] wntn lh yhw‹h› klbbh*

1 Whatever he asks from a man, may it be favored [ ] and let YHW‹H› give to him as he wishes (=according to his heart).

6.1.15 LACHISH

Lachish 1

1 *gmryhw . bn . hṣlyhw .*	1 Gemaryahu, son of Hiṣṣilyahu
2 *yʾz̊nyhw . bn ṭbšlm .*	2 Yaazanyahu, son of Tobshalem
3 *ḥgb . bn. yʾznyhw .*	3 Ḥagab, son of Yaazanyahu
4 *mbṭḥyhw . bn . yrm̊ẙh̊ẘ*	4 Mibṭahyahu, son of Yirmeyahu
5 *mtnyhw . bn . nryhw*	5 Mattanyahu, son of Neriyahu

Lachish 2

1 *ʾl ʾdny . yʾwš yšmʿ*
2 *yhwh . ʾt ʾdny . šm̊ʿt šl*
3 *m .ʿt . kym ʿt kym my .ʿbd*
4 *k klb ky . zkr ʾdny .ʾt .*
5 *[ʿ]bdh . ybkr . yhwh ʾt ʾ*
6 *[dn]y dbr . ʾšr lʾ . ydʿth*

1 To my lord Yaush: May YHWH
2 give you good news
3 (but) a dog that my lord has remembered
5 his [se]rvant? May YHWH favor my
6 l[or]d with knowledge of anything you do not already know.

Lachish 3

1 *ʾbdk . hwšʿyhw . šlḥ. l*
2 *hg[d lʾd]ny y[ʾ]w[š] . yšmʿ.*
3 *yhw[h ʾt] ʾdny šmʾt . šlm*
4 *w[ ]s̊[ ]w[ʿt] hpqḥ*
5 *[nʾ] ʾt ʾzn ʿbdk̥ . lspr .ʾšr .*
6 *šlḥ ʾdny lʿbdk ʾmš . ky . lb*

Lachish 3 (continued)

7 *ʿbd̊[k] d̊ẘh . mʾz . šlḥk .ʾl .ʿbd*
8 *k wky ʾmr .ʾdny . lʾ . ydʿth .*
9 *qrʾ . spr ḥyhwh . ʾm . nsh .ʾ*
10 *yš . lqrʾ ly spr lnṣḥ. wgm .*
11 *kl s̊pr ʾšr ybʾ .ʾly ʾm .*
12 *qrʾty .ʾth [ʾḥ]r ʾtnnhw*
13 *[ʾ]l . mʾwm̊[h] ẘlʿbdk . hgd .*
14 *lʾmr . yrd śr . hṣbʾ .*
15 *knyh̊ẘ bn ʾlntn lbʾ .*
16 *mṣrymh . wʾ[t]*
17 *hwdwyhw bn ʾḥyhw w*

Reverse

18 *ʾnšw šlḥ. lqḥt . mzh .*
19 *wspr . ṭbyhw ʿbd . hmlk . hbʾ*
20 *ʾl . šlm . bn ydʿ . mʾt . hnbʾ . lʾm*
21 *r . hšmr . šlḥh . ʿb‹d›k . ʾl . ʾdny .*

1 Your servant Hoshayahu (hereby) [re]po[rts]
2 to my [lor]d Y[a]u[sh]: May YHW[H] cause
3 my lord to hear good news.
4 and [ ] And [now], please explain
5 to your servant (the meaning of) the letter which
6 [my lo]rd sent to your servant yesterday. For [your]
7 servant has been sick at heart ever since you sent (it) to your servant.
8 And as for what my lord said, "You do not know how
9 to read a letter!," as ‹Y›HWH lives, no one has ever tried
10 to read a letter to me! Moreover,
11 any letter which might come to me,
12 I can read and recount
13 every det[ail] (contained in it). Now, it has been reported to your servant
14 that the commander of the army,
15 Konyahu, the son of Elnatan has gone down in order to enter
16 Egypt. He has sent (messengers) to take
17 Hawdawyahu, the son of Ahiyahu and
18 his men from here.
19 With regard to the letter of Tobyahu, servant of the king, which was sent
20 to Shallum, son of Yada, from the prophet and which begins
21 "Beware," your ser‹vant› has sent (=forwarded) it to my lord.

Lachish 4

1 *yšmʿ . yhw[h ʾt ʾdn]y . ʿt kym .*
2 *šmʿt ṭb . wʿt kkl ʾšr . šlḥ . ʾdny.*
3 *kn .ʿśh . ʿbdk ktbty ʿl hdlt kkl .*
4 *ʾšr šlḥ[th ʾ]ly . wky . šlḥ . ʾ*
5 *dny .ʿl . dbr byt hrpd . ʾyn šm . ʾ*
6 *dm wsmkyhw lqḥh . šmʿyhw w*
7 *yʿlhw . hʿyrh wʿbdk . ʾy[nn]*
8 *y šlḥ šmh ʾt hʿ[d hym]*

Reverse

9 *ky ʾm . btsbt . hbqr [y]b[ʾ]*
10 *wydʿ . ky ʾl . mśʾt lkš . nḥ*
11 *nw šmrm . kkl . hʾtt . ʾšr ntn*
12 *ʾdny . ky lʾ . nrʾh ʾt ʿz*
13 *qh*

1 May YHW[H] cause my [lord] to hear
2 good tidings at this time! And now, your servant has done
3 everything my lord sent (word to do). I have posted everything
4 my lord has written to me. In regard to what my lord has written
5 about the matter of Beth-HRPD, there is no one there.
6 As for Semakyahu, Shemayahu has seized him and
7 taken (=brought) him up to the city. Your servant is [not] able
8 to send the wit[ness] there [today].
9 For if he [co]me[s around] during the morning tour
10 he will know that we
11 are watching the Lachish (fire-)signals, according to all the signs which my lord
12 gave us, for we cannot see
13 Azeqah.

Lachish 5

1 *yšmʿ [yhwh ʾt ʾd]ny*
2 *[šmʿt šl]m wṭb [ʿt]*
.3 *[kym ʿt kym] my .ʿbdk*
4 *klb . [ky] .šlḥth ʾl ʿbd*
5 *k .ʾ[t] . hs[prm] kzʾ*

1 May [YHWH cause my lo]rd to hear
2 [tidings of pea]ce and good, [at this]
3 [very time]. Who is your servant
4 (but) a dog that you have sent your servant
5 the[se lette]rs?

Lachish 5 (continued)

6	*[t] . hšb .ʿbdk . hspr*	6	Your servant (now) returns the letters
7	*m .ʾl ʾdny . yr̊ʾ̊k y*	7	to my lord. May YHWH allow my lord to witness
8	*hwh . hq̊ṣr̊ . bṭ̊b̊*	8	a good harvest
9	*hym . hʾl .ʿbdk . y‹b›ʾ*	9	today. Will Tobyahu be bringing
10	*ṭbyhw . zrʿ lmlk̊*	10	royal grain to your s servant?

Lachish 6

1 *ʾl ʾdny yʾwš . yrʾ . yhwh ʾ*
2 *t̊. ʾdny ʾt hʿt hzh . šlm my*
3 *ʿbdk̊. klb ky . šlḥ . ʾdny ʾ[t sp]*
4 *r hmlk [wʾt] spry hśr[m lʾm]*
5 *r qrʾ nʾ whnh . dbry . h[śrm]*
6 *lʾ ṭbm lrpt ydyk [wlhš]*
7 *qṭ . ydy hʾ[nšm] ydʿ[ ]*
8 *[ ]ʾnk[y]ʾdny hlʾ tk*
9 *tb ʾl[yhm] l[ʾmr lm]h̊ tʿśw .*
10 *kzʾt w[ ] šlm [ ] hl*
11 *mlk [ ] w [ ] d*
12 *[ ] ḥy . yhwh .ʾlh*
13 *yk k[y m]ʾz qrʾ ʿb*
14 *dk ʾt hspr[m] l[ʾ] h[y]h*
15 *lʿb[dk]*

1 To my lord Yaush. May YHWH cause my lord to see
2 this season in peace (= may he make this time a good one for you). Who is
3 your servant (but) a dog that my lord should have sent (him) th[e]
4 king's [lett]er [and tho]se of the official[s]
5 [tellin]g (me) to please read (them)? Well, the [officials'] statements
6 are not good-- they are the kind which would weaken you [and slack]en
7 (the courage of) the pe[ople.] (My lord) will know
8 I My lord, won't you write
9 to [them] a[sking, "Wh]y are you doing
10 this?" to the
11 king
12 As YHWH your God lives,
13 ev[er si]nce your servant read
14 the letter[s],
15 he has [been able to think of] nothing [else].

Lachish 7

1	traces only	1	
2	traces only	2	
3	*[ ] spr [ ]*	3	letter
4	*[ ] k [ ]*	4	
5	*[ ] yhw . spr. b[ṭ]*	5	yahu, a letter
6	*bšlm h[ ]*	6	[To]bshalem

Lachish 8

1	*yšmʿ y[hwh]ʾt .ʾdn[y šm]*	1	May Y[HWH] cause [my] lord to hear
2	*ʿt ṭb [ʿt kym]*	2	good [ne]ws [at this time.]
3	*h[ ]n[ ]ʾ[ ]mʾ*	3	Moab
4	*b[ ] rḥ[ ]yh[*	4	
5	*[ ]r[*	5	
Reverse			
6	*[ ]y[ ]ʾkzb*	6	Akzib
7	*[ ]ʾdny . šmh*	7	my lord there

Lachish 9

1 *yšmʿ yhwh .ʾt ʾd*
2 *ny š[mʿt] šlm . w[ṭb]*
3 *[wʿ]t tn . lḥm* ⊢— *w*
4 *[yy]n // hšb .*
5 *[l]ʿbdk d*
6 *br b*
Reverse
7 *yd šlmyhw .ʾ*
8 *šr nʿśh . m*
9 *ḥr*

1 May YHWH give my lord
2 [gre]at n[ews].
3 [And n]ow, give 10 (loaves of) bread and
4 two *bat*-measures ?) of [win]e (to bearer). Retur[n]
5 word [to] your servant
6 through the
7 intermediary of Shelemyahu
8 about what we are to do
9 tomorrow.

Lachish 11

1	traces only	1	
2	traces only	2	
3	*ʾl̊n̊t̊n̊ [ ]*	3	Elnatan
4	*mkyhw [ ]*	4	Mikayahu
5	*sm̊kyhw*	5	Semakyahu
6	*ṣ̊[d]qẙ[hw]*	6	Ṣe[de]qya[hu]
7	traces only	7	

Lachish 12

1	*[ ]klb .ʾdny . h[ ]*	1	dog my lord
2	*[s]pr [ ]*	2	[le]tter
3	*[ḥ]y yhwh [k]y[ ]ʾy[]*	3	[A]s YHWH lives
4	*q[r]ʾty [ʾ]th ʿbd[k]*	4	I r[e]ad [i]t. Your servant
5	*[ ]*	5	
6	*[ ]ʾdny [ ]*	6	my lord
7	*[ ]h̊ . ʿbdk [ ]*	7	your servant

Lachish 13

1	*[ ]qm lʿśt mlʾkh .*	1	arise and do work
2	*[ ]wsmk[yhw]h[ ]*	2	and Semak[yahu]
3	*[ ]ʾt .ʾšpt ////*	3	quivers, four

Lachish 16

1	*[ ]ḥm[ ]*	1	
2	*[ ]h hy [ ]*	2	
3	*[š]lḥ hʿ[ ]*	3	[s]end the
4	*[sp]r. bny[ ]*	4	[the let]ter of the sons of (or:my son's letter)
5	*[y]hw hnbʾ [ ]*	5	[-ya]hu the prophet [ ]
6	*[ ]m [ ]*	6	
Reverse			
7	*[ ]ʾ [ ]*	7	
8	*[ ]ʿ [ ]*	8	
9	*[ ] šlḥʾ [ ]*	9	send
10	*[d]br wḥ[ ]*	10	[w]ord and

Lachish 17

1	*[ ]ʿbd̊[k]*	1	[your] servant
2	*[]ʾdny [ ]*	2	my lord
3	*[ʾ]dny g[ ]*	3	my [l]ord

Lachish 18

1 *ʿd . hʿrb[ ] šlm yšl̊ḥ [ʿ]b[dk h]spr ʾšr*
2 *šlḥ. ʾdny . [lʿ]zr[y]hẘ*

1 until evening [Your se]rv[ant] will send [the] letter which
2 my lord sent [to] Azar[ya]hu.

Lachish 19

1	*bn ʿzr* ⊢	1	son of Ezer, ten
2	*pq̊ḥ̊.* ı⊢	2	Peqaḥ, eleven
3	*m̊kl̊ .* ⲭ	3	Mikal, twenty
4	*šmʿ[yhw] .* ⲭ	4	Shema[yahu], twenty
5	*ẙb̊š*	5	Yabesh
6		6	six
7	ı⊢	7	eleven
8		8	
9	ı⊢	9	eleven

Lachish 20

1	*btšʿyt byt [ ]ẙhw*	1	In the ninth (year), house of [ ]yhw
2	*ḥkly[hw bn ʾ]zn̊[y] /*	2	Ḥaka[lyahu, son of A]zni, 1

Lachish 21

1	*ʾl ʾdny*	1	To my lord
2	*ʾt ʿbd*	2	your servant
3	*k klb ywṣ*	3	(but) a dog, he will bring
4	*ʾ*	4	forth
5	*whʾ*	5	
Reverse			
6	[ ]	6	
7	[ ]	7	
8	*m̊r̊ḥ̊ẙn̊*	8	
9	*ḥ̊r̊ʾ̊*	9	
10	*[ ]r̊ḥ̊[ ]*	10	

Lachish 22

1	*l[ ]*	1	Belonging to
2	*l[ ]*	2	Belonging to
3	*lʾl[ ]*	3	Belonging to El [ ]
4	*ldl[yhw]*	4	Belonging to Dela[yahu]
5	*lsmkyhw[ ]*	5	Belonging to Semakyahu
6	*lʾš[yhw]* ⊣	6	Belonging to Esh[yahu] *homer*

Lachish 22 (continued)

7	*lʿśyhw bn []ʾ[ ]* ∟	7	Belonging to Asayahu, son of [ ] *seah*
8	*lʾlyš[b]*	8	Belonging to Elyashi[b]
9	*l[ ]*	9	Belonging to
10	*lbyt ʾkzy[b]*	10	Belonging to Beth-Akzi[b]

Lachish 23

1	*[ ]gdhwzḥt . g /*	1	
2	*[ ] sʿpṣqr . ʾk*	2	
3	*[ ]št .*	3	

Lachish 24

1	*ʾbgd*	1	Abigad (PN) or Abecedary

Lachish 25

1	*yyn .ʿšn .*	1	strong (=vintage, fermented: red) wine

Lachish 26

1	*[n/ʾ]ryhw*	1	[Neri]yahu (or [Uri]yahu (?))

Lachish 27

1	*[lyhw]bnh*	1	[Belonging to Yeho]banah

Lachish 28

1	*[ly]hwbnh*	1	[Belonging to Ye]hobanah

or Lemaire:

1	*[y]hw bn r[ ]*	1	yahu, son of

Lachish 29

1	*brbʿt*	1	In the fourth (year)
2	*qlm . pkmt .*	2	(?)
3	*[ ]b /*	3	one *bat*(-measure)

Lachish 30

1	*mz . ṣmqm . šḥrt .*	1	extract (=wine (?)) of black raisins

Lachish 31

1	*[ ]*	1	
2	*[b]n . ybrk[ ]*	2	[so]n of YBRK

Lachish 31 (continued)

3	*[ ]bgy[ ]*	3	
4	*[b]n . qr̥[ ]*	4	[so]n of
5	*[b]n . ygr .*	5	[so]n of Yagur

Lachish 32

1	*lʾlyrb*	1	Belonging to Elyarib

6.1.16 MEṢAD ḤASHAVYAHU

Meṣad Ḥashavyahu 1

1 *yšmʿ ʾdny . hśr*
2 *ʾt dbr ʿbdh .ʿbdk*
3 *qṣr . hyh .ʿbdk . bḥ*
4 *ṣr ʾsm . wyqṣr ʿbdk*
5 *wykl wʾšm kymm . lpny šb*
6 *t kʾšr kl [ʿ]bdk ʾt qṣr wʾ*
7 *sm kymm wybʾ . hwšʿyhw bn šb*
8 *y . wyqḥ . ʾt bgd ʿbdk kʾšr klt*
9 *ʾt qṣry zh ymm lqh .ʾt bgd ʿbdk*
10 *wkl ʾhy . yʿnw ly . hqṣrm ʾty bḥm*
11 *h̊šm̊š̊ ʾḥy . yʿnw ly .ʾmn nqty . mʾ*
12 *[šm hšb nʾ ʾt] bgdy wʾm lʾ . lśr lhš*
13 *[b ʾt bgd] ʿ̊b̊[dk wtt]n ʾlw . rḥ*
14 *[mm whš]b̊t ʾt̊ [bgd ʿ]bdk wlʾ tdhm [ ]*
15 *[ ]*

1 May the official, my lord, hear
2 the plea of his servant. Your servant
3 is working at the harvest. Your servant was in Ḥaṣar-
4 Asam. Your servant reaped,
5 finished, and stored (the grain) a few days ago before stopping.
6 When your [se]rvant had finished his reaping and had stored
7 it a few days ago, Hoshayahu ben Shabay came
8 and took your servant's garment. When I had finished
9 my reaping, at that time, a few days ago, he took your servant's garment.
10 All my companions will testify for me, all who were reaping with me in the heat of
11 the sun-- they will testify for me that this is true. I am guiltless of an
12 in[fraction. (So) please return] my garment. If the official does (= you do) not consider it an obligation to retur[n]

Meṣad Ḥashavyahu 1 (continued)

13 [your] ser[vant's garment, then hav]e pi[ty] upon him
14 [and ret]urn your [se]rvant's [garment]. You must not remain silent
15

Meṣad Ḥashavyahu 2

1	*lhšbyhw bn ẙʾ[ ]*	1	Belonging to Hashavyahu, son of

Meṣad Ḥashavyahu 3

1-6	traces only	1-6	
7	*[ʿ]bdẙhw*	7	[O]badyahu
8	*[ ]n̊phm̊[ ]*	8	(?)
Reverse			
9	*ʿl[ ]*	9	

Meṣad Ḥashavyahu 4

1	*//// š(qlm)*	1	Four she(kels)

Meṣad Ḥashavyahu 5

1	*šq‹l›*	1	Sheke‹l›

Meṣad Ḥashavyahu 6

1	*ʿ̊ṣ̊bʿl*	1	Uṣbaʿal
2	*[ ] ksp š* 	2	eighty (?) shekels of silver

6.1.17 MOUSSAÏEFF OSTRACA

Moussaïeff Ostracon 1

1 *kʾšr ṣwk . ʾšy*
2 *hw . hmlk . ltt byd*
3 *[z]kryhw . ksp tr*
4 *šš . lbyt yhzh .̊*
5 š *///*

1 According as Ashyahu the king commanded you
2 to give to
3 [Ze]karyahu silver from Tar-
4 shish for the house of YHYW:
5 three shekels.

Moussaïeff Ostracon 2

1 *ybr̊kk ̊. yhwh bšl̊m . wʿt . yšm*
2 *ʿ . ʾdny . hš̊r̊ ʾt ʾmtk̊ mt*
3 *ʾyšy . lʾ bnm . whyh . ydk*
4 *ʿmy . wntth . byd . ʾmtk . ʾt . h*
5 *nḥlh ʾšr . dbrth . lʿms*
6 *yhw . wʾt . śdh . hḥṭm . ʾš*
7 *r bnʿmh . ntth . lʾḥ*
8 *yw .*

1 May YHWH bless you in peace, And now: May
2 my lord the commander listen to your maidservant. My husband
3 died without sons. (I request politely that the following) happen: (let) your your hand be
4 with me and entrust to your maidservant the
5 inheritance about which you spoke to Amas-
6 yahu. As for the wheat field that
7 is in Naamah, you have (already) given (it) to
8 his brother.

6.1.18 MURABBAʿAT

papMur 17a

1 *ʾ̊m̊r̊ . [ ]yhw . lk . [š]lḥ. šl̊ḥ̊t .ʾt šlm bytk*
2 *7wʿt .ʾl . tšmʿ lk[l] d̊b̊r̊ .ʾšr ydbr .ʾlyk*

1 [X-]yahu (hereby) says to you: I hereby [s]end heartfelt greetings to your household.
2 And now, don't listen to w[hat X] will say to you

papMur 17b

1	*n̊m̊ṭ̊r . hwšʿ*	1	NMṬR Hoshea; fourteen *ephah*
2	*ʾby . ṣʿby*	2	Abi Ṣebi; ten *ephah*
3	*ʾ̊l̊ʿd̊h kršn*	3	Eladah Karshan; five *ephah*
4	*šmʿyhw . ywʿzr*	4	Shemayahu Yawezer; six *ephah*

6.1.19 NAḤAL YISHAI

Naḥal Yishai

1	*ʾrr .ʾšr . ymḥh̊*	1	Cursed be he who effaces
2	*[ ]nh̊*	2	
3	*[ ]yh̊[ ]*	3	
4	*brk . yhw[ ]*	4	Blessed be Yehaw-
5		5	
6	*brk . bgy [ ]mlk [ ]*	6	Blessed be Bagi king
7	*brk .ʾdnẙ .*	7	Blessed be my lord
8		8	

6.1.20 OPHEL

Ophel 1

1 *ḥ̊[z]qyhw bn qrʾh . bśd‹h› šrʿqʿm̊ yhw[ ]*
2 *ʾḥyhw bn hśrq bʿm̊q ẙd̊t̊.*
3 *ṣ̊p̊[n]ẙhw bn qrṣ̊ bʿm̊q ẙd̊t̊*
4 *[ṣd]qyhw*
5 traces only
6 traces only
7 traces only
8 *ʾ̊ẘryhw h[ ]*

1 Ḥi[z]qiyahu, son of Qoreh, in the fiel‹d of› ŠR̊Q̊M̊
2 Aḥiyahu, son of Hashoreq, in the valley of monuments
3 Ṣepa[n]yahu, son of Qeres, in the valley of monuments
4 [Ṣid]qiyahu
5
6
7
8 Uriyahu

Ophel 2 (see Shiloh in *BA* 42 (1979): 170)

1	*[ ] ṣbr . h[ ]*	1	accumulate
2	*[ ]b šbʿ ʿśr[ ]*	2	seven ten
3	*[ ]rbʿy . w[ ]*	3	fourth

Ophel 3 (see Naveh in *IEJ* 32 (1982): 195-98)

1	*mṭht . lz[ ]*	1	under
2	*rk . hmym̥[ ]*	2	the water

Ophel 3 (see Naveh in *IEJ* 32 (1982): 195-98) (continued)

3	*byrkty h̊[ ]*	3	in the back of the (?)
4	*nsḥh ks[ ]*	4	(?)

Ophel inscription 675b (see Lemaire in *Levant* 10 (1978): 156-58)

1	*[ś]d̊h[ ]*	1	f[ield]
2	*h̊m . whnh̊ r̊[ ]*	2	and behold
3	*d̊m . l̊m . lkr[ ]*	3	to the people
4	*m̊. hʿz̊b̊. h̊[ ]*	4	
5	*h . ẘʿr̊ẘ .ʿl[ ]*	5	
6	*śdh . w[ ]*	6	field and
7	*ʾt̊ . nb̊l[ ]*	7	jar
8	*ṣ[ ]*	8	
9	*n̊b̊[l]*	9	jar

Ophel a (see Lemaire in *Levant* 10 (1978): 156-61)

1	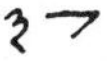 *šmnm*	1	fifty-seven (jars of) oil
2	//// *šbr̊m*	2	four (jars of) grain

Ophel b (see Lemaire in *Levant* 10 (1978): 156:61)

1		1	two hundred
2	*mnw .* 	2	they counted (numbered) eighteen
3	*lʿśr .*	3	to give a tenth

Ophel c (see Lemaire in *Levant* 10 (1978): 156:61)

1	*šmnm .*	1	oil
2	*šm̊n̊m̊ .*	2	oil
3	*šmn̊m*	3	oil
4	 *šmnm̊*	4	five (jars of) oil
5	////////	5	eight
Reverse			
6	*g̊t̊ . p̊r̊ḥ̊.*	6	Gat Peraḥ

6.1.20 RAMAT RACHEL

1	*ʾḥyhw*	1	Aḥiyahu
2	*ḥsdyhw*	2	Ḥasadyahu

6.1.21 SAMARIA

Samaria 1

1	*bšt . hʿśrt . lšm*	1	In the tenth year. Belonging to Shemaryaw
2	*ryw . mbʾrym . nbl [yn]*	2	from Beerayim a jar of
3	*yšn .*	3	old [wine]
4	*rgʿ . ʾlyšʿ . //*	4	Raga Elisha, two
5	*ʿzʾ . q[d]bš /*	5	Uzza Qadbes, one
6	*ʾlbʾ [ ] /*	6	Eliba one
7	*bʿlʾ . ʾlyš[ʿ]*	7	Baʿala Elisha
8	*ydʿyw*	8	Yedayaw

Samaria 2

1	*bšt . hʿś*	1	In the tenth year
2	*rt . lgdyw .*	2	Belonging to Gaddiyaw
3	*mʾzh .*	3	from Azah.
4	*ʾbbʿl . //*	4	Abibaʿal, two
5	*ʾḥz . //*	5	Ahaz, two
6	šbʿ . .	6	Sheba, one
7	*mrbʿl . /*	7	Maribaʿal, one

Samaria 3

1	*bšt . hʿśrt . l[ ]*	1	In the tenth year, belonging to
2	*ʾ . mšmydʿ . nbl [yn y] .*	2	from Shemida, a jar of
3	*šn . lbʿlʾ . ʿ[ ] .*	3	old [wine] . Belonging to Baʿala

Samaria 4

1	*[b]št . htšʿt . mq*	1	[In the] ninth year, from Qo[ṣeh].
2	*[ṣh .] lgdyw . nbl .*	2	Belonging to Gaddiyaw, a jar
3	*yn . yšn*	3	[of old wine.]

Samaria 5

1	*bšt . ht[šʿt .]*	1	In the nin[th] year
2	*mqṣh . l[gd]ẙw*	2	from Qoṣeh. Belonging to [Gaddi]yaw,
3	*nbl . yn . yšn .*	3	a jar of old wine.

Samaria 6

1	*b̊št . htšʿt .*	1	In the ninth year,
2	*m̊qṣh . lgd*	2	from Qoṣeh. Belonging to Gaddiyaw,
3	*yw . nbl . yn*	3	a jar of
4	*ysn .*	4	old wine.

Samaria 7

1	*bšt . [mqṣ]*	1	In the [-th year, from Qoṣe]h
2	*h . lgdẙ[w . nbl . yn . y]*	2	Belonging to Gaddiya[w, a jar of]
3	*šn .*	3	[o]ld [wine].

Samaria 8

1	*[bšt . h]t̊šʿt . mgb*	1	[In the] ninth [year], from Geba.
2	*[ʿ . lʾdn]ʿm . nbl .*	2	[Belonging to Adoni]am, a jar of
3	*[yn . yš]n .*	3	[o]ld [wine].

Samaria 9

1	*bšt . htšʿt . my*	1	In the ninth year, from Yaṣit
2	*ṣt . lʾdnʿm .*	2	Belonging to Adoniam,
3	*[n]bl . y[n .] yšn .*	3	[a ja]r of o[ld] wine.

Samaria 10

1	*bšt . htšʿt . m*	1	In the ninth year, from
2	*yṣt . lʾd̊nʿ*	2	Yasit. Belonging to Adoniam,
3	*m . nbl . yn . .*	3	a jar of
4	*yšn . .*	4	old wine.

Samaria 11

1	*[n]bl . yn .*	1	[a ja]r of wine
2	*[lʾd]n̊ʿm .*	2	[Belonging to Ado]niam.

Samaria 12

1	*bšt . htšʿt .*	1	In the ninth year,
2	*mšptn . lbʿl*	2	from Shiptan. Belonging to Baʿal
3	*zmr . nbl . yn .*	3	Zamar, a jar of
4	*yšn*	4	old wine.

Samaria 13

1	*bšt . hʿśrt . mʾbʿ*	1	In the tenth year, from Abiezer.
2	*zr . lšmryw . nbl .*	2	Belonging to Shemaryaw, a jar of

Samaria 13 (continued)

3	*yn . yšn lʾš̊[ḥr]*	3	old wine. Belonging to As[ḥur]
4	*[ ] mtwl [ ]*	4	from Tawil

Samaria 14

1	*bšt[.]h̊tš[ʿt .] mg̊*	1	In the nin[th] year, from Gat-
2	*t prʾn . lšmryw .*	2	Paran. Belonging to Shemaryaw,
3	*nbl . yn . yšn .*	3	a jar of old wine.

Samaria 15

1	*[mḥ]ṣrt . l[ ]*	1	[From Ḥa]ṣerot. Belonging to
2	*[n]bl . y[n . yšn .]*	2	[a j]ar of [old] w[ine]

Samaria 16a

1	*b̊št . hʿśrt . ms*	1	In the tenth year, from Seper.
2	*pr . lgdyw . nbl .*	2	Belonging to Gaddiyaw, a jar of
3	*šmn . rḥṣ*	3	refined oil.

Samaria 16b

1	*bšt . hʿśrt . ms*	1	In the tenth year, from Seper.
2	*pr . lgdyw . nbl .*	2	Belonging to Gaddiyaw, a jar of
3	*šmn . rḥṣ .*	3	refined oil.

Samaria 17a

1	*bšt . hʿśrt . mʾz*	1	In the tenth year, from Azah.
2	*h . lgdyw . nbl . šm*	2	Belonging to Gaddiyaw, a jar of
3	*n . rḥṣ .*	3	refined oil.

Samaria 17b

1	*[bšt . hʿ]śrt . mʾz[h .]*	1	[In the t]enth [year] from Aza[h].
2	*[lgdy]ẘ . nbl . šmn*	2	[Belonging to Gaddiya]w, a jar of
3	*[rḥṣ .]*	3	[refined] oil.

Samaria 18

1	*bšt . hʿśrt . mḥṣrt*	1	In the tenth year, from Ḥaṣerot.
2	*lgdyw . nbl . šmn .*	2	Belonging to Gaddiyaw, a jar of
3	*rḥṣ .*	3	refined oil.

Samaria 19

1	*bšt . hʿśrt .*	1	In the tenth year,
2	*myṣt . nbl .*	2	from Yaṣit, a jar of
3	*šmn . rḥṣ . l*	3	refined oil belonging to
4	*ʾd̊nʿm .*	4	Adoniam.

Samaria 20

1	*bšt . h̊ʿ[śrt . yn .]*	1	In the ten[th] year, [wi]ne
2	*mkrm . ḥt̊[l . nbl . š]*	2	of Kerem-Hat[el, a jar of]
3	*mn . rḥṣ̊*	3	refined [oi]l.

Samaria 21

1	*bšt . hʿśrt . lšmr*	1	In the tenth year. Belonging to Shemaryaw,
2	*yw . mtwl . nbl . š*	2	from Tawil, a jar of
3	*mn . rḥṣ .*	3	refined oil.

Samaria 22

1	*bšt .* ˥∧ *mḥ*	1	In the fifteenth year, from
2	*lq . lʾšʾ .ʾḥ̊*	2	Ḥeleq. Belonging to Esha
3	*mlk .*	3	Aḥimelek.
4	*ḥlṣ . mḥṣrt̊*	4	Ḥeleṣ from Ḥaṣerot.

Samaria 23

1	*bšt .* ˥∧ *mḥlq .*	1	In the fifteenth year, from Ḥeleq.
2	*lʾšʾ .ʾḥmlk .*	2	Belonging to Esha Aḥimelek.
3	*ḥlṣ . mḥṣrt .*	3	Ḥeleṣ from Ḥaṣerot.

Samaria 24

1	*bšt . h*˥∧*[mḥ]lq . lʾš[ʾ] ʾḥ̊ml̊[k .]*	1	In the fifteenth year, [from Ḥe]leq. Belonging to Esh[a] Aḥimele[k.]
2	*rpʾ .ʿnmś . m̊[ḥ]ṣ̊rt̊*	2	Rapa Animes, from [Ḥa]ṣerot.

Samaria 25

1	*[ ] m̊ḥ̊[ ]*	1	
2	*[ʾ]ḥml[k]*	2	[A]ḥimele[k]
3	*ʾḥzy . m*	3	Aḥzay, from
4	*ḥṣrt*	4	Ḥaṣerot

Samaria 26

1	*[bšt . ˥Λ mḥl]q . lʾšʾ*	1	[In the fifteenth year, from Ḥele]q. Belonging to Esha
2	*[ ] . hẙn . mḥ[ṣrt .]*	2	the wine from Ḥaṣerot.

Samaria 27

1	*bšt . ˥Λ mḥlq . lʾšʾ .*	1	In the fifteenth year, from Ḥeleq. Belonging to Esha
2	*ʾḥmlk .*	2	Ahimelek.
3	*bʿlʾ . bʿlmʿny .*	3	Baʿala the Baʿalmeʿonite.

Samaria 28

1	*bšt . ˥Λ mʾbʿzr . lʾš*	1	In the fifteenth year, from Abiezer. Belonging to Esha
2	*ʾ . ʾḥmlk .*	2	Ahimelek.
3	*bʿlʾ . mʾlmtn .*	3	Baʿala from Elmattan.

Samaria 29

1	*bšt . ˥Λ mš̊[mydʿ . l]ʾšʾ*	1	In the fifteenth year, from She[mida.] [Belonging to] Esha
2	*ʾḥmlk .*	2	Ahimelek
3	*ʾ̊m̊r . mspr .*	3	Amar from Seper.

Samaria 30

1	*bšt . ˥Λ mšmyd̊ʿ*	1	In the fifteenth year, from Shemida.
2	*lḥl̊ṣ . gdyw .*	2	Belonging to Ḥeleṣ Gaddiyaw.
3	*grʾ . ḥnʾ . [ ]*	3	Gera Hanna.

Samaria 31a

1	*bšt . h ˥Λ mšmydʿ .*	1	In the fifteenth year, from Shemida.
2	*lḥlṣ .ʾpṣḥ.*	2	Belonging to Heleṣ Epeṣaḥ.
3	*bʿlʾ . zk̊r .*	3	Baʿala Zakkur.

Samaria 31b

1	*bšt . [h ˥Λ mšmyd]ʿ .*	1	In the [fifteenth] year, from Shemida].
2	*l[ḥlṣ .ʾpṣḥ] .*	2	Belonging to [Heleṣ Epeṣaḥ].
3	*bʿlʾ[.]z[kr .]*	3	Baʿala Za[kkur].

Samaria 32

1	*bšt . ⅂∧ mš‹m›ydᶜ .*	1	In the fifteenth year, from She‹m›ida
2	*lḥlṣ .*	2	Belonging to Heleṣ
3	*ʾḥmʾ .*	3	Ahima.

Samaria 33

1	*[bšt . h] ⅂̊∧ mšmy*	1	[In the fifteenth year], from Shemi[da].
2	*[dᶜ . lḥ]l̊ṣ̊ . gdyw .*	2	Belonging to Ḥe]leṣ Gaddiyaw.
3	*[ ] m̊n̊t .*	3	MNT

Samaria 34

1	*[bš]t . h ⅂∧ m̊[š]m̊ẙ[dᶜ .]*	1	In the fifteenth year, from [She]mi[da],
2	*[lḥlṣ . g]d̊yw . ṣ[ ]*	2	[Belonging to Ḥeleṣ Ga]ddiyaw

Samaria 35

1	*bšt . ⅂∧ mš[mydᶜ .]*	1	In the fifteenth year, from She[mida.]
2	*lḥlṣ . gd[yw .]*	2	Belonging to Ḥeleṣ Gaddi[yaw].
3	*yw[ ]*	3	Yaw

Samaria 36

1	*[bšt . h ⅂∧ m]šmyd[ᶜ]*	1	[In the fifteenth year, from] Shemida.
2	*[ ]*	2	
3	*[g]rʾ . ywyšᶜ[ ]*	3	[Ge]ra Yawyasha

Samaria 37

1	*bšt . ⅂∧ mšmydᶜ .*	1	In the fifteenth year, from Shemida.
2	*lʾḥmʾ.*	2	Belonging to Ahima.
3	*ʾšʾ . bᶜl{ᶜ}zkr .*	3	Esha Baᶜal-Zakkur.

Samaria 38

1	*bšt . ⅂∧ mšmy*	1	In the fifteenth year, from Shemida.
2	*dᶜ . lʾḥmʾ .*	2	Belonging to Ahima.
3	*d̊lh .ʾlʾ .*	3	Dalah Ela.

Samaria 39

1	*bšt . ⅂Λ mšmydʿ .*	1	In the fifteenth year, from Shemida.
2	*[l]ʾḥmʾ.*	2	[Belonging to] Ahima.
3	*[ʾš]ʾ .*	3	[Esha].

Samaria 40

1	*[m]š̊mydʿ . lʿ[ ]*	1	[from] Shemida. Belonging to

Samaria 41

1	*[ʾly]šʿ . ʿglẙẘ*	1	[Eli]sha Egelyaw

Samaria 42

1	*[b]š̊t . ⅂Λ m‹ʾ›śr̊ʾ[l]*	1	[In the] fifteenth year, from ‹A›srie[l].
2	*l̊ydʿyw .*	2	Belonging to Yedayaw
3	*ʾdnyw . gdy[w]*	3	Adoniyaw Gaddiya[w]
4	*mʿšrt*	4	from Asheret

Samaria 43

1	*bšt . h[⅂Λ]*	1	In the [fifteenth] year
2	*ḥnn b̊[ʿrʾ]*	2	Ḥanan Ba[ʿara]
3	*ʾl[ ]*	3	El

Samaria 44

1	*[bšt] . h ⅂Λ mškm .*	1	[In] the fifteenth [year], from Shekem.
2	*[ ]hp[ʾ]r .*	2	HP[ʾ]R
3	*[ ] . hyn .*	3	the wine

Samaria 45

1	*bšt . h ⅂Λ mḥgl̊[h]*	1	In the fifteenth year, from Ḥogla[h].
2	*lḥnn . bʿ̊r̊ʾ*	2	Belonging to Ḥanan Baʿara.
3	*ywntn . myṣ̊[t]*	3	Yawnatan from Yaṣi[t].

Samaria 46

1	*bšt . ⅂Λ*	1	In the fifteenth year
2	*lḥnn . b[ʿr]*	2	Belonging to Ḥanan Ba[ʿar]a
3	*ʾ*	3	

Samaria 47

1	*[bšt . ˥Λ m]ḥ̊glh . lḥnn . bʿrʾ . m*	1	[In the fifteenth year, from] Ḥoglah. Belonging to Ḥanan Baʿara, from
2	*[ ] . myṣt .*	2	from Yaṣit.

Samaria 48

1	*bšt . ˥Λ mśr[ʾl] . l̊ẙd̊ʿ̊yw*	1	In the fifteenth year, from Asri[el]. Belonging to Yedayaw
2	*ʾḥmlk .*	2	Aḥimelek.
3	*yʿś . myšb .*	3	Yaʿas from Yosheb.

Samaria 49

1	*bš̊[t . mšmyd]*	1	In the [-th] y[ear, from Shemid]a.
2	*ʿ . lḥ̊[lṣ]*	2	Belonging to Ḥe[leṣ].
3	*mzy[ ]*	3	from (?)
4	*m̊kẘr .*	4	from Kur.

Samaria 50

1	*bšt . ˥Λ lgmr . mnʿh .*	1	In the fifteenth year, belonging to Gomer, from Neʿah.
2	*ʿbdyw . lʾryw .*	2	Obadyahu. Belonging to Uriyaw.

Samaria 51

1	*bšt . hʿśrt . l[ ]*	1	In the tenth year, belonging to
2	*[ ]*	2	
3	*ʾḥʾ . hyhd[y]*	3	Aḥa, the Judean.

Samaria 52

1	*b ˥Λ m̊n̊ʿ̊[h]*	1	On the fifteenth, from Neʿa[h]
2	*ʾbyw . [ ]*	2	Abiyaw

Samaria 53

1	*bšt . hʿśrt . yn .*	1	In the tenth year, wine of
2	*krm . htl . bnbl . šmn .*	2	Kerem Hatel, in a jar of
3	*rḥṣ .*	3	refined oil.

Samaria 54

1	*bšt . hʿśrt . yn . k*	1	In the tenth year, wine of Kerem
2	*rm . htl . nbl . šmn . rḥ*	2	Hatel, a jar of
3	*ṣ .*	3	refined oil.

Samaria 55

1	*bšt . hʿśrt . kr*	1	In the tenth year, the vineyard
2	*m . yḥwʿly . nbl .*	2	of Yehaweli; a jar of
3	*šmn . rḥṣ .*	3	refined oil.

Samaria 56

1	*bšt .̊ ᒣΛ m̊ht̊[l .]*	1	In the fifteenth year, from Hate[l].
2	*lnmš[ ]*	2	Belonging to Nemesh
3	*[ ]d̊l̊[ ]ʿ̊d̊*	3	

Samaria 57

1	*[ ]ʿbdʾ . yw[ ]*	1	Abda Yaw
2	*[ ]nʾ . šm‹y›dʿ*	2	Shem‹i›da
3	*[ ]yg*	3	

Samaria 58

1	*bšt . ᒣΛ lb̊dyw*	1	In the fifteenth year. Belonging to Bedyaw.
2	*krm . htl .*	2	Kerem Hatel.

Samaria 59

1	*nbl . šmn . r̊[ḥ]*	1	A jar of
2	*ṣ . bšt . [ ]*	2	re[fi]ned oil. In the year

Samaria 60

1	*krm . yḥwʿl[y]*	1	Vineyard of Yehawel[i]

Samaria 61

1	*krm . htl .*	1	Kerem Hatel,
2	*bšt . ᒣΛ*	2	In the fifteenth year.

Samaria 62

1	*yn . šmyd[ʿ]*	1	Wine of Shemida

Samaria 63

1	*bšt . // tΛ*	1	In the twelfth (?) year,
2	*mšmyd̊ʿ*	2	from Shemida.

Samaria 64

1	*m̊n̊ʿ̊h̊ l[ ]*	1	From Neʿah, belonging to
2	*ʿ̊[ ]*	2	

Samaria 66

1	*ḥ̊g̊l̊[h]*	1	Ḥogla[h]

Samaria 67

1	ᒣΛ *m̊ẙṣ̊[t]*	1	fifteen, from Yaṣit.

Samaria 72

1	*bšt . hʿśrt . yn . krm .*	1	In the tenth year, wine of Kerem
2	*htl . bnbl . šmn . rḥṣ .*	2	Hatel, in a jar of refined oil.

Samaria 73

1	*bšt . [hʿśrt]*	1	In the [tenth] year
2	*yn . kr̊[m htl bnbl]*	2	wine of Kere[m Hatel, in a jar of]
3	*šmn . [rḥṣ]*	3	[refined] oil

Samaria 78

1	*r̊g̊ʾ̊ . sr̊*	1	Ragga (?) SR

Samaria 80

1	*[y]ṣ̊t̊*	1	[Ya]ṣit

Samaria 82

1	*šmn . rḥ*	1	refined oil
2	*ṣ .*	2	

Samaria 89

1	*n̊b̊l . y[n]*	1	a jar of wi[ne]

Samaria 90

1	*[ ]m̊šmydʿ*	1	from Shemida
2	*[ ]ṣ̊ ʾ̊p̊ṣ̊ḥ̊*	2	Epeṣah (?)

Samaria 97

1	ᒣΛ	1	fifteen

Samaria 99

1	*htl*	1	Hatel (the mound)

Samaria 100

1	*bšt . hts̊̌[ʿt]*	1	In the nin[th] year

Samaria 101

1	*yn . yšn*	1	old wine

Samaria 102

1	*l[ʾ]š[ʾ]*	1	Belonging to Esha (?)

Samaria 689

1	*lpḥʾ*	1	Belonging to Paḥa

Samaria C1012

1	*mḥ[syw]*	1	Maḥ[seyaw]
2	*qlyẘ*	2	Qolayaw
3	*smk[yw]*	3	Semak[yaw]
4	*ʾry[w]*	4	Uriya[w]
5	*mn[ḥm]*	5	Mena[ḥem]

Samaria C1101 (Barley Ostracon)

1	*brk šlm̊[ ]*	1	Baruk Shallum
2	*brk hd̊ʿm hqšbw[ ]*	2	(O) Baruk, inform them to pay attention
3	*ymnh śʿrm* ///	3	he should count out three *seah*-measures (?) of barley

Samaria C 1142

1	*lʿzr . h[ ]r̊[ ]*	1	Belonging to Ezer

Samaria C 1220

1	*brk ʾḥz*	1	Baruk Aḥaz

Samaria C 1265

1	*lywyšʿ*	1	Belonging to Yawyasha

Samaria C 1307

1	*ldmlʾ .*	1	Belonging to Domla

Samaria Asher Fragment

1	*ʾšr .*	1	Asher

6.1.22 SILOAM

Siloam Tunnel

1 *[tmt .]hnqbh . wzh . hyh . dbr . hnqbh . bʿwd [hḥṣbm . mnpm .ʾt .]*
2 *hgrzn .ʾš .ʾl . rʿw . wbʿwd . šlš .ʾmt . lhn[qb wyšm]ʿ . ql .ʾš . q*
3 *[r]ʾ . ʾl . rʿw . ky . hyt . zdh . bṣr . mymn . ẘm̊[śm]ʾ̊l̊ . wbym . h*
4 *nqbh . hkw . hḥṣbm .ʾš . lqrt . rʿw . grzn .ʿl . grzn . wylkw[.]*
5 *hmym . mn . hmwṣ .ʾl . hbrkh . bmʾtym̊ ẘʾlp .ʾmh . wm[ʾ]*
6 *t .ʾmh . hyh . gbh . hṣr .ʿl . rʾš . hḥṣb[m .]*

1 Its tunneling [is through]. And this was the way in which it was tunneled out. While
2 the picks were still (in motion), each man toward his fellow worker, and while there were yet three cubits (of rock) to be tun[neled through], the voice of a man [could be hea]rd
3 ca[ll]ing to his fellow gang-member, for there was a fissure in the rock on the right and on [the le]ft. Now, on the day that the
4 tunneling (was completed), the hewers struck (the rock), each man toward his fellow worker, (with) pick against pick, and (then)
5 the water flowed from the spring to the pool a distance of twelve hundred cubits. (At that point), the rock was one [hun]dred
6 cubits high over the head(s) of the hewer[s].

6.1.23 SILWAN

Silwan 1

1 *ḥd[r] b̊k̊tp hṣ̊[r]*

1 (Tomb)-cham[ber] in the side of the ro[ck].

Silwan 2

1 *zʾt̊ [qbrt šbn]ẙhw ʾš̊ʿ̊l hbyt .ʾyn̊ [p]h̊ ksp . wz̊h̊b*
2 *[ky] ʾm̊ [ʿṣmtw] ẘʿ̊ṣm[t] ʾm̊th ʾ̊[t]h ʾrwr hʾdm̊ ʾšr*
3 *yp̊th̊ ʾ̊t z̊ʾ̊t*

1 This is the [tomb of Sheban]yahu, royal steward. There is neither silver nor gold [he]re,
2 [on]ly [his bones] and his servant-wife's bon[es] w[ith] him. Cursed be the man who
3 opens this (tomb).

Silwan 3

1	*[ ]qb̊ʿt . z[ ]*	1	the tomb of
2	*ʾ̊šr yp̊[tḥ]*	2	who o[pens]
3	*[ ]d̊ʿ*	3	

6.1.24 TELL AMAL

Tell Amal Jar Inscription

1	*lnmš*	1	Belonging to Nemesh

6.1.25 TELL BEIT MIRSIM

Tell Beit Mirsim Sherd 2

1	*bt*	1	*bat*-measure

Tell Beit Mirsim Sherd 3

1	*lʿz[yhw]*	1	Belonging to Uzzi[yahu]

Tell Beit Mirsim Sherd 4

1	*lḥz̊q̊[yhw]*	1	Belonging to Ḥizqi[yahu]

Tell Beit Mirsim Sherd 5

1	*[lg]rʾ*	1	[Belonging to Ge]ra

Tell Beit Mirsim Sherd 6

1	*[ln]ḥm*	1	Belonging to Naḥum

6.1.26 TELL IRA

Tell Ira 1

1	*mpqd . brkyhw*	1	Roll call: Berekyahu
2	*gbḥ*	2	Gibbaḥ
3	*mwqr*	3	Mowqir
4	*šlmyhw*	4	Shelemyahu

Tell Ira 2 (jar inscription)

1	*lgbr mgn*	1	Belonging to Geber Magen

Tell Ira 3 (jar inscription)

1	*ʾhd*	1	measure of volume (?)

6.1.27 TELL QASILE

Tell el Qasile 1

1	*lmlk ʾl̊[p]*	1	For the King: one thou[sand]
2	*šmn wmʾh̊*	2	one hundred (units of) oil.
3	*ḥ̊yhw*	3	Ḥiyahu

Tell el Qasile 2

1	*z̊hb .ʾpr . lbyt . ḥrn .*	1	Gold of Ophir for Beth-ḤRN
2	*š* ≡	2	thirty shekels

6.2 Seals

6.2.1 ARAD

Arad 105

1	*lʾlyšb*	1	Belonging to Elyashib,
2	*bn ʾšyhw*	2	son of Eshyahu

Arad 106

1	*lʾlyšb*	1	Belonging to Elyashib,
2	*bn ʾšyhw*	2	son of Eshyahu

Arad 107

1	*lʾl‹y›šb*	1	Belonging ‹to› El‹ya›shib,
2	*‹b›n ʾšyh‹w›*	2	[so]n of Eshyah[u]

Arad 108

1	*lbrkyhw*	1	Belonging to Berekyahu,
2	*bn [y]hw*	2	son of [ya]hu
3	*bn šlmyhw*	3	son of Shelemyahu

Arad 109

1	*ldršyh*	1	Belonging to Derashyahu,
2	*w bn ʿ[ ]*	2	son of

6.2.2 AVIGAD

Avigad HB 1

1	*lʾdnyhw*	1	Belonging to Adoniyahu
2	*ʾšr ʿl hbyt*	2	royal steward

Avigad HB 2

1	*lʾdnyhw*	1	Belonging to Adonyiahu
2	*ʾšr ʿl hbyt*	2	royal steward

Avigad HB 3

1	*lntn ʾšr*	1	Belonging to Natan
2	*[ʿ]l ‹h›byt*	2	[royal] steward

Avigad HB 4

1	*lʾlšmʿ*	1	Belonging to Elshama
2	*[ʿ]bd hmlk*	2	[ser]vant of the king

Avigad HB 5

1	*lgdlyhw*	1	Belonging to Gedalyahu
2	*ʿbd hmlk̊*	2	servant of the king

Avigad HB 6

1	*lgʾlyhw b*	1	Belonging to Gealyahu son
2	*n̊ hmlk̊*	2	of the king

Avigad HB 7

1	*lnry[hw b]*	1	Belonging to Neriyahu son
2	*n hmlk*	2	of the king

Avigad HB 8

1	*lyrḥmʾl*	1	Belonging to Yerahmeʾel
2	*bn hmlk*	2	son of the king

Avigad HB 9

1	*lbrkyhw*	1	Belonging to Berekyahu
2	*bn nryhw*	2	son of Neriyahu
3	*hspr*	3	the scribe

Avigad HB 10

1	*śr hʿr*	1	Leader of the city

Avigad HB 11

1	*lʾdnyhw b*	1	Belonging to Adonyahu son
2	*n yqmyhw*		of Yeqamyahu

Avigad HB 12

1	*lp̊d̊yhw*	1	Belonging to Pedayahu
2	*yhwqm*	2	Yehoqam

Avigad HB 13

1	*[lʾ]h̊yhw*	1	[Belonging to A]ḥiyahu
2	*[ʾ]byhw*	2	[A]biyahu

Avigad HB 14

1	*lʾḥqm b[n]*	1	Belonging to Aḥiqam so[n of]
2	*ṭbyhw*	2	Tobyahu

Avigad HB 15

1	*lʾḥqm*	1	Belonging to Aḥiqam
2	*nryhw*	2	Neriyahu

Avigad HB 16

1	*ʾḥqm*	1	Aḥiqam
2	*ʾḥʾb*	2	Ahab

Avigad HB 17

1	*lʾlʿz*	1	Belonging to Eliʿaz
2	*bn ʾḥʾb*	2	son of Ahab

Avigad HB 18

1	*lʾlʿz bn*	1	Belonging to Eliʿaz son of
2	*ʾḥʾb*	2	Ahab

Avigad HB 19

1	*lʾḥʾb*	1	Belonging to Ahab
2	*bnʾ prḥ*	2	son of Ephroaḥ

Avigad HB 20

1	*[lʾ]prḥ bn*	1	[Belonging to E]phroaḥ son of
2	*yhwšʿ*	2	Yehoshua

Avigad HB 21

1	*lʾprḥ b*	1	Belonging to Ephroaḥ son
2	*n yhwšʿ bn*	2	of Yehoshua son of
3	*mtnyhw*	3	Mattanyahu

Avigad HB 22

1	*[lʾ]pr̊ḥ*	1	[Belonging to E]phroaḥ
2	*[bn] šḥr*	2	[son of] Shaḥar

Avigad HB 23

1	*lʾprḥ*	1	Belonging to Ephroaḥ
2	*[bn šḥ]r bn*	2	[son of Shaḥa]r son of
3	*[g]dyhw*	3	[Ga]dyahu

Avigad HB 24

1	*lšḥr bn*	1	Belonging to Shaḥar son of
2	*gdyhw*	2	Gadyahu

Avigad HB 25

1	*lšḥr [b]*	1	Belonging to Shaḥar [so]n
2	*n gdy*	2	of Gaddi

Avigad HB 26

1	*lšḥr [bn]*	1	Belonging to Shaḥar [son of]
2	*[g]dyh[w]*	2	[Ga]dyah[u]

Avigad HB 27

1	*[l]ʾlyhw b̊*	1	[Belonging to] Eliyahu son
2	*[n] mykh*	2	[of] Mikah

Avigad HB 28

1	*lʾlyʿz*	1	Belonging to Eliʿaz
2	*bn hwšʿy[hw]*	2	son of Hoshaya[hu]

Avigad HB 29

1	*lʾlyrm̊*	1	Belonging to Eliram
2	*šmʿyhw*	2	Shemayahu

Avigad HB 30

1	*lʾln[t]n*	1	Belonging to Elna[ta]n
2	*bn yʾš*	2	son of Yaush

Avigad HB 31

1	*[l]ʾmryhw*	1	[Belonging to] Amaryahun
2	*[b]n*	2	[so]n
1	*yhwʾb*	3	Yehawab

Avigad HB 32

1	*lʾšḥ̊r b*	1	Belonging to Eshhor son
2	*[n]ʿśyhw*	2	[of] Asayahu

Avigad HB 33

1	*lʾšyhw*	1	Belonging to Eshyahu
2	*bn šmʿyhw*	2	son of Shemayahu

Avigad HB 34

1	*[lʾš]rḥy*	1	Belonging to [Ashe]rḥay
2	*ʿśyhw*	2	Asayahu

Avigad HB 35

1	*lbnyhw*	1	Belonging to Benayahu
2	*ʿlyhw*	2	Alayahu

Avigad HB 36

1	*lbʿdyhw*	1	Belonging to Beʿadyahu

Avigad HB 37

1	*lbʿdyhw*	1	Belonging to Beʿadyahu
2	*śryhw*	2	Saryahu

Avigad HB 38

1	*[l]brkyhw*	1	[Belonging to] Berekyahu
2	*[bn š]mʿyhw*	2	[son of She]mayahu

Avigad HB 39

1	*lgʿly b*	1	Belonging to Gaʿali son
2	*n ʾlysmk*	2	of Elyismak

Avigad HB 40

1	*lgʿly b*	1	Belonging to Gaʿali son
2	*n ʾlsmk*	2	of Elsamak

Avigad HB 41

1	*lgd[ly]hw*	1	Belonging to Geda[lya]hu
2	*hw[š]ʿyhw*	2	Ho[sha]yahu

Avigad HB 42

1	*ldmlyhw*	1	Belonging to Domlayahu
2	*bn rpʾ*	2	son of Rapha

Avigad HB 43

1	*ldmlyhw [b]*	1	Belonging to Domlayahu [so]n
2	*n hwšʿyh[w]*	2	of Hoshayah[u]

Avigad HB 44

1	*[ld]mlyhw*	1	[Belonging to Do]mlayahu
2	*[bn h]wšʿyhw*	2	[son of Ho]shayahu

Avigad HB 45
1	*ld[mlyhw]*	1	Belonging to Do[mlayahu]
2	*bn hw[šʿ]*	2	son of Ho[shea]

Avigad HB 46
1	*ldmly[hw]*	1	Belonging to Domlaya[hu]
2	*hwš[ʿyhw]*	2	Hosha[yahu]

Avigad HB 47
1	*lhwšʿyhw*	1	Belonging to Hoshayahu
2	*ḥlṣyhw*	2	Ḥelesyahu

Avigad HB 48
1	*lhwšʿyhw*	1	Belonging to Hosayahu
2	*šmʿ*	2	Shema

Avigad HB 49
1	*lhṣlyhw*	1	Belonging to Hiṣṣilyahu
2	*bn šbnyhw*	2	son of Shebanyahu

Avigad HB 50
1	*lzkr bn*	1	Belonging to Zakar son of
2	*nryhw*	2	Neriyahu

Avigad HB 51
1	*[lz]kr bn*	1	[Belonging to Za]kar son of
2	*[ ]yhw*	2	yahu

Avigad HB 52
1	*lhbʾ b*	1	Belonging to Haba son
2	*n mtn*	2	of Mattan

Avigad HB 53
1	*lḥgb bn*	1	Belonging to Ḥagab son of
2	*ṣpnyhw*	2	Ṣepanyahu

Avigad HB 54
1	*lḥgb bn*	1	Belonging to Ḥagab son of
2	*ṣpny[hw]*	2	Ṣepanya[hu]

Avigad HB 55

1	*[l]ḥgy bn*	1	Belonging to Ḥaggi son of
2	*hwdwyhw*	2	Hawdawyahu

Avigad HB 56

1	*lḥṭš*	1	Belonging to ḤṬŠ
2	*špṭyhw*	2	Shephatyahu

Avigad HB 57

1	*lḥlq b*	1	Belonging to Ḥeleq son
2	*n ʿzr*	2	of Azar

Avigad HB 58

1	*lḥlqyhw* b	1	Belonging to Ḥeleqyahu son
2	*[n] yhw*	2	[of] -yahu

Avigad HB 59

1	*lḥlqyhw*	1	Belonging to Ḥeleqyahu
2	*bn [ ]*	2	son of

Avigad HB 60

1	*[l]ḥlṣ b[n]*	1	[Belonging to] Ḥeles [son of]
2	*ʾḥʾb*	2	Ahab

Avigad HB 61

1	*lḥnnyhw*	1	Belonging to Ḥananyahu
2	*nḥmy[hw]*	2	Neḥemyah[hu]

Avigad HB 62

1	*ḥnnyh̊ẘ*	1	Ḥananyahu
2	*zrḥ*	2	Zeraḥ

Avigad HB 63

1	*[lḥ]nn bn*	1	[Belonging to Ḥa]nan son of
2	*[ʿ]zyhw bn*	2	[A]zayahu son of

Avigad HB 64

1	*[l]ḥnn bn*	1	[Belonging to] Ḥanan son of
2	*šmʿyhw*	2	Shemayahu

Avigad HB 65

1	*lṭby[hw]*	1	Belonging to Tobya[hu]
2	*ʿbdʾ*	2	Abda

Avigad HB 66

1	*lyʾš bn*	1	Belonging to Yaush
2	*ʾlšmʿ*	2	Elshama

Avigad HB 67

1	*lyʾš*	1	Belonging to Yaush
2	*[b]n pdyhw*	2	[so]n of Pedayahu

Avigad HB 68

1	*lydʿyhw*	1	Belonging to Yedayahu
2	*bn krmy*	2	son of Karmi

Avigad HB 69

1	*lydʿyhw*	1	Belonging to Yedayahu
2	*bn šʿl*	2	son of Shual

Avigad HB 70

1	*lyhwʾ*	1	Belonging to Yahu
2	*b n*	2	son of
3	*mšmš*	3	Mishmesh

Avigad HB 71

1	*lyhwʾḥ*	1	Belonging to Yehoaḥ
2	*ʾlyʿz*	2	Eliaz

Avigad HB 72

1	*[l]yhwʾḥ*	1	[Belonging to] Yehoaḥ
2	*ʾlʿz*	2	El‹i›az

Avigad HB 73

1	*[lyh]wʾḥ b*	1	[Belonging to Yeh]oaḥ, son
2	*[n] ʾlʿz*	2	[of] El‹i›az

Avigad HB 74

1	*lyhwʿz*	1	Belonging to Yehoaz
2	*bn mtn*	2	son of Mattan

Avigad HB 75

1	*lyqmyhw*	1	Belonging to Yeqamyahu
2	*bn mšlm*	2	son of Meshullam

Avigad HB 76

1	*lyqm[yhw]*	1	Belonging to Yeqam[yahu]

Avigad HB 77

1	*lyqmyhw*	1	Belonging to Yeqamyahu
2	*bn nḥm*	2	son of Nahum

Avigad HB 78

1	*lyrm̊[yhw]*	1	Belonging to Yerem[yahu]
2	*yšmʿʾ[l]*	2	Yishmae[l]

Avigad HB 79

1	*lyšmʿʾl*	1	Belonging to Yishmael
2	*[b]n̊ šʿl bn*	2	[so]n of Shual son of
3	*[ḥl]ṣyh[w]*	3	[Hele]syah[u]

Avigad HB 80

1	*lyšm[ʿʾl]*	1	Belonging to Yishm[ael]
2	*[b]n̊ mḥsy[hw]*	2	[so]n of Maḥseya[hu]

Avigad HB 81

1	*lyšm[ʿʾl]*	1	Belonging to Yishma[el]

Avigad HB 82

1	*lyšm[ʿʾl]*	1	Belonging to Yishma[el]

Avigad HB 83

1	*lyšʿyhw*	1	Belonging to Yeshayahu
2	*bn ḥml*	2	son of Ḥamal

Avigad HB 84

1	*[ly]šʿyhw b*	1	[Belonging to Ye]shayahu so[n]
2	*[n ʾ]lṣd[q]*	2	[of E]lṣede[q]

Avigad HB 85

1	*lmḥsyhw*	1	Belonging to Maḥseyahu
2	*ʾlyhw*	2	Eliyahu

Avigad HB 86

1	*lmḥ[sy]hw*	1	Belonging to Maḥ[seya]hu
2	*bn plṭyhw*	2	son of Pelatyahu

Avigad HB 87

1	*[lmʿ]śyhw*	1	[Belonging to Maʿa]seyahu
2	*myʾmn*	2	Miyamin

Avigad HB 88

1	*[lm]yʾmn*	1	[Belonging to Mi]yamin
2	*[bn] ʿpy*	2	[son of] Opay

Avigad HB 89

1	*lmyr[b]*	1	Belonging to Mera[b]
2	*yšmʿʾl*	2	Yishmael

Avigad HB 90

1	*lmkyhw*	1	Belonging to Mikayahu
2	*bn ʾlʿz*	2	son of Eliaz

Avigad HB 91

1	*lmkyh[w]*	1	Belonging to Mikayah[u]
2	*yšʿy[hw]*	2	Yishaya[hu]

Avigad HB 92

1	*lmkyhw*	1	Belonging to Mikayahu
2	*bn mšlm*	2	son of Meshullam

Avigad HB 93

1	*[ls]mky[hw]*	1	[Belonging to Se]makya[hu]
2	*bn ʿmdyh[w]*	2	son of Amadyah[u]

Avigad HB 94

1	*lmky[hw]*	1	Belonging to Mikaya[hu]
2	*plṭyhw*	2	Peletyahu

Avigad HB 95

1	*lmky[hw] b*	1	Belonging to Mikaya[hu] son
2	*n šḥ[r]*	2	of Shaḥa[r]

Avigad HB 96-97

1	*lmkyhw*	1	Belonging to Mikayahu
2	*šbnyhw*	2	Shebanyahu

Avigad HB 98

1	*[l]mlkyhw*	1	[Belonging to] Melekyahu
2	*ḥlq*	2	Ḥeleq

Avigad HB 99

1	*lmlkyhw*	1	Belonging to Melekyahu
2	*bn pdyhw*	2	son of Pedayahu

Avigad HB 100

1	*[l]mnḥm*	1	[Belonging to] Menaḥem
2	*ḥnnyhw*	2	Ḥananyahu

Avigad HB 101

1	*lmnhm bn*	1	Belonging to Menaḥem son of
2	*yšmʿʾl*	2	Yishmael

Avigad HB 102

1	*lmn[ḥm bn]*	1	Belonging to Mena[ḥem son of]
2	*yš[mʿʾl]*	2	Yish[mael]

Avigad HB 103

1	*lmnḥm b*	1	Belonging to Menaḥem son
2	*n mnš*	2	of MNŠ

Avigad HB 104

1	*lmnḥm*	1	Belonging to Menaḥem
2	*pgy*	2	PGY

Avigad HB 105

a:

1	*lmʿśy[hw]*	1	Belonging to Maʿaseya[hu]
2	*ʾšyh[w]*	2	Eshyah[u]

b:

1	*[l]mʿśy[hw]*	1	[Belonging to] Maʿaseya[hu]
2	*ʾšyhw*	2	Eshyahu

Avigad HB 106

1	*lmspr bn*	1	Belonging to Mispar son of
2	*[ ]ywʿ[ ]*	2	

Avigad HB 107

1	*lmʿśy[hw]*	1	Belonging to Maʿaseya[hu]
2	*ḥlqyhw*	2	Ḥeleqyahu

Avigad HB 108

1	*mṣr [b]*	1	MṢR [so]n
2	*n šlm*	2	of Shallum

Avigad HB 109

1	*lmqnmlk*	1	Belonging to Miqnemelek

Avigad HB 110

1	*lmšlm*	1	Belonging to Meshullam
2	*ʾšyhw*	2	Eshyahu

Avigad HB 111

1	*lmšlm [b]*	1	Belonging to Meshullam [son]
2	*[n] rpʾyhw*	2	of Rapayahu

Avigad HB 112

1	*lmšʿn b[n]*	1	Belonging to Mishan so[n of]
2	*šḥr*	2	Shaḥar

Avigad HB 113

1	*lmtn bn*	1	Belonging to Mattan son of
2	*[ʾ]dnyḥy*	2	[A]doniḥay
3	*[bn š]ḥr*	3	[son of Sha]ḥar

Avigad HB 114

1	*lmtn bn*	1	Belonging to Mattan son of
2	*plṭyhw*	2	Peletyahu

Avigad HB 115

1	*lmtn bn*	1	Belonging to Mattan son of
2	*[p]lṭyhw*	2	[Pe]letyahu

Avigad HB 116

a:

1	*lmtn b[n]*	1	Belonging to Mattan so[n of]
2	*plṭyh[w]*	2	Peletyah[u]

b:

1	*lmtn b[n]*	1	Belonging to Mattan so[n of]
2	*[p]lṭy[hw]*	2	[Pe]letya[hu]

Avigad HB 117

1	*lmtn bn*	1	Belonging to Mattan
2	*hwdwyhw*	2	Hawdawyahu

Avigad HB 118

1	*lmtn b[n]*	1	Belonging to Mattan so[n of]
2	*yhwzrḥ*	2	Yehozeraḥ

Avigad HB 119

1	*lmtnyhw b*	1	Belonging to Mattanyahu son
2	*n smkyhw*	2	of Semakyahu

Avigad HB 120

1	*lngby b*	1	Belonging to Negbi son
2	*n mlkyhw*	2	of Melekyahu

Avigad HB 121

1	*ln̊[ḥ]m bn*	1	Belonging to Na[ḥu]m son of
2	*rpʾ[yhw]*	2	Rapa[yahu]

Avigad HB 122

1	*lnmš b[n]*	1	Belonging to Nemesh so[n of]
2	*n̊ryh̊w*	2	Neriyahu

Avigad HB 123

1	*lnmšr*	1	Belonging to NMŠR
2	*bn šʿl*	2	son of Shuʿal

Avigad HB 124

1	*lnmšr bn*	1	Belonging to NMŠR son of
2	*šbnyhw*	2	Shebanyahu

Avigad HB 125

1	*lnryhw*	1	Belonging to Neriyahu
2	*ʾdny[hw]*	2	Adoniyahu

Avigad HB 126

1	*lnryhw*	1	Belonging to Neriyahu
2	*ʾšrḥy*	2	Asherhay

Avigad HB 127

1	*lnryhw*	1	Belonging to Neriyahu
2	*[ʾ]šryḥt*	2	[A]sheryaḥat

Avigad HB 128

1	*lnryhw b*	1	Belonging to Neriyahu son
2	*n hṣlyhw*	2	of Hiṣṣilyahu

Avigad HB 129

1	*lntn ʾḥ*	1	Belonging to Natan
2	*mlk*	2	Aḥimelek

Avigad HB 130

1	*lntn*	1	Belonging to Natan
2	*pdyhw*	2	Pedayahu

Avigad HB 131

1	*lsʾl b*	1	Belonging to SʾL son
2	*n ysp*	2	of Yasap

Avigad HB 132

1	*[l]slʾ b*	1	[Belonging to] Sallu son
2	*n kslʾ*	2	of Kisla

Avigad HB 133

a:

1	*lsʿdyh[w]*	1	Belonging to Saʿadyah[u]

b:

1	*lsʿd[yhw]*	1	Belonging to Saʿadyahu
2	*[b]n z[ ]*	2	[so]n of

Avigad HB 134

1	*lʿbdyhw*	1	Belonging to Abadyahu
2	*b̊n mtn*	2	son of Mattan

Avigad HB 135

1	*lʿzr*	1	Belonging to Ezer
2	*plṭyhw*	2	Peletyahu

Avigad HB 136

1	*lʿzryh[w]*	1	Belonging to Azaryah[u]
2	*bn s[mk]*	2	son of Sa[mak]

Avigad HB 137

1	*lʿzryhw*	1	Belonging to Azaryahu
2	*b̊n̊ pdyhw*	2	son of Pedayahu

Avigad HB 138

1	*lʿzrqm*	1	Belonging to Azarqam
2	*bn prpr*	2	son of Parpar

Avigad HB 139

1	*[l]ʿzrqm*	1	[Belonging to] Azarqam
2	*[bn] ṣdqʾ*	2	[son of] Ṣidqa

Avigad HB 140

1	*lʿkb[r]*	1	Belonging to Akba[r]

Avigad HB 141

1	*lʿlyhw*	1	Belonging to Alayahu
2	*rpʾ*	2	Rapa

Avigad HB 142

1	*l̊ʿlyhw*	1	Belonging to Alayahu
2	*ḥlṣ̊*	2	Ḥeleṣ

Avigad HB 143

1	*lplṭyhw b*	1	Belonging to Pelatyahu son
2	*n hwšʿyhw*	2	of Hoshayahu

Avigad HB 144-145, 147

1	*lpḷtyhw*	1	Belonging to Pelatyahu
2	*hwšʿyhw*	2	Hoshayahu

Avigad HB 146

1	*lpḷtyhw*	1	Belonging to Pelatyahu
2	*[ ]ẙhw*	2	yahu

Avigad HB 148

1	*lpḷtyhw*	1	Belonging to Pelatyahu
2	*bn hwšʿyhw*	2	son of Hoshayahu

Avigad HB 149

1	*lpḷtyhw*	1	Belonging to Pelatyahu
2	*bn ḥlq*	2	son of Heleq

Avigad HB 150

1	*lpn[ ]b[ ]*	1	Belonging to PN s‹on of›
2	*ḥnny*	2	Ḥanani

Avigad HB 151

1	*lpšḥr bn*	1	Belonging to Pasḥur son of
2	*ʾḥʾmh*	2	Aḥamah

Avigad HB 152

1	*lpšhr bn*	1	Belonging to Pashur son of
2	*mnḥm*	2	Menaḥem

Avigad HB 153

1	*lptḥ b*	1	Belonging to Pataḥ son
2	*n nḥm*	2	of Naḥum

Avigad HB 154

1	*lṣpn[yhw]*	1	Belonging to Ṣepan[yahu]
2	*mqnyhw*	2	Miqneyahu

Avigad HB 155

1	*lṣpnyhw*	1	Belonging to Ṣepanyahu
2	*šʾlh*	2	Sheʾalah

Avigad HB 156

1	*lqrbʾr*	1	Belonging to Qerabor
2	*bn̊ ʿzrʾl*	2	son of Azarel

Avigad HB 157

1	*lr̊ʾyhw*	1	Belonging to Reʾayahu
2	*ḥ̊lṣyhw*	2	Ḥeleṣyahu

Avigad HB 158

1	*lšlm b*	1	Belonging to Shallum son
2	*n ʾlšm̊[ʿ]*	2	of Elshama

Avigad HB 159

1	*[lšl]m bn*	1	[Belonging to Shallu]m son of
2	*[ʾl]šmʿ*	2	[El]shama

Avigad HB 160

1	*lšl[m bn]*	1	Belonging to Shallu[m son of]
2	*ʾ[l]š̊[mʿ]*	2	E[l]sha[ma]

Avigad HB 161

1	*lšlm b[n]*	1	Belonging to Shallum so[n of]
2	*hwšʿyhw*	2	Hoshayahu

Avigad HB 162

1	*[l]šmʿyhw*	1	[Belonging to] Shemayahu
2	*yʾzn*	2	Yaʾazan

Avigad HB 163

1	*lšmʿyhw*	1	Belonging to Shemayahu

Avigad HB 164

1	*lšʿl bn*	1	Belonging to Shuʿal son of
2	*yšmʿʾl*	2	Yishmael

Avigad HB 165

1	*lšp̊ṭy[hw]*	1	Belonging to Shephatya[hu]
2	*ʾdnyhw*	2	Adoniyahu

Avigad HB 166

1	*lšp̊t b[n]*	1	Belonging to Shaphat so[n of]
2	*ʾḥ̊yhw*	2	Aḥiyahu

Avigad HB 167

1	*lšbny[hw]*	1	Belonging to Shebanya[hu]
2	*śryhw*	2	Saryahu

Avigad HB 168

1	*ltnḥ̊[m]*	1	Belonging to Tanḥu[m]
2	*hṣl[yhw]*	2	Hissil[yahu]

Avigad HB 169

1	*[ ] bn*	1	son of
2	*gryhw*	2	Geriyahu

Avigad HB 170

1	*[ ]*	1	
2	*dmlyhw bn[ ]*	2	Domlayahu son of

Avigad HB 171

1	*[ ]*	1	
2	*yhwq[m]*	2	Yehoqa[m]

Avigad HB 172

1	*[ ]*	1	
2	*yqmyh[w]*	2	Yeqamyah[u]

Avigad HB 173

1	*[ ]*	1	
2	*yšmʿʾl*	2	Yishmael

Avigad HB 174

1	*lš[ʿ]l b[n]*	1	Belonging to Shu[ʿa]l so[n of]
2	*ml[k]y[hw]*	2	Mele[k]ya[hu]

Avigad HB 175

1	*[ ]*	1	
2	*mlk[yhw]*	2	Melek[yahu]

Avigad HB 176

1	*[ ]*		
2	*bn nḥm*	1	son of Naḥum

Avigad HB 177

1	*[ ]*	1	
2	*ʿzyh[w]*	2	Azayah[u]

Avigad HB 178

1	*[ ]*	1	
2	*pdyhw*	2	Pedayahu

Avigad HB 179

1	*[ ]yhw*	1	yahu
2	*šmʿyh[w]*	2	Shemayah[u]

Avigad HB 180

1	*[ ]*	1	
2	*bn špṭ[yhw]*	2	son of Shephat[yahu]
3	*[ ]*	3	
4	*bn [šp]ṭyhw*	4	son of [Shepha]tyahu

Avigad HB 183

1	*[ ]yhw*	1	yahu
2	*[pš]ḥr*	2	[Pas]ḥur

Avigad HB 195

1	*[ ]ʿml[ ]*	1	Amal

Avigad Aroer Seal; *EI* 14 (1978)

1	*lqwsʾ*	1	Belonging of Qawsa

Avigad Seal 1 (Manesseh); *IEJ* 13 (1963)

1	[ ]	1	
2	*lmnsh bn*	2	Belonging to Manesseh son of
3	*hmlk*	3	the king

Avigad Seal 2 (Akbor); *IEJ* 13 (1963)

1	*ʿkbr*	1	Akbor
2	*ʾḥqm*	2	Aḥiqam

Avigad Seal 3 (Kiryat Yearim); *IEJ* 13 (1963)

1	*lyš‘yh*	1	Belonging to Yeshayahu
2	*w ’mryhw*	2	Amaryahu

Avigad Seal 4 (Samaria); Priest of Dor Seal; *IEJ* 25 (1975)

1	*lṣdq*	1	Belonging to Ṣadoq
2	*bn mk’*	2	son of Mika
3	*[lz]kryw*	3	[Belonging to Ze]karyaw
4	*khn d’r*	4	Priest of Dor

Avigad Seal 5 (Ornamented Seal); *IEJ* 4 (1954)

1	*lš’l*	1	Belonging to Shaul

Avigad Seal 6; *IEJ* 4 (1954)

1	*l‘z’*	1	Belonging to Uzza
2	*bn ḥts*	2	son of ḤTS

Avigad Seal 7; "Seven Hebrew Seals,"*BIES* 18 (1954)

1	*šbn’*	1	Shubna

Avigad Seal 8; "Seven Hebrew Seals;" *BIES* 18 (1954)

1	*lšm‘ b*	1	Belonging to Shema son
2	*n zkryw*	2	of Zekaryaw

Avigad Seal 9; "Seven Hebrew Seals;" *BIES* 18 (1954)

1	*yw‘śh*	1	Yawasah
2	*zkr*	2	Zakkur

Avigad Seal 10; "Seven Hebrew Seals;" *BIES* 18 (1954)

1	*yw’mn*	1	Yawaman
2	*‘bdy*	2	Abdi

Avigad Seal 11; "Seven Hebrew Seals;" *BIES* 18 (1954)

1	*lyr’*	1	Belonging to Yere

Avigad Na‘ar Seal 1

1	*mlkyhw*	1	Malkiyahu
2	*n̊r špṭ*	2	steward of Shaphat

Avigad Na‘ar Seal 2

1	*l̊bnyh*	1	Belonging to Benayahu
2	*w n̊r ḥgy*	2	steward of Haggi

Avigad Sheʿyabab Seal; "Seals and Sealings," *IEJ* 14 (1964)

1	*lšʿybb*	1	Belonging to Sheyabab

Avigad Seal 2; "Seals and Sealings," *IEJ* 14 (1964)

1	*l̊ḥnnyhw b*	1	Belonging to Ḥananyahu son
2	*n gdlẙhw*	2	of Gedalyahu

Avigad "Baruk the Scribe and Jerahmeel the King's Son," Bulla 1 *IEJ* 28 (1978)

1	*lbrkyhw*	1	Belonging to Berekyahu
2	*bn nryhw*	2	son of Neriyahu
3	*hspr*	3	the scribe

Avigad "Baruk the Scribe and Jerahmeel the King's Son," Bulla 2 *IEJ* 28 (1978)

1	*lyrḥmʾl*	1	Belonging to Yeraḥmeʾel
2	*bn hmlk*	2	the King's son

Avigad Hecht Seal 1 (Festschrift Reʿuben R. Hecht, 1979)

1	*[l]ydw ʾšr*	1	Belonging to Yiddo
2	*[ʿ]l hbyt*	2	royal steward

Avigad Hecht Seal 2 (Festschrift Reʿuben R. Hecht, 1979)

1	*[lʾ]šnʾ*	1	[Belonging to U]shna

Avigad Hecht Seal 3 (Festschrift Reʿuben R. Hecht, 1979)

1	*lyšʿyhw*	1	Belonging to Yeshayahu
2	*ʿmlyhw*	2	Amalyahu

Avigad Hecht Seal 4 (Festschrift Reʿuben R. Hecht, 1979)

1	*l[̥]yhw*	1	Belonging to yahu
2	*bn̊ ʿmlyhw*	2	son of Amalyahu

Avigad Hecht Seal 5 (Festschrift Reʿuben R. Hecht, 1979)

1	*ldlyhw bn*	1	Belonging to Delayahu son of
2	*gmlyhw*	2	Gemalyahu

Avigad Hecht Seal 6 (Festschrift Reʿuben R. Hecht, 1979)

1	*lʾḥyqm*	1	Belonging to Aḥiqam
2	*mtn*	2	Mattan

Avigad Hecht Seal 7 (Festschrift Reʿuben R. Hecht, 1979)

1	*lʿzr*	1	Belonging to Azar

Avigad Hecht Seal 8 (Festschrift Reʿuben R. Hecht, 1979)

1	*lʾbgyl b*	1	Belonging to Abigail
2	*t ʾlḥnn*	2	daughter of Elḥanan

Avigad Hecht Seal 9 (Festschrift Reʿuben R. Hecht, 1979)

1	*lklkl*	1	Belonging to Kilkel
2	*mnḥm*	2	Menaḥem

Avigad Hecht Seal 10 (Festschrift Reʿuben R. Hecht, 1979)

1	*lywʾl b*	1	Belonging to Yoel son
2	*n yhwkl*	2	of Yehukal

Avigad Hecht Seal 11 (Festschrift Reʿuben R. Hecht, 1979)

1	*lydnyhw*	1	Belonging to Yedanyahu
2	*bn ntnyhw*	2	son of Netanyahu

Avigad Hecht Seal 12 (Festschrift Reʿuben R. Hecht, 1979)

1	*lʿzr*	1	Belonging to Azar

Avigad Sar HaʿIr Seal 1; *IEJ* 26 (1976)

1	*śr hʿr*	1	governor of the city

Avigad *EI* 14 (1978)

1	*lśryhw*	1	Belonging to Serayahu
2	*nryhw*	2	Neriyahu

Avigad Lyre Seal; *IEJ* 28 (1978)

1	*lmʿdnh*	1	Belonging to Maʿadanah
2	*bt hmlk*	2	the King's daughter

Avigad "New Names" Seal 1; *EI* 12 (1975)

1	*lḥmyʿdn*	1	Belonging to Ḥamiaddan
2	*bt ʾḥmlk*	2	daughter of Aḥimelek

Avigad "New Names" Seal 2; *EI* 12 (1975)

1	*lḥlqyhw*	1	Belonging to Ḥilqiyahu
2	*bn ddyhw*	2	son of Dodiyahu

Avigad "New Names" Seal 3; *EI* 12 (1975)

1	*lmlkyhw*	1	Belonging to Malkiyahu
2	*bn ḥylʾ*	2	son of Ḥayla

Avigad "New Names" Seal 4; *EI* 12 (1975)

1	*lšknyh*	1	Belonging to Shekanyahu
2	*w ḥylʾ*	2	Ḥayla

Avigad "New Names" Seal 5; *EI* 12 (1975)

1	*yrʾwyhw*	1	Yiruyahu
2	*ʾrʾ*	2	Ara

Avigad "New Names" Seal 6; *EI* 12 (1975)

1	*lklkly*	1	Belonging to Kilkelyahu
2	*hw zkr*	2	Zeker

Avigad "New Names" Seal 7; *EI* 12 (1975)

1	*lʾbr*	1	Belonging to Abiryahu
2	*yhw*	2	

Avigad "New Names" Seal 8; *EI* 12 (1975)

1	*ldltyhw*	1	Belonging to Deletyahu
2	*bn ḥlq*	2	son of Ḥeleq

Avigad "New Names" Seal 9; *EI* 12 (1975)

1	*lšbnyhw*	1	Belonging to Shebanyahu
2	*bṣr*	2	Beṣer

Avigad "New Names" Seal 10; *EI* 12 (1975)

1	*lšlmyh*	1	Belonging to Shelemyahu
2	*w śrmlk*	2	Sarmelek

Avigad "New Names" Seal 11; *EI* 12 (1975)

1	*lśryhw*	1	Belonging to Serayahu

Avigad "New Names" Seal 12; *EI* 12 (1975)

1	*yhwqm*	1	Yehoqim

Avigad "New Names" Seal 13; *EI* 12 (1975)

1	*yhwqm*	1	Yehoqim
2	*yhwndb*	2	Yehonadab

Avigad "New Names" Seal 14; *EI* 12 (1975)

1	*lšbʿ y*	1	Belonging to Sheba
2	*ḥmlyhw*	2	Yaḥmolyahu

Avigad "New Names" Seal 15; *EI* 12 (1975)

1	*ldršy*	1	Belonging to Derashyahu
2	*hw ḥml*	2	Ḥamal

Avigad "New Names" Seal 16; *EI* 12 (1975)

1	*lʾḥyw*	1	Belonging to Aḥyaw
2	*bn šʾl*	2	son of Shaul

Avigad "New Names" Seal 17; *EI* 12 (1975)

1	*lʿzr*	1	Belonging to Ezer
2	*ʾlʿš*	2	Elash

Avigad "New Names" Seal 18; *EI* 12 (1975)

1	*ldmlʾ*	1	Belonging to Domla

Avigad "New Names" Seal 19; *EI* 12 (1975)

1	*lzqn*	1	Belonging to Zaqan
2	*ʾḥzyhw*	2	Aḥazyahu

Avigad "New Names" Seal 20; *EI* 12 (1975)

1	*lšʿnp*	1	Belonging to Shenaph
2	*bn nby*	2	son of Nabi

Avigad "Avigad" Seal; *IEJ* 18 (1968)

1	*lʾbgd*	1	Belonging to Abigad

Avigad Locust Seal; *IEJ* 16 (1966)

1	*lʿzry*	1	Belonging to Azaryaw
2	*w hgbh*	2	Haggebah

Avigad Seal 1; *EI* 9 (1969)

1	*lpdyhw*	1	Belonging to Pedayahu
2	*bn psḥ*	2	son of Paseaḥ

Avigad Seal 2; *EI* 9 (1969)

1	*l̊ḥnn*	1	Belonging to Ḥanan
2	*ydlyh̊ẘ*	2	Yidleyahu

Avigad Seal 3; *EI* 9 (1969)

1	*ldlh*	1	Belonging to Dalah

Avigad Seal 4; *EI* 9 (1969)

1	*lʾprḥ*	1	Belonging to Ephroaḥ
2	*b[n] smkyh̊w*	2	so[n of] Semakyahu

Avigad Seal 5; *EI* 9 (1969)

1	*lgdlyhw*	1	Belonging to Gedalyahu
2	*bn smk*	2	son of Samak

Avigad Seal 6; *EI* 9 (1969)

1	*lyʾznyh̊[w]*	1	Belonging to Yaʾazanyah[u]
2	*[b]n g̊dl*	2	[so]n of Giddel

Avigad Seal 7; *EI* 9 (1969)

1	*lʾlyqm̊*	1	Belonging to Elyaqim
2	*bn mʿśyh̊*	2	Maʿaseyah

Avigad Seal 8; *EI* 9 (1969)

1	*lʿśy*	1	Belonging to Asi
2	*gryhw*	2	Geriyahu

Avigad Seal 9; *EI* 9 (1969)

1	*lnḥm*	1	Belonging to Naḥum
2	*ʾlšm̊ʿ*	2	Elishama

Avigad Seal 10; *EI* 9 (1969)

1	*lʾply bn*	1	Belonging to Ephli son of
2	*šmʿ*	2	Shama

Avigad Seal 11; *EI* 9 (1969)

1	*ʾḥyhw*	1	Aḥiyahu
2	*šm*	2	Shem

Avigad Seal 12; *EI* 9 (1969)

1	*lyrmyhw*	1	Belonging to Yirmeyahu

Avigad Seal 13; *EI* 9 (1969)

1	*lywʾr*	1	Belonging to Yawur

Avigad Seal 14; *EI* 9 (1969)

1	*llḥš*	1	Belonging to Loḥesh

Avigad Seal 15; *EI* 9 (1969)

1	*lyhwʾḥz*	1	Belonging to Yehoaḥaz
2	*bn̊ hmlk*	2	the King's son

6.2.3 BARKAY

Barkay Sar HaʿIr Seal 1; *Qadmoniot* 10 (1977)

1	*s̊r̊ h̊ʿr*	1	governor of the city

6.2.4 BETH-SHEMESH

Beth-Shemesh (Ain Shems) Seal 1

1	*lḥsdʾ*	1	Belonging to Ḥasda
2	*yrmyhẘ*	2	Yirmeyahu

Beth-Shemesh (Ain Shems) Seal 2

1	*lʾlyqm*	1	Belonging to Elyaqim
2	*[n]ʿr ywkn*	2	[ste]ward of Yawkin

Beth-Shemesh (Ain Shems) Seal 3

1	*ṣpn*	1	Ṣapan
2	*ʿzr*	2	Ezer

Beth-Shemesh (Ain Shems) Seal 4

1	*lʿdyhw*	1	Belonging to Adayahu
2	*ʾḥmlk*	2	Aḥimelek

Beth-Shemesh (Ain Shems) Seal 5

1	*mnḥm*	1	Menahem
2	*wyhbnh*	2	and Yahbanah

Beth-Shemesh (Ain Shems) Seal 6

1	*l{n}mlk*	1	Belonging to the King
2	*mmšt*	2	MMŠT

Beth-Shemesh (Ain Shems) Seal 7

1	*lbky*	1	Belonging to Baki
2	*šlm*	2	Shallum

Beth-Shemesh (Ain Shems) Seal 8

1	*lṣdq*	1	Belonging to Ṣedeq
2	*smk*	2	Samak

Beth-Shemesh (Ain Shems) Seal 9

1	*ltnḥ*	1	Belonging to Tanḥum
2	m *ngb*	2	Negeb

Beth-Shemesh (Ain Shems) Seal 10a

1	*lk̊s̊ʾ*	1	Belonging to Kesa
2	*zkʾ*	2	Zakka

Beth-Shemesh (Ain Shems) Seal 10b

1	*lksʾ*	1	Belonging to Kesa
2	*zkʾ*	2	Zakka

6.2.5 BORDREUIL

Bordreuil Seal 1 (*Catalogue*, 1986, no. 40)

1	*lʾbyw ʿbd ʿzyw*	1	Belonging to Abyaw servant of Uzziyaw

Bordreuil Seal 5 (*Catalogue*, 1986, no. 44)

1	*lʾbšʿl*	1	Belonging to Abishuʿal

Bordreuil Seal 6 (*Catalogue*, 1986, no. 45)

1	*lšbnyhw*	1	Belonging to Shebanyahu
2	*bn*	2	son of

Bordreuil Seal 10 (*Catalogue*, 1986, no. 50)

1	*lʿzʾ b*	1	Belonging to Uzza son
2	*n bʿlḥnn*	2	of Baʿalḥanan

Bordreuil Seal 12(*Catalogue,* 1986, no. 52)

1	*lplṭh bn*	1	Belonging to PLṬH son of
2	*yšmʿʾl*	2	Yishmael

Bordreuil Seal 13 (*Catalogue,* 1986, no. 53)

1	*lḥnnyhw b*	1	Belonging to Ḥananyahu son of
2	*n qwlyhw*	2	of Qawlayahu

Bordreuil Seal 15 (*Catalogue,* 1986, no. 55)

1	*lšmʿ b*	1	Belonging to Shema son
2	*n ywstr*	2	of Yawsatar

Bordreuil Seal 17 (*Catalogue,* 1986, no. 57)

1	*[l]ṣpnyh*	1	[Belonging to] Ṣepanyah
2	*mtnyh*	2	Mattanya

Bordreuil Seal 19 (*Catalogue,* 1986, no. 59)

1	*l̊dmlyhw b*	1	Belonging to Domlayahu son
2	*n yhw[ ]*	2	of Yehaw-

6.2.6 BORDREUIL/LEMAIRE

Bordreuil/Lemaire Seal 2; *Semitica* 24 (1974)

1	*lʾšʾ*	1	Belonging to Esha

Bordreuil/Lemaire Seal 1a; *Semitica* 26 (1976)

1	*lšʿryhw*	1	Belonging to Sheʿaryahu
2	*bn ḥnyhw*	2	son of Ḥanniyahu

Bordreuil/Lemaire Seal 1b; *Semitica* 26 (1976)

1	*lhwdyhw*	1	Belonging to Hawdiyahu
2	*šʿryhw*	2	Shearyahu

Bordreuil/Lemaire Seal 2; *Semitica* 26 (1976)

1	*lṣpn*	1	Belonging to Ṣapan
2	*nryhw*	2	Neriyahu

Bordreuil/Lemaire Seal 3; *Semitica* 26 (1976)

1	*[ ]*	1	
2	*lyrymwt*	2	Belonging to Yeremot
3	*bnyhw*	3	Benayahu

Bordreuil/Lemaire Seal 4; *Semitica* 26 (1976)

1	*lʿzryhw b*	1	Belonging to Azaryahu son
2	*n šmryhw*	2	of Shemaryahu

Bordreuil/Lemaire Seal 5; *Semitica* 26 (1976)

1	*lšmryhw*	1	Belonging to Shemaryahu
2	*bn pdyhw*	2	son of Pedayahu

Bordreuil/Lemaire Seal 6; *Semitica* 26 (1976)

1	*lyrmyhw*	1	Belonging to Yirmeyahu
2	*bn mnḥm*	2	son of Menaḥem

Bordreuil/Lemaire Seal 7; *Semitica* 26 (1976)

1	*lʿśyhw*	1	Belonging to Asayahu
2	*bn ḥwyhw*	2	son of Ḥawayahu

Bordreuil/Lemaire Seal 8; *Semitica* 26 (1976)

1	*lʾḥʾmh*	1	Belonging to Aḥiama
2	*bn yqmyhw*	2	son of Yeqamyahu

Bordreuil/Lemaire Seal 9; *Semitica* 26 (1976)

1	*lhwdyhw*	1	Belonging to Hawdiyahu
2	*mtnyhw*	2	Mattanyahu

Bordreuil/Lemaire Seal 10; *Semitica* 26 (1976)

1	*lmkyhw*	1	Belonging to Mikayahu
2	*bn šlm*	2	son of Shallum

Bordreuil/Lemaire Seal 11; *Semitica* 26 (1976)

1	*lʿzr bn*	1	Belonging to Ezer son of
2	*mtnyhw*	2	Mattanyahu

Bordreuil/Lemaire Seal 12; *Semitica* 26 (1976)

1	*lʾšyh*	1	Belonging to Eshyahu
2	*w ʿzr*	2	Ezer

Bordreuil/Lemaire Seal 13; *Semitica* 26 (1976)

1	*lywzn b*	1	Belonging to Yawzan so[n]
2	*[n] ʿd*	2	

Bordreuil/Lemaire Seal 14; *Semitica* 26 (1976)

1	*lʿdyhw b*	1	Belonging to Adayahu son
2	*n šptyhw*	2	of Shephatyahu

Bordreuil/Lemaire Seal 15; *Semitica* 26 (1976)

1	*lšlm b*	1	Belonging to Shallum son
2	*n nḥm*	2	of Naḥum

Bordreuil/Lemaire Seal 16; *Semitica* 26 (1976)

1	*lmtn*	1	Belonging to Mattan

Bordreuil/Lemaire Seal 17; *Semitica* 26 (1976)

1	*lʾlyšb*	1	Belonging to Elyashib
2	*bn šʿl*	2	son of Shuʿal

Bordreuil/Lemaire Seal 18; *Semitica* 26 (1976)

1	*lṭbʾ*	1	Belonging to Tobel
2	*l pdy*	2	Padi

Bordreuil/Lemaire Seal 19; *Semitica* 26 (1976)

1	*lrpʾ*	1	Belonging to Rapha

Bordreuil/Lemaire Seal 20; *Semitica* 26 (1976)

1	*l[ ]*	1	Belonging to
2	*bn̊ r̊pʾ*	2	son of Rapha

Bordreuil/Lemaire Seal 21; *Semitica* 26 (1976)

1	*lplṭyhw*	1	Belonging to Pelatyahu
2	*ḥlqyhw*	2	Ḥilqiyahu

Bordreuil/Lemaire Seal 22; *Semitica* 26 (1976)

1	*l̊d̊lh̊*	1	Belonging to Dalah
2	*[ ]m̊lk*	2	melek

Bordreuil/Lemaire Seal 1; *Semitica* 29 (1979)

1	*lgdyhw*	1	Belonging to Gadyahu
2	*bn*	2	son of
3	*hmlk*	3	the king

Bordreuil/Lemaire Seal 2; *Semitica* 29 (1979)

1	*lmlkyhw*	1	Belonging to Malkiyahu
2	*bn mtn*	2	son of Mattan

Bordreuil/Lemaire Seal 3; *Semitica* 29 (1979)

1	*lʾlyhw*	1	Belonging to Elyahu
2	*ʾḥmlk*	2	Aḥmelek

Bordreuil/Lemaire Seal 4; *Semitica* 29 (1979)

1	*lʾlyʾr b*	1	Belonging to Elyaʾir son
2	*n yrmyhw*	2	of Yirmiyahu

Bordreuil/Lemaire Seal 5; *Semitica* 29 (1979)

1	*ʾḥqm̊*	1	Aḥiqam
2	*plṭyh̊ẘ*	2	Peleṭyahyu

Bordreuil/Lemaire Seal 6; *Semitica* 29 (1979)

1	*lntn*	1	Belonging to Natan
2	*mʾ̊s*	2	Mʾš

Bordreuil/Lemaire Seal 7; *Semitica* 29 (1979)

1	*lytm*	1	Belonging to Yotam
2	*bn ʾlzkr*	2	son of Elzakar

Bordreuil/Lemaire Seal 8; *Semitica* 29 (1979)

1	*l[s]m̊k̊*	1	Belonging to [Sa]mak
2	*[pd]y*	2	[Pad]i

Bordreuil/Lemaire Seal 1; *Semitica* 32 (1982)

1	*lʾlyʾr*	1	Belonging to Elyair
2	*pdyhw*	2	Pedayhu

Bordreuil/Lemaire Seal 2; *Semitica* 32 (1982)

1	*lnryhw mtn*	1	Belonging to Neriyahu Mattan

Bordreuil/Lemaire Seal 3; *Semitica* 32 (1982)

1	*lyknyhw*	1	Belonging to Yekanyahu
2	*bn ḥkl*	2	son of Ḥakal

Bordreuil/Lemaire Seal 4; *Semitica* 32 (1982)

1	*lntn*	1	Belonging to Natan
2	*ʾlyhw*	2	Eliyahu

Bordreuil/Lemaire Seal 5; *Semitica* 32 (1982)

1	*lmnšh mlkyhw*	1	Belonging to Manessah Melekyahu

Bordreuil/Lemaire Seal 6; *Semitica* 32 (1982)

1	*lmkr mkyhw*	1	Belonging to Makir Mikayahu

Bordreuil/Lemaire Seal 7; *Semitica* 32 (1982)

1	*lh̊[ ]yh*	1	Belonging to
2	*pdyhw*	2	Pedayahu

Bordreuil/Lemaire Seal 8; *Semitica* 32 (1982)

1	*lsʿdyhw mlkyhw*	1	Belonging to Saʿadyahu Melekyahu

Bordreuil/Lemaire Seal 9; *Semitica* 32 (1982)

1	*lʿṣlyhw*	1	Belonging to Aṣelyahu
2	*bn ydw*	2	son of Yiddo

Bordreuil/Lemaire Seal 10; *Semitica* 32 (1982)

1	*š̊l̊m bn špṭ̊yhw*	1	Shallum son of Shephatyahu

Bordreuil/Lemaire Seal 11; *Semitica* 32 (1982)

1	*lmrymwt*	1	Belonging to Meremot

Bordreuil/Lemaire Seal 12; *Semitica* 32 (1982)

1	*lʾlšmʿ śrmlk*	1	Belonging to Elshama Sarmelek

Bordreuil/Lemaire Seal 13; *Semitica* 32 (1982)

1	*lḥzq*	1	Belonging to Ḥazaq

Bordreuil/Lemaire Seal 14; *Semitica* 32 (1982)

1	*lmšlm̊*	1	Belonging to Meshullam
2	*ʾspẙ*	2	Aspi

Bordreuil/Lemaire Seal 15; *Semitica* 32 (1982)

1	*lmnr*	1	Belonging to MNR

6.2.7 TELL DAN

Tell Dan 1; Biran

1	*lʾmṣ̊*	1	Belonging to Amoṣ

6.2.8 DAYAN

Dayan Seal 1; Aharoni, *Tel Aviv* 1 (1974)

1	*bnyhw*	1	Benayahu
2	*gry*	2	Geri

Dayan Seal 2; Aharoni, *Tel Aviv* 1 (1974)

1	*lʾldg*	1	Belonging to Eldago[n]
2	*[n]*	2	

Dayan Seal 3; Aharoni, *Tel Aviv* 1 (1974)

1	*lzry*	1	Belonging to Zeriyaw
2	*w hr*	2	the Rabbatite
3	*bt*	3	

6.2.9 DRIVER

Driver Seal 1; *PEQ* (1955)

1	*lhwšʿ̊*	1	Belonging to Hoshea

6.2.10 EN GEDI

En Gedi Seal 1

1	*lʾryhw*	1	Belonging to Uriyahu
2	*ʿzryhw*	2	Azaryahu

En Gedi Seal 2

1	*ln̊r̊ʾ*	1	Belonging to Nera

En Gedi Seal 3

1	*ṭbšlm*	1	Tobshalem

6.2.11 GEZER

Elijah Seal; Graesser, *BASOR* 220 (1975)

1	*lʾlyhw*	1	Belonging to Eliyahu
2	*yqmyhw*	2	Yeqamyahu

6.2.12 GIBEON

Gibeon Seal 1

1	*msh*	1	Mosah

Gibeon Seal 2

1	*lnḥm*	1	Belonging to Nahum
2	*hṣlyhw*	2	Hiṣṣilyahu

Gibeon Seal 3

1	*ltnḥ*	1	Belonging to Tanḥum
2	*m ngb*	2	Negeb

Gibeon Seal 4

1	*[ʿ]zryh[w]*	1	[A]zaryah[u]

Gibeon Seal 5

1	*lmšl*	1	Belonging to Meshullum
2	*mʾlntn*	2	Elnatan

Gibeon Seal 6

1	*lm[šl]*	1	Belonging to Me[shullu]m
2	*m ʾl[ntn]*	2	El[natan]

Gibeon Seal 7

1	*ltnḥm*	1	Belonging to Tanḥum
2	*mgn*	2	Magen

6.2.13 HEBRON

Hebron Seal 1; Herr #3; *IEJ* 24 (1974)

1	*lyhwzr̊*	1	Belonging to Yehozaraḥ
2	*ḥ bn ḥlq*	2	son of Ḥilqi[ya]hu
3	*[y]hw ʿbd ḥ*	3	servant of
4	*z̊q̊ẙh̊ẘ*	4	Ḥizqiyahu

6.2.14 HERR

Herr 4

1	*lšbnyw*	1	Belonging to Shebanyaw
Reverse			
2	*lšbnyw ʿ*	2	Belonging to Shebanyaw
3	*bd ʿzyw*	3	servant of Uzziyaw

Herr 39

1	*lgʾlyhw*	1	Belonging to Gealyahu
2	*bn hmlk*	2	son of the king

Herr 40

1	*l̊ḥʾh̊*	1	Belonging to ḤʾH̊
2	*bʿdʾl*	2	Baʿadel

Herr 41

1	*lḥgy*	1	Belonging to Ḥaggi
2	*yšʾl*	2	Yishal

Herr 43

1	*lḥmn*	1	Belonging to Ḥaman

Herr 44

1	*lḥn̊nyhw*	1	Belonging to Ḥananyahu
2	*nrẙhw*	2	Neriyahu

Herr 48

1	*yšmʿʾl̊*	1	Yishmael
2	*ʾ̊ryhẘ*	2	Uriyahu

Herr 53

1	*mnḥ̊m*	1	Menaḥem

Herr 56

1	*pqḥ*	1	Peqaḥ

Herr 60

1	*lqnyw*	1	Belonging to Qenayaw

Herr 62

1	*lrm̊ʿ*	1	Belonging to RMʿ

Herr 63

1	*lrpʾ*	1	Belonging to Rapha
2	*yhwkl*	2	Yehukal

Herr 64

1	*lšbn*	1	Belonging to Shebanyahu
2	*yh̊w*	2	

Herr 65

1	*š̊bnyhw*	1	Shebanyahu
2	*[ʿ]zryhw*	2	[A]zaryahu

Herr 66

1	*l̊šlm*	1	Belonging to Shallum
2	*ʾḥʾ̊*	2	Aḥa

Herr 67

1	*šmryw*	1	Shemaryaw

Herr 68

1	*lśr*	1	Belonging to the Governor

Herr 70

1	*lḥgy b*	1	Belonging to Ḥaggi son
2	*n p[ ]*	2	of

Herr 74

1	*lʾldlh*	1	Belonging to Eldalah

Herr 75

Herr 75

1	*lʾlyṣr*	1	Belonging to Elyaṣar

Herr 79

1	*lʾry*	1	Belonging to Uriyahu
2	*hw*	2	

Herr 80

1	*lblgy*	1	Belonging to Bilgay
2	*smk*	2	Samak

Herr 81

1	*lbn*	1	Belonging to Ben

Herr 89

1	*lzkr*	1	Belonging to Zakkur
2	*hwšʿ*	2	Hawshea

Herr 90

1	*lḥwrṣ*	1	Belonging to Ḥawreṣ
2	*bn pqll*	2	son of PQLL

Herr 93

1	*lḥnnyhw*	1	Belonging to Ḥananyahu
2	*bn ʿzryhw*	2	son of Azaryahu

Herr 94

1	*lḥnnyhw*	1	Belonging to Ḥananyahu
2	*b̊n ʿkbr*	2	son of Akbor

Herr 99

1	*lyhwʿzr b*	1	Belonging to Yehoezar son
2	*n ʿbdyhw*	2	of Obadyahu

Herr 100

1	*lyhwšʿ b*	1	Belonging to Yehawshua son
2	*n ʿśyhw*	2	of Asayahu

Herr 104

1	*lyḥṣ*	1	Belonging to Yaḥaṣ

Herr 105

1	*l yqm*	1	Belonging to Yeqamyahu
2	*yh w*	2	

Herr 107

1	*lyrm*	1	Belonging to Yerem
2	*zmryhw*	2	Zemaryahu

Herr 109

1	*lkšy*	1	Belonging to Kushi
2	*ydʿyhw*	2	Yedayahu

Herr 110

1	*lmʾš*	1	Belonging to MʾŠ
2	*bn mnḥ*	2	son of Manoaḥ
3	*hspr*	3	the scribe

Herr 116

1	*lmqnyhw ‹b›*	1	Belonging to Miqneyahu son
2	*n yhwmlk*	2	of Yehomelek

Herr 117

1	*lnʾhbt b*	1	Belonging to Neʾehebet daughter
2	*t dmlyhw*	2	of Domlayahu

Herr 118

1	*ln̊ḥ̊m̊ b*	1	Belonging to Naḥum son
2	*n ḥ̊mn̊*	2	of Ḥaman

Herr 119

1	*lnḥmyhw*	1	Belonging to Neḥemyahu
2	*b̊n mykyhẘ*	2	son of Mikayahu

Herr 120

1	*lntnyhw*	1	Belonging to Netanyahu
2	*bn bwzy*	2	son of Buzi

Herr 121

1	*lntnyhw b*	1	Belonging to Netanyahu son
2	*n ʿbdyhw*	2	of Obadyahu

Herr 122

1	*lsylʾ b*	1	Belonging to Silla son
2	*n hwdyh*	2	of Hawdayah

Herr 124

1	*lʿbdyhw*	1	Belonging to Obadyahu
2	*šḥrḥ‹r›*	2	Sheḥarḥo‹r›

Herr 128

1	*ʿzryhw*	1	Azaryahu
2	*ḥlqyhw*	2	Ḥilqiyahu

Herr 131

1	*lʿśyw*	1	Belonging to Asayaw
2	*bn ywqm̊*	2	son of Yawqim

Herr 133

1	*lqlyhw*	1	Belonging to Qolayahu
2	*dmlʾl*	2	Domlael

Herr 135

1	*lšḥrḥr bn*	1	Belonging to Sheḥarḥor son of
2	*ṣpnyhw*	2	Ṣepanyahu

Herr 137

1	*lšmʿ*	1	Belonging to Shema

Herr 140

1	*lšʿl*	1	Belonging to Shuʿal
2	*yšʿyhw*	2	Yeshayahu

Herr 141

1	*lšpṭ*	1	Belonging to Shqphat

Herr 143

1	*lʿmdyhw*	1	Belonging to Amadyahu
2	*bt šbnyhw*	2	daughter of Shebanyahu

Herr 144

1	*lzkr*	1	Belonging to Zakkur
2	*ʿzr*	2	Ezer

Herr 145

1	*lʿbdyhw*	1	Belonging to Obadyahu
2	*bn yšb*	2	son of Yashab

Herr 146

1	*l‹ʾ›ḥmlk*	1	Belonging to ‹A›ḥimelek

Herr 148

1	*lʾlšmʿ b*	1	Belonging to Elishama son
2	*n hmlk*	2	of the king

Herr 149

1	*lyḥmlyh*	1	Belonging to Yaḥmolyahu
2	*w mʿśyhw*	2	Maʿaseyahu

Herr 151

1	*ldmlyhw*	1	Belonging to Domlayahu
2	*bn nryhw*	2	son of Neriyahu

Herr 152

1	*lʾlšmʿ b*	1	Belonging to Elishama son
2	*n gdlyhw*	2	of Gedalyahu

Herr 153

1	*lʾlrm*	1	Belonging to Eliram
2	*ḥsdyhw*	2	Ḥasadyahu

Herr 156

1	*lʾsp*	1	Belonging to Asap

Herr 159

1	*lḥym*	2	Belonging to Ḥayyim

Herr 162 (forgery ?)

1	*ʾbš*	1	Abishua
2	*wʿ*	2	

6.2.15 HESTRIN

Hest. 57

1	*lyšm̊ʿ̊ʾl b*	1	Belonging to Yishmael son
2	*n ḥlqyhw*	2	of Ḥilqiyahu

Hest. 59

1	*lhṣlyh*	1	Belonging to Hissilyahu
2	*w ḥnnyhw*	2	Ḥananyahu

Hest. 60

1	*lhṣlyhw*	1	Belonging to Hissilyahu
2	*yšʿyhw*	2	Yeshayahu

Hest. 61

1	*lyhwʿzr*	1	Belonging to Yehoezer
2	*ygdlyhw*	2	Yigdalyahu

Hest. 65

1	*lʿzyhw b*	1	Belonging to Uzziyahu son
2	*n nryhw*	2	of Neriyahu

Hest. 72

1	*lhwšʿyhw*	1	Belonging to Hoshayahu
2	*ʾlšmʿ*	2	Elishama

Hest. 73

1	*lhwšʿyh*	1	Belonging to Hoshayahu
2	*wʾḥmlk*	2	Aḥimelek

Hest. 74

1	*lʿbdyhw*	1	Belonging to Obadyahu
2	*yšʿʾ*	2	Yisha

Hest. 77

1	*lmʿśyh*	1	Belonging to Maʿaseyah
2	*yšmʿʾl*	2	Yishmael

Hest. 78

1	*lmnḥm*	1	Belonging to Menaḥem
2	*bn hwšʿ*	2	son of Hoshea

Hest. 79

1	*lʾryhw*	1	Belonging to Uriyahu
2	*ḥnnyhw*	2	Ḥananyahu

Hest. 80

1	*lʾryhw*	1	Belonging to Uriyahu
2	*ʾlntn*	2	Elnatan

Hest. 82

1	*lbnyhw b*	1	Belonging to Benayahu son
2	*n ṣbly*	2	of Ṣibli

Hest. 83

1	*smk*	1	Samak
2	*bqš*	2	Baqqesh

Hest. 90

1	*ṣpn*	1	Ṣaphan

Hest. 91

1	*lʾlyqm*	1	Belonging to Elyaqim
2	*ʿz*	2	Uzza

Hest. 94

1	*myʾmn*	1	Miyamin
2	*b‹n› ʿdd*	2	so‹n of› Oded

Hest. 96

1	*lšpṭyhw*	1	Belonging to Shephaṭyahu
2	*smk[yh]w*	2	Semak[yah]u

6.2.16 JERUSALEM

Jerusalem Citadel Seal 1; *Qadmoniot* 3 (1970)

1	*lmtnyhw*	1	Belonging to Mattanyahu
2	*ʿzryhw*	2	Azaryahu

Jerusalem Seal 2; *Mountain of the Lord*, p. 181

1	*hwšʿm*	1	Hoshaʿam
2	*ḥgy*	2	Ḥaggi

Jerusalem Seal 3; Avigad, *IEJ* 20 (1970)

1	*lṣpn ʾ*	1	Belonging to Ṣapan
2	*bmʿṣ*	2	Abimaaṣ

Jerusalem Seal 4; Mazar, *Jerusalem Revealed* (1975),pp . 38-39

1	*lmnḥm*	1	Belonging to Menaḥem
2	*ywbnh*	2	Yawbanah

Jerusalem Seal 5; Mazar, *Jerusalem Revealed* (1975), pp . 38-39

1	*lḥgy b*	1	Belonging to Ḥaggi son
2	*n šbnyhw*	2	of Shebanyahu

Jerusalem Seal 6; Mazar, *Jerusalem Revealed* (1975), pp . 38-39

1	*[l]nḥm*	1	[Belonging to] Naḥum
2	*hṣlyhw*	2	Hiṣṣilyahu

Jerusalem Bulla 1; Shiloh, *IEJ* 36 (1986)

1	*lblgy b*	1	Belonging to Bilgai son
2	*n dlyh[w]*	2	of Delayah[u]

Jerusalem Bulla 2; Shiloh, *IEJ* 36 (1986)

1	*lgmryhw*	1	Belonging to Gemaryahu
2	*[b]n ṣpn*	2	[so]n of Ṣapan

Jerusalem Bulla 3; Shiloh, *IEJ* 36 (1986)

1	*lḥ̊nmlk̊*	1	Belonging to Hanimelek
2	*yšmʿʾl*	2	Yishmael

Jerusalem Bulla 4; Shiloh, *IEJ* 36 (1986)

1	*[lṭbšlm]*	1	[Belonging to Tobshallem]
2	*bn zkr*	2	son of Zakkur
3	*hrpʾ*	3	the healer

Jerusalem Bulla 5; Shiloh, *IEJ* (1986)

1	*lšmʿyhw*	1	Belonging to Shemayhu
2	*bn yʾzny[h]*	2	son of Yaazanya[h]

Jerusalem Bulla 7; Shiloh, *IEJ* 36 (1986)

1	*lʾlšmʿ b*	1	Belonging to Elishama son
2	*n smkyh*	2	of Semakyah

Jerusalem Bulla 8; Shiloh, *IEJ* 36 (1986)

1	*lmky[hw]*	1	Belonging to Mikaya[hu]
2	*bn ḥsy*	2	son of Ḥasi

Jerusalem Bulla 9; Shiloh, *IEJ* 36 (1986)

1	*lʾprḥ*	1	Belonging to Ephroaḥ
2	*ʾḥyhw*	2	Aḥiyahu

Jerusalem Bulla 10; Shiloh, *IEJ* 36 (1986)

1	*lʾlšmʿ*	1	Belonging to Elishama
2	*bn yhwʾb̊*	2	son of Yehoab

Jerusalem Bulla 12; Shiloh, *IEJ* 36 (1986)

1	*lydʿyhw*	1	Belonging to Yedayahu
2	*bn mšlm*	2	son of Meshullam

Jerusalem Bulla 13; Shiloh, *IEJ* 36 (1986)

1	*lgdyhw*	1	Belonging to Gaddiyahu
2	*bn ʿzr*	2	son of Azar

Jerusalem Bulla 14; Shiloh, *IEJ* 36 (1986)

1	*lšmʿy[hw]*	1	Belonging to Shemaya[hu]
2	*mḥsy[hw]*	2	Mahseya[hw]

Jerusalem Bulla 17; Shiloh, *IEJ* 36 (1986)

1	*lrpʾyhw*	1	Belonging to Rapayahu
2	*bn ʾprḥ*	2	son of Ephroḥ

Jerusalem Bulla 19; Shiloh, *IEJ* 36 (1986)

1	*lgmryh*	1	Belonging to Gemaryah
2	*bn mgn*	2	son of Magen

Jerusalem Bulla 20; Shiloh, *IEJ* 36 (1986)

1	*[l]ʾlntn*	1	[Belonging to] Elnatan
2	*bn blgy*	2	son of Bilgai

Jerusalem Bulla 23; Shiloh, *IEJ* 36 (1986)

1	*lšmʿyhw*	1	Belonging to Shemayahu
2	*[b]n plṭyhw*	2	[so]n of Pelatyahu

Jerusalem Bulla 27; Shiloh, *IEJ* 36 (1986)

1	*lʿzryhw b*	1	Belonging to Azaryahu son
2	*n ḥlqyhw*	2	of Ḥeleqyahu

Jerusalem Bulla 28; Shiloh, *IEJ* 36 (1986)

1	*lṭbšlm̊*	1	Belonging to Tobshallem
2	*bn zkr*	2	son of Zakkur

Jerusalem Bulla 29; Shiloh, *IEJ* 36 (1986)

1	*lʾlyqm̊*	1	Belonging to Elyaqim
2	*bn ʾwhl*	2	son of Ohel

Jerusalem Bulla 31; Shiloh, *IEJ* 36 (1986)

1	*lbnyhw b*	1	Belonging to Benayahu son
2	*n hwšʿyhw*	2	of Hawshayahu

Jerusalem Bulla 32; Shiloh, *IEJ* 36 (1986)

1	*lʿzrqm*	1	Belonging to Azarqam
2	*mkyhw*	2	Mikayahu

Jerusalem Bulla 33; Shiloh, *IEJ* 36 (1986)

1	*lbrkyhw*	1	Belonging to Berakyahu
2	*bn mlky*	2	son of Malki

Jerusalem Bulla 34; Shiloh, *IEJ* 36 (1986)

1	*lḥnnyh[w] b*	1	Belonging to Ḥananyah[u] son
2	*n ʾhʾ*	2	of Aha

Jerusalem Bulla 35; Shiloh, *IEJ* 36 (1986)

1	*lsylʾ b*	1	Belonging to Silla son
2	*n ʾlšmʿ*	2	of Elshama

Jerusalem Bulla 36; Shiloh, *IEJ* 36 (1986)

1	*lnryhw*	1	Belonging to Neriyahu
2	*dmlyhw*	2	Domlayahu

Jerusalem Bulla 39; Shiloh, *IEJ* 36 (1986)

1	*lšpṭyhw*	1	Belonging to Shephaṭyahu
2	*bn ṣpn*	2	son of Ṣapan

Jerusalem Bulla 45; Shiloh, *IEJ* 36 (1986)

1	*lʾḥymh̊*	1	Belonging to Aḥimah
2	*ḥnnyh*	2	Ḥananyah

Jerusalem Bulla 48; Shiloh, *IEJ* 36 (1986)

1	*lyʾznyh[w]*	1	Belonging to Yaʾazanyah[u]
2	*[b]n mʿśyhw*	2	[so]n of Maʿaseyahu

Jerusalem Bulla 50; Shiloh, *IEJ* 36 (1986)

1	*lšpṭyhw*	1	Belonging to Shephatyahu
2	*bn dmlẙ[hw]*	2	son of Domlaya[hu]

Jerusalem Bulla 51; Shiloh, *IEJ* 36 (1986)

1	*[l]nḥm bn*	1	[Belonging to] Naḥum son of
2	*šʾlh*	2	Sheʾalah

6.2.17 LACHISH

(Near) Lachish Seal 1; Bartlett, *PEQ* 108 (1976)

1	*lḥnh*	1	Belonging to Ḥannah

Lachish Seal 1; Driver, *PEQ* 70 (1938)

1	*ṣpn ʿ*	1	Ṣapan
2	*zryhw*	2	Azaryahu

Lachish Seal 2; Diringer, *PEQ* 73 (1941); see Hestrin Seal 27 (*Inscribed Seals*, p. 42)

1	*lḥlqyhw*	1	Belonging to Ḥilqiyahu
2	*bn mʾs*	2	son of MʾS

Lachish Seal 3; Diringer, *PEQ* 73 (1941)

1	*smk*	1	Samak
2	*lʾḥmlk*	2	Belonging to Aḥimelek

Lachish Seal 4; Diringer, *PEQ* 73 (1941)

1	*lšbnʾ*	1	Belonging to Shubna
2	*ʾḥʾb*	2	Aḥab

Lachish Seal 5; Diringer, *PEQ* 73 (1941)

1	*lšpṭyh*	1	Belonging to Shephaṭyahu
2	*w ʿśyhw*	2	Asayahu

Lachish Seal 6; Diringer, *PEQ* 73 (1941)

1	*lgdlyhw*	1	Belonging to Gedalyah
2	*[ʾ]šr ʿl hbyt*	2	royal steward

Lachish Seal 7; Diringer, *PEQ* 73 (1941)

1	*lšlm*	1	Belonging to Shallum
2	*ʿhʿš*	2	ʿḤʿŠ

Lachish Seal 8; Diringer, *PEQ* 73 (1941)

1	*hwšʿ*	1	Hawshea
2	*ṣpn*	2	Ṣapan

Lachish Seal 9; Diringer, *PEQ* 73 (1941)

1	*mšlm*	1	Meshullam
2	*ʾḥmlk*	2	Aḥimelek

Lachish Seal 10; Diringer, *PEQ* 73 (1941)

1	*ltnḥm*	1	Belonging to Tanḥum
2	*mgn*	2	Magen

Lachish Seal 11; Diringer, *PEQ* 73 (1941)

1	*lšlm*	1	Belonging to Shallum
2	*ʾḥʾmr*	2	Aḥamar

Lachish Seal 12; Diringer, *PEQ* 73 (1941)

1	*lnḥm*	1	Belonging to Naḥum
2	*ʿbdy*	2	Abdi

Lachish Seal 13; Diringer, *PEQ* 73 (1941)

1	*lʿbd*	1	Belonging to Abdi
2	*y*	2	

Lachish Seal 14; Diringer, *PEQ* 73 (1941)

1	*lšbn*	1	Belonging to Shubna
2	*ʾ šḥ[r]*	2	Shaḥa[r]

Lachish Seal 15; Diringer, *PEQ* 73 (1941)

1	*lśwk*	1	Belonging to SWK
2	*šbn*	2	Shubna
3	*ʾ*	3	

Lachish Seal 16; Diringer, *PEQ* 73 (1941)

1	*lnḥm*	1	Belonging to Naḥum
2	*ḥṣlyhw*	2	Ḥiṣṣilyahu

Lachish Seal 17; Diringer, *PEQ* 73 (1941)

1	*ls[ ]*	1	Belonging to
2	*šbnẙh̊*	2	Shebanyah

Lachish Seal 18; Diringer, *PEQ* 73 (1941)

1	*šbnẙh̊*	1	Shebanyah

Lachish Seal 19; Diringer, *PEQ* 73 (1941)

1	*l̊pn b̊n*	1	Belonging to Pan son of
2	*yḥ̊ny*	2	Yaḥani

Lachish Seal 20; Diringer, *PEQ* 73 (1941)

1	*kr̊my*	1	Karmi
2	*ypẙh̊ẘ*	2	Yophiyahu

Lachish Seal 21; Diringer, *PEQ* 73 (1941)

1	*ls‹m›ky*	1	Belonging to Sa‹m›ki
2	*ṣ̊p̊n̊ẙhw*	2	Ṣepanyahu

Lachish Seal 22; Diringer, *PEQ* 73 (1941)

1	*ṣ̊pny[hw]*	1	Ṣepany[ahu]

Lachish V Seal 1

1	*lyhwkl*	1	Belonging to Yehukal
2	*bn yhwḥ̊y*	2	son of Yehoḥay

Lachish V Seal 2

1	*lnḥm b*	1	Belonging to Naḥum son
2	*n̊nnyhẘ*	2	of Ananyahu

Lachish V Seal 3

1	*[l]n̊ryhẘ*	1	Belonging to Neriyahu
2	*prʿš*	2	Parosh

Lachish V Seal 4

1	*l̊ẙh̊wʾl*	1	Belonging to Yehoel
2	*myʾmn*	2	Miyamin

Lachish V Seal 5

1	*[l]šbnyhw*	1	[Belonging to] Shebanyahu
2	*[ ]hmlk*	2	the King

Lachish V Seal 6

1	*lyrmyhw*	1	Belonging to Yirmeyahu
2	*bn ṣpnyhw*	2	son of Ṣepanyahu
3	*bn̊ nby*	3	son of Nabi

Lachish V Seal 7

1	*lyrmyhw*	1	Belonging to Yirmeyahu
2	*bn spnyhw*	2	son of Sepanyahu

Lachish V Seal 9

1	*[l]yhwrm*	1	[Belonging to] Yehoram

Lachish V Shekel Weight 1

1	*l̊n̊d̊b*	1	Belonging to Nedabyah
2	*yh*	2	

6.2.18 LEMAIRE

Lemaire Seal 1; "Sept sceaux nord-ouest sémitiques inscrits," *EI* 18 (1985)

1	*lywʿlyh̊ẘ*	1	Belonging to Yoelyahu
2	*yšmʿʾl*	2	Yishmael

Lemaire Seal 2; *EI* 18 (1985)

1	*lsmkyh̊*	1	Belonging to Semakyah[u(?)]
2	*ʿms*	2	Amas

Lemaire Seal 3; *EI* 18 (1985)

1	*s̊ʿ̊dyh*	1	Saʿadyah
2	*ʾlsmk*	2	Elsamak

Lemaire Seal 4; *EI* 18 (1985)

1	*l̊n̊r̊yhẘ*	1	Belonging to Neriyahu
2	*g̊šmy*	2	GŠMY

Lemaire Seal 5; *EI* 18 (1985)

1	*lʿzryhw*	1	Belonging to Azaryahu
2	*ḥlqʾ*	2	Ḥilqa

Lemaire Seal 6; *EI* 18 (1985)

1	*lʾlšmʿ*	1	Belonging to Elshama
2	*ḥlṣyhw*	2	Ḥeleṣyahu

6.2.19 MAʿASEYAHU

Maʿaseyahu Seal; Stieglitz, *IEJ* 23 (1973)

1	*lmʿśyhw*	1	Belonging to Maʿaseyahu
2	*yšʿyh[w]*	2	Yeshayah[u]

6.2.20 MEGIDDO

Megiddo Seal

1	*lšmʿ*	1	Belonging to Shema
2	*ʿbd yrbʿm*	2	servant of Yeroboam

6.2.21 NAVEH

Naveh Seal 1; *Qadmoniot* 1 (1968-69); *IEJ* 15 (1965)

1	*lyhwyšmʿ*	1	Belonging to Yehoyishma
2	*bt šwššrʾṣr*	2	daughter of Shawas-shar-uṣur

6.2.22 RAMAT RACHEL

Ramat Rachel Seal 1

1	*lnrʾ*	1	Belonging to Nera
2	*šbnʾ*	2	Shubna

Ramat Rachel Seal 2

1	*lmnḥm ywbnh*	1	Belonging to Menaḥem Yawbanah

Ramat Rachel Seal 3

1	*l[ ]*	1	Belonging to
2	*ʾlšmʿ*	2	Elishama

Ramat Rachel Seal 4

1	*l[ ]*	1	Belonging to
2	*brʾ*	2	Bara

Ramat Rachel Seal 5

1	*štl*	1	Shatal

Ramat Rachel Seal 6

1	*ẙh̊ẘḥl*	1	Yehoḥel
2	*šḥr*	2	Shaḥar

Ramat Rachel Seal 7

1	*yhwḥyl*	1	Yehoḥayl
2	*šḥ[r]*	2	Shaḥa[r]

Ramat Rachel Seal 8

1	*lʾlyqm*	1	Belonging to Elyaqim
2	*[n]ʿr ywkn*	2	[ste]ward of Yawkin

Ramat Rachel Seal 9

1	*lšbnʾ*	1	Belonging to Shubna
2	*šḥr*	2	Shaḥar

6.2.23 REIFENBERG

Reifenberg Seal 1

1	*lʾlsm̊ʿ̊y*	1	Belonging to Elsemaki

Reifenberg Seal 2

1	*lʾbyw*	1	Belonging to Abiyaw

Reifenberg Seal 3

1	*lhwšʿyhw*	1	Belonging to Hoshayahu
2	*bn šlmyhw*	2	son of Shelemyahu

Reifenberg Seal 4

1	*lʾẙdh*	1	Belonging to Iadah

Reifenberg Seal 5

1	*lgdyhw*	1	Belonging to Gaddiyahu
2	*bn bṣy*	2	son of Beṣay

Reifenberg Seal 7

1	*lʾdtʾ ʾ*	1	Belonging to Adata
2	*št pšḥr*	2	wife of Pasḥur

Reifenberg Seal 8

1	*lšnẙẘ*	1	Belonging to Shenayaw

Reifenberg Seal 9

1	*mky*	1	Maki
2	*šq̊n̊yh*	2	Sheqanyah

Reifenberg Seal 11

1	*lšlm*	1	Belonging to Shallum

Reifenberg Seal 12

1	*lyhwʿz̊*	1	Belonging to Yehoaz
2	*ʾh̊ʾb̊*	2	Ahab

Reifenberg Seal 17

1	*lrbyhw*	1	Belonging to Rabbiyahu
2	*hglnyh*	2	Higlaniyah

Reifenberg Seal 18; *IEJ* 4 (1954)

1	*lʿzryh*	1	Belonging to Azaryah
2	*bn nḥm*	2	son of Naḥum

Reifenberg Seal 19; *IEJ* 4 (1954)

1	*lmlkyhw*	1	Belonging to Malkiyahu
2	*ḥlṣyhw*	2	Ḥeleṣyahu

Reifenberg Seal 20; *IEJ* 4 (1954)

1	*lḥṣy b*	1	Belonging to Ḥaṣi son
2	*n gmlyhw*	2	of Gamliyahu

Reifenberg Seal 21; *IEJ* 4 (1954)

1	*lyprʿyw*	1	Belonging to Yiprayaw

6.2.24 SHECHEM

Shechem Seal 1

1	*lmbn*	1	Belonging to Miben

6.2.25 TELL AMAL

Tell Amal Seal Impression; Hestrin, *IEJ* 24 (1974)

1	*lyhwzr̊ḥ*	1	Belonging to Yehawzaraḥ
2	*bn ḥlq[y]hw*	2	son of Ḥilqiyahu
3	*ʿbd ḥzqẙh̊ẘ*	3	servant of Ḥizqiyahu

6.2.26 TELL BEIT MIRSIM

Tell Beit Mirsim 1

1	*lʾlyqm*	1	Belonging to Elyaqim
2	*nʿr ywkn*	2	steward of Yawkin

6.2.27 TELL EN-NASBEH

Tell en-Nasbeh 1

1	*lšbnʾ*	1	Belonging to Shubna
2	*šḥr*	2	Shaḥar

Tell en-Nasbeh 2

1	*ʾḥ̊zyh̊[w]*	1	Aḥazyah[u]
2	*mt̊nyh̊[w]*	2	Mattanyah[u]

Tell en-Nasbeh 3

1	*lyʾznyhw*	1	Belonging to Yaʾazanyahu
2	*ʿbd hmlk*	2	servant of the king

6.2.28 TORREY

Torrey Ushna Seal 1; *BASOR* 79 (1940)

1	*lʾšnʾ ʿ*	1	Belonging to Ushna
2	*bd ʾḥz*	2	servant of Aḥaz

SELECTED BIBLIOGRAPHY

Aartun, Kjell. *l. Teil. Adverbien, Verneinungspartikeln, Bekräftigungspartikeln, Hevorhebungspartikeln.* Alter Orient und Altes Testament 21/1. Kevelaer: Butzon & Bercker; Neukirchen-Vluyn: Newkirchener Verlag, 1974.

____. *Die Partikeln des Ugaritischen 2 Teil. Präpositionen, Konjunktionen.* Alter Orient und Altes Testament 21/2. Kevelaer: Butzon & Bercker; Newkirchen-Vluyn: Neukirchener Verlag, 1978.

Aharoni, Yohanan. "*ṭbyʿwt-ḥwtm ʿbrywt mrmt-rḥl* [Hebrew Jar-Stamps from Ramat Rahel]." *Eretz Israel* 6 (1960): 56-60.

____. "Excavations at Ramat Rahel, Seasons 1959 and 1960." *Rome Universita Centro Di Studi Semitici, Serie Archaeologica* 2 (1962): 1-91.

____. "The Samaria Ostraca—An Additional Note." *Israel Exploration Journal* 12 (1962): 67-69.

____. "Chronique archéologique: Ramat Rahel." *Revue Biblique* 70 (1963): 572-74.

____. "The Use of Hieratic Numerals in Hebrew Ostraca and the Shekel Weights." *Bulletin of the American Schools of Oriental Research* 184 (1966): 13-19.

____. "*ḥwtmwt šl pqydym mmlktyym mʿrd* [Seals of Royal Functionaries from Arad]." *Eretz Israel* 8 (1967): 101-3.

____. "The 'Persian Fortress' at Lachish—An Assyrian Palace?" *Bulletin of the Israel Exploration Society* 31 (1967): 80-91.

____. "*hʾwstrqwnym šl ʿrd* [The Arad Ostraca]." *Qadmoniot* 1 (1968): 101-4.

Aharoni, Yohanan. "Trial Excavation in the 'Solar Shrine' at Lachish, Preliminary Report." *Israel Exploration Journal* 18 (1968): 157-69.

_____. "Rubute and Ginti-kirmil." *Vetus Testamentum* 19 (1969): 137-45.

_____. "Three Hebrew Ostraca from Arad." *Bulletin of the American Schools of Oriental Research* 197 (1970): 16-40.

_____. *Beer-Sheba I, Excavations at Tel Beer-Sheba, 1969-1971 Seasons*. Tel Aviv: Tel Aviv University, 1973.

_____. "Three Hebrew Seals." *Tel Aviv* 1 (1974): 157-58.

_____. *Investigations at Lachish, the Sanctuary and the Residency 8 (Lachish V)*. Tel Aviv: Gateway Publishers, Inc., 1975.

_____. *ktwbwt ʿrd* [Arad Inscriptions]. Jerusalem: Bialik Institute, 1975.

_____. *Arad Inscriptions*. Edited by Anson R. Rainey. Jerusalem: Israel Exploration Society, 1981.

Ahlström, G.W. *Aspects of Syncretism in Israelite Religion, Horae Soederblomianae* V. Lund: C.W.K. Gleerup, 1963.

_____. *Royal Administration and National Religion in Ancient Palestine.* Leiden: E.J. Brill, 1982.

Albright, William Foxwell. "A Revision of Early Hebrew Chronology." *Journal of the Palestine Oriental Society* 1 (1920-1921): 49-79.

_____. "Egypt and the Early History of the Negeb." *Journal of the Palestine Oriental Society* 4 (1924): 131-62.

_____. "Notes on Early Hebrew and Aramaic Epigraphy." *Journal of the Palestine Oriental Society* 6 (1926): 75-86.

_____. "The Site of Tirzah and the Topography of Western Manasseh." *Journal of the Palestine Oriental Society* 11 (1931): 241-51.

_____. "The Seal of Eliakim and the Latest Preëxilic History of Judah, with some Observations on Ezekiel." *Journal of Biblical Literature* 51 (1932): 77-106.

_____. "The North-Canaanite Poems of AlʾEyan Baʿal and the 'Gracious Gods.'" *Journal of the Palestine Oriental Society* 14 (1934): 101-15.

_____. "A Supplement to Jeremiah: The Lachish Ostraca." *Bulletin of the American Schools of Oriental Research* 61 (1936): 10-16.

Albright, William Foxwell. "Ostracon C 1101 of Samaria. "*Palestine Exploration Fund Quarterly Statement* 68 (1936): 211-15.

_____. "A Reexamination of the Lachish Letters." *Bulletin of the American Schools of Oriental Research* 73 (1939): 16-21.

_____. "The Lachish Letters after Five Years." *Bulletin of the American Schools of Oriental Research* 82 (1941): 18-24.

_____. "The Gezer Calendar." *Bulletin of the American Schools of Oriental Research* 92 (1943): 16-26.

_____. Review of *The Babylonian Genesis: The Story of Creation*, by Alexander Heidel. *Journal of Biblical Literature* 62 (1943): 366-70.

_____. "The Oracles of Balaam." *Journal of Biblical Literature* 63 (1944): 207-33.

_____. "Postscript to Professor May's Article." *Bulletin of the American Schools of Oriental Research* 97 (1945): 26.

_____. "Palestinian Inscriptions." In *Ancient Near Eastern (Supplementary) Texts (and Pictures)*, pp. 320-22, 568-69. Edited by J.B. Pritchard. Princeton: Princeton University, 1969.

Andersen, Francis I. *The Hebrew Verbless Clause in the Pentateuch. Journal of Biblical Literature Monograph Series XIV*. Nashville: Abingdon Press, 1970.

Andersen, Francis I. and A. Dean Forbes. *Spelling in the Hebrew Bible*. Biblica et Orientalia 41. Rome: Biblical Institute Press, 1986.

Avigad, Nahman. "The Epitaph of a Royal Steward from Siloam Village." *Israel Exploration Journal* 3 (1953): 137-52.

_____. "Seven Ancient Hebrew Seals." *Bulletin of the Israel Exploration Journal* 18 (1954): 147-53.

_____. "Three Ornamental Hebrew Seals." *Israel Exploration Journal* 4 (1954): 235-38.

_____. "*šbʿh ḥwtmwt ʿbryym* [Seven Hebrew Seals]." *Bulletin of the Israel Exploration Society* 18 (1954): 147-53.

_____. "The Second Tomb-Inscription of the Royal Steward." *Israel Exploration Journal* 5 (1955): 163-66.

_____. "New Light on the *Mṣh* Seal Impressions." *Israel Exploration Journal* 8 (1958): 113-19.

Avigad, Nahman."'A Seal of Manasseh Son of the King.'" *Israel Exploration Journal* 13 (1963): 133-36.

_____. "Seals and Sealings." *Israel Exploration Journal* 14 (1964): 190-94.

_____. "Seals of Exiles." *Israel Exploration Journal* 15 (1965): 222-32.

_____. "A Hebrew Seal with a Family Emblem." *Israel Exploration Journal* 16 (1966): 50-53.

_____. "The Seal of Abigad." *Israel Exploration Journal* 18 (1968): 52-53.

_____. "*ʿbn-mšql mgwlpt wʿlyh ktwbt ʿbryt* [A Sculptured Stone Weight with Hebrew Inscription]." *Qadmoniot* 2 (1969): 60-61.

_____. "*qbwṣt ḥwtmwt ʿbryym* [A Group of Hebrew Seals]." *Eretz Israel* 9 (1969): 1-9.

_____. *šyšh ḥwtmwt ʿbryym ʿtyqym* [Six Ancient Hebrew Seals]." In *Sepher Shmuel Yeivin*, pp. 305-8. Jerusalem: Kiryat Sepher, 1970.

_____. "Ammonite and Moabite Seals." In *Near Eastern Archaeology in the Twentieth Century: Essays in Honor of Nelson Glueck*, pp. 284-95. Edited by James A. Sanders. Garden City, NY: Doubleday, 1970.

_____. "Excavations in the Jewish Quarter of the Old City, 1970 (Second Preliminary Report)." *Israel Exploration Journal* 20 (1970): 129-40.

_____. "Excavations in the Jewish Quarter of the Old City of Jerusalem, 1971 (Third Preliminary Report)." *Israel Exploration Journal* 22 (1972): 193-200.

_____. "Two Hebrew Inscriptions on Wine-Jars." *Israel Exploration Journal* 22 (1972): 1-9.

_____. "*šmwt ḥdšym bḥwtmwt ʿbryym* [New Names on Hebrew Seals]." *Eretz Israel* 12 (1975): 66-71.

_____. "The Priest of Dor." *Israel Exploration Journal* 25 (1975): 101-7.

_____. "The Governor of the City." *Israel Exploration Journal* 26 (1976): 178-82.

_____. "New Light on the Naʿar Seals." In *Magnalia Dei: The Mighty Acts of God, Essays on the Bible and Archaeology in Memory of G. Ernest Wright*, pp. 294-300. Edited by F. M. Cross, W.E. Lemke, and P.D. Miller. New York: Doubleday, 1976.

_____. "*śr-hʿyr* [The Governor (Śar Ha-ʿir)]." *Qadmoniot* 10, no. 2-3/38-39 (1977): 68-69.

Avigad, Nahman. "*bwlh šnyyh šl śr-hʿyr* [On 'A Second Bulla of a Śar Haʿir']." *Qadmoniot* 11, no. 1/41 (1978): 34-35.

_____. "Baruch the Scribe and Jerahmeel the King's Son." *Israel Exploration Journal* 28, no. 1-2 (1978): 52-56, plate 15.

_____. "The King's Daughter and the Lyre." *Israel Exploration Journal* 28 (1978): 146-51.

_____. "Baruch the Scribe and Jerahmeel the King's Son." *Biblical Archaeologist* 42, no. 2 (1979): 114-18.

_____. "A Group of Hebrew Seals from the Hecht Collection." In *Festschrift Reuben R. Hecht*, pp. 119-26. Jerusalem: Koren Publishers, 1979.

_____. *bwlwt ʿbrywt mymy yrmyhw* [Hebrew Bullae From the Time of Jeremiah]. Jerusalem: *hḥbrh lḥqyrt ʾrṣ-yśrʾl wʿtyqwtyh*, 1986.

_____. *Hebrew Bullae from the Time of Jeremiah. Remnants of a Burnt Archive.* Jerusalem: Israel Exploration Society, 1986.

_____. "The Inscribed Pomegranate from the 'House of the Lord.'" In *The Israel Museum Journal VIII*, pp. 7-16. Jerusalem: The Israel Museum, 1989.

_____. *Corpus of West Semitic Stamp Seals.* Edited by Benjamin Sass. Jerusalem: Hebrew University of Jerusalem, Israel Exploration Society, 1997.

Bange, L.A. *A Study of the Use of Vowel-Letters in Alphabetic Consonantal Writing*. Munchen: Verlag UNI-druck, 1971.

Bar-Adon, P. "An Early Hebrew Inscription in a Judean Desert Cave." *Israel Exploration Journal* 25 (1975): 226-32.

Bar-Asher, Moshe. *qwbṣ mʾmrym blšwn ḥzl* [Anthology of Articles Concerning Rabbinic Hebrew], 1972.

Barkay, Gabriel. "*bwlh šnyhh šl śr-hʿyr* [A Second Bulla of a Śar Haʿir]." *Qadmoniot* 10 (1977): 69-71.

_____. *Ketef Hinnom: A Treasure Facing Jerusalem's Walls.* Jerusalem: The Israel Museum, 1986.

_____. "The Priestly Benediction on Silver Plaques from Ketef Hinnom in Jerusalem." *Tel Aviv* 19 (1992): 139-92.

Barr, James. "St Jerome and the Sounds of Hebrew." *Journal of Semitic Studies* 12 (1967): 1-36.

Barr, James. "Philo of Byblos and his 'Phoenician History.' " *Bulletin of the John Rylands University Library* 57 (1974-1975): 17-68.

Barth, J. *Die Pronominalbildung in den semitischen Sprachen*. Hildesheim: Georg Olms, 1967. Reproduced from the first ed., Leipzig, 1913.

Bartlett, John R. "The Seal of *Hnh* from the Neighborhood of Tell ed-Duweir." *Palestine Exploration Quarterly* 108 (1976): 59-61.

Bauer, Hans and Pontus Leander. *Historische Grammatik der hebräischen Sprache des Alten Testamentes*. Hildesheim: Georg Olms, 1965.

Beeston, A.F.L. *A Descriptive Grammar of Epigraphic South Arabian*. London: Luzac, 1962.

Beit-Arieh, Itzhaq. "A First Temple Period Census Document." *Palestine Exploration Quarterly* 115/2 (1983): 105-8.

_____. "*ʾstrqwn ʾḥqm mḥwrbt ʿwzh* [The Ostracon of Aḥiqam from Ḥorvat ʿUza]." In *Eretz Israel: Archaeological, Historical, Geographical Studies*. Vol. 18, pp. 94-96. Edited by B. Mazar and Y. Yadin. Jerusalem: The Israel Exploration Society, 1985.

_____. "The Ostracon of Ahiqam from *Ḥorvat ʿUza*." *Tel Aviv* 13/14 (1987): 32-38.

Beit-Arieh, Itzhaq and Bruce C. Cresson. "An Edomite Ostracon from *Ḥorvat ʿUza*." *Tel Aviv* 12 (1985): 96-101.

_____. "*Ḥorvat ʿUza*. A Fortified Outpost on the Eastern Negev Border." *Biblical Archaeologist* 54 (1991): 126-35.

Benz, Frank L. *Personal Names in the Phoenician and Punic Inscriptions*. Rome: Biblical Institute Press, 1972.

Bergstrasser, Gotthelf. *Hebräische Grammatik I*. 2 vols. Leipsig: Hinrichs, 1918; Brd. 19d; revised ed., Hildesheim: Georg Olms, 1962.

Berlejung, Angelika and Andreas Schüle. "Erwägungen zu den neuen Ostraka aus der Sammlung Moussaïeff." *Zeitschrift für Althebraistik* 11 (1998): 68-73.

Beyer, Klaus. *Althebräische Grammatik*. Gottingen: Vandenhoeck & Ruprecht, 1969.

Birnbaum, Solomon Asher. "The Dates of the Gezer Tablet and of the Samaria Ostraca." *Palestine Exploration Quarterly* 74 (1942): 104-8.

Blau, Joshua. "*dkdwq mśwwh ḥdš šl hlšwnwt hšmywt* [Review of S. Moscati *et alia*, An Introduction to the Comparative Grammar of the Semitic Languages]." *Lešonenu* 30 (1966): 136-56.

_____. *On Pseudo-Corrections in Some Semitic Languages.* Jerusalem: Israel Academy of Sciences and Humanities, 1970.

_____. *A Grammar of Biblical Hebrew.* Wiesbaden: Harrassowitz, 1976.

_____. "'Weak' Phonetic Change and the Hebrew *Śîn.*" *Hebrew Annual Review* 1 (1977): 67-119.

_____. "Short Philological Notes on the Inscription of Mešaᶜ." *Maarav* 2/2 (Spring, 1980): 143-57.

Boehmer, Julius. "Ein alphabetisch-akrostichisches Rätsel und ein Versuch es zu lösen." *Zeitschrift für die Alttestamentliche Wissenschaft* 28 (1908): 53-57.

Bordreuil, Pierre. "Inscriptions sigillaires ouest-sémitiques I: Épigraphie ammonite." *Syria* 50 (1973): 181-95.

_____. "Inscriptions sigillaires ouest-sémitiques II. Un cachet hébreu récemment acquis par le Cabinet des Medailles de la Bibliothèque Nationale." *Syria* 52 (1975): 107-18.

_____. *Catalogue des sceaux ouest-sémitiques inscrits de la Bibliothèque Nationale du Musée du Louvre et du Musée biblique de Bible et Terre Sainte.* Paris: Bibliothèque Nationale, 1986.

Bordreuil, Pierre and André Lemaire. "Trois sceaux nord-ouest sémitiques inédits." *Semitica* 24 (1974): 25-34.

_____. "Nouveaux sceaux hébreux, araméens et ammonites." *Semitica* 26 (1976): 45-63.

_____. "Nouveau groupe de sceaux hébreux, araméens et ammonites." *Semitica* 29 (1979): 71-84.

_____. "Nouveaux sceaux hébreux et araméens." *Semitica* 32 (1982): 21-34.

Bordreuil, Pierre, Felice Israel and Dennis Pardee. "Deux ostraca paléo-hébreux de la collection Sh. Moussaïeff." *Semitica* 46 (1997): 49-76.

_____. "King's Command and Widow's Plea. Two New Hebrew Ostraca of the Biblical Period." *Near Eastern Archaelogy* 61:1 (1998): 2-13.

Borée, Wilhelm. *Die alten Ortsnamen Palästinas.* Hildesheim: Georg Olms Verlagsbuchhandlung, 1968.

Brown, Francis, S.R. Driver, and Charles A. Briggs. *A Hebrew and English Lexicon of the Old Testament.* Oxford: Clarendon Press, 1st ed., 1907, 3rd printing, 1976).

Bruton, Pamela. A Review of *Matres Lectionis in Ancient Hebrew Epigraphs,* by Ziony Zevit." *Journal of Near Eastern Studies* 42 (1983): 163-65.

Chase, Debra A. "A Note on an Inscription from Kuntillet ᶜAjrud." *Bulletin of the American Schools of Oriental Research* 246 (1982): 63-67.

Claassen, Walter Theophilus. "The Hiphᵓil Verbal Theme in Biblical Hebrew." Ph.D. dissertation, University of Stellenbosch, 1971.

Cody, A. "A New Inscription from Tell al-Rimah and King Jehoash of Israel." *Catholic Biblical Quarterly* 32 (1970): 325-40.

Cohen, Rudolph. "*hḥpyrwt bqdš brnᶜ bšnym* 1976-1982 [The Excavations at Qadesh Barnea, 1976-1982]." *Qadmoniot* 16, no. 1/16 (1983): 2-14.

Coogan, Michael David. *West Semitic Personal Names in the Murašû Documents.* Missoula, MT: Scholars Press, 1976.

Corpus Inscriptionum Semiticarum, Part I: Phoenician Inscriptions. Paris: Académie des Inscriptions et Belles-Lettres, 1881-.

Cowley, A.E. *Aramaic Papyri of the Fifth Century B.C..* Oxford: Clarendon Press, 1923.

_____. *Gesenius' Hebrew Grammar as Edited and Enlarged by the Late E. Kautzsch.* Oxford: Clarendon Press, 2nd Eng. ed. 1910, 15th impression, 1980.

Cross, Frank Moore. "Lachish Letter IV." *Bulletin of the American Schools of Oriental Research* 144 (1956): 24-26.

_____."Epigraphic Notes on Hebrew Documents of Eighth-Sixth Centuries B.C.: I. A New Reading of a Placename in the Samaria Ostraca." *Bulletin of the American Schools of Oriental Research* 163 (1961): 12-14.

_____. "Epigraphic Notes on Hebrew Documents of the Eighth-Sixth Centuries, B.C.: III. The Inscribed Jar Handles from Gibeon." *Bulletin of the American Schools of Oriental Research* 168 (1962): 18-23.

_____. "Epigraphic Notes on Hebrew Documents of the Eighth-Sixth Centuries B.C.: II. The Murabbaᶜat Papyrus and the Letter found Near Yabneh-Yam." *Bulletin of the American Schools of Oriental Research* 165 (1962): 34-46.

Cross, Frank Moore. "The Cave Inscriptions From Khirbet Beit Lei." In *Near Eastern Archaeology in the Twentieth Century*, pp. 299-306. Edited by James A. Sanders. Garden City: Doubleday & Co., 1970.

_____. "The Seal of Miqneyaw the Servant of Y-H-W-H." *Proceedings of the Sixth World Congress of Jewish Studies in Jerusalem*, 1973.

_____. "Ammonite Ostraca from Heshbon. Hesbon Ostraca IV- VIII." *Andrews University Seminary Studies* 13 (1975): 1-20.

_____. "Newly Found Inscriptions in Old Canaanite and Early Phoenician Scripts." *Bulletin of the American Schools of Oriental Research* 238 (1980): 1-20.

_____. "The Ammonite Oppression of the Tribes of Gad and Reuben: Missing Verses from 1 Samuel 11 Found in 4Q Samuel[a]." In *History, Historiography and Interpretation. Studies in Biblical and Cuneiform Literatures*, pp. 148-58. Edited by H. Tadmor and M. Weinfeld. Jerusalem: Magnes, 1983.

_____. "A Literate Soldier: Lachish Letter III." In *Biblical and Related Studies Presented to Samuel Iwry*, pp. 41-47. Edited by Ann Kort and Scott Morschauser. Winona Lake, Ind.: Eisenbrauns, 1985.

Cross, Frank Moore and David Noel Freedman. *Early Hebrew Orthography: A Study of the Epigraphic Evidence.* American Oriental Series 36. New Haven: American Oriental Society, 1952.

_____. *Studies in Ancient Yahwistic Poetry.* A dissertation submitted to John Hopkins University, Baltimore, MD. 1950. Society of Biblical Literature Dissertation Series 21. Missoula, MT: Scholars Press, 1975.

Cross, Frank Moore and R.J. Saley. "Phoenician Inscriptions on a Plaque of the Seventh Century B.C. from Arslan Tash in Upper Syria." *Bulletin of the American Schools of Oriental Research* 197 (1970): 42-49.

Davies, G. I. *Ancient Hebrew Inscriptions. Corpus and Concordance.* Cambridge: Cambridge University Press, 1991.

de Vaux, Roland. "Les ostraca de Lachis." *Revue Biblique* 48 (1939): 181-206.

de Vogue, Melchior. *Intailles at legende sémitiques* (=*Mélanges d'archéologie orientale*). Part III. Paris, 1968.

Delekat, L. "Ein Bittschriftentwurf eines Sabbatschanders (*KAI* 200)." *Biblica* 51 (1970): 462.

Delavault, B. and A. Lemaire, "Les inscriptions phéniciennes de Palestine." *Rivista di Studi Fenici* 7 (1979): 1-33.

Delitzsch, Friedrich. *Assyrisches Handwörterbuch*. Leipzig: J.C. Hinrichs'sche Buchhandlung, 1896.

Demski, Aaron. "A Proto-Canaanite Abecedary Dating from the Period of the Judges and its Implications for the History of the Alphabet." *Tel Aviv* 4 (1977): 14-27.

Demski, Aaron and Moshe Kochavi. "An Alphabet from the Days of the Judges." *Biblical Archaeology Review* 4, no. 3 (1978): 22-25.

Deutsch, R. and M. Heltzer. *Forty New Ancient West Semitic Inscriptions*. Tel Aviv: Archaeological Center Publication, 1994.

_____. *New Epigraphic Evidence from the Biblical Period*. Tel Aviv: Archaeological Center Publication, 1995.

Dever, William G. "Iron Age Epigraphic Material from the Area of Khirbet el-Kôm." *Hebrew Union College Annual* 40/41 (1970): 139-205.

_____. "Asherah, Consort of Yahweh? New Evidence from Kuntillet ʿAjrûd." *Bulletin of the American Schools of Oriental Research* 255 (1984): 21-37.

Diem, Werner Von. "Das Problem von *śim* Althebräischen und die Kanaanaische Lautvershiebung." *Zeitschrift der Deutschen morgensländischen Gesellschaft* 124 (1974): 221-52.

Dion, Paul E. (collaborator). In *Handbook of Ancient Hebrew Letters* by Dennis Pardee. Chico, CA: Scholars Press, 1982.

Diringer, David. *Le iscrizioni antico-ebraiche palestinesi*. Florence, Italy: Felice le Monnier, 1934.

_____. "On Ancient Hebrew Inscriptions Discovered at Tell ed-Duweir (Lachish)-I." *Palestine Exploration Quarterly* 73 (April, 1941): 38-56.

_____. "On Ancient Hebrew Inscriptions Discovered at Tell ed-Duweir (Lachish)-II." *Palestine Exploration Quarterly* 73 (July, 1941): 89-106.

Diringer, David and S.P. Brock. "Words and Meanings in Early Hebrew Inscriptions." In *Words and Meanings: Essays Presented to David Winton Thomas*, pp. 39-45. Edited by Peter R. Ackroyd and Barnabas Lindars. Cambridge: University Press, 1968.

Donner, H., and W. Röllig. *Kanaanäische und aramäische Inschriften*. Band I and II. Wiesbaden: Otto Harrassowitz, 1962.

Dossin, G. "Signaux lumineux au pays de Mari." *Revue d'assyriologie et d'archéologie orientale* 35 (1938): 174-86.

Dotan, Aron. "New Light on the ʿIzbet Ṣarṭah Ostracon," *Tel Aviv* 8, no. 2 (1981): 160-72.

Driver, Godfrey Rolles. "Old and New Semitic Texts." *Palestine Exploration Quarterly* 70 (1938): 188-92.

_____. "Hebrew Seals." *Palestine Exploration Quarterly* (1955): 183.

Eisler, Robert. *Die Kenitischen Weihinschriften der Hyksoszeit in den Sinaibergwerken und der Ursprung des Alphabets* (Freiburg: Herdersche Verlagshandlung, 1919), p. 32; new rev. ed., *Die Kenitischen Weihinschriften der Hyksoszeit im Bergbaugebiet der Sinaihalbinsel und einige andere unerkannte Alphabet denkmaler aus der Zeit der XII. bis XVIII. Dynastie.* Hildesheim: Verlag. Dr. H.A. Gerstenberg, 1975.

Emerton, J.A. "New Light on Israelite Religion: The Implications of the Inscriptions from Kuntillet ʿAjrud." *Zeitschrift für die alttestamentliche Wissenschaft* 94 (1982): 2-20.

Encyclopaedia Biblica. S.v. "Shebnaʾ"' (Hebrew), by Aaron Demski.

Encyclopaedia Britannia, 1911 ed. S.v. "Semitic Languages," by Theodor Nöldeke.

Encyclopaedia Judaica, 4th ed., vol. 2. S.v. "Alphabet, Hebrew," by Joseph Naveh.

Février, James G. "Remarques sur le calendrier de Gézer." *Semitica* 1 (1948): 33-41.

_____. "Le *waw* conversif en punique." In *Hommages à André Dupont-Sommer*, pp. 191-92. Paris: Librairie d'Amérique et d'Orient, 1971.

Finkelstein, Louis. "A Talmudic Note on the Word for Cutting Flax in the Gezer Calendar." *Bulletin of the American Schools of Oriental Research* 94 (1944): 28-29.

Fischer, A. "Zur Siloahinschrift." *Zeitschrift des deutschen morgenländischen Gesellschaft* 56 (1902): 800-809.

Frankel, Zacharias. *Vorstudien zu der Septuaginta* Leipsic: F.C. Vogel,1841.

Freedman, David Noel. "The Massoretic Text and the Qumran Scrolls: A Study in Orthography." *Textus* 2 (1962): 87-102.

_____. "The Orthography of the Arad Ostraca." *Israel Exploration Journal* 19 (1969): 52-56.

Galling, Kurt. "Beschriftete Bildsiegel des ersten Jahrtausends v. Chr. vornehmlich aus Syrien und Palastine." *Zeitschrift des deutschen Palastina Vereins* 64 (1941): 121-202.

Garbini, Giovanni. "Note sul 'calendrio' di Gezer." *Annali dell'istituto orientale di Napoli* 6 (1954-56): 123-30.

____. "Note epigrafiche 3. Le iscrizioni ‹‹protocananaiche›› del XII e XI secolo a.C." *Annali dell'istituto Orientale di Napoli* 34 (1974): 584-90.

____. "Recensioni [Review of *Inscriptions hébraïques. Tomb I. Les ostraca* by André Lemaire]." *Annali dell'istituto Orientali di Napoli* 37 (1977): 241-43.

____. "Sull'alfabetario di ʿIzbet Ṣarṭah." *Oriens Antiquus* 17 (1978): 286-95.

____. "Il Cantico di Debora." *Parole de Pasato* 33 (1978): 5-31.

____. *Storia e problemi dell'epigrafai Semitica.* Napoli, 1979.

____. "Le serie alfabetiche semitiche e il loro significato." *Annali Orientale Istituto Orientale di Napoli* 42 (1982): 403-11.

____. "I sigilli del Regno di Israele." *Oriens Antiqvvs* 21 (1982): 163-76.

Gevirtz, S. "West Semitic Curses and the Problem of the Origins of Hebrew Law." *Vetus Testamentum* 11 (1961): 137-58.

Gibson, John C.L. *Textbook of Syrian Semitic Inscriptions, Vol I: Hebrew and Moabite Inscriptions.* Oxford: Clarenden Press, 1971.

Gilula, M. "*lyhwh šmrn wlʾšrth* [To Yahweh Shomron and his Asherah]," *Shnaton: An Annual for Biblical and Ancient Near Eastern Studies*, vol. 3. Edited by Moshe Weinfeld (1978-9): 129-37.

Ginsberg, H.L. "Review." *Bulletin of the Jewish Palestine Exploration Society* 2 (1935): 49.

____. "*ʾl tʿwdwt lkyš* [Observations on the Lachish Documents]." *Bulletin of the Jewish Palestine Exploration Society* 3 (1935): 77-86.

____. "Lachish Notes." *Bulletin of the American Schools of Oriental Research* 71 (1938): 24-26.

Glueck, Nelson. "The First Campaign at Tell el-Kheleifeh (Ezion-Geber)." *Bulletin of the American Schools of Oriental Research* 71 (1938): 3-17.

____. "Tell el-Kheleifeh Inscriptions." In *Near Eastern Studies in Honor of William Foxwell Albright*, pp. 237-39. Edited by Hans Goedicke. Baltimore and London: John Hopkins Press, 1971.

Gordon, Cyrus H. *Ugaritic Textbook.* Roma: Pontificium Institutum Biblicum, 1965.

Goshen-Gottstein, Moshe Henry. *Text and Language in Bible and Qumran.* Jerusalem: Orient Pub. House, 1960.

_____. "Hebrew Bible Manuscripts: Their History and Their Place in the *HUBP* Edition." *Biblica* 48 (1967): 243-90.

Gottwald, Norman Karol. *Studies in the Book of Lamentations.* Chicago: Allenson, 1954.

Graesser, Carl, Jr. "The Seal of Elijah." *Bulletin of the American Schools of Oriental Research* 220 (1975): 63-66.

Grant, Elihu and Wright, G. Ernest. *Ain Shems Excavations V.* Haverford: J.H. Furst, Co., 1939.

Grelot, Pierre. *Documents araméens d'Egypte. Littératures anciennes du Proche-Orient* (LAPO) 5. Paris: Les Editions du Cerf, 1972.

Hadley, Judith M. "Some Drawings qnd Inscriptions on Two Pithoi from Kuntillet ʿAjrud," *Vetus Testamentum* 37 (1987): 180-211.

Harris, Zelig S. *A Grammar of the Phoenician Language.* New Haven: American Oriental Society, 1936.

_____. *Development of the Canaanite Dialects.* American Oriental Series 16. New Haven: American Oriental Society, 1939.

Heltzer, Michael. "Some North-west Semitic Epigraphic Gleanings from the XI-VI Centuries b.c." *Annali dell'istituto orientali di Napoli* 21 (1971): 183-98.

Heltzer, Michael and Michael Ohana. *Massōret ha-šĕmōt ha-ʿibriyyīm ha-ḥūṣ-miqrāʾyīm mitteqūp̄at Bayt Riʾšōn ʿad hătīmat ha-Talmūd* [Extra-biblical Hebrew Names from the Period of the First Temple through the Talmudic Period]. *Studies in the History of the Jewish People and the Land of Israel.* Monograph Series, vol. II. Haifa University Press,

Herr, Larry. *The Scripts of Ancient Northwest Semitic Seals.* Harvard Semitic Monographs 18. Missoula, MT: Scholars Press, 1978.

Hestrin, Ruth and Michal Dayagi-Mendels. "A Seal Impression of a Servant of King Hezekiah." *Israel Exploration Journal* 24 (1974): 27-29.

_____. *Inscribed Seals, First Temple Period, Hebrew, Ammonite, Moabite, Phoenician and Aramaic.* Jerusalem: Israel Museum, 1979.

Hoftijzer J. and K. Jongeling. *Dictionary of the North-West Semitic Inscriptions*. Leiden: Brill, 1995.

Holladay, J.S. "Of Sherds and Strata: Contributions toward an Understanding of the Archaeology of the Divided Monarchy." In *Magnalia Dei, The Mighty Acts of God. Essays on the Bible and Archaeology in Memory of G. Ernest Wright*, pp. 253-93. Edited by Frank Moore Cross, Werner E. Lemke, and Patrick D. Miller. Garden City, NY: Doubleday, 1976.

Honeyman, A.M. "A Note on the Names Shebaniah, Shebna, Etc." *Palestine Exploration Quarterly* 76 (1944): 168-69.

_____. "The Syntax of the Gezer Calendar." *Journal of the Royal Asiatic Society* (1953): 53-58.

Horn, Siegfried H. "An Inscribed Seal from Jordan." *Bulletin of the American Schools of Oriental Research* 189 (1968): 41-43.

The Interpreter's Dictionary of the Bible, 1962 ed., vol. 1. S.v. "Buzite."

The Interpreter's Dictionary of the Bible, Vol. 3. S.v. "Name," by R. Abba.

_____. Vol. 4. S.v. "Silla."

Israel, Felice. "Studi di lessico ebraico epigrafico I: I materiali del Nord." *Langues Orientales Anciennes Philologie et Linguistique* 2 (1989): 36-67.

_____. "Inventaire préliminaire des sceaux paléo-hébreux (Études de lexique paléo-hébraïque III)." *Zeitschrift für Althebraistik* 7 (1994): 51-80.

Israel Museum, *ktwbwt msprwt* [Inscriptions Reveal], Catalogue no. 100. Edited by Efrat Carmon. Jerusalem: Israel Museum, 1973.

Jackson, Kent P. *The Ammonite Language of the Iron Age*." Chico, CA: Scholars Press, 1983.

Janssens, Gerard. *Studies in Hebrew Historical Linguistics Based on Origen's Secunda*. Orientalia Gandensia 9. Leuven: Belgium: Uitgeverij Peeters, 1982.

Jean, Charles F., and Jacob Hoftijzer. *Dictionnaire des inscriptions sémitiques de l'ouest*. Leiden: E.J. Brill, 1965.

Kahle, Paul E. *The Cairo Geniza*. Oxford: Oxford University Press, 1959.

Katz, P. "The Meaning of the Root *QNH*." *Journal of Jewish Studies* 5, no. 3 (1954): 126-31.

Kaufman, Ivan Tracy. "The Samaria Ostraca: A Study in Ancient Hebrew Palaeography." Ph.D. dissertation, Harvard University, 1966.

Kaufman, Stephen A. *The Akkadian Influences on Aramaic.* Assyriological Studies, no. 19. Chicago and London: The Univerity of Chicago Press, 1974.

_____. "The History of Aramaic Vowel Reduction." In *Arameans, Aramaic and the Aramaic Literary Tradition*, pp.47-55. Edited by Michael Sokoloff. Ramat-Gan: Bar Ilan University Press, 1983.

_____. "On Vowel Reduction in Aramaic." *Journal of the American Oriental Society* 104, no. 1 (1984): 87-95.

Kedar-Kopfstein, Benjamin. "Semantic Aspects of the Pattern *Qôṭēl*." *Hebrew Annual Review* 1 (1977): 155-76.

Kittel, Rudolf. *Biblia Hebraica.* Stuttgart: Wurttembergische Bibelanstalt, 1937.

Kochavi, Moshe. "An Ostracon of the Period of the Judges from ʿIzbet Ṣarṭah." *Tel Aviv* 4 (1977): 1-13.

Koehler, Ludwig and Walter Baumgartner. *Lexicon in Veteris Testamenti Libros.* Leiden: E.J. Brill, 1958.

Konnecke, C. *Die Behandlung der hebräischen Namen in der Septuaginta.* Programm des d.u.g. Gymnasiums zu Stargard in Pommern, 1885.

Kutscher, Edward Yechezkel. "Inscriptions of the First Temple Period." In *Sepher Yerushalayim*, p. 169. Edited by M. Avi-Yonah. Jerusalem: Bialik Institute, 1956.

_____. "Contemporary Studies in North-Western Semitic." *Journal of Semitic Studies* 10 (1965): 21-51.

_____. *The Language and Linguistic Background of the Isaiah Scroll (IQIsa[a]).* Hebrew Original, 1969. Leiden: Brill, 1974.

_____. *A History of the Hebrew Language.* Leiden: E.J. Brill & Jerusalem: Magnes Press, 1982.

Lambdin, Thomas. *Introduction to Biblical Hebrew.* New York: Charles Scribner's Sons, 1971.

Lang, Bernard. "The Decalogue in the Light of a Newly Published Palaeo-Hebrew Inscription (Hebrew Ostracon Moussaïeff no. 1)." *Journal for the Study of the Old Testament* 77 (1998): 21-25.

Layton, Scott C. "The Steward in Ancient Israel: A Study of Hebrew (*ʾĂŠER*) *ʿAL-HABBAYIT* in its Near Eastern Setting." *Journal of Biblical Literature* 109/4 (1990): 633-49.

Leiman, Sid Z., ed.. *The Canon and Masorah of the Hebrew Bible: An Introductory Reader*. New York: Ktav Pub. House, 1974.

Lemaire, André. "L'ostracon de Meṣad Ḥashavyahu (Yavneh-Yam) replacé dans son contexte." *Semitica* 21 (1971): 64-8.

____. "L'ostracon C 1101 de Samarie. Nouvel essai." *Revue Biblique* 79 (1972): 565-70.

____. "Les ostraca hébreux de l'époque royale israelite." Ph.D. dissertation; Université de Paris, 1973.

____. "Remarques sur la datation des estampilles lmlk." *Vetus Testamentus* 25 (1975): 678-82.

____. "*Zamīr* dans la tablette de Gezer et le Cantique des Cantiques." *Vetus Testamentum* 25 (1975): 15-26.

____. "Prières en temps de crise: Les inscriptions de Khirbet Beit Lei." *Revue Biblique* 83 (1976): 558-68.

____. "Les inscriptions de Khirbet el-Qôm et l'Ashérah de YHWH." *Revue Biblique* 84 (1977): 595-608.

____. *Inscriptions hébraïques, tomb I: Les ostraca. Littératures anciennes du Proche-Orient* 9. Paris: Editions du Cerf, 1977.

____. "Inscription paléo-hébraïque sur une assiette." *Semitica* 27 (1977): 20-22.

____. "Archaeological Notes. 1: Les ostraca paléo-hébreux des fouilles de l'Ophel." *Levant* 10 (1978): 156-61.

____. "Abécédaires et exercises d'écolier en épigraphie nord-ouest sémitique." *Journal Asiatique* 266 (1978): 221-35.

____. "A Note on Inscription XXX from Lachish." *Tel Aviv* 7, no. 1/2 (1980): 92-94.

____. "Une inscription paléo-hébraïque sur grenade en ivoire." *Revue Biblique* 88, no. 2 (1981): 236-39.

____. "Who or What was Yahweh's Asherah?" *Biblical Archaeology Review* 10/no. 6 (1984): 42-51.

____. "Date et origine des inscriptions paléo-hébraïques et phéniciennes de Kuntillet ʿAjrud." *Studi Epigrafici e linguistici* 11 (1984): 131-43.

Lemaire, André. "Sept sceaux nord-ouest sémitiques inscrits." In *Eretz-Israel: Archaeological, Historical and Geographical Studies.* Vol. 18, pp. 29-32. Edited by B. Mazar and Y. Yadin. Jerusalem: The Israel Exploration Society, 1985.

_____. Review of *Handbook of Ancient Hebrew Letters: A Study Edition* by Dennis Pardee, S. David Sperling, J. David Whitehead, and Paul E. Dion. *Journal of Near Eastern Studies* 45, no. 2 (1986): 152-54.

Levi della Vida, Giorgio. "The Shiloaḥ Inscription Reconsidered." *Beihefte zur Zeitshrift für die alttestamentliche Wissenschaft* 103 (1968): 162-66.

Levine, B.A. "The Netînîm." *Journal of Biblical Literature* 82 (1963): 207-12.

_____. "Notes on a Hebrew Ostracon from Arad." *Israel Exploration Journal* 19 (1969): 49-51.

Lewy, Julius. "The Old West Semitic Sun-God Ḥammu." *Hebrew Union College Annual* 18 (1944): 429-88.

Lidzbarski, M. *Ephemeris für semitische Epigraphik III.* Giessen: Verlag von Alfred Topelmann, 1915.

Lindenberger, James M. *Ancient Aramaic and Hebrew Letters.* Atlanta: Scholars Press, 1994.

Lipinski, E. Review of *Textbook of Syrian Semitic Inscriptions, I*, by J.C.L. Gibson. In "North-west Semitic Inscriptions." *Orientalia Lovaniensia Periodica* 8 (1977): 81-117.

_____. "Etudes d'onomastique ouest-sémitique." *Bibliotheca Orientalis* 37 no. 1/2 (1980): 3-12.

Livni, Izhak. "*lktbt hšlḥ* [The Siloam Inscription]." *Bulletin of the Jewish Palestine Exploration Society* 9 (1942): 114-15.

Löhr, Max. "Alphabetische und alphabetisierende Lieder im Alten Testament." *Zeitschrift für die alttestamentliche Wissenschaft* 25 (1905): 173-98.

McCarter, Peter Kyle. "Yaw, Son of Omri: A Philological Note on Israelite Chronology." *Bulletin of the American Schools of Oriental Research* 216 (1974): 5-7.

_____. In *Anchor Bible I Samuel.* Garden City, NY: Doubleday, 1980.

_____. *Ancient Inscriptions: Voices from the Biblical World.* Washington, DC: Biblical Archaeology Society, 1996.

McCown, Chester Charleton. *Tell en-Nasbeh I.* Berkeley: Palestine Institute of Pacific School of Religion and the American Schools of Oriental Research, 1947.

Maisler, Benjamin. "Excavations at Tell Qasile." *Bulletin of the Jewish Palestine Exploration Society* 15:1-2 (1949): 8-18.

_____. "Two Hebrew Ostraca from Tell Qasile." *Journal of Near Eastern Studies* 10 (1950): 265-67.

Malamat, A. "On the Akkadian Transcription of the Name of King Joash." *Bulletin of the American Schools of Oriental Research* 204 (1971): 37-40.

Martin, M.F. "Six Palestinian Seals." *Rivista degli Studi Orientali* 39 (1964): 203-10.

Mazar, Benjamin. *The Excavations in the Old City of Jerusalem Near the Temple Mount, Preliminary Report of the Second and Third Seasons 1969-1970.* Jerusalem: Israel Exploration Society, 1971.

Mazar, Benjamin, Trude Dothan and I. Dunayevsky. "En-Gedi, the First and Second Seasons of Excavations 1961-1962." *Atiqot* 5 (1966): 35-38.

Meshel, Zeev. *Kuntillet ʿAjrud: A Religious Centre from the Time of the Judean Monarchy on the Border of Sinai.* Israel Museum Cat. No. 175, 1978.

_____. "Did Yahweh Have a Consort?" *Biblical Archaelogy Review* 5, no. 2 (1979): 24-35.

_____. "*Kuntillet ʿAjrud.*" In the *Anchor Bible Dictionary*, vol. 4, pp. 103-9. Edited by David Noel Freedman. New York: Doubleday, 1992.

Meshel, Zeev and Carol Meyers. "The Name of God in the Wilderness of Zin." *Biblical Archaeologist* 39/1 (1976): 6-10.

Mettinger, Tryggve N.D. *Solomonic State Officials: A Study of the Civil Government Officials of the Israelite Monarchy.* Lund: CWK Cleerups Forlag, 1971.

Michaud, Henri. "Le témoignage des ostraca de Tell Douweir concernant le prophète Jérémie." *Revue des Etudes Sémitiques* (1941): 42-60.

_____. "Les ostraca de Lakiš conservés à Londres." *Syria* 34 (1957): 39-60.

_____. *Sur la Pierre et L'Argile.* Neuchatel: Delachaux and Niestle, 1958.

Milik, J.T. "Notes d'épigraphie et de topographie palestiniennes." *Revue Biblique* 66 (1959): 550-53.

Milik, J.T. In P. Benoit *et al. Discoveries in the Judean Desert II. Les Grottes de Murabbaʿât.* Oxford: Clarendon, 1961.

Millard, A. R. "Assyrian Royal Names in Biblical Hebrew." *Journal of Semitic Studies* 21 (1976): 1-14.

_____. "*YW* and *YHW* Names." *Vetus Testamentum* 30, fasc. 2 (1980): 208-12.

Miller, Patrick D., Jr., "Psalms and Inscriptions." *Supplements to Vetus Testamentum* 32 (1981): 311-32.

Moran, W. L. "Early Canaanite *yaqtula.*" *Orientalia* n.s. 29 (1960): 1-19.

Moscati, Sabatino. *L'Epigrafia ebraica antica 1935-1950*. Roma: Pontificio Istituto Biblico, 1951.

_____. *An Introduction to the Comparative Grammar of the Semitic Languages*. Weisbaden: Harrassowitz, 1964.

Munch, P.A. "Die alphabetische Akrostichie in der jüdischen Psalmendictung." *Zeitschrift der deutschen morgenländischen Gesellschaft* 90 (Neue Folge Band 15, 1936): 703-10.

Naveh, Joseph. "A Hebrew Letter from the Seventh Century B.C.." *Israel Exploration Journal* 10 (1960): 129-39.

_____. "More Hebrew Inscriptions from Meṣad Ḥashavyahu." *Israel Exploration Journal* 12 (1962): 27-32.

_____. "Old Hebrew Inscriptions in a Burial Cave." *Israel Exploration Journal* 13 (1963): 74-92.

_____. "*ktwbwt knʿnywt wʿbrywt* (1960-1964)" [Canaanite and Hebrew Inscriptions]. *Lešonenu* 30 (1965): 65-80.

_____. "A Paleographic Note on the Distribution of the Hebrew Script." *Harvard Theological Revue* 61 (1968): 68-74.

_____. "*šny ḥwtmwt ʿbryym* [Two Hebrew Seals]." *Qadmoniot* 1 (1968-69): 105.

_____. "The Scripts in Palestine and Transjordan in the Iron Age." In *Near Eastern Archaeology in the Twentieth Century: Essays in Honor of Nelson Glueck*, pp. 277-83. Edited by J.A. Sanders. Garden City, NY: Doubleday, 1970.

_____. "New Light on the Naʿar Seals." In *Magnalia Dei: The Mighty Acts of God, Essays on the Bible and Archaeology in Memory of G. Ernest Wright*, pp. 294-300. Edited by F.M. Cross, W.E. Lemke, and P.D. Miller. New York: Doubleday, 1976.

Naveh, Joseph. "Some Considerations on the Ostracon from ʿIzbet Ṣarṭah." *Israel Exploration Journal* 28 (1978): 31-35.

_____. "Graffiti and Dedications." *Bulletin of the American Schools of Oriental Research* 235 (1979): 27-30.

_____. Review of *The Scripts of Ancient Northwest Semitic Seals,* by Larry Herr. *Bulletin of the American Schools of Oriental Research* 239 (Summer, 1980): 75-76.

_____. "*lmkbrm ʾw lmkbdm* ?['Belonging to Makbiram' or 'Belonging to the Food-servers'?]." *Eretz Israel* 15 (1981): 301-2.

_____. "The Greek Alphabet: New Evidence." *Biblical Archaeologist* 43, no. 1 (1980): 22-25.

_____. "A Fragment of an Ancient Hebrew Inscription from the Ophel." *Israel Exploration Journal* 32 (1982): 195-98.

Norin, Stig. "Jô-Namen und J^{e}hô-Namen." *Vetus Testamentum* 29 (1979): 87-97.

Noth, Martin. *Die Israelitischen Personennamen im Rahmen der Gemeinsemitischen Namengebung.* Stuttgart: Kohlhammer, 1928.

Nylander, C. "A Note on the Stonecutting and Masonry of Tel Arad." *Israel Exploration Journal* 17 (1967): 56-59.

Pardee, Dennis. "The Preposition in Ugaritic." *Ugarit-Forschungen* 8 (1976): 215-322.

_____. "A New Ugaritic Letter." *Bibliotheca Orientalis* 34 (1977): 3-20.

_____. "Letters from Tel Arad." *Ugarit-Forschungen* 10 (1978): 289-336.

_____. "The Judicial Plea from Meṣad Ḥashavyahu (Yavneh-Yam): A New Philological Study." *Maarav* 1/1 (1978): 33-66.

_____. "Literary Sources for the History of Palestine and Syria II: Hebrew, Moabite, Ammonite, and Edomite Inscriptions." *Andrews University Seminary Studies* 17 (1979): 47-69.

_____. "A Brief Note on Meṣad Ḥashavyahu Ostracon, l. 12: *wʾmlʾ*." *Bulletin of the American Schools of Oriental Research* 239 (1980): 47-48.

_____. *Handbook of Ancient Hebrew Letters.* Chico, CA: Scholars Press, 1982.

_____. Review of *Matres Lectionis in Ancient Hebrew Epigraphs*, by Ziony Zevit. *Christian Biblical Quarterly* 44 (1982): 503-4.

Pardee, Dennis. The 'Epistolary Perfect' in Hebrew Letters." *Biblische Notizen* 22 (1983): 34-40.

_____. Review of *Arad Inscriptions* by Yohanan Aharoni. *Journal of Near Eastern Studies* 44/1 (1985): 67-71.

_____. Review of *Spelling in the Hebrew Bible: Dahood Memorial Lecture* by Francis I. Andersen and A. Dean Forbes. *Catholic Biblical Quarterly* 50 (1988): 276-80.

_____. Review of *Biblical and Related Studies Presented to Samuel Iwry* by Ann Kort and Scott Morschauser. *Journal of Near Eastern Studies* 49/1 (1990): 88-94.

_____. Review of *Hebrew Bullae from the Time of Jeremiah : Remnants of a Burnt Archive* by Nahman Avigad. *Journal of Near Eastern Studies* 50/3 (1991): 222-24.

Pardee, Dennis and Whiting, Robert M. "Aspects of Epistolary Verbal Usage in Ugaritic and Akkadian." *Bulletin of the School of Oriental and African Studies* 50 (1987): 1-31.

Pennacchietti, Fabrizio A. "'Sono già due anni che nel paese c''è carestia' (Gen. XLV, 6): i sintagmi temporali ebraici introdotti dal pronome *ze* e la loro traduzione in siriaco, arabo ed etiopico." *Vicino Orient* 3 (1980): 225-42.

Porten, B. "'Domlaʾel' and Related Names." *Israel Exploration Journal* 21 (1971): 47-49.

Prignaud, J. "Un sceau hébreu de Jérusalem et un ketib du livre d'Esdras." *Revue Biblique* 71 (1964): 372-83.

_____. "Scribes et graveurs à Jérusalem vers 700 av. J.C." In *Archaeology in the Levant: Essays for Kathleen Kenyon*, pp. 136-48. Edited by Roger Moorey and Peter Parr. Warminster, England: Aris & Phillips LTD, 1978.

_____. *Hebrew Inscriptions and Stamps from Gibeon.* Philadelphia: University of Pennsylvania Museum, 1959.

Rahtjen, B.D. "A Note Concerning the Form of the Gezer Tablet." *Palestine Exploration Quarterly* 93 (1961): 70-72.

Rainey, Anson F. "Administration in Ugarit and the Samaria Ostraca." *Israel Exploration Journal* 12 (1962): 62-63.

_____. "The Samaria Ostraca in the Light of Fresh Evidence." *Palestine Exploration Quarterly* 99 (1967): 32-41.

Rainey, Anson F. "Semantic Parallels to the Samaria Ostraca." *Palestine Exploration Quarterly* 102 (1970): 42-51.

_____. "The Word *Ywm* in Ugaritic and in Hebrew." *Lešonenu* 36 (1972): 186-89.

_____. "Three Additional Hebrew Ostraca from Tel Arad." *Tel Aviv* 4 (1977): 97-104.

_____. "The *Sitz im Leben* of the Samaria Ostraca." *Tel Aviv* 6 (1979): 91-94.

_____. *Arad Inscriptions* by Yohanan Aharoni. Jerusalem: The Israel Exploration Society, 1981.

_____. Review of *Matres Lectionis in Ancient Hebrew Epigraphs* by Ziony Zevit. *Journal of Biblical Literature* 102 (1983): 629-34.

Ranke, Hermann. *Early Babylonian Personal Names*. Philadelphia: University of Pennsylvania, 1905.

Reifenberg, A. "Some Ancient Hebrew Seals." *Palestine Exploration Quarterly* 70 (1938): 113-16.

_____. "Ancient Hebrew Seals III." *Palestine Exploration Quarterly* 70 (1942): 109-12.

_____. "Discovery of a New Hebrew Inscription of the Pre-Exilic Period." *Bulletin of the Journal of the Palestine Exploration Society* 13 (1947): 80-83.

_____. "A Newly Discovered Hebrew Inscription of the Pre-Exilic Period." *Journal of the Palestine Oriental Society* 21 (1948): 134-37.

_____. *Ancient Hebrew Seals*. London: The East and West Library, 1950.

_____. "Hebrew Seals and Stamps IV." *Israel Exploration Journal* 4 (1954): 139-42.

Reisner, George Andrew. *Israelite Ostraca from Samaria*. Boston: E.O. Cockayne, 1924.

Reisner, George Andrew, Clarence Stanley Fisher and David Gordon Lyon. *Harvard Excavations at Samaria*, 2 vols. Cambridge: Harvard University Press, 1924.

Renz, Johannes and Wolfgang Röllig. *Handbuch der althebräischen Epigraphik*. Band I: *Die althebräischen Inschriftenn*, Teil 1: *Text und Kommentar*. Band II/I: *Die althebräischen Inscriften*, Teil 2: *Zusammenfassende Erörterungen, Paläographie und Glossar*. Band III: *Texte und Tafeln*. Darmstadt: Wissenschaftliche Buchgesellschaft, 1995.

Richter, Wolfgang. *Grundlagen einer althebräischen Grammatik. B. Die Beschreibungsebenen. II. Die Wortfügung (Morphosyntax).* St. Ottilien: EOS Verlag, 1979; *III. Der Satz (Satztheorie).* St. Ottilien: EOS Verlag, 1980.

Sarfatti, Gad B. "Hebrew Inscriptions of the First Temple Period—A Survey and Some Linguistic Comments." *Maarav* 3/1 (Jan., 1982): 55-83.

Sasson, Victor. "An Unrecognized Juridical Term in the Yabneh-Yam Lawsuit and in an Unnoticed Biblical Parallel." *Bulletin of the American Schools of Oriental Research* 232 (1978): 57-63.

_____. "Studies in the Lexicon and Linguistic Usage of Early Hebrew Inscriptions." Ph.D. dissertation, New York University, 1979. Ann Arbor: MI: University Microfilms International 7925520, 1980.

_____. "*šmn rḥṣ* in the Samaria Ostraca." *Journal of Semitic Studies* 26 (1981): 1-5.

_____. "The Siloam Tunnel Inscription." *Palestine Exploration Quarterly* 114 (1982): 111-16

Savignac, R.M. Review of *Le Iscrizioni antico-ebraiche Palestinesi*, by David Diringer. *Revue Biblique* 44 (1935): 291-94.

Segal, J.B. "'YRḤ' in the Gezer 'Calendar.'" *Journal of Semitic Studies* 7 (1963): 212-21.

Segert, Stanislav. *A Grammar of Phoenician and Punic.* Munchen: C.H. Beck, 1976.

Sérandour, A. "'Remarques complémentaires sur la contribution ordonnée par le roi *ʾšyhw* pour le temple de YHWH.'" *Semitica* 46 (1997): 77-80.

Shanks, Hershel. "'Three Shekels for the Lord.'" *Biblical Archaeology Review* 23 (1997): 28-32.

Shea, William H. "The Date and Significance of the Samaria Ostraca." *Israel Exploration Journal* 27 (1977): 16-27.

Rainey, Anson F. "City of David: Excavation 1978." *Biblical Archaeologist* 42 (1979): 165-71.

_____. *City of David I. Monographs of the Institute of Archaeology.* Jerusalem: Hebrew University, 1984.

Rainey, Anson F. "*qbwṣt bwlwt ʿbrywt mʿyr dwd* [A Group of Hebrew Bullae from the City of David]." In *Eretz-Israel: Archaeological, Historical and Geographical Studies.* Vol. 18, pp. 73-87. Edited b y B. Mazar and Y. Yadin. Jerusalem: The Israel Exploration Society, 1985.

____. "A Group of Hebrew Bullae from the City of David." *Israel Exploration Journal* 36 (1986): 16-38.

Siegel, Jonathan. "The Evolution of Two Hebrew Scripts." *Biblical Archaeology Review* 5, no. 3 (1979): 28-33.

Sivan, Daniel. "On the Grammar and Orthography of the Ammonite Findings." *Ugarit-Forschungen* 14 (1982): 219-34.

von Soden, Wolfram. *Grundriss der akkadischen Grammatik.* Pontifical Biblical Institute Analecta Orientalia. Rome, 1931- . 33/47, rev. ed., 1969.

Soggin, J. Alberto. "Un passage difficile dans l'inscription de Siloe." *Vetus Testamentum* 8 (1958): 297-302.

Speiser, Ephraim Avigdor. "The Pronunciation of Hebrew According to the Transliterations in the Hexapla." *Jewish Quarterly Review* 16 (1925-1926): 343-82.

____. "The Pronunciation of Hebrew Based Chiefly on the Transliterations in the Hexapla." *Jewish Quarterly Review* 23 (1932-33): 233-65.

____. "Progress in the Study of the Hurrian Language." *Bulletin of the American Schools of Oriental Research* 74 (1939): 4-7.

Sperber, Alexander. "Hebrew Based Upon and Greek and Latin Transliterations," *Hebrew Union College* 12/13 (1937-38): 103-274.

____. *A Historical Grammar of Biblical Hebrew.* Leiden: E.J. Brill, 1966.

Stager, Lawrence E. "The Finest Olive Oil in Samaria." *Journal of Semitic Studies* 28/2 (1983): 241-45.

Stamm, J.J. "Hebräische Ersatznamen." In *Studies in Honor of Benno Landsberger on his Seventy-fifth Birthday*, April 1965, pp. 59-79. *Assyriological Studies* 16. Chicago: University of Chicago Press, 1965.

____. "Ein Problem der altsemitischen Namengebung." *Fourth World Congress of Jewish Studies* (1967): 141-47.

____. "Hebräische Frauennamen." In *Hebräische Wortforschung. Festschrift zum 80. Geburtstag von Walter Baumgartner*, pp. 301-39. *Supplements to Vetus Testamentum XVI*. Leiden: Brill, 1967.

Stamm, J.J. "Eine Gruppe hebräischer Personennamen." In *Travels in the World of the Old Testament. Studies Presented to Prof. M.A. Beek on the Occasion of His 65th Birthday*, pp. 230-40. Assen: Van Gorcum, 1974.

Stieglitz, R.R. "The Seal of Maʿaseyahu." *Israel Exploration Journal* 23 (1973): 236-37.

Sukenik, E.L. "Inscribed Hebrew and Aramaic Potsherds from Samaria." *Palestine Exploration Quarterly* 65 (1933): 152-54.

Talmon, Shmaryahu. "The Gezer Calendar and the Seasonal Cycle of Ancient Canaan.*" *Journal of the American Oriental Society* 83 (1963): 177-87.

Talmon, Shmaryahu and Frank Moore Cross, eds.. *Qumran and the History of the Biblical Text.* Cambridge: Harvard University Press, 1975.

Teixidor, Javier. "Bulletin d'épigraphie sémitique." *Syria* 56 (1979): 353-405.

_____. *Bulletin d'épigraphie sémitique* (1964-1980). Paris: Librairie Orientaliste Paul Geuthner, 1986.

Torczyner, Harry. *Lachish I, The Lachish Letters.* London: Oxford University Press, 1938.

_____. "*ktwbt hšlwḥ, lwḥ gzr wḥrs hʿwpl* [The Siloam Inscription, Gezer Calendar, and Ophel Ostracon]," *Bulletin of the Jewish Palestine Exploration Society* 7 (1939): 1-9.

_____. *tʾwdwt lkyš: mktbym mymy yrmyhw hnbʾ* [Documents (Testimony) of Lachish. Letters from the Days of the Prophet Jeremiah]. Jerusalem: Jewish Palestine Exploration Society, 1940.

Torrey, Charles C. "A Few Ancient Seals." *Annual of the American Schools of Oriental Research* 3 (1923): 103-8.

_____. Brief Communications-Hebrew and Aramaic from Beth Shemesh." *Journal of the American Oriental Society* 55 (1935): 307-10.

_____. "A Hebrew Seal from the Reign of Ahaz." *Bulletin of the American Schools of Oriental Research* 79 (1940): 27-28.

_____. "The Seal from the Reign of Ahaz Again." *Bulletin of the American Schools of Oriental Research* 82 (1941): 16-17.

Ulrich, Eugene Charles. "4 QSam^c : A Fragmentary Manuscript of 2 Samuel 14-15 from the Scribe of *Serek Hay-yahad* (1QS)." *Bulletin of the American Schools of Oriental Research* 235 (1979): 1-25.

Ussishkin, David. "On the Shorter Inscription from the 'Tomb of the Royal Steward.'" *Bulletin of the American Schools of Oriental Research* 196 (1969): 16-22.

_____. "Royal Judean Storage Jars and Seal Impressions." *Bulletin of the American Schools of Oriental Research* 223 (1976): 1-13.

_____. "Excavations at Tel Lachish, 1973-1977, Preliminary Report." *Tel Aviv* 5, no. 1-2 (1978): 1-97.

_____. "Excavations at Tel Lachish 1978-1983: Second Preliminary Report." *Tel Aviv* 10, no. 2 (1983): 97-175.

_____. *The Village of Silwan.* Jerusalem: Israel Exploration Society, 1993.

Van Dyke Parunak, H. "The Orthography of the Arad Ostraca." *Bulletin of the American Schools of Oriental Research* 230 (1978): 25-31.

Vattioni, Francesco. "I sigilli ebraici." *Biblica* 50 (1969): 357-88.

_____. "I sigilli ebraici II." *Augustinianum* 2 (1971): 447-54.

_____. "Sigilli ebraici. III." *Annali dell'istituto orientali di Napoli* 28

Vinnikov, I.N. "O vnov' otkrytoj nadpisi k jugu ot Jaffy." *Archiv Orientalni* 33 (1965): 546-52.

Waterman, Leroy. *Royal Correspondence of the Assyrian Empire.* Ann Arbor: Univ. of Michigan, 1931.

Weinfeld, Moshe. "ywmn prswmym. Review of Z. Meshel, *kwntylt- ʿgrwd, ʾtr mqwdš mtqwpt hmlwkh bgbwl syny [Kuntillet ʿAjrud: A Religious Centre from the Time of the Judean Monarchy on the Border of Sinai]."* In *Shanaton* 4 (1980): 280-84.

_____. *"ywmn prswmym. nwspwt lktwbwt ʿgrwd* [Further Remarks on the Ajrud Inscriptions]." *Shanaton* 5-6 (1982): 233-39, esp. pp. 237-39.

_____. "Kuntillet ʿAjrud Inscriptions and Their Significance." *Studi Epigrafici e Linguistici* 1 (1984): 121-43.

Wevers, J.W. "Ḥeth in Classical Hebrew." In *Essays on the Ancient Semitic World,* pp. 110-12. Edited by J.W. Wevers and D.B. Redford. Canada: University of Toronto, 1970.

Williams, Ronald J. *Hebrew Syntax: An Outline.* Toronto and Buffalo: University of Toronto Press, 1967.

Wirgin, Wolf. "The Calendar Tablet from Gezer." *Eretz Israel* 6 (1960): 9-12.

Yadin, Yigael. "Aḥa of Yahud." *Bulletin of the Israel Exploration Society* 16 (1951): 61-63.

_____. "Recipients or Owners: A Note on the Samaria Ostraca." *Israel Exploration Journal* 9 (1959): 184-87.

_____. *The James A. de Rothschild Expedition at Hazor, Hazor II, An Account of the Second Season of Excavations, 1956.* Jersusalem: Magnes Press of the Hebrew University, 1960.

_____. "A Hebrew Seal from Tell Jemmeh." *Eretz Israel* 6 (1960): 53-55.

_____. "A Further Note on the Samaria Ostraca." *Israel Exploration Journal* 12 (1962): 64-65.

_____. "A Note on the Stratigraphy of Arad." *Israel Exploration Journal* 15 (1965): 180.

_____. "A Further Note on the Lamed in the Samaria Ostraca." *Israel Exploration Journal* 18 (1968): 50-51.

_____. *Jerusalem Revealed, Archaeology in the Holy City 1968-1974.* Jerusalem: Israel Exploration Society, 1975.

_____. "The Lachish Letters-- Originals or Copies and Drafts?" In *Recent Archaeology in the Land of Israel,* pp. 179-86. Edited by Hershel Shanks (English ed.) and Benjamin Mazar (Hebrew ed.). Washington, D.C.: Biblical Archaeology Society, 1984 (Eng. edition, Jerusalem: Israel Exploration Society, 1981 (Hebrew edition).

Yeivin, Samuel S. The History of the Jewish Script I. Jerusalem, 1939.

_____. "The Judicial Petition from Meẕad Ḫashavyahu." *Bibliotheca Orientalis* 19 (1962): 3-10.

_____. "A Hieratic Ostracon from Tel Arad." *Israel Exploration Journal* 16 (1966): 153-59.

_____. "Ostracon A1/382 from Hazor and its Implications." *Eretz Israel* 9 (1969): 86-87.

Zadok, Ran. *On West Semites in Babylonia during the Chaldean and Achaemenian Periods. An Onomastic Study.* Jerusalem: J. H. & Z. Wanaarta and Tel Aviv University, 1977.

_____. Review of *West Semitic Personal Names in the Murašû Documents*, by Michael David Coogan. *Israel Exploration Journal* 28, no. 4 (1978): 290-92.

Zadok, Ran. *The Jews in Babylonia during the Chaldean and Achaemenian Periods according to the Babylonian Sources.* Studies in the History of the Jewish People and the Land of Israel. Monograph Series. Vol. 3. Haifa: Haifa University Press, 1979.

Zevit, Ziony. "The Linguistic and Contextual Arguments in Favor of a Hebrew 3 m.s. Suffix -Y." *Ugarit-Forschungen* 9 (1977): 315-28.

_____. *Matres Lectionis in Ancient Hebrew Epigraphy.* American Schools of Oriental Research Monography Series, no. 2. Cambridge, Mass.: American Schools of Oriental Research, 1980.

_____. "A Chapter in the History of Israelite Personal Names." *Bulletin of the American Schools of Oriental Research* 250 (1983): 1-16.

_____. "The Khirbet el-Qôm Inscription Mentioning a Goddess." *Bulletin of the American Schools of Oriental Research* 255 (1984): 39-47.